Praise for *A Jew in the Street*

"*A Jew in the Street* fully bears out the adage that 'nothing is as unpredictable as the past.' In this array of intellectually sparkling essays, a select group of this generation's leading Jewish historians pay handsome tribute to their teacher and colleague, Michael Stanislawski. The book showcases acute cameo portraits of major and minor personalities and events, spanning over three centuries of Jewish history. The authors regale us with new insights, quite in the spirit of Stanislawski's own method of upending received wisdom. The chapters, grouped into four parts, traverse the Central and Eastern European terrain and sometimes glance further afield to Israel and the Americas. This rich volume attests to the ways in which contemporary scholars are revamping popular images of the European Jewish past and creating new traditions of historiography."
—Eli Lederhendler, academic director of the Leonid Nevzlin Research Center for Russian and East European Jewry at The Hebrew University of Jerusalem

"Michael Stanislawski is an exemplary historian. His works encompass events and ideas within Jewish and Zionist history of the nineteenth and twentieth centuries. He combines professionalism with classical liberalism. This collection by his colleagues and former students greatly and freshly adds to Jewish historiography. It proves again that the research gates are widely open and open ended."
—Elyakim Rubinstein, former vice president, Supreme Court of Israel

"The essays in this volume offer a stunning array of innovative perspectives on the history of European Jewry in modern times. The essays' range, erudition, and originality are a worthy homage to Michael Stanislawski's distinguished career as a scholar and teacher."
—Derek Penslar, Harvard University

"These sparkling essays are a fitting tribute to Michael Stanislawski, a scholar who has done so much to make us rethink what were once long-held assumptions about the Jews of Eastern Europe. These articles are also a homage to Stanislawski, the inspiring teacher. Having trained a generation of leading scholars, many of whom have contributed to this important volume, his legacy is here for all to see."
—John Efron, Koret Professor of Jewish History, University of California–Berkeley

"Michael Stanislawski's extraordinary impact on the writing of modern Jewish history is well known, but this volume allows for appreciating his enormous influence as a colleague and teacher. Those in his debt have learned to take a second look at received truths and, in fidelity to the evidence, to raise self-critical historiography to the status of a high art. This volume does so at every turn."
—Samuel Moyn, Yale University

"This collection of works by noted scholars challenges convincingly the condescending attitudes sometimes shown towards Festschrift volumes. All the chapters are products of solid research dealing with a broad range of topics in European Jewish history."
—Gennady Estraikh, professor in the Skirball Department of Hebrew and Judaic Studies, New York University

A JEW IN THE STREET

A JEW IN THE STREET

NEW PERSPECTIVES ON EUROPEAN JEWISH HISTORY

Edited by Nancy Sinkoff, Jonathan Karp,
James Loeffler, and Howard Lupovitch

IN HONOR OF MICHAEL STANISLAWSKI

Wayne State University Press
Detroit

© 2024 by Wayne State University Press, Detroit, Michigan 48201. All rights reserved. No part of this book may be reproduced without formal permission.

ISBN 9780814349670 (paperback)
ISBN 9780814349687 (hardcover)
ISBN 9780814349694 (e-book)

Library of Congress Control Number: 2023945967

On cover: Street scene in Lask, ca. 1939, from the Archives of the YIVO Institute for Jewish Research, New York; Moshe Vorobeichic, "Ulica Jatkowa" (Butchers Street) in the Jewish Quarter of Vilna, courtesy of the Moi-Ver Raviv-Vorobeichic Collection and the Ghetto Fighters' House Archives. Cover design by Mindy Basinger Hill.

Grateful acknowledgment is made to the Institute for Israel and Jewish Studies at Columbia University and the Cohn-Haddow Center for Judaic Studies at Wayne State University for the generous support of the publication of this volume.

Wayne State University Press rests on Waawiyaataanong, also referred to as Detroit, the ancestral and contemporary homeland of the Three Fires Confederacy. These sovereign lands were granted by the Ojibwe, Odawa, Potawatomi, and Wyandot Nations, in 1807, through the Treaty of Detroit. Wayne State University Press affirms Indigenous sovereignty and honors all tribes with a connection to Detroit. With our Native neighbors, the press works to advance educational equity and promote a better future for the earth and all people.

Wayne State University Press
Leonard N. Simons Building
4809 Woodward Avenue
Detroit, Michigan 48201-1309

Visit us online at wsupress.wayne.edu.

Contents

Introduction: Michael Stanislawski and the
Reenvisioning of the European Jewish Past 1
Jonathan Karp and James Loeffler

I. Encounters and Translations in History, Law, and Memory

1. A Convert's Yiddish Translation of *Yeven Meẓulah* 29
   Edward Fram and Jonathan Gribetz

2. Chiefly on Translation and Timekeeping in Dov Ber
   Birkenthal's *Memoirs* 55
   Gershon David Hundert

3. When the Rebbe "Met" the Tsar: History or Folklore? 77
   David Assaf

4. In Search of the Three Sisters: The Genealogy of a
   Jewish Magical Incantation 101
   Natan M. Meir

5. Big Stakes for Small Claims: An Early Modern Jewish
   Court Between Civil and Religious Law 121
   Elisheva Carlebach

II. Rethinking National Consciousness

6. Cosmopolitan, International, and Jewish: '48ers in Exile   149
   Michael L. Miller

7. Hungarian Jews or Jews in Hungary:
   The Jews of Munkács and Ungvár   167
   Howard Lupovitch

8. Nation and Emancipation   201
   Olga Litvak

III. The Displacements of Europe's Great Wars

9. East, West, and a Gendering of Jewish Tradition
   During the First World War   227
   Nils Roemer

10. The Yiddish Chair in Weimar Germany That Wasn't   241
    Kalman Weiser

11. The Jewish Postwar   267
    Gil Rubin

12. Temporalities of Postwar Jewish Emigration   289
    Rebekah Klein-Pejšová

IV. Legacies of European Jewish Culture and History

13. The Rise of Yiddish Religious
    Revolutionary Socialism, 1926–1941   317
    Daniel B. Schwartz

14. The Fires of Hell, or *azoy vi got in ades*?
    Revisiting Jewish Odessa from Mendoza, Argentina, 1964   345
    Israel Bartal

15. Biography as *Hesped*: S. L. Shneiderman's Homage
    to Ilya Ehrenburg   373
    Nancy Sinkoff

16. The Wall and the Mountain: Symbols of Two Israels   399
    Michael Brenner

17. Past and Present: Modern Jewish Historiography,
    Premodern History, and the Politics of History   419
    Magda Teter

    Acknowledgments   447
    Contributors   449
    Index   453

Introduction

Michael Stanislawski and the
Reenvisioning of the European Jewish Past

Jonathan Karp and James Loeffler

Awake, my people! How long will you sleep?
The night has passed, the sun shines through.
Awake, cast your eyes hither and yon
Recognize your time and place.

These lines open the most misunderstood poem in modern Jewish history. In his 1866 Hebrew verse manifesto, "Awake, My People!" (*Hakizah ami*), the poet Judah Leib Gordon (1830–1892) exhorts his fellow Eastern European Jews to grasp the new world that lay at hand, one far different from any that their ancestors could ever have imagined. After urging enlightenment, literal and spiritual, upon his readers, Gordon then offers his famous prescription for Jewish modernity: "Be a Jew in the home and a man in the street." Gordon's poem went on to become an iconic anthem of modern Jewish culture, memorized by generations of schoolchildren the world over. Yet its most celebrated line is often read incorrectly as a plea for cultural assimilation and strict compartmentalization of Jewish difference in the modern world. Only in 1988 did Michael Stanislawski demonstrate that Gordon's poem was not intended as an expression of embarrassed deference but a confident vision of Eastern European Jewish self-assertion. As Stanislawski revealed, the phrase "Be a man in the street and a Jew at home" was a call not for the bifurcation of Jewish identity but for its integration; it advocated being both a full-fledged man—a free, modern, enlightened, Russian-speaking mensch—and a Jew at home in the creative spirit of Hebrew heritage.[1]

Gordon's phrase provides the starting point for this book. We invited a distinguished roster of historians to share new perspectives based on original research on the making of key aspects of European Jewish modernity. Our title, "A Jew in the Street," gestures playfully to the way in which these historians tug at the images and texts of the past to tease out deeper understandings of modern Jewish history and to challenge shopworn historiographic assumptions. It is often the categories that we take most for granted in the study of European Jewish history—Jew and non-Jew, particular and universal, East and West, private and public, individual and community, religious and secular, traditional and modern—that, on closer scrutiny, begin to dissolve into a marvelously rich picture of dynamic historical change. As Stanislawski showed in his study of Gordon, the movement of Jewish Enlightenment (Haskalah) that the Russian Hebrew poet epitomized marked one of the earliest modern efforts to integrate Jewish and European culture. Although certainly controversial in Gordon's day, it was only in the late nineteenth century, amid new and more hostile circumstances for Russian Jews, that the Haskalah came to be criticized as outmoded, indeed as a tragic mistake. A new, more confrontational Jewish politics emerged, one characterized by an open, public assertion of Jewish cultural and national prerogatives as played out on what was termed "the Jewish street." One of the effects, ironically, was to further extend the Haskalah's notion of Jewish socialization more directly into the mainstream of European society. But this new Jewish politics also led to the challenging of liberal individualism and the public-private dichotomy on which it was premised. In many ways this Jewish street politics would constitute a dominant strain of contentious Jewish public activity into the first half of the twentieth century. Our title thus speaks to multiple phases in modern European Jewish history: that marked by the original meaning of Gordon's prescription to be a "Jew in the home" and by the subsequent emergence of a range of new political and cultural activism characterized by the notion of a "Jew in the street." Michael Stanislawski has brilliantly illuminated aspects of both phases; hence it is appropriate that our title honors the man whose own writing and teaching inspire the work presented in these pages.

* * *

The field of Russian Jewish historiography lay in a moribund state in 1983 when Stanislawski published his masterful first book, *Tsar Nicholas I and the Jews: The Transformation of Jewish Society in Russia, 1825–1855*, based on his 1979 Harvard dissertation.[2] The wartime and postwar destruction of Jewish communities as well as Cold War geopolitics frustrated scholarly investigations, especially after a generation of European Jewish historians had been decimated in the Shoah. Pious memory and romanticized literary recollections dominated public understanding of the Russian Jewish past. Undeterred by these challenges, Stanislawski creatively built his own source base from which to launch a bracing revision of the historical record. Against the myth of a merciless tsarist regime terrorizing its docile Jewish population, he showed how Russian Jewish modernity began with a complex negotiation between a "reform"-minded authoritarian state and a Jewish society riven with conflicts over communal authority, Enlightenment knowledge, and the promise of modern citizenship. It was in dialogue with the state and amid bitter struggle within its own ranks that Russian Jews began their path into the modern world.[3] Writing in the late Cold War period, at a time when Western scholars had continued to view life in the Pale of Settlement as little more than a bitter prologue to the dramas of Stalinist persecution, Nazi decimation, Zionist liberation, and American deliverance, Stanislawski helped transform the field of Russian Jewish history. Taking the past on its own terms, Stanislawski also navigated through a research environment in which many archives remained closed to scholars and unfettered academic inquiry into Soviet society was effectively precluded. In doing so, he set a new standard for the use of literary and other cultural sources in the writing of modern Jewish history.

In rejecting ideologies and teleologies in the treatment of the Russian Jewish past, Stanislawski's *Tsar Nicholas* also began the work of revising the larger master narratives of modern Jewish historiography in several critical ways. First and foremost was his treatment of antisemitism. Historians of Europe and European Jewry long favored a dark metanarrative in which anti-Jewish hatred functioned as an undifferentiated, eternalist presence in modern Jewish life. True, Salo Baron, who established the study of Jewish history at Columbia University, where Stanislawski later made his academic home, had famously challenged this pervasive "lachrymose conception," but Baron aimed his revision principally at the historical depiction of the Jewish Middle Ages rather than the modern era.[4] It was Stanislawski who extended and deepened Baron's insights, especially as regards the nineteenth century's largest Jewish community: the Jews of the Russian Empire. Before Stanislawski's intervention, this community was frequently presented as double victims. Physically brutalized by merciless neighbors and hateful regimes and deprived of the glories of Western civilization and progress, they were living symbols of the unremitting face of antisemitism. They existed in a supposed state of geographic seclusion, which also implied a civilizational boundary between Europe's east and west, despite the fact that the boundaries of Central, East-Central, and Eastern Europe were porous and frequently changing.[5]

This image of isolation offered a simple and convenient but ultimately superficial causal explanation for the rise of Jewish politics, whether as a political revolt expressed through Zionism and socialism or by Jews "voting with their feet" in the mass migrations of the late nineteenth century. As Stanislawski would write in *For Whom Do I Toil?*, "We have an image of an ideological development of East European Jewry as a neat case of doctrinal succession: traditional Judaism yielding to the Haskalah whose naive, optimistic view of the world crashes on the shores of anti-Semitism and radicalism and is transmuted into the more realistic and long-lived ideologies of modern Jewish nationalism and socialism."[6] The terror of the Holocaust and the Stalinist attack on Jewish life served to confirm that lachrymose view. Yet from *Tsar Nicholas* onward, Stanislawski challenged this facile metanarrative in a number of ways. He showed how the Russian autocratic regime attempted to engage and improve its Jewish population, much like the Habsburg and Prussian regimes to its west, if in a more brutally heavy-handed fashion.[7] Moreover, some of the worst anti-Jewish policies of persecution were shaped with the connivance of Jewish communal leaders and official experts, reflecting a profound internal Jewish conflict over authority and economics. Consequently, Stanislawski was able to offer a far more sophisticated understanding of how antagonism did and did not translate into state practices. In addition, he showed how the image of Jewish suffering became an important tool for Jewish Enlightenment intellectuals to deploy in promoting the ideals of Western liberalism.[8]

If antisemitism did not exist as a generic condition or permanent feature of Jewish experience, neither did it serve as a causal trigger for the radically new Jewish politics that emerged out of late nineteenth-century Eastern Europe. Stanislawski made this point in his second book, *For Whom Do I Toil?*, a biography of Judah Leib Gordon. There, he dispelled the myths surrounding this transformative cultural figure, which had depicted him as a naïve idealist whose Enlightenment panacea was quickly superseded by Jewish realpolitik. Instead, Stanislawski portrayed Gordon as a tough-minded realist who was deeply engaged in the politics of the day. The result was a more rounded picture of modern Jewish culture that had emerged out of a dialectical interplay between European Enlightenment and Jewish nationalism. Furthermore, this dynamic had functioned to provide a kind of response to the decline of Jewish legal sovereignty that had been undermined by the slow encroachment of centralized state political authority.[9] Framing this history through a literary biography, Stanislawski showed how a bookish Jewish man grew into a symbol of an entire Jewish world in flux and an avatar of historical progress whose words and phrases would define Eastern European Jewish self-understanding for generations.

Stanislawski's third major book, *Zionism and the Fin de Siècle: Cosmopolitanism and Nationalism from Nordau to Jabotinsky*, was a pioneering study of Zionism's relationship to antisemitism and aesthetics in the European fin de siècle.[10] Peeling past layers of myth and ideology, Stanislawski demonstrated how a political movement premised on radical Jewish collective liberation owed its very imagination to the same European world against which it rebelled. Against generations of scholars who depicted Zionism as an inevitable response to European oppression, Stanislawski insisted that the modern Jewish nationalism of its founders was neither predetermined by religious messianism nor the product of defiant reaction against the depredations of antisemitism or assimilation. On the contrary, Jewish nationalism emerged from the legacy of a premodern Jewish corporate identity that sought a new existence as a discrete nation in the framework of the European nationalisms in the nineteenth century. Hence Jewish nationalism paradoxically represented both an organic expression of a preexisting ethnoreligious identity and a self-conscious process of acculturation into European political culture. Neither a wholesale rejection of Europeanness nor merely its belated imitation, Jewish nationalism emerged through the complex interplay of premodern Jewish politics, Hebrew Enlightenment, and European Romanticism. Stanislawski went on to trace the historical arc of Zionism through the establishment of the State of Israel in 1948 to the present day in his definitive concise chronicle, *Zionism: A Very Short Introduction*.[11]

The question of politics and violence in Zionism's present led Stanislawski back to a different corner of Eastern European Jewish history in *A Murder in Lemberg: Politics, Religion, and Violence in Modern Jewish History*. There he showed that intra-Jewish political violence hardly began with the 1995 assassination of Israeli prime minister Yitzhak Rabin and that the battle between the liberal and Orthodox wings of Judaism had taken place in Eastern Europe too.[12] Much of Stanislawski's work is preoccupied with the entrenched conflict between Jewish liberalism and ultra-Orthodoxy, as shown in traditionalists' fierce struggle against the maskilic-backed tsarist educational reforms described in *Tsar Nicholas*, Gordon's own dystopian fears of a future resurgence of militant and politicized Orthodoxy discussed in *For Whom Do I Toil?*, and especially in the bloody conflict chronicled in *A Murder in Lemberg*. At the same time, that particular book also doubled as an historiographic argument that the sharp dichotomies between Russia and the rest of Jewish Central and Eastern Europe have been overstated, a point that has become important to the understanding of the larger imperial dimensions of Eastern European Jewish history and of the origins of the Ashkenazic Jewish community in North America.[13]

Puncturing the myths of rabbinic nonviolence was of a piece with Stanislawski's resolute refusal to indulge in cliches and facile labels when characterizing modern Jewish identities, hence his insistence on interrogating one of the most misused words in the lexicon of modern Jewish history: *assimilation*.[14] In *Zionism and the Fin de Siècle* and elsewhere, Stanislawski showed that European acculturation did not mean Jewish deracination; indeed, the expletive *assimilationist* was lobbed by all manner of Jews against one another: cultural nationalists against *maskilim*, Bundists against Jewish Bolsheviks, secular Russian Zionists against German Orthodox rabbis, and so on. More crucially, modern European Jews did not necessarily bifurcate themselves neatly into Jewish and non-Jewish parts. As our title suggests, the private and the public often commingled in European Jewry, just as the lines blurred between the universal and the particular, the individual and the collective, even the Jewish and the Christian.

One way in which Stanislawski has demonstrated this complex mélange of identities and ideas in the fashioning of modern Jewish selves has been through his pioneering work on Jewish biography. From his life of Gordon through his revelatory smaller-scale studies on Vladimir Jabotinsky, Max Nordau, and Theodor Herzl down to his trenchant monograph *Autobiographical Jews*, Stanislawski has used the study of biography and memoir to show the constant interplay of culture and politics. *Zionism and the Fin de Siècle* set a new standard for the critical biographical study of key Zionist figures such as Herzl and Jabotinsky, exposing the full role of literature and the literary craft in the imagination of Jewish nationhood.[15] *Autobiographical Jews*, in its turn, took aim at the literary fictions of selfhood that lie at the root of so many individual icons and monumental texts populating the canon of Jewish cultural history and structuring the Jewish imagination of the self.[16] This book likewise showed the crucial importance of multilingualism in the manufacture of modern Jewish culture and Jewish lives. In his studies Stanislawski helped launch a trend of the history of iconography, the study of how Jewish historical figures come to be turned into iconic symbols of the Jewish past and present. That legacy can be seen inter alia in the biographical turn in contemporary Jewish historiography and letters.[17]

Many of these same themes can be detected in the chapters of this book. For instance, Stanislawski's careful contextualization and demythologizing of antisemitism is evident today in the new historiography of antisemitism, including Olga Litvak's contribution to this volume, which, like other contemporary scholarship, challenges the eternalist paradigm and substitutes in its place a textured account of continuities and discontinuities in anti-Jewish animus across time and space; Litvak also carefully parses the various meanings attached to such terms as *antisemitism* and *Judeophobia*.[18] Stanislawski's insight that perhaps the most ferocious of modern Jewish internecine struggles are not the obvious ones, pitting nationalists against assimilationists or Yiddishists against Hebraists, but those that array liberal Jews against forms of politicized religious Orthodoxy is echoed in the contributions of Howard Lupovitch and Michael Brenner, among others. Stanislawski's arguments regarding the subterranean survival of forms of premodern Jewish sovereignty find support in the analysis of Jewish small claims courts provided by Elisheva Carlebach. Stanislawski's focus on biography, the historical utility of ego documents, and Jewish iconography are evident in the contributions of Gershon David Hundert, David Assaf, Israel Bartal and Nancy Sinkoff, and his attentiveness to the complex agendas of translation surface in the studies by Edward Fram and Jonathan Gribetz (as well as those of Hundert and Sinkoff). Finally, the constructed nature of Jewish east-west dichotomies provides a central theme in the chapters by Nils Roemer and Rebekah Klein-Pejšová. This volume is therefore not simply an example of scholars paying tribute to a mentor and colleague but a rich expression of Michael Stanislawski's signal impact on a generation of Jewish historians.

* * *

Stanislawski once remarked in the course of a graduate seminar, "Everyone else seems to know everything about [the past]," breezily asserting its self-evident truths, yet this certitude all too frequently rests on a shaky foundation of myth and supposition. Accordingly, the task of the historian is not only to ignore conventional wisdom in pursuit of truth but also to explain the manufacture and persistence of illusion. In his long, distinguished career, Stanislawski modeled this lesson both through his research and writing and in the classroom. He taught it to the generations of undergraduates who passed through Columbia University history and core curriculum courses and to the doctoral students who joined him in his weekly graduate seminar room.

The editors of this volume are all veterans of that classroom. There, Stanislawski dared us to join him in learning history in a radically transgressive way. Rather than requiring us to pay deference to preceding generations of scholars (and pseudo-scholars), Stanislawski insisted on a more Cartesian approach to the study of the past: He proposed that, each time, we discard our inherited assumptions and theoretical blinders and instead start from scratch. What did the sources reveal when read without the overlay of secondary interpretations? What did the authors sound like without the filters of myth and memory? How should we capture the past knowing our knowledge would always remain inconsistent and incomplete? For us students, it was a liberating and even exhilarating experience. He imbued us with a sense that doing history is a rigorous *and* creative enterprise. It was a crucial lesson that we took with us into our own classrooms and scholarship.

This volume is likewise inspired by Stanislawski's fresh and iconoclastic approach but also by four specific themes that have shaped his own writings in the field of European Jewish history: encounters and translations in history, law, and memory; rethinking national consciousness; the displacements of Europe's great wars; and legacies of European Jewish culture and history. The contributors to this volume, who include both Stanislawski's students and his colleagues, take up these themes in their chapters. Because of limited space, the editors could include essays only by those who were his direct doctoral students and whose principal research systematically engages Central, East-Central, and Eastern Europe (with a nod to those civilizations' impact on modern Israel), as well as a handful of his closest colleagues in that field. Unfortunately, this limitation cannot do full justice to Stanislawski's expansive legacy, one that encompasses such diverse fields as Jewish legal history,[19] the study of modern conversion and apostasy,[20] literary and art history,[21] the history of Jewish Enlightenment in comparative perspective,[22] and the history of modern Orthodoxy.[23]

Part I, "Encounters and Translations in History, Law, and Memory," opens with two chapters that nod to Stanislawski's deep concern with language and translation as markers of acculturation and registers of self-description. In his own contribution to a 1998 festschrift in honor of his teacher and colleague Yosef Hayim Yerushalmi, Stanislawski penned a remarkable essay on Yiddish translations of the classic work of early modern Jewish history writing, the *Shevet yehudah* of Solomon ibn Verga (c. 1460–1554).[24] Here Edward Fram and Jonathan Gribetz deploy similar literary forensic skills to examine the agendas involved in the 1686 Yiddish translation of *Yeven mezulah* (The Abyss of Despair), Natan Neta Hanover's iconic Hebrew chronicle of the 1648 Khmelnytsky uprising, which resulted in the deaths of tens of thousands of Jews in Ukraine and a massive refugee crisis.[25] Hanover was a refugee himself when he penned the chronicle. But given the narrow stratum of Hebrew readers, it was only through the translation by Moses ben Abraham that most Jewish men and women could access this history. Fram and Gribetz ask what excisions and additions the translator made and for what reasons (ranging from production costs to religious sensibilities). Their account is particularly intriguing because, as they detail, the translator was a Christian convert to Judaism whose former identity led him to inject theological assumptions that were largely alien to the original.

Similar issues arise in Gershon David Hundert's chapter on Dov Ber Birkenthal's *Memoirs*. Birkenthal (1723–1805), better known to Jewish historians as Ber of Bolechów, was a merchant who produced both an autobiography (a rare genre for Jews in this period) and a history of Jewish messianism, *Divrei binah*. As Hundert shows, these two works overlapped, inasmuch as, by his own account, the central episode of Birkenthal's life was his role as the translator into Polish of Rabbi Hayyim Rappoport's Hebrew responses to the blood libel accusations leveled by the messianic pretender and apostate Jacob Frank against the Polish Jewish community. The fact that Birkenthal knew Polish well enough to fulfill this role begs the question of what status foreign language learning enjoyed among premodern Eastern European Jews. Indeed, this is a question Birkenthal—who learned German in addition to Hebrew, Yiddish, and Polish—takes up directly in his writings. Birkenthal's memoirs reveal a mind curious about general learning; he was eager for discussions with the learned non-Jewish merchants he encountered in his travels but also defensive about the controversial nature of his language studies. In his memoir he is at pains to show that his mastery of Polish enabled him to play a vital role in defending the Jews from Frank's calumnies, although Birkenthal's history of messianism deploys selective and polemical Hebrew translations of the works of Christian historians to demonstrate how God's plan always works in the Jews' favor, evidence to the contrary notwithstanding. In rather striking contrast to the case of Moses ben Abraham, Hundert avers that Birkenthal's translation projects aimed to Judaize Christian historical knowledge in a way that largely resisted the homogenizing effect of incipient modernity in Eastern Europe.

A similar theme emerges in David Assaf's lively chapter on the vexing question of the place of Hasidism in the transition to Jewish modernity. Assaf approaches the question in relation to folktales posing as actual history, in which the teller relates the nature and consequences of meetings between Hasidic zaddikim and Gentile leaders (statesmen, kings, and emperors included). Ostensibly presented as true-life events and sometimes containing kernels of historical fact, these stories aimed to send the message that what might seem like mundane interactions, ones that essentially leave in place the status quo with Gentiles on top and Jews on the bottom, are revealed on deeper analysis to mirror cosmic struggles between divine and demonic forces.[26] One Hasidic master discussed by Assaf studied the genealogies of Polish noblemen not (or not just) as a measure of shrewd diplomacy but to harness the kabbalistic forces underlying all mundane appearances to protect his flock while simultaneously advancing the process of redemption. Clearly, Hasidic genealogy has never been a trivial pursuit!

A second contribution devoted to Jewish folklore, Natan Meir's history of the folk incantation invoking "three women sitting on a crag," shows this particular folk remedy to have medieval roots as well as a cultural provenance shared by Jews and Christians. The incantation was variously deployed to ward off the evil eye or to protect an infant boy on the eve of his circumcision from the depredations of the demon Lilith. Here too we find a gendered linguistic dualism at play, but now between Hebrew and Yiddish. The Hebrew version, which often included biblical verses, was associated with *ba'alei shem*, whereas female healers and spell-casters (*opshprekherkes*) favored the Yiddish version, sometimes interpolating Slavic rhymes. Besides its nuanced reconstruction of vernacular religion, Meir's excavation underscores an important point Stanislawski has often made himself, specifically, that although Jewish historians tend to emphasize revolutionary change and transformation affecting Eastern European Jews, there is also an "impressive continuity" of traditions and folklore that reached into the twentieth century. The remarkable durability and afterlife of this half-submerged channel of Ashkenazic imaginative vernacular constitutes an important feature of modern Jewish culture.

In fact, the theme of blurred borderlines between premodern and modern, or between early modern and modern, was anticipated early on in Stanislawski's work. Recent scholarship has followed his lead in challenging assumptions about the periodization of Jewish modernity and the indexes of tradition and change.[27] Institutions once thought to serve as absolute markers of modernity in the Weberian sense, such as the state monopoly on licit violence, have been shown to admit too many exceptions to retain such a status. In the 1920s Salo Baron famously argued that Jews owed their emancipation to the logic of the state that could not tolerate corporatist competitors to its centralized sovereignty.[28] Baron's student Yerushalmi stressed the impact of these ruptures on the interiority of Jewish identity in the early modern European world. Yet Stanislawski, in his first book, showed how long traditional corporate structures persisted in European Jewish history and how much Jewish leaders sought to negotiate the terms of their acquiescence to absolutist state authority.

In this volume Elisheva Carlebach's chapter highlights another partial exception to Baron's dominant theory. Examining the rich source of eighteenth-century records for the Jewish small claims court in Altona, Carlebach establishes that the early modern state—which in other respects sought gradually to curtail the autonomous institutions of the Jewish community—allowed and even encouraged local Jewish authorities to operate courts for petty financial disputes. Carlebach explains that small claims courts in Europe were a distinctly post-medieval phenomenon, designed to defuse conflicts over competing financial claims that might previously have been settled by informal mechanisms, including at times violent ones. Given the significant Jewish presence in small trade, these courts suited Jewish communities particularly, although their extant records have yet to be mined for the data they contain on Jewish business matters, employer-servant contracts, and the like. Interestingly, the Jewish small claims court system reflected a high degree of collaboration between rabbinic and lay leadership, strata that have often been depicted as at odds during this period. Carlebach provides an overview of the records pertaining to Altona Jewry during a short period in the late eighteenth century. But she also extends her discussion forward to show that, in the Jewish case at least, the small claims courts continued to function with state approval into the second half of the nineteenth century.

Even as early modern corporate structures persisted well into the nineteenth century, including the *kahal*, not formally abolished in tsarist Russia until 1844, modern national identities began to develop among European Jewish populations. Part II, "Rethinking National Consciousness," takes up questions of how Jewish self-identification and political imagination changed across the long nineteenth century in response to revolution and reform. In Central Europe the 1848 revolutions brought nationality to the forefront of politics, highlighting the complex and often ambiguous national identities of the many Jewish revolutionaries, such as Adolf Fischhof, Joseph Goldmark, Gabriel Riesser, and Moses Hess. In his overview of the cohort of Jewish participants in the Vienna Uprising of that year, Michael Miller shows that such figures as Moritz Hartmann, Karl Tausenau, Sigmund Engländer, Sigmund Kolisch, Simon Deutsch, Adolf Buchheim, and Adolf Chaisés made up a fairly coherent cohort. All born around the year 1820 and all migrating to Vienna from regions such as Bohemia, Galicia, Moravia, and Hungary, they found careers as journalists and literati, at first covering the arts and only in the aftermath of the Paris uprising shifting to politics. They all also espoused essentially similar views, favoring a constitutional monarchy (though a few were outright republicans) and a *Grossdeutsch* solution to the problem of German unification. Miller is as much attuned to the consequences as to the causes of this Jewish "political debut" into European politics, as Baron labeled it.[29] First, 1848 marked the ominous inception of the public's antisemitic association between Jews collectively and political subversion. "The whole revolution was nothing but a Jewish revolution," as one Habsburg minister suggested at the time. Second, Miller traces the subsequent lives and careers of those who managed to escape arrest (or in one case, execution) and relocate to London or Paris, often settling in close quarters with fellow revolutionary refugees. Some gradually weaned themselves from politics, but others, for example, Simon Deutsch and Sigmund Englander, became lifelong professional revolutionaries. Unsure of what importance to attribute to the Jewish component of their backgrounds, historians, Miller notes, have all too often chosen to ignore it; in contrast, Miller takes it on directly.

A quite different Central European Jewish experience is detailed in Howard Lupovitch's overview of the Jews of Munkács and Ungvár, towns with markedly high Jewish populations whose location made them subject to shifting boundaries from the eighteenth through the twentieth centuries. As Lupovitch notes, "Jews in Munkács and Ungvár and in the region generally were at one time or another defined—and saw themselves—as Hungarian, Polish, Ukrainian, Slovak, and Karpato-Rus' Jews; and as *Galizianers*, Ashkenazim, and *Ostjuden*." They therefore form an ideal sample with which to trace the dynamics of emerging national consciousness across Central European states. The experiences of Jews living under Magyar Hungarian rule demonstrate how communities effectively balanced the goals of preserving identity, maintaining religious observance, and signaling loyalty to the state and its Magyar elite. Not that there was a singular exclusive path that all Jews in these towns and region pursued, Lupovitch shows. On the contrary, strategies differed between Hasidic and non-Hasidic ultra-Orthodox Jews as well as between these two groups and the Neolog Jews whose approach was akin to that of the Reform Judaism evolving in nineteenth-century Germany. As in so many of the contributions in this volume, here too the language question looms large. With Magyars less than a majority of the population, their rule under nominally democratic auspices could be facilitated by allying with the significant Jewish population through the mechanism of Magyarization, which entailed Jews acquiring an adequate command of the Magyar language. And although Hasidic and non-Hasidic Orthodox Jews generally made common cause against the Neologs, the non-Hasidic Orthodox were more amenable to Magyarization, so long as it did not intrude on religious observance.

This pattern of accommodation, so characteristic of European Jewish modernization during the first two-thirds of the nineteenth century, came under intense criticism from the 1880s on, especially in Eastern Europe. Historians traditionally attribute the waning belief in the possibility of reconciling Jewish and modern European national identities through adaptation and compromise to the outbreak of violent antisemitism in Russia starting in 1881. Olga Litvak challenges this long-standing assumption by asking whether *Autoemancipation*, the pathbreaking 1882 pamphlet by Leo Pinsker that first helped galvanize Zionist sentiment, was really inspired by its author's response to antisemitism, as has long been assumed. Rather than identifying antisemitism as the cause and core of the work's argument on behalf of Zionism, Litvak proposes a revisionist reading. She insists that Pinsker's supposedly secular analysis of the disease of *Judeophobia* was little more than a rhetorical ruse that masked an attack on emancipation for its destructive assault on Jewish authenticity. Litvak's virtuosic interrogation of the background, sources, and semiotics of Pinsker's pamphlet, set against the backdrop of contemporary Jewish thought and European nationalist ideology, is a fierce rejection of long-standing historiographic assumptions and a challenge to one of the master narratives of modern Jewish politics.

If the Jewish world was not remade by the Russian pogroms of 1881, it was certainly transformed by the twentieth century's global wars, the subject of the third part, "Displacements of Europe's Great Wars." World War I resulted in the collapse of the imperial system (Russia, Austria-Hungary, the Ottoman Empire, and Germany), under which most Jews had lived for centuries, and its replacement by an array of nation-states. The Balfour Declaration marked a turning point for Zionist fortunes in Palestine. But the war also provided the opportunity, arguably more than in previous military conflicts, for Jews of all combatant states to demonstrate their loyalty and military prowess, virtues long questioned by their detractors. Oddly, until recently, World War I has not been a topic high on the research agendas of Jewish historians. This is due in part to the overwhelming impact of the war's sequel and its genocidal destruction of European Jewry, which has led historians to consider World War I almost entirely in terms of how it led to the later conflagration. Yet recent scholarship has rejected this limited perspective and has sought instead to treat World War I and the Jews as a topic in its own right rather than a foreshadowing of the Holocaust.[30]

In his chapter Nils Roemer explores how German Jewish men involved in the Eastern campaign reacted to their face-to-face encounters with (more) traditional Jewish life in Poland and Russia. Scholars have long understood the so-called renaissance of Jewish sensibility in Weimar Germany, associated with such figures as Franz Rosenzweig, Martin Buber, Bertha Pappenheim, and Gershom Scholem, as influenced, even in the decade before World War I, by the migration of *Ostjuden* to Germany and the positive perception of their more "authentic" and "spiritual" Jewish character. Roemer extends this analysis by focusing particularly on the topic of gender, asking specifically how German Jews stationed in the East perceived their coreligionists in terms of masculine and feminine constructs. His analysis suggests, first, that these German Jewish men brought with them the same gendered preconceptions concerning traditional Russian Jews that they had formed before the war and, second, that they tended to favorably compare the more traditional Jewish women they encountered in the east, whom they viewed as rooted in humble home and naïve faith, with Jewish women back home, whom they cast as worldly, deracinated, and materialistic.

A subsequent if equally fraught encounter of West and East is explored in Kalman Weiser's chapter. Just as it is necessary for historians to suspend foreknowledge when it comes to examining the impact of World War I on Jews, so too should we recognize that German scholarly interest in Eastern European Jews before the Nazi regime was not invariably or inevitably motivated by antisemitism. Weiser's examination of a little-known episode during the Weimar period concerning the establishment of an academic Yiddish chair is a case in point. The episode involves a peculiar encounter and partnership between a non-Jewish German-language researcher named Heinz Kloss and the foremost contemporary scholar of Yiddish, Solomon Birnbaum. Kloss sought Birnbaum's assistance in establishing a chair in Yiddish language at a proposed institute for the study of cognate Germanic languages that he hoped to create.

Weiser reminds us that not only had Yiddish been a topic of interest to some Christians (largely for Hebraist and missionary purposes) since at least the eighteenth century but also that academic Yiddish study had first emerged in Weimar Germany, with more than 10 doctoral dissertations produced there in the decade after the war. Relations between Kloss and Birnbaum were strained throughout their nearly 10 years of planning and correspondence, with disagreement centering on Kloss's intent to harness Yiddish linguistic study to the goal of elucidating the development of modern German and on Birnbaum's conviction that Yiddish must be treated as a full-fledged, autonomous, and integral language in its own right. Despite this difference, the plan—which involved practical applications as well as scholarly ones—was not as far-fetched as it might retrospectively appear. The Weimar government was interested in asserting its role as the protector not just of German speakers in other lands but also of speakers of endangered languages more generally. Still, whatever realistic hope the unlikely collaborators might have entertained was crushed by the advent of National Socialism, which forced Birnbaum to flee to London and Kloss to accommodate himself (all too comfortably, it turns out) to the new regime.

From Birnbaum's vantage point, regime change meant profound dislocation and despair over the future. But Gil Rubin's chapter on the Jewish postwar experience shows that as late as 1939 or even 1940, Jewish leaders in Palestine, London, and New York believed that the future was still uncertain. They planned optimistically for the situation that would arise after Hitler's presumed defeat with a range of possibilities that would only later be foreclosed. Their plans date back to the 1920s, when leaders anticipated the future existence of two principal regions of Jewish demographic concentration: the Yishuv in Palestine and Eastern Europe within and adjacent to the former Pale of Settlement.

In fact, the war seemed to offer a ray of hope that the doldrums of the Depression era would give way to something better, even or especially for Jews. A number of American Jewish organizations established planning institutes to make detailed preparations for the postwar, starting in late 1940. Even when news began to surface of systematic Nazi mass killings of Jews, planners did not yet imagine a full-scale genocide. Most Jewish statesmen assumed that a significant remnant of 2 million or more would outlast the Nazis. Hence the concept of minority rights as well as migration to Palestine remained mutually operative until quite late in the conflict. Yet when the full magnitude of the destruction did finally become apparent, the same planners descended into despair. Zionists in particular worried that their movement might soon become effectively defunct, at least in terms of the goal of achieving some kind of majority status in a part of Palestine. The final note of Rubin's tale is the most ironic: Despite the war's impossibly grim outcome for Jews, it did in the end fulfill a semblance of the planners' most hopeful expectations. World War II's apotheosis was the dual outcome of collective destruction and national rebirth. But it is only by recapturing the brief moment between the war's outbreak and full awareness of the Holocaust that the planners' misplaced yet ironically fulfilled optimism can be understood.

Although 1948 appears as a year of triumph for Zionists, the interval between Germany's surrender and the announcement of statehood was exceedingly grim. This was due not only to the realization of how completely the Final Solution had succeeded but also to the evident failure of the global community to consider any kind of restitution to the Jews. Unlike the diplomatic negotiations in Paris following World War I, there was hardly any official discussion of Jewish status or rights in the immediate aftermath of World War II.

As Rebekah Klein-Pejšová examines in her chapter, international organizations came to see Jewish survivors as a nonrepatriable group by the end of 1946. In other words, survivors could not, for the most part, return to their former homes, nor were sufficient avenues opened to them for emigration. Klein-Pejšová provides a big-picture overview of the enormous hardships faced by occupants of the displaced person (DP) camps following the war. Emigration was an exhausting waiting game, as countries of destination constantly shifted admissions policies in the face of diplomatic maneuvering—or evasion. Jewish DPs coined the phrase "black aliyah" to refer to a desperate exit without certainty of a specific destination. Even when opportunities arose, the bureaucratic hurdles to emigration could prove maddening. The resulting frustration led to a raft of forgeries (and consequently to familiar charges of Jewish criminality) and to occasional violent incidents. Often, only the intervention of such agencies as HIAS (the Hebrew Immigrant Aid Society) cleared the path to exit. When the dust had settled and the long period of uncertainty ended, "a new diaspora," in Klein-Pejšová's words, had willy-nilly come into existence, with refugees relocating to Brazil, Chile, Venezuela, Sweden, Egypt, and the Belgian Congo among other locales.

Our volume's final part, "Legacies of European Jewish Culture and History," moves from the vibrant lifeworlds and devastating destructions of Jewish Europe to their broader cultural and political echoes across the rest of the twentieth-century Jewish world. Daniel Schwartz's chapter brings to light a little discussed aspect of the modern Jewish association with socialism: self-conscious efforts to synthesize leftist thought with the Jewish religious tradition. Certainly, there are numerous examples of Christian socialists, from R. H. Tawney to liberation theology. But parallel instances in the Jewish world are surprisingly hard to find. Although countless efforts have been made to link socialism with some alleged Jewish spirit or doctrine, most Jewish socialists did little more than seek out superficial historical linkages by identifying biblical precedents, such as Deuteronomic laws relating to the remission of debts on the jubilee year. In his essay Schwartz examines three prominent Jewish socialists who believed that Judaism as a religion was integral not just to the roots of socialism but also to its current practice: Isaac Naḥman Steinberg (1888–1957), William Nathanson (1883–1963), and Abraham Bick (1913–1990). As Schwartz notes, "Their work shared certain themes—an embrace of Jewish messianism as a prototype or model for socialism, an insistence on the need for 'religiosity' over mere religion, and a mining of classical sources for socialist prooftexts—but they varied in the degree to which they were activists, in the concreteness of their programs, and in the nature of the radical Judaism they pursued. Together, however, they served as an alternative to freethinking anarchism, reformist socialism and trade unionism, and Bolshevik (increasingly Stalinist) communism."

The contributions of Israel Bartal and Nancy Sinkoff return us to the question of the languages of modern Eastern European Jews, a core theme in this volume. Bartal offers a fascinating excavation of a little known *maskil* whose path, despite its idiosyncrasies, contains elements that are representative of a generation of Russian Jews. Israel Ze'ev Spivakoff (1874–1968) was an Odessa-born businessman, Hebraist, and literary figure. He lived much of his later life in Mendoza, a provincial Argentinean city, where he published both a Spanish-Hebrew dictionary and his own memoirs written in an antiquated Hebrew style. But in Bartal's telling, the city of Odessa looms much larger than Mendoza.

Unlike many *maskilim* who migrated to Odessa as part of their journey to modern Jewish consciousness, Spivakoff was born there. He embodied its spirit of both provincialism and cosmopolitanism, and these contradictions become evident in his literary output. A sort of amateur ethnographer, Spivakoff used his extensive business travels as opportunities to conduct research and reportage on the condition and mentalities of local Jews throughout the Pale of Settlement. The oddity of this practice, Bartal emphasizes, is that Spivakoff wrote his highly realistic accounts in a biblical style of Hebrew reminiscent of the early Haskalah but by his day long outmoded. In this manner he rendered his kaleidoscopic portrait of the pre–World War I Eastern European Jewish world as though it was a Hebrew-speaking realm.

A similar disjuncture is found in Spivakoff's memoirs, produced in Argentina and also written in an archaic Hebrew style. Unlike many Odessans of his generation, Spivakoff chose not to emigrate to Palestine, where he might have experienced the modernization of the Hebrew language. Despite this anomaly, Bartal concludes that Spivakoff was in some ways quite representative of the world left behind: "His is a collective biography of the ethnic-religious community into which he was born, whose spirit he imbibed, and whose collapse, over which the Jews had no control, swept him away, along with everyone else. In short, these personal memories are part of the historical story shared by the largest Jewish community in the world." What Bartal is pointing to here is the role that Hebrew played for Eastern European *maskilim* in mediating their journey from Yiddish traditionalism to the absorption of modern European culture.

Nancy Sinkoff's chapter considers both the surprising parallels and disjunctions between a Jewish leftist nationalist and Yiddishist, on the one side, and a cosmopolitan Russian Jewish communist writer, on the other. Her chapter focuses on S. L. Shneiderman's little-known 1968 biography of the famously controversial Soviet writer Ilya Ehrenberg. Given Ehrenberg's complicated relationship to Stalinism, the accusations leveled against him of complicity in the liquidation of the Jewish Anti-Fascist Committee specifically and more generally Stalin's destruction of Jewish culture in the postwar Soviet Union, one might have expected Shneiderman to produce an indictment of Ehrenberg rather than the nuanced and sympathetic portrait of him that Sinkoff explicates here. Beyond the fact of the two writers' personal relationship (mutually respectful, if not close), Sinkoff argues that Shneiderman's benign account of Ehrenberg's activities—what amounts to an exoneration—is rooted in a post-Shoah spirit of reconciliation between two wings of Eastern European Jewry: the Polish, Yiddish-oriented, and nationalist side; and the Russian, assimilationist, and Sovietized branch. Their radically different experiences dating to the Polish partitions of the eighteenth century but especially to the Bolshevik Revolution of 1917 could not entirely eradicate the common origins and essential integrity of Eastern European Jews. In the aftermath of the Holocaust, Shneiderman's personal admiration for Ehrenberg's literary accomplishments and his appreciation of the ways in which Ehrenberg successfully navigated a treacherous tightrope between accommodation and resistance, animated at all times by a profound hatred of antisemitism, led him to compose a biography that displays a distinctly post–Cold War if not revisionist spirit of tolerance. That such a work was published in Yiddish, almost guaranteeing it a small readership and gearing it to the community that had lost so much by its identification with communism, underscores the almost miraculous nature of Shneiderman's feat.

No such spirit of reconciliation emerges in Michael Brenner's account of two alternative symbols of modern Jewish statehood for preeminence: Mount Herzl, a newly designated memorial site housing the remains of the "father of Zionism," Theodor Herzl; and the Kotel, otherwise known as the Wailing Wall or, later, the Western Wall. Brenner describes how these two sites have signified competing agendas in the evolution of Israeli national myths. The highest elevation in Jerusalem became "Mt. Herzl in 1950, shortly after Herzl's remains were reinterred there." The founders of Israel sought out a unifying symbol that would focus the loyalties of the nation's disparate constituencies on a universally admired figure. As Brenner details, numerous other contenders for preeminent national memorial or monument were considered before Mount Herzl was awarded that distinction. And, as he further describes, though never truly a beloved site of pilgrimage, Mount Herzl adequately fulfilled its function between 1949 and 1967, when Israel's regnant ideology was that of *mamlakhtiyut* statism, a view of the Israeli state apparatus as the all-important guardian of collective Jewish interests.

Brenner notes ironically that Herzl himself was no "lover of Zion," insofar as Zion meant Jerusalem, and would have preferred to be buried in

Haifa, overlooking the Mediterranean. But such inconvenient facts could not be allowed to interfere with the agenda of national consolidation effected during the formative era in Israel's development. Yet after 1967 Israel's stunning military victory could not disguise the fact that statism no longer sufficed to bind the centrifugal forces fragmenting Israeli society. In this context the Western Wall, which had been captured during the Six Day War, proved to be the more powerful national symbol. With the expansion of the political right and its messianic ethos, the wall was the perfect symbol of an indomitable and providential Jewish history, despite the fact that it had never actually been a part of the ancient Jerusalem Temple and had only begun to take on a profound religious symbolism during the Ottoman period. In encapsulating the story of Israel's shifting national iconography by capturing the meanings variously attributed to the mountain and to the wall, Brenner has deployed an effective heuristic device for representing Israel's changed identity over time.

Finally, Magda Teter's reflection on the state of the field of modern Jewish historiography provides a fitting conclusion to this volume. Teter's central concern in her essay is a basic question that Jewish historians have always consciously or unconsciously asked: What is the purpose of Jewish history? Beginning and concluding with different iterations of the mission statement of the Association of Jewish Studies, one from the time of its founding in 1969 and another from several years ago, Teter sees Jewish historians as perpetually caught between the contending agendas of scientific objectivity on the one hand and interested communal and political engagement on the other. With these two poles in mind, she traces the development of Jewish historiography not just through its most monumental accomplishments and eminent practitioners but also through the smaller scale, more localized, more amateur expressions that have actually constituted much of its substance. Teter concludes that a historiography adhering rigorously to precepts of objectivity and one unapologetically committed to engagement and advocacy do not constitute mutually exclusive and purely distinct archetypal approaches but have combined or alternated in a condition of fruitful if tense hybridity.

Michael Stanislawski, whose work is marked not just by great rigor but by a wholesale rejection of ideological dogma and doctrinal orthodoxy coupled with a strong empathy for his historical subjects, would surely concur.

Notes

1 Michael Stanislawski, *For Whom Do I Toil? Judah Leib Gordon and the Crisis of Russian Jewry* (Oxford, UK: Oxford University Press, 1988), 52. See also Michael Stanislawski, "Gordon, Yehudah Leib," in *The YIVO Encyclopedia of Jews in Eastern Europe*, 9 August 2010, yivoencyclopedia.org/article.aspx/Gordon_Yehudah_Leib (accessed 17 April 2023); and the remarks in Gershon Bacon, "An Anthem Reconsidered: On Text and Subtext in Yehuda Leib Gordon's 'Awake, My People!'" *Prooftexts* 15, no. 2 (1995): 194. Although Gordon used the male pronoun, his commitment to women's equality was well attested, not only in his poem "Kotso shel yod" (The Tip of the Yud), which condemned the rabbinic establishment's mistreatment of *agunot* (literally "anchored wives," i.e., women denied divorce bills by their husbands), but also in his encouragement of Jewish female writers, particularly Miriam Markel-Mosessohn, to whom he dedicated the poem. One could therefore read "man" as "human being." See Stanislawski, *For Whom Do I Toil*, 127–28. For more on Markel-Mosessohn, see Carole Balin, *"To Reveal Our Hearts": Russian-Jewish Women Writers in Imperial Russia* (Cincinnati: Hebrew Union College Press, 2001). It is also worth mentioning here the curious fact that Gordon's couplet "Jew in the home / man in the street" has been (and is often still) regularly misattributed to the eighteenth-century Jewish philosopher Moses Mendelssohn. See, for example, Isaac Deutscher, *The Non-Jewish Jew and Other Essays* (London: Oxford University Press, 1968), 31.

2 Michael Stanislawski, *Tsar Nicholas I and the Jews: The Transformation of Jewish Society in Russia, 1825–1855* (Philadelphia: Jewish Publication Society, 1983); Michael Stanislawski, "The Transformation of Jewish Society in Russia, 1825–1855," PhD diss., Harvard University, 1979. The book was published in Russian as *Tsar Nikolai I i evrei: transformatsiia evreiskogo obshchestva v Rossii (1825–1855)* (Moscow: Knizhniki, Text/Tekst, 2014).

3 Stanislawski further transformed our understanding of Russian Jewish emancipation in Michael Stanislawski, "Russian Jewry, the Russian State, and the Dynamics of Jewish Emancipation," in *Paths of Emancipation*, ed. Pierre Birnbaum and Ira Katznelson (Princeton, NJ: Princeton University Press, 1995), 262–83.

4 See David Engel, "Crisis and Lachrymosity: On Salo W. Baron, Neobaronianism, and the Study of Modern European Jewish History," *Jewish History* 20, nos. 3–4 (2006): 243–64. Ironically, Baron did not internalize his own

insights in his work on Eastern Europe; his *The Russian Jew Under Tsars and Soviets* (New York: Macmillan, 1964) was marred by its lachrymosity, setting the stage for the correctives offered by Stanislawski.

5 Central, East-Central, and Eastern Europe connote a geography and nomenclature that have resisted constancy. We define them as the lands between Russia and German Central Europe, from the Baltics south to the Balkans. On the construction of Europe's west and east, see Larry Wolff, *Inventing Eastern Europe: The Map of Civilization on the Mind of the Enlightenment* (Redwood City, CA: Stanford University Press, 1994).

6 Stanislawski, *For Whom Do I Toil*, 5.

7 In this Stanislawski preceded and anticipated by several years the important work of John Klier, who extended and elaborated on Stanislawski's nuanced approach to tsarist Jewish policy in the late eighteenth and early nineteenth century. See, especially, John Klier, *Russia Gathers Her Jews: The Origins of the Jewish Question in Russia, 1772–1825* (DeKalb: Northern Illinois University Press, 1986).

8 On the construction of Russian Jewish suffering as a manifestation of political ideology, see Olga Litvak, *Conscription and the Search for Modern Russian Jewry* (Bloomington: Indiana University Press, 2006).

9 This theme is also explored in Michael Stanislawski, "Haskalah and Zionism: A Reexamination," in *Vision Confronts Reality: Historical Perspectives on the Contemporary Jewish Agenda*, ed. Ruth Kozodoy, David Sidorsky, and Kalman Sultanik (Madison, NJ: Fairleigh Dickinson University Press, 1989), 56–67.

10 Michael Stanislawski, *Zionism and the Fin de Siècle: Cosmopolitanism and Nationalism from Nordau to Jabotinsky* (Berkeley: University of California Press, 2001).

11 Michael Stanislawski, *Zionism: A Very Short Introduction* (Oxford, UK: Oxford University Press, 2016).

12 Michael Stanislawski, *A Murder in Lemberg: Politics, Religion, and Violence in Modern Jewish History* (Princeton, NJ: Princeton University Press, 2007), published in Hebrew as *Reẓaḥ bi-Levov* (Jerusalem: Merkaz Zalman Shazar, 2010) and in Swedish as *Ett mord i Lemberg: politik, religion och våld i modern judisk historia* (Stockholm: Dialogos, 2008).

13 On Stanislawski's exploration of the contours of Ashkenazic identity, see Michael Stanislawski, "Towards an Analysis of the 'Bi'ur' as Exegesis: Moses Mendelssohn's Commentary on the Revelation at Sinai," *Neti'ot Ledavid:*

Jubilee Volume for David Weiss Halivni, ed. Yaakov Elman, Ephraim Bezalel Halivni, and Zvi Arie Steinfeld (Jerusalem: Orhot, 2004), 135–52; and Michael Stanislawski, "The Yiddish *Shevet Yehudah*: A Study in the 'Ashkenization' of a Sephardic Classic," in *Jewish History and Jewish Memory: Essays in Honor of Yosef Hayim Yerushalmi*, ed. Elisheva Carlebach, John M. Efron, and David M. Myers (Hanover, NH: University Press of New England, 1998), 134–49. For the insights as to the common Ashkenazic identity of "German" and "Russian" Jewish immigrants to the United States, see Hasia Diner, *The Jews of the United States, 1654–2000* (Berkeley: University of California Press, 2004). On the complexities of Eastern European Ashkenazic identity stretched across modern empires following the partitions of Poland, see Eli Lederhendler, "Did Russian Jewry Exist Prior to 1917?" in *Jews and Jewish Life in Russia and the Soviet Union*, ed. Yaacov Ro'i (Tel Aviv: Cummings Center Series, 1994), 15–27; and Scott Ury, "Who, What, When, Where, and Why Is Polish Jewry? Envisioning, Constructing, and Possessing Polish Jewry," *Jewish Social Studies*, n.s., 6, no. 3 (2000): 205–28.

14 Stanislawski, *Zionism and the Fin de Siècle*, 6–9.

15 Also of note are Stanislawski's introduction to Vladimir Jabotinsky, *The Five*, trans. Michael R. Katz (Ithaca, NY: Cornell University Press, 2005), ix–xiv; and Michael Stanislawski, "Jabotinsky as Playwright: New Texts, New Subtexts," *Studies in Contemporary Jewry* 12 (1997): 40–54.

16 Michael Stanislawski, *Autobiographical Jews: Essays in Jewish Self-Fashioning* (Seattle: University of Washington Press, 2004). Additional related studies include Michael Stanislawski, with Barbara Kirshenblatt-Gimblett and Marcus Moseley, "Introduction," in *Awakening Lives: Autobiographies of Jewish Youth in Poland Before the Holocaust*, ed. Jeffrey Shandler (New Haven, CT: Yale University Press, 2002), xi–xlii; Michael Stanislawski, "Simone Weill et Raïssa Maritain," *Les Cahiers du Judaisme* 11 (2002): 97–107; and Michael Stanislawski, "Louise Nevelson's Self-Fashioning: The 'Author of Her Own Life,'" in *The Sculpture of Louise Nevelson: Constructing a Legend*, ed. Louise Nevelson, Brooke Kamin Rapaport, Arthur C. Danto, and Gabriel de Guzman (New Haven, CT: Yale University Press, 2007), 27–35.

17 Note, for instance, the two important series: Penguin's Schocken/Nextbook Jewish Encounters sequence of biographies and Yale University Press's Jewish Lives series.

18 "AHR Roundtable: Rethinking Anti-Semitism," special section of *American Historical Review* 123, no. 4 (October 2018): 1122–245; Sol Goldberg, Scott

Ury, and Kalman Weiser, eds., *Key Concepts in the Study of Antisemitism* (London: Palgrave Macmillan, 2020); Guy Miron, Verd Noam, Miriam Frankel, Nadav Ne'eman, Scott Ury, and Shmuel Feiner, *Antisemitism: Historical Concept, Public Discourse*, special issue of *Zion* 75, nos. 1–4 (2020) (Hebrew); and David Engel, "Away from a Definition of Antisemitism: An Essay in the Semantics of Historical Description," in *Rethinking European Jewish History*, ed. Jeremy Cohen and Moshe Rosman (Liverpool, UK: Liverpool University Press / Littman Library of Jewish Civilization, 2009), 30–53.

19 Michael Stanislawski, "A Jewish Monk? A Legal and Ideological Analysis of the Origins of the 'Who Is a Jew' Controversy in Israel," in *Text and Context: Essays in Modern Jewish History and Historiography in Honor of Ismar Schorsch*, ed. Eli Lederhendler and Jack Wertheimer (New York: Jewish Theological Seminary, 2005), 547–77.

20 Michael Stanislawski, "Jewish Apostasy in Russia: A Tentative Typology," in *Jewish Apostasy in the Modern World*, ed. Todd M. Endelman (New York: Holmes & Meier, 1987), 189–205.

21 Besides the studies already cited, note also Michael Stanislawski, "Von Jugendstil zum 'Judenstil': Universalismus und Nationalismus in Werk Ephraim Moses Liliens," in *Zionistische Utopie-israelitische Realität*, ed. Michael Brenner and Yfaat Weiss (Munich: C. H. Beck, 1999), 68–101; and Michael Stanislawski, "The Jews and Russian Culture and Politics, 1881–1991," in *Russian Jewish Artists in a Century of Change, 1890–1990*, ed. Susan Goodman (New York: Prestel, 1995), 16–27. Mention should also be made of Stanislawski's pioneering work in developing a Jewish historical canon for pedagogical purposes. See Michael Stanislawski, William Hallo, and David Ruderman, eds., *Heritage: Civilization and the Jews—Study Guide* (New York: Praeger, 1984); and Michael Stanislawski, William Hallo, and David Ruderman, eds., *Heritage: Civilization and the Jews—Source Reader* (New York: Praeger, 1984).

22 Michael Stanislawski, "The Tsarist Mishneh Torah: A Study in the Cultural Politics of the Russian Haskalah," *Proceedings of the American Academy for Jewish Research* 50 (1983): 165–83; Michael Stanislawski, "The Jewish and Muslim Enlightenments in Russia: Judah Leib Gordon and Ismail Bey Gasprinskii," in *Jews and Muslims in the Russian Empire and the Soviet Union*, ed. Franziska Davies, Martin Schulze Wessel, and Michael Brenner (Göttingen: Vandenhoeck & Ruprecht, 2015), 31–46.

23 Michael Stanislawski, "Reflections on the Russian Rabbinate," in *Jewish Religious Leadership: Image and Reality*, ed. Jack Wertheimer (New York: Jewish

Theological Seminary, 2004), 2: 429–46; Michael Stanislawski, "Paradoxes of Leniency: Rabbi Moshe Feinstein on Conservative Marriages and Divorces," in *Let the Old Make Way for the New: Studies in the Social and Cultural History of Eastern European Jewry, Presented to Immanuel Etkes*, ed. David Assaf and Ada Rapoport-Albert (Jerusalem: Merkaz Shazar, 2009), 2: 261–79.

24 Stanislawski, "Yiddish *Shevet Yehudah.*"

25 See, most recently, Adam Teller, *Rescue the Surviving Souls: The Great Jewish Refugee Crisis of the Seventeenth Century* (Princeton, NJ: Princeton University Press, 2020).

26 On this topic, see also Ada Rapoport-Albert, "Hagiography with Footnotes: Edifying Tales and the Writing of History in Hasidism," *History and Theory* 27, no. 4 (1988): 119–59.

27 See, for instance, David B. Ruderman, *Early Modern Jewry: A New Cultural History* (Princeton, NJ: Princeton University Press, 2010), 202–6.

28 Salo W. Baron, "Ghetto and Emancipation," *Menorah Journal* 14 (1928): 515–26.

29 Salo W. Baron, "The Impact of the Revolution of 1848 on Jewish Emancipation," *Jewish Social Studies* 11, no. 3 (July 1949): 211.

30 For general overviews, see Marsha L. Rozenblit and Jonathan Karp, eds., *World War I and the Jews: Conflict and Transformation in Europe, the Middle East, and America* (New York: Berghahn, 2017); and Edward Madigan and Gideon Reuveni, eds., *The Jewish Experience of the First World War* (London: Palgrave Macmillan, 2019).

PART I

ENCOUNTERS AND TRANSLATIONS IN HISTORY, LAW, AND MEMORY

1

A Convert's Yiddish Translation of *Yeven Meẓulah*

Edward Fram and Jonathan Gribetz

In "The Yiddish *Shevet Yehudah*: A Study in the 'Ashkenization' of a Spanish-Jewish Classic," Michael Stanislawski analyzed the first Yiddish translation of *Shevet yehudah*, the Hebrew text of Jewish suffering and persecution written in the wake of the expulsion of the Jews from the Iberian Peninsula. Uncovering important differences between the Hebrew original, printed in 1553, and the Yiddish translation that appeared in Cracow in 1591, Stanislawski, our teacher, linked these changes to the translator's worldview and ideology, which were different from those of the Hebrew author who experienced the Spanish Expulsion.

Adapting a text to the sensibilities of the Yiddish target audience was not an innovation of the translator of *Shevet yehudah*. Yiddish translations of medieval and Renaissance epics often suppressed or modified references that were overtly Christian or deemed inappropriate for Jewish readers.[1] In the case of the Yiddish *Shevet yehudah*, Stanislawski exposed the cultural rifts between Sephardic and Ashkenazic societies that the translation reflected. Stanislawski identified several rubrics under which he categorized the Yiddish translator's additions, emendations, and excisions. The otherwise unknown Yiddish translator was careful to attribute events to divine retribution rather than natural causes, to remove references to Jewish usury, and to defend the Talmud and rabbinic Judaism. The translator omitted references to Christian miracles and claims of supersession and excised accounts of Jewish conversion to Christianity. "Until the secrets of the dozens of yet unstudied premodern Yiddish texts are revealed," Stanislawski noted, "it is impossible to know how typical this process," which he termed Ashkenization, was in "the annals of early modern Jewish folk literature."[2]

Responding to this call for further scholarship on Yiddish translations of Hebrew texts in the early modern period, in this essay we look at a different pair of texts. We examine some of the changes made in the course of "translating" into Yiddish Nathan Neta (alternatively rendered Note or Nata) Hannover's *Yeven meẓulah*, a Hebrew chronicle of the events that have come to be known in Jewish memory as the Khmelnytsky massacres (1648–1649).[3] The slaughter of Jews was just one element of a broader rebellion—with religious, economic, and social underpinnings—led by Cossacks under Bogdan Khmelnytsky against the domination of the Polish nobility. The violent deaths of tens of thousands of Jews were, for many Jews then and since, the central and most salient feature of the uprising.[4]

Originally published in 1653, Hannover's narrative appeared in a significantly emended form in Yiddish translation in 1686.[5] Although this pair of texts is not exactly parallel to that which Stanislawski analyzed, because in our case both the Hebrew and the Yiddish were presumably written for Ashkenazic Jews, we nevertheless identify some fascinating transformations that resulted from the Yiddish translator's deletions, additions, and emendations. These changes were not due to Ashkenization, but they were, we argue, informed both by the distinct assumptions that seventeenth-century authors had about readers of Hebrew prose as opposed to Yiddish poetry and, just as important, by the translator's quite different background, and his correspondingly distinct education and assumptions, from that of the original author.

Nathan and Moses

Nathan Neta Hannover spent his early life in Ostroh, Volhynia.[6] He became an itinerant preacher and probably a successful one at that, for he was invited to give a public address in Cracow during the holiday of Sukkot in 1645. In 1648 Hannover was living in Zasław, where his in-laws resided. In the wake of the events in Eastern Europe, Hannover fled westward and spent several years traveling through the German lands, where he gave homiletical lectures "every Sabbath" to support himself and his family.[7] By 1652 Hannover had settled in Venice, where *Yeven meẓulah* was first published. Hannover would go on to serve as a rabbi in Livorno in 1654 and later in Iași and Uherský Brod (now in the Czech Republic), where he, together with more than 350 Jews and Christians, was killed by Hungarian Kuruc rebels in July 1683.[8] During his lifetime Hannover succeeded in printing a reworking of the sermon that he delivered in Cracow; a Hebrew-German-Latin-Italian conversation lexicon, text, and guidebook for travelers; and a collection of prayers for Lurianic kabbalistic rituals. He mentioned that he had prepared other rabbinic works but Hannover did not succeed in having them printed before he was killed.[9]

The translator of *Yeven meẓulah* was also well traveled but had a different personal background from Hannover. Moses ben Abraham was from Mikulov (Nikolsburg), where there was an important Jewish community in the mid-seventeenth century.[10] Moses, however, was not part of this community; he was born a Christian and presumably grew up on the other side of town under a different name.[11] We know nothing of his life as a Christian and do not know what moved him to convert, a dangerous decision in the Holy Roman Empire, where conversion to Judaism was deemed an act of apostasy and punishable by death.[12] Apparently after deciding to convert and perhaps after spending some time in Poland, Moses emigrated to the Netherlands, where he could live openly as Moses ben Abraham the Jew.[13] In 1680 Moses married a Jewish woman, and by the mid-1680s he was the compositor (and possibly the translator and editor) of the Yiddish newspaper *Dinstagishe un Fraytagishe Kurant* in Amsterdam.[14] Eventually he would leave Amsterdam and move to Berlin, Dessau, Frankfurt an der Oder, and Halle, but while still in Amsterdam he translated Hannover's *Yeven meẓulah* into Yiddish and later set up his own publishing business, where he published both Hebrew and Yiddish works.[15]

Moses ben Abraham's Yiddish translation was published by David Segel, who was involved in financing, editing, and, later, correcting works produced at the Amsterdam printing house of his father, Uri Phoebus.[16] The family printing house focused on selling books to Polish Jews. Moses ben Abraham's small book about the tragedy of 1648–1649 would certainly have spoken to Polish Jews both in the East and to those who had migrated westward in the wake of the upheavals of the midcentury.[17]

Why Translate *Yeven Meẓulah* into Yiddish?

Hebrew was the universal language of educated Jews, and a text written in Hebrew transcended any one locale. This was no small matter for Hannover, who published *Yeven meẓulah* in Venice, far away from the scene of the events described.[18] No less important, traditionally, Hebrew texts had much greater staying power than those written in local vernaculars.[19] But because only a small segment of Eastern European Jewry was able to understand a Hebrew text such as Hannover's, the original Hebrew *Yeven meẓulah* was directed at a relatively limited, erudite male readership. Thus the 1686 project of translating the Hebrew text into Yiddish must be viewed as a popularization aimed at making the book accessible to the broad Yiddish-reading audience, men and women alike. After all, a Yiddish book's readers would include women and men who lacked formal education. A talented Hebrew-to-Yiddish translator could transform the original into something that the Jewish masses would appreciate.

That, in our case, the translator was neither a native Yiddish speaker nor the beneficiary of lifelong Jewish education makes Moses ben Abraham's ability to produce such a translation all the more impressive and, at the same time, helps account for some of the ways that his Yiddish *Yeven metsulah* differs from Hannover's Hebrew original.

Moreover, there was an art to Yiddish translation. Like many other Yiddish texts, and unlike Hannover's original work of prose, Moses ben Abraham's translation was written almost entirely in rhymed couplets.[20] Although there was no set meter, the translation generally followed an AABBCC rhyme scheme.[21] Presenting Yiddish texts in rhyme, whether biblical translations, heroic epics, or, later, even legal instruction, was a well-established tradition in Yiddish literature that went back to at least the fourteenth century.[22] The use of rhyme should be seen not only as part of a convention but also as an effort to make the Yiddish *Yeven metsulah* more mellifluous for the Yiddish reader.[23] The use of rhyme was not without its pitfalls, as sometimes the need to maintain the rhyme scheme compelled the translator to take poetic license.²⁴ For instance, describing the sociopolitical situation before the massacres, Hannover wrote,

> *Ve-am ha-yevanim hayu holkhim ve-dalim* [2 Samuel 3:1] *ve-hayu nivzim u-shefalim* [Malachi 2:9] *ve-hayu la-avadim ve-li-shefaḥot* [Deuteronomy 28:68] *le-am polin ve-le-yehudim, lehavdil.*²⁵

> And the Greek [Orthodox] nation became poorer and poorer, and they were vile and base, and they became slaves and maidservants to the Polish people and the Jews, not to compare [Gentiles and Jews].

The Yiddish translation rendered this somewhat differently.

> *Ober di yevonim ir priẓim un hern zayn geblibn far akht un dos folk di yevonim hobin gemuzt zayn ẓu di polkn knekht / un zayn nokh der ẓu gehaltin gevorn gor shlekht. Un hobn gam ken di yehudim iber di yevonim moshel gevezn / nur draysik toyzint man hot zikh der melekh unter di yevanim oys gelozn.*²⁶

> But the Greek [Orthodox] were scorned by the [Polish] nobles and lords and the Greek [Orthodox] people were forced to be slaves to the Poles. And they were consequently treated very badly. And the Jews too lorded over the Greek [Orthodox]. The king only liberated thirty thousand of these Greek [Orthodox].²⁷

Moses ben Abraham separated the fact that Poles and Jews ruled over the population Hannover and he both referred to as "Greek" (we will refer to them as "Greek Orthodox") into two sentences, the second of which could then rhyme with the following sentence's *gelozn*, "were liberated." As a result, the word *lehavdil*, a pious convention that accentuated the difference between Jews and Gentiles, had no place.²⁸ Here, as in other instances, the rhyme scheme dictated some of the translator's editorial choices.

In producing his text, Moses ben Abraham did not merely translate Hebrew into Yiddish, nor did he simply transform prose into verse. By analyzing other sorts of changes in the text, we are able more clearly to discern Moses's innovations and, perhaps, motivations. In comparing Moses ben Abraham's text to Hannover's, we find three sorts of differences. The most common differences are excisions, that is, details that appear in the Hebrew but that were not translated into the Yiddish. The least common differences are additions, that is, details that appear in the Yiddish but have no parallel in the Hebrew. The third type of differences are alterations, that is, points in the Yiddish that are different from details in the Hebrew. As we seek to account for the differences between the texts, we are on firmest ground concerning the second and third types, that is, the additions and alterations. We can see clearly, in the case of alterations, the disjuncture between Moses ben Abraham's raw materials and his final product, and we can try to explain changes that the translator/adaptor deliberately made. For the additions we know that Moses ben Abraham chose to add to the original text. We are on shakier ground, however, when it comes to excisions, because Moses ben Abraham's text is much shorter than Hannover's and it is difficult to ascertain whether an excision was motivated by a particular issue in the text that Moses sought to avoid or simply by his need to cut words wherever possible because of the mundane costs of printing. As we will show, certain patterns appear in the excisions and we regard some as significant, but we recognize that arguments from absence are, perforce, methodologically knotty.

Political History or Chronicle of Persecution?

Moses ben Abraham's translation projected a different frame of reference from Hannover's work. Whereas Hannover provided his readers with numerous details about the Polish monarchy and internal politics and intrigues, these facts were excised from the Yiddish text.[29] Moses ben Abraham focused more narrowly on the persecution of the Jews; internecine conflicts between non-Jews did not contribute to his tale of Jewish suffering.[30] Hannover's introduction and, in particular, his glowing description of Jewish life in Poland before 1648 that made the magnitude of what was lost so much more poignant were not included in the translation, because these too added little to the tale and took up significant space.[31] Even Hannover's emphasis on Jewish martyrdom was rarely transmitted to the Yiddish reader.

In trying to explain the cause of these violent events, Hannover recognized that Polish Jews had mistreated the local population and explicitly acknowledged that the Greek Orthodox had legitimate reasons to resent the Jews. Yet in keeping with traditional Jewish historiography, Hannover ultimately saw the destruction of synagogues and the killing of about 200 Jews in the Pavlyuk uprising (1637) as a divine punishment.[32] Where Hannover emphasized the role of Israel's sins, Moses ben Abraham spoke of God's mercy and prayed for immediate redemption.[33] Despite the fact that the frontispiece of the Yiddish translation attributed the fate of Polish Jewry in 1648–1649 to sin, in the body of the translation Moses ben Abraham never assigned the fate of the Jews to sin or any other cause.[34] He reported the events of 1648–1649 without attempting to explain them.[35]

Moses ben Abraham's translation did not incorporate most of the biblical verses and rabbinic idioms that Hannover used, some of which alluded to experiences that were central to Jewish self-identity and helped create a sense of cultural and historical continuity.[36] Playing on the word *Greek*, for instance, Hannover connected the Greek Orthodox of his time with the ancient Seleucid Greeks who, according to a midrash, forced the Jews to choose between apostasy and death.[37] Hannover's partial citation of the midrash lacked context, but wording from a Hebrew prayer recited on Hanukkah alerted liturgically literate readers to the nexus between the persecutions and heroism of the present and those of the past.[38] As a recent convert, Moses ben Abraham may not have recognized these somewhat opaque allusions and thus left them aside.[39]

Among the most troubling passages in *Yeven mezulah* is an eyewitness report that Hannover said he received from a survivor of the attack on Narol. According to the woman, "For five days they had no food, and they ate human flesh and they cut limbs from the bodies of the dead, roasted them, and ate them."[40] Hannover wanted to convey to his readers the extent of Jewish suffering. Moses ben Abraham omitted these gruesome details in his translation as well as the report that "several hundred Jews" who had taken refuge in the synagogue in the town were killed by the attackers and then the synagogue and the bodies in it were set ablaze. Moses ben Abraham was certainly acutely aware of the horrors of war and, in other contexts, did not shy away from relaying them to readers. Indeed, almost three-quarters of the articles in his *Kurant* focused on war and sometimes included graphic descriptions, such as the decapitation of the bodies of Turks by imperial forces, who then hung them up around the city of Ofen (Buda) as a message to the local population.[41] Perhaps Moses ben Abraham did not want to include such horrifying, disturbing details about Jews in his translation. It seems more likely, though, that these excisions were, again, a consequence of practical publishing exigencies. As in the *Kurant*, in translating *Yeven mezulah* Moses ben Abraham constantly had to make editorial decisions because of limited space.[42] His publisher was often strapped for cash, and the local Ashkenazic population of about 1,500 adults was among the poorest in all of Amsterdam.[43] The final product had to be affordable for this audience if the publisher was to see a return on his investment.[44]

From time to time the Yiddish text contained embellishments of the Hebrew original. For example, in describing the events in Bar, Hannover explained that the town was strongly fortified and that the Poles and Jews were able to hold the Greek Orthodox and Tatars at bay for a few days. However, according to Hannover, the Greek Orthodox residents of the town betrayed the Poles and Jews and dug a tunnel to let the attackers into the town. Moses ben Abraham added, without any apparent source, that the Greek Orthodox residents of Bar had previously taken an oath that they would help the Poles defend the town.[45] This made Greek Orthodox duplicity even viler to the Yiddish reader.

Moses ben Abraham's translation altered some of the most moving passages in *Yeven mezulah*. The events in Tulczyn are a case in point. Hannover described how the Jews and Poles joined in a mutual defense pact. However, the Poles reneged on their promise and turned the Jews over to the Cossacks, who led the military efforts of the rebellion, when the Poles believed that they had an opportunity to save themselves at the Jews' expense. Incensed by the betrayal, the Jews wanted to attack the Poles but, according to Hannover, the head of the local yeshiva, Rabbi Aaron, spoke to his co-religionists and said, "Hear my brothers and my nation. We are in the Diaspora among the nations. If you will lay a hand on the princes, all the kings of Edom [i.e., Catholic Christendom] will hear of it and they will take their revenge on all our brethren who are in the Diaspora, God forbid! Therefore, if it is a heavenly decree, let us accept our sentence with joy."[46] The Yiddish translation made no mention of "all the kings of Edom" and referred only to the princes of Poland, who would punish local Jews if they rebelled.[47] Tulczyn Jewry's self-sacrifice in solidarity with Ashkenazic Jewry was reduced to solidarity with the Jews of Poland. Perhaps Moses ben Abraham, the convert from Christianity, did not appreciate the latent valence of the term *Edom*.[48]

Martyrdom and Paradise

In Hannover's portrayal of the events, when the Jews of Tulczyn understood that they were about to face a choice between conversion and death, three of the leading rabbis warned the "holy people" that they should die martyrs' deaths. The people unanimously affirmed their commitment to God in the most resounding way possible: "Hear Israel, the Lord is our God, the Lord is One" (Deuteronomy 6:4), tying them to perhaps the archetypical Jewish martyr, Rabbi Akiva, who, according to the Talmud, died as these words left his mouth.[49] This must have sent a chill up the spine of some readers, yet it was lost in translation. Rather than emphasize the steadfast belief of Jews, Moses ben Abraham altered the discourse and had the rabbis remind the people that if they died for the sanctification of God's name, they would immediately inherit the next world. Hannover made no mention of such an idea in his story of 1648–1649. For him, martyrdom declared the truth of Jewish belief and the steadfastness of the Jewish people. It was an end in and of itself.

Similarly, in the continuation of the Tulczyn story, an intermediary was said to have approached the Jews and placed a flag in the ground. Reminiscent of a talmudic story of a mother and her seven sons who were killed during the Hadrianic persecutions, the messenger called out for any Jews who wanted to save their lives by converting to come forward and sit under the flag.[50] In Hannover's text the refusal of the Jews of Tulczyn to do so said all that was necessary to be said. They unanimously accepted the divine decree.[51] In the Yiddish too, no Jew came forward, but in Moses ben Abraham's telling the Jews' rejection of the offer had a clear motivation. Moses ben Abraham attributed this resilience to their desire to enter the Garden of Eden after death. Martyrdom, for Moses ben Abraham, was again a means to reach Paradise rather than a selfless statement of belief in a fundamental Jewish dogma.

The idea that Jewish martyrs have a place in Paradise appeared in Jewish sources in the wake of the First Crusade, and the notion that the righteous took their place in the heavenly world almost directly after death was found in some medieval Jewish sources.[52] Perhaps this was all known to Moses ben Abraham. However, his view of martyrdom and heaven likely had a different source. In the book of Luke 16:19–23, Lazarus and the rich man who shunned him in life appear to have gone to their respective places in Heaven and Hell immediately after death. This well-established Christian idea may already have been deeply embedded in Moses's consciousness and found expression in his translation. In this instance of translation from Hebrew into Yiddish, we may be witnessing not Ashkenization but rather Christianization—or, more precisely, the introduction of Christian sensibilities and concepts into a Jewish text.

If in certain cases Moses ben Abraham emphasized the reward of Paradise for Jewish martyrdom, in other instances he avoided the language of martyrdom altogether. Hannover described the cases of two Jewish maidens who were captured by individual Cossacks during the attack on Niemirów. Trapped by their captors and forced to marry, Hannover portrayed each as being determined to maintain her Jewish identity to the end.[53] One of the young women tricked her Cossack captor into killing her just before consummating the marriage, thus, Hannover said, avoiding defilement and instead dying for the sanctification of God's name.[54] The second woman was on her way to her nuptials in a church on the other side of a river when she jumped from a bridge to her death. Hannover labeled this too an act of martyrdom. In both cases Hannover called on God to avenge these self-inflicted deaths.[55] Moses ben Abraham did not use the language of martyrdom in his narration of these events, nor did he note the first woman's specific desire not to be defiled. Yiddish readers were left to draw their own conclusions about the character of these women's deaths.

To be sure, Moses ben Abraham was aware of the Jewish notion of dying for the sanctification of God's name. Hannover described how the kabbalist and local preacher Rabbi Samson ben Pesaḥ of Ostropole and 300 men huddled in the synagogue in Polonne in fervent prayer, wearing shrouds and prayer shawls, the clothes in which adult Jewish males were generally buried, outwardly demonstrating their readiness to die as Jews. In Hannover's depiction of the events, their enemies entered the synagogue and simply slaughtered them. They never faced an immediate choice between apostasy and death.[56] Confusing Rabbi Samson with the sixteenth-century Safed kabbalist, "our master and teacher, Rabbi Isaac Luria," Moses ben Abraham narrated this story and added that each person died for the sanctification of God's name.[57] In this instance, Hannover did not share the sentiment. Hannover asserted that all these men were killed on holy ground (i.e., in the synagogue) and called on God to avenge their deaths, but he did not label them martyrs.[58] As a relatively recent convert, Moses ben Abraham may not have been sensitive to all the nuances of Jewish life and law. He understood that there was a concept of martyrdom in Judaism, but he does not seem to have appreciated its classic definition in Ashkenazic culture since at least the time of the First Crusades: the choice between life as a Christian and death as a Jew. That is, faced with a demand to accept idolatry—and medieval Ashkenazic Jews generally viewed Christianity with its icons and belief in the Trinity as a form of idolatry—or be killed, Jewish law demanded that a Jew give up his or her life.[59] However, if one did not face a choice and was simply killed as or for being a Jew, one did not generally qualify as a martyr in classical medieval Jewish sources. Moses ben Abraham's Yiddish translation, then, reveals the recent convert's only partial appreciation for—or acceptance of—contemporary Jewish concepts.

Another case in point is found in Moses ben Abraham's translation of the Hebrew term *nefesh* (soul) in Hannover's *Yeven meẓulah*. During the events of 1648, Hannover lived in Zasław, and when the community there heard of what had happened in nearby Polonne, some left behind all their worldly goods and fled "to save our souls and the souls of our sons and daughters."[60] Hannover's use of the Hebrew term for "soul" (*nefesh*) evokes a depth of connotations from biblical and Jewish thought. Psalm 33:19–20 ("to save their soul from death . . . our souls waited for the Lord") makes it clear that saving one's soul (*nefesh*) from death implies more than just rescuing one's body.[61] The multifaceted nature of the soul seems to have been lost on Moses ben Abraham, who wrote that everyone who fled only wanted "to save their bodies [*guf*]," omitting the mix of corporeal and spiritual that Hannover's term had implied.[62]

Moreover, Hannover did not criticize those who fled; in fact, he and his family were among them. By contrast, and without any apparent source in Hannover's text, Moses ben Abraham added that some men left their wives behind, a violation of God's command that husband and wife should be "one body [*ayn layb*]," a reference to Genesis 2:24 ("and they should be one flesh").[63] From a traditional Jewish perspective, this was a rather strange interpretation of the biblical text. Based on his understanding of the Talmud, the classic medieval Jewish commentator Rashi (d. 1105) had explained this verse to mean that a man and a woman together are a union that can create one flesh, that is, a child.[64] The idea that a husband could not leave his wife behind may have been unpalatable from a moral perspective, but, according to the rabbinic tradition, this was not the meaning of the biblical command in Genesis. However, Christian understandings of Genesis 2:24—and of Matthew 19:5–6—spoke of making two people into one flesh. The Vulgate translated Genesis 2:24 as "erunt duo in carne una," suggesting that husband and wife cannot be divided. Matthew 19 echoed this: "Itaque jam non sunt duo, sed una caro [so they are no longer two, but one flesh]." Similarly, Martin Luther spoke of husband and wife becoming one, "und se warden sein ein Fleisch." The remainder of the verse in Matthew 19:6 only strengthened the notion that husband and wife cannot be separated: "Quod ergo Deus conjunxit, homo non separet [what God has joined together let no man separate]." Moses ben Abraham may have converted to Judaism, but, at least in the years shortly after his conversion, he continued to be informed by a Christian frame of reference and, perhaps unwittingly, introduced it into his Yiddish translation of *Yeven meẓulah*. Indeed, Moses ben Abraham also occasionally softened anti-Christian terminology. Where Hannover referred to the eve of an upcoming Christian festival as the holiday of apostasy or destruction (*simḥat ha-shemad*), Moses ben Abraham translated it as the eve of "an important holiday."[65]

Wiping Out the Memory of, or Not Forgiving, Enemies

Moses ben Abraham's frame of reference is further revealed in a short comment in his description of the killing of the Jews of Zasław. According to Hannover, about 200 Jews who were too sick to flee the town were slaughtered by the Greek Orthodox mob.[66] Moses ben Abraham took some minor liberties in his translation of this section and left out some of the most gruesome and agonizing details of the story. Not only did he not mention that the Jews requested to be killed at the cemetery, where they were said to have been crowded into a building—perhaps the cleansing house where the bodies of Jews were generally prepared for burial—and that they were murdered and burned there, but he left out the hair-raising fate of the local Catholic priests who, Hannover reported, were skinned alive. What Moses ben Abraham did do was add something that was totally out of context: a short prayer that God should not forgive the perpetrators.[67] Surely Hannover, who invoked the phrase "may his name be blotted out" whenever referring to Khmelnytsky, would never have considered the possibility that God might forgive the Cossacks, their leaders, or their allies for what they did to the Jews. (Moses ben Abraham also never added "may his name be blotted out" after mentioning Khmelnytsky's name, although Moses surely had no fondness for the leader, whom he once labeled "an evil man.")[68] In another instance Hannover wrote "May God avenge their blood" after describing how, in Krzemieniec, the Cossacks slaughtered Jewish children like animals. Here, as earlier, Moses ben Abraham wrote, "May God, may He be blessed, not forgive them," the perpetrators, that is.[69] "May God not forgive them" is a substantially different wish, based on a different set of assumptions, from either "May his name be blotted out" or "May God avenge their blood." One would only pray for one's persecutor not to be forgiven by God if one had reason to think that, ordinarily, God would forgive the persecutor. This thought likely never crossed Hannover's mind, because the notion of forgiving one's enemies was not a normative Jewish idea. It was, however, very much a Christian idea. In the Sermon on the Mount, Jesus said to his followers, "Pray for those who persecute you" (Matthew 5:44).[70] According to Luke 23:34, as Jesus was led to the crucifixion, he was reported to have said, "Father, forgive them [i.e., those who called for his death] for they know not what they do."[71] Seventeenth-century Jews did not call for any type of pity, compassion, or clemency for those whom Hannover called "the haters of Israel."[72] In praying for God *not* to forgive the perpetrators, Moses ben Abraham's Christian sensibilities crept into his translation project.

Popularization and Sanitization

In his study of the Yiddish *Shevet yehudah*, Stanislawski pointed to the Yiddish version's "censorship of virtually every reference in this long chronicle of Jewish suffering and persecution to the conversion of Jews to Christianity, either voluntarily or by force."[73] This was not the case in Moses ben Abraham's text. Although Hannover's *Yeven meẓulah* is not nearly as filled with references to Jewish conversion to Christianity as Solomon ibn Verga's *Shevet yehudah*—not least because of the distinct nature of the respective historical events chronicled—when Hannover did write about conversion, our translator often translated faithfully.

Moses ben Abraham did, however, prefer to excise key elements of a crucial discussion about conversion—especially about its subsequent societal implications—that appears in Hannover's original. In his chapter on the massacres at Ostrog, Hannover wrote about the Polish king's ordinance that "whoever had been forced to change his faith, may return to his former faith."[74] Hannover continued:

> Also the women whom the Cossacks married by force, fled to the cities which were populated by Jews. Thus hundreds of forced converts became Jews again. In the places where severe carnage took place, hundreds of boys and girls and infants had been converted. The Jews took them back by force from the hands of the Gentiles. After thorough investigation, they provided them with identifying tags giving the names of the families to which they belonged. These were hung on the neck of each child. Many women had become *agunot* [here, a reference to women who could not remarry because it was unclear whether their husbands were still alive], and many widows who had become subject to levirate marriage, became *agunot* because the levir [a widow's former brother-in-law required by biblical law to marry or renounce marriage to her] had departed from the land.[75]

Moses ben Abraham's version of this story retained the discussion of Jewish conversion to Christianity, but all details related to the familial and social consequences of these conversions disappeared.

> At the same time the king called out. Whichever Jew deserted his faith. And whichever Jew was coerced [to convert]. Because the non-Jews had convinced many hundred to convert. Everyone should again be free to be a Jew. Many hundred people returned. And again, embraced Judaism [*yehud*]. And again, came under Israel. And many hundred small children were taken back from the non-Jews by force. They had to give back both young and old.[76]

In the Yiddish there was no mention of women being forced to marry Cossacks, and there was no question about the identity of the true parents of the rescued children or any discussion of the process of returning them to their proper parents; nor was there any reference to *agunot*. Whereas

Hannover stressed the problems that these events posed for Jewish families and the implicit doubts about the Jewish lineage of many children, Moses ben Abraham cleansed the text of these issues.

Discerning the translator's motivation for this excision, as for the others we have already discussed, is necessarily speculative, but we would like to propose several possibilities for consideration (beyond the overarching practical economic need for greater concision throughout the text). Insofar as Moses ben Abraham understood his role to be not only translator but also popularizer—producing a text that would be read by classes of Jews far beyond the elite readership of the Hebrew—he may have preferred to avoid controversial issues, especially religious-genealogical ones. If there were doubts about the Jewishness of children who were returned to Jewish families after the massacres, perhaps Moses ben Abraham reasoned that these were not for the masses to worry about. Moreover, Moses ben Abraham prepared his translation more than three decades after the events of 1648–1649 transpired. Those children who had been returned to their families after the massacres were now adults, indeed potential readers of this translation. Their personal status had already been determined by the rabbinic leadership and the community, and there was no reason, Moses ben Abraham may have believed, to raise the question again in a popularization. Finally, we can only wonder whether Moses ben Abraham's identity as a convert to Judaism may have informed his preference to avoid discussing matters of lineage in Judaism. It is certainly possible that, as the biological child of Christian parents, Moses ben Abraham was uncomfortable addressing problems associated with genealogical "impurity" in Jewish society. For whatever reason or assortment of reasons, Moses ben Abraham removed this entire discussion from his text.

*   *   *

As we have seen, Hannover's *Yeven meẓulah* and Moses ben Abraham's translation are different texts. Moses ben Abraham's work was carefully prepared in rhyme, but he had different assumptions and a different background and wrote for a different audience than Hannover did. He also had limited space to work with. Just as the late sixteenth-century translator of *Shevet yehudah* adapted the text for his audience, so too did Moses ben Abraham. Yet the importance of the popularization of *Yeven meẓulah* should not be underestimated. Whereas *Shevet yehudah* was reprinted in

Hebrew not long after its original publication and gained an almost immediate foothold, the Hebrew *Yeven meẓulah* did not fare quite so well.[77] After the events of 1648–1649 it was Me'ir ben Samuel of Szczebrzeszyn's chronicle *Ẓok ha-itim* that was published in Cracow (1650), Saloniki (1652), and then plagiarized and republished in Venice in 1656.[78] Hannover's *Yeven meẓulah* was not reprinted until 1727. Moses ben Abraham's Yiddish translation and popularization may have helped to raise the profile of Hannover's work above those of other Hebrew chronicles and contributed to its being republished and retranslated and ultimately becoming the most popular chronicle of the fate of the Polish Jewry in 1648–1649. That this was the work of a recent convert to Judaism makes the project all the more remarkable.

Notes

1. See, among many others, Arnold Paucker, "Yiddish Versions of Early German Prose Novels," *Journal of Jewish Studies* 10, nos. 3–4 (1959): 151–67; and Jean Baumgarten, *Introduction to Old Yiddish Literature*, trans. Jerold C. Frakes (Oxford, UK: Oxford University Press, 2005), 135–37, 160–62.
2. Michael Stanislawski, "The Yiddish *Shevet Yehudah*: A Study in the 'Ashkenization' of a Spanish-Jewish Classic," in *Jewish History and Jewish Memory: Essays in Honor of Yosef Hayim Yerushalmi*, ed. Elisheva Carlebach, John Efron, and David Myers (Hanover, NH: University Press of New England, 1998), 146.
3. For an English translation, see Nathan Nata Hannover, *Abyss of Despair: The Famous 17th Century Chronicle Depicting Jewish Life in Russia and Poland During the Chmielnicki Massacres of 1648–1649*, trans. Abraham J. Mesch (New Brunswick, NJ: Transaction, 1983).
4. The number of Jewish casualties during the uprising has been the source of much disagreement. For a discussion and reassessment, see Shaul Stampfer, "What Actually Happened to the Jews of Ukraine in 1648?" *Jewish History* 17, no. 2 (2003): 207–27.
5. There have been various claims of an earlier Yiddish translation. Israel Zinberg cited a 1655 edition by the very same translator with the exact same introductory piece as the 1686 edition; see Israel Zinberg, *A History of Jewish Literature*, trans. Bernard Martin (Cincinnati: Hebrew Union College Press;

and New York: Ktav, 1975), 6: 126, 7: 231. Isaac Benjacob and Chaim Friedberg suggested that there was a 1676–1677 edition, also by the same translator as the 1686 printing; see Isaac Benjacob, *Oẓar ha-sefarim: sefer arukh li-tekhunat sifrei Yisra'el nidpasim ve-kitvei yad* (Vilnius: Romm, 1880), 2: 217, no. 130; and Chaim Friedberg, *Beit eked sefarim* (Tel Aviv: Bar-Juda, 1951), v. 2, no. 400. The 1676–1677 edition was included in Yeshayahu Vinograd, *Oẓar ha-sefer ha-ivri: reshimat ha-sefarim she-nidpesu be-ot ivrit me-reishit ha-defus ha-ivri bi-shenat 229 (1469) ad shenat 623 (1863)* (Jerusalem: Ha-makhon le-bibliografiyah memuḥshevet, 1993), Amsterdam, no. 427; and Mirjam Gutschow, *Inventory of Yiddish Publications from the Netherlands, c. 1650–c. 1950* (Leiden: Brill, 2006), 28, no. 72. Jacob Shatzky had already questioned Benjacob's and Friedberg's dating; see Jacob Shatzky, "Historish-kritisher araynfir tsum 'Yeven meẓulah' fun R. Natan Neta Hanover," in *Gzeyres takh*, by Nathan Neta Hannover (Vilnius: YIVO, 1938), 93. No physical evidence of any pre-1686 edition has been found; see Chone Shmeruk, "Yiddish Literature and Collective Memory," *Polin* 5 (1990): 181, no. 20.

6 For a biographical sketch, see Mesch's introduction to Hannover, *Abyss of Despair*, 13–22.

7 Nathan Neta Hannover, *Sefer ta'amei sukkah* (Amsterdam: Samuel ben Moses and Reuben ben Elyakum, 1652), fol. 2b.

8 See David Kaufmann, "Die Verheerung von Ungarisch Brod durch den Kuruzzenüberfall vom 14. Juli 1683," *Monatsschrift für Geschichte und Wissenschaft des Judentums* 37, nos. 6–7 (1893): 319–20.

9 See Hannover, *Abyss of Despair*, 25; Hannover, *Sefer ta'amei sukkah*, fol. 2b; Nathan Neta Hannover, *Sefer sha'arei ẓiyyon* (Amsterdam: Uri Phoebus ben Aaron ha-Levi, 1671), fol. 2b; and Y. Joseph Cohen, "Ha-sifrut ha-toranit be-Romanyah ad sof ha-me'ah ha-19," *Kiryat sefer* 44 (1969): 141–43.

10 The frontispiece of the Yiddish translation lists the translator as "the rabbi, our teacher Moses ben Abraham of blessed memory" without further specification. There was a Rabbi Moses ben Abraham who was head of the rabbinic court in Grodno and who died in 1681 (see his grandson's introduction to Moses ben Abraham of Grodno, *Tiferet le-Mosheh*, ed. Solomon ben Ḥayyim of Grodno [Berlin, 1776]). This Moses ben Abraham signed his name by noting that his father had died a martyr's death, which our translator did not do; see the rabbi's approbation to David ben Aryeh, *Sefer migdol David* (Amsterdam: Uri Phoebus ben Aaron ha-Levi, 1680), fol. 2a; as well as the entries in Israel Halperin and Israel Bartal, eds., *Pinkas va'ad arba araẓot*, 2d

ed. (Jerusalem: Mosad Bialik, 1990), 116 (no. 288) and 177 (no. 392). The frontispiece of Solomon ben Eliezer ha-Levi, *Sefer moreh ẓedek*, ed. Zadok ben Asher Wahl (Amsterdam: Moses ben Abraham, 1690), identifies Moses ben Abraham as being from Nikolsburg.

11 Moses was likely born a Catholic. Nikolsburg was a haven for Anabaptists and later Bohemian Brethren in the sixteenth century, but by the mid-seventeenth century it was again a Catholic stronghold. See J. Loserth, "Der Communismus der mährischen Wiedertäufer im 16. and 17. Jahrhundert: Beiträge zu ihrer Lehre, Geschichte und Verfassung," *Archiv für österreichische Geschichte* 81, no. 1 (1895): 286–91. Although some seventeenth-century non-Jews spoke Yiddish, particularly in the German-speaking lands, Aya Elyada has pointed out that this "was predominantly" a Protestant phenomenon; see Aya Elyada, *A Goy Who Speaks Yiddish: Christians and the Jewish Language in Early Modern Germany* (Stanford, CA: Stanford University Press, 2012), 6–7. When in Amsterdam, Moses, like the local Dutch, favored the Huguenots in their struggles against Louis XIV of France. See Hilde Pach, "Moushe's Choices: Was the Compositor of the Oldest Yiddish Newspaper a Creator or an Epigone?" *Studia Rosenthaliana* 40 (August 2007): 202.

12 See Allison P. Coudert, "Judaizing in the Seventeenth Century: Francis Mercury van Helmont and Johann Peter Späth (Moses Germanus)," in *Secret Conversions to Judaism in Early Modern Europe*, ed. Martin Mulsow and Richard Popkin (Leiden: Brill, 2004), 84, 84n33.

13 On possible time spent in Poland, see I. H. Van Eeghen, "Moses Abrahamsz, Boekdrukker in Amsterdam," *Studia Rosenthaliana* 6, no. 1 (1972): 58.

14 I. H. Van Eeghen noted that Moses married a Jewish woman in 1680, probably before coming to Amsterdam (Van Eeghen, "Moses Abrahamsz," 58). Whether she or members of her family assisted Moses in translating material remains an open question. Lajb Fuks and Renate Fuks-Mansfeld listed a Moses ben Abraham as a compositor of the Amsterdam 1680 liturgical Bible; however, this is an error. The compositor's name was Moses ben Aaron. See Lajb Fuks and Renate Fuks-Mansfeld, *Hebrew Typography in the Northern Netherlands, 1585–1815: Historical Evaluation and Descriptive Bibliography* (Leiden: Brill, 1987), 2: 273, no. 343.

15 Regarding his work at the *Kurant* and further biographical information, see, most recently, H. Pach-Oosterbroek, "Arranging Reality: The Editing Mechanisms of the World's First Yiddish Newspaper, the *Kurant* (Amsterdam, 1686–1687)," PhD diss., University of Amsterdam, 2014, pp. 79, 83–88.

16 See Fuks and Fuks-Mansfeld, *Hebrew Typography*, vol. 2, nos. 307, 337, 345.4, and 359, for examples of financing; no. 354, as an editor, and, later, no. 367, as a corrector.

17 On the importance of the Polish market for the publishing house, see Fuks and Fuks-Mansfeld, *Hebrew Typography*, 2: 236–43. Uri Phoebus eventually moved to Poland, where he founded a Hebrew printing house in Żółkiew. On Polish and Lithuania Jews in the west in the wake of the events of 1648 and the ensuing years, see Adam Teller, *Rescue the Surviving Souls: The Great Jewish Refugee Crisis of the Seventeenth Century* (Princeton, NJ: Princeton University Press, 2020), 259–71. Regarding Amsterdam in particular, see Yosef Kaplan, "Amsterdam and Ashkenazic Migration in the Seventeenth Century," *Studia Rosenthaliana* 23 (1989): 35–44.

18 In the sixteenth century there were numerous Yiddish speakers in the Italian lands and Venice was a hub of Yiddish publishing. However, as the seventeenth century progressed, Yiddish publishing generally moved eastward to Poland and later, after 1648, to Amsterdam.

19 For example, both Moses Maimonides's *Guide for the Perplexed* and his commentary on the Mishnah were written in Judeo-Arabic. The *Guide* was translated into Hebrew during Maimonides's lifetime, and the commentary was translated after his death. The works gained wide recognition only after they were translated into Hebrew.

20 Hannover's Hebrew introduction, which Moses ben Abraham did not include in his translation, was written in rhyme.

21 From time to time there were breakdowns in the rhyme scheme. See, for example, Nathan Neta Hannover, *Sefer yeven metsulah*, trans. Moses ben Abraham (Amsterdam: David ben Uri Phoebus Segel, 1686), fol. 7b.

22 See Chone Shmeruk, *Sifrut Yiddish: perakim le-toldoteihah* (Tel Aviv: Porter Institute, 1978), 118 (regarding the history of the phenomenon) and 117–36 (more generally regarding biblical translations).

23 For a sense of the pervasiveness of the use of rhyme at this time, see Ruth von Bernuth, *How the Wise Men Got to Chelm: The Life and Times of a Yiddish Folk Tradition* (New York: New York University Press, 2016), 104–5.

24 See Stefanie Stockhorst, "Defining Conventions for the Verse Epic in German: Notes on the Relationship Between Codified Poetics and Poetological Paratexts in the Baroque Poetry Reform," *Yale University Library Gazette* 82, nos. 1–2 (2007): 39–50.

25 Nathan Neta Hannover, *Sefer yeven meẓulah* (Venice: Commissaria Vendramina, 1653), fol. 2b.

26 Moses ben Abraham's translation, Hannover, *Sefer yeven metsulah* (1686), fol. 2a.

27 We have included this last sentence simply to show the rhyme; this detail is found in the Hebrew as well shortly after the passage we have quoted.

28 It is not that Moses ben Abraham was not willing to emphasize the distinction between Jews and Gentiles, because elsewhere he used the word *lehavdil* in this very way ("bay areyli[m] un lehavdil bay yehudi[m] in polin"). See Moses ben Abraham's translation of Hannover, *Sefer yeven metsulah* (1686), fol. 3b.

29 Pach-Oosterbroek noted that political and royal news was usually left out of the *Kurant*. See Pach-Oosterbroek, "Arranging Reality," 122.

30 See, for example, Hannover, *Sefer yeven meẓulah* (1653), fol. 2b (Hannover, *Abyss of Despair*, 27). Moses ben Abraham's translation (Hannover, *Sefer yeven metsulah* [1686]), fol. 2a, omitted the details about the king's marriage and the ancestry of the new queen. Similarly, compare Hannover's (1653), fol. 2b (Hannover, *Abyss of Despair*, 30), with Moses ben Abraham's (1686), fol. 2b, where, again, details of the royal family were left out of the Yiddish translation. Moses ben Abraham did include Hannover's tale of Tatar revenge on the Greek Orthodox but radically abridged it. Perhaps it merited inclusion because Hannover, playing on Numbers 31:2, where Moses was commanded to avenge the people of Israel on the Midianites, said that this represented God avenging Polish Jewry. This was something that even a Christian would not have denied, for both Psalms 94:1 and Romans 12:19 specifically said that vengeance was God's.

31 Subsequent Yiddish translations of *Sefer yeven meẓulah* in 1739 (Wandsbek) and 1849 (Lemberg) also did not include Hannover's description of Jewish life in Poland.

32 On traditional historiography, see Yosef Hayim Yerushalmi, *Zakhor: Jewish History and Jewish Memory* (Seattle: University of Washington Press, 1982), 21–24. Also see Adam Teller, "Jewish Literary Responses to the Events of 1648–1649 and the Creation of a Polish-Jewish Consciousness," in *Culture Front: Representing Jews in Eastern Europe*, ed. Benjamin Nathans and Gabriella Safran (Philadelphia: University of Pennsylvania Press, 2014), 23–24.

33 Moses ben Abraham's translation of Hannover, *Sefer yeven metsulah* (1686), fol. 16b. Cf. Hannover, *Sefer yeven meẓulah* (1653), fol. 11a (Hannover, *Abyss of Despair*, 109).

34 Following Hannover, Moses maintained that the fate of the Jews was a "decree [Yid. *gzeyreh*]" from God. The Jews gave charity, did good deeds, and prayed to try to avert it but to no avail (compare Moses ben Abraham's translation of Hannover, *Sefer yeven metsulah* [1686], fol. 7a–b, with Hannover, *Sefer yeven meẓulah* [1653], fol. 4b). The *gezerah* was a negative event in human eyes, but God's reasoning could not be fathomed. Note that the frontispiece of the Yiddish translation, which was unlikely to have been written by Moses ben Abraham, did say that "because of our many sins, thousands of rabbis and learned men, men and women, young men, and young women, were killed in all sorts of strange ways. May God avenge their blood."

35 It is possible that Moses did not understand the Hebrew abbreviation that Hannover used to say "in our many sins," yet he deciphered others, such as the abbreviation for "may his name be wiped out." Moreover, the idea appeared a few times in Hannover's text and was spelled out in some detail at the end of the chronicle (Hannover, *Sefer yeven meẓulah* [1653], fol. 11a [Hannover, *Abyss of Despair*, 109]).

36 See, for example, *Avot* 3:2 and Hannover, *Sefer yeven meẓulah* (1653), fol. 4b; Genesis 21:27, the covenant between Abraham and Abimelech, and Hannover, *Sefer yeven meẓulah* (1653), fol. 5a, compared with Moses ben Abraham's translation, Hannover, *Sefer yeven metsulah* (1686), fol. 9a (although Moses ben Abraham did use two Hebrew words, *koret berit*); and Genesis 34:25, when Simeon and Levi attacked the residents of the town in which Shechem lived, and Hannover, *Sefer yeven meẓulah* (1653), fol. 5b, compared with Moses ben Abraham's translation, Hannover, *Sefer yeven metsulah* (1686), fol. 9a. Also see Adam Teller, "A Portrait in Ambivalence: The Case of Natan Hanover and His Chronicle, *Yeven Metsulah*," in *Stories of Khmelnytsky: Competing Literary Legacies of the 1648 Ukrainian Cossack Uprising*, ed. Amelia M. Glaser (Palo Alto, CA: Stanford University Press, 2015), 24. Note that Moses ben Abraham followed Hannover's linking of the Cossack leader Maksym Kryvonis to the biblical Haman by using the same biblical adjective to describe him. Compare Esther 3:10, 8:1, 9:10, and 9:24 with Hannover, *Sefer yeven meẓulah* (1653), fol. 5a; and with Moses ben Abraham's translation, Hannover, *Sefer yeven metsulah* (1686), fol. 8b.

37 For example, *Bereshit Rabbah* 2:4, 16:4, and 44:17.

38 Hannover, *Sefer yeven meẓulah* (1653), fol. 2b.

39 See Moses ben Abraham's translation, Hannover, *Sefer yeven metsulah* (1686), fol. 2b.

40 Hannover, *Sefer yeven meẓulah* (1653), fol. 8b. This information did not appear in other contemporary Hebrew chronicles that Hannover sometimes relied on. See Me'ir ben Samuel of Szczebrzeszyn, *Ẓok ha-itim* (Cracow, 1650), fol. [8b]; and Gabriel Schussberg, *Petaḥ teshuvah* (Amsterdam: Emanuel Benvenisti, 1651), fol. 12a.

41 See Pach-Oosterbroek, "Arranging Reality," 113.

42 Pach, "Moushe's Choices," 202; Pach-Oosterbroek, "Arranging Reality," 202–6. Helmer Helmers noted that war reports were basic components of articles in Amsterdam newspapers from the beginning of Dutch corantos and, later, during the Thirty Years War. See Helmer Helmers, "Foreign News in Times of Domestic Crisis: The Truce Conflicts, the Thirty Years' War, and the Rise of the Dutch Newspaper," in *Negotiating Conflict and Controversy in the Early Modern Book World*, ed. Alexander Samuel Wilkinson and Graeme Kemp (Leiden: Brill, 2019), 265.

43 Pach-Oosterbroek, "Arranging Reality," 62, 77–78.

44 The octavo Yiddish book is 16 pages long, ending rather neatly on the verso page of the sixteenth page of text. The frontispiece was simply an added sheet. It would seem that Moses ben Abraham had to watch his word count.

45 Moses ben Abraham's translation, Hannover, *Sefer yeven metsulah* (1686), fol. 13a. Cf. Hannover, *Sefer yeven meẓulah* (1653), fol. 8a.

46 Hannover, *Sefer yeven meẓulah* (1653), fol. 5b. On the reference as specifically to Roman Catholics, see Malachi Haim Hacohen, *Jacob and Esau: Jewish European History Between Nation and Empire* (Cambridge, UK: Cambridge University Press, 2019), 137–38.

47 Me'ir ben Samuel of Szczebrzeszyn did say that this would be heard in all of Poland and that Jews in Edom would suffer. See Me'ir ben Samuel of Szczebrzeszyn, *Ẓok ha-itim*, fol. 3b. However, there is nothing to suggest that Moses ben Abraham altered his translation of Hannover based on other versions of the events.

48 The word *Edom* appeared three times in Hannover's text. In one instance, based on Exodus 15:15, Hannover used *Edom* to refer to military leaders involved in the conflict, a clear reference to Poles (Hannover, *Sefer yeven meẓulah*, 1653, fol. 6b). However, the "kings of Edom" (fols. 4b, 5b) demanded a broader definition of the term, because there were not multiple kings of Poland.

49 BT *Berakhot* 61b.

50 BT *Gittin* 57b. In the talmudic story the youngest and only surviving son was told to pick up the king's signet ring rather than worship the idol directly. He refused to do so. The story of the mother and her sons may have begun with 2 Maccabees 7, but as Gerson Cohen noted, Jews probably learned of it through rabbinic literature. Gerson Cohen, "Hannah and Her Seven Sons in Hebrew Literature," in his *Studies in the Variety of Rabbinic Cultures* (Philadelphia: Jewish Publication Society, 1991), 39–40.

51 See Zevi Hirsch Koidanover, *Kav ha-yashar* (Frankfurt: Johann Vaust, 1705), sec. 37.8.

52 The idea that the righteous would gain a place in Paradise or the Garden of Eden was talmudic. See, for example, JT *Pe'ah* 1:1; BT *Berakhot* 16b; and *Shabbat* 119b. On medieval martyrs attaining a place in Paradise, see Shmuel Shepkaru, *Jewish Martyrs in the Pagan and Christian Worlds* (Cambridge, UK: Cambridge University Press, 2009), 198–205. The idea of immediate transfer to Heaven or Hell appeared in rabbinic literature, but it was attributed to the view of a non-Jew; see Reuven Hammer, ed., *Sifre: A Tannaitic Commentary on the Book of Deuteronomy* (New Haven, CT: Yale University Press, 1986), 312. Earlier in the same section, *Sifre* says that souls must first be judged by God before being assigned to their place in the afterlife. The notion of immediate transfer was later expressed by Naḥmanides in his *Sha'ar ha-gemul*; see Moses ben Naḥman, *Kitvei Rabbeinu Mosheh ben Naḥman*, ed. Charles Ber Chavel (Jerusalem: Mosad Ha-Rav Kuk, 1964), 2: 288–89, 2: 294–97. *Sha'ar ha-gemul* first appeared in print in 1490 (Naples) and was republished in 1518 (Constantinople) and 1595 (Venice). A search of "Footprints: Jewish Books Through Time and Place," an online bibliographic database, shows that copies of the work were found in the homes of Ashkenazic Jews in the sixteenth century and later. The text was also cited by seventeenth-century Polish rabbis such as Samuel Eidels and Isaiah Horowitz. That the righteous immediately passed into Paradise appeared in Yiddish ethical literature of the seventeenth and early eighteenth centuries; see, for example, Koidanover, *Kav ha-yashar*, secs. 71 and 100. Koidanover's work was very much dependent on Joseph of Dubnow's *Sefer yesod Yosef* (sections 30 and 67), but the latter work was published in 1785; see Jacob Elbaum, "Kav ha-yashar: keẓat devarim al mivneihu, al inyanav ve'al mekorotav," in *Ḥut shel ḥen: shay le-Ḥava Turni'anski*, ed. Israel Bartal, Galit Hasan-Rokem, Ada Rapoport-Albert, Claudia Rosenzweig, Vicky Shifriss, and Erika Timm (Jerusalem: Shazar, 2013), 15n3, 19n10, 30–48, 53–56. Later in life, Moses ben Abraham believed that the Garden of

Eden was an earthly paradise. See Chone Shmeruk and Israel Bartal, "'Tela'ot Mosheh': sefer ha-gei'ografit ha-rishon be-yidish ve-te'ur erez Yisra'el shel R. Mosheh bar Abraham ha-ger," *Cathedra* 40 (July 1986): 126.

53 See Teller, "Jewish Literary Responses," 29.

54 Earlier in the Niemirów story, Hannover described Jewish women of the town who drowned themselves in order not to be defiled (Hannover, *Sefer yeven mezulah* [1653], fol. 5a). This act and the motive were mentioned in Moses ben Abraham's translation, Hannover, *Sefer yeven metsulah* (1686), fol. 8a. Moses may have felt that this would suffice for all the related stories. If so, he may have misjudged the significance of the stories of the two women that Hannover highlighted.

55 On the story of these women, see Adam Teller, "Jewish Women in the Wake of the Chmielnicki Uprising: Gzeires Taḥ-Tat as a Gendered Experience," in *Jewish Culture in Early Modern Europe: Essays in Honor of David B. Ruderman*, ed. Richard Cohen, Natalie B. Dohrmann, Adam Shear, and Elchanan Reiner (Cincinnati: Hebrew Union College Press; and Pittsburgh: University of Pittsburgh Press, 2014), 41 with note 16; and Teller, "Jewish Literary Responses," 28–31.

56 Teller wrote, regarding Hannover's original book, "Martyrdom is therefore the central theme of this text and is here given an unambiguous definition. It is the choice of death over conversion to Christianity" (Teller, "Jewish Literary Responses," 27). Also see Teller, "Jewish Literary Responses," 30.

57 Compare Hannover, *Sefer yeven mezulah* (1653), fol. 6b, with Moses ben Abraham's translation, Hannover, *Sefer yeven metsulah* (1686), fol. 10b. Both rabbis were mentioned by Hannover in this passage, because Rabbi Samson had written a commentary on the *Zohar* according to Luria's interpretations. Moses ben Abraham confused the two in his translation.

58 Yehuda Liebes, "Mysticism and Reality: Towards a Portrait of the Martyr and Kabbalist, R. Samson Ostropoler," in *Jewish Thought in the Seventeenth Century*, ed. Isadore Twersky and Bernard Septimus (Cambridge, MA: Harvard University Press, 1987), 221–55, esp. 245–55 with note 98, in which Liebes persuasively argues that Rabbi Samson saw his death as a martyr's death, akin to the deaths of talmudic rabbis during the Hadrianic persecutions. Based on kabbalistic sources, Rabbi Samson may have idealized human self-sacrifice and ultimately performed it. Hannover may not have appreciated this, or, if he did, he did not condone it.

59 Hannover's use of the term *aku"m* to refer to non-Jews (e.g., Hannover, *Sefer yeven mezulah* [1653], fol. 10b) should not be taken as a sure sign that he saw

the Greek Orthodox as idolators; the use of the term may have been dictated by the Venice printing house. Nowhere in *Yeven meẓulah* did Hannover specifically refer to Christians as idolators. Not all sixteenth- and seventeenth-century Ashkenazic Jews saw Christians as idolators. David ben Manasseh Hadarshan thought that non-Jews were no longer idolators and were simply following in the ways of their ancestors; see David ben Manasseh Hadarshan, *Shir Hama'alot l'David = (Song of the Steps) and Ktav Hitnazzelut l'darshanim = (In Defense of Preachers)*, ed. Hayim Goren Perelmuter (Cincinnati: Hebrew Union College Press, 1984), 81. The same responsum appears in Moses Isserles, *She'elot u-teshuvot ha-Rema*, ed. Asher Siev (Jerusalem: Mosad Ha-Rav Kuk, 1970), no. 62. See also Joel Sirkes, *Sefer she'elot u-teshuvot bayit ḥadash ha-ḥadashot* (Koretz, Poland: Johann Anton Krieger, 1784), no. 29; the discussion in Elijah Judah Schochet, *Bach Rabbi Joel Sirkes: His Life, Works, and Times* (Jerusalem: Feldheim, 1971), 124–25; and the view cited in the name of Rabbi Johanan in BT *Ḥullin* 13b. There was an evolving redefinition of Jewish martyrdom taking place in Ashkenazic society that came to see any Jew killed by a non-Jew, no matter what the circumstances, as a martyr. See Edward Fram and Verena Kasper-Marienberg, "Jewish Martyrdom Without Persecution: The Murder of Gumpert May, Frankfurt am Main, 1781," *AJS Review* 39, no. 2 (2015): 290–98.

60 Hannover, *Sefer yeven meẓulah* (1653), fol. 6b.
61 In the context of Psalm 33:20, the word *soul* cannot simply mean "body." Also see Koidanover, *Kav ha-yashar*, sec. 37.8, who said that one who dies a martyr's death gives up body and soul.
62 Moses ben Abraham's translation, Hannover, *Sefer yeven metsulah* (1686), fol. 10b.
63 Hannover, *Sefer yeven meẓulah* (1653), fol. 10b. *Layb* was not the standard seventeenth-century Yiddish or German translation of the word *basar* in this verse. See, for example, the two Yiddish translations of the Bible published in Amsterdam in 1679 and 1687; or *Bibel, das ist die Heilige Schrifft Alten und Neuen Testaments, nach der uhralten, gemeinen Lateinischen von der Catholischen Kirchen bewährten und in derselbigen bisshero allzeit gebrauchten Version* (Mainz: Johan Andrea Endter, Christoph Wust, 1661). However, *layb* was used in a Bavarian translation of Genesis 2:24 and Matthew 19:6. This may offer a further clue into Moses ben Abraham's background. See https://bibeltext.com/bairisch/genesis/2.htm (accessed 19 July 2021).
64 BT *Sanhedrin* 58a, with Rashi's comments. Also see Naḥmanides on Genesis 2:24 compared with 37:27.

65 Hannover, *Sefer yeven meẓulah* (1653), fol. 4b; Moses ben Abraham's translation, Hannover, *Sefer yeven metsulah* (1686), fol. 5a.

66 Hannover, *Sefer yeven meẓulah* (1653), fol. 7a.

67 Moses ben Abraham's translation, Hannover, *Sefer yeven metsulah* (1686), fol. 11a. See also fols. 12a and 14a.

68 Hannover, *Sefer yeven meẓulah* (1653), fol. 15b. The Wandsbek and Lemberg translations of *Yeven meẓulah* placed the curse next to each mention of Khmelnytsky's name. Moses did say of Kryvonis, "May his name be blotted out" (Moses ben Abraham's translation, Hannover, *Sefer yeven metsulah* [1686], fol. 8b).

69 Hannover, *Sefer yeven meẓulah* (1653), fols. 8b–9a; Moses ben Abraham's translation, Hannover, *Sefer yeven metsulah* (1686), fol. 14b.

70 See John P. Meier, *Matthew* (Collegeville, MN: Liturgical Press, 1990), 53–55.

71 See Hermann Strack and Paul Billerbeck, *Kommentar zum Neuen Testament aus Talmud und Midrasch* (Munich: Beck, 1969), 2.2: 264. See also Samuel Tobias Lachs, *A Rabbinic Commentary on the New Testament: The Gospels of Matthew, Mark, and Luke* (Hoboken, NJ: Ktav, 1987), 108.

72 Hannover, *Sefer yeven meẓulah* (1653), fol. 7b.

73 Stanislawski, "The Yiddish *Shevet Yehudah*," 145.

74 Hannover, *Sefer yeven meẓulah* (1653), fol. 10a (Hannover, *Abyss of Despair*, 103).

75 Hannover, *Sefer yeven meẓulah* (1653), fols. 10a–10b (Hannover, *Abyss of Despair*, 103–4). On the topic of *agunot* in the Ashkenazic realm in this period, see Noa Shashar, *Gevarim ne'elamim: agunot be-merḥav ha-Ashkenazi, 1648–1850* (Jerusalem: Karmel, 2020).

76 Moses ben Abraham's translation, Hannover, *Sefer yeven metsulah*, (1686), fol. 16a.

77 Although Yeshayahu Vinograd included a possible Salonika edition (1570?), Jeremy Cohen noted only the 1554 Adrianople and the 1567 Sabbioneta editions. See Vinograd, *Oẓar ha-sefer ha-ivri*, no. 89; and Jeremy Cohen, *A Historian in Exile: Solomon Ibn Verga, "Shevet Yehudah," and the Jewish-Christian Encounter* (Philadelphia: University of Pennsylvania Press, 2016), 2.

78 Online scans of all three editions can be found through the catalogue of the National Library of Israel. The plagiarism was already noticed by Moritz Steinschneider, *Catalogus librorum Hebraeorum in Bibliotheca Bodleiana* (Hildesheim: Olms, 1964), sec. 6324.4.

2

Chiefly on Translation and Timekeeping in Dov Ber Birkenthal's *Memoirs*

Gershon David Hundert*

This chapter is part of a case study of Dov Ber Birkenthal (1723–1805) of Bolechów (Bolekhiv, today in western Ukraine), a wine merchant and communal leader.[1] Birkenthal wrote two books in Hebrew: a history of messianism called *Divrei binah* (Understanding Words)[2] and another work conventionally referred to as his *Memoirs*.[3] Although he hoped to publish both books, they remain substantially in manuscript. That Birkenthal wrote books is unusual, because we have few books by eighteenth-century Polish or Lithuanian burghers and because few books composed by Jewish authors who were not rabbis exist from that period. Both of Birkenthal's books include extended passages translated into Hebrew from books published in Polish and German. I focus mainly on those translations, following some introductory remarks.

The first editor of Birkenthal's *Memoirs*, Mark Wischnitzer, omitted the first 43 pages of the 187-page manuscript. Although Wischnitzer did

---

* Editors' note: We all mourn the untimely death of our valued colleague and friend, Gershon David Hundert (1946–2023), whose contribution to this volume illustrates his erudition, boundless intellectual curiosity, and collegial generosity.

publish a few autobiographical passages from those pages, he declared the rest to be "only translations from printed books, and therefore not worth reproducing."[4]

Birkenthal's history of messianism treats mainly the Sabbatean movement and its aftermath. Shabbetai Tsevi was acclaimed by Jews all over the world as the messiah in 1665, but by 1666 he had converted to Islam under pressure from the Ottoman government and his followers overwhelmingly abandoned him. However, despite bans of excommunication and general condemnation, some of them were not willing to give up the conviction of living in a redeemed world and persisted in their beliefs. One center of such people was the Polish province of Podolia. Communal leaders tolerated these secret heretics—there were no real secrets—so long as they behaved in public in accordance with accepted norms. Jacob Frank (1726–1791) returned to Podolia in 1755 from the Sabbatean center in Salonika and disturbed this tacit agreement between rabbinic authorities and Sabbatean heretics.[5] He advocated public behaviors that defied communal norms and led to a ban of excommunication against them. The Sabbateans sought protection in the Catholic hierarchy and ultimately engaged in two public debates (1757 and 1759) with the rabbis over the purported blasphemies in the Talmud. The last point debated in 1759 saw the Sabbateans seeking to substantiate the libel that Jews are required to use Christian blood in their ceremonies. As Birkenthal attests in *Divrei binah*, it was he who recorded and translated into Polish the answers provided by Ḥayim Rapoport (d. 1771), the chief rabbi of Lwów and its region, regarding the blood libel accusation. In other words, Birkenthal's role in the confrontation with sectarian Jews who not only rejected the Talmud and the Oral Torah but also accused Jews of the ritual murder of Christians and the ceremonial use of Christian blood was a central event in his life. It propelled him to write his 329-page history of messianism, *Divrei binah*.

In *Divrei binah* there are translations from two books that Birkenthal used to reconstruct the events in connection with the Sabbatean Frankist scandal in the 1750s. One, Franciszek Kleyn's *Coram iudicio*, includes records of the events in 1756–1757 and is written partly in Latin and partly in Polish.[6] The other, *Złość żydowska* by Gaudenty Pikulski, written only in Polish, documents mainly the events of 1759.[7] As was the case with the *Memoirs*, Abraham Brawer, who published excerpts from *Divrei binah*, did not deem Birkenthal's translations worthy of publication. Indeed, in his autobiography Brawer boasts that he successfully blocked publication of the whole manuscript by "a young scholar."[8]

My topic here is precisely what can be learned from the omitted passages that make up Birkenthal's translations. I focus on his choice of texts, the manner of his translation, their significance, and what they can tell us about the translator and the era in which he lived. I begin with an extended description of Birkenthal's translation work followed by an analysis of its historical significance, broadly viewed.

The surviving manuscript of the *Memoirs* lacks both its cover page and the author's introduction. It begins in medias res with an account of how Birkenthal came to learn Polish and German and why he chose to translate and include passages from two books in his own works.

As noted earlier, Birkenthal wrote both his books in Hebrew. Yiddish words are rare in the surviving manuscripts and are used primarily to explain certain terms. In *Divrei binah* Birkenthal occasionally compiles long passages excerpted from earlier Hebrew books. On one occasion, he translated into Hebrew a section of a book published in Yiddish—*Sheyris Yisroyel*—without informing his readers that he had done so.[9] I would note that, in contrast to Birkenthal, this work characteristically refers only vaguely to non-Jewish sources as "scholars of the nations" but specifies the titles of Jewish books. It does mention Jacques Basnage, but only once. The issue of why Birkenthal so rigorously used Hebrew to the virtual exclusion of his own vernacular is not one that he addresses.

Most of the surviving pages of the *Memoirs* are from various drafts, but we do have a few pages of what seems to be the fair copy of his book. It is here that we can observe the visual and other influences of his forays into European historical literature. There are manicules and asterisks and even an attempt at a marginal illustration. In addition, Birkenthal uses the size and boldness of individual words for emphasis. Throughout both of his books, with few exceptions, Birkenthal is careful to cite his sources, often including the edition dates and page numbers. This was somewhat unusual because "early modern Jewish authors ... often ... attempted to conceal or obfuscate their [non-Jewish] sources in order to create the chimera of a purely-domestic Jewish library."[10]

Birkenthal informs us that he learned Polish in 1737 when he was 14 years old and still living in his father's house. He declares that he intends to "sanctify the Name of Heaven" by providing answers to the challenges of Christians. To do so, he was obliged to read many of their books. Thus, far from wasting time that should have been spent in Torah study, he was performing the loftiest of commandments: sanctifying God's name in the world. Whether this rationale was his original or even true motivation for learning languages is an open question. What is clear here, however, is that in the intensely intimate, visible, and surveilled communal life of an eighteenth-century Eastern European Jew, Birkenthal felt the need to justify his unusual course of study and to present himself in the best possible light.[11] There were rarely any secrets in these communities; privacy was not an available concept in that era.

Notwithstanding his first declaration, later in the *Memoirs* Birkenthal gives a different account of the circumstances in which he learned Polish. In this explanation he did so to please his father, who, knowing Polish and other languages himself, hired a Polish gentleman to tutor Birkenthal. In that same time, he also studied Latin "and understood the principal part of its grammar."[12]

Birkenthal reports that he learned German in 1749, soon after he left home and took up residence in an inn in Lwów where there were many Gentile merchants, "Germans, Saxons, and Frenchmen."[13] They showed him many books, most of which were in German, and so, he says, he was obliged to learn this language as well. He agreed to teach Hebrew to a young Saxon merchant's clerk in exchange for the clerk teaching him German. He also learned "some French."[14] These intellectual exchanges, as Birkenthal conveys them, belie notions of rigid confession-based insularity in this region and historical period.

Birkenthal signals the importance of his acquisition of German by linking it to his reading of a biblical verse his eyes came upon during the New Year of 1748–1749.

> Just as I completed the morning prayers [for the New Year], my eye fell on the verse in Psalms 81:6: "He made it a decree in Joseph, when he went out through the land of Egypt. I heard a language that I understood not." And this was fulfilled in that year. I went to Lwów to take up the trade in Hungarian wine and I learned the German language and some French, as I shall describe below in the proper place.[15]

In his *Memoirs* Birkenthal translated passages from a Polish translation of Giovanni Botero's *Relazioni Universali* (Universal Relations) and from a German translation of Humphrey Prideaux's *The New and Old Testament Connected in the History of the Jews*.[16] Birkenthal translated from a German version published in the 1720s.[17] Giovanni Botero's *Universal Relations* appeared in four volumes between 1591 and 1598 (Botero died in 1617). Widely influential, his books set out to demonstrate the "universal" extent of the Catholic Church in all parts of the world.[18] Birkenthal tells us that, because he was known among "all the Gentiles, the nobles, and the other people" for his interest in and understanding of Christian writings regarding their doctrines and the history of the world, a nobleman brought him a copy of *Theatrum świata*,[19] a Polish translation of Botero's work, and encouraged him to read it, "since it is fitting that I know more about the history of our people."[20]

Birkenthal translated only 11 pages from two parts of Botero's book that dealt specifically with the kingdom of Abyssinia/Ethiopia.[21] In introducing this section, Birkenthal writes that the author was a "believer in the Pope" and a great hater of Jews but also that "he admits the truth."[22] He declares that he will focus on passages concerning Jews and their lands, and on

> the honor of their kings, first among the monarchs of antiquity. His lineage reaches a son of Solomon the son of David, King of Israel. In addition to him, there are many other Jews in their land under mighty kings. [And I copied] everything that would benefit the people of Israel, that they might know that we also can await and hope for full redemption by a righteous redeemer who will arrive speedily in our days.
>
> The author, in his book, *Theatrum*, writes about the essentials of the states and lands of the four corners of the world. After writing about Egypt, the lands and states of Kush, called Nubia, and Meroe and other states of that region, he goes on to write about the region of Ethiopia. It has a great king who rules many states and kingdoms as can be seen from his book; in Part 1, Book 3, at the end of page 224, this people is called Abyssinian. And the author calls their king Prester John [Papiyan],[23] but this name is mistaken. The author himself says this: that it is an error to call the king by this name. I will

explain, in the proper place, that other books on the nature of the nations of the world written in German also testify that no king of the state of Abyssinia was ever called Prester John. All that has been in written to that effect is in error.[24]

As Birkenthal himself asserted, his interest in these pages was to demonstrate that a dynasty of Jewish kings together with a large Jewish population had existed in the African kingdom. To bolster this proposition, he was less than literal in his translation. Where Botero wrote, "The Abyssinians . . . are of the opinion that their king is a descendant of one of the sons of Solomon and the Queen of Sheba, whose name was Melilah," Birkenthal omitted the words "are of the opinion."[25] Despite his cautionary note of skepticism as to the veracity of the Abyssinian narrative, Botero further noted that after reaching maturity in Jerusalem, Melilah went to join his mother in Abyssinia. Consequently, he adds, Abyssinians preserve certain Jewish customs, including circumcision, the Sabbath, and a loathing of the flesh of swine. Birkenthal reproduces this passage in Hebrew, adding that, with the arrival of Solomon's son, all the residents of the state became Jews.

Botero's text describes the Ethiopian state and its rulers, its crops and its mines, its army, and its population. Birkenthal reproduces all of this in Hebrew but alters it along the way. Birkenthal routinely substitutes the Hebrew months for those of the Christian calendar, thus Elul replaces August, a silver scepter stands in for a silver crucifix, and the three Jewish pilgrimage festivals (*sheloshet ha-regalim*) replace the holy days Christmas, Easter, and the Exaltation of the Holy Cross. Tellingly, when he reaches a passage in Botero's book that mentions limits on the king of Abyssinia's jurisdiction over priests and sacramental matters, Birkenthal writes, "Here [Botero] writes about the king's jurisdiction in the matter of the property of priests. This is clearly a lie and a falsehood, and I have not copied it for this reason."[26]

A further example of Birkenthal's commentary on Botero's veracity is worth noting. Botero writes that the Abyssinian ruler likely descended from Melilah, one of the sons of King Solomon and the Queen of Sheba, and that during the reign of Queen Candaces, the Abyssinians converted to Christianity. A subsequent ruler, King John, who was childless, gave the kingdom to his nephews: "Thus, the royal blood was divided among three families: Balthazar, Gaspar, and Melchior." Birkenthal renders this passage in the following way: "And the king is a descendent of one of the sons of Solomon, King of Israel, and the Queen of Sheba. The name of that son of Solomon was Elimelekh. Here the priest-author writes lies and falsehood in the matter of the three kings who visited Jesus the Nazarene when he was born. And he seeks to support the lie with falsehood. These words are not worthy of being recorded."[27] Because Botero nowhere connected the names of the three kings with the Christian legend of the Magi, Birkenthal's knowledge of this association clearly came from another source.[28]

We find similar sorts of alterations, comments, and omissions in the much longer extract that Birkenthal translated from Humphrey Prideaux's *The New and Old Testament Connected in the History of the Jews*. Prideaux (1648–1724) was a late Stuart Anglican divine and historian.[29] He knew Hebrew well but disdained rabbinic Judaism, Islam, Catholicism, and deism, polemicizing in print against all of them.[30] On the other hand, in his eyes, the biblical text was infallible. In *The New and Old Testament Connected*, Prideaux's central concern was to resolve apparent contradictions in chronology between the biblical account and those of ancient historians such as Herodotus and Xenophon, who themselves give divergent accounts of Persian history.[31] Birkenthal is not interested in the problem of resolving chronological accounts that seem to contradict Scripture. He knows the truth must accord with the biblical version. He introduces the section from Prideaux as follows:

> In addition, there came to me a book translated from English [and] written by a great and wise author who gathered many passages from our Holy Torah, the Prophets and the Writings, and other holy books that mention historical and worldly matters and combined these with histories of the nations. For they have many collections of the books of many nations, which are called archives and libraries, particularly in the capital city of London, where this author, Humphrey Prideaux, dwells. I found [in his book] much concerning the good and the bad that befell our people of Israel at the hands of their neighbours and other nations near and far, as I will explain, if God wills it, the great profit that arises for us to [help us] understand well many contradictory passages in the Prophets since many of them are clarified by these stories. These were not known to us from the books of our Tradition.[32]

Birkenthal was familiar with all of Prideaux's book, but his translation is restricted to the first part of Book 2. Roughly 50 pages long, it treats the period between the destruction of Jerusalem by Nebuchadnezzar and the Edict of Cyrus that permitted Jews to return from Babylon to the Holy Land. Birkenthal refers to this section as "The Kings of Babylon and Persia."[33] He omits some passages and summarizes others. He occasionally grows impatient with what seems to him to be needless detail. He complains, "One author writes about how many houses there were in Babylon at the time of Alexander the Great. There is no need to translate this because it matters not at all."[34] Sometimes Birkenthal shortens Prideaux's summaries of debates over chronology by omitting most of the discussion, noting that obviously the account of Josephus Flavius or of the biblical text is to be preferred.[35] As was the case with his treatment of Botero's text, the names of months are given as Hebrew months.[36] Passages that Birkenthal deemed offensive, such as one that says that the Temple in Babylon exceeded the size of the Temple in Jerusalem, are left out.[37] He calls that temple in Babylon a *beit tifleh*, which is a punning derogatory term often used by Jewish writers to designate a church.[38] Whereas Prideaux tends simply to cite biblical chapters and verses in support of what he is saying—writing, for example, that Cyrus was "famous in Holy Writ not only for being the restorer of the Kingdom of Israel but especially in being there appointed for it (Isaiah 44:28; 45:1) by name many years before he was born. Which is an honour therein to none, only to him and Josiah, King of Judah (I Kings 13:2)"—Birkenthal actually quotes the key verse. He writes that Cyrus was "famous in the Holy Writings themselves, not only for restoring the Kingdom of Israel, but that many years before his birth, Isaiah the Prophet foresaw [this] and mentioned him by name. He was obliged to do this as written in Isaiah 44:28, who says of Cyrus 'He is my shepherd, and he shall fulfill all my purpose,' saying of Jerusalem, 'She shall be built,' and of the Temple, 'your foundation shall be laid.' Such an honour is given to no other except Yoshiyahu, King of Judah."[39]

In the materials reviewed thus far, we see that Birkenthal found little to quarrel with in the sources he consulted, because they largely did not represent a challenge to his understanding of Judaism's tradition and history. Indeed, as he noted, these works had supplemented his knowledge. But at the core of his translation project was a serious and fraught issue: the question of whether Jews continued to retain their sovereignty in the wake of their defeat by the Romans in 70 CE. Key here is the church's reading of Genesis 49:10 in which the patriarch Jacob blessed his son Judah, saying, "The scepter shall not depart from Judah, nor the ruler's staff from between his feet until Shiloh comes." This verse, a longtime locus classicus in Christian-Jewish debate, was often cited in early modern Poland-Lithuania. The Christian reading held this to be a prophecy affirming the supersession of Israel in flesh (i.e., the Jews) by Israel in spirit (i.e., the church).[40] Here, Judah stood for the Jewish people and Judea for the Jews' land, and the scepter signified sovereignty or political independence and, by extension, the Jews' Temple. Shiloh was taken to refer to Jesus. Thus, the Christian reading contended, the prophecy anticipated that Jews would lose their sovereignty and that their scepter would depart upon the arrival of Shiloh/Jesus. With the defeat and exile of the Jews from their land and the destruction of their temple at the hands of the Romans, the prophecy had been fulfilled.

Birkenthal's desire to refute this claim, "she'en li-yehuda memshalah" (roughly, "that Jews lack sovereignty"), was a key element underlying his choice of what to translate and substantially explains his selection of this passage in Prideaux's book.[41]

With minor exceptions, Birkenthal faithfully translated Prideaux's refutation of Jewish claims of sovereignty that turned on the *resh galuta* (exilarch), a descendant of King David who served as the leader and representative of Jews in Babylonia from the second century. Prideaux argued that Jews answered the Christian reading of Genesis 49:10 by referring to the continuity of the Davidic royal family, but given that this office had ceased to exist, the prophecy was returned to its full force, adding, "Why do they then any longer resist the power of it?"[42]

At this point in the translation, Birkenthal interpolates a paragraph headed "My Answer on This," in which he announces that he is writing a separate composition on what he has found in "their books."[43] He notes that he has translated Jakub Radliński's version of *Rabbi Samuel*, referring to the first Polish-language anti-Jewish publication (1536), from "their secular language to our holy tongue."[44] In a passage elsewhere in the *Memoirs*, Birkenthal notes that he read the book in 1753, the year the third Polish edition was published in Lublin.[45] Declaring the book to be full of stultification and lies and its author unworthy of being considered a scholar, Birkenthal emphasizes that, notwithstanding their mendacity, Radliński's words have aroused hatred against Jews among Christians.[46]

Radliński's influential book was an augmented version of the Polish *Letter of Rabbi Samuel*, which, in turn, was a Polish version of a work that circulated widely in Europe beginning in the fourteenth century. One scholar calls it an anti-Jewish "best seller."[47] This was true in Poland-Lithuania too: Radliński's version was published in Lublin six times between 1725 and 1753. The core text is "a full-scale Christian work analyzing the Jewish exile as evidence of God's rejection of the Jews."[48] The chapter that Birkenthal cites is devoted to interpreting Genesis 49:10.

In the passages introducing his translations from Botero, Birkenthal asserts that the Christians "have invented a prophecy" about Jesus of Nazareth based on the testament of the patriarch Jacob, and they stubbornly and falsely claim that Jews have lacked sovereignty since the coming of Jesus.[49] Introducing passages from Botero that he believed proved that there were Jewish kings long after Jesus, he wrote, "[And I copied] everything that would benefit to the people of Israel, that they might know that we also can await and hope for full redemption by a righteous redeemer who will arrive speedily in our days."[50] In the visual presentation of his text Birkenthal highlights in large bold letters the words "the powerful armies of the king of Abyssinia," underscoring his belief that, despite what Christians maintain, the messiah has not yet come and Jews did not lose sovereignty in the time of Jesus.[51] Furthermore, he had done so by using the writings of Christian scholars themselves to confute their reading of Genesis 49:10.

As we have seen, Birkenthal framed his justification for learning foreign languages as arising from his desire to successfully represent the Jewish side in debates against Christians. In addition to his concern with refuting the church's interpretation of Genesis 49:10 is his insistence on the truth of the existence of a written Torah and an oral Torah. In maintaining that both were sacred and revealed to Moses on Sinai, he sought to defend the Talmud from its Christian detractors. His purpose, as he expressed it, was "to sanctify the Name of Heaven in all of my answers to the questions of Christians and other unbelievers regarding the Lord's Torah transmitted orally by Moses from God's mouth."[52] Birkenthal's insistence on the necessity of responding to the questions of Christians and his ability to do so point to an immediate sense of urgency on his part. He understood that Christianity posed a real threat and must be countered. His insistent disavowal of its claims speaks both to his devotion to the truth claims of Judaism and to his willingness to cross boundaries to acquire the skills necessary to be successful. Christianity did pose a threat; his energetic contestation amounts to an attribution of power.

Birkenthal notes that there were those who disapproved of his learning languages and reading foreign works. We could posit that stretching or testing the norms of a regimented society is a way of establishing individual identity. In this case, language learning was not a universal taboo among European Jews, but it clearly evoked anxiety in Birkenthal in his Ruthenian context. Thus he devotes considerable space to citing passages from rabbinic authorities, all of them Sephardic, who endorsed such wide reading precisely as preparation for defending Judaism.[53]

Still, Birkenthal is not consistent in his explanation of his acquisition of languages. As noted earlier, he claimed that he learned Polish because his father wanted him to and that, at the same time, he learned some Latin. He adds that he had to desist from his language studies because people began to murmur that his studies were not for the sake of Heaven.[54] Elsewhere he stresses the utility of his knowledge of Polish for his people because he can prepare properly worded petitions and other documents on their behalf. All the reasons he gives could easily coexist in his mind and come to the fore at different times. Interestingly, he never explicitly mentions the most obvious benefit of acquiring linguistic skills: the commercial advantage he gained by being multilingual.

Almost certainly, Birkenthal's own experience was crucial in the formation of his preoccupation with theological debate over the claims of Christianity and Judaism. Just after asserting that he has read "their books," Birkenthal alludes to what must have been a critical and fateful moment in his life: His reward for that "distasteful study" was the reward of all of Israel.[55] Here Birkenthal is referring to an event he described in detail in *Divrei binah*.[56] As he tells us, he had been the translator from Polish to Hebrew and Hebrew to Polish at the great debate "with the evil sect of believers in Shabbetai Zvi (may his name be blotted out)" in the cathedral in Lwów in 1759.[57] The believers to whom he refers, the Sabbatean Frankists, were a millenarian, nihilist sectarian Jewish group that, having been ostracized by the Jewish community and seeking the protection of the Catholic Church, engaged in public debates against the Jews.[58] In the first debate, held in Kamieniec-Podolsk in 1757, the Sabbatean Frankists condemned the Talmud, the Oral Law. In a subsequent debate—the one in which Birkenthal played a role—held in the cathedral of Lwów in 1759, they accused Jews of ritual murder and the ceremonial use of Christian blood.

Birkenthal's translation work, both as a general project and in terms of its particulars, calls for some reflection as to its historical significance. Translation in the way Birkenthal carried it out did not leave the text unchanged, not only because of omissions and emendations but also because of the selection of the particular passages and their inclusion in a text that included passages translated from other writings. This sort of translation produces work that is at once not original at all and, at the same time, entirely original. They are not "only translations," as Wischnitzer would have it.[59] As we have seen, Birkenthal did not hesitate to interfere in the texts he was translating. These interventions take two forms. At times they are part of a domestication or Judaization of the text for his readers. In the case of the texts in the *Memoirs*, the most obvious example is the presentation of dates in which the original text reads, for example, August but is transcribed as Elul in the Hebrew translation. The conundrum of all translation is how much to domesticate the foreign, bringing the original author's cultural world closer to the reader rather than bringing the reader to confront what is foreign. In this case an issue arises related to the measurement of time as seen in Birkenthal's work. On the one hand, it is true that when Birkenthal translates Prideaux, he skips the historical debates over chronology between Herodotus and Xenophon, for example, presumably because he believes the only true chronology is the one found in the Hebrew Bible. From another vantage point, however, such a position stands in sharp contrast to what many historians mark as a significant shift in consciousness: the emergence of a shared homogeneous measurement of the day and of the year. The tendency was toward Europeans sharing the same calendrical and clocked time. Thus the standardization of time became a marker of modernity.[60]

Birkenthal's translating the names of the months is thus not only domestication but also a possible signal of resistance to the beginnings of the homogenizing tendencies in the measurement of time. His inconsistency signals at least a certain ambivalence on his part. There are about 30 dates in the texts. In a third of them he does not change the text, that is, January remains January; in about a third he domesticates the date, and August becomes Elul; and in about a third of the cases, we get this blending: the Christian month, called "their month," and the Hebrew year. Elsewhere, when he records the year, he sometimes calls it "of Jesus" or "of the Christians." Moreover, when he is writing in the first person and not translating, Birkenthal notes dates almost exclusively in parochial Hebrew ways, such as the day of the month, the weekly Torah reading, or holidays. The saddle time—or *Sattelzeit*, what the historian Reinhart Koselleck called the end of the eighteenth century, a period when ideas about history, about the nature of time itself, changed[61]—finds expression in Birkenthal's writing. In Birkenthal's mind, the calendar is "other" and Christian. He refers to "their month" and the year of the Christians. When it comes to clocked time, there is no such problem.[62] I am using a rather loose version of Koselleck's term to characterize the multiple contradictions in this period and their reflection in Birkenthal's writings.

Outside the translated texts, in his own writing, Birkenthal refers to clock time, generally regarding events that involve him with Gentiles and/or those that are momentous in one way or another, such as the debate with the Sabbatean Frankists or his meeting with a Russian military officer.[63] The notation of the exact time marks the solemnity and importance of the occasion. It might also serve as a status marker. Such importance is accorded not only to meetings with Gentiles. In his *Memoirs* Birkenthal also notes the hour of his mother's death and adds that it was the precise anniversary of the day and hour of his own birth. The epitaph on his wife's grave, unusually, marks the precise hour of her death.[64] This certainly reflects Birkenthal's concern with accuracy and details, and it might also have afforded him a sense of some sort of control over what could not be controlled.

The other form of authorial interference in Birkenthal's translations is one that might be characterized as polemical but was, it should be noted, quite commonplace in early modern European translations, particularly of religious history texts. Here, the translator alters or rewrites the text to serve his own theological position.[65] Birkenthal's selective method of translation and his interventions in the text reflect this tactic well. He is more than willing to use Christian writers as authorities when they buttress his claims and, equally, to brand them as liars when their assertions threaten to undermine his polemical purposes.

Birkenthal believed that he was serving a higher purpose in rendering these texts in Hebrew and that he had discovered in them "matters that are not known to any of our traditional texts." And here we come to the heart of the matter that arises from Birkenthal's translation work: the question of the nature of knowledge. Changes in what is known and how one knows involve new sets of credentials and/or new sources of authority. As noted earlier, Birkenthal learned that there were libraries and archives in the great capital city of London that contain histories of many nations. He understood also that these archives were forms of epistemic authority, other, and outside his own. It is certainly the case that different (sometimes contradictory) orders of knowledge can coexist in a society or a culture. Birkenthal's express avowal of his non-Jewish sources and his explicit citation from those texts in his work were extremely unusual in his place and time. That he undertook such a project, despite legitimate concerns about his reputation and status—witness his temporary abandonment of his studies of Polish when his neighbors began to mutter—represents his clear recognition of a broadening of the sources of authority and knowledge.

In selecting and translating from specific history texts, Birkenthal made himself an arbiter of what was useful and perhaps even "true" knowledge. To be clear, he was not engaged in systematic research, comparing sources to establish a correct record. Rather, Birkenthal cited the books he used as authorities to help him verify the one truth that he already knew: the truth of the Jewish tradition.[66] What was worth preserving and conveying was whatever served that larger purpose.

Even though Birkenthal's devotion to his community's normative beliefs is unquestionable, nonetheless there is a subversive element in what he does in his books: His acts of translation, in and of themselves, accord authority to sources outside the canon. Although he adamantly rejected anything that seemed to him to contradict the truth, he still thought that what they said strengthened the authority of the received truth. He was not interested in alternative ways of understanding history, but he was attracted to the way history was done in "their books" both in terms of their content and their form.

In choosing to learn languages and to read noncanonical books, Birkenthal—despite his legitimate anxieties about status and reputation—chose to exercise agency, even as he treated this "new knowledge" conservatively. Living in a saddle time, Birkenthal's translations reveal some of the inner tensions of the age concerning authority and truth and illustrate the small changes, the complexities, and the ambiguities of the day. It is not ideology that animates his actions, nor does he advocate any program for change. On the contrary, in his view, his endeavors were defensive and conservative as he sought to preserve the basic beliefs in divine providence, the election of Israel, and the sanctity of the Talmud that he had inherited. His writings illustrate that categorical ethnic and religious distinctions did not preclude contact and exchange of information and that such boundaries could often be maintained at the same time as stable, persisting, and often vitally important social relations across dichotomized statuses.[67]

Notes

1 Dov Ber ben Yehuda Leib would have adopted the name Birkenthal to conform to the Austrian name laws introduced in Galicia beginning in 1785. In archival sources before that time, he appears sometimes as Brezer and in variations such as Brzozowy, all meaning "birch." Birkenthal translates the Polish cognomen. On Birkenthal, see Gershon David Hundert, "Language Acquisition as a Criterion of Modernization Among East Central European Jews," in *Reappraisals and New Studies of the Modern Jewish Experience: Essays in Honor of Robert M. Seltzer*, ed. Brian Smollett and Christian Wiese (Leiden: Brill, 2014), 13–28.

2 *Divrei binah*, MS B964, 28°7507, Israel National Library, Jerusalem (hereafter cited as DB). Avraham Ya'akov Brawer published portions of 61 pages drawn from pages 185–328 of the manuscript. However, in that version there are some important elisions and alterations to the text, even in the passages presented as quotations. A. Y. Brawer, "Makor ḥadash le-toledot Frank vesi'ato," *Ha-shiloaḥ* 23 (1917–1918): 146–56, 330–42, 439–49; and 38 (1921): 231–38; reprinted in A. Y. Brawer, *Galiẓiyah viyehudeihah* (Jerusalem: Mosad Bialik, 1965), 197–275. The title page of the manuscript indicates that Birkenthal completed *Divrei binah* in 1800.

3 Although Birkenthal's memoir cannot by any definition be classified as an autobiography, it is self-writing. My approach to this text is informed in significant ways by Michael Stanislawski's strictures and analysis on how to approach such texts, as set forth in Michael Stanislawski, *Autobiographical Jews: Essays in Jewish Self-Fashioning* (Seattle: University of Washington Press, 2004). Two manuscript collections include portions of the *Memoirs*. One is in New York at the Jewish Theological Seminary Library, MS 10775 (hereafter, S). The other is in the John Rylands Research Institute and Library

at the University of Manchester, Marmorstein ms. 1 (hereafter, R). Dov Ber Ben Yehuda Birkenthal, *Divrei binah, Zikhronot*, ed. Gershon Hundert (Jerusalem: Mosad Bialik, 2023).

4 Dov Ber Birkenthal, *The Memoirs of Ber of Bolechow (1723–1805)*, trans. M. Vishnitzer (Wischnitzer) (London: Oxford University Press, 1922), iv.

5 A. Kraushar, *Frank i Frankiści Polscy 1726–1816: Monografia historyczna osnuta na źródłach archiwalnych i rękopismienych* (Kraków: U. G. Gebethner i spółki, 1895), vol. 2 (no. 1312), 329–30.

6 Franciszek Kazimierz Kleyn, *Coram iudicio recolendae memoriae Nicolai de stemmate Jelitarum a Dembowa Góra Dembowski, Dei & Apostolicae Sedis Gratia Episcopi Camenecenis, Postulati Archi-Episcopi Metropolitani Leopoliensis, Praepositi Generalis Commendatorii Michoviens Aequitis Aquilae Albae*, Pars III, *De decisoriis Processus inter infidels Iudaeos Diocesis camenecensis, in material iudaicae eorum perfidiae, aliorumque muto obiectorum AD 1757 expedita ac in executes pendens* (Lwów: 1758). DB, 193–227.

7 Gaudenty Pikulski, *Złość żydowska Przeciwko Bogu y bliźniemu Prawdzie y Sumnieniu na obiaśnienie Talmudystów. Na dowód ich zaślepienia. y Religii dalekiey od prawa Boskiego przez Moyżesza danego. Rozdzielona na trzy części opisana* (Lwów: Jan Szlichtyn, 1760); DB, 229–76, 287–92. Part III of Pikulski's book replicates without acknowledgment verbatim material from a book by the Jesuit Jakub Radliński, *Prawda chrześcijańska od nieprzyjaciela swego zeznana, to iest traktat Rabina Samuela.* DB, 229–76, 287–92.

8 Mikhaʾel Ha-kohen Brawer and Avraham Yaʿakov Brawer, *Zikhronot av u-veno* (Jerusalem: Mosad Ha-Rav Kuk, 1966), 404; cf. Brawer, *Galiẓiyah viyehudeihah*, 208–9.

9 Menaḥem Man Ben Solomon Amelander Ha-Levi, *Keter kehunah, ve-hu, Sefer Yosipon, bi-leshon Ashkenaz* (Amsterdam: Naftali Herts Rofe and Kosman ben Yosef Barukh, 1743); first Hebrew ed., *Sheʾerit Yisraʾel* (Lemberg: Shlomo Yaris Rapaport, 1804). See H. Hominer, ed. and trans., *Sefer sheʾerit Yisrael ha-shalem* (Jerusalem: Hominer, 1964); Bart Wallet, "Hidden Polemic: Josephus's Work in the Historical Writings of Jacques Basnage and Menaḥem Amelander," in *Josephus in Modern Jewish Culture*, ed. Andrea Schatz (Leiden: Brill, 2019), 42–61; Bart Wallet, "Ongoing History: The Successor Tradition in Early Modern Jewish Historiography," *Studia Rosenthaliana* 40 (2007): 183–94; and Andrea Schatz, "A Tradition in the Plural: Reframing *Sefer Yosippon* for Modern Times," in *Josephus in Modern Jewish Culture*, ed. Andrea Schatz (Leiden: Brill, 2019), 62–84.

10 Iris Idelson-Shein, "Shabbethei Bass and the Construction—and Deconstruction—of a Jewish Library," *Jewish Culture and History* 22, no. 1 (2021): 2.
11 Hundert, "Language Acquisition," 13–28.
12 S, 56.
13 R, 1.
14 R, 14.
15 R, 14.
16 Giovanni Botero, *Theatrum świata wszytkiego, na ktorem Europa, Asia, Afryka i Ameryka, także narodow, krajow, miast, nacji obyczaje, bogactwa i insze przymioty są wystawione, po włosku naprzod przez Jana Botera Benesiusa opisane*, trans. Paweł Łęczycki (Krakow, 1659).
17 Humphrey Prideaux, *The Old and New Testament Connected in the History of the Jews and Neighbouring Nations from the Declension of the Kingdoms of Israel and Judah to the Time of Christ*, 9th ed. (London: Printed for R. Knaplock in St. Paul's Church-Yard, and J. Tonson in the Strand, 1725). Birkenthal translated from one of the German editions: *Alt- und Neues Testament: in eine Connexion mit der Jüden und benachbarten Völcker Historie gebracht, von Verfall der Reiche Israel und Juda an biß auf Christi Himmelfarth, worinnen die biblische Geschichte durch die weltliche vortrefflich bestätiget* (Dresden: Lobecken, 1721; and Johann Wilhelm Harpeter, 1726).
18 Robert Bireley, *The Counter-Reformation Prince: Anti-Machiavellianism or Catholic Statecraft in Early Modern Europe* (Chapel Hill: University of North Carolina Press, 1990), ch. 3; Victoria Ann Kahn, *Machiavellian Rhetoric: From the Counter-Reformation to Milton* (Princeton, NJ: Princeton University Press, 1994), 60–84.
19 Blythe Alice Raviola, *Giovanni Botero: un profile fra storia e storiografia* (Milan: Bruno Mondador, 2020); Stefan Bielański, *Giovanni Botero: historyk i pisarz polityczny epoki kontrreformacj* (Krakow: Universitas, 1995).
20 R, 1.
21 Botero, *Theatrum świata wszytkiego*, 224–29, 145–46, 229–30, and then back to 147.
22 S, 2.
23 Meir Bar-Ilan, "Prester John: Fiction and History," *History of European Ideas* 20, nos. 1–3 (1995): 291–98; Robert Silverberg, *The Realm of Prester John: With a New Afterword* (London: Phoenix Press, 2001).
24 S, 2–3.

25 "Jest opinia u Abissinow poddanych Popa Jana iakby ich Pan miał isdż z iednego syna Salomonowego y z krolowey Sabby nazwanego Melilech" (Botero, *Theatrum świata wszytkiego*, 226).

26 S, 7[1] 8; Botero, *Theatrum świata wszytkiego*, 146.

27 S, 8; Botero, *Theatrum świata wszytkiego*, 146–47.

28 More examples of Birkenthal seeking to present Abyssinia as a glorious *Jewish* kingdom are the following: Botero's text criticizes the exaggeration of the number of soldiers of Prester John given by Franciscus Alvarez (100,000) and asserts that the ruler, when he needed them, could not produce nearly so many. He notes that there was one group of knights, under the protection of St. Anthony, drawn from every third son of a noble house. Birkenthal omits the criticism, calls the ruler king and not Prester John, and omits the reference to the patron saint of the equestrian order. See S, 10; and Prideaux, *Old and New Testament Connected*, 147. Later, where Botero speaks of the war of a Muslim kingdom against "the Christian Abyssinians, subjects of Prester John," Birkenthal simply records a war "against the Abyssinians." See S, 12; and Prideaux, *Old and New Testament Connected*, 150.

29 On the "Anglican Enlightenment," see William J. Bulman, *Anglican Enlightenment: Orientalism, Religion, and Politics in England and Its Empire, 1648–1715* (Cambridge, UK: Cambridge University Press, 2015). On Prideaux and Jews, see David B. Ruderman, *Jewish Enlightenment in an English Key: Anglo-Jewry's Construction of Modern Jewish Thought* (Princeton, NJ: Princeton University Press, 2000).

30 See, for example, Prideaux, *Old and New Testament Connected*; and Humphrey Prideaux, *The Life of Mahomet, or, the History of That Great Impostor, from His Birth, A.D. 571, to His Death, A.D. 632: To Which Is Added, a Discourse, Shewing That the Gospel of Jesus Christ Is No Imposture . . . Addressed to the Deists of the Present Age* (Glasgow: Printed by E. Miller for W. Stewart, 1799).

31 Prideaux's book largely follows James Ussher, and his preoccupation with chronology was characteristic of many scholars of the early modern period. See Anthony T. Grafton, *Joseph Scaliger: A Study in the History of Classical Scholarship* (Oxford, UK: Oxford University Press, 1983), 1: 36.

32 R, 1.

33 S, 23.

34 "It is unnecessary to translate more insignificant matters." S, 15; Prideaux, *Old and New Testament Connected*, 125.

35 S, 27, 28.
36 For example, S, 19; S, 22; and Prideaux, *Old and New Testament Connected*, 131, 136.
37 S, 17; Prideaux, *Old and New Testament Connected*, 127.
38 *Beit tifleh* in S, 15, instead of *Tempel* in Prideaux, *Old and New Testament Connected*, 125. *Tifleh* connotes superstition and vapidity, echoing the Hebrew word *tefilah* (prayer), with the same spelling, but different vowel points.
39 S, 24; Prideaux, *Old and New Testament Connected*, 139.
40 There is a vast literature on this verse and its interpretation in the context of Jewish-Christian debate. The classic work is Adolf Poznański, *Schiloh: Ein Beitrag zur Geschichte der Messiaslehre*, Erster Teil, *Die Auslegung von Gen. 49,10 Im Altertume bis zu Ende des Mittelalters* (Leipzig: Hinrichs, 1904). See David Berger, *The Jewish-Christian Debate in the High Middle Ages: A Critical Edition of the Niẓẓahon Vetus* (Philadelphia: Jewish Publication Society of America, 1979), 249–51; and Judith Kalik, "The Attitudes Towards the Jews in Christian Polemic Literature in Poland in the 16th–18th Centuries," *Jews and Slavs* 11 (2003): 61–63.
41 S, 1.
42 S, 22; Prideaux, *Old and New Testament Connected*, 137–38.
43 S, 23.
44 Samuel Marochitanus, *Prawda chrześcijańska od nieprzyiaciela swego zeznana, to iest traktat rabina Samuela pokazuiący błędy żydowskie około zachowania prawa Moyżeszowego, y przyiścia Messyaszowego, ktorego Żydzi czekaią . . . od Alfonsa Bonohomine, Hiszpana . . . około roku 1339 z arabskiego ięzyka na łaciński przeniesiony . . .; przez pewnego teologa Zakonu s. Franciszka Re. Obser. Prowincyi Ruskiey przedrukowany w Lublinie roku [. . .] 1725 z łacinskiego iezyka na polski przetłumaczony roku pańskiego 1733. przez Jakoba Radlinskiego* (Lublin: Collegium Societatis Jesu, 1753). The oldest version presents itself as a translation from Arabic by a Spanish Dominican. On the history of the reception of this work, see Ora Limor, "The Epistle of Rabbi Samuel of Morocco: A Best-Seller in the World of Polemics," in *Contra Iudaeos: Ancient and Medieval Polemics Between Christians and Jews*, ed. Ora Limor and Guy Stroumsa (Tübingen: Mohr, 1996), 177–94; and Magda Teter, *Blood Libel: On the Trail of an Antisemitic Myth* (Cambridge, MA: Harvard University Press, 2020), 191–92. On Jakub Paweł Radliński, see *Polski Słownik Biograficzny* (Wrocław: Zakład Narodowy im. Ossolińskich, 1989), 29: 708–10.
45 R, 1.

46 S, 23. The pagination of *Prawda chrześcijańska* is different in each of the three editions I have examined: 1733, 1740, and 1753. Birkenthal's reference is correct. Altogether six editions were published between 1725 and 1753.

47 Limor, "Epistle of Rabbi Samuel."

48 David Berger, "The Problem of Exile in Medieval Jewish-Christian Polemic," in *"In the Dwelling of a Sage Lie Precious Treasures": Essays in Jewish Studies in Honor of Shnayer Z. Leiman*, ed. Yitzhak Berger and Chaim Milikowsky (New York: Yeshiva University Press, 2020), 190.

49 S, 1.

50 S, 2.

51 S, 9. In S, 10, the rulers near the king.

52 R, 1.

53 After a gap of some 300 years, the basic compositions of medieval Sephardic talmudic scholarship were republished in a short period: 100 different books in the space of 33 years in the eighteenth century. This, and other dimensions of a renewed Sephardic influence on Ashkenazic culture, is a key development in this period, but there is no space to explore it here.

54 S, 57.

55 S, 1.

56 DB, 185–329.

57 DB, 231, 292–93.

58 Paweł Maciejko, *The Mixed Multitude: Jacob Frank and the Frankist Movement, 1755–1816* (Philadelphia: University of Pennsylvania Press, 2011); Ada Rapoport-Albert, *Women and the Messianic Heresy of Sabbatai Zevi: 1666–1816*, trans. Deborah Greniman (Oxford, UK: Littman Library of Jewish Civilization, 2011). The term *Frankism* did not appear until the nineteenth century. Rachel Elior, "Israel ba'al Shem Tov and Jacob Frank: Hasidism and Shabateanism," in her *The Mystical Origins of Hasidism* (Oxford, UK: Littman Library of Jewish Civilization, 2006), 173n1.

59 See Birkenthal, *Memoirs* (trans. Wischnitzer), iv.

60 Although not concerned particularly with culture, the standard work on this topic is David Landes, *Revolution in Time: Clocks and the Making of the Modern World*, rev. ed. (Cambridge, MA: Harvard University Press, 2000).

61 Reinhart Koselleck, *The Practice of Conceptual History: Timing History, Spacing Concepts* (Stanford, CA: Stanford University Press, 2002), 154–69.

62 Jewish timekeeping is not at issue here. On issues related specifically to Poland, see, for example, David Zvi Kalman, "Unequal Hours: The Jewish

Reception of Timekeeping Technology from the Bible to the Twentieth Century," PhD diss., University of Pennsylvania, 2019, pp. 235, 254, 259, 260, 264, 269–70, 320, 331–33.

63 DB, 237, 276, 280, 286, 287, 293, 297, 298; S, 49, 87–88, 118; R, 95.

64 Michael Nosonovsky, *Hebrew Epitaphs and Inscriptions from Ukraine and Former Soviet Union* (Washington, DC: Lulu, 2006).

65 Andre Lefevere, *Translation, Rewriting, and the Manipulation of Literary Fame* (London: Routledge, 1992); Peter Burke, "Cultures of Translation in Early Modern Europe," in *Cultural Translation in Early Modern Europe*, ed. Peter Burke and R. Po-chia Hsia (Cambridge, UK: Cambridge University Press, 2007), 7; Susan Bassnet, "When Is a Translation Not a Translation?" in *Constructing Cultures: Essays on Literary Translation*, ed. Susan Bassnet and André Lefevere (Clevedon, UK: Multilingual Matters, 1998), 25–40.

66 Anthony Grafton, *The Footnote: A Curious History* (Cambridge, MA: Harvard University Press, 1997), 33.

67 Fredrik Barth, *Ethnic Groups and Boundaries: The Social Organization of Culture Difference* (Boston: Little, Brown, 1969), 9–10.

3

When the Rebbe "Met" the Tsar

History or Folklore?

David Assaf

Did the Rebbe Ever Meet the Tsar?

In the treasure of legends and folklore of the Jews one can find many stories of meetings, dialogues, or polemic encounters between prominent Jewish sages in ancient times and non-Jewish kings or rulers, some even identified by name. These alleged meetings are documented in the talmudic and the midrashic literature[1] and in rabbinic medieval writing.[2] It is doubtful that such meetings ever took place in reality, but the literary motifs and exegetical patterns that shaped these early tales remained potent, influencing later descriptions from the nineteenth century to the present.

This study deals with encounters between Hasidic leaders (known as rebbes or zaddikim) and the authorities in the territories where they lived and were active. According to the Hasidic sources, the exchanges were not just with government representatives. The Hasidic leaders confronted face to face and prevailed over real kings and emperors. But is that what really happened? Did these admired and venerated rabbis truly wage war against the almighty tsar or supremely eminent Holy Roman Emperor? If indeed such events had transpired, why did their echoes never reach the ears of historians?

In fact, such confrontations never actually took place. The struggles or "wars" occurred exclusively in the Hasidim's imagination and folklore.

Nevertheless, the imagined events were based on partial truths padded with archetypal myths whose objective was to consolidate the Hasidic communal identity and bolster the image of its persecuted leader, who was suffering at the hands of the emissaries of a despised government. Hence what we have here is a literary device, a way to shape a complex reality into a legendary struggle between two opposing forces: the dark and the light, symbolized by the Gentile ruler and the Hasidic zaddik.

The sources that recount these confrontations are clearly hagiographic. The hagiographic sources have three basic and interconnected characteristics, which the researcher must disentangle to render them "usable" and able to yield reliable information: (1) typological patterns of traditional or kabbalistic thinking and hermeneutics, (2) aspects of popular folklore and legend, and (3) historical reality, or at least fragments of it that have been organized and interpreted according to the typological patterns.[3]

Many tales that have come down to us consist of eminent zaddikim struggling with the Russian tsar, the Austrian emperor, or holders of government positions identified with or acting in the place of these powers. (From the Hasidim's perspective, the person sending the envoy and the envoy himself, even the local police officer, could be equated with the mighty ruler.) In the rest of this chapter I try to demonstrate the interweaving of these elements with a few episodes connected to three different personalities.[4]

Leib Surehs "Meets" with Emperor Joseph II

There is little reliable information about the real life of Leib Surehs (1730–1791). Leib Surehs (meaning "Leib, Sarah's son") was a "hidden zaddik." His enigmatic life was fertile ground for the sowing of legends and myths that supported his image as a popular holy saint with unique supernatural powers. He was supposedly active in supporting his fellow hidden zaddikim, ransoming Jewish captives, rectifying the souls of dead sinners, and, above all, wandering at will among the palaces of emperors and kings.[5]

The maskil Michael Levi Rodkinson (Frumkin), who collected, wrote, and published Hasidic tales for a living and was himself descended from a prominent Chabad family, was the first to spread and perhaps even invent the Leib Surehs tales.[6] Another maskil who spread legends about Leib Surehs was Abraham Ber Gottlober, who also had been a Hasid in his youth. He documented some legends in his memoirs, including Leib Surehs's encounter with the last king of the Poland-Lithuanian Commonwealth, Stanisław August Poniatowski, at his coronation ceremony: "It was in the year 1764, and I heard about this event in 1833 from an old man in Warsaw who was about ninety years old or more. He saw with his own eyes Leib Surehs enter among the rows of the guards in the king's court. And no one stopped him or protested, for (according to this old man) the guards didn't see him, only the Jews, and it was a miracle."[7]

What was the purpose of Leib Surehs's visit to the palace? Gottlober does not elaborate, but it seems it was the very fact of the visit. Thanks to his supernatural power of invisibility, this Jew in Hasidic dress succeeded in infiltrating a non-Jewish event. We can speculate that this retrospective tale relates to a significant event that had transpired a few months before: the Polish Sejm's abolishment of the Council of Four Lands, the central representative body of Jewish autonomy in Poland. Polish Jews viewed this as not only a real danger to their autonomy but also a personal affront, because the council was a symbol of their honor and independence. Perhaps behind Leib Surehs's miraculous tale lies the true story of a failed attempt at intercession against this decree.[8]

Gottlober recounts another strange matter regarding Leib Surehs. Apparently, at the third Sabbath meal, instead of delivering the customary Torah teaching expected of a zaddik, he would recite the genealogy of the Polish nobility.

> He would go about figuring out the family lineage of some Polish lords like Potocki, Radziwiłł, Czartoryski, and the like. He would say: Lord so and so Radziwiłł, son of so and so, son of the son of so and so, who also had sons by the names of so and so, and these were the names of his daughters. And the eldest became the wife of this lord, and the second to the other, and this son married that one's daughter and so on and so forth—the entire family tree with all its branches and extensions. And when he would get to the end of one he would begin with another family. . . . That is what he did all the time.[9]

This unusual teaching is not utter nonsense, however. It is a type of mystical theurgical practice, analogous to the customary ritual reading or memorizing of lists of names of biblical figures, sages, and zaddikim practiced in the circle of Rabbi Nahman of Bratslav.[10] In the case of Leib Surehs, it had an inverted meaning: familiarity with "the Lords of Esau and the Ishmaelites," a type of delving into the impure. Knowledge of the royal genealogy was likely highly important, as Hasidic legend attributes to Leib Surehs miracles of leaping from one place to another and supernatural acts of invisibility. These virtues enabled him to meet with the Habsburg emperor Joseph II and to pressure him against issuing decrees unfavorable to the Jews.

According to the legend, Leib Surehs traveled back in time to the palace of the Austrian emperor in Vienna, where he demanded that Joseph II abolish his 1782 Edict of Tolerance (*Toleranzpatent*), which had aimed to redefine the legal status of Jews within the majority society. For traditional Jewish society this was an evil decree intended to shake Judaism's very foundations. Clearly, the folk legend created the hero who could battle this wicked plot. With his supernatural powers, Leib Surehs was able to bypass the palace guards, enter the emperor's chambers, and torment him. Armed with a knife, Leib Surehs slashed the emperor and threatened to kill him if he did not repeal the decree. The emperor refused, and, according to the tale, "Josef hardened his heart, like the Pharaoh of Egypt." The emperor cried out in pain, but his guards were unable to apprehend the invisible zaddik. Leib Surehs's "war" against Emperor Joseph II continued for seven years, "and as he fought with him on earth, the Emperor's angel fought with Leib in heaven. And for that reason Leib was ill seven years, the same number of years the Emperor was ill." The terrestrial and celestial battle was resolved only with the deaths of both men on the same day and year.[11]

In an attempt to reconcile the historical background with this tale, Gottlober asserted that Leib Surehs was actually a spy who disguised himself as a holy man and thus was able to gain entry into the palaces of kings, where he would gather sensitive information.[12] Naturally, there is no basis for such a claim. In fact, Gottlober's account preserved a maskilic interpretation originally intended to not only temper the fantastic elements of the Hasidic tales but also give them a rational explanation that would at the same time point out the Hasidim's lack of loyalty to their homeland.

In the end, despite his supernatural powers, Leib Surehs's mission failed. He was unable to bend the emperor's will. However, the failure did not derive from the zaddik's lowly position; on the contrary, he was revealed to possess extraordinary powers even greater than the emperor's, and the battleground simply moved from earth to heaven. The reason for his failure had nothing to do with his power or its limits but with God's will. Hence the echo of the biblical story of the Pharaoh, whose heart God purposely hardens, in the legend of Leib Surehs is significant. After all, even Hasidic legend cannot change the historical fact of the issuing of the edict. At most, it can plant the hope in the heart of the listener that redemption will come, just as it did in the days of Moses.

Another important aspect of Leib Surehs's legend is the mystical element linking the two opposed personalities. Both Leib Surehs and Emperor Joseph II were ill for seven years before they died (seven being a typological number), and they both expired on the same exact date.[13] This trope (which connects two polar personalities, usually a Jew and a Gentile) recurs in the discussion of the Hasidic tale involving Tsar Nicholas I and Rabbi Israel of Ruzhin, who apparently also shared the same birthdate.

The myth of Leib Surehs was so enduring that even at the beginning of the twentieth century, the elders of the remote town of Jałtuszkiw (Podolia Province), where the zaddik lived in his last days, still repeated tales about him and the emperor. One maintained that a beautiful carriage arrived in the town once, and out of it stepped the emperor Joseph II, who asked to be escorted to Leib Surehs's dwelling. Leib was not at home, and the emperor said to those gathered around him, "When he comes, tell him that I can no longer stand such terrible suffering. I am going to die, but he too will not live." When the zaddik returned from his travels, he sensed the event immediately and rent his garments, saying, "If this is what was decreed to me from heaven, then I lovingly accept it."[14]

The words of the Jałtuszkiw-born writer Jacob Wasserman, who attempted to find reliable information on Leib, can perhaps serve as evidence of the historian's helplessness in the face of such legends: "It is impossible to know anything about the real life of this unique man whom people consider a saint. It is doubtful whether any scholar will solve this enigma. Thousands of legends continue to veil the man that was Leib Surehs, and even from all the 'information,' we know nothing at all about him."[15]

Rabbi Schneur Zalman of Lyady "Meets" with Tsar Paul I

Unlike the legendary personality of Leib Surehs, the life of Rabbi Schneur Zalman of Lyady (1745/49–1812), founder of Chabad Hasidism, is well documented. He had the misfortune to be active when the controversy between Hasidim and Mitnagdim reached its peak. Based on the false informing of Jewish opponents of Hasidism to the Russian authorities, he was jailed in St. Petersburg in 1798 and again in 1800. Each time, he was interrogated and quickly released. The fact of his having been in prison at all created a situation whereby the exalted zaddik was subordinate to a person of the lowest rank, in this instance a drunk prison guard. This inverted status—where the elevated is inferior and the inferior is elevated—is fertile ground for spinning a countermyth that maintains that what appears to be true is only a small, distorted portion of the actual truth. It is an optical illusion of a momentary triumph of evil over good. The real struggle does not take place in the prison cell; it happens in entirely different spheres—the ethical, metahistorical, and cosmic—in which the zaddik prevails.

Already by the nineteenth century, stories had spread among Chabad Hasidim about Tsar Paul I's interest in Schneur Zalman and his request to meet with him. Aleksander Zederbaum, editor of the Hebrew journal *Ha-meliz*, quotes these tales in his book *Keter kehunah*, published in 1867.

> And they [the Hasidic tales] added another embellishment, that the emperor himself came in disguise to talk with him. And according to them he found favor in the emperor's eyes who bantered him a bit and told him a few riddles, shared with him some pieces of wisdom, and the rabbi was able to hold his own throughout. The page is not long enough to describe all the miracles the Hasidim have exaggerated, even the testimony that once the rabbi came (from the jail?) to the emperor's court and the young fellow rapped his scepter on the Rabbi's clothes, and the rabbi cried out, saying that in his time there will be trouble for the Jews.[16]

Michael Levi Rodkinson, mentioned earlier, was one of the disseminators of this legend. He was also the first to write a systematic semimodern account of the history of Chabad. According to him, Tsar Paul I visited the prisoner Schneur Zalman in disguise, but the rabbi, in his wisdom, immediately saw through the ruse.

> And he paid the appropriate respect to the emperor, hailing him: "My lord Emperor!" And Paul, berating him, thus denied: "I am not the Emperor, and why would you show me the honor reserved for the Emperor?" And the rabbi answered: "The kingdom on earth is like the kingdom in heaven, and when I beheld my lord Emperor, I was seized by fear, and I understood immediately that I now stand before the Emperor." After this, he tested the Rabbi's erudition in many aspects and found him to be completely knowledgeable in every wisdom.[17]

Another very late but highly influential source tells of the tsar's "head of interrogation," who entered Schneur Zalman's prison cell and began a conversation that veered toward issues of faith. The learned Christian official was bothered by the question of how the all-knowing God could have asked Adam, who was hiding from him in Paradise, "Where art thou?" The following is the purported verbal exchange between the two:

> The rabbi answered him: "Do you believe that the Torah is eternal, recounted to every man, in every time and generation?" The official replied, "This I do believe." "If so," the zaddik said, "This is what the Almighty calls out to every man, in every time, in every era: Where art thou? Where are you in your own world? This and this many days and years have passed in your life span, and where have *you* gotten to in *your* world? Thus, the Almighty calls out: you have lived forty-six years until today, and where are you on your journey?" When the official heard the zaddik utter his exact age, he became animated and placed his hand on the rabbi's shoulder and said, "Man of Valor!" but his heart was fluttering in his chest.[18]

Martin Buber's rephrasing of this alleged conversation suggests that the rabbi was not interested in a direct answer to the officer's question. He viewed it as a provocative interfaith polemic and therefore seized on the opportunity to show the officer the emptiness of his life. The question "Where art thou?" the rabbi interpreted, did not refer to a man's physical location but to the mysteries of his soul, his future deeds and willingness to take responsibility for his life. The Hasidic legend thus drew on the real incident of the zaddik's incarceration and interrogation but ascribed to it an incisive saying of deep and profound ethical significance, which, in fact, he could have uttered at any routine encounter with a Hasidic adherent. The implanting of this dialogue within the dramatically charged setting of the prison, featuring a confrontation between a Gentile interrogator and Jewish interrogatee, strengthens the moral lesson and places the weaker party being questioned in a superior position in relation to the powerful interrogator.

More than a few authentic documents relating to the interrogation have been preserved, and they reflect Schneur Zalman's unique personality. There is no reference to any open dialogue such as that described; for corroboration we can lean on Yehoshua Mondshine, a Chabad Hasid and prominent scholar of Hasidism, who published the original documents of the imprisonment and interrogation. Mondshine states, "As regards the many tales about what happened to our rabbi in jail and the wisdoms he demonstrated in front of the king and ministers—we know nothing. It is clear that there is no hint of it in the documents, and there is no sign in those documents that our rabbi met the tsar face to face during his imprisonment."[19]

A particularly interesting passage from Schneur Zalman's response to his interrogators during his first incarceration (1798) is noteworthy. In answer to the interrogators' query, he described the background of Hasidism's growth, which he saw as mainly connected to the decline of the previous generation's spiritual leadership. There were, in his opinion, corrupt rabbis who bought their rank through monetary payments to Polish noblemen. They were pretentious, status-seeking, ignorant boors who despised devotional prayer.

> Until God showed mercy upon us and awoke the spirit of rulership of the Empress of All Russia [Catherine the Great], may her glory be exalted, to govern and expand throughout all of the land of Poland. And before there was crowned by her there the last king,[20] at which time the decline of the rulership of the aforementioned Rabbis began, little by little, until the time the land of Poland was partitioned and the rulership of the Rabbis collapsed completely, particularly in White Russia [Belarus]. For a terrible decree called *Ukaz* was issued, to

abolish absolutely these aforementioned Rabbis [status], so that they will no longer buy rabbinates from the lords. And then [our] people were liberated and made free in our country Russia, where each and every one has the permission and ability, whoever so desires in our land, to prolong their prayers as they see fit, singly or in a group, in the study hall or in another place, and no one in our land can protest this.[21]

It is difficult to determine whether this response should be understood as the apologetics of a person under interrogation who is attempting to flatter his interrogators or as an authentic expression of the zaddik's positive attitude toward Russian rule. At any rate, it is clear that Schneur Zalman attributed a positive effect to the partitions of Poland with regard to the collapse of the old, corrupted rabbinate and the spread of Hasidism. The problem of the Hasidim was therefore not the merciful Russian government but rather an internal hatred within Jewish society that causes the haters of Hasidism to make false accusations about its leaders and incite the government authorities against them. It is not by accident that Chabad remained loyal to Russian rule until the Communist revolution. During the Napoleonic wars, Schneur Zalman unequivocally supported Russia and, as a result, was forced to flee with his family in 1812 from Lyady further southwest into the Russian interior, escorted by a Russian military convoy. He despised the French and saw in Napoleon's rule a great danger to the future of traditional Jewish society. He was quoted by his son Dov Ber as saying:

> But this is a great tragedy for the Jews, because not one will remain with his faith or his assets. For I feel toward him [Napoleon] an absolute hatred, because he is the devil . . . and because of this hate, he [Schneur Zalman] made the decision to escape, saying, it is better for me to die than to live under him . . . and he did not want, under any circumstance, to stay even one day under his rule.[22]

The demonic figure then, is not the compassionate Russian tsar but the liberal French king. Schneur Zalman's son and heir Dov Ber (known as the Mitteler Rebbe) continued this tradition of loyalty, even though he himself was imprisoned for two months as a result of being informed on (in 1826).²³ So too did the third rebbe, Menachem Mendel (known as the Zemach Tzedek), who was awarded the honorary Russian title of Honored Citizen for Generations. He was registered in the third merchant's guild and was keenly involved in various government projects to improve conditions for Russia's Jews—from the conference of rabbis in St. Petersburg to the encouragement of Jewish agricultural colonies in the New Russia provinces. We can conclude that, despite the personal sufferings that both the older rebbe and his son, the Mitteler Rebbe, experienced at the hands of the tsarist regime, among them and their descendants and heirs there was never a tendency toward confrontation with the authorities but rather instances of cooperation and attempts at intercession and negotiation.²⁴

Rabbi Israel of Ruzhin "Meets" with Tsar Nicholas I

Hasidic legend interweaves historical reality in the life of Israel Friedman of Ruzhin (1796–1850) in a most interesting manner. Rabbi Israel, who was the great-grandchild of Dov Ber of Mezeritch, ascended to leadership in 1813 at the young age of 17, and in a short time he was the leader of thousands of Hasidim in Ukraine. He was known for his regal way, characterized by an extravagant lifestyle of unprecedented wealth and magnificence in emulation of the customs of the Polish lords and charismatic Hasidic leadership that sought to present his way as a unique method of religious worship.²⁵

There is no evidence that his wealth or ostentatious lifestyle was offensive to the Russian authorities. On the contrary, he was registered in the second merchant's guild, and there are no signs of any tension between him and the authorities before 1836, when the saga known as the Ushits case erupted. In that year, following the murders of two Jewish informers who had been sanctioned by a secret court composed of some community elders in Podolia, 80 Jews were arrested and put on trial in military court. Among them was the zaddik from Ruzhin, who allegedly had given his consent to the murders. Rabbi Israel was under investigation for more than four years and was even imprisoned (for about two years) in Kiev. Eventually, of all the accused, he was the only one who was acquitted at trial and allowed to return to his home in Ruzhin. Despite his acquittal, he was placed under police surveillance and was not permitted to host Hasidim at his court. Unable to tend to his adherents and fearing expulsion from the Pale of Settlement, the zaddik fled Russia in 1840 in a daring escape. After many adventures and ordeals, he successfully reconstituted his court permanently in Sadagora (Sadigura in Yiddish), in Austrian Bukovina. Russia's continued efforts to convince the Austrian authorities to extradite the Jewish fugitive failed. Israel Friedman and his family left Russia for good and eventually established new Hasidic courts in Austrian Bukovina and Galicia and later in Moldavia and Romania.[26]

A significant Hasidic hagiography developed around the dramatic events of the rabbi's investigations, imprisonment, and flight. These tales attempted to interpret the meaning of the rabbi's sufferings and endow them with heroic and metahistoric meaning that would strengthen his image as a royal descendent of the seed of David, who tried to redeem the Jews and paid a price for his messianic role. This hagiography fluctuates between two parallel poles that blur the real events.

The first pole presents the story of the murders as a cover for the real reason for the rabbi's incarceration: Tsar Nicholas I's fear of a Jew, descended from the royal house of King David, who does not recognize the tsar's legitimate rule and threatens to rule in his stead. Added to the tsar's fear was his jealousy of the zaddik's veneration by thousands of Jews. The tsar was so convinced of the danger the zaddik posed to him that he devoted his entire agenda to the destruction of the royal Jewish seed and the messianic hope that lay within it. Hasidic lore thus interprets these events as a political struggle between the tsar and the zaddik on the question of who was the real ruler of the Russian Empire.[27]

The second pole interprets the tension between the zaddik and the tsar as an earthly manifestation of a heavenly struggle between the forces of impurity and the forces of holiness. Because the zaddik was guiltless in the murder case, the entire legal procedure was nothing but an illusion, a pretext to conceal a heavenly plan meant to bring about an encounter between two extreme foes: the demonic Nicholas, who represents the great empire of evil, and the righteous zaddik, who is the force of good in the world. This was apparently a contemporary interpretation, as the Polish zaddik Menachem Mendel of Kotsk, who was usually quite critical of Israel of Ruzhin's ways, supposedly said of him that "he stood up in public in order to subdue the power of that *kelipah* [demon] of the famous evil king who reigned in his time."[28]

Although we know that details of the Ushits case were brought to the personal attention of Nicholas and that he personally ordered Israel of Ruzhin's expulsion from the Pale, these facts should not be misconstrued.[29] Nicholas's regime dealt with thousands of similar cases. The entire tsarist bureaucratic system was recruited to quell Nicholas's paranoia, and it is doubtful that the rabbi of Ruzhin (whose name appears in many Russian documents, mainly after his escape from Russia) was a more significant threat than other professional troublemakers of all ethnicities throughout the vast Russian Empire. The fact that the rabbi was indeed persecuted and humiliated by government officials surely turned him into a hero in the eyes of his community, but it is doubtful that his fame exceeded that sphere and became a serious national issue that actually disrupted the tsar's sleep.

On the other hand, it is logical that political and religious issues lie at the heart of Hasidic lore. With the consolidation of the Jewish Pale, forced conscription into the tsar's army, and the 1835 statute on the Jews, among other government steps taken in relation to the Jews, Nicholas I was seen as the Jews' ultimate enemy, who planned for their destruction instead of their welfare.[30] When the Hasidic legend describes how Nicholas could not sleep because of his fear of the zaddik from Ruzhin, it hints at the figure of Ahasuerus but actually evokes Haman, who sought to annihilate the entire Jewish people. From a religious perspective, it did not escape the Jews' notice that Nicholas, like all Russian tsars and particularly his predecessor and brother, Alexander I, promoted the status of the tsar as a Christian messianic figure.

In the spirit of the conflict between these two leaders, Hasidic hagiography had them meet in person. When Nicholas allegedly came to the prison in Kiev to visit the rabbi, he looked at the Jewish king and said, "He is surely not an ugly man, but his eyes look like the eyes of a rebel against the monarchy."[31] After World War I, when S. An-sky visited the destroyed town of Sadagora, he heard the following story from a local Jew: "Nicholas hated the Ruzhiner intensely and persecuted him all his life. This amazed the Russian ministers, and once they asked Nicholas: Is it proper for a great king like yourself to constantly persecute this lowly *zhid*? Nicholas jumped up and called out in great anger: What you say, that he is a lowly *zhid*, is not true. For all my life I have been weighing down the world in one direction and he weighs it down in the other, and I have never been able to prevail!"[32]

Rabbi Israel himself once said, "I was born on the same day as he, but three hours later, and I cannot catch him." This Jew continued to tell An-Sky, "The Ruzhiner did not want to reveal himself and sit upon the zaddik's throne as long as Nicholas was reigning as tsar. He stipulated a condition: He or I! And he raised a commotion in all the palaces and it almost happened that Nicholas was deposed from his royal throne."[33] Nicholas was born in June 1796, and Israel of Ruzhin was born in October of that year—three months, not hours, later. But Hasidic lore, as we saw with Leib Surehs and Emperor Joseph II, is not particular with inconsequential details.

Nicholas's negative attitude toward the Jews was not a secret, nor was the paranoid nature of his rule, which led to informing and the Third Department's (the political secret service) endless questioning and inquiry of every real and imagined tale.[34] It is not surprising that, because of the investigation of the Ushits case and Israel of Ruzhin's subsequent escape from Russia, more and more tales spread about the monarchic and adventurous nature of zaddikim. Thus, for example, in 1846 an investigation was initiated into the claim of a Jew from Zhitomir that he had found a letter on a street in Berdichev that testified to a meeting in Sadagora (that never took place) between the rabbi of Ruzhin and Moses Montefiore. The letter described how the zaddik will be the king of Israel and bring about a revolution against the tsar with the aid of Polish lords.[35]

Hasidic hagiography connected the meeting between the rabbi and the tsar also to the purchase of land in the Old City of Jerusalem, where the Tiferet Israel Synagogue would eventually be erected. This synagogue was built long after the deaths of the rabbi and the tsar, but the Hasidic tale claimed that already in 1843, the zaddik had discovered that Nicholas was intending to purchase a plot next to the Western Wall in order to erect a church. The rabbi responded quickly and granted a large sum of money to the printer Nissan Bak, his main representative in Palestine, to buy the plot from the Arabs before the Russian deal went through and build a synagogue for the Sadagora Hasidim on it. When Nicholas discovered that Bak had preempted the Russian consul, he said in anger, "This one [Rabbi Israel] always stands in my way."[36]

In fact, a plot was purchased for the building of a synagogue in 1843, after Rabbi Israel declared that his Hasidim in Jerusalem must pray separately from the other Hasidic communities. However, construction did not begin until after 1859, when an official Ottoman license (*firman*) was finally procured. We have no evidence that Nicholas was interested in purchasing a plot in the Old City during the same period. Russian land purchases in Jerusalem began only in the second half of the 1850s, mainly after the Crimean War and the death of Nicholas. Building activity centered almost entirely in the western part of Jerusalem, outside the walls of the Old City, because the needs of Russian pilgrims required the establishment of a large and imposing compound. It is clear, therefore, that the story of an alleged competition regarding the purchase of the plot in the Old City has no historical basis.[37] The Russians did eventually build a church and pilgrim hostel, known as the Russian Compound, in the western part of Jerusalem.

Depicting Rabbi Israel as someone who was in constant struggle with the tsar served, paradoxically, the purposes of the maskilim, Hasidism's opponents, who wanted to portray Hasidism as a provocative, dangerous, and politically unstable entity that was disloyal to the regime under which the Hasidim lived. However, this subversive image contradicts the historical reality in which Hasidism functioned as a steady and conservative force that had no interest in unnecessary provocation against the government or in destabilizing the old political order.

In another Hasidic tale we read that Nicholas sent a converted Jew disguised as a Hasid to spy on Rabbi Israel in order to find some pretext against him. This is a familiar literary motif in Hasidic hagiography: In the eyes of its opponents, Hasidism is a secretive, difficult-to-infiltrate sect, and the only way to discover its mystery and political intentions is through espionage. However, the zaddik, in his wisdom, is able to uncover the spy's identity, whether he be a non-Jew or a *maskil*, and teach him a moral lesson.[38] Here too, the spy comes to the Hasidic court in the guise of a wealthy Hasid, who tells the rabbi of his failing business as a result of the tsar's edicts and pleads for him to curse the tsar to die so that a better ruler will replace him. Of course, the zaddik discovers the plot and says nothing against the tsar; instead, he tells a roundabout tale that concludes with a teaching that the tsar is in no way responsible for the persecution of the Jews, for "the king's heart [is] in the hand of the Lord" (Proverbs 21:1). Like Pharaoh, God hardens Nicholas's heart on purpose. The hidden lesson is that the great and all-powerful tsar is actually a small pawn in the divine plan.[39]

The most recent version of this Hasidic tale comes from a Chabad internet website. The teller, Rabbi Nissan Mindel, picks up the folk tradition of Nicholas's fear of the zaddik of Ruzhin, who behaved like a king and did not recognize the tsar's authority. The ending and moral lesson of this version is noteworthy.

> "Your majesty, our Torah teaches us that the heart of kings and princes is in the hand of God. When Jews faithfully keep the Torah and *mitzvos*, they are treated kindly, when they neglect the Torah and *mitzvos*, God hardens the heart of their king. Jews always realize that whether they fare well or badly, it is entirely up to them, and *they never pray for a new king, because there is no certainty that the new king will be any better.*" . . .
>
> Having concluded his story, the Ruzhiner looked straight into the eyes of his visitor and said to him: "Go and tell those who have sent you here that all accusations against Jews of being unfaithful to the king are false. *Jews are always loyal citizens* and pray for the welfare of the rulers and of the country in which they live."[40]

Despite the modern wording and the fact that it is a complete invention, the author perfectly summarizes the authentic Hasidic worldview: The survival of traditional Jewish society, sheep surrounded by 70 wolves (Gentiles and unfaithful Jews), can be assured only through absolute loyalty to the ruler and not by provocation, demonization, or struggle. This statement clearly reflects Hasidism's nature as an exilic movement in the deepest sense of the word. Hasidism sees the answer to the Jews' troubles not through modern solutions (such as the national radicalism of Zionism or the social radicalism of the worker movements) but rather in a realpolitik framework, where the Jews' ability to reshape the world order is small. Apparently, this conservative position, which demands loyalty to the authorities that be, is contrary to the militant message of the Hasidic tales that call for a cosmic struggle between the forces of light and the forces of darkness. Nevertheless, the truth in these conflicting attitudes is not contradictory. They reflect different dimensions: the realistic world, where it is preferable to get along with the harsh ruler in power; and the mythic world, with its ongoing war between the "angel of Esau" and the "angel of Jacob."[41]

Conclusion

Hasidic tales that describe encounters between the righteous zaddikim and the authorities who represent the empire of evil are influenced also by kabbalistic theories that identify the human evil with demons and spiritual impurity infiltrating the world. Religious thought, both popular and elite, was not satisfied with an interpretation of the political reality as it was but saw in it a reflection of hidden cosmic events understandable only according to traditional exegetical patterns. The Gentile rulers are not merely representatives of a political regime with which it is necessary to get along in the real world, in the spirit of talmudic expressions such as "Pray for the welfare of the government" (*Avot* 3:2) or *dina de-malkhuta dina*, meaning "the law of the government is the law" (BT *Gittin* 10b). They are pawns on the Almighty's primordial chessboard along with the zaddikim of the generation. In this game, though, the standard rules keep changing. This game is a struggle between the forces of evil and the forces of goodness and a competition between spiritual impurity and those whose mission it is to destroy it and bring the captured sparks to redemption. In these interpretive patterns that characterized the thought of kabbalistic circles, folktales became integrated with fragments of reality.

There is another telling aspect of the stories of meetings between zaddikim and rulers: Judeo-centrism. This outlook finds expression, paradoxically, not only in Hasidic lore but also in the modern imagery of antisemites, who likewise exaggerate the importance of Jews and their influence, both monetary and mystical, on the non-Jewish government system. The memory traditions of the Hasidim reflect, of course, their moral and educational needs, and these, as far from reality as they may be, sometimes find their way to the ears of those who are interested, for entirely different reasons, in magnifying the power of the Jews.

From a Hasidic perspective, the typological conflict between the zaddik and the tsar is not a kind of folklore. Contemporary Hasidim viewed actions that to the outsider appeared mystical and irrational as practical. In Poland in 1757, Israel Ba'al Shem Tov (the Besht) attempted to cope with the decree to burn the Talmud following the controversy with the Frankists, through a special way of praying.[42] In 1804 Rabbi Nahman of Bratslav sought to abolish the "Jewish statute" of Tsar Alexander I through ecstatic dancing.[43] Abraham Ber Gottlober recounts in his memoirs that in

1827, when Nicholas I's army conscription decree reached his hometown of Starokonstantynów, the Jewish inhabitants, to stave off the evil, used a method recommended by a local magician (*ba'al shem*): They sent a corpse with a signed petition addressed to God, pleading that he take away this iniquity from them.[44] To those on the sidelines, this scene appears absurd, and, in fact, Gottlober brought this story to show his readers "how far belief in the dead had penetrated among our folk due to the crimes of the Hasidim." Yet, in the eyes of the Hasidim, this was a practice equivalent in importance to using an intercessor, bribery, or any other practical-activist means.[45] The secular viewpoint, which sees this act as "passive resistance," is not exact;[46] it would be more correct to view it as "traditional activism."

This unique activism might be better understood through the story of the zaddik Abraham Twersky of Turisk (1806–1889), who "absolutely despised the Russian Tsar Alexander the Second, and countless times aggressively cursed him; not only in front of his confidants but also in front of strangers." He would openly preach against the tsar and explicitly voice his hope for his demise. His sons cautioned him that in doing so he was endangering his own life and the lives of the Hasidim who listened to him, "for among those who listen to the teachings are all sorts of people, some of them who are unknown to us, and who knows if among them may be found informers." The rabbi responded to his sons with wonder tinged with naïveté and the pretense of innocence: "It had not crossed my mind that my sons would think that I organize my Torah teachings. Am I aware of how my words are taken? Am I to be guilty if such expressions as these are heard coming from my mouth?"[47]

From the zaddik's point of view, the preaching of Torah, which by chance includes curses against the ruler, is not a political act of rebellion but a mystical move for which he is not responsible. From our perspective, there is no doubt that this mysticism contains clear political aspects.

The attitude toward the Austrian emperors was no different, as the following two strange tales, which also highlight the term *traditional activism*, reveal. According to a nineteenth-century Hasidic tradition, the *maggid* Israel of Koznicz (1736–1814) called his attendant during the third Sabbath meal and asked him to bring him his cane: "And he gave it to him. And he [the *maggid*] got up from the table and stood in the middle of the room, and called out these words to a tune: Frants, Frants, ker zich iber mit dem shwants [Franz, Franz flip over with your penis] . . . and he held his cane up in his hand . . . and he did this a number of times."[48] The song's vulgarity, which, surprisingly, was preserved in a Hasidic source, points to its authenticity. But who is this Franz? We must conclude that it relates to Franz II (1768–1835), the grandchild of Empress Maria Theresa and the last emperor of the Holy Roman Empire, who in 1804 established the Austrian Empire and was known since then as Franz I. We have no idea how the name of Franz I came to the attention of the *maggid* and what was the specific event that caused the *maggid* to rhyme *Frants* with *shwants*. Perhaps it is connected to the Napoleonic wars in Russia.

Another strange tale that relates to Emperor Franz Joseph (1830–1916) is attributed to the zaddik Haim of Kosov (1795–1854).

> In his time . . . Emperor Franz Joseph ascended to the throne [1848]. . . . When he was anointed king, he [Rabbi Haim] requested . . . that they bring him a picture of this young Franz Joseph [who was then 18 years old], and they brought him, and he placed it inside the *maḥzor*, at the back of the book between the pages and the cover. And on Rosh Hashanah he flipped through the pages to that place a number of times and looked at the image of the young Franz Joseph, and every time he would land a sharp blow on the nose of the young emperor in the picture, and this was a mystery. After Rosh Hashanah he said . . . to his close associates: there are three things I wish to impart to you about the Emperor: . . . that he live a long life . . . that he not be a hater of the Jews . . . and that another king shall not rise in his stead in Austria. . . . And the Hasidim interpreted this . . . to mean that the rabbi, in his holy spirit, had seen that this same Emperor would be a great hater of the Jews and would distress them; but with the strength of the rabbi's hands, who struck the Emperor's nose, he sweetened the *Dinim* [heavenly decrees].[49]

This retrospective story, which sticks close to the historical facts (Franz Joseph's reign indeed lasted for 68 years and after his death the Austro-Hungarian Empire indeed was dismantled), seeks mainly an explanation for the fact that this emperor was not only good for the Jews of the empire but also gained their love and admiration. The answer is that, because of his real nature, this emperor was supposed to hate the Jews, but that, thanks to the zaddik's mystical act (slapping Franz Joseph's picture), he was able to sweeten the *dinim* and change the course of history.

Treating these stories as "children's fairy tales," in which "Hasidism would cause the angry mob to nod off," as the historian Simon Dubnow understood the folktales on Leib Surehs, misses the point.[50] Not only does it fail to see the connection to real historical events, but it also mainly elides the unique status of Hasidic folklore, both oral and printed, as, first, the foundation of popular myths that form the structure of the imagery connected with zaddikim and, second, as a fashioner of moral and political patterns of thinking and reaction to historical events of upheaval.

Notes

1. For example, the meeting between Simeon the Just and Alexander the Great (Meir Ben Shahar, "Jews, Samaritans and Alexander: Facts and Fictions in Jewish Stories on the Meeting of Alexander and the High Priest," in *Brill's Companion to the Reception of Alexander the Great*, ed. Kenneth Royce Moore [Leiden: Brill, 2018], 403–26); the meeting between Yohanan ben Zakkai and Vespasian (Gedalyahu Alon, "Rabban Joḥanan B. Zakkai's Removal to Jabneh," in *Jews, Judaism, and the Classical World*, trans. Israel Abrahams [Jerusalem: Magnes, 1977], 269–313; Jeffrey L. Rubenstein, *Talmudic Stories: Narrative Art, Composition, and Culture* [Baltimore: Johns Hopkins University Press, 1999], 139–75); and the meeting between Judah ha-Nasi and Antoninus (Aharon Oppenheimer, *Rabbi Judah ha-Nasi* [Tübingen: Mohr Siebeck, 2017], 48–58).
2. Such as the imaginable meeting between Rashi and Godfrey of Bouillon (Gedaliah ibn Yahya, *Shalshelet ha-kabbalah* [Amsterdam, 1697], 38a) or that between the Maharal of Prague and Emperor Rudolf II (David Gans, *Sefer Ẓemaḥ David*, ed. Mordechai Breuer [Jerusalem: Magnes, 1983], 145).
3. On the term *usable* in the study of Hasidic hagiographic sources, see Moshe Rosman, "Hebrew Sources on the Baal Shem Tov: Usability vs. Reliability," *Jewish History* 27 (2013): 153–69.
4. See also David Assaf, "When the Rabbis 'Met' Napoleon," *Tradition* 54, no. 2 (2022): 55–63.
5. The legendary figure of Surehs influenced the poet Shimshon Meltzer (born in Tłuste in 1909), who devoted a few ballads to him. See Shimshon Meltzer, *Or zaruʿa: sefer ha-shirot ve-ha-baladot* (Tel Aviv: Dvir, 1966), 73–80, 114–26.
6. See *Sipurei ẓadikim meha-ḥut ha-meshulash* (Lemberg, 1864); and Gedaliyah Nigal, ed., *Sipurei Mikhaʾel Levi Rodkinson* (Jerusalem: Hamakhon Leḥeker

Ha-sifrut Ha-ḥasidit, 1988), 102–14. On Rodkinson and his project in the field of Hasidic tales, see Yonatan Me'ir, *Shivḥei Rodkinson: Mikha'el Levi Frumkin-Rodkinson veha-ḥasidut* (Tel Aviv: Hakibuẓ Hame'uḥad, 2012); and the expanded English translation, Jonatan Meir, *Literary Hasidism: The Life and Works of Michael Levi Rodkinson* (Syracuse, NY: Syracuse University Press, 2016).

7 Abraham Ber Gottlober, *Zikhronot umasa'ot*, ed. Reuven Goldberg (Jerusalem: Mosad Bialik, 1976), 1: 180. Gottlober's memoir on Hasidism ("Memoir of My Youth") was originally published in his journal *Ha-boker or* 5–6 (1880–1881).

8 The Polish Sejm's approved abolishment of the Jewish council on 6 June 1764. The decree went into effect on 2 January 1765; see Israel Halperin, ed., *Pinkas va'ad arba araẓot* (Jerusalem: Mosad Bialik, 1945), 440–41. Poniatowski was elected on 7 September 1764, and the coronation ceremony took place on 13 November 1764.

9 Gottlober, *Zikhronot*, 1: 179.

10 *Sefer shmot ha-ẓadikim* ([Mahlov], 1811). The first list, which comprised hundreds of names, was prepared by Rabbi Nahman's disciple Nathan of Nemirov and updated in later editions with the addition of many new names. See David Assaf, *Bratslav: Bibliografiyah mu'eret* (Jerusalem: Merkaz Zalman Shazar, 2000), no. 5.

11 The legend about Leib Surehs's meetings with Joseph II was published first in Gottlober, *Zikhronot*, 1: 181–83, but was hinted in Hasidic sources as well; see Aharon Walden, *Shem ha-gedolim he-ḥadash* (Warsaw, 1864), ma'arekhet gdolim, 43a, no. 42. After Gottlober, such tales were published also by Shmuel Abba Horodezky, "Lekorot ha-hasidut," *Ha-shilo'aḥ*, 13 (1903–1904): 339–43 (a revised version was published in his book *Ha-ḥasidut veha-ḥasidim* [Berlin: Dvir, 1923], 2: 7–12). Consequently, new comments with corrections and new material were published in *Ha-shilo'aḥ*: Yaakov Wasserman, "Le-toldotav shel reb leib surehs," *Ha-shilo'aḥ*, 13 (1903–1904): 481; Yaakov Wasserman, "Le-toldot reb leib surehs [Part I]," *Ha-shilo'aḥ*, 13 (1903–1904): 579–80; and S. A. Kardimon, "Le-toldot reb leib surehs [Part II]," *Ha-shilo'aḥ*, 13 (1903–1904): 580–82. Simon Dubnow wrote in a letter sent to Horodezky in 1903: "On Reb Leib Surehs, we almost have no historical material, unless you add some empty tales from *Adat ẓadikim*, *Sipurei zadikim* and late tales. In my opinion, to devote a special study to this 'riddle' is unnecessary" (S. A. Horodezky, *Zikhronot* [Tel Aviv: Dvir, 1957], 212).

12 Gottlober, *Zikhronot*, 1: 179–84. On the continuity of Leib Surehs's myth among Hasidim during the second half of the nineteenth century, see Mordecai Spector, *Mayn lebn* (Warsaw: Ahisefer, 1927), 3: 44–49; and Yehuda Leib Maimon, *Midei ḥodesh be-ḥodsho* (Jerusalem: Mosad Ha-Rav Kuk, 1958), 4: 181–96. Among Yiddish speakers of that time, there was the expression *Leib surehs krom*, which refers to a very poor shop. The source of this expression is based on a popular tale that, during the big Polish fairs, Leib used to rent an empty store and sit there and rectify the souls of the wandering dead who approached him; see Horodezky, *Ha-ḥasidut veha-ḥasidim*, 2: 8; and Martin Buber, *Or ha-ganuz: sipurei ḥasidim* (Jerusalem: Schocken, 1946), 171–72. Based on this legend, S. Ben-Ẓiyon wrote his story "Be-khanuto shel reb leib surehs" (published in *Prudot: kovez le-divrei sifrut* 1 [1934]: 13–20) and Shimshon Meltzer composed his poem "Takhrikhim" (published in his *Or zaru'a*, 73–76).

13 This is a folk fabrication with no connection to real history. The emperor Joseph II died on 20 February 1790 after being ill for two years; Leib Surehs died a year later, on 10 March 1791, and we do not know how many years he was actually ill. The inscription on Leib's tombstone was copied and published by Wasserman, "Le-toldot reb leib surehs," 579.

14 Horodezky, *Ha-ḥasidut veha-ḥasidim*, 2: 12.

15 Wasserman, "Le-toldot reb leib surehs," 580.

16 Aleksander Zederbaum, *Keter kehunah* (Odessa, 1867), 114–15. We can assume that the "young fellow" refers to Tsar Alexander I.

17 Michael Levi Rodkinson, *Toldot amudei Ḥabad* (Königsberg, 1876), 50. In the book Rodkinson provides more tales about Schneur Zalman's wisdom, which became clear to the Russian ministers during his imprisonment.

18 Mordechai Martin Buber, *Darko shel adam al pi torat ha-ḥasidut* (Jerusalem: Mosad Bialik, 1957), 8 (or, in a slightly different version, Buber, *Or ha-ganuz*, 278). The origin of this tale is Haim Meir Heilman, *Beit rabbi* (Berdichev, 1902), 1: 57–58 (attributed to "one of the rabbis, decedents of our rabbi [Schneur Zalman]"). Interestingly, the age 46 is not mentioned in the original source (*Beit rabbi*), and it is probably Buber's addition, which was later adopted in the Chabad sources; see Shlomo Yosef Zevin, *Sipurei ḥasidim* (Tel Aviv: A. Zioni, 1955), 12–13. Such tales inspired the imaginations of writers and poets—for example, Aaron Zeitlin's 1936 poem "Der tsar un der 'tanya,'" published in his book *Gezamelte lider* (New York: Matanot, 1947), 2: 372–77; and Zalman Shneur's story "Ha-ga'on ve-ha-rav," in his collection *Kitvei Zalman*

Shneur (Tel Aviv: Dvir, 1960), 194–99 (this story is the short version of Zeitlin's five-volume Yiddish novel *Keyser un rebi: historisher roman* [New York: Tsiko Bikher, 1944–1952]).

19 Yehoshua Mondshine, *Ha-ma'asar ha-rishon* (Jerusalem: Knizhniki, 2012), 12.
20 This refers to Stanisław August Poniatowski, the last king of the Poland-Lithuanian Commonwealth (1764–1795), who was appointed to his rule with the intervention of Catherine the Great (who was also the mother of his daughter).
21 Yehoshua Mondshine, *Kerem Ḥabad* 4, no. 1 (1992): 46–47; Mondshine, *Ha-ma'asar ha-rishon*, 62–64.
22 Yehoshua Mondshine, *Ha-masa ha-aḥaron* (Jerusalem: Knizhniki, 2012), 10–16.
23 Shalom Dover Levin, ed., *Ma'asar ve-ge'ulat admor ha-emẓa'i* (Brooklyn: Kehot, 1997).
24 Ilya Luria, *Milḥamot Lyubavitsh: Ḥasidut ḥabad be-Rusya ha-tsarit* (Jerusalem: Merkaz Zalman Shazar, 2018), 180–86.
25 David Assaf, *The Regal Way: The Life and Times of Rabbi Israel of Ruzhin* (Stanford, CA: Stanford University Press, 2002).
26 For an extensive survey of the Ushits case, the conflict between Rabbi Israel and Tsar Nicholas, and the flight from Russia, see Assaf, *Regal Way*, 105–35. For the Hebrew translation of the protocol of the military court's final verdict in the Ushits case, see David Assaf, *Derekh ha-malkhut: Rabbi Yisra'el me-Ruzhin umekomo be-toldot ha-ḥasidut* (Jerusalem: Merkaz Zalman Shazar, 1997), 467–76.
27 This interpretation even made its way into the writing of *maskilim* and historians (such as Simon Dubnow); see Assaf, *Regal Way*, 366–67n46.
28 Shmuel of Sochaczew, *Shem mi-Shmu'el: Bereshis* (Pioterkov: Henech Follman, 1928), 212, 221; Assaf, *Regal Way*, 119n24.
29 See the Russian documents (in Hebrew translation) in Assaf, *Regal Way*, 477–78 (nos. a and e).
30 Eliahu Tcherikower, "He-hamon ha-yehudi, ha-maskilim veha-memshalah biymei Nikolai I," *Zion*, 4 (1939): 150–69; Michael Stanislawski, *Tsar Nicholas I and the Jews: The Transformation of Jewish Society in Russia, 1825–1855* (Philadelphia: Jewish Publication Society, 1983).
31 Isaac Even, *Fun'm rebin's hoyf: zikhroynes un mayses* (New York, self-published, 1922), 29; Aaron Marcus, *Ha-hasidut*, trans. Moshe Shenfeld (Tel Aviv: Netsakh, 1954), 210–11.

32 S. An-sky, *Gezamelte shriftn* (Warsaw, 1928), 6: 135–37; S. Ansky, *The Dybbuk and Other Writings*, trans. Golda Werman, ed. David G. Roskies (New York: Schocken, 1992), 207–8.
33 An-sky, *Gezamelte shriftn*, 6: 135–37; Ansky, *Dybbuk*, 207–8.
34 The Third Department was established in 1826. On this, see Sidney Monas, *The Third Section: Police and Society in Russia Under Nicholas I* (Cambridge, MA: Harvard University Press, 1961); and P. S. Squire, *The Third Department: The Establishment and Practices of the Political Police in the Russia of Nicholas I* (Cambridge, UK: Cambridge University Press, 1968).
35 Saul Ginzburg, *Ketavim historiyim*, trans. Y. L. Baruch (Tel Aviv: Dvir, 1944), 168–71.
36 Abraham Isaac Bromberg, *Mi-gedolei ha-ḥasidut*, vol. 6, *Ha-admor rabbi Israel Fridman me-Ruzhin* (Jerusalem: Mosad Ha-Rav Kuk, 1953), 155–56.
37 Assaf, *Regal Way*, 298–99. For more on the synagogue and its history, see Reuven Gafni, Yochai Ben-Ghedalia, and Uriel Gellman, eds., *Gavoha me-al gavoha: Beit ha-keneset tif'eret yisra'el veha-kehilah ha-ḥasidit bi-Yerushalayim* (Jerusalem: Yad Yitzhak Ben-Zvi, 2016).
38 On this pattern, see David Assaf, "Nifgeshu al yedei eize hitvakhut: masorot zikaron pulmusim al pegishatam shel ribal ve-ha-rabi me-apta," in *Ḥut shel ḥen: shay le-Ḥava Turni'anski*, ed. Israel Bartal, Claudia Rosenzweig, Ada Rapoport-Albert, Viki Shifris, Galit Hasan-Rokem, and Erika Timm (Jerusalem: Merkaz Shazar, 2013), 247–69.
39 Dov Erman, *Devarim arevim* (Munkatsh: Kahn & Fried, 1903), 1: 122; Shlomo Telingator, *Tiferet Yisra'el* (Jerusalem: Kineret, 1945), 45–47.
40 Nissan Mindel, "Rabbi Yisroel Friedman of Ruzhin," chabad.org, www.chabad.org/library/article_cdo/aid/112494/jewish/Rabbi-Yisroel-Friedman.htm (accessed 6 September 2023); emphasis mine.
41 Compare to the writing of Lubavitsh Hasid Rabbi Haim Eliezer Bikhovsky (d. 1924): "But we know in our sense that the *alter rebbe* [Schneur Zalman] replaced Paul and surely replaced his Angel before, and also later during the French war, he replaced Napoleon and surely replaced his Angels before. And the Tzemach Tzedek [the third rebbe of Habad] also replaced Nicholas the First with Alexander the Second, and surely replaced his Angel before too" (Haim Eliezer Bikhovsky, *Kitvei ha-Rakha Biḥovski* [Brooklyn, 1990], 67).
42 Avraham Rubinstein, ed., *Shivḥei ha-Besht* (Jerusalem: Rubin Mass, 1991), 91–94.

43 Nathan Sternhartz of Nemirov, *Sefer ḥayei moharan* (Jerusalem: Keren had-pasa De-ḥasidei Braslav, 1976), siḥot ha-shayakhim la-torot, 15–16, no. 10.
44 Gottlober, *Zikhronot*, 1: 155–58.
45 On the unique nature of Hasidic intercession (*shtadlanut*), see David Assaf and Israel Bartal, "Shtadlanut ve-ortodoksiya: tsadikei Polin be-mifgash im ha-zemanim ha-ḥadashim," in *Ẓadikim ve-anshei Ma'ase: Meḥkarim be-ḥasidut Polin*, ed. Rachel Elior, Israel Bartal, and Chone Shmeruk (Jerusalem: Mosad Bialik, 1994), 65–90; and Marcin Wodziński, "Hasidism, *Shtadlanut*, and Jewish Politics in Nineteenth-Century Poland: The Case of Isaac of Warka," *Jewish Quarterly Review* 95 (2005): 290–320.
46 Tcherikower, *He-hamon ha-yehudi*, 150–54.
47 Mordechai Twersky, *Gedulat Mordekhai [. . .] mi-Kozmir* (Warsaw: Mefiẓei Torah ve-Dat, 1938), 1: 10–11. The same story was told about his son, Mordechai of Kuzmir (1840–1917), regarding Tsar Alexander III (Twersky, *Gedulat Mordekhai*, 20–21). See Gadi Sagiv, "Ḥasidut Tshernobil: toldoteihah ve-torotehah me-reshitah ve-ad erev milḥemet ha-olam ha-rishonah," PhD diss., Tel Aviv University, 2009, 414.
48 Zevi Hershke, "Shemu'ot, mesorot, ve-sipurim mi-ẓadikei Polin," *Heikhal ha-Ba'al Shem Tov* 14 (2006): 96.
49 Hayim Kahana, *Even shetiyah ha-shalem* (New York: Peri Eẓ Ḥayim, 1993), 84.
50 Simon Dubnow, *Toldot ha-ḥasidut* (Tel Aviv: Dvir, 1930), 176.

4

In Search of the Three Sisters

The Genealogy of a Jewish Magical Incantation

Natan M. Meir

In 1909 the ethnographer and writer S. An-sky published a short article in the journal *Evreiskaia Starina* (Jewish Antiquities) about incantations against the evil eye that he had collected from Jews in the northern provinces of the Pale of Settlement.[1] An-sky included in his piece transcriptions of four variants—three in Hebrew and a fourth in Yiddish—of a common incantation beginning with the words "Three women stand on the crag of a rock" (*shalosh nashim omdot al shen selah*; or *dray vayber zitsen oyf a shteyn*). This charm was apparently widespread among Eastern European Jews.[2] What follows is a preliminary attempt to explore the origins of this peculiar incantation, which has deep roots in both Jewish textual traditions and European magical motifs shared by Christians and Jews.[3]

Magical charms and remedies were just one aspect of the larger realm of Jewish vernacular or folk religion that was an integral part of the religious landscape of Jews wherever they lived until the coming of modernity and in many cases well into the modern era. In the late nineteenth century and into the twentieth, Jewish historical writing usually treated folk religious practices as superstitions and thus found them unworthy of attention. One notable exception was Simon Dubnow, founder of Russian Jewish historiography, who encouraged Russian Jews to collect all artifacts of folk culture for an all-encompassing understanding of the Jewish people's historical experience.[4] It was folklorists and ethnographers like An-sky who collected evidence of such practices and, in some cases, attempted to analyze them, often in comparison with similar rituals and customs in other religious cultures.[5]

The Evil Eye

The concept of the evil eye—"the belief that someone can project harm by looking at another's property or person"—is shared by many cultures, especially in the Near East, the Mediterranean basin, Europe, parts of sub-Saharan Africa, and South Asia.[6] In biblical and rabbinic sources the evil eye (Hebrew, *ayin ha-ra*; Aramaic, *eina bisha*) is frequently associated with ill-will, jealousy, stinginess, and selfishness and sometimes with sinfulness and destructive intent.[7] Ancient and medieval rabbinic literature also frequently blamed sickness and death on the evil eye, as in an oft-quoted passage from the Babylonian Talmud (*Bava Mezia* 107b) in which the sage Rav went to a cemetery and divined that 99 out of 100 of those buried there had died by the evil eye.[8] In kabbalistic thought, as it was developed by Hasidic teachers, if one admired with avarice an item belonging to someone else, one could unwittingly sever that item from its supernal roots, thus contributing to the power of evil in the world.[9]

In traditional Jewish culture the evil eye generally took two forms. The first form originated with a specific person who had the power to "cast" the evil eye—in other words, to cause harm to others by his or her powerful gaze—often motivated by envy or greed. But the evil eye could also be cast unwittingly simply by admiring a neighbor's child or domestic animal or even by staring. The second kind of evil eye was a more general notion of danger emanating from the invisible but very real world of demons that was interwoven with the ordinary visible world.[10] Sometimes the two were linked; as William Sumner wrote of the evil eye in his cross-cultural analysis, "It is the demons who are irritated by human luck and prosperity who inflict calamity, pain, and loss, at the height of good luck."[11]

Defenses against the evil eye included both preventive and counteractive measures.[12] Preventive measures often consisted of avoiding praising or counting one's family members or wealth, as in the Yiddish expression *keneyn[eh]ore* ("no evil eye"), often inserted in speech after referencing one's own or someone else's good fortune.[13] Some would attempt to hide or veil beauty, which was understood to attract the evil eye; in traditional Eastern European Jewish culture, this could take the form of describing children as ugly instead of beautiful and even dirtying their faces with coal dust.[14] Euphemisms were also considered an effective prophylaxis, as in referring to the cemetery as "the house of life."[15] Standard methods of counteracting the evil eye once it had been cast included deploying scriptural verses, various names of God, and spells.[16]

The concept of the evil eye held a central place in the folk cultures of both Ashkenazic and Sephardic Jews, and prophylactic measures and counteractive remedies, including incantations, amulets, and hand gestures, circulated freely between the two cultural spheres in the premodern era (and to an even greater extent today in contemporary Israel).[17] So too did aspects of folk magic move across the boundaries of faith communities, often more easily than we might imagine.[18]

In collections of magical remedies and charms that featured *Shalosh nashim*, the incantation was often ascribed to the early Hasidic master Shemuel Shmelke Halevi Horowitz of Nikolsburg (Poland/Moravia, 1726–78).[19] Because the incantation appears in an Italian collection of magical charms that probably dates to the fifteenth century, it seems impossible that Horowitz had a hand in its crafting, though he may have had an authentic association with it (e.g., if he recommended its use to his followers). It may be of note that one of Horowitz's disciples, Israel Hopstein, known as the Maggid of Kozhniz (Kozienice), was known for his familiarity with magic and used "amulets and similar accoutrements to heal the sick, exorcise demons, cure sterility, and the like."[20] It would certainly not have been at all unusual for a Hasidic rabbi like Horowitz to engage in magical practices.

Shalosh Nashim: The Text

The charm circulated in two versions: Hebrew and Yiddish. The Hebrew version, which was usually replete with biblical verses, was usually used by *ba'alei shem* (magico-religious healers), whereas the Yiddish version, which sometimes replaced the verses with rhymes borrowed from Slavic charms, was used by female healers and spell casters (*opshprekherkes*). The Yiddish version sometimes also included information (magical metadata, as it were) on performative practices that were supposed to attend the charm, such as spitting and yawning; both of these actions were associated in many traditional cultures with the evil eye or the defense against it (sympathetic magic often prescribed as an antidote to a particular evil an imitation of that very evil).

The following tale is a representative version of the Hebrew charm, synthesized from several sources:

> Three women are sitting on the crag of a rock: The first says "So-and-so [N., son/daughter of N.] is sick," the second says, "So-and-so is not sick," and the third says, "So-and-so is not sick and will never be sick." If a man cast this evil eye on him, may the hair of his head and his beard fall out. And if a woman cast this evil eye on him, may her teeth fall out and her breasts fall off. Just as the sea is uncharted and fish and ants have no kidneys, may so-and-so not be touched by any evil, pain, or damage, and may the evil eye have no power over him. For he is of the seed of Joseph. As it is written, "Joseph is a fruitful bough, a fruitful bough by a well, whose branches run over the wall" [Genesis 49:22, NJPS translation]. "Then Israel sang this song: 'Spring up, O well! Sing unto it!' The well the leaders sank, dug by the nation's nobles, by the lawgiver, with their staves. And from the wilderness they went to Mattanah, from Mattanah to Nahaliel, from Nahaliel to Bamoth, and from Bamoth in the valley that is in the country of Moab, to the top of Pisgah, which looks down on the wasteland" [Numbers 21:17–20]. Just as Hezekiah King of Judah was healed from his illness, so may so-and-so be healed quickly and return to his former strength by the force of the Name that emerges from the acrostic A-G-L-A [*atah gibor le-olam Adonai*; You are forever powerful, Lord].[21]

The Yiddish version was often similar to the Hebrew, though it usually began as follows: "Tfu! Tfu! Tfu! So-and-so is under an evil eye [i.e., under a spell] [said three times]. Three women sit on a rock. The first says, So-and-so has an evil eye; the second says, No; the third says, Wherever it came from, let it go back there."[22] One Yiddish variant omits the biblical verses altogether, substituting an imprecation for banishing the evil eye that referred to empty fields and forests "where people do not venture and where wild animals roam."[23]

Apparently, the incantation was often used for a person who fell ill suddenly, where the cause of the illness was assumed to be an evil eye that had been cast upon him or her.[24] In some cases the charm was recited by three elderly women, as a kind of performance of the text of the formula itself. According to one description, the women murmured the words quietly, and at a certain point they began to yawn; the patient then invariably began to yawn as well. Yawning was understood to be efficacious against the evil eye.[25]

The imprecation directed at the unknown caster of the evil eye is not, as it might seem at first blush, an incidental element of the charm. "If a man cast this evil eye on him, may the hair of his head and his beard fall out. And if a woman cast this evil eye on him, may her teeth fall out and her breasts fall off." The phrases are almost identical to those found in other folk cultures. For example, folk healers on a Greek island studied by anthropologist Regina Dionisopoulos-Mass in the 1970s would recite the following: "If it is a woman who has cast the eye, then destroy her breasts. If it is a man who has cast the eye, then crush his genitals."[26] In his pathbreaking essay "Wet and Dry, the Evil Eye," Alan Dundes argues that the notion of the evil eye rests on the concept that "life depends on liquid" and that the evil eye threatens to drain the life force out of an individual, leaving it dry. Life and the continuation of life are integrally linked to human sexuality and the reproductive organs, which in turn are associated with various forms of liquid—semen, blood, and breast milk. Thus the person casting the evil eye is assumed to want to "steal" the life force away from their victim. Indeed, in another incantation against the evil eye that was used by Eastern European Jews, the prophet Elijah encounters a dark angel (in one version Dumah/Dume, the angel with authority over souls in hell) who says that he is on his way to eat the flesh and drink the blood of the person who has been struck by the evil eye. (This may be the evil angel that was sometimes said to be generated by a gaze of anger or envy.)[27] In response, Elijah intones, "Just as you do not have permission to drink all the waters of the sea [alternative version: all the waters of the Jordan River], so may you not have permission to harm" that individual.[28] The motif of liquid is clear here: The adjuration draws a link between human blood and the waters of the sea. In the *Shalosh nashim* charm, the man's hair and beard are symbols of masculinity and virility, and the woman's teeth symbolize feminine beauty; all these are associated with sexuality and the life force. And as we shall see, the topos of water plays a central role in the spell.

Medieval Antecedents

Deep in the substratum of European folk culture lies the motif of the three sisters, who appear in many Christian magical incantations across the European continent. Giuseppe Veltri locates the origins of the sisters in Greco-Roman culture: the three *Parcae*, or Fates. The Fates "originally were goddesses of birth, and . . . were also considered to be deities of fortune. . . . The sisters' function is to decide one's fate and to protect the infants during birth."[29] Whereas pre-Christian traditions gave the Fates a positive valence, Christianity saw in them "demons of the afterlife."[30]

Two of the earliest incantations to feature the three female figures were charms against uterine or abdominal pain that Marcellus Empiricus (Marcellus of Bordeaux; fourth–fifth centuries) reproduced in his *De Medicamentis*.[31] In this case the incantations revolve around three virgins in the middle of the sea. In one charm they have placed a marble table (a symbol we will discuss later) in the middle of the sea. In the other the virgins are circumambulating a tree standing in the middle of the sea, from whose branches hangs a bucket of human intestines; two of the women knot them and the other unravels them.[32] The contradictory nature of the maidens' actions—two of them cause pain by knotting the entrails while the third relieves the pain by unraveling them—might be a symptom of their hybrid valence: The Fates were pagan goddesses but took on a demonic character (or at least partly so) in the Christian era. As Edina Bozóky explains, this kind of magical formula revolves around the historiola, a mythical story that "invoke[s] from the past a miraculous incident—most commonly a miraculous healing—that presents analogous circumstances to the situation of the patient."[33]

In the High Middle Ages the charm of the three virgins usually found expression in historiolas in which the three figures undertake three separate actions, the last of which is decisive for the healing nature of the spell, as in the charm from *De Medicamentis*.[34] A typical pattern is as follows: "The first says, 'I see blood'; the second says, 'I want to draw back the blood' [*reculer le sang*]; the third says, 'I stop so-and-so's blood.'"[35] These charms frequently included river or water imagery: "Three Marys passed over the holy bridge" (Spain, 1486); "There were three Maryes went over the floude [river]" (England, 1684).[36]

One of the earliest pieces of evidence that we have for Jewish use of the trope of the three sisters lies in a womb incantation—a charm meant to ease childbirth or uterine pain—in medieval Judeo-German, which opens with the words, "Womb, lie down! You are as old as me. If you take me down to the earth, you must be buried with me." The text, which was written (as magical incantations often were) on the margins of an existing manuscript, was originally brought to light by the rabbi and historian Moritz Güdeman in the late nineteenth century and was more recently reconsidered by Veltri and John Howard, who dated the text to the fourteenth century.[37] The charm speaks of a fish without scales (which Veltri identifies as a dolphin, an allusion to the womb) swimming in a "bottomless sea" and then of three mermaids sitting on the sand with the supplicant's entrails.[38] The first mermaid beats the intestines, the second straightens them out, and the third moves them into the right place. The desired effect is clear: Whereas the first maiden is the putative cause for the uterine pain, the second and third ease the symptoms by counteracting the action of their sister.

Womb incantations could of course be recited at childbirth, and a related set of charms and rituals were intended to appease the spirits who might harm or kidnap a newborn. One such ritual was preparing a table for the three sisters or similar demonic spirits after the birth of the child.[39] Among the Jews of medieval Ashkenaz, this took the form of the Wachnacht, an opportunity for relatives and friends of the family of the newborn, especially women, to gather the night before the circumcision for a festive meal. The goal was to fend off demons, particularly Lilith, the demoness who was understood to kidnap Jewish babies before the circumcision, at this intensely vulnerable moment.[40] The Wachnacht became a widespread tradition in medieval Jewish communities, though it did not gain that name until the early modern period.[41] The custom paralleled the Christian vigil on the night before a child's baptism, which also incorporated a special meal, a practice linked to the tradition of leaving food out for spirits such as Frau Holle to dissuade them from kidnapping the unbaptized child.[42] In a medieval ritual similar to the Wachnacht in which a Jewish child received her or his non-Jewish name, medieval Ashkenazic

Jews called out to Holle and asked her what that name should be. The ritual came to be called Hollekreisch or holekrash.[43]

As evidence that medieval Ashkenazic Jews had the custom of preparing a table with food the night before the circumcision, we have the description of Rabbi Yeruḥam ben Meshullam, active in early- to mid-fourteenth-century Provence and Spain, of just such a practice.[44] Apparently, the explanation that was often provided was that the meal would ensure luck for the newborn. The custom was found among Polish Jews in the sixteenth century, because in his glosses on the *Shulḥan Arukh* Moses Isserles noted that there were places where the custom was to set a table and place food on it the evening before the circumcision. In theory, this kind of practice was forbidden because it was tantamount to setting the table for idolatrous purposes, the prooftext for which was Isaiah's reference to those "who set a table for Luck" (*le-orekh le-gad shulḥan*; Isaiah 65:11, NJPS translation). The Hebrew term *gad* can mean "luck" as well as a god of fortune—not a coincidence, I would suggest: Isserles was almost certainly referring to the Fates or their contemporary European equivalent. But he added that some recent authorities had permitted the custom for the good fortune of the infant (*le-mazal ha-tinok*).[45] Whether or not rabbinic authorities gave their approbation, at least some Jews maintained the practice; in the seventeenth century the Polish-Lithuanian rabbi Shabbetai ben Meir HaKohen, author of the *Siftei Kohen*, emphasized that, although having a special meal the evening before the circumcision, called a *vakh*, was not forbidden, placing food on the table with the intention that it be left there overnight was.[46]

There was Jewish textual precedent for the idea of three supernal beings protecting the baby from Lilith. The *Alphabet of Sirach*, an early medieval collection of proverbs and fables, includes a legend in which three angels engage in a battle with the demonic Lilith, whose entire purpose of existence is to harm children and, in some texts, to suck their blood.[47] Ultimately, Lilith gives up, saying, "I swear unto you by the name of the living and great God, that whenever I shall see either you or your names or your images on an amulet, I will not hurt that child."[48] This trope was undoubtedly linked to a common magical formula in medieval Christian Europe that referred to three angels—often Raphael, Gabriel, and Michael—impeding seven demons of illness from doing harm to an individual.[49]

The motif of the three sisters spread far and wide throughout Europe, including Poland, where, as was true in much of Eastern Europe, the three were often grouped together with a mother figure.[50] This might be St. Sophia with her three martyred daughters, Faith, Hope, and Charity, or St. Odile (Polish, Otylija). According to legend, Odile, patron saint of Alsace, was born blind, and her sight was miraculously restored thanks to baptismal water. The cult of Odile is thus associated not only with sight and the eyes—she is the patron saint of the blind—but also with water, and many hagiographic accounts of her life recount that Odile "made numerous springs flow."[51] Hagiographic accounts of Odile's life mention no daughters, but a common Polish magical incantation still recounted that "St. Odile had three daughters." For the charm to be effective, of course, it did not matter whether it had any relationship to historical reality; what was important was that it listed the three sisters and their actions, one after another. In this case: "Saint Odile had three daughters: / One spun, / The second embroidered, / The third cast charms with the help of the Lord."[52] In this particular case the action of spinning is analogous to the knotting that we saw in the earlier charm; the first sister is symbolically twisting the patient's innards, which the rest of the charm would then undo.

Although there is generally little variation in the core phrase of the charm—"Three women stand on the crag of a rock"—among the different versions that circulated, the few we have are significant. The text usually begins with "Three women," but an Italian collection of practical Kabbalah dating probably to the late Middle Ages has "three sisters" instead, as does a medico-magical text from the eighteenth or nineteenth century preserved in manuscript.[53] Given that these are likely among the earliest extant versions of the incantation, this difference is significant and may point to an earlier version that is closer to the Christian "three sisters" charms discussed earlier.

Another important variation can be found in an article on Jewish religious customs in which Samuel Rappoport reproduced the text of *Shalosh nashim*, noting that when the healer is reciting the last verse from Numbers 21 ("from Bamoth [the heights] to the valley"), "it is important to think about the abovementioned three women."[54] But why? This may give us an important insight into the oral tradition of how the charm was supposed to be recited and may also be a remnant of the Christian substratum of the text, in which the women functioned as intercessors or even goddesslike figures. It also provides a clear linkage between the "heights" of the biblical verse and the stony outcropping on which the three women were imagined to be standing. That the women were sometimes perceived as intercessory figures is made even more explicit in the variant that we find in Avrom Rechtman's account of the ethnographic expedition organized by S. An-sky in the Pale of Settlement in 1913–1914, which includes the assurance that "the three women will intercede for you" (*Di dray vayber zoln zikh far dir miyen*).[55]

Biblical Texts and Their Networks of Meaning

Now that we have examined the core phrase of the charm, let us take some time to understand the biblical verses that were usually included in the second half of the conjuration. Because the earliest versions of the charm that we have date to the early modern period or even the late Middle Ages, it is possible to cast our net quite wide in searching for any subtextual symbolic meanings that may have had significance for premodern Jews. These textual allusions may refer to classical midrash, kabbalistic teachings, medieval tales, and other components of the Jewish textual corpus that were in many cases accessible only to learned men, but in other cases they could be available to ordinary men and women through popularized versions of the original texts.

The first biblical passage quoted in the charm is from Jacob's blessing of Joseph in Genesis 49:22: *ben porat yosef, ben porat alei ayin*, often translated as "Joseph is a fruitful bough, a fruitful bough by a well" (NKJV translation). A midrash in the Babylonian Talmud, noting that *ayin* means "eye" in addition to "well," renders *alei* as *olei*, yielding, "transcending the influence of the [evil] eye" (BT *Berakhot* 20a). For that reason, this phrase frequently appears in spells against the evil eye. In some versions of the three-women charm, the quotation includes the next few words in the verse: *banot tsa'adah alei shur*, traditionally rendered as "His branches run over the wall." The medieval French commentator Rashi, drawing on a midrash in *Bereshit Rabbah* 98:18, explains that the word *banot* can actually be understood literally as "daughters," a reference to the Egyptian princesses (kings' daughters) who peeked through the lattices in pharaoh's palace to get a glimpse of Joseph. Even when they threw their jewelry at him to get his attention, he did not look at them, the midrash notes with satisfaction—a reference to Joseph's purity and virtuous character. From a literary perspective it is internally consistent that a spell that revolves around the trope of three (supernatural?) women contains a biblical passage referring to princesses.

We now move on to the long quote from Numbers 21 referring to the well of the chieftains: "Then Israel sang this song: 'Spring up, O well! Sing unto it!'" As Tuszewicki suggests, this passage is clearly a reference to Miriam's Well, which according to a rabbinic legend magically followed the Israelites, sustaining them with fresh water during their 40-year trek through the wilderness.[56] The well, identified in some sources with the water source created when Moses struck the rock in Exodus 17, had such great power in the rabbinic imagination that it was considered one of the ten items created on the eve of the first Sabbath (*Avot* 5:6)—in other words, the last things to be created ex nihilo during the first week of Creation. Because the topos of water was a central one for charms against the evil eye and demons, it makes some sense that among the additional items that some rabbis added to the list of those created on the eve of the first Sabbath were the demons.

According to one midrash, the well miraculously revealed to the Israelites wandering in the desert the wonderous victories that God had wrought for them over their enemies without their knowledge. It did so by sending its water into the caves where enemy troops had assembled, and from which they planned to ambush the Israelites, but where they ultimately met their doom at the hand of God. The well's water then returned to the Israelites in a geyser of severed limbs.[57] Miriam's Well is thus a potent symbol of God's protection of his people from evil and of their triumph over their enemies—an apt association for a charm against the evil eye.

The Jewish mystical tradition also linked Miriam's Well with the notion of combating evil in the following way. In kabbalistic imagery one of the many symbols for *malkhut*, the lowest *sefirah*, was the well, because *malkhut* was figured as a vessel receiving the flow of divine energy from the other *sefirot* by means of the *sefirah* of *yesod*.[58] The *Zohar Ḥadash* comments on Numbers 21 that the song that the Israelites sang to the well (i.e., Miriam's Well) was intended to mystically link the tangible well of this world with the supernal well, *malkhut*. Thus, when they sang, "Spring up, well!" they were actually enjoining *malkhut*, the lower mother, to rise up and join with *binah*, the third *sefirah*, also known as the "upper mother."[59] When that took place, the serpent—symbol of evil—departed from the world.

There is also a tradition associating Miriam's Well with magical healing. *Sefer ha-orah*, a medieval work attributed to the eleventh-century commentator Solomon ben Isaac (Rashi), recounts a tale in which the waters of Miriam's Well magically surge in arbitrary fashion into all the springs and wells in the world at the close of the Sabbath. Thus, if one draws water at that time, one may be lucky enough to dip into the magical waters of the well, which heal maladies of the skin instantaneously.[60]

The incantation's reference to King Hezekiah is obviously an allusion to an instance of wondrous healing: when Hezekiah fell gravely ill, prayed to God for healing, and was answered.[61] But there is more to it than that. Hezekiah is associated in several ways with water, which we have already seen is a consistent motif in the *Shalosh nashim* charm and its antecedents. II Chronicles recounts that during the Assyrian siege of Jerusalem, Hezekiah diverted the spring of Gihon from its usual path into a channel that fed a manmade pool.[62] Rabbinic legend related that Hezekiah hid a list of healing springs that circulated among the common folk because they resorted to the springs rather than praying to God for assistance.

The Stone and the Water

In our charm the three women are always described as standing or sitting "on the crag of a rock" (Hebrew version) or "on a stone" (Yiddish version). The Hebrew phrase *shen ha-selah* (Job 39:28) was probably borrowed from the biblical text to give the charm a more traditionally Jewish cast, especially in its initial phrase, where the reference to "three women" has no clear Jewish textual referent. The original context of the phrase in Job bears no relationship to the incantation against the evil eye.[63] On the other hand, the rock or stone is a magical symbol that reappears in many European charms. A figure sitting or standing on a stone, especially of marble, is a widespread trope in magical charms. The mountain, of course, is an intermediary between heaven and earth.[64]

As Edina Bozóky writes, "In folklore charms, water and stone are also often associated."[65] In Slavic medico-magical texts, the stone is usually pictured submerged in the sea.[66] A Yiddish spell to stop a nosebleed is reminiscent of the charm in *De Medicamentis* that we saw earlier: "Under the black sea lies a white stone. Under the stone [the waters] flow."[67] We have already seen a medieval charm that refers to "the bottomless sea." Although our incantation does not picture the stone on water, in one Yiddish-language version the three women stand on a stone in the middle of the desert, ontologically similar to the sea in its expansiveness, seeming endlessness, and sublimity.[68] (The image is similar to that evoked by the biblical reference in the charm to "the top of Pisgah, which looks down on the wasteland.") Perhaps an older version had the three women standing on a rock in the middle of the sea, and that latter portion was lost over time. It is certainly true that most variants of the charm include a reference to the uncharted sea (*keshem she'eyn la-yam derekh*), and we have already noted the significance of the reference to Miriam's Well.

Why, then, is the motif of water so central to *Shalosh nashim*? Returning to Dundes's theory of wet and dry, we note that the quest to combat the evil eye is fundamentally about countering the forces of evil and death, which sought to drain the vitality out of the patient. In the end, although the text opens with a crag of a rock as the setting for the incantation, it is water, in both direct references and biblical allusions—the sea, the well, the Spring of Gihon, the healing pools—that occupies pride of place in the incantation.

Conclusion

A cursory survey reveals that *Shalosh nashim* is apparently still in use among contemporary Israeli Jews, though a more thorough exploration of its persistence in contemporary Israeli society is outside the scope of this study. In 2019, for example, a framed Israeli amulet for protection against the evil eye was offered for auction on the European Catawiki website; the text included the three-women incantation. According to the description provided by the seller, the amulet was given as a gift to donors to Yeshivat Ha-mekubbalim, a center of kabbalistic study in Jerusalem.[69] In March 2020 the website of Breslav Meir, a Jerusalem-based religious and charitable organization with roots in Breslav Hasidism, published two incantations ("prayers") against the evil eye by Pinḥas of Korets and Shmelke of

Nikolsburg; the latter was a version of the three-women charm.[70] This is only one page of many on the website with advice on and charms against the evil eye.[71]

But the most interesting recent version of *Shalosh nashim*—with slight but significant variations from the text we have examined—appeared in a 2009 article on charms against the evil eye on the popular ultra-Orthodox Israeli website Kikar Ha-shabbat. The most notable interpolation was a passage from another adjuration about the meeting on the road between Elijah and Lilith and her hosts in which the prophet forbids the demoness from harming the individual she has set out to harm by means of the evil eye.[72] This latest version of the charm, though preserving the core text about the three women, evidently does away with some of the enigmatic character of the classic version by introducing the figure of Lilith. As we have seen, Lilith and other demonic figures may well have hovered just beneath the visible text of the spell, but they rarely surfaced. Here, however, Lilith enters into the text and the three women are subsumed into her shadow, as it were. Nonetheless, they persist: nameless, faceless, standing on the crag of a rock. Their staying power after so many centuries is remarkable indeed and a testament to the lasting potency of the image of the three women and their millennia-old roots in Jewish and European cultures.

Notes

It is a privilege to contribute to this volume in honor of my teacher Michael Stanislawski. His sophisticated historical thinking, attention to minute details in the historical source, and compassion and empathy for historical actors have served as models to me since the start of my career as a historian. Among the many things he taught me—in the classroom, on the printed page, and in our tête-à-têtes—perhaps the one that has influenced me the most is his advice to not hide the unknowns or blank spaces in one's research. If you're not sure about something or don't have the evidence to substantiate a point, tell your readers! They'll appreciate your frankness.

1 On An-sky's ethnographic activities, see Gabriella Safran, *Wandering Soul: The Dybbuk's Creator, S. An-sky* (Cambridge, MA: Harvard University Press, 2010), 142–46, 187–96; and Nathaniel Deutsch, *The Jewish Dark Continent:*

Life and Death in the Russian Pale of Settlement (Cambridge, MA: Harvard University Press, 2011).

2 Abraham Rechtman, *Yidishe etnografye un folklor; zikhroynes vegn der etnografisher ekspeditsye, ongefirt fun Sh. An-ski* (Buenos Aires: Yidisher visnshaftlekher institut, 1958), 293.

3 COVID-19 restrictions on interlibrary loan activity during the writing of this piece meant that I did not have access to the full scope of literature that I would ordinarily have consulted. I am grateful to Marek Tuszewicki and Shaul Stampfer for sharing material with me and to Admiel Kosman, Elly Moseson, and John Ott for helpful references.

4 Dan Ben-Amos, "Jewish Studies and Jewish Folklore," *Proceedings of the World Congress of Jewish Studies* 10, Division D (Art, Folklore, and Music), 2 (1989): 5–11; Simon Dubnow, *Ob izuchenii istorii russkikh evreev i ob uchrezh-denii russko-evreiskago obshchestva* (St. Petersburg: A. E. Landau, 1891), 73.

5 On the study of Jewish folklore in Eastern Europe, see Haya Bar-Yitzhak, *Pioneers of Jewish Ethnography and Folkloristics in Eastern Europe* (Ljubljana, Slovenia: Scientific Research Center of the Slovenian Academy of Sciences and Art, 2010); Itzik Nakhmen Gottesman, *Defining the Yiddish Nation: The Jewish Folklorists of Poland* (Detroit: Wayne State University Press, 2003); and Barbara Kirshenblatt-Gimblett, "Folklore, Ethnography, and Anthropology," *The YIVO Encyclopedia of Jews in Eastern Europe*, yivoencyclopedia.org/article.aspx/Folklore_Ethnography_and_Anthropology (accessed 2 September 2021).

6 Clarence Maloney, "Introduction," in *The Evil Eye*, ed. Clarence Maloney (New York: Columbia University Press, 1976), v, xi.

7 Rivka Ulmer, *The Evil Eye in the Bible and in Rabbinic Literature* (Hoboken, NJ: KTAV, 1994), 5, 9–15, 105–15; "Evil Eye," *Encyclopaedia Judaica*, 2nd ed., link.gale.com/apps/doc/CX2587506167/GVRL?u=oregon_portland&sid=bookmark-GVRL&xid=2839eb11 (accessed 2 September 2021).

8 Ulmer, *Evil Eye*, 24–27.

9 Marek Tuszewicki, *A Frog Under the Tongue: Jewish Folk Medicine in Eastern Europe* (London: Littman Library of Jewish Civilization, 2021), 264.

10 Joshua Trachtenberg, *Jewish Magic and Superstition: A Study in Folk Religion* (New York: Atheneum, 1970 [1939]), 54–56; Regina Lilientalowa, "Eyn hore," trans. Nekhome Epshteyn, *Yidishe filologye* 1, no. 4–6 (1924): 270–71.

11 William Graham Sumner, *Folkways: A Study of Sociological Importance of Usages, Manners, Customs, Mores, and Morals* (Boston: Ginn, 1906), 515.

12 "Evil Eye," *Encyclopaedia Judaica*.
13 "Talk: Blessings, Curses, and Other Expressions," *The YIVO Encyclopedia of Jews in Eastern Europe*, yivoencyclopedia.org/article.aspx/Talk/Blessings_Curses_and_Other_Expressions (accessed 2 September 2021); Trachtenberg, *Jewish Magic and Superstition*, 55; Tuszewicki, *Frog Under the Tongue*, 266.
14 Lilientalowa, "Eyn hore," 248–50.
15 Trachtenberg, *Jewish Magic and Superstition*, 57.
16 Ulmer, *Evil Eye*, 139–40.
17 "Evil Eye," *Encyclopaedia Judaica*.
18 See Marek Tuszewicki, "Non-Jewish Languages of Jewish Magic: On Homeliness, Otherness, and Translation," in *Jewish Translation—Translating Jewishness*, ed. Magdalena Waligórska and Tara Kohn (Berlin: De Gruyter, 2018), 135–50.
19 Ẓevi Joshua ben Samuel Shmelke Horowitz, *Semikhat moshe* (Lemberg, 1869), 32v; Avraham Ḥayim Simḥah Bunem Mikhalzohn, *Shemen ha-tov* (Piotrków, 1905), 79; Yehudah Yudel Rozenberg, *Refa'el ha-malakh* (Piotrków, 1907), 106; Sh. (Shelomoh) Spivak, ed., *Sefer zikaron = Andenk-bukh, k. k. Zaviertshe veha-sevivah* (Tel Aviv: Irgun yozei Zavirtsah veha-sevivah, 1957), 100–101.
20 David Biale, David Assaf, Benjamin Brown, Uriel Gellman, Samuel Heilman, Moshe Rosman, Gadi Sagiv, and Marcin Wodziński, *Hasidism: A New History* (Princeton, NJ: Princeton University Press, 2018), 150.
21 Based on S. An-ski, "Zagovory ot durnogo glaza, boleznei i neschastnykh sluchaev (Obsprecheniss, Verreidung) sredi evreev severo-zapadnago kraia," *Evreiskaia Starina* 1 (1909): 75–76; Lilientalowa, "Eyn hore," 262–64; Rechtman, *Yidishe etnografye un folklor*, 293; and Rozenberg, *Refa'el ha-malakh*, 105–6. Most of these versions of the incantation were gathered by ethnographers from informants in prewar Eastern Europe; the Rozenberg text was published in a 1907 collection of remedies and charms. All are nearly identical with the exception of minor words or phrases.
22 Lilientalowa, "Eyn hore," 264; Tuszewicki, "Non-Jewish Languages," 139.
23 For an explanation of these motifs relating to Slavic magical incantations, see Tuszewicki, "Non-Jewish Languages," 143.
24 Tuszewicki, *Frog Under the Tongue*, 274.
25 Lilientalowa, "Eyn hore," 269.
26 Regina Dionisopoulos-Mass, "The Evil Eye and Bewitchment in a Peasant Village," in *The Evil Eye*, ed. Clarence Maloney (New York: Columbia

University Press, 1976), 46. Dundes lists several other parallels. See Alan Dundes, "Wet and Dry, the Evil Eye: An Essay in Indo-European and Semitic Worldview," in *The Evil Eye: A Folklore Casebook*, ed. Alan Dundes (New York: Garland, 1981), 265–66.

27 Tuszewicki, *Frog Under the Tongue*, 264; Trachtenberg, *Jewish Magic and Superstition*, 56.

28 Lilientalowa, "Eyn hore," 266–67; Bar-Yitzhak, *Pioneers of Jewish Ethnography*, 171–72.

29 Giuseppe Veltri, "The Meal of the Spirits, the Three *Parcae*, and Lilith," in his *A Mirror of Rabbinic Hermeneutics: Studies in Religion, Magic, and Language Theory in Ancient Judaism* (Berlin: De Gruyter, 2015), 189.

30 Veltri, "Meal of the Spirits," 189.

31 On magical charms and remedies for uterine pain in antiquity, see Jean-Jacques Aubert, "Threatened Wombs: Aspects of Ancient Uterine Magic," *Greek, Roman, and Byzantine Studies* 30, no. 3 (1989): 421–49.

32 Veltri, "Meal of the Spirits," 190n472.

33 Edina Bozóky, "Medieval Narrative Charms," in *The Power of Words: Studies on Charms and Charming in Europe*, ed. James Alexander Kapaló, Éva Pócs, and William Ryan (Budapest: Central European University Press, 2013), 101.

34 Bozóky, "Medieval Narrative Charms," 111. On the question of the origins of the three virgins in pre-Christian Germanic myth, see Matthias Zender, "Die Verehrung von drei heiligen Frauen im christlichen Mitteleuropa und ihre Vorbereitungen in alten Vorstellungen," in *Matronen und verwandte Gottheiten*, ed. Gerhard Bauchhenß and Günter Neumann (Köln: Rheinland-Verlag, 1987), 213–28.

35 Patrice Lajoye, "Quelques considérations cosmologiques dans deux formules de Marcellus de Bordeaux," Academia.edu (2017), p. 95, www.academia.edu/43515070/Quelques_consid%C3%A9rations_cosmologiques_dans_deux_formules_de_Marcellus_de_Bordeaux (accessed 14 May 2021).

36 Lajoye, "Quelques considérations cosmologiques," 94–95.

37 Moritz Güdeman, "Vermischung von Jüdischem und Heidnischem aus neuer und alter Zeit," *Monatsschrift für Geschichte und Wissenschaft des Judentums* 24, no. 6 (1875): 269–73; Veltri, "Meal of the Spirits," 194–95; John A. Howard, "Der 'Bärmuttersegen': Ein mittelhochdeutscher Spruch," *Colloquia Germanica* 11 (1978): 211–32.

38 In kabbalistic imagery the sea is perceived as the dwelling place of demonic forces. According to the *Zohar*, God cast Lilith into the depths of the sea after

the creation of man. Raphael Patai, *The Hebrew Goddess*, 3rd ed. (Detroit: Wayne State University Press, 1990), 231.
39 Veltri, "Meal of the Spirits," 190–91.
40 For an amulet intended to protect the parturient from Lilith and the evil eye in the medieval magical compilation known as *Sefer Raziel Ha-malakh*, see Patai, *Hebrew Goddess*, 237–39. It is possible that premodern Jews linked the three sisters to Na'amah, Agrat, and Maḥlat, three demonesses described in the *Zohar*, but there is no firm evidence for this hypothesis.
41 On the Wachnacht in the early modern period and especially among Italian Jews, see Elliott S. Horowitz, "The Eve of the Circumcision: A Chapter in the History of Jewish Nightlife," *Journal of Social History* 23, no. 1 (1989): 45–69.
42 Elisheva Baumgarten, *Mothers and Children: Jewish Family Life in Medieval Europe* (Princeton, NJ: Princeton University Press, 2004), 100; Herman Pollack, *Jewish Folkways in Germanic Lands (1648–1806): Studies in Aspects of Daily Life* (Cambridge, MA: MIT Press, 1971), 27–28. Holle was a Janus-faced spirit who protected some children but stole others. Max Weinreich, "Holekrash: A Jewish Rite of Passage—A Preliminary Statement," in *Folklore International: Essays in Traditional Literature, Belief, and Custom in Honor of Wayland Debs Hand*, ed. D. K. Wilgus (Hatboro, PA: Folklore Associates, 1967), 246. Jill Hammer argues for a more holistic understanding of Holle as an awesome and sometimes frightening mother figure whose power embraced both life and death. Jill Hammer, "Holle's Cry: Unearthing a Birth Goddess in a German Jewish Naming Ceremony," *Nashim: A Journal of Jewish Women's Studies and Gender Issues* 9 (2005): 62–87.
43 Baumgarten, *Mothers and Children*, 97–99; Weinreich, "Holekrash."
44 Jehuda Bergmann, "Zur Geschichte religiöser Bräuche," *Monatsschrift für Geschichte und Wissenschaft des Judentums* 71, no. 4 (1927): 169.
45 *Shulḥan Arukh*, Yoreh De'ah 178.
46 Christian authorities were also annoyed at the persistence of customs related to the Fates. See, for example, the decree issued by the Bishop of Worms in the eleventh century rebuking Christians for setting out a table for the three sisters. Veltri, "Meal of the Spirits," 188.
47 See also the ancient adjuration against Lilith on a magic bowl in which Elijah meets Lilith "and all her band" on the way to the house of a parturient in Patai, *Hebrew Goddess*, 227.
48 Moritz Steinschneider, *Alphabetum Siracidis utrumque cum expositione antiqua (narrationes et fabulas continente)* (Berolini: A. Friedlaender, 1858), 23b;

Moses Gaster, "Two Thousand Years of a Charm Against the Child-Stealing Witch," *Folklore* 11 (1900): 156–57.
49 Bozóky, "Medieval Narrative Charms," 102.
50 Ukrainian folk charms also included the motif of the three virgins or sisters. See Andriy Temchenko, "Mifolohema 'try divytsi/try sestry/try ptashky' v obryadovykh tekstakh ukraïintsiv (na materiali zamovlyan')," *Etnichna istoriia narodiv IEvropy* 45 (2015): 5–11.
51 Quoted in Odile Kammerer, "Odile," *Encyclopedia of the Middle Ages*, www.oxfordreference.com/view/10.1093/acref/9780227679319.001.0001/acref-9780227679319-e-2021. See also David Farmer, "Odile," *The Oxford Dictionary of Saints*, www.oxfordreference.com/view/10.1093/acref/9780199596607.001.0001/acref-9780199596607-e-1221.
52 Henryk Biegeleisen, *Lecznictwo ludu polskiego* (Krakow: Polska Akademja Umiejętności, 1929), 243. My thanks to Magda Teter for her help in translating this text.
53 "Koveẓ be-kabalah ma'asit," thirteenth–fourteenth century, MS 8114, Jewish Theological Seminary Library, Special Collections, fol. 16b (second pagination); and "Segulot, kemi'ot, u-refu'ot," eighteenth–nineteenth century, MS 10082, Jewish Theological Seminary Library, Special Collections, fol. 5b.
54 Samuel Rappaport, "Aus dem religiösen Leben der Ostjuden," *Der Jude* 6 (1921): 115.
55 Rechtman, *Yidishe etnografye un folklor*, 293.
56 See Howard Schwartz, *Tree of Souls: The Mythology of Judaism* (New York: Oxford University Press, 2004), 387 and the references there.
57 *Bamidbar Rabbah* 19:25.
58 Arthur Green, *A Guide to the Zohar* (Stanford, CA: Stanford University Press, 2004), 52–53; Yeruḥam Fishel Lachower, Isaiah Tishby, and David Goldstein, eds., *The Wisdom of the Zohar: An Anthology of Texts* (Oxford, UK: Oxford University Press, 1989), 1, 393n50.
59 *Zohar Ḥadash*, *Ḥukat* 12. On supernal mother and lower mother in the *Zohar*, see Oded Yisraeli, "Honoring Father and Mother in Early Kabbalah: From Ethos to Mythos," *Jewish Quarterly Review* 99, no. 3 (2009): 400–402.
60 Salomon Buber, ed., *Sefer ha-orah* (Lvov: A. Salat, 1905), 230–31; Trachtenberg, *Jewish Magic and Superstition*, 195.
61 II Kings 20:1–7.
62 II Chronicles 32.

63 It is intriguing, however, that the book of Job ends with an enumeration of Job's children, who include seven children and *three daughters*—of whom only the latter are named (Job 42:14).

64 Bozóky, "Medieval Narrative Charms," 105.

65 Bozóky, "Medieval Narrative Charms," 105.

66 Tuszewicki, "Non-Jewish Languages," 145.

67 Rozenberg, *Refa'el ha-malakh*, 104; Tuszewicki, "Non-Jewish Languages," 145.

68 M. Fried, "Volksmedizinisches und Diätetisches aus Ostgalizien," *Mitteilungen der Gesellschaft für Jüdischen Volkskunde* 13 (1910): 168.

69 "A Jewish Kabalistic Amulet for Protection and Good Luck," Catawiki, www.catawiki.com/en/l/25508831-a-jewish-kabalistic-amulet-for-protection-good-luck-paper (accessed 19 November 2021). Since the writing of this article, the amulet has been sold and the listing removed from the website.

70 "2 tefilot neged ayin ha-ra mirabi pinḥas mikoriẓ ve-rabi shmelke minikolsburg" (advice article on a religious website), Breslav Meir, 18 March 2020, www.breslevmeir.com/2-תפילות-נגד-עין-הרע-של-רבי-פנחס-מקורי/ (accessed 4 September 2021).

71 "Tefilot neged ayin ha-ra" (n.d.) (list of effective prayers and charms against the evil eye), Breslav Meir, www.breslevmeir.com/category/סגולה-נגד-עין-הרע/ (accessed 4 September 2021).

72 Hayim Fuchs, "Beli ayin ha-ra: Yesh bikhlal davar kazeh?" Kikar Ha-shabbat, 12 August 2009, www.kikar.co.il/בלי-עין-הרע-יש-בכלל-דבר-כזה.html (accessed 5 May 2023).

5

Big Stakes for Small Claims

An Early Modern Jewish Court Between
Civil and Religious Law

Elisheva Carlebach

Selig the meat seller must pay the widow of Samuel bar Goetschlik 8 Mark, 8 Schilling; that is, four measures [*litra'ot*] of meat until the debt of 8 Mark, 8 Schilling, above mentioned, is fully repaid.

This routine ruling is one of many in a summary register of cases, *Protocol of the Acts of the Bet Din in Altona*, that came before a Jewish court in the third quarter of the eighteenth century.[1] From winter 1768 through spring 1771, hundreds of Jewish plaintiffs and defendants with small claims had their cases heard by the court. In this chapter I focus on the record of those cases. Although it is true that "histories of justice . . . cannot be written from the perspective of . . . case summaries alone" and that they certainly cannot offer deep insight into the motives of "the consumers of the law," the record opens a window into the workings of a Jewish institution that scholarly literature has barely touched.[2] Few similar civil "small claims" court records have survived from Jewish courts in the premodern period. Recent analyses of two rabbinic court records from the late eighteenth century, those of Frankfurt and of Metz, have opened a window into the jurisprudential values, parameters, and accommodations to non-Jewish civil law in these two Ashkenazic Jewish rabbinic courts in Western Europe.[3] Evelyne Oliel-Grausz's study of a "community forum" for adjudicating disputes in eighteenth-century Sephardic Amsterdam continues to expand the basis for historical analysis of Jewish judicial autonomy in premodern Europe.[4]

The Altona record presents an opportunity to revisit questions about the meaning of Jewish courts, their archives, and the tenor of Jewish communal life in a late eighteenth-century urban enclave in northwestern Europe. The adjudication of disputes between Jews in Jewish courts according to Jewish law was central to the perception and claim of Jewish autonomy before emancipation. The protocol allows us to test this claim by using it to pose several important questions: How autonomous were Jewish courts in early modern Europe? What were the parameters of their jurisdiction, and how did they change over time? What can the existence of such courts and their records illuminate about Jewish life? How and why did centralizing states of the seventeenth and eighteenth centuries tolerate these courts? How "Jewish" was the law applied in them? This chapter contributes to the ongoing discussion about Jewish legal institutions in the early modern period by providing context for and analysis of a record from a Jewish court in Altona that was civil in nature and primarily, though not exclusively, concerned with small claims.

Altona, neighbor and rival of Hamburg, was a Danish port city. The Danish kings granted the right to arbitrate small claims to the triple Altona-Hamburg-Wandsbek Jewish community in 1641 and 1664.[5] By the early decades of the eighteenth century, the policy and politics of the Senate in Hamburg began to diverge from that of the crown in Copenhagen. The Senate sought to limit the power of semi-autonomous bodies, whereas the Danish kings confirmed the right of Altona's Jews to self-adjudication (albeit limited to some degree) multiple times throughout the mid-nineteenth century.

The Altona Jewish community housed the administrative seat of Ashkenazic Jews living in neighboring Hamburg, Wandsbek, and, for some of the time, Glückstadt.[6] The earliest privileges for Jewish civil jurisdiction in Altona, from the mid-seventeenth century, granted the Jewish community the right to arbitrate small claims cases.[7] By the 1730s the right to autonomous adjudication for Jews was granted by the king of Denmark; it was renewed several times.[8] A remarkable anomaly, the court functioned officially until the period of the unification of Germany in the 1860s. It was to be the last standing state-recognized Jewish court in German lands.

Andreas Gotzmann has laid the conceptual foundations and illuminated the theoretical complexities surrounding concepts of religious versus civil law and the political parameters of judicial autonomy for German Jews of the Habsburg Empire and its neighbors. He argues that, from the late seventeenth century and through the eighteenth century, the centralizing (and often) absolutist authorities defined precisely the types of adjudication they permitted to Jewish courts.[9] As the privileges of toleration (*Geleitbriefe*) in German lands granted to Jewish communities demonstrate, every location and its government had different policies and characteristics; no two Jewish communities operated under the exact same conditions. By the eighteenth century many German authorities permitted Jewish courts to continue adjudicating in limited realms: ceremonial law (including some areas of family and inheritance law) and civil cases involving small claims.[10]

As the eighteenth century progressed, states became more vigilant and restrictive over the power of Jewish courts to adjudicate. Although most granted rabbinic courts the right to continue litigating religious law, they increasingly reserved to the states the exclusive right to judge civil cases.[11] Authorization for Jewish courts to adjudicate small claims, variously defined, is an interesting exception to this trend. This exception to the states' gradual withdrawal of Jewish courts' right to engage in civil law betrays an internal contradiction on their path toward consolidation of political power. It shows that the states' interest in curtailing the right of civil jurisdiction for Jews lay primarily in cases where they stood to gain financially rather than purely consolidating their own authority. The language of the powers granted to these exceptional Jewish civil courts shifted over time, from referring to them as courts of conciliation (the weakest terminology), to courts of arbitration (a stronger legal term), to courts of adjudication (the most legally potent).[12]

The relegation of Jews' small claims to Jewish courts coincided with the emergence of such courts in Europe generally. The small claims court as a separate and permanent entity within a larger judicial system arose slowly in early modern Europe. Disputes that might have been settled by street brawls, vendettas, or informal mediation came to be "juridified" (*Verrechtlichung*) in ever more disciplined court systems.[13] In parts of Germany small claims courts as such did not exist in the late medieval to early modern period, but there were various "lower courts" based more on locale than on significance of cases. It is likely that small claims came before the town, village, or municipal courts; however, jurisdictional variations were territory specific.[14] Regardless of their origin, such courts served important symbolic and practical purposes. In the first instance, they could be seen as resolving quarrels among people of little social consequence over matters of no general importance. According to that view, these courts existed at considerable cost to society—in officials' salaries and in space and record keeping—in order to unclog a more important court system. The lower courts segregated the petty from the more complex cases where the financial and social stakes were higher. Eric Steele argues that the public investment in small claims courts opened up a primary point of contact for common people with the justice system. They granted a certain equity to the poor, because without such courts the barriers to access the justice system were simply too high.[15] Such factors were certainly at play in Jewish court systems, with separate courts delimited by the value of the case.[16]

Jewish small claims courts served multiple parties and purposes. They served the purposes of governments that were just opening their courts to all classes of people and were afraid that the additional burden of Jewish cases would overwhelm the courts. At a time when toleration of Jews, individual or collective, was still a precarious matter, Jews feared that petty cases or nuisance traffic to non-Jewish courts would jeopardize their tenuous legal status. These courts allowed the jurists to focus on high-stakes cases and allowed the Jewish communities to maintain some claim of autonomous authority over their members. Finally, unlike in almost every other Jewish communal institution, most Jews—including the poorest, women as well as men, teenagers, servants, and others not generally accorded prominent places in society—found a forum in this venue from which they could have their day in court. Because the largest percentage of disputes fell under the rubric of small claims, these courts allowed the community direct contact with the least economically visible members.[17]

Standing Courts Versus Ad Hoc Courts

As a rule, evidence for the existence of a Jewish court did not necessarily mean that it was a standing court (*bet din kavu'a*) with a fixed rotation of judges, a regular space in which to function, and the creation and maintenance of records. Before the eighteenth century fixed courts in Western European Jewish communities were scarce. Instead, ad hoc courts, in which each party chose one judge and the judges chose a third, were preferred and were far more common.[18] An ad hoc court might issue a decision in writing that the parties could produce in the event of future dispute; however, because the court itself dissolved with the disposition of the case, there was no mechanism by which to maintain records of decisions. As communities grew larger, this system became more unwieldy; without records, rulings could not be enforced. Litigants were often hard put to find copies of decisions handed to them by the ad hoc court years or even decades earlier. Larger populations meant that individual memory of judgments could not be relied on. The lack of a basic enforcement mechanism, such as a central repository for written records, weakened the institution of Jewish courts in the eyes of Jewish litigants. This is one of several reasons that Jews at times preferred non-Jewish standing courts over Jewish adjudication, despite rabbinic prohibitions against seeking justice in non-Jewish courts.[19] Standing courts provided by the Jewish community were a far more viable way to adjudicate disputes and preserve the outcomes. Yet, as Jay Berkovitz has noted, Jewish courts did not generally become standing institutions until later in the eighteenth century, and few records from Jewish courts have survived from before the last third of the eighteenth century.[20] This could be due to the expense of standing courts; communal budgets were always strained. The community would have to retain and pay judges, scribes, and secretaries; it would have to provide space for the hearings and for retrievable storage of the documentation. Many of the rabbis who adjudicated cases kept their own personal records, a precedent that dates back to the medieval period.[21] The existence of court-owned records, as opposed to rulings handed to individual litigants, could not be taken for granted even for nation-state courts in the eighteenth century. See, for example, the lament of one historian of English criminality: "The dossiers left by the prosecutors and judges of the royal courts of France have no counterparts in England, where almost all the important evidence was given orally at the trial and never recorded."[22] Official recording and archiving of the decisions of a Jewish civil court in the second half of the eighteenth century can be seen as a means for the Jewish community to preserve its raison d'être in an age of new challenges to its existence. The maintenance of written records turned the court into a nexus of justice, communal memory, and the perpetuation of some form of Jewish autonomy.

The *Bet Din Zuta*

As the size of urban Jewish populations in Europe grew from the mid-sixteenth century forward, several larger Jewish communities established and maintained a layered system of Jewish courts.[23] It is important to bear in mind that every one of these courts functioned with the explicit consent of the state authority. Although the courts' jurisdictional boundaries could be based on the region of the litigants' residence, the value of the cases often determined the *level* of court that would adjudicate it. Cases that were legally complex, such as personal status cases, inheritance, and large commercial disputes, were assigned to the highest courts, which were presided over by the chief rabbi and the most advanced scholars. The lowest level of such a multitiered division was the equivalent of the small claims court. Across early modern Europe, larger Jewish communities adopted similar arrangements. In Frankfurt am Main, Fürth, and Prague similar stratified court systems were established.[24] The regulations of Krakow in 1595 stipulated a tripartite judicial system in which the value of the case determined which court heard the claims.[25] The Senate of Hamburg approved the Jewish court system in a meeting on 8 September 1721, perhaps modeled on its own long-standing multitiered judicial system.[26] The court convened in Altona, seat of the chief rabbi of the triple community, and representatives from the other communities attended and sat on cases on a regular rotation basis. The court in Altona, then, was from the outset the product of a complex relationship between jurisdictions. The lowest level of the court, referred to as the *bet din zuta*, literally "small court," or popularly as *Gröschel bet din* (penny court), heard small claims and minor disputes.[27] The chief rabbi oversaw the court and staffed it with members of his rabbinic court as well as with others, including local scholars and learned lay leaders, on rotation.

The Court Record

When litigants appeared before the Jewish small claims court, they generated many forms of written record. Plaintiffs contacted the court officials, who prepared written summonses and entered information into a court docket.[28] Both sides prepared and presented to the court various types of written evidence over the course of a hearing. The court scribe wrote a summary of each side's arguments and claims, along with the verdict, in the running record. Receipts confirming the judgments were often handed to the litigants, slips of paper in cursive writing and hand-signed by a judge or court official, that gave the plaintiff and/or defendant evidence of the court's ruling.[29] A hypothetical judgment might say, "Berel must pay Shmerl 10 marks within fourteen days of today. If he fails to pay on time, the judgment is doubled." Both sides would be given a copy of the ruling, and it worked like a promissory note, payable upon presentation when due, sometimes used in lieu of cash if Shmerl traded it to another person, included it in his papers, and or included it in his property value, to be inherited and activated by his estate if he died before collecting on it. Occasionally, such a slip of paper is still preserved in the pages of the summary record.[30]

When the court scribe initially created a record, he included a condensed version of the arguments of each side, a history of the case if warranted, additional testimony or evidence, and the ruling. The entry would be signed by the judge or judges. This formed the basic account of the court's proceedings. At least three volumes containing full proceedings of the court for the late eighteenth century survive from the Altona Jewish community.[31] The section discussed here represents a further level of record creation.[32] After a number of years the volumes of fuller deliberations of the court became cumbersome to access. Scribes compressed the large amount of material to its bare outline, numbering each case and creating an index (by Hebrew alphabetical order of the litigants' first names) and thus providing basic finding aids to the disposition of the cases. Several different hands and styles of recording can be discerned in the summary section.[33] Eventually, after 1,458 cases, numbered cases gave way to a new scribal regime. The scribe who succeeded to the position announced that he would enter into the summary only cases that were still pending. He saw no reason to keep a record of those cases that had already been resolved. This is a greater intervention into the record maintenance process than the previous minor variations in the summary volume that betrayed the change from one scribal hand to the next. It bespeaks a different perception of the primary function of the record, the first aiming for an archival inscription of every case and the second a more limited utilitarian conception that reached only to the immediate future.

Here I focus on the section of the first 1,458 numbered summaries. Each précis usually contained the judgment and sometimes the positions of the plaintiff and defendant in brief; they do not convey any of the arguments or the reasoning of the judges. The names of the judges are never mentioned (with one exception), making it extremely difficult to ascribe judicial temperament or particular characteristics to any individual party.[34] Although it represents a distillation of the court's proceedings, it is a quite different type of document from the original rulings or their first full transcription.[35] Bound in one codex volume and supplied with a rudimentary finding aid, the summary record was intended to serve as an enduring retrievable archive. The written records were not ancillary to the function of the small claims court; they were a crucial element of the performance of justice before the litigants and the community. Court records guaranteed recourse if original rulings were not honored, and they constituted the final stage in the transformation from an ad hoc court to a standing court. Eventually, the records that originated as a living and active resource for members of the community would be preserved as a part of its historical patrimony.

Logistics of the *Bet Din*

The Jewish court in Altona met twice a week, on Mondays and Thursdays; on most court days the docket contained up to 10 cases, with a double session before some Jewish holidays in which the court heard twice that number of cases. The Jewish community of Altona maintained a dual court system: a civil lay court alongside a rabbinic court. The protocol before us is that of the *kahal* court, that is, the civil court that provided arbitration that did not have the weight of Jewish law. The chief rabbi, as head of the rabbinic court system, presided over the court in spirit; he was invoked in some cases, and he was named as a guarantor or safe keeper for payments to be held in escrow several times in this record.[36] The community as a whole operated both courts, and it did not make the sharpest distinction between them. To illustrate this, I cite an entry from the notes of the secretary (*shamash*) to the lay leadership: "Today, Friday 17 Elul [1767] I was sent by the *parnas* of the month, Hirsch Breslau, to the wife of Eisik ben Meir to tell her that, as Mr. Feyvish, son of R. Yakov Rey is complaining that he has 'no peace from her in the streets,' she should desist from [such behavior] in the future. If she has claims against him, she should go before the *bet din* or the *kahal*."³⁷ The latter two Hebrew terms refer to the two court systems, rabbinic or lay. Communal officials repeatedly emphasized that disputants should go to the Jewish courts and not fight on the streets and that there was a choice between rabbinic and lay Jewish courts. Thus the community acknowledged that the lay court did not claim to be ruling according to rabbinic law (Halakha), yet it still qualified as a Jewish court. By referring to the choice of Jewish courts, the official was conspicuously excluding non-Jewish courts, where Jews intent on forum shopping could have sought justice as well.³⁸ In effect, the community offered a modified form of legal pluralism, one that existed within the Jewish community itself.

Because the purpose of the small claims court was to streamline procedure and resolve conflict as efficiently as possible, the rules in many small claims courts differed from those of higher courts. Most litigants represented themselves, the burden of evidence and witnesses was lighter, and the judges often attempted to mediate a compromise rather than issue a formal judgment.³⁹

As in the case of rabbinic courts, when no compelling evidence or testimony emerged, the court imposed an oath on one or both of the litigants. Taking an oath often decided the case; the refusal to do so could lead to forfeiture of the claim. Evidence of how seriously oaths were regarded comes from the many instances in which litigants preferred to forgo serious sums of money to avoid taking an oath.⁴⁰ The court prescribed an array of oaths in varying degrees of severity. When there was reason to doubt the litigants' word, the court asked her or him to swear in the presence of a Torah scroll or to produce credible witnesses. Some oaths were to be taken in specific synagogues, to put the proceedings under the watchful eye of a local public. Unlike rabbinic courts, in which women could testify only under specific circumstances, the small claims court accepted the unmediated testimony of women, and they testified under oath or swore in the presence of the entire synagogue, as did the men. Thus the court ordered Fogel Windmill to bring two silver items to be appraised by the court. "She must swear in the Altona [main] synagogue that Ephraim, son of Anshel Katz, owes her at least the value of the [silver] items. If she refuses to take an oath, she must return to him both items under threat of *herem* [ban]."⁴¹ In the course of the 1,458 numbered cases, 2,463 men and 414 women appeared as plaintiffs and defendants before the court; 14.5%

of those who appeared were women.[42] In multiple cases women appear as independent actors and in partnerships with others, men and women, who do not appear to be related to them.

Many of the entries record the decision of the court in brief: *A must pay B a certain sum within a certain number of days*. A surprising number of decisions appear to be open-ended, leaving the litigants with no final resolution and a number of possible, sometimes contradictory, options. An example of this can be seen in the following resolution:

> R. Joel H'b [Halberstadt], regarding the matter of his debt of 200 R't [Reichsthaler] toward the dowry of his daughter: a compromise was reached between him and the groom. He can remove the debt of the amount owed within three months; if not, he can pay a fine of a third of the dowry, according to the terms of the contract; unless some clause can be found within it to exempt him completely.[43]

The case notes conclude with three options, presented as a compromise agreed to by both parties: The defendant could pay the outstanding amount over extra time; he could pay the fine stipulated by the contract; or if he could find a loophole in the contract, he could free himself of any obligation entirely. This pattern appears in a number of cases in which the record makes clear that there is no guarantee that a particular compromise or outcome will be enforced. The fact that a future date is set as a new deadline or that a contractual loophole is still a possibility leaves the door open for further litigation. In some cases litigants appealed to the court for a more definitive (or positive) result than what had been granted in a prior appearance. The summary record repeats an earlier decision with the conclusion, "the judgment is upheld" (*ha-pesak nitkayem*).[44] Decisions such as these mark the court as a venue to arbitrate disputes and record attempts to settle and mediate between parties; it did not render formal, binding legal decisions in all cases.

Agency

About 50 of the cases, slightly less than 3%, involved an agent or representative (*mursheh*) before the court who would have had the power to argue and to collect the amount of a judgment or to pay it in the place of or in addition to the litigant who hired him. This is a far lower rate than would have been likely in the case of larger sums that would be adjudicated before rabbinic courts, where learned litigators (*to'anim*) often represented litigants who needed someone with expertise in the law to represent them.[45] The cases brought here are of another order. From the entries in the record, we can learn several things regarding the use of representation. Several men in the community made a career (or at least part of a living) acting as agents to the small claims court, as the same names reappear numerous times. At least five different people appear in the capacity of agents representing their clients before the court.[46] They were paid a set fee for their services. Even poor people sometimes hired an agent to improve their chances of a favorable outcome. Occasionally, the agents themselves appear as plaintiffs over denial or delinquency in payment of their fees.[47] One agent, Reuven bar Zalman Schreiber, had to apologize to the court for not having the writ of agency (*harsha'a*) with him at the court; he obligated himself to bring it before the court in a timely manner.[48] In one case the agent took a woman to court, complaining that he had not been paid the customary fee for bringing about reconciliation between her and her husband; the woman denied promising the agent even one penny for mediating between them.[49]

Rabbinic courts in the early modern period dealt with a wide range of issues, notably with personal status matters such as divorce, inheritance cases, and business disputes with large sums at stake.[50] No such cases are included in the civil court record. The conflicts recorded by the small claims civil court concerned modest sums of money, small investment partnerships, or items of limited commercial value. Th civil court adjudicated several categories of contract disputes as well: those between employers and their male and female servants, those between employers and tutors of children, and those with voluntary societies (*hevrot*), often over delinquent payment of membership dues. The concerns of the small claims court were decidedly civil rather than religious or even moral. No Sabbath violators, adulterers, or other religious law breakers are to be found in the pages of this record, although they assuredly could be found in the community and in the pages of its other contemporaneous records. The court did not judge cases of libel and violation of honor, nor did it hear cases in which the community itself was the aggrieved party, such as the violation of a communal regulation or nonpayment of taxes. Such cases would have resulted in the levy of a punitive fine; they were recorded in a separate logbook for the office of the communal treasurer. Fines and monetary penalties were generally allocated for communal needs (often marked as charity) and for the king's treasury, and therefore careful tracking of that income in a separate ledger was warranted.[51]

Commerce

Business disputes in the small claims civil court record generally concerned investments, purchase and sale of commodities, and a vigorous microcredit market. The microcredit cases often revolved around the conditions and facts of loan and repayment or the current ownership of a single item, such as a garment, a watch, or a vessel, that served as security for a loan.[52] If the value of an item was unclear, the court performed its own appraisal, and in the case of specialized goods such as watches and jewelry, it ordered an appraisal by an expert.

Altona's Jews invested in the wide array of commodities that coursed through the port city. Presumably, they bought wholesale and sold retail, often dividing their investments among multiple partners with complex payout arrangements. Virtually all the commodities mentioned in the court cases were imported into Hamburg/Altona rather than exported.[53] The disputes pertained to an array of textiles and items related to the production of clothing, such as buttons, indigo, feathers, and hosiery. Durable foodstuffs of all kinds circulated through the hands of Jewish merchants: coffee, wine, pickled meat, lox, cocoa, cheese, and chocolate; in addition, they dealt in manufactured goods, such as mirrors, watches, porcelain dishes, and all types of printed books. A considerable number of disputes concerned the pooled purchase of lottery tickets and the distribution of payouts. Lottery drawings had become a popular spectacle conducted with great fanfare in the streets of Altona. One early nineteenth-century visitor described the public entertainment.

> In Altona, the drawing is done openly on the street. The wheel, which was richly ornamented, and appeared to be of glass, was placed on a stage in front of the Stadthaus, and was flanked by two boys in scarlet

uniform, with hat and feather, who drew from the wheel, and produced the numbers to an anxious and excited populace. The foreground was guarded by soldiers, while a band of very tolerable musicians kept saluting the smiles of dame Fortune, or drowning the sighs of her unsuccessful worshippers.[54]

Contracts

Beyond petty commerce, a second major area of cases before the small claims civil court concerned contractual agreements over wages, labor conditions, terms of employment, or other unwritten obligations. Disputes between maidservants and employers alone made up 9% of all the cases in this record, which allows historians to engage with new aspects of the employment conditions of the Jewish "working poor."[55]

Although contracts, conditions of employment, wages and tips, and suspicion of theft were the primary causes of litigation, it is worth pausing to note that detailed and thorough regulations governing domestic service, though presumed by the court and the community to exist, do not seem to have been widely promulgated or available in the late eighteenth century, either to the litigants or to the court itself. One of the earliest extant sets of Altona community regulations from the late seventeenth century includes several paragraphs specifically about the hiring, firing, and working conditions of maidservants.[56] Servants were free to hire themselves out to any householder they pleased, but each party had to give at least four weeks' notice before the season ended if they wished to part ways. A later hand added to the regulations:

> Even prior to the four weeks, one who hires a maidservant [away from a current employer] must notify the father or the current employer of the girl, via the *shamash* or other reliable agent, that he had given *meydel geld* [a maidservants' fee as a binder]. This small sum was given to confirm the existence of an arrangement with the new employer. If within eight days of notification of his will to the householder or to the father of the maidservant, she wished to remain with her first employer, she may do so. After eight days, the binder could not be revoked.[57]

I was unable to locate more detailed eighteenth-century regulations governing the hiring of Jewish servants in Altona, but it is possible to piece together the intricate rules and customs governing the relationship between employers and domestic servants from the litigation itself. The procedures practiced by the Jewish community were modeled on local German regulations.[58] Oddly, the parties to the Jewish court hearings, including the court itself, could not locate the written regulations either. Although the basic outlines remained in place throughout the eighteenth century and became fixed as communal norms, the text of the regulations appears to have fallen into disuse by the time of the small claims court record.

A few examples illustrate this. Hirsch Fanheim or his wife would be entitled to deduct a sum from the security deposited by a maidservant who left their employ, equal to the amount he had to pay the new servant over the first one, "unless the ordinance [*ha-takkanah*] stipulated otherwise." The record then continues in the first-person voice of the (apparently) court scribe or *shamash*: "Lo, I saw the ordinance, and [it stipulates] that [this transaction] can only be valid if it had been mediated by the *shamash*." Because the parties acted without the communal functionary as a go-between, "Hirsch must refund the entire security to the maidservant."[59] Thus the court issued a provisional ruling, dependent on the regulations that were not accessible to the judges to consult. Once the *shamash* checked the regulations (in a rare first-person voice), the ruling had to be reversed.[60] In other cases where the court referred to the regulations, it did so in an apologetic tone. When a maidservant was granted her petition for wages owed to her but was forced by the court to pay a fee of 6 shillings for the summons, the ruling noted that this was "as mandated by communal statute [*takkanat ha-kahal*]."[61] Similarly, the court ordered Samuel Posner to pay his maidservant the entire wage for the seasons she worked for him, but he was permitted to deduct the expenses he paid for her stay at the infirmary (*hekdesh*) during her illness as well as additional costs she incurred during said illness (presumably doctor fees and/or medicine) because this was the community regulation (*takkanat ha-kehillah*).[62] Hirsch Feuer had to prove within eight days that it was the communal ordinance (*she-takkanat ha-kahal hu*) that one may not hire a non-Jewish maidservant without asking the current (Jewish) employer for consent through the communal *shamash*. If he provided evidence of the regulation, the security in the transaction would be returned.[63] The record does not specify how a litigant could go about producing evidence of a communal ordinance if the court itself did not have a copy of the ordinance to consult. Perhaps Altona's ordinances governing specific occupations were copied by hand or printed in a limited run.[64]

In another type of case the court ruled that an employer who evicted a maidservant from his home before the contractual term of employment ended, contrary to the community regulations (*neged takkanat kahal*), must forward the entire amount of the contract to the court. If the maidservant managed to find other employment, the amount of her new salary would be deducted from the amount held by the court; if not, the court would award the entire sum to her.[65] This case is one of many in which the court itself acted as guarantor for the specific sums owed to litigants. Maidservants, many of whom were migrants from the countryside, would likely end up on the community charity rolls if they did not find steady employment. By protecting the contractual rights of the servants, the community protected its own interests as well.[66]

Cases involving young men who served as teachers of boys (*melamdim*) came before the court regularly, and their arrangements with individual householders regarding the religious education of their children were also governed by communal norms and regulations. The small claims court heard disputes about delinquent payments; teachers accused of not paying their assistants (*behelfers*), as stipulated in their contract; parents claiming to have seen their children playing in the streets during the time they should have been studying; additional fees for teaching writing or Torah cantillation; providing firewood for heat in the study room; and similar matters. As in the case of servants, many of the teachers were migrants from other communities or from the countryside. The court served as the community's instrument for imposing discipline from the urban center over a young and mobile population.

A final prominent cluster of cases involved the regulations and contractual agreements related to membership in voluntary societies (*hevrot*) that played a role in the welfare and intellectual life of the community. Originally, membership in these societies was a sign of belonging and prestige. Members of the community vied for the honor of a place in the societies and paid dues and carried out duties with alacrity. Loss of status would have sufficed to enforce the provisions of the voluntary societies among members. The societies taking delinquent members to court included those named Visiting the Sick, Bread for the Poor, Torah Study, Carrying the Bier, and the like. Societies took their members to court over missed membership dues, irregular attendance at meetings, and missing equipment. These cases point to a social problem in the community. The value of former markers of honor and belonging had eroded to become financial and time-consuming burdens that community members no longer cared to uphold.

* * *

Jewish communal life and legislation can never be seen in isolation from the surrounding society and its goals and norms. Scholarship on both Jewish and German court records reinforces the argument that Jews were at home in multiple legal venues and that Jewish courts functioned in many ways as proxies for a state or imperial entity.[67] Gotzmann notes that the Jewish community in Altona constituted something of an exception to the rule of greater encroachment of non-Jewish norms into Jewish communal legislation and adjudication. Although this is true regarding the very existence of royally recognized Jewish courts in Altona through the mid-nineteenth century, it is unclear whether this is the case with regard to the internal jurisprudence of the Jewish courts.[68] But dwelling on that aspect, though it is significant, would obscure a primary feature of this record.

The small claims court record reveals the profound entanglement of the community itself as a corporate entity—the authors of its regulations, its numerous officials, its enforcers, and its members (all adult, male, tax paying members)—in the minute details of the economic life of its permanent members and its temporary residents (the latter often young, poor, and transient). The existence of ramified sets of regulations and mechanisms for adjudication shows the determination of the community leaders to provide justice to the middle and poorer classes of Jews who had settled in Altona. Nevertheless, settlement of disputes and cessation of quarreling were in themselves a desired goal to ensure social stability in the community and its political future within Altona.[69] In cases such as employer-employee disputes, the framers of the regulations created a system from which the employers benefited most, but they still advanced the interests of the community at large and those of the poorest litigants.

Even the illusion that justice was dispensed contributed to a reduction of social friction that would otherwise be expressed in less peaceable ways.

A significant portion of the cases revolved around recent communal regulation of spheres of life that had not been subjected to such detailed oversight before this period. For example, it is difficult to find any communal statutes governing employer-servant relationships before the early modern period. The hypertrophy of detailed regulation is intertwined with the development of an arbitration court to adjudicate disputes and with the intricate record-keeping mechanisms that this development demanded. Both reflect developments in German legal thought and practice at this time as well.[70]

The small claims court record constitutes an archive of dailiness, of ordinary social habits and the material culture of the lower economic ranks of Altona's Jews. But it is important to remember that every written record is a fragment that conceals far more than it reveals. To illustrate this, we can point to one population that makes a robust appearance in the small claims court: female domestic servants. The record conveys the sense that servants and their employers were scrupulous about adhering to contractual conditions. The court heard disputes over contracts, wages, handkerchiefs and pairs of socks, a range of tips, and small sums of money. Other records for these years from Jewish Altona open an entirely different aspect of its maidservant life. The semiprivate record of a communal scribe reveals an ongoing crisis of illegitimate pregnancies among the Altona Jewish maidservants.[71] Mary Lindemann has documented something similar for neighboring Hamburg in just these years, and the phenomenon was common across Europe and centuries old in various configurations.[72] Yet not one case out of the entire 1,458 in the small claims court record concerns maidservants fired for pregnancy, demands for paternity support, or the disposition of babies born to maidservants during a period of service. Such matters were not part of the purview of this particular court. Had the court record been the only archival record to survive from this period and place, our perception of the lives of the community and its maidservants would be utterly different and entirely wrong (as it still surely must be). Reading the literature of archival criticism alongside the dissonant perspectives provided by two archival sources emanating from the same stratum within the same society in the same years raises many questions: about the nature of the community and its morals, about definitions of equity and justice, and, above all, about the nature of our sources and how to read them.

The investment in the court by the community in the form of time, expertise, space, and record keeping speaks not only to the communal need to maintain peace but also to its self-perception as a center of justice. This was so as a matter of general reputation of the community as an embodiment of Jewish virtues of mercy, charity, justice, and the like.[73] In addition, it was meant as a veiled threat to Jews who contemplated taking their cases to the non-Jewish courts, a matter of great importance in the course of the eighteenth century as Jewish civil adjudication came to be seen as one of the major impediments to the full emancipation of Jews.[74]

The joint responsibility of lay leadership and rabbinate in administering the court challenges a long-standing assumption that these two classes formed antagonistic poles in Jewish communities.[75] Although there was no shortage of contentiousness in this period within and between these groups, as Jewish communal institutions came under criticism and attack during the debates over Jewish civil emancipation in the eighteenth century, Jews who still cared about these communal institutions realized how interdependent they were and made common cause over their concern to see them survive.[76]

Notes

I thank the volume editors and the audiences at the University of Wisconsin–Madison Mosse Center, the Princeton University Davis Center, and the Research Group on Rethinking Early Modern Jewish Legal Cultures of the Israel Institute for Advanced Studies, Jerusalem, for their constructive comments on earlier drafts of this paper. I dedicate this essay to Michael Stanislawski, my teacher and colleague of many years, for his contributions to untangling the issues of religion, state, and the individual throughout his many works.

1 The central record in this article is the *Protokoll ma'aseh bet din beAltona* (hereafter AHW). It can be found at the National Library of Israel, Jerusalem, Central Archives for the History of the Jewish People, MS AHW 121/1. The cited ruling is at AHW 121/1, 77, case no. 993.

2 Daniel Lord Smail, *The Consumption of Justice: Emotions, Publicity, and Legal Culture in Marseille, 1264–1423* (Ithaca, NY: Cornell University Press, 2003), 4.

3 Edward Fram, *A Window on Their World: The Court Diaries of Rabbi Hayyim Gundersheim Frankfurt am Main, 1773–1794* (Cincinnati: Hebrew Union College Press, 2012); Jay Berkovitz, *Protocols of Justice: The Pinkas of the Metz Rabbinic Court, 1771–1789* (Leiden: Brill, 2014).

4 Evelyne Oliel-Grausz, "Dispute Resolution and *Kahal Kadosh Talmud Torah*: Community Forum and Legal Acculturation in 18th Century Amsterdam," in *Religious Changes and Cultural Transformations in the Early Modern Sephardi Communities*, ed. Yosef Kaplan (Leiden: Brill, 2018), 228–57.

5 Günter Marwedel, *Die Privilegien der Juden in Altona* (Hamburg: Hans Christians, 1976), 134, 144.

6 On the judicial relationship between the Jews of Hamburg and those of Altona in the mid-eighteenth century, see David H. Horowitz, "Fractures and Fissures in Jewish Communal Autonomy, 1710–1782," PhD diss., Columbia University, 2010.

7 Andreas Gotzmann, "Strukturen jüdischer Gerichtsautonomie in den deutschen Staaten des 18. Jahrhunderts," *Historische Zeitschrift* 267, no. 2 (1998): 338.

8 Marwedel, *Privilegien*, 80–88.

9 Gotzmann, "Strukturen," 337.

10 For a comparative analysis of the French Jewish and civil courts, see Jay Berkovitz, *Law's Dominion: Jewish Community, Religion, and Family in Early Modern Metz* (Leyden: Brill, 2020), 99–143.

11 Most states did not allow Jewish courts to adjudicate criminal cases.

12 Gotzmann, "Strukturen," 338–40.

13 On the processes indicated by the term *juridification*, see Winfried Schulze, "Die veränderte Bedeutung sozialer Konflikte im 16. und 17. Jahrhundert," in *Der Deutsche Bauernkrieg*, ed. Hans-Ulrich Wehler (Göttingen: Vandenhoeck & Ruprecht, 1975), 277–302; and David Saunders, "Juridifications and Religion in Early Modern Europe: The Challenge of Contextual History of Law," *Law and Critique* 15 (2004): 99–118. I thank Yair Mintzker for illuminating discussions of the intersecting developments of *Verrechtlichung* and *Verschriftlichung* in this period.

14 See, for example, Maria Rita Sagstetter, *Hoch- und Niedergerichtsbarkeit im Spätmittelalterlichen Herzogtum Bayern* (Munich: Beck'sche, 2000); and

Susanna Burghartz, "Disziplinierung oder Konfliktregelung? Zur Funktion städtischer Gerichte im Spätmittelalter: Das Zürcher Ratsgericht," *Zeitschrift für historische Forschung* 16, no. 4 (1989): 385–407. I thank Tamar Menashe for helpful discussions on the court systems in the Habsburg Empire. England established a small debt court in 1606 and local courts of request over the course of the eighteenth century. Barbara Yngvesson and Patricia Hennessey, "Small Claims, Complex Disputes: A Review of the Small Claims Literature," *Law and Society Review* 9, no. 2 (1975): 223.

15 Eric Steele, "The Historical Context of Small Claims Courts," *American Bar Foundation Research Journal* 6, no. 2 (1981): 296, 300–301.

16 From the point of view of internal Jewish law and practice, see the discussion by Yiẓḥak Beret, "He'omnam din pruta kedin me'ah?" *Da'at: Limudei Yahadut veru'aḥ* 435 (1994), https://www.daat.ac.il/mishpat-ivri/skirot/skira.asp?id=236 (accessed 12 December 2023). Thanks to Menachem Butler for assistance with this reference.

17 Gotzmann, "Strukturen," 344–45.

18 Moshe Frank, *Kehilot Ashkenaz uvatei dineihen meha-me'ah ha-12 ad sof ha-me'ah ha-15* (Tel Aviv: Dvir, 1938), 96–99; Simcha Assaf, *Batei hadin vesidreihen aḥare ḥatimat ha-talmud* (Jerusalem: Dfus hapo'alim, 1923), 54–56. These ad hoc courts were known as *zabl'a* courts, a Hebrew acronym for *zeh borer lo eḥad*, and in them each litigant chose one judge and the two judges appointed a third.

19 Among the many works attesting to Jewish use of non-Jewish courts despite rabbinic injunctions, see Uriel Simonsohn, *A Common Justice: The Legal Allegiances of Christians and Jews Under Early Islam* (Philadelphia: University of Pennsylvania Press, 2011); and Rena Lauer, *Colonial Justice and the Jews of Venetian Crete* (Philadelphia: University of Pennsylvania Press, 2019).

20 Jay Berkovitz, "Competing Perspectives on Legal Decision Making in Early Modern Ashkenaz," *Jewish History* 31, nos. 1–2 (2017): 149–71. The *pinkas takanot* of the Friedberg Jewish community (1664) refers to an ad hoc system operating in the mid-seventeenth century. Individual plaintiffs could convene a group of *parnassim*, with or without the *av bet din*, and could alternatively convene a group of men who were not part of the *kahal*. The range of options were intended to ensure that justice could be sought within a small community where many of the leaders could have relationships, positive or negative, with the plaintiff. Stefan Litt, ed., *Protokollbuch und Statuten der Jüdischen Gemeinde Friedberg (16–18 Jahrhundert)* (Friedberg: Bindernagel, 2003), 168.

21 On medieval lay and ad hoc Jewish courts, see Rachel Furst, "Marriage Before the Bench: Divorce Law and Litigation Strategies in Thirteenth-Century Ashkenaz," *Jewish History* 31 (2017): 7–30, esp. 11–14; and Pinchas Roth, *In This Land: Jewish Life and Legal Culture in Late Medieval Provence* (Toronto: Pontifical Institute of Medieval Studies, 2021), 34–48.

22 Douglas Hay, "War, Dearth, and Theft in the Eighteenth Century: The Record of the English Courts," *Past and Present* 95 (1982): 118.

23 On the exponential growth of some Jewish urban populations, see Jonathan Israel, *European Jewry in the Age of Mercantilism, 1550–1750*, 3rd ed. (Portland: Littman Library, 1998), 134–40. On changes in Jewish ritual and communal practice designed to accommodate larger populations, see Elhanan Reiner, "On the Roots of the Urban Jewish Community in Poland in the Early Modern Period," *Gal-Ed* 20 (2006): 13–37 (Hebrew).

24 Michael Brocke, Julius Carlebach, and Carsten Wilke, *Biographisches Handbuch der Rabbiner*, Teil 1, *Die Rabbiner der Emanzipationszeit in den deutschen, böhmischen und großpolnischen Ländern, 1781–1871* (Munich: Saur, 2004), 65.

25 Majer Balaban, "Die Krakauer Judengemeinde-Ordnung von 1595 und ihre Nachträge," *Jahrbuch der Jüdisch-Literarischen Gesellschaft* 10 (1912): 331–38.

26 See, for example, Beate Binder, *Illustriertes Recht: die Miniaturen des Hamburger Stadtrechts von 1497* (Hamburg: Verlag Verein fur Hamburgische Geschichte, 1988), esp. 113, lower court, "neddersten gherichtes."

27 Brocke et al., *Biographisches Handbuch der Rabbiner*, 65n113. A decade later, the Senate began to limit its power over Hamburg Jews.

28 Plaintiffs paid the *shamash* (communal secretary) a fee for issuing and delivering a summons. For an example of a log of the *bet din* docket, see AHW 126. (I was able to see only a photocopy of this manuscript), covering the years 1767–1769. It contains only names of the plaintiff and the defendant, according to a formula of "defendant [summoned by] plaintiff" under each Monday or Thursday date.

29 For the more formal records of the Metz *bet din* and the role of scribes in condensing and recording the judgments, see Berkovitz, *Law's Dominion*, 53–55.

30 For example, AHW 121/1, 38, par. 263: "*he'etek min ps'd (pesak din) min yud gimel Tammuz 5528*, copy of the ruling of 13 Tamuz 1768." A later volume, AHW 121/2, preserved an original slip of paper with a ruling (at p. 234) which is copied on p. 11. It pertains to the amount the community would

pay to support the widow of noted scholar Rabbi Jacob Emden. The texts are almost, but not exactly, identical.

31 AHW 121/2, AHW 121/3, and AHW 121/4. The Central Archives for the History of the Jewish People hold continuous records from the Altona Jewish court through the late nineteenth century. The full series awaits scholarly analysis.

32 AHW 121/1.

33 For example, AHW 121/1, 81a, par. 1083, where the style and handwriting change abruptly.

34 One précis, AHW 121/1, 36, par. 229, notes that Seligman Hahn and his maidservant agreed to be heard by a panel of two judges (as opposed to the usual three judges to hear each case), not named here, because one of the three, "R. Yosef" was related to Seligman Hahn and had to recuse himself.

35 The brief entries accord with Gotzmann's description of "summary, one-sided description of trials," which are different from the "external documentation of the legal proceedings committed to writing." Andreas Gotzmann, "At Home in Many Worlds? Thoughts About New Concepts in Jewish Legal History," *Jahrbuch des Simon Dubnow Institute* 2 (2003): 424. Berkovitz, "Competing Perspectives," notes that, by definition, court records issued by *dayanim* (judges) of whatever status do not give reasons, whereas the purpose of rulings by *poskim* (jurists) is to establish the law and clarify it.

36 For example, AHW 121/1, 51, par. 501.

37 AHW 20, 9.

38 On forum shopping in general, see the contributions in Lauren Benton and Richard Ross, eds., *Legal Pluralism and Empires, 1500–1850* (New York: New York University Press, 2013). For Hamburg Jews, see Horowitz, "Fractures and Fissures."

39 Yngvesson and Hennessey, "Small Claims," 223.

40 Stefan Litt discusses taxpayers who added to the value they declared, out of fear that the amounts they had declared under oath might inadvertently cause them to have sworn falsely, thus violating a biblical prohibition. See Stefan Litt, *Jüdische Gemeindestatuten aus dem aschkenasischen Kulturraum, 1650–1850* (Göttingen: Vandenhoeck & Ruprecht, 2014), 42.

41 AHW 121/1, 52a, par. 536.

42 These numbers do not take into account multiple appearances by the same party over time.

43 AHW 121/1, 51a, par. 508. I thank Albert Kohn for pointing out the distinctive features of such open-ended rulings to me.

44 AHW 121/1, 39, par. 264. See similarly AHW 121/1, 41, par. 324; 42a, par. 359.
45 Berkovitz, *Protocols of Justice*, 2: 60, estimates that approximately one-third of the litigants hired agents to represent them before the rabbinic court in Metz. By contrast, the much earlier and distant Krakow *takanot* forbade any litigants before the small claims court to be represented by a *mursheh*, with the exception of widows, orphans, and any party deemed in exceptional need of representation. Their *mursheh* would be assigned by the court. Balaban, "Die Krakauer," 334, par. 52.
46 Among the people designated as *mursheh* numerous times are Rabbis Yehezkel, Juzpa, Itzik, Reuven b. Zalman Schreiber, Leyb Furst, and Leyb Prager.
47 For example, *Samuel vs. Itzik mursheh*, AHW 121/1, 52a, par. 534, in which the agent claimed fees for representing the defendant in two separate cases for a total of 6 Reichsthaler.
48 AHW 121/1, 41a, par. 333.
49 AHW 121/1, 84a, par. 1142.
50 Printed editions of Jewish court records include Fram, *Window on Their World*; and Berkovitz, *Protocols of Justice*. Records of an Alsatian Jewish court in Nidernai, in a somewhat damaged manuscript, can be viewed at the Library of the Jewish Theological Seminary, Digitized Collections, MS 8135, SHF 1668:17 (1775–79), MS 8133, SHF 1668:17 (1781–84), and MS 8538, SHF 1672:50 (1787–91).
51 For a ledger of fines assessed for violations of honor and other infractions, see AHW 15. Although the Talmud expressed grave reservations about the permissibility of Jewish courts to levy fines as compensation for violence and dishonor, halakhic attitudes changed over time. See Ephraim Kanarfogel, "The Adjudication of Fines in Ashkenaz During the Medieval and Early Modern Periods and the Preservation of Communal Decorum," *Diné Israel* 32 (2018): 159–87.
52 For example, AHW 121/1, 90a, par. 1249: Edel, wife of Mann, must bring the frock (*malbush rok*) of Zanvil b. Moses for the court to appraise and to adjudicate between them.
53 John Strang, in Theodore Foster, *Foster's Cabinet Miscellany* (New York: Theodore Foster, 1837), 4: 50.
54 Foster, *Foster's Cabinet Miscellany*, 4: 73.
55 Debra Kaplan, *The Patrons and Their Poor: Jewish Community and Public Charity in Early Modern Germany* (Philadelphia: University of Pennsylvania Press, 2020), esp. 80–86.

56 Heinz Mosche Graupe, ed., *Die Statuten der drei Gemeinden Altona, Hamburg und Wandsbek: Quellen zur jüdischen Gemeindeorganisation im 17. und 18. Jahrhundert* (Hamburg: Hans Christians, 1973), 53, 67–69.
57 AHW 9, 17, par. 95.
58 For examples of contemporaneous regulations in German lands, see Rainer Schröder, "Gesinderecht im 18. Jahrhundert," in *Gesinde im 18. Jahrhundert*, ed. Gotthardt Frühsorge, Rainer Gruenter, and Beatrix Freifrau Wolff Metternich (Hamburg: F. Meiner, 1995), 13–39.
59 AHW 121/1, 47, par. 406.
60 An almost identical occurrence appears at AHW 121/1, 47, par. 409, where again the scribe says, "After I checked the regulations," the ruling had to be changed. Such forgetfulness was not unique to Altona. The Amsterdam Ashkenazic communal record keeper noted, concerning sumptuary regulation, that the old set had been forgotten in the mists of time. The leaders revived it because such regulation was still necessary to avoid competitive consumption. Elchanan Tal, *Ha-kehilah ha-Ashkenazit beAmsterdam bame'ah ha-18* (Jerusalem: Shazar Center, 2010), 151, par. 21.
61 AHW 121/1, 36, par. 229.
62 AHW 121/1, 42a, par. 359. The term *takanat ha-kehilah* (ordinances of the community) and *takkanat ha-kahal* (ordinances of the communal leaders) are used interchangeably here.
63 AHW 121/1, 83a, par. 1124.
64 Examples of single-leaf or broadsheet printed *takanot* from Altona can be found in the folder AHW 27. Even if several copies circulated and others were stored in the communal record room, they might have been lost over time. When one of the litigants represented the community itself, the records were more accessible. In an entry in an Altona *pinkas* from 1797, the *shamash* of Altona says about a case against a Jewish resident of Hamburg, "I stood before the court again with the above mentioned [party] and I showed the court a copy of the *pinkas takanot*, at number 129." AHW 21.1, 3.
65 AHW 121/1, 81, case nos. 1075 and 1076.
66 On the migrant status of many servants in Jewish communities in Germany, see Monika Richarz, "Mägde, Migration und Mutterschaft: Jüdische Frauen der Unterschicht im 18. Jahrhundert," *Aschkenas* 28, no. 1 (2018): 39–69.
67 Gotzmann, "At Home," 413–36. Gotzmann's pioneering article has been followed by many studies of Jewish legal pluralism and embeddedness of Jewish communal courts into larger non-Jewish judicial frameworks.

The focus of this chapter is the existence of legal pluralism *within* the Jewish communal framework, a small sphere embedded within a larger political constellation.

68 Marwedel, *Privilegien*, 334–69, contains increasingly intrusive decrees concerning Jewish civil jurisdiction from the late eighteenth century forward.

69 Late medieval cities similarly strove to establish themselves as centers of justice in order to strengthen their autonomy from imperial and royal interference. See, for example, Dietrich W. Poeck, ed., *Das älteste Greifswalder Stadtbuch (1291–1332)* (Cologne: Böhlau, 2000), xx.

70 Andreas Gotzmann, *Jüdische Autonomie in der Frühen Neuzeit: Recht und Gemeinschaft im deutschen Judentum* (Göttingen: Wallstein, 2008).

71 E. Carlebach, "Fallen Women and Fatherless Children: Jewish Domestic Servants in Eighteenth-Century Altona," *Jewish History* 24 (2010): 295–308.

72 Mary Lindemann, "Love for Hire: The Regulation of the Wet-Nursing Business in Eighteenth Century Hamburg," *Journal of Family History* 6, no. 4 (1981): 379–95.

73 Elisheva Carlebach, "'For We Jews Are Merciful': Emotions and Communal Identity," *Early Modern Workshop* 13 (2016): 72–78, fordham.bepress.com/cgi/viewcontent.cgi?article=1152&context=emw (accessed 7 May 2023).

74 For example, when a rumor that a member of Altona's Jewish community planned to litigate in the local Gentile court, the community leader sent a warning "that they should not do this, for justice is to be found in Jewish courts, there are judges in the land and the truth will emerge." Jewish Theological Seminary, MS 10772, fol. 27a, 4 Tammuz 1766. In Hamburg, in 1732, a Jew named Isaac recounted a dire warning issued to him by the secretary of the Jewish court of Altona if he did not desist from his intention to take a case to the non-Jewish court. When Isaac asked the secretary why he was being singled out persistently, he answered that "if such a ban were not strictly upheld, the reputation of the Jewish council would completely diminish, for if [Isaac] were not dealt with so harshly, then everyone would go to the Christian authorities and complain, and then our courts would entirely collapse [*gäntzlich zu Grunde gehen*]." The secretary warned Isaac that the communal elders would spend as much as was necessary to defeat him so that resistance was futile. See, in general, Horowitz, "Fractures and Fissures," and the example cited on p. 64.

75 See, for example, David Ruderman, *Early Modern Jewry: A New Cultural History* (Princeton, NJ: Princeton University Press, 2010), 74–81.

76 On the emancipation debates, see David Sorkin, *Jewish Emancipation: A History Across Five Centuries* (Princeton, NJ: Princeton University Press, 2019); for a discussion of Central Europe, see Sorkin, *Jewish Emancipation*, chaps. 3, 4, 8, 11–14. Rabbinic decisors had championed the rights of the community and its duly elected lay leaders since the medieval period; for an early modern example, see the discussion in Jay Berkovitz, "The Persona of a Poseq," *Modern Judaism* 32, no. 3 (2012): 262.

PART II

RETHINKING NATIONAL CONSCIOUSNESS

6

Cosmopolitan, International, and Jewish

'48ers in Exile

Michael L. Miller

If you walk into the reading room of the Széchenyi National Library in Budapest, you will see an entire bookshelf devoted to the so-called *emigráció*, with scores of books devoted to freedom fighters and revolutionaries who fled Hungary in 1849, when the Habsburg army quashed the Hungarian War of Independence (with the help of the Russian army). Nineteenth-century memoirs by political émigrés such as György Klapka and Ferenc Pulszky intermingle with more recent scholarship, such as Lajos Lukács's *Hungarian Political Emigration* (*Magyar politikai emigráció*), Sándor Veress's *The Hungarian Emigration in the East* (*A magyar emigráció a Keleten*), and Dénes Jánossy's two-volume magnum opus, *The Kossuth Emigration in England and America* (*A Kossuth-emigráció Angliában és Amerikaban, 1851–1852*). The *emigráció* represents a distinct period in Hungarian historiography and can be dated from 1849 to 1867 (the year of the Austro-Hungarian Compromise) or perhaps even to 1894, when Lajos Kossuth's corpse was repatriated to Hungary following his death in Italian exile. The Hungarian émigrés numbered in the thousands, and their memory has been immortalized on the urban landscape of Hungary in the form of street signs and, in some cases, statues. In 1864 one of these émigrés, K. M. Kertbeny (who is best known today for coining the term *homosexual*), published a directory of almost 2,000 Hungarian émigrés living across the globe, with the largest concentrations in England, France, Italy, and "the Orient" (meaning the Ottoman Empire).[1]

Similarly, there is a sizable, though smaller, literature on German (or German-speaking) émigrés, especially those who found refuge in the United States following the defeat of the Revolutions of 1848. Notable works on these "Forty-eighters" (or *Achtundvierziger*), as they were commonly called, include Georg von Skal's *Die Achtundvierziger in Amerika* (1923), A. E. Zucker's *Political Refugees of the German Revolution of 1848* (1950), Carl Wittke's *Refugees of Revolution: The German Forty-Eighters in America* (1952), and Josephine Goldmark's colorful memoir, *Pilgrims of '48* (1930). By and large, these works assume a rather hagiographic character, praising the German refugees' contributions to the economic and associational life of America and, above all, their participation in the Civil War on the side of the North. Indeed, their fight against slavery in America was often portrayed as a continuation of their struggle for freedom in Central Europe (and consequently the scholarship generally ignores the '48ers fighting on the side of the Confederacy).[2] Monuments to these '48ers dot the American Midwest, where many of them settled in the 1850s.

More recently, historians have turned their attention to the German refugees in Great Britain, focusing on Karl Marx, Friedrich Engels, and a slew of other lesser-known exiles and examining their role in the development of German socialism. Rosemary Ashton's pioneering work, *Little Germany: German Refugees in Victorian Britain* (1989), provides a colorful, in-depth social history of the Germany colony in Britain, and Christine Lattek's *Revolutionary Refugees: German Socialism in Britain, 1840–1860* (2006) explores the social and cultural environment of the German colony with an eye toward understanding the role of exile in the development of socialist political theory. Sabine Freitag's *Exiles from European Revolutions: Refugees in Mid-Victorian England* (2003) and Heléna Tóth's *An Exiled Generation: German and Hungarian Refugees of Revolution, 1848–1871* (2014) are among the rare works that adopt a comparative perspective, occasionally transcending national categories.

In the Hungarian case and, perhaps to a lesser extent, the German American and Anglo-German cases, the mid-nineteenth-century emigration is embedded in a collective national (or ethnic) narrative. However, in Austria, where the revolution erupted on 13 March 1848, the emigration has remained as peripheral as Vienna's Achtundvierzigerplatz ('48er Square), a small square that is situated in the 14th District, right next to the cemetery where the victims of the March Revolution were buried. Achtundvierzigerplatz was dedicated in 1929, along with 24 small streets, each named after a victim of the revolution.[3] In 1929, of course, the Social Democratic Party had a majority in the Austrian capital, which was popularly known as Red Vienna, and it is hardly surprising that the memory of 1848 in Austria was preserved by the party, which viewed itself as the ideological heir to the revolution.[4] The memory of the emigration, however, was not preserved by a political party but rather by a state institution, namely, the Informationsbüro (Bureau of Information). This was the Habsburg Empire's central intelligence agency, whose web of spies and informants kept track of the émigrés, or fugitives (*Flüchtlinge*), as the files generally call them.[5]

In this chapter I examine a small group of Jewish revolutionaries who actively participated in the Viennese revolution of 1848—so actively, in fact, that they found themselves on the Informationsbüro's "Most Wanted" list and were forced to find refuge beyond the reach of the Habsburg Empire. As Salo W. Baron has pointed out, the Revolutions of 1848 marked a "political debut" for Europe's Jews, above all in Central Europe, where Adolf Fischhof, Joseph Goldmark, Ludwig August Frankl, Johann Jacoby, Gabriel Riesser, Ignatz Kuranda, and other Jewish intellectuals played prominent roles in the revolutionary movement, mostly as liberal centrists or moderate leftists.[6] The British historian G. M. Trevelyan famously characterized 1848 as "the turning point at which history failed to turn," but for the Jews of Central Europe, the Revolutions of 1848 had far-reaching consequences, not only setting the stage for Jewish emancipation but also unleashing pernicious new forms of Judeophobia.[7] Indeed, the conspicuous participation of Jews in the Revolutions of 1848 helped shape the invidious antisemitic image of the Jew as revolutionary conspirator, which crystallized in the early twentieth century as the myth of Judeo-Bolshevism.

The revolutionaries examined in this chapter were young Jewish students and literati from Bohemia, Moravia, Galicia, and Hungary who lived in Vienna before 1848 and became quickly radicalized in the early heady days of the revolution. They vehemently (and verbally) opposed Habsburg "tyranny" and "despotism" and ardently supported the so-called "Greater German Solution" (*Grossdeutsche Lösung*), which envisioned a unified democratic Germany from the Elbe to the Rhine as a bulwark against Russian "tyranny." (The envisioned Greater Germany included Bohemia, Moravia, and Austrian Silesia, which were under Habsburg rule at the time.) All these individuals publicized their views in the newspapers and journals that proliferated after press censorship was lifted in March 1848, and some of them even incited the population to armed insurrection against the Austrian army in October 1848. After fleeing the Habsburg Empire, they drew on their personal networks from before the revolution and on the more extensive network of European revolutionaries who congregated in London, Paris, and, to some extent, Brussels, Geneva, and Constantinople.

The group of Jewish revolutionaries included Moritz Hartmann and Karl Tausenau from Bohemia; Sigmund Engländer, Sigmund Kolisch, Simon Deutsch, and Adolf Buchheim from Moravia; and Adolf Chaisés from Galicia. Most of them were born around 1820 and had come to Vienna in the 1840s, often to study at Vienna's university. Before the revolution they participated in a kind of Jewish republic of letters, a highly interconnected network of young men in Berlin, Prague, Leipzig, Breslau, Dresden, Pest, and elsewhere who wrote and published in German-language periodicals. Sigmund Engländer published a cultural journal in Vienna called *Der Salon* (The Salon), and many others contributed to *Sonntagsblätter* (Sunday Papers), a cultural journal founded and edited by Ludwig August Frankel, a Bohemia-born writer who had studied medicine in Padua, Italy, before taking a job as the secretary of Vienna's Jewish community. Before March 1848 their journalistic activity focused to a large extent on theater, literature, and the arts, steering clear of politically charged topics.

With the outbreak of revolution and with the newly granted freedom of the press, these cultural critics swiftly metamorphosed into political journalists, publishing some of the most radical newspapers of 1848, with articles that even called for the elimination of the ruling Habsburg dynasty and the murder of Count Latour, the minister of war, who was eventually lynched by a mob on 6 October 1848. During the revolution, Sigmund Engländer edited the satirical journal *Wiener Katzenmusik* (Viennese Caterwauling), Adolf Buchheim coedited the *Politischer-Studenten-Courier* (Political Student Courier), Adolf Chaisés coedited the *National-Zeitung* (National Newspaper), and Sigmund Kolisch briefly edited *Der Radikale* (The Radical), a fiercely antimonarchist paper that also published articles by Karl Tausenau and Simon Deutsch. In the words of R. John Rath, a leading historian of the Viennese revolution of 1848, these papers vied with each other for "irresponsibility and radicalism," often bordering on obscenity and demagoguery.[8] They all identified themselves as "democratic," a term associated with political radicalism and popular sovereignty in midcentury Central Europe.[9]

As self-declared democrats, these Jewish journalists pilloried reactionaries and counterrevolutionaries, lampooned aristocrats and clergymen, and relentlessly agitated against the emperor's advisers, the so-called Camarilla. Above all, they tried to push the revolution further and further to the left, exhorting the *Volk* to rise up and "destroy traitors to the cause of freedom."[10] As a rule, they supported a constitutional monarchy—with representative government, ministerial responsibility, and expanded suffrage—but as the revolution radicalized and their attacks on the Camarilla grew ever more vituperative, some of these journalists, especially those connected to *Der Radikale*, advocated abolishing the monarchy and proclaiming a republic.[11] Many of these papers also advocated the creation of a democratic Greater Germany, unifying all the German speakers—and all German-speaking lands—into one state under the leadership of Austria. (Supporters of Lesser Germany, or *Kleindeutschland*, tended to favor a constitutional monarchy under the leadership of Prussia.)

These Jewish journalists also played an active role in the associational life of the revolution. Many of them took the lead in organizing political clubs, which a contemporary English observer derided as "the rendezvous of all the agitators."[12] These clubs, a feature of all the European revolutions in 1848, from France and Italy to Austria, Hungary, and the German lands, were meeting places for like-minded people, who staged debates, drafted petitions, printed pamphlets, and took to the streets to hasten political change and promote social reform, especially on behalf of workers, artisans, and students.[13] Karl Tausenau was an impassioned speaker at the Society of the Friends of the People (Gesellschaft der Volksfreunde) and president of the Demokratenverein (Democrats Association), where he was succeeded by Adolf Chaisés, also a member of the Society of Friends of the People and a leader of the Liberal Club on the Wien; Simon Deutsch belonged to Der Deutsche Adler (the German Eagle), the Wiener demokratische Klub (Viennese Democratic Club), and the Verein der Deutschen in Österreich (Association of Germans in Austria) and was one of the leaders of the Wiener akademische Legion (Viennese Academic Legion), a volunteer student corps that came into being at the outbreak of the revolution. These associations were standard-bearers of German liberal nationalism, advocating democratic government and, quite often, a union with Germany.

These journals and associations flourished until the Vienna Uprising (or October Revolution) was crushed by the Habsburg army. The Vienna Uprising (6–31 October 1848) marked the most radical stage of the Viennese revolution. As Austrian troops were being mobilized to suppress the Hungarian revolution, radicalized workers and students tried to prevent them from leaving Vienna, leading to street battles, the lynching of Count Latour, the evacuation of Emperor Ferdinand and his court to Olmütz (Olomouc), Moravia, and the relocation of the recently convened parliament to Kremsier (Kroměříž), Moravia. During the early days of the uprising, Tausenau established the Central Committee of Radical Clubs (Central-Comité der radikalen Vereine) to coordinate the activities of the radical associations. In the words of a later historian, the Central Committee constituted a "secret government, whose dangerousness was fortunately attenuated due to the fact that, aside from Tausenau, none of its members were at all serious."[14] (The "unscrupulous agitator" Adolf Chaisés was one of its less serious members.)[15] The October Revolution ended with the court martial and execution of 19 instigators of the insurrection, including Alfred Julius Becher, editor of *Der Radikale* (before Sigmund Engländer), and Hermann Jellinek, a frequent contributor. Jellinek and Becher were accused of "open incitement to armed insurrection" after calling on their readers to fight the imperial troops who were suppressing the Vienna Uprising, and they were both hanged in November 1848 (and buried in the cemetery near today's Achtundvierzigerplatz). Hermann Jellinek, and his older brother Adolf Jellinek, a preacher in Leipzig at the time, were Jewish. As the Austrian poet Eduard von Bauernfeld quipped, Hermann Jellinek was put to death "because they needed a Jew and there was no one else at hand!"[16]

The noticeable participation of so many Jews in the Viennese revolution, especially among the radical democratic journalists, contributed to the perception that "the whole revolution was nothing but a Jewish revolution" (in the words of Ernst von Schwarzer, minister of public works at the time).[17] Joseph Alexander von Helfert, a chronicler of the Viennese press in 1848, observed that the "overwhelming prominence of the Jewish element" in the revolutionary leadership, above all in the radical press, irked the general populace so much that it filled them with "righteous anger and disgust."[18] During the revolution, anti-Jewish leaflets and broadsides regularly attacked Deutsch, Chaisés, Engländer, Jellinek, Kolisch, Tausenau, and others, decrying them as "Vienna's radical-mosaic scribblers" (*radikal-mosaischen Federhelden Wiens*) and denouncing them as shameless, treacherous, and talentless Jacobins who had radicalized the revolution and damned it to failure.[19] "Had our troops not been victorious on October 31, 1848," wrote an antirevolutionary journalist some six months later, "then these [Jews] would have surely given us the guillotine as a gift."[20]

Aside from Jellinek, most of the Jews who stood accused of high treason managed to flee Vienna at the end of the October Revolution. Adolf Fischhof, president of the Committee of Public Safety—and "practically the uncrowned emperor of Austria," in Salo W. Baron's hyperbolic terms—was one of the few exceptions.[21] He was arrested and imprisoned but released after seven months because of a lack of evidence.[22] Many of the others found themselves on a most wanted list of "political criminals and capital traitors" (*Staatsverbrecher und Hochverräther*), which detailed their crimes, and, if known, their current location (in June 1851).[23]

- **Adolf Buchheim** was accused of "inciting the masses and using violent means for the aggressive resistance to the executive power of the state."
- **Karl Tausenau** was accused of "agitating for the violent alteration of the constitution, for the eradication of the dynasty, and [for] the public incitement of the masses for the murder of Count Latour."
- **Adolf Chaisés** was also accused of striving for the "eradication of the dynasty" and engaging in "armed resistance" against the Habsburg army during the October uprising.[24]
- **Moritz Hartmann** was accused of "publicly praising the October uprising in the name of the Left in Frankfurt and participation in the armed resistance against [Habsburg] troops."
- **Simon Deutsch** was accused of "publicly advocating the establishment of a republic" and strengthening the revolution

through "his publicly known connections with German Democrats." He was also accused of haranguing the masses, together with Hermann Jellinek and Sigmund Kolisch, during the October Revolution.
- **Sigmund Kolish** was accused of haranguing the masses, together with Simon Deutsch and Hermann Jellinek, during the October Revolution.
- **Sigmund Engländer** appeared on a separate wanted list as a "preeminent (fugitive) participant in the October events."[25]

Jellinek, of course, had already been executed, so he was not among the wanted fugitives, but Buchheim, Chaisés, Deutsch, Engländer, Kolisch, and Tausenau were, together with dozens of other revolutionaries who had fled the Habsburg Empire in October 1848.

According to the most wanted list, Chaisés, Kolisch, and Engländer were in Paris in 1851 and Tausenau was in London. As for the other fugitives, their locations were not known at the time. We now know that Hartmann fled first to Germany, where he participated in the Baden Revolution (which lasted until July 1849), before taking refuge in Switzerland and then Paris. Adolf Buchheim made his way to London by way of Leipzig, Brussels, and Paris. Simon Deutsch (who used the alias Berthold Schwarz) traveled to Breslau, Leipzig, Dresden, and Frankfurt, and he eventually joined the likes of Chaisés, Engländer, and Kolisch in the French capital. During the perilous peregrinations, these fugitives found refuge with other revolutionaries, who helped them escape to the safety of England, France, and sometimes America.

Paris and London were the primary destinations for these Austrian fugitives. Paris, with a revolutionary—and republican—tradition going back to 1789, had been a place of refuge for Central and Eastern European revolutionaries, going back to the Polish uprising of 1830. Furthermore, the February Revolution of 1848 led to the creation of the Second French Republic, which lasted until 2 December 1851 (when Louis Bonaparte's coup d'état ushered in the Second Empire). Many fugitives found refuge in France, where they could expect to find kindred spirits not only among politicians (e.g., Pierre-Joseph Proudhon and Henri-Louis Tolain) but also among Parisian intellectuals, such as the historian Jules Michelet, who welcomed Simon Deutsch, Sigmund Kolisch, and other Central

European refugees into his salon.[26] Although France might seem a natural place of refuge, England—one of the few places that did not experience a revolution in 1848—seems a less likely destination for these refugees. A police report from 1853 reflected on precisely this conundrum, speculating that England's "unique legislative system" and its "isolated state" could explain why more than 5,000 Hungarian, Polish, German, Italian, and French émigrés had made London their home.[27] The police report also explained why the English people "protected" these refugees. First, England's freedom and security enabled the country to tolerate "the most dangerous elements of all other nations" without danger or harm. Second, it served England's economic interests to absorb and nurture these revolutionaries, because, so long as the Continent remained unstable, English industrialists would retain a competitive edge. Whatever the reasons, London became home to the Italian revolutionary Giuseppe Mazzini, the Hungarian revolutionary Ferenc Pulszky, and of course, Karl Marx and Friedrich Engels. As the police report noted, "This mass of refugees lives in no way separate from one another, but rather they stay in close contact with each other and in well-ordered organizations."

In Paris and London these refugees, who often arrived without knowledge of French or English, helped each other find work. They worked as private tutors, waiters, bookkeepers, servants, and peddlers, and, quite often, they resumed their writing activities, penning newspaper articles for German-language newspapers or authoring books on the revolution (or other related topics). Moritz Hartmann was a correspondent for the *Kölnische Zeitung*, editor of the Stuttgart-based journal *Freya*, and founder of the Parisian *Revue Germanique*. Sigmund Kolisch wrote articles for the Stuttgart-based *Morgenblatt* and the Leipzig-based *Gartenlaube*, including a piece on his friend Jules Michelet; he also wrote a historical novel about the Revolutions of 1848, *Ludwig Kossuth und Clemens Metternich*.[28] Sigmund Engländer became editor of the *Londoner Deutsche Zeitung* and the *Journal de Londres* and also assumed a leading position at the newly established Reuter's Telegraphic Agency in London; in 1864 he published a four-volume history of the French workers' movement (which Walter Benjamin quoted extensively in his *Paris, Capital of the Nineteenth Century* [1935]).[29]

Engländer, like many of his fellow refugees, became involved in the workers' movement, seeing it as a natural continuation of the revolutionary activity in 1848. In 1851 Karl Tausenau, together with the German refugee and Young Hegelian Arnold Ruge, helped establish the German Agitation Union in London.[30] In the same year the French government sought to expel Simon Deutsch, Sigmund Engländer, Sigmund Kolisch, Adolf Buchheim, and several other refugees for their alleged participation in the Franco-German communist plot, which aimed to overthrow the government. Deutsch and others also became active in the International Workingmen's Association, which was established in London in 1865. The International Workingmen's Association, and, as we will see, the Social Democratic movement in Austria, attracted many '48ers, drawing them together in transnational political movements with genealogies stretching back to the Revolutions of 1848. Indeed, many of our protagonists are mentioned in the correspondence of Karl Marx, Friedrich Engels, Moses Hess, and other members of the ramified network of European Communists and Social Democrats in the second half of the nineteenth century.

They are not always mentioned in a positive light, however. The surreptitious activities of Communist agitators, combined with the watchful eye of the state (and its paid informants) often bred suspicion and distrust among members of the often fractious émigré communities in Paris, London, and elsewhere. In 1852 Marx informed Engels that Simon Deutsch was an informant for the French police who had been sent to London to interrogate Karl Tausenau (literally, "to pull the worms out of his nose").[31] An 1853 police report called Adolf Chaisés the "Hauptspion" (chief spy) in Paris and also referred to Paul Julius Reuter, founder of the Reuter's Telegraph Agency, as "a spy of first rank." Not surprisingly, Sigmund Engländer, who worked for Reuter's, was also suspected of being an informant. In 1852 Marx vilified him as a "notorious police spy" in Paris and blamed him for revealing the Franco-German plot to the French authorities.[32] In 1855 he referred to Engländer's *Londoner Deutsche Zeitung*, which had just gone to press, as a "German rag" and identified its editor as "the ill-famed Sigmund Engländer, of Paris police memory."[33] In 1860 Marx informed Engels that Engländer was in the pay of both France and Russia and was "at present editing European world history in Reuter's name."[34]

Marx may have cast doubts on many of the '48ers, but the group of refugees remained rather tight-knit, despite the large distances that often separated them. Johann(es) Nordmann, a '48er who had written for Frankl's *Sonntagsblätter*, visited Moritz Hartmann in Belgium in 1858, and together they traveled to Paris to visit Simon Deutsch and Sigmund Kolisch.[35] Many of the refugees remained in contact with Ludwig August Frankel, who remained in Vienna, and his correspondence serves as an invaluable source for tracing the network of Viennese revolutionaries in exile. Moritz Hartmann corresponded with Simon Deutsch and Sigmund Kolisch during his sojourn in the Ottoman Empire as a correspondent for the *Kölnische Zeitung* during the Crimean War. A letter from Kolisch to Hartmann from June 1854 expresses a sentiment that must have been on the minds of many refugees: a general amnesty that would allow them to return to the Habsburg Empire.[36]

In this respect, 1857 constitutes a turning point in the history of the emigration. In that year Emperor Franz Joseph granted a general amnesty, allowing most "political criminals and capital traitors" to return to the Habsburg Empire. Simon Deutsch began visiting Vienna quite regularly in the 1860s, but he never moved back. On the other hand, Moritz Hartmann and Sigmund Kolisch moved back in 1868, and they both began writing for the *Neue Freie Presse*, a newspaper that was founded during the Revolutions of 1848 and had become the newspaper of record in the Habsburg Empire. Tausenau and Buchheim remained in London for the rest of their lives, Tausenau as a language tutor and Buchheim as a professor of German language and literature at King's College and a translator of German poems and literature into English. In London neither of them engaged in the firebrand political activism of their Viennese youth. Tausenau mastered the art of being English—tailored suits, self-deprecating humor, and almost no accent—and rarely spent time with other political refugees.[37] He kept his distance, according to one '48er, mostly because of the lingering suspicion that "he had betrayed the good cause."[38] Likewise, Buchheim also remained politically aloof. According to his obituary in *The Modern Language Quarterly* (July 1900), "Ever since 1852 Buchheim has devoted himself solely to educational and literary work, but he followed with the keenest interest the great political transformations which Germany and Austria underwent during the last forty years." Like many other '48ers, Buchheim "had hailed the dawn of a more liberal era" in 1848 but then steered clear of politics in its aftermath.[39]

This was not the case with Simon Deutsch, who split his time between Paris and Constantinople and from the late 1860s onward became involved in the politics of his native land.[40] Deutsch had become a banker in Paris, and he used his fortune to support the Austrian Social Democratic movement, financing demonstrations in Vienna, paying the deposit for the *Volkswille* (Will of the People), the main newspaper of Austrian Social Democracy, and serving as the treasurer of the workers' compensation fund. Deutsch was monitored by the Austrian police, and he was interrogated in a treason trial of Austrian Social Democrats that took place in 1870. At the trial, when asked about the movement, he insisted that the workers' party did not aim to "bring about a violent upheaval, but rather to improve the plight of [the workers] in general through peaceful means." Another witness at the trial noted that Deutsch supported social democracy on idealistic grounds, because he believed it embodied the democratic spirit of 1848. This may also explain Deutsch's active participation in the Paris Commune of 1871 ("essentially a working-class government," in the words of Karl Marx), for which he was briefly imprisoned.[41]

Even Deutsch's involvement in the activities of the Young (or New) Ottomans can be understood as a continuation of the revolutionary struggle against tyranny and despotism. The Young Ottomans were a loosely organized group of liberal Westernized intellectuals who wanted to introduce constitutional government to the Ottoman Empire. In the 1860s many of its members were in Parisian exile, where they came into contact with Simon Deutsch and other '48ers (as well as refugees from earlier European revolutions, such as Wladyslaw Plater, who fled to Paris after his involvement in the 1830 Polish insurrection against tsarist Russia). Deutsch and Plater had the rare distinction of being the only non-Ottoman signatories to the statutes of the Young Ottoman Society, which was founded in Paris on 30 August 1867. As a historian of the Young Ottomans has observed, the new society was committed to "the destruction of Russian influence . . . in the East" by fighting for the emancipation of Ottoman Christians "from the Muscovite protectorship" and the reestablishment of independent Poland. The Young Ottomans, he argues, were part of a ramified group of "disenchanted radicals, exiled democrats, and cosmopolitan nationalists" who saw Deutsch and other '48ers as kindred spirits and fellow travelers.[42] Deutsch, for his part, saw the Young Ottomans as partners in the larger struggle against tyranny, be it Russian, Habsburg, or Ottoman. In 1877, the year of Deutsch's death, it was rumored that Midhat Pasha, the reformist grand vizier who had just introduced the Ottoman Empire's first constitution, was even planning to appoint Deutsch, an old friend, as *vali* (governor) of Ottoman Bulgaria.[43]

Sigmund Engländer, who worked for Reuters in London, Constantinople, and Paris for nearly half a century (1854–1902), remained politically active, even though he promised his employer in 1871 to "abstain from all public connection with political associations," lest he compromise the agency's "character for impartiality."[44] Indeed, his history of the French workers' movement, published in German in 1864, was more of an impassioned political treatise than a history of a social movement.[45] Spanning more than 1,300 pages, Engländer's four-volume magnum opus was heavily influenced by Pierre-Joseph Proudhon's mutualist philosophy, which envisioned workers' councils and associations as the building blocks of a more equitable future society. Proudhon himself had participated in the February Revolution in France, and many of the Austrian refugees in Paris had a natural affinity for his ideas. Engländer's history of the French workers' movement draws extensively on Proudhonist thought, calling for the reform of society "through the synthesis of capital and labor" and the reform of the state "through the transformation of state sovereignty into pure self-governance [by the people]."[46] In 1873, two years after promising to "abstain from all public connection with political associations," Engländer published a book (in English) titled *The Abolition of the State: An Historical and Critical Sketch of the Parties Advocating Direct Government, a Federal Republic, or Individualism*, which was basically a distillation of Proudhon's "individualist anarchism." Engländer introduced his book as follows:

> As soon as unrestrained individual liberty maintains itself, and all the political and social functions are performed without the aid of any power—whether that power be legislative, executive, or judicial—and are exercised by a common and national association, from that moment the traditional idea of the State or Government ceases to exist. The State is then reduced to a simple realization of the will of the people by delegates, elected for a certain period of time and for certain specified objects.[47]

As an expression of popular sovereignty, Proudhon's antistatism (as articulated by Engländer) was certainly more radical than any of the democratic ideologies propagated in Vienna in 1848, but Engländer viewed Proudhonism—and its emphasis on "unrestrained individual liberty"—as the true heir to the "democratic and revolutionary movement on the Continent."[48]

Engländer's commitment to the international workers' movement was not atypical for Austrian '48ers, nor was Deutsch's commitment to social democracy. Engländer, Deutsch, and many other '48ers in exile were part of a larger international movement that often transcended national narratives and emphasized class narratives instead. To the extent that these refugee '48ers are dealt with in Habsburg or Austrian history, it is in the context of the international workers' movement and its local iterations. Some are mentioned in Walter Pollak's *Sozialismus in Österreich* (Socialism in Austria) and in Wolfgang Häusler's *Von der Massenarmut zur Arbeiterbewegung: Demokratie und soziale Frage in der Wiener Revolution von 1848* (From Mass Poverty to the Workers' Movement: Democracy and the Social Question in the Viennese Revolution of 1848), both published in 1979.[49] This was the year in which Bruno Kreisky and the Social Democratic Party won their fourth straight election (and fifty years after the dedication of Achtundvierzigerplatz by an earlier Social Democratic government).

Still, the "emigration," like the worker's movement and the Social Democratic movement, retained its international character, which may explain why it remains peripheral in histories of Austria or the Habsburg Empire, whose authors do not quite know what to do with the cosmopolitan, transnational, and often Jewish refugees who fled the Revolutions of 1848 but in many cases tried to perpetuate their ideals beyond the political boundaries of the empire or nation-state.

Notes

My teacher, Michael Stanislawski, first piqued my interest in the Revolutions of 1848 and, in particular, their impact on the Jews of the Habsburg lands. The Revolutions of 1848 became the fulcrum of my first book, *Rabbis and Revolution: The Jews of Moravia in the Age of Emancipation* (Stanford, CA: Stanford University Press, 2010), and they served as the dramatic backdrop for Michael Stanislawski's *A Murder in Lemberg* (Princeton, NJ: Princeton University Press,

2007), which investigates the assassination of Abraham Kohn, a progressive rabbi in Lemberg, Galicia (today Lviv, Ukraine), who was poisoned on 6 September 1848 and died the following day.

1 K. M. Kertbeny, *Alphabetische Namenliste ungarischer Emigration, 1848-1864, mit Einschluss der ausserhalb Ungarn Internirten: Sammt vorläufigen biographischen Andeutungen in Abreviaturen* (Brussels: Kiessling, 1864).
2 Michael L. Miller, "From Central Europe to Central America: Forty-Eighters in the Filibuster Wars of the Mid-Nineteenth Century," in *Transatlantic Revolutionary Cultures, 1789-1861*, ed. Charlotte A. Lerg and Heléna Tóth (Leiden: Brill, 2018), 193-208.
3 "Nach den Märzgefallenen werden Straßen benannt," *Arbeiter Zeitung* (30 April 1929), 4.
4 Wolfgang Häusler, *Von der Massenarmut zur Arbeiterbewegung: Demokratie und soziale Frage in der Wiener Revolution von 1848* (Vienna: Jugend & Volk, 1979).
5 On the Informationsbüro, see Tibor Frank, *From Habsburg Agent to Victorian Scholar: G. G. Zerffi, 1820-1892* (Boulder, CO: East European Monograph, 2001). *Flüchtling* can also be translated as "refugee," but the Informationsbüro clearly saw them as "fugitives" from the law.
6 Salo W. Baron, "The Impact of the Revolution of 1848 on Jewish Emancipation," *Jewish Social Studies* 11, no. 3 (July 1949): 195-248.
7 The scholarly literature on Jews and the Revolutions of 1848 is quite extensive, and here I cite the most important works, with particular emphasis on German-speaking Central Europe: Salo W. Baron, "The Revolution of 1848 and Jewish Scholarship: Part II: Austria," *Proceedings of the American Academy for Jewish Research* 20 (1951): 1-100; Jacob Toury, *Mehumah u-mevukhah be-mahapekhat 1848: peraʾot "Shenat ha-Ḥerut" vezikatan la-antishemiyut ha-ḥadashah* (Tel Aviv: Moreshet, 1968); Wolfgang Häusler and Werner J. Cahnman, eds., *Das Judentum im Revolutionsjahr 1848* (Vienna: Herold, 1974); Werner E. Mosse, Arnold Paucker, and Reinhard Rürup, eds., *Revolution and Evolution 1848 in German-Jewish History* (Tübingen: J. C. B. Mohr, 1981); Walter Grab and Julius H. Schoeps, eds., *Juden im Vormärz und in der Revolution von 1848* (Stuttgart: Burg, 1983); Elisabeth Campagner, *Judentum, Nationalitaetenprinzip und Identität: Die Juedische Revolutionspresse von 1848* (Frankfurt: Peter Lang, 2004); Ernst Wangermann, "1848

and Jewish Emancipation in the Habsburg Empire," in *1848, The Year the World Turned*, ed. Jay Boardman and Christine Kinealy (Newcastle, UK: Cambridge Scholars, 2007), 70–82; Michael L. Miller, *Rabbis and Revolution: The Jews of Moravia in the Age of Emancipation* (Stanford, CA: Stanford University Press, 2010); Ulrich Michael Rasche, *Die Revolution von 1848/49 und die europäischen Juden: Im Spannungsfeld zwischen Antisemitismus und "Emanzipation"* (Munich: Grin, 2020).

8 R. John Rath, *The Viennese Revolution of 1848* (Austin: University of Texas Press, 1957), 224.

9 Pieter Judson, *Exclusive Revolutionaries: Liberal Politics, Social Experiment, and National Identity in the Austrian Empire, 1848–1914* (Ann Arbor: University of Michigan Press, 1996), 38.

10 Rath, *Viennese Revolution*, 338.

11 Wolfgang Häusler, "Hermann Jellinek (1823–1848): Ein Demokrat in der Wiener Revolution," *Jahrbuch des Instituts für Deutsche Geschichte* 5 (1976): 125–75.

12 William H. Stiles, *Austria in 1848–49: A History of the Late Political Movements in Vienna, Milan, Venice, and Prague; with a Full Account of the Revolution in Hungary [&c.]* (New York: Harper & Brothers, 1852), 1: 122.

13 Judson, *Exclusive Revolutionaries*, 38.

14 Anton Springer, *Geschichte Oesterreichs seit dem Wiener Frieden 1809: Zweiter Theil—Die österreichische Revolution* (Leipzig: S. Hirzel, 1865), 519.

15 See Baron, "Impact of the Revolution of 1848," 218.

16 Walter Grab, "Das Wiener Judentum: Eine historische Überlick," in his *Zwei Seiten einer Medaille: Demokratische Revolution und Judenemanzipation* (Cologne: PapyRossa, 2000), 203.

17 "Was Minister von Schwarzer von der Revolution hält," *Wiener Charivari (Katzenmusik)*, no. 70 (9 September 1848), 273.

18 Joseph Alexander Freiherr von Helfert, *Die Wiener Journalistik im Jahre 1848* (Vienna: Manz, 1877), 147.

19 See, for example, [Sebastian Brunner], *Die jüdischen Feder-Helden oder: Das politisch-literarische Schabesgärtle in Wien* (Vienna: Gedruckt bei M. Lell, [1848]), Wienbibliothek im Rathaus, Rb 3412. This leaflet attacked Hermann Jellinek, Sigmund Kolish, Sigmund Engländer, Simon Deutsch, Moritz Mahler, August Silberstein, and Mathias Emanuel Löbenstein, among others.

20 "Wiener Tagesberichte," *Wiener Zuschauer* 130 (8 June 1849): 1038–39.

21 Baron, "Impact of the Revolution of 1848," 213.
22 Heinrich Friedjung, *Österreich von 1848 bis 1860* (Stuttgart: J. G. Cotta, 1912), 2: 192.
23 "Verzeichniß flüchtiger k.k. österr. Staatsangehöriger, welche sich an den revolutionären Unternehmungen in den Jahren 1848 und 1849 schwer betheiligt haben und von dem Wiener Kriminalgericht steckbrieflich verfolgt werden," *Allgemeiner Polizei-Anzeiger* 32, no. 52 (30 June 1851): 280–82.
24 For Chaisés, see also *Allgemeiner Polizei-Anzeiger* 30, no. 33 (25 April 1850): 165–66.
25 "Verzeichniß der von der k.k. österreichischen Militair-Untersuchungs-Commission in Wien als hervorragene (flüchtlige) Theilnehmer an den Octoberereignissen bezeichnete Individuen," *Allgemeiner Polizei-Anzeiger* 32, no. 52 (30 June 1851): 286.
26 See Jules Michelet, *Journal*, 4 vols. (Paris: Gallimard, 1959–76).
27 A. Vandermeulen, *Enthüllungen aus der höheren Region der politischen Spionage, in Berichten eines ungarischen Judas Ischarioth* (Berlin: Reinhold Schlingmann, 1862), 77–91.
28 Sigmund Kolisch, "Pariser Bilder und Geschichten: Eine Stunde bei Michelet," *Die Gartenlaube* 26 (1863): 408–10; Sigmund Kolisch, *Ludwig Kossuth und Clemens Metternich*, 2 vols. (Leipzig: Keil, 1850).
29 Sigmund Engländer, *Geschichte der französischen Arbeiter-Associationen*, 4 vols. (Hamburg: Hoffmann, 1864); Michael B. Palmer, *International News Agencies: A History* (Basingstoke, UK: Palgrave Macmillan, 2021), 41.
30 Christine Lattek, *Revolutionary Refugees: German Socialism in Britain, 1840–1860* (London: Routledge, 2016), 87.
31 Letter from Karl Marx to Friedrich Engels, 3 July 1852, in Karl Marx and Friedrich Engels, *Collected Works*, Vol. 39, *Letters, 1852–55* (Moscow: Progress, 1983), 126.
32 Karl Marx to Friedrich Engels, 3 July 1852.
33 Letter from Karl Marx to Friedrich Engels, 6 September 1855, in Karl Marx and Friedrich Engels, *Collected Works*, Vol. 39, *Letters, 1852–55* (Moscow: Progress, 1983), 547.
34 Letter from Karl Marx to Friedrich Engels, 12 April 1860, in Karl Marx and Friedrich Engels, *Collected Works*, Vol. 41, *Letters, 1860–64* (Moscow: Progress, 1985), 121–22.
35 Johannes Nordmann, "Simon Deutsch: Ein Gedenkblatt," *Allgemeine Zeitung des Judentums* (1 May 1883), 293–96.

36 Sigmund Kolisch (Paris) to Moritz Hartmann, 23 June 1854, Wienbibliothek im Rathaus, Nachlass Moritz Hartmann.
37 Rosemary Ashton, *Little Germany: Exile and Asylum in Victorian England* (Oxford, UK: Oxford University Press, 1986), 183.
38 "Weil er . . . im Geruche der Abtrünnigkeit von der guten Sache stund." M. C. Gritzner, *Flüchtlingsleben* (Zurich: Verlag der Schabelitz'schen Buchhandlung, 1867), 198–99.
39 Karl Breul, "Karl Adolf Buchheim," *Modern Language Quarterly* 3, no. 1 (July 1900): 1–4.
40 Michael L. Miller, "From Liberal Nationalism to Cosmopolitan Patriotism: Simon Deutsch and 1848ers in Exile," *European Review of History / Revue européenne d'histoire* 17, no. 3 (2010): 379–93.
41 Karl Marx, "The Civil War in France," in *The First International and After*, ed. David Fernbach (London: Penguin, 1992), 212.
42 Andrew Arsan, "The Strange Lives of Ottoman Liberalism: Exile, Patriotism, and Constitutionalism in the Thought of Mustafa Fazil Paşa," in *Mediterranean Diasporas: Politics and Ideas in the Long 19th Century*, ed. Maurizio Isabella and Konstantin Zanou (London: Bloomsbury, 2016), 159.
43 "A Jewish Governor," *Jewish Chronicle* (9 February 1877), 9.
44 Michael B. Palmer, "European News-Agency Beginnings: The Role of S. Engländer," *Media History* 22, no. 1 (2016): 33.
45 Wolfgang Häusler, "Sigmund Engländer: Kritiker des Vormärz, Satiriker der Wiener Revolution und Freund Friedrich Hebbels," in *Juden im Vormärz und in der Revolution von 1848*, ed. Walter Grab and Julius H. Schoeps (Stuttgart: Burg, 1983), 83–137.
46 Engländer, *Geschichte der französischen Arbeiter-Associationen*, 4: 212.
47 S. Engländer, *The Abolition of the State: An Historical and Critical Sketch of the Parties Advocating Direct Government, a Federal Republic, or Individualism* (London: Trübner, 1873), 2.
48 Engländer, *Abolition of the State*, 1.
49 Walter Pollak, *Sozialismus in Österreich: Von der Donaumonarchie bis zur Ära Kreisky* (Vienna: Econ, 1979); Häusler, *Von der Massenarmut*.

7

Hungarian Jews or Jews in Hungary

The Jews of Munkács and Ungvár

Howard Lupovitch

Munkács is a Jewish metropolis where more than half of the inhabitants are Jewish.... When we arrived at four in the afternoon, the streets were full of black-caftaned men, most of whom sported the ritual mop of hair and stood in small groups transacting business.... The cities of Ruthenia are made up of Hungarian Jews, and one hears only Hungarian speech.[1]

A classic Eastern European joke describes an elderly Jewish man being interviewed about his life. When asked where he is from, he explains that he was "born in Austria-Hungary, went to school in Czechoslovakia, married in Hungary, worked most of his life in the Soviet Union, and now lives in Ukraine." When the interviewer follows up, "Traveled a lot, then?" the man answered, "No, I have never moved from Munkács."[2] This apocryphal anecdote underlines the geographic fluidity of this quintessential border region that complicates even the most elemental taxonomy of European Jewry. Situated at the juncture of Hungary, Slovakia, Poland, Ukraine, and Romania—five states whose boundaries fluctuated considerably during the first half of the twentieth century—Jewish and other inhabitants of this region found themselves at one time or another living in all five of these states.

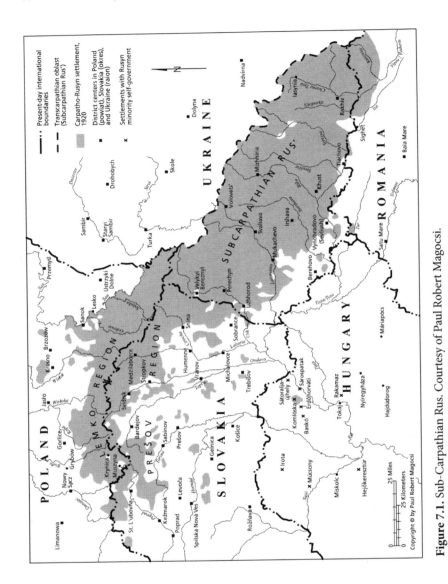

Figure 7.1. Sub-Carpathian Rus. Courtesy of Paul Robert Magocsi.

These fluctuating borders resulted from the changes to the map of East-Central Europe following the collapse of the Habsburg monarchy in 1918 and from efforts by the nation-states that emerged out of the ruins of the Habsburg monarchy—notably Hungary, Czechoslovakia, Romania, Ukraine, and Poland—to claim this and other border regions as part of their own national homeland.³ The endless shifting of boundaries, much like the ethnic diversity of this region, is exemplified by the fact that the region and its major cities were identified not by one but by multiple names. The region was known at one time or another as Subcarpathian (or Transcarpathian) Ruthenia, Subcarpathian Rus', Karpato-Rus, and, currently, Zakarpatska Ukraina. Munkács, one of the two major cities in the region that are the subject of this chapter, has alternatively been called Munkatsch (German and Yiddish), Mukacevo (Czech), and, today, Mukacheve (Ukrainian); and Ungvár (Hungarian), the other major city, is today known as Uzshorod (Ukrainian). For Jews who lived in these towns and in this region generally, the multiplicity of languages and cultures, often competing for political and cultural hegemony, complicated the ways that these Jews self-identified and were identified by their non-Jewish neighbors and the state. Jews in Munkács and Ungvár and in the region generally were at one time or another defined—and saw themselves—as Hungarian, Polish, Ukrainian, Slovak, and Karpato-Rus' Jews; and as *Galizianers*, Ashkenazim, and *Ostjuden*.⁴

For this reason, the Jewish communities of Munkács and Ungvár provide a useful case study in which to explore the complexities of defining the connection between communities of Jews and the development of a national consciousness based on the state in which they lived. A useful time frame in this respect is the long nineteenth century, from 1772 through 1918, when the region belonged to the Kingdom of Hungary, that is, to what was later known as the Transleithanian part of the Habsburg monarchy.⁵ Throughout this period its varied populace continued to maintain strong connections—economic, social, cultural, religious—with family and compatriots in neighboring states and provinces. Most Jews who lived in these towns during the nineteenth century were either themselves immigrants or the descendants of immigrants from Poland, Ukraine, or Slovakia. As such, even after residing in Hungary for years or even decades, they still had strong cultural, religious, familial, and communal ties to the towns, regions, and states where they or their forbears had lived previously. Hungarian state policies toward the end of the nineteenth century fortified the ties between these Jews and Hungary—or at least attempted to—but, even at the turn of the twentieth century, many Jews in the region still resembled their coreligionists in Galicia and other neighboring regions as much as they resembled Jews elsewhere in Hungary.

170 Howard Lupovitch

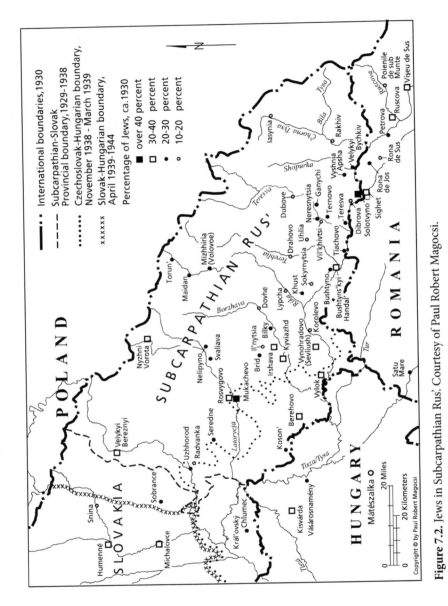

Figure 7.2. Jews in Subcarpathian Rus'. Courtesy of Paul Robert Magocsi.

The task of fleshing out the connection between Jews in this region and their host state is complicated by the fact that most Jews who lived in Munkács and Ungvár, like the majority of Jews in Subcarpathian Ruthenia, were intensely observant Jews who lived in relatively insular communities. For these Jews a connection and sense of belonging to Hungary or some other state or province was secondary to the fact that they were Jewish, part of the local Jewish community, and, more broadly, part of *klal yisrael*. It manifested more locally on the mundane level of daily predominantly commercial interactions between Jews and other denizens. Jewish economic activity, as will be discussed, was more a common thread than a distinguishing factor between Jews in the hinterland regions of Hungary and Poland. Moreover, most Jews acknowledged the authority of the state that governed them, obeyed its laws, and even evinced a deep sense of patriotism; beyond that, they tried to minimize the intrusion of the state into internal Jewish communal life. Whether or not they defined themselves or were seen by others as Hungarian Jews ranked a distant second to their self-identity as Halakha-abiding Jews. The relatively small number of Jews who lived in the Carpathian region had largely been ignored by Hungarian state officials so long as they paid their taxes and supplied the requisite "gifts" to the appropriate bureaucrats and nobles. The prevalence of Yiddish as the language of Jews was similarly of little or no concern to Hungarian officialdom or state policy.

The region has aptly been described as a catchment, where a hodgepodge of Jews from neighboring regions settled during the century before 1860.[6] This was true not only in terms of immigration but also in terms of the religious world these Jews inhabited, situated between the Hasidic-dominated world of Poland (and, later, Galicia) and the Orthodox- and ultra-Orthodox-dominated nineteenth-century Hungary. During the first half of the nineteenth century, proponents of these two religious and spiritual influences vied for hegemony in the Subcarpathian region, with neither emerging victorious. Ultimately, the preeminent position of one or the other in a particular community resulted from the arrival of a leading family from one world or the other. Thus the arrival of the Shapira family in Munkács eventually brought the Jews there into the Hasidic orbit; and in Ungvár the arrival of the disciples of Orthodox founder and leader Moses Sofer brought the Jews there into the world of Hungarian Orthodoxy.

The balance between a sense of Jewishness and Hungarianness (*magyarság*) began to shift toward Hungarianness in the 1860s, when Hungarian state policy, for reasons having less to do with Jews than with broader Magyar political and national aspirations, intensified state efforts to Magyarize all Jews in Hungary, including those in Munkács, Ungvár, and the surrounding towns and villages.[7] At the end of the 1860s Hungarian state policy elevated more deliberately the status of the Magyar language and

Magyar culture over rival national languages and cultures. Before then, demonstrations of Jewish loyalty in the form of explicit, public, and overt support for the Magyar nation had satisfied the expectations of state officials and Magyar nationalists. By 1870 these expectations demanded more concrete displays of loyalty and patriotism, in particular, the embrace of the Magyar language as the primary language of the Jewish street and as the language of instruction in Jewish schools.

In general, Hasidic and ultra-Orthodox Jews responded to these expectations as "a much more restrained and defensive acculturation process" that "formed a dynamic, insistent counterpoint" to broader patterns of Hungarian Jewish acculturation, to paraphrase one historian's conceptualization of Orthodox Jewish responses in Poland.[8] Moreover, the growing pressure to acculturate revealed fault lines within the Jewish communities of Munkács and Ungvár, not only between the more observant Jewish majority and the more acculturated Jewish minority but within the observant majority itself.

This fault line appeared differently in the two cities. In Ungvár the fault line divided an Orthodox and ultra-Orthodox majority from a Modern Orthodox and Neolog minority.[9] This more straightforward intracommunal division was comparable to intracommunal divisions elsewhere between more and less acculturated Jews. By contrast, the Jewish community of Munkács divided into a Hasidic majority that remained connected and oriented to their Hasidic counterparts in Galicia, and a community of non-Hasidic Orthodox and ultra-Orthodox Jews who were increasingly oriented toward the Orthodox leadership emanating from the disciples of Moses Sofer in Pressburg/Pozsony. The dividing line that unfolded in Munkács was less clearly defined at first, but it was eventually clarified by the response of each part of the community to the demands of increasingly aggressive Magyarization policies during the second half of the nineteenth century. The Hasidic response reflected a more rejectionist approach to Magyarization that sought, above all, to minimize the influence of any non-Jewish culture; although some Hungarian Hasidim became Magyar speakers by the twentieth century, the broader wariness toward things non-Jewish remained largely intact. The non-Hassidic ultra-Orthodox response reflected a more synthesizing attitude toward non-Jewish culture, which used the tools of Magyarization (language and secular education) to fortify the hallowed beliefs and practices of ultra-Orthodox Jews.

The disparities between the two outlooks thus delineated between a Magyarized and non-Magyarized Orthodoxy.[10]

Wasser-Polaken: Jewish Immigrants Under Magnate Tutelage

Munkács and Ungvár are located about 40 kilometers from each other and about 340 kilometers northeast of Budapest, in the heart of the Carpathian region. This region was noted by nineteenth-century Hungarian geographer Elek Fényes for its scenic beauty and rustic character. Each town was a county seat: Munkács of Bereg County and Ungvár of Ung County. According to Fényes, at the end of the 1830s the overall population of Ungvár was twice that of Munkács, but the two towns were populated by a similar composite of ethnic and religious groups. The 4,001 inhabitants of Munkács included 980 Roman Catholics, 1,388 Greeks, 87 Calvinists, 895 Lutherans, and 651 Jews; the 8,015 denizens of Ungvár included 2,800 Catholics, 2,214 "Greeks," 437 Calvinists, and 624 Jews.[11] Accordingly, Fényes described Munkács as a "Hungarian-Russian-German market town" and Ungvár as "a composite of Russian, Magyar, and, to a lesser extent German speakers."[12]

Most Jewish settlers in the region were immigrants or children of immigrants from Poland. Jewish migrants and other travelers crossed the border from Poland (and, after 1772, Austrian Galicia) into Hungary with few impediments. These Jews were commonly referred to as *finiatsy* (Yiddish, "those from," as in *fin Poyln*, "those from Poland") or *wasser-polaken* (literally "water Jews" in Yiddish), in reference to their having crossed the river from Galicia into Hungary. From the eighteenth to the early twentieth century, the number of Jews in the region increased, initially mainly through immigrants and later more through biological increase and internal migration, from 890 in 1735 to nearly 130,000 by 1910. Concurrently, the percentage of Jews in the overall population increased from 11% in 1869 to more than 15% by 1910.[13]

Most of these Jewish immigrants settled in privately owned towns and villages, including Munkács and Ungvár. As elsewhere in East-Central Europe, the landlords who owned and ruled these towns and villages were magnate families who formed part of the upper tier of Hungarian nobility.

Neither Munkács nor Ungvár was a chartered town (*szabad király város*) with the right to exclude Jews *de non tolerandis judeus*. Jews were able to settle in both towns under the aegis of the ruling magnate families, though more easily in Munkács than in Ungvár. Ungvár was a royal market town (*kamarai mezőváros*), a sort of corporate hybrid between chartered and privately owned town.[14] Since the fourteenth century, the town had been ruled by the Drugeth family on behalf of the royal crown. Hungarian king Robert Charles awarded them the town in recognition of military bravery and loyalty to the crown. Among other things, this meant that any initiative to admit or exclude Jews required the approval of both the royal crown and the magnate family. After 1840, when the Hungarian State Assembly removed restrictions on Jewish residence in most cities, the Jewish communities in Ungvár grew at a more accelerated rate.[15]

Munkács was more like a standard magnate-owned market town (*mezőváros*) where permission from and protection of magnate rulers enabled Jews to settle there. Until the end of the seventeenth century, Jews were involved in tax farming and flour milling for magnate families, especially for the Rákóczi estates in and around Munkács. In 1680 three Jews received a license from the Rákóczi family to brew liquor and run a tavern in Szent Miklos, a small, magnate-owned town near Munkács; from Szent Miklos, Jewish traders occasionally visited Munkács to conduct business. In 1687 Emperor Leopold I transferred Munkács to the jurisdiction of the Schonborn family following the defeat of Ferenc Rákóczi by the Habsburg dynasty. In 1687 the new lords of the town granted Abraham the Jew permission to import cloth and to reside in Munkács. The Schonborn family continued to encourage Jewish settlement more enthusiastically than their predecessors had, granting more Jews permission to settle there, mainly as arrendators, tavern keepers, and vendors of meat, grain, candles, and soap and a few as cattle breeders and artisans. By 1741, 80 Jewish families lived in Munkács as an organized community.[16]

In 1772 the first partition of Poland brought Galicia under Habsburg jurisdiction and made it easier to cross the border from Poland into northeastern Hungary. Thereafter a plurality of these Jews settled in Munkács and Ungvár, the two largest cities in the region, along with the next two largest cities, Beregszász and Máramarossziget.[17] A steady influx of Jews from Galicia increased the Jewish communities of Munkács and Ungvár further.[18]

The Jewish Economy: Between Polish and Hungarian Paradigms

The economic life of Jews in Munkács and Ungvár and in the region generally is perhaps the vivid commonality between Jews living in Hungary and Poland. Much like Jews in prepartitioned Poland and then Galicia and in neighboring regions of Hungary, Jews in the region were officially classified as either *Schutzjuden* (protected Jews, i.e., Jews granted special permission to live in one of the major cities) or *Dorfjuden* (village Jews). For Jews arriving in one of these major towns, the principal impediment to remaining was obtaining a commercial license. Although Jews were under the sponsorship of a magnate patron, the burghers who made up the local town council had to approve the application. One such applicant, who was requesting a license to sell explosives, went to great lengths to demonstrate his economic utility to local commerce. The applicant noted his membership in the local hunters' club and the endorsement of several local nobles. He also noted that, in addition to explosives, he was also able to procure matches, hunting equipment, food, and chemicals. Finally, he pointed out that his was a highly profitable venture.[19]

In smaller towns and villages too, most Jews in the area engaged in some form of commerce. Here, though, this meant a more hybrid combination of farming a small plot of land, consuming some of the produce, and selling the rest to eke out enough of a living to cover basic household expenses. Most small town and village Jews were simply *luftmenschen*, wandering from place to place and supporting themselves and their families as day laborers with the help of the communal dole. As one historian noted, "Only a small proportion of the Jews earned their living as middlemen, renting pastures from the landowners and leasing them to the Ruthenian peasants. Side by side with the productive manual laborers, there was a striking number of chronically unemployed loafers, as well as professional beggars of all ages."[20] Yekutiel Grunwald, a leading rabbi in the region during the first half of the twentieth century, homiletically recalled this widespread Jewish poverty: "Ten measures of poverty were given to the world: nine were taken by the town of Máramaros."[21]

The minority of Jews who were better off economically lived mainly in Munkács and Ungvár. They were divided into four categories according to their commercial relationship either with a (mainly noble and magnate) patron, if they were fortunate enough to have a patron, or with their rank-and-file customers: *Hausjuden*, Jews who managed a lord's financial affairs; *Kornjuden* (also known as *Produktenhandler*), Jews who bought and sold agricultural produce; *Handlerjuden*, Jews who sold retail products; and *Möbeljuden*, Jews who sold furniture and other basic supplies to military officers stationed in or near Munkács or Ungvár.[22]

The role of Jewish merchants in building and sustaining the local and regional economy became a source of historical debate at the end of the nineteenth century. Hungarian historians, who hitherto paid little attention to this region and its Jews, increasingly included Jews but selectively tailored their inclusion to a specific ideological agenda. Champions of Magyar national hegemony over rival Slovak, Polish, and proto-Ukrainian national movements weaponized an image of Subcarpathian Jews to suit their Magyar national goals. In some cases this meant redefining Jews in the region, along with Jews elsewhere in Hungary, as "Magyars of the Jewish persuasion" to help enlarge the Magyar population of Hungary (which made up 45% of the total population) into a national majority and to enlist Jews as "magyarizing agents" to help enlist other national minorities into the ranks of the Magyars. In general, this outlook worked to the benefit of Jews in the Carpathian region and elsewhere in Hungary.[23]

Other Magyar nationalist writers, though, disparaged and demonized Jews in the region to appease "awakening Ruthenians" by diverting their discontent toward Jews.[24] Foremost among these writers was Miklós Bartha (1848–1905). Bartha based his information on the findings of the "Highlands Commission" (Hegyvidéki akció) conducted by Ede Egan, a Hungarian economist of Irish origin who had been appointed by the minister of agriculture to draw up an economic plan to improve the living conditions of the Ruthenians. In *Kazár Földön* (In the Land of the Khazars), Bartha spun these data to refute the notion, popular among patriotic Hungarian Jews, that the first Jews who settled in Hungary were Khazar Jews who had arrived in the Danube basin a millennium earlier with the original Magyars.[25] Bartha rejected this ancient pedigree, emphasizing instead that most Jews in Subcarpathian Ruthenia were recent immigrants from Poland and Galicia. In itself, this claim was historically accurate in its portrayal of Jews. Yet Bartha, echoing the views of Győző Istóczy (1842–1915) and other leading Hungarian racial antisemites, added that these recent Jewish arrivals were "parasitic leeches and bloodsuckers who invaded the Ruthenian nation, carrying the Talmud on their backs and hatred for Christians in their hearts." He referred to Munkács derisively as *La Rome Juive* and, later, the Czechoslovakian Jerusalem.[26]

This disparaging appraisal of Jews, compounded by concerns over the less than upright behavior of *Ostjuden* who crossed the border, lingered throughout the nineteenth century and into the twentieth. This attitude intensified as the number of Jews crossing the Carpathians into Hungary increased from the 1880s onward. A particular concern was the presumed prevalence of Jewish smugglers undermining efforts to regulate commerce from Galicia into Hungary. Beginning in 1909, the captain of the guards who patrolled the border area required all those traveling near the border between Hungary and Galicia to carry identification papers and a birth certificate.[27]

However, such concerns had more to do with perception than an actual threat posed by Jewish immigrants. In sharp contrast to Bartha, other observers attributed to Jews a more constructive impact on the region's commercial growth and development. Qualifying the disparaging appraisal of Bartha, Hermann Bidermann noted that

> in any event it will be unfair to deny the Jews of Upper Hungary [i.e., Subcarpathian Ruthenia] the credit due them as the prime mover in the advancement of local trade. Indeed, without them, local industry would never have reached such a high level of development; from the salt mines in Maramaros—a branch which represents a worth of many millions and which is managed by Jews—to the smallest workshops, all the commerce in the area of Ruthenia is in their hands.[28]

Such observations were more in sync with the reality of the situation. By the end of the eighteenth century a clear division of activity had emerged within the realm of local and regional commerce. Balkan merchants dominated larger-scale and international trade, whereas Jewish merchants, most of whom were petty traders and dealers in second-hand goods, dominated local trade. State and local officials agreed that Jewish peddlers played an essential role in the local economy, bringing basic items such as matches and kerosene to remote Ruthenian villages whose inhabitants had little or no access to markets and trade fairs.[29] They noted also that Jewish peddlers often spoke Ruthenian and that there was a mutual dependence between

Jews and Ruthenian peasants. A police report from 1890 underlined this view.

> Except for their daily bread, the peasants are dependent on the Jew at every stage of their lives. He serves as their consumer counselor, agent and factotum, in the full sense of the word. And if we wanted to banish them, the peasants would be the first to demand their return. The Jews exploit the full the advantages accruing from this status and, by granting interest-bearing loans, control not only the peasants but also the clergy; yet it would be a mistake to speak of the prevalence of antisemitism in the sense of racial hatred.[30]

The growing importance of Munkács and Ungvár as commercial centers was paralleled by the growing role of Jews in local and regional commerce and industry. By the turn of the nineteenth century the most successful Jewish merchants were invited each year to participate in the deliberations of the local city council. By 1815 many Jews in Munkács could be described as well-off or, at least, upwardly mobile. By 1822 Jews in Munkács owned 67 houses and 24 places of business.[31]

By the end of the nineteenth century Jews in the two towns made up the bulk of leading entrepreneurs and professionals, not only in these two cities but also across Bereg and Ung Counties. In Ungvár Mor Kaufmann founded the city's first steam works and liquor and yeast factories. In Beregszaz Lipót Moskovits, Sándor Vári, Manó Kont, and József Winkler founded brickworks factories that were essential to the construction of buildings and roads. Most of the leading lumber merchants were also Jews.[32] The Munkács and Ungvár Commercial Association, founded in 1876 with a branch in each city, was made up predominantly of upper-middle-class Jewish merchants, who accounted for more than three-quarters of the 180 members and for more than half of Jewish commerce in Bereg and Ung Counties.[33] Out of 146 shareholders in the Munkácsi népbank (Munkács People's Bank), 115 were Jewish. By 1900 the largest bank in Ungvár had a majority of Jewish officers.[34] Moreover, by the turn of the twentieth century, Jews made up a substantial part of the liberal professions, with half of all lawyers in Ung County and nearly half in Bereg County belonging to the Jewish confession. Two-thirds of physicians and more than half of all pharmacists in the two counties were Jews, as were more than half of all engineers, nearly two-thirds of industrial clerks, and three-quarters of commercial clerks.[35]

State Protection and Antisemitism

The growing influx of Jewish immigrants into Subcarpathian Ruthenia beginning in the 1880s eventually elicited a surge of anti-Jewish agitation, a combination of an older, local, more traditional Polish-style, theologically based Jew hatred and the more novel xenophobic racial antisemitism of the late nineteenth century that emanated, above all, from Viktor Istóczy (1842–1915), a vigorous antisemite and member of the National Assembly.[36] Although largely polemical, such views crystallized into more menacing and violent outbursts of antisemitism. The most notorious incident was a blood libel accusation that took place in 1882 in the small town of Tiszaeszlár in Szabolcs County, about 70 miles from Ungvár and 90 miles from Munkács.[37] This incident began locally but eventually became a cause célèbre not only for anti-immigration advocates such as Istóczy but also for defenders of liberalism who generally supported Jewish integration.[38] For the latter, this incident was not only the first major challenge to the Emancipation Law of 1867, which had granted Jews civic equality only a decade and a half earlier, but also a litmus test of whether or not Jewish civic equality extended to immigrants, especially to unacculturated *Ostjuden*. As such, for Jews in Munkács and Ungvár, most of whom were unacculturated or *Ostjuden*—or both—the outcome of the ensuing trial resonated deeply and personally. That the Jews accused of this crime were defended by the leading attorney in Hungary, Károly Eötvös, and were eventually exonerated strengthened not only a new sense of belonging in Hungary but also the notion that, contrary to the claims of some advocates of Jewish citizenship, civic equality was not predicated on assimilation.[39]

For Hungarian Jews, including those in Subcarpathian Ruthenia, a sense of security was preserved, among other things, by a confidence in the stability of state and society. They believed that the rule of law prevailed in Hungary, antisemitic incidents notwithstanding. Less dramatic events further tested and ultimately fortified this outlook. For example, in 1883 a crowd of anti-Jewish demonstrators marched through the main square of Ungvár chanting "Hungary for Hungarians" (*Magyarország a Magyarnak*) and calling for all Jews in Ungvár to be evicted from their homes and expelled from Ung County.[40] The local gendarmes in Ungvár prevented this demonstration from precipitating anti-Jewish violence. Several years later, in 1903, a reporter from the *Allgemeine Zeitung des Judentums* noted how the rule of law could overcome the lawless event of law enforcement officers: "Last Monday night in the town of Ungvár, two gendarmes killed a local peasant and took the corpse to the Jewish cemetery to bury it there so as to incite a blood libel against Jews. Fortunately, a Jewish wagon driver happened to be passing by, [and he] called out loudly until others assembled; the two gendarmes were taken away and arrested by the police. The next day they were led in prison clothing and taken to prison in Beregszaz."[41]

The fact that other ethnic minorities were seen as less reliable and trustworthy than Jews benefited the Jews, sometimes even preempting a blood libel accusation from gaining traction. A Greek Orthodox resident of Munkács claimed that two missing girls had been abducted by "caftaned blokes" (*kaftanos alapok*). When the local police investigated, they concluded that "since only the Greek Orthodox residents mentioned it, the authorities need not investigate."[42] The combination of confidence in the rule of law and economic upward mobility created a sense of stability for Jews in pre–World War I Hungary. This stability allowed Jewish communities not only to expand and flourish but also to mediate internal disputes and tensions without a sense of urgency and concern over the image of Jews in the eyes of their non-Jewish neighbors and the state.

Competing Traditionalist Outlooks

The Jewish communities of Munkács and Ungvár matured during the course of the nineteenth century against this economic backdrop. In contrast to other parts of East-Central Europe, the upward mobility, commercial success, and rise of a Jewish haute bourgeoisie and intelligentsia in Subcarpathian Rus' were not paralleled by any widespread move away from traditional Judaism or the traditional Jewish community. The traditional community remained entrenched and continued to dominate all facets of Jewish life. Indicative in this regard is a distilled description of the Jewish community of Munkács in 1929: "Already in the eighteenth century the community was one of the strongest in Torah and daily and weekly religious observance."[43] The late Elie Wiesel made a similar observation in his recollections of growing up in the Subcarpathian town of Sziget.

> You went out into the street on Saturday and felt Shabbat in the air. Stores were closed, business centers at a standstill, municipal offices deserted. For the Jews as well as their Christian neighbors it was a day of total rest. The old men gathered in synagogues and houses of study to listen to itinerant preachers, the young went strolling in the park, through the woods, along the riverbank. Your concerns, anxieties and troubles could wait: Shabbat was your refuge.[44]

Hyperbole and nostalgia notwithstanding, such observations and recollections capture the predominantly traditional character of Jewish life in the region, in larger cities such as Munkács and Ungvár no less than in smaller towns and villages. The array of communal institutions that were erected in each town during the eighteenth century to manage and regulate all facets of Jewish life remained not only vibrant but also dominant into the twentieth century. The emergence of pockets of Neolog Judaism, elsewhere a measure of religious change as a result of acculturation and economic upward mobility, did little to alter the overall picture of Jewish communal life. In this regard, the ways that Hasidic and ultra-Orthodox Jews in Munkács and Ungvár engaged with the growing pressures of Magyarization reflect the limited impact that Magyarization had on traditionalist communities, which remained vibrant and entrenched in the face of changing conditions. To paraphrase Glenn Dynner's broader appraisal of traditional Jewish life in late nineteenth-century East-Central Europe, in Munkács and Ungvár Jewish traditionalism became more focused, dynamic, and assertive as a result of the encounter with Magyarization.[45]

The development of the formal institutions of Jewish life began in earnest during the eighteenth century in Munkács and a century later in Ungvár. Before the 1760s, though the two towns were already emerging as important commercial centers, many Jews who did business there lived elsewhere in nearby—or not so nearby—towns and villages, at times because of local restrictions and impediments but also because there was little in the way of organized Jewish communal life in the two towns. This situation began to change during the last decades of the eighteenth century. By 1760 there were enough Jews in Munkács to found a synagogue in a local home (and incur a synagogue tax). In 1778 the Munkács Jewish community established its first synagogue (*bet midrash*) in the home of Paul Farkas, a local Christian, which they leased for thirty years at an annual rate of 30 forints.

During the first half of the nineteenth century, first Munkács and then Ungvár increasingly resembled a fully functioning Jewish community. In 1827 Jews in Munkács erected an *eruv* for the first time, with permission of the city. By the 1880s both Jewish communities had established a full network of institutions that served the ritual, educational, and charitable needs of their constituencies, culminating in both cases with the founding of women's associations: the Bereg County Jewish Women's Aid Society (Bereg Megyei Izraelita Magyar Nőegylet) in Munkács in 1881 and the Ungvár Israelite Women's Mutual Sick Aid Society (Ungvári Izraelita Kölcsönös Betegsegélyező Nőegylet) in Ungvár in 1888.[46] The emergence of these two organizations epitomized the broader relationship between economic change and traditional Jewish life. The women's associations were founded and led by women from middle-class and affluent families who had both the financial means and the acumen to excel at philanthropy and become the heart of their community's charitable activities. In neither community, however, did this translate into a change in the religious status of these women, whose role in public Jewish life—in the synagogue and in the schools—changed little, if at all, until the twentieth century.[47]

More broadly, the emergence of these communal networks fortified the traditional and relatively insular character of each community. Noting an identity that reinforced Jewish separateness, which he considered an obstacle to feelings of belonging to the state, the deputy sheriff of Bereg County, Gyula Jobbaszty, commented, "It is clear that in Bereg County associations strengthened the social barrier that exists between Jews and Christians. . . . In Munkács this means especially the Jewish immigrants from Galicia whose behavior shows movement toward the concept of the Hungarian state with the greatest passivity and who struggle to fence in their niche schools from the area of public education."[48]

The coming of age of the two communities and the full triumph of traditional Jewish life there crystallized with the arrival of Meir Eisenstadter (aka MaHaRaM Eysh, 1780–1852) in Ungvár in 1835 and the Shapira Hasidic dynasty in Munkács a half-century later. Although the two shared an intractable commitment to meticulous adherence to Jewish law and custom and a fierce opposition to religious innovation, they were the bearers of different and, at times, conflicting outlooks, which included a different attitude toward Magyarization. Eisenstadter was a disciple of the Hatam Sofer and a champion of Hungarian Orthodoxy; he came to Ungvár from elsewhere in Hungary. The Shapira family was a champion of the Hasidic life of their erstwhile home in Poland and Galicia. Each elevated their community from a marginal to a prominent and influential Hungarian Jewish community by the end of the nineteenth century; yet each remained oriented in a different geographic and spiritual direction: Eisenstadter westward toward Pressburg and the Shapira family eastward toward Galicia. Both regarded Hungarian language and culture with wariness and looked askance at its ubiquity; for Eisenstadter and his followers, though, it was a more familiar and hence less menacing vernacular than it was for more recently arriving immigrants from Poland, who were accustomed to an entirely different vernacular.

Moreover, before the 1880s Munkács and Ungvár were very much guided by the Orthodox leaders of Pressburg. Until the 1880s both communities were accurately described as northeastern branches of Pressburg Orthodoxy—and Ungvár retained this distinction into the twentieth century. From as early as 1810 both communities began to engage the services of students of Moses Sofer, or students of his students. Abraham Gottesman, communal rabbi of Munkács at the turn of the nineteenth century until his death in 1814, corresponded with Meir Barbi, a disciple of Moses Sofer in Pressburg. Meir Eisenstadter himself was the son in-law of David Deutsch of Vagujhely, another disciple of Moses Sofer.[49]

Before Meir Eisenstadter's arrival in Ungvár, the community had engaged a series of capable but unremarkable rabbis. Eisenstadter was the first with a reputation as a first-rate scholar that extended into Galicia and across Hungary to Pressburg. Eisenstadter and his son and successor, Menachem Eisenstadter, served as chief rabbi of the community during the nearly four decades when the community emerged as a leading Hungarian Jewish community. Moreover, Eisenstadter was the first rabbi in the region who was well paid. Previously, rabbis in the region typically had been recruits from Galicia who lived from hand to mouth; one historian described them as a "clerical proletariat."[50]

The rise of the Shapira family in Munkács was more protracted.[51] The first family member to serve as rabbi of Munkács, Zvi Elimelech

Shapira (1785–1841), arrived in 1824. After an extended clash with the lay-dominated *kehilla* board that objected to excessive Hasidic influence, he returned to Galicia in 1829, lamenting "the obstinate nature of those in this county, who are defiant and listen to no one."[52] This situation in Munkács ebbed and flowed until the 1880s. By the end of the 1850s anti-Hasidic sentiment abated briefly. A decade later, most synagogues used the Hasidic prayer book and liturgy. However, the hiring of Chaim Sofer, a disciple of Moses Sofer (but no relation), as community rabbi in 1868 reasserted the influence of Pressburg over that of rival Hasidic rabbis. Sofer's departure for Budapest in 1880 left a vacuum in the rabbinate that was filled by Shlomo Shapira, grandson of Zvi Elimelech. From this point on, a member of the Shapira family would be community rabbi until 1928, and the community would become one of the central bastions of Hasidic Judaism in the region, indeed, in all of Hungary.[53]

Under the leadership of the Eisenstadters in Ungvár and the Shapiras in Munkács, the region became a stronghold not only of Orthodox and Hasidic life in Hungary in general but also a major center of yeshiva learning worldwide. Meir Eisenstadter founded a new yeshiva in Ungvár not long after his arrival; within two decades the yeshiva had 240 permanent students and dozens of part-time students. Supported by an annual gift of 60,000 forints from the Jewish community, this yeshiva attracted first-rate students and scholars, most notably perhaps Solomon Ganzfried (1804–1886), the author of the broadly influential law code *Kitzur Shulhan Aruch*.[54] In 1851 Jews in Munkács founded a yeshiva there. Initially this yeshiva paled beside Eisenstadter's. Beginning under the leadership of Chaim Sofer, the yeshiva began to rival its counterpart in Ungvár. Under the tutelage of the Shapira family, it was transformed into a first-rate Hasidic yeshiva. By the end of the nineteenth century the yeshivot in Munkács and Ungvár rivaled their Hasidic and Orthodox counterparts in the region, indeed, throughout Hungary.

By the end of the 1880s both communities were major centers of vibrant traditional Jewish life. A century earlier, in the second half of the eighteenth century, noted Jewish merchant and intercessor Dov Ber Birkenthal of Bolechów visited the region three times.[55] He visited Munkács each time, but only briefly, for specific commercial purposes: to pick up fresh horses in one case and to conclude a business transaction in another. More tellingly, he spent the Sabbath elsewhere, in Máramaros or some other town, where there was already a more established synagogue and other communal institutions.⁵⁶ By the end of the 1880s both cities were perceived as fully developed Jewish communities; a recurring advertisement in the Orthodox newspaper *Kol maḥazikei ha-dat* placed by Abraham David Weiser, an innkeeper in Munkács, announced weekly, "I wish to let our *meticulously observant coreligionists* who come here on business to our city of Munkács know that I have clean rooms to rent and provide food per the request of the tenant.... Available upon request are the fresh produce of our region, including walnuts, hazelnuts, and plums."⁵⁷

Selective Magyarization: Education and Vernacular Language

The preeminent positions of Hasidism in Munkács and Orthodoxy in Ungvár were tested during the second half of the nineteenth century by state-sponsored Magyarization policies and attempts by progressive Neolog Jews to infiltrate these communities and expand their presence there. On the whole, attempts to establish a Neolog community were far less successful than efforts to Magyarize the local Jews. The small Neolog congregation that had formed during the 1860s attempted to secede from the main Jewish community in 1868. Its leaders were excommunicated by Meir Eisenstadter, whose edict was defended by Moses Schick, the renowned and influential rabbi of Huszt.

> I have heard and it turns my stomach that the horn of Torah has descended in the holy community of Ungvár, frivolous individuals have incited the people to arbitrarily follow the offspring of Gentiles on an evil path toward desecration, and consumed the meat prepared by a *shochet* [Hebrew for "ritual slaughterer"] who was banned by the community; and lest these frivolous individuals say that their preacher gave permission to the *shochet*—know that the preacher himself is not authorized.⁵⁸

The combined objection by the two leading rabbis undermined subsequent attempts by Neolog Jews to expand beyond a small minority.

In Munkács the communal leadership preempted any attempts by Neolog Jews to establish even a small enclave. Even the slightest inkling of nonobservance elicited fierce condemnation from the communal rabbinate. For example, in 1868 two local Jewish doctors were seen smoking on the Sabbath. When the recently arrived Chaim Sofer heard about this transgression, he condemned the two doctors the following Saturday morning in his weekly sermon in severe terms: "I did not believe that anyone would be so shameless to do something like this in Munkács. . . . I thought that if it did happen, people would assail the perpetrators until they had to be carried away. . . . I cannot promise that if I were to come upon such a Jew I would not trade my life for his."[59]

At times, though, Sofer and other Hasidic and Orthodox rabbis in the two communities condemned each other no less vehemently than they condemned religious laxity and Neolog Judaism. For example, Hasidic Jews in Munkács repeatedly criticized Chaim Sofer, despite his piety, because they refused to accept his non-Hasidic customs, such as strolling publicly side by side with his wife on Shabbat and holidays. (This was one of the reasons Sofer left for Budapest in 1880.) Moreover, until the 1850s, Munkács was the site of an ongoing turf war between Belz Hasidim and the disciples of Menachem Mendel in Kosov. Hasidic Jews in Ungvár vehemently opposed the Orthodox rabbi Eleazar Löw even after he built them a *kloiz* and allowed them to operate largely autonomously.[60]

The mere possibility of Neolog Judaism infiltrating their communities, however, led Orthodox and Hasidic leaders in the two towns to lay aside their differences. For example, in July 1865 Hasidic leaders from Subcarpathian Ruthenia and Galicia met in Munkács in a conference presided over by the Rabbi of Belz. While reiterating their objections to "rigid rabbis" (i.e., non-Hasidic Orthodox rabbis), they emphasized that their primary aim had to be unity and initiating a "defensive alliance" (*Schutzbundnis*) between rabbis of Poland and northern Hungary against religious innovation.[61] Five years later, Chaim Sofer, still rabbi in Munkács, expressed his preference for Hasidic Jews over Neolog Jews in a letter to the president of the ultra-Orthodox Shomrei Ha-Dat (Guardians of the Faith) society in Budapest: "It is a great principle to distance oneself from the reformers . . . such that the separation between Jews and reformers should be like the distance between Heaven and Earth. . . . And even if this costs us a few communities, it is still better to have a complete Judaism."[62] By 1880 this willingness to join forces against Neolog Jews culminated in the rabbis of Munkács and Ungvár forming a sort of anti-Reform coalition that lasted for more than a half-century.[63]

In contrast to their untrammeled rejection of religious innovation, the Hasidic and Orthodox rabbis in Munkács and Ungvár, to varying degrees, responded less definitely and objected more tepidly to state policies and initiatives to improve communal education and replace Yiddish with Magyar as the language of the Jewish street. The rabbis held back their opposition so long as these policies and initiatives steered clear of religious innovation. For example, in 1848 communal leaders in Munkács supported a statewide initiative to support Edward Einhorn's Pest-based Magyarization society. The rabbinate approved so long as it was clear that this was a pro-Magyarization but anti-Reform project.[64]

State involvement in internal Jewish matters intensified during the 1850s and 1860s as first proponents of Habsburg neoabsolutism and then Magyar nationalism pressured Jews in Hungary to acculturate more rapidly. For Habsburg neoabsolutists this meant adopting the German language; for Magyar nationalists, Magyar. From the outset, officials in charge of this endeavor regarded revamped Jewish education as an indispensable first step toward acculturation. In 1851 the Habsburg regime passed the National Education Fund Act. This new law commuted the large debt that Hungarian Jews owed the royal crown—a combination of arrears from the Toleration Tax that had been abrogated in 1845 and the large indemnity imposed on Hungarian Jews for siding against the Habsburg dynasty during the Hungarian Revolution of 1848 and war of independence in 1849—into a fund that established a network of state-sponsored dual-curriculum schools for Hungarian Jews. In addition, the new law stipulated that all Jewish children were required to attend these schools or acquire a general education in some other way. After 1860 rabbis in Hungary were required to be able to read, speak, and write Hungarian fluently in order to have the title of rabbi.

The 1851 law and subsequent laws elicited varied responses from rabbis in Hungary. Modern Orthodox rabbis such as Esriel Hildesheimer and Neolog rabbis embraced the law immediately. Far less accommodating and more varied were the responses of Hasidic and Orthodox rabbis to the proposed innovation in education. Hasidic and Orthodox rabbis were suspicious both of state schools and Jewish *Normalschulen*, albeit for different reasons. Regarding state schools, the Hasidic and Orthodox rabbis worried about students being required to attend school on Saturday and Jewish holidays and, even more so, about students and their parents being willing to attend school on these holy days for the material benefit of attaining a secular education. They also worried that children using their non-Jewish names might lead to religious laxity or indifference. Hasidic rabbis outright forbade their followers from sending their children to state schools. By contrast, Orthodox rabbis never explicitly forbade their followers from sending their children to state schools but discouraged the practice.[65]

Not surprisingly the number of Jewish students in the two communities who attended state schools diminished steadily during the latter half of the nineteenth century. In Munkács, for example, the number of Jewish boys attending one local gymnasium dropped from 18 in 1844 to 6 by 1869. In Ungvár there were 242 Jewish children in public schools in 1878; by 1908 there were only 19.[66] In 1912 the percentage of Jewish children who attended state schools in Munkács, Ungvár, Beregszaz, and Maramarossziget was less than 2% of the number of Jewish children attending public schools in all of Hungary, despite the fact that these children made up more than 10% of all Jewish children in Hungary.[67]

The reluctance to allow Jewish children to attend public schools delineated the limit of immersion into mainstream society. Jewish leaders in these communities evinced a similar reluctance to allow Jews to enlist for military service. When Jewish emancipation at the end of the 1860s introduced the possibility of Hungarian Jews being conscripted into the Hungarian National Guard, communal leaders in Munkács and Ungvár took immediate steps to preempt from the outset what they regarded as an ominous threat to Jewish identity. In March 1867 Jews in Ungvár petitioned for the exemption of yeshiva students from military service in the name of religious freedom. The petition was granted several weeks later, prompting the local correspondent of *Hamagid* to comment, "Liberty has been declared for all those boys who streamed to Ungvár to study with Rabbi Eisenstadt—exemption from military service; this is the good fortune that the king has bestowed on our yeshiva."[68]

Rabbinic disapproval of public schools prompted a minority of Jewish laity to advocate more enthusiastically for changes in local Jewish schools that, in their estimation, were in disarray and badly in need of improvement. As one community member noted in 1860:

> The Ungvár Jewish community badly needs a richer educational life.... Education is the indisputable measure of progress, so we need the community to undertake these measures.... Hitherto community schools have been the stepchild of the community, left to sustain itself. While other community institutions, and schools in other communities, were cared for more richly and provided more resources, our schools have often been neglected for months and tossed a few crumbs from time to time.[69]

In response to these concerns, affluent Jews in the two communities looked for ways to circumvent the rabbi-dominated community board. In 1866 wealthy Jews funded and founded a new, secular school in each community. A year later they convinced the county government of Bereg County to establish an artisan training institute for 16-year-old boys. Initially, local rabbis refused to approve these schools, mainly because of an unwillingness to employ non-Orthodox Jewish teachers to teach secular subjects and a dearth of Orthodox teachers who could teach these classes.[70] Gradually these determined parents overcame rabbinic resistance with limited success. In 1866 a new elementary school opened in Munkács, with "three classes and three proficient teachers."[71]

The firm resistance to educational reforms evinced by rabbis in Munkács and Ungvár did not preclude some of the same rabbis from sanctioning certain aspects of Magyarization, specifically the use of Magyar as a vernacular language. In a sense, Meir Eisenstadter and Chaim Sofer, the two most prominent Orthodox leaders in the two communities, articulated what was, in retrospect, an exegetical basis for this outlook. In a sermon he delivered on *Shabbat Shuva*, Eisenstadter defined a crucial distinction between two approaches to observing Jewish law.

> For many years there have been two types of pious Jews who share in common a fear of God.... The one group claims that the only way to worship God is to accept the ways of our forebears . . . and that any inquiry into the roots of religious practice and belief will only lead to permissiveness and are nearly akin to losing faith and distancing oneself from reward; and this is the reason why God commanded us "and you shall not follow your hearts and your eyes": "Your hearts" meaning heresy and "your eyes" meaning infidelity.... Thus no one

should be enticed by his limited knowledge to imagine that his thinking can oversee the pursuit of the truth. . . . Yet a person is also obligated to investigate using knowledge to clarify the truth of his reality through inquiry and argument using intellectual abilities. Thus, the Torah also taught, "You shall know in your heart that the Lord is God." Accordingly, we must explain what is meant by "Do not follow your heart." The answer, according to Maimonides: only when it leads you to uproot essential teachings of the Torah.[72]

Along complimentary lines, Chaim Sofer, in a commentary on Psalms 19:11, alluded to the importance of engaging with the outside world.

> The Holy one, blessed is He created man to eat and to sate his soul from that which is permitted to him and to strengthen his body [to be] strong and bold in the service of the creator; but he need not be an ascetic [*nazir 'olam*] and separate himself from the pleasures of the world by fashioning wings of separation and subsisting only on the joys of looking upon the countenance of the living king, for he will become empty and lost from the world . . . because he cannot tolerate the burden of abstinence and asceticism.[73]

In tandem, Eisenstadter and Sofer provided a justification for those among their disciples who regarded the Magyar language as a necessary and useful means to engage with the world. Eisenstadter's implicit criticism of those who reject "any inquiry into the roots of religious practice" and lauding of those who "investigate using knowledge to clarify the truth of his reality through inquiry and argument using intellectual abilities" allowed for the possibility of using Magyar language as a tool for inquiry, argument, and investigation that would help prevent the uprooting of essential Torah teachings. Moreover, embedded in these ideas was a thinly veiled criticism of Hasidic tendency to see any and all aspects of the non-Jewish world as impure, including the replacement of sacred Yiddish *mamaloshen* with the impure Magyar *Anyanyelv* (mother tongue or vernacular). Instead, Eisenstadter and Sofer advocated a selective engagement with mainstream society that would include adopting Magyar as one's daily language. This absolved their followers from having to choose between adherence to a Jewish custom and complying with a state regulation.[74]

To be sure, this did not mean full embrace of the Magyar language. Sofer and other rabbis in the two communities were fierce advocates of the rabbinic ruling (*psak din*) of Mihalovce in 1865, a hallmark of burgeoning Hungarian ultra-Orthodoxy, that prohibited changes in the synagogue service, including the use of any vernacular language as part of the service. Yet the fine line drawn by Eisenstadter and Sofer resonated with a subtle distinction in the language of this ruling's opening clause: "It is forbidden for a sermon in the synagogue to be given in vernacular language and it is forbidden for people to listen to these sermons. Henceforth any Jew who hears a rabbi or anyone else speaking a non-Jewish language is required to leave and resign from the synagogue. Sermons must be given only in a Jewish language that are deemed kosher in this country." Strictly speaking, this was not a ban on the adoption of the Magyar language generally; rather, it was the use of Magyar or another vernacular as part of the synagogue service that was forbidden.[75]

The distinction between delivering a sermon in Magyar and speaking the language outside the synagogue in nonreligious situations dovetailed with a core aim of advocates of Magyar nationalism. These advocates' primary concern at the turn of the twentieth century was transforming the Magyars in Hungary (who made up 45% of the total population) from an ethnic minority into an ethnic majority. They saw transforming or, at least, redefining Hungarian Jews (who made up 4% of the total population) as Magyars as the most straightforward means to accomplish this all-important task. Magyar nationalists had little interest in the cultural behavior of Jews beyond their embrace of the Magyar language, if not as their only language, then at least as one of their spoken languages. In this way, as Miklós Konrád has shown, "Yiddish speakers were counted in the census by their alternative language—Magyar—and many more Magyar-speaking Jews were suddenly 'discovered' in Bereg and Ung Counties (62% by 1910)."[76]

Hasidic leaders in Munkács were less favorably disposed to the introduction of the Magyar language in any forum. The selective openness to adopt Magyar without upsetting Jewish tradition eventually permeated Munkács with the founding of the Bereg Megyei Izraelita Magyar Egylet (The Bereg County Magyar Society), which formed in Munkács in 1881. The aims of this organization resonated with state and communal aims: spreading Magyar nationalism and patriotism, cultivating

Magyar language, and stressing public culture while defending religious belief from spiritual and moral attacks.[77] Yet this organization sparked a backlash from Hasidic leaders in Munkács, who condemned any use of Magyar as unacceptable. In response, Aaron Reinberger, the president of the Jewish community, defended the use of Magyar in daily Jewish life and demanded that the rabbi of Belz and other Hasidic leaders outside Munkács cease interfering in the affairs of the Jewish community.[78]

By limiting the influence of the Magyar language, even the most stentorian and vehement objections from Hasidic leaders were unable to prevent Hasidic Jews in Munkács from eventually learning to speak Magyar by the beginning of the twentieth century. As one journalist observed:

> The Jews of Munkács have always been devoted to and been bold advocates of Magyar civilization [*muvelődés*].... Jewish homes always have Magyar books and daily newspapers.... There you have it, Jews in Munkács speak Hungarian, only Hungarian. What is puzzling is that there is no advantage, no preference, no advancement from speaking this language. On the contrary, even when they are dragged through the mud, imprisoned, or even face bayonets and rent asunder because of it, Hungarian Jews still speak Hungarian.[79]

* * *

In the redrawing of the map of East-Central Europe following World War I, Munkács and Ungvár became part of the new state of Czechoslovakia. For the inhabitants of the two cities, Jewish and non-Jewish alike, this meant acclimating to a new political and cultural reality. No longer part of the now defunct Kingdom of Hungary and the Habsburg Empire, the population of the two towns and their entire Subcarpathian Ruthenia region had to reorient themselves to a new dominant national culture. Yet it was far from clear what that culture was or would be. The ensuing years consisted in no small part of a culture and language war between Czechs, Slovaks, and Hungarians.[80] The last, in particular, saw in their language and culture the last bastion of a golden age that had collapsed with the Kingdom of Hungary itself.

In a sense, though, Jews in the region had unknowingly prepared themselves for this tumultuous moment. For decades before this change, they had navigated the tortuous path between competing languages and cultures. Only a generation or two removed from transplanting themselves from Galicia to Hungary—from a Polish to a Hungarian mainstream—these Jews had recently dealt with the challenge of juggling vernacular languages and balancing these vernaculars with their own Jewish languages and cultures. Jews in the region maintained strong ties to their erstwhile homes, family, and friends in Galicia—Hasidic Jews above all. Yet Jews in the region also forged a connection not only with the Hungarian state but also with Magyar culture by means of the Magyar language. By the beginning of World War I, Jews in the region lived between worlds: not only with one (larger) foot in the Jewish community and the other (smaller) foot in the mainstream community, but also with one hand embracing a sense of being part of Hungarian Jewry and the other still grasping a connection to Polish Jewry. Like other Jews in East-Central Europe, the worldview of these Jews was a mishmash of connections and affiliations that challenge present-day scholars to unravel. For these Jews themselves, who cared little about whether they were Hungarian and Polish so long as their Jewish lives were undisturbed, this challenge was of little importance.

By the end of the 1920s, though, an interesting variation on this story took shape. Before World War I, most Jews in Munkács and Ungvár preferred their own Jewish culture in one fashion or another to a full embrace of a vernacular culture and language. As the traditional Jewish world of their youth and that of their parents began to erode after World War I, a growing number of the younger generation of Jews in Munkács and Ungvár gravitated toward a different Jewish alternative: the nationalism of Zionism. Although rejecting the religious traditionalism of their forebears in favor of a secular identity, this younger generation nonetheless recreated the relative insularity of those forebears. Like them, young Jews in post–World War I Munkács and Ungvár reinforced their identity as Hungarian Jews by maintaining a social and cultural distance from the Hungarian mainstream. This would become an increasingly difficult posture to maintain in the growing political and social complexity of interwar East Central Europe.

Notes

Michael Stanislawski once remarked that his knowledge of Hungarian Jewry "ends at Munkács and Ungvár." I acknowledge with deep gratitude not only the wit and humility of this bon mot but also his commitment to explore the messy complexity of Jewish identity in East-Central Europe.

1 Raymond Recouly, "Le carrefour de races," *Le Figaro* (3 September 1920).
2 Timothy Garten Ash, "Hail Ruthenia," *New York Review of Books* (22 April 1999), www.nybooks.com/articles/1999/04/22/hail-ruthenia (accessed 5 May 2023). Another version is quoted by Anna Berger: "It is possible to have been born in Austria-Hungary, have been married in Czechoslovakia, have given birth in Hungary, have lived with your family in the Soviet Union, reside currently in Ukraine . . . and never to have left the city of Mukacheve." Anna Berger, "The Jews of Munkács: A Minority Among Minorities," *Australian Journal of Jewish Studies* 19 (2005): 11.
3 See Joseph Rothschild, *East Central Europe Between the Two World Wars* (Tacoma: University of Washington Press, 1974), especially the chapters on Poland, Czechoslovakia, Romania, and Hungary; and Paul Robert Magocsi, *Historical Atlas of Central Europe: Third Revised and Expanded Edition* (Toronto: University of Toronto Press, 1918), 118–25.
4 Paul Robert Magocsi, *The Shaping of National Identity: Subcarpathian Rus', 1848–1948* (Cambridge, MA: Harvard University Press, 1978); Paul Robert Magocsi, *With Their Back to the Mountains: A History of Carpathian Rus' and Carpatho-Rusyns* (Budapest: Central European University Press, 2015). Because the focus of this essay is the period when these cities were part of the Kingdom of Hungary, I am using Munkács and Ungvár and refer to the region as Subcarpathian Ruthenia.
5 The redrawing of the map of East-Central Europe after World War I and, in particular, the truncating of the Kingdom of Hungary by the Treaty of Trianon and the transfer of parts of the region to a newly formed Ukraine and Czechoslovakia, introduced a different context and an ethnic and political dynamic that are beyond the scope of the present study.
6 See Levi Cooper, "Polish Hasidism and Hungarian Orthodoxy in a Borderland: The Munkács Rabbinate," *Polin: Studies in Polish Jewry* 31 (2019): 119–20. See also Levi Cooper, "Yivo rabanim yivo tarbut: Rabane Munkács ke-mikre mivḥan le-meta narrativ shel Yahadut Hungariya" [Import

Rabbis, Import Culture: The Rabbis of Munkács as a Case Study Meta Narrative of Hungarian Jewry], in *Tamid Hungarim: Yehude Hungariya Be-Temurot ha'et ha-Ḥadasha* [Always Hungarian: The Jews of Hungary Through the Vicissitudes of the Modern Era], ed. Guy Miron, Shlomo Spitzer, and Anna Szalai (Ramat Gan: Bar Ilan University Press, 2021), esp. 122–23.

7 "Magyarize" refers to the adoption of Magyar as a primary language and the embrace of other aspects of Magyar culture, for example, literature, music, poetry, and cuisine.

8 Glenn Dynner, "Replenishing the 'Fountains of Judaism': Traditionalist Jewish Education in Interwar Poland," *Jewish History* 31, nos. 3–4 (2018): 230.

9 Neolog refers to the religiously progressive wing of Hungarian Jewry. At times mistaken for the Hungarian wing of German-style Reform Judaism, Neolog was in fact a less ideological version of Positive-Historical or Conservative Judaism, which allowed for broad innovation in Jewish life and practice so long as it was rooted in halakhic precedent. After 1870 Neolog had a second valence: affiliation with a Neolog community or congregation apart from observance. Thus a sizable portion of the Neolog movement was composed of religiously indifferent, nonobservant Jews for whom Neolog was nothing more than a state-required affiliation. For a more detailed explanation, see Howard Lupovitch, "Neolog: Reforming Judaism in a Hungarian Milieu," *Modern Judaism* 40, no. 3 (2020): 328–31.

10 Fittingly, the distinction between rejectionist and synthesizing Orthodoxy was a central theme in a graduate seminar taught by Michael Stanislawski, "Traditional Responses to Modernity."

11 "Greeks" was both an official and a colloquial term for merchants and other residents who hailed from the Balkan Peninsula and were affiliated with a form of Eastern Orthodox Christianity, including not only Greeks but also Turks, Armenians, and Serbs.

12 Elek Fényes, *Magyar országnak, és a hozzá kapcsolt tartományoknak mostani álla̋otja statistikai és geographiai tekintetben* (Pest: Trattner-Károlyi, 1843), 3: 374–75; Elek Fényes, Magyar *Geografiai szotar* (Pest: Nyomatott Kozma Vazulnál, 1851), 119–20.

13 Yeshayahu Jelinek, *The Carpathian Diaspora: The Jews of Subcarpathian Rus' and Mukachevo, 1848–1948* (New York: Columbia University Press, 2007), 13.

14 In this sense, Ungvár was like Miskolc. For a comparison, see Howard Lupovitch, *Jews at the Crossroads: Tradition and Accommodation During the Golden Age of the Hungarian Nobility, 1729–1878* (Budapest: Central European University Press, 2007), 23–25.

15 Miklós Konrád, "Demographic Changes," in *Zsidók Kárpátalján: Történelem És Örökség a Dualizmus Kor Átol Napjainkig*, ed. Bányai Viktória, Fedinec Csilla, and Komoróczy Szonja Ráhel (Budapest: Aposztróf, 2013), 15–19. The specific Jewish population figures are 890 in 1735, 6,311 in 1787, 41,323 in 1850, 64,903 in 1869, 78,424 in 1880, 94,444 in 1890, 112,400 in 1900, and 128,791 in 1910. The percentage of Jews was 11.2% in 1869, 13.7% in 1880, 14.3% in 1890, 14.9% in 1900, and 15.2% in 1910.

16 "Munkács," in *Magyar Zsidó Lexikon*, ed. Péter Ujvári (Budapest: Magyar Zsido Lexikon kiadasa, 1929), 619; S. HaKohen Weingarten, "Munkács," in *Arim ve-imahot beYisraël*, ed. Y. L. Maimon (Jerusalem: Mosad Ha-Rav Kuk, 1946), 1: 346 (Hebrew).

17 Jelinek, *Carpathian Diaspora*, 36–39.

18 Weingarten, "Munkács," 1: 345–47.

19 Jelinek, *Carpathian Diaspora*, 42.

20 Livia Rothkirchen, "Deep-Rooted yet Alien: Some Aspects of the History of the Jews in Subcarpathian Ruthenia," *Yad Vashem Studies* 12 (1977): 150.

21 Rabbi Yekutiel Y. Grunwald, *Maẓevet kodesh le-kehilot Yisraël she-neḥrevu* [In Memory of the Destroyed Jewish Communities] (New York, 1952), 2. Grunwald was paraphrasing the aphorism in BT *Kiddushin* 49b: "Ten measures of poverty descended on the world—Nine were taken by Babylonia and the remainder by the rest of the world."

22 Grunwald, *Ma ẓevet Kodesh*, 54–55.

23 For a succinct but more detailed expression of this outlook, see Ezra Mendelsohn, *The Jews of East Central Europe Between the World Wars* (Bloomington: Indiana University Press, 1987), 91–99.

24 Rothkirchen, "Deep-Rooted yet Alien," 160. *Ruthenian* was the Habsburg term for Ukrainians who were Uniate Christians.

25 On this, see Miklós Konrád, "Narrating the Hungarian-Jewish Past: The 'Khazar Theory' and the Integrationist Jewish Scientific Discourse," in *Cultural Nationalism in a Finnish-Hungarian Historical Context*, ed. Gábor Gyáni and Anssi Halmesvirta (Budapest: MTA Bölcsészettudományi Kutatóközpont Történettudományi Intézet, 2018), 49–61. On the Khazar

myth generally, see Shaul Stampfer, "Did the Khazars Convert to Judaism," *Jewish Social Studies* 19, no. 3 (2014): 1–72.

26 Bartha Miklós, *Kazár Földön* (Budapest: Ellenzék Könyvnyomda, 1901), 81–82.

27 Sándor Komáromi, "Minta: Orosz," *Egyenlőség* (18 April 1909), 3.

28 Hermann I. Biderman, *Die ungarischen Ruthenen, ihr Wohngebiet, ihr Erwerb, und ihre Geschichte* (Innsbruck: Wagner'schen Universitäts-Buchhandlung, 1862), 131. See also Rothkirchen, "Deep-Rooted yet Alien," 160.

29 René Martel, "La Ruthénie subcarpethetique au temps du servage féodal," *Le Monde Slav* (January 1938), 144–47. On the Ruthenian economy generally, see Alexander Bonkáló, "Die ungarlandsiche Ruthenen," *Ungarischer Jahrbücher* 1 (1922): 2–6.

30 *Uber den Stand der ungarischen und galizischen Ruthenen-Bewegung*, Osterreichisches Staatsarchiv, Vienna, Informationsbtiro, Annexe 27, 150–163, cited in Rothkirchen, "Deep-Rooted yet Alien," 163.

31 "Munkács," in *Magyar Zsidó Lexikon*, 620.

32 Konrád, "Demographic Changes," 29–30.

33 Tamás Csíki, "Vállasi élet, Önszerveződés: Egyletek, Szervezetek," in *Zsidók Kárpátalján: Történelem És Örökség a Dualizmus Kor Átol Napjainkig*, ed. Bányai Viktória, Fedinec Csilla, and Komoróczy Szonja Ráhel (Budapest: Aposztróf, 2013), 101.

34 Jelinek, *Carpathian Diaspora*, 46–47.

35 Viktor Karády, "Értelmiség, iskolázás, és elitképzés," in *Zsidók Kárpátalján: Történelem És Örökség a Dualizmus Kor Átol Napjainkig*, ed. Bányai Viktória, Fedinec Csilla, and Komoróczy Szonja Ráhel (Budapest: Aposztróf, 2013), 83.

36 On traditional Polish-style antisemitism, see Magda Teter, *Jews and Heretics in Catholic Poland: A Beleaguered Church in the Post-Reformation Era* (Cambridge, UK: Cambridge University Press, 2005), 107–112. On Istóczy and racial antisemitism in Hungary, see Gyorgy Szabad, "A polgári jogegyenlőség elleni támadás és kudarca a század végi Magyarországon" [The Attack on Equal Rights and Its Failure in Hungary at the End of the Nineteenth Century], *Tarsadalmi Szemle* 37, nos. 8–9 (1982): 69–71; Árpád Welker, "'Jew' Versus Antisemite: The Dual Between Mor Warhmann and Győző Istóczy, 1882," *Jewish Studies at the Central European University* 5 (2005–2007): 158–61; and Nathaniel Katzburg, "The Antisemitic Party in Hungary and Its Place in Political Life, 1883–1887," *Zion* 30 (1975), esp. 83–85 (Hebrew).

37 On late nineteenth-century blood libels, see Hillel Kieval, "Death and the Nation: Ritual Murder as Political Discourse in the Czech Lands," *Jewish History* 10, no. 1 (1996): 75–91.
38 Most noteworthy perhaps in this regard was Károly Eötvös, a leading proponent of Liberalism in Hungary and the lead defense attorney at the Tisza-Eszlar trial.
39 On the Tisza Eszlar blood libel and its aftermath, see Daniel Véri, "The Tiszaeszlár Blood Libel: Image and Propaganda," in *Antisemitismus im 19. Jahrhundert aus internationaler Perspektive*, ed. Mareike König and Oliver Schulz (Göttingen: V & R Unipress, 2019), 263–90. On the riots, see Robert Nemes, "Hungary's Antisemitic Provinces: Violence and Ritual Murder in the 1880s," *Slavic Review* 66, no. 1 (2007), esp. 22–26. On antisemitic parties before World War I, see Paul Hanebrink, *In Defense of Christian Hungary: Religion, Nationalism, and Antisemitism, 1890–1944* (Ithaca, NY: Cornell University Press, 2009), esp. 12–40.
40 The demonstration was reported in the Orthodox weekly *Kol maḥazikei ha-dat* on 13 September 1883.
41 *Allgemeine Zeitung des Judentums* (16 August 1901), 6.
42 "Glosszak a hétről," *Egyenlőség* (21 November 1915), 2.
43 Peter Ujvári, ed., *Magyar Zsidó Lexikon* (Budapest: Magyar Zsido Lexikon kiadasa, 1929), 619.
44 Elie Wiesel, *One Generation After* (New York: Random House, 1970), 14.
45 Glenn Dynner, "Jewish Traditionalism in Eastern Europe: The Historiographical Gadfly," in *Writing Jewish History in Eastern Europe*, ed. Natalia Aleksiun, Brian Horowitz, and Antony Polonsky (Oxford, UK: Littmann Library of Jewish Civilization, 2017), 299.
46 Csíki, "Vállasi élet," 96.
47 The founding of a Bais Ya'akov school in Munkács after World War I was a limited first step toward changing this role.
48 Csíki, "Vállasi élet," 103.
49 Weingarten, "Munkács," 1: 347; "Ungvár," in *Magyar Zsidó Lexikon*, ed. Peter Ujvári (Budapest: Magyar Zsido Lexikon kiadasa, 1929), 926.
50 Cooper, "Polish Hasidism'" 121–24; Jelinek, *Carpathian Diaspora*, 52; Y. Spiegel, "Ungvár," *Arim ve-imahot beYisra'el* 4 (1950): 6. Before Eisenstadter, the closest any rabbi of Ungvár approached fame or notoriety was his immediate predecessor, Rabbi Zvi Hirsch Heller, who was asked by the Jews of Csaba to intervene against Yonatan Alexanderssohn in 1832. See Jacob Katz, "Parasha

Stuma be-ḥaye ha-Ḥatam Sofer: Parashat Alexanderssohn," *Zion* 55, no. 1 (1990): 85–88.

51 Cooper, "Yivo rabanim yivo tarbut," esp. 125–26.

52 Netanel Katzburg, "The History of the Hungarian Jews," in *Pinkas ha-kehilot-Hungariyah: enẓiklopediyah shel ha-yishuvim ha-yehudiyim le-min hivasdam ve'ad le-aḥer sho'at milḥemet ha-olam ha-sheniya*, ed. Theodor Levi (Jerusalem: Yad va-shem, 1975), 33 (Hebrew); Weingarten, "Munkács," 1: 351.

53 "Munkacs," *Ben Chananja* 5 (5 May 1862): 306; Erzsebet Mislóvics, "The Appearance and Spread of Hasidism," in *Zsidók Kárpátalján: Történelem És Örökség a Dualizmus Kor Ától Napjainkig*, ed. Bányai Viktória, Fedinec Csilla, and Komoróczy Szonja Ráhel (Budapest: Aposztróf, 2013), 62 (Hungarian).

54 Ujvári, *Magyar Zsidó Lexikon*, 620. On the *Kitzur* and its impact in Hungary, see Howard Lupovitch, "The *Kitzur Shulchan Aruch* and Its Impact in Hungary and Beyond," *Studies in Judaism, Humanities, and the Social Sciences* 1, no. 2 (2018): 84–86.

55 On Birkenthal, see Gershon Hundert's chapter in this volume (Chapter 2).

56 Dov Ber Birkenthal, *The Memoirs of Ber of Bolechow*, trans. and ed. M. Vishnitzer (Oxford, UK: Oxford University Press, 1922), 93, 117, 171.

57 *Kol maḥazikei ha-dat* (12 November 1885), 7; emphasis mine.

58 Quoted in Spiegel, "Ungvár," 14–15.

59 Quoted in Weingarten, "Munkács," 1: 353.

60 Katzburg, "History of the Hungarian Jews," 34; Spiegel, "Ungvár," 20–21.

61 "Munkacs," *Ben Chananja* 8 (1865): 565.

62 Y. Y. Sofer, *Sefer Kan Sofer* (London: 1963), 35.

63 Erzsebét Mislóvics, "Rabbis, Trends, Communities," in *Zsidók Kárpátalján: Történelem És Örökség a Dualizmus Kor Ától Napjainkig*, ed. Bányai Viktória, Fedinec Csilla, and Komoróczy Szonja Ráhel (Budapest: Aposztróf, 2013), 48 (Hungarian).

64 Weingarten, "Munkács," 1: 351–52.

65 Weingarten, "Munkács," 1: 356.

66 Viktória Banyai and Bálint Varga, "Traditional and Modern Education," in *Zsidók Kárpátalján: Történelem És Örökség a Dualizmus Kor Ától Napjainkig*, ed. Bányai Viktória, Fedinec Csilla, and Komoróczy Szonja Ráhel (Budapest: Aposztróf, 2013), 76 (Hungarian).

67 Viktor Karády, "Intelligentsia, Schooling, Specialization," in *Zsidók Kárpátalján: Történelem És Örökség a Dualizmus Kor Ától Napjainkig*, ed. Bányai

Viktória, Fedinec Csilla, and Komoróczy Szonja Ráhel (Budapest: Aposztróf, 2013), 79 (Hungarian).

68 "Ungvár," *Hamagid* (20 March 1867), 9. Here it is important to note that, in general, Hungarian and Habsburg Jews, unlike their Russian Jewish counterparts, did not regard conscription into the Habsburg army as the beginning of a miserable life or as a threat to Jewish identity; rather, they viewed it more as a means of social opportunity. Franz Jozef was beloved to Hungarian and other Habsburg Jews—the opposite of Tsar Nicholas I. Thus the reluctance to allow ultra-Orthodox Jews in Ungvár or Hasidic Jews in Munkács to be conscripted was a narrower concern about limiting contact with non-Jews and nonobservant Jews. The attitude of ultra-Orthodox and Hasidic Jews toward military service is a desideratum.

69 "Ungvár," *Ben Chananja* 9, no. 3 (17 January 1866): 60–61.

70 Jelinek, *Carpathian Diaspora*, xx.

71 "Munkacs," *Ben Chananja* 9, no. 13 (1866): 264.

72 Meir Eisenstadter, *Imre Yosher* (Ungvár, 1864), 8a–b.

73 Chaim Sofer, *Sefer Tehillim 'im Perush Shaare Ḥaim* (Pressburg: Abraham David Alkalay, 1893), 28b.

74 Ayala Fader noted a similar use of Yiddish among Hasidic Jews in New York City. See Ayala Fader, "Learning Faith: Language Socialization in a Community of Hasidic Jews," *Language in Society* 35, no. 2 (2006): 223–27.

75 Quoted in Sonyja Ráhel Komoróczy, "Use of Language," in *Zsidók Kárpátalján: Történelem És Örökség a Dualizmus Kor Ától Napjainkig*, ed. Bányai Viktória, Fedinec Csilla, and Komoróczy Szonja Ráhel (Budapest: Aposztróf, 2013), 38–39.

76 Miklós Konrád, "Az államhatalom és a régió más népességeinek viszonya a zsidósághoz," in *Zsidók Kárpátalján: Történelem És Örökség a Dualizmus Kor Ától Napjainkig*, ed. Bányai Viktória, Fedinec Csilla, and Komoróczy Szonja Ráhel (Budapest: Aposztróf, 2013), 108.

77 Csíki, "Vállasi élet," 103.

78 Weingarten, "Munkács," 1: 359.

79 Ferenc Fábián, "What Language Do the Jews of Munkács Speak?" *Egyenlőség* (2 October 1920), 4 (Hungarian).

80 On this, see Rebekah Klein-Pejšová, *Mapping Jewish Loyalties in Interwar Slovakia* (Bloomington: Indiana University Press, 2015), esp. 23–25.

8

Nation and Emancipation

Olga Litvak

The first astonishing thing that I ever heard Michael Stanislawski say was that Russian Jews did not come to America because they were victims of antisemitism. They came, he said, for the same reason that large numbers of people usually leave one continent for another: because they were poor. He said it during one of the lectures of the first course I ever took with him; this was in the fall of 1992, and I had just started graduate school. The room, filled with students who must have been raised on stories of Eastern European ancestors plunging directly into the freezing Atlantic to escape charging Cossacks, seemed to be positively vibrating. Apparently, no one wanted to know that their great-grandmother was not so much a heroic political refugee as an ordinary economic migrant—and probably also a liar. I distinctly heard the sound of pitchforks being sharpened.

I heard the same sound several years later when Michael informed a roomful of people that the French philosopher Simone Weil (1909–1943), who was born into a Jewish family, was ignorant of Judaism and had not much use or concern for Jews unless they were Catholic, at a time, it should be said, when Jewish life in Europe hung by a thread. This might have been an unexceptionable remark, except that Michael made it at a French department conference celebrating the wisdom and compassion of none other than Simone Weil. To annoy two constituencies that view the historical problem of antisemitism from such different perspectives takes uncommon analytical percipience and a Promethean degree of chutzpah. The hostility of the audience would not have been so unsettling had

Michael not been right. Because, of course, he *was*, both about the unfortunate myopia of the French Jewish humanitarian and about the impulse behind the Great Migration.[1] I must confess that my interest in the person and the politics of Simone Weil was pretty much exhausted by that conference; but I have been thinking about the etiological function of antisemitism in modern Jewish historiography on and off since the fall of 1992. In the last thirty years the subject seems to have lost none of its interpretive traction or intellectual cachet.[2] Professional interest in modern anti-Jewish violence shows no signs of waning.[3] To historians trying to account for specific features of modern Jewish experience, antisemitism is a gift that keeps on giving.[4]

Nowhere is the etiological usefulness of antisemitism more conspicuous than in the history of Zionism, where scholarship continues to take for granted that the recourse to antisemitism *in* Zionist reasoning provides a sufficient explanation *of* Zionism's origins.[5] In the first instance, the term *antisemitism* is a rhetorical construction—a way of talking about the Jewish condition—intended to convince the reader to embrace the Zionist point of view. It is debatable whether or not a capacious and imprecise neologism derived from a fallacious philological theory that manages to be both racist (anti-Jewish) *and* Christian (anti-Judaic) at the same time can perform any explanatory function independent of the political discourse in which it is embedded.[6] All we can really say is that the creative and highly emotional deployment of *antisemitism* as a literary trope has proven effective in mobilizing public support for Zionism; this is far from demonstrating that "modern anti-semitism, pogroms and government persecution" gave "birth to the Jewish national movement."[7] It is undoubtedly true that many Jews find the Zionist narrative persuasive, but this does not mean that Zionist history has gotten it right; similarly, although Marxist literature has persuaded at least an equal number of readers, no historian of Marxism, I think, would draw from this powerful rhetorical effect the conclusion that Marxist claims about the accuracy of its conjectures on the causes of major historical events, such as the French Revolution, must therefore be self-evident. At the same time, arguing about whether antisemitism accounts for the appearance and the appeal of Zionism—in the same way that it does or does not account for the Russian Jewish migration to the United States—will not get us very far in challenging a comprehensive narrative structure that still commands impressive uncritical assent in many quarters. Identifying an alternative set of causes for the origins of Zionism (and other tectonic shifts in Jewish life) will not displace arguments from antisemitism, no matter how thin or conceptually flawed they may be. If classroom experience is any indication, counterarguments seem to have the opposite of their intended effect. To shift the ground in which current consensus is so firmly planted, historians need to figure out how commonplace explanations work and why people continue to find them convincing. What we should be trying harder to understand is the "meaning" of *antisemitism* in Jewish historical reasoning, "relative to a linguistic context or [Wittgensteinian] 'language game'" that makes sense of even the most bizarre or apparently irrational statements. Their "intention to persuade presupposes such a framework of shared meanings in which certain concepts and rules for applying them in argument have a conventional life."[8] Being right, it seems, is not enough.

With this dispiriting concession in mind, what I undertake in this chapter is a rhetorical analysis of the first publicly persuasive text in the history of Zionism: *Autoemancipation*, a German tract written by the Odessa physician and public activist L. S. Pinsker (1821–1891).[9] Insofar as this text motivated a sufficient number of its readers to create an institution dedicated to the achievement of Zionist aims, *Autoemancipation* can be considered the first document in the history of the Zionist movement, even though the Zionist idea was in circulation for a decade before its publication.[10] Throughout the 1870s the prospects of Jewish national awakening were continuously discussed in the Russian Jewish press, chiefly by the Hebrew writer Perez Smolenskin (1842–1885) but not least by Pinsker himself.[11] Still, Zionism did not congeal into an organization until *Autoemancipation* rallied "Lovers of Zion" (Hebrew, *hovevei-ẓiyon*) to form themselves into "societies." What had changed? According to most historians who have, of course, read Pinsker, the answer is antisemitism.[12] In the late spring of 1881, following the assassination of Tsar Alexander II (r. 1856–1881) in March of that year, the southwestern provinces of the Pale of Settlement were hit with a wave of violent and terrifying urban disturbances (later christened with the evocative and now ubiquitous term *pogroms*) aimed chiefly, it seems, at the destruction of Jewish property.[13] The shock, so the familiar story goes, alerted Pinsker to the epochal significance of antisemitism and set the course for the awakening of Jewish political conscience.[14] *Autoemancipation* spelled out the nature of the connection between antisemitism and this political awakening; Pinsker's foundational contribution to the history of Zionism lies in his immediately assessing (as is assumed, correctly) the implications of antisemitism for the future of the Jews. The coincidence between this story and the story of the second coming of Zionism in the person of Theodor Herzl (1860–1904), as recounted by Herzl himself, is uncanny, not to say suspicious. Herzl's Damascus moment came some twenty years after Pinsker's, when, having witnessed the political martyrdom of Alfred Dreyfus at the Place de la Concorde, he went home and wrote *Der Judenstaat* (1896).[15] A pattern began to emerge.

The neat conjunction of event with text presents historians with an irresistible teleology. It would be easy to conclude that the pogroms of 1881–1882 rendered Pinsker's treatment of antisemitism self-evident. In this view the most significant thing about *Autoemancipation* would be its timing. If history itself, rather than what he had made of it, convinced Pinsker's first readers, historians might have every reason to concur, even though the specific aspect of his argument that had to do with antisemitism rested, as we shall see in a moment, on singularly questionable assumptions about human behavior that are not so easy to accept. Indeed, modern Jewish scholarship has thoroughly digested the idea that antisemitism jolted Zionism into being; for historians, the reality of "modern antisemitism, pogroms and government persecution"[16] in late imperial Russia underwrites the ineluctable truth of Pinsker's claims, just as the Dreyfus affair once underwrote Herzl's. This is why *Autoemancipation* has entered into Jewish historiography not as a document that locates antisemitism at the center of Zionist ideology but as a "trenchant analysis"[17] of the Jewish condition (and *that*, presumably, is the reason that Pinsker succeeded where his predecessors had failed). In the standard reading of *Autoemancipation*, the rise of antisemitism both informed Pinsker's argument *and* proved him right. But contiguity is not causality. If one is waiting for a bus and it arrives just as it starts raining, one does not, no matter how wet one gets, immediately leap to the conclusion that the rain caused the bus to arrive. The relationship between the violence of 1881, no matter how appalling it was, and the timely arrival of Zionism was not implicit in the events themselves. Before it could be reproduced, with only modest variations, in the writing of modern Jewish history, this connection had to be made; credit for making it is typically given to Pinsker.[18]

In this essay my chief concern is to show that Pinsker did not make this connection by appealing to political reason or to historical evidence but to a "framework of shared [Jewish] meanings." In other words, Pinsker's argument appeared so convincing not because it was striking in its immediacy or radical in its implications but because it was already familiar to its Jewish readers. When we look closely at *Autoemancipation*, we find that what is new does not persuade, and what persuades is not new. Indeed, Pinsker's intellectual contribution to Zionism—his explanation of "Jew-hatred" (German, *Judenhass*) by reference to the concept of Judeophobia—has also proven the most refractory; although the substance of Pinsker's argument has become conventional Zionist wisdom, Zionist historiography has quietly dropped the term *Judeophobia* from its vocabulary.[19] The principal point of Pinsker's case for the connection between antisemitism and the urgency of national regeneration did not, in fact, originate with him. About a year before the appearance of *Autoemancipation*, it was already the subject of an article by M. L. Lilienblum, published in St. Petersburg's Russian-language Jewish weekly *Razsvet*.[20] Lilienblum also lived in Odessa and frequented the same social circles as Pinsker. Although the connection has never, to my knowledge, been made, *Autoemancipation* is clearly indebted to its long-forgotten predecessor. Moreover, it is entirely possible that Lilienblum, a ubiquitous presence in the Russian Jewish press throughout the 1870s and the author of a popular autobiographical novel called *Hattot ne'urim* (1876), actually reached more Russian readers than Pinsker. Unlike Pinsker, Lilienblum actually used the term *antisemitism* and characterized it essentially as a social and economic phenomenon.

Pinsker departed from Lilienblum chiefly in adopting a "scientific" approach to the historical necessity of Zionism. His version of Lilienblum's argument rested on a diagnosis of anti-Jewish hostility as a permanent feature of Jewish life among the nations. Traceable to "fear of the Jewish ghost," this "prejudice," says Pinsker, "paved the way for Judeophobia," a pathological hatred of Jews and the tendency to hold the Jewish people collectively responsible for the "real and supposed misdeeds of its individual members" (*AE*, 5–6; Blondheim, 3). Identified with the fear of ghosts, which Pinsker accepts as a brute fact of human existence (a fact, that is to say, without a rational explanation), "Judeophobia" belongs together "with a number of other subconscious and superstitious ideas, instincts and idiosyncrasies." It is a "form of demonopathy" that "has become fully naturalized among all of the people of the earth with whom the Jews have had intercourse." A "psychic disorder . . . transmitted for two thousand years," Judeophobia is to be treated as a hereditary incurable disease, a "blind natural force of nature" (*AE*, 7; Blondheim, 4) against which it is useless to reason or expostulate.

The formative connection between antisemitism and Zionism that Pinsker appears to have introduced into Zionist ideology has become so embedded in contemporary ways of thinking about Jewish modernity that his unprecedented translation of political antisemitism into biological terms (an exercise without empirical foundation and alien to scientific opinion of Pinsker's *own* time, to say nothing of ours) goes unremarked, in the hopes, I think, that the difference between Judeophobia and antisemitism will be ignored. In his acutely intelligent article on the relationship between Zionism and antisemitism, Scott Ury reproduces Pinsker's strangest idea without a single qualifying word: "Trained as a physician, Pinsker understood Judeophobia to be 'a form of demonopathy' that had been transformed from 'a psychic aberration' into a hereditary social disease that would then be 'handed down and strengthened for generations and centuries.'"[21] It is difficult to accept that the description of Jew hatred as a "form of demonopathy" was merely a by-product of Pinsker's medical training.[22] Equally questionable is the proposition that Pinsker's representation of antisemitism as a "hereditary social disease" and a "blind natural force" constitutes evidence of rational "understanding" and not the work of an extravagant and highly idiosyncratic imagination. The assumption that Pinsker's conclusions are reasonable and even intuitive diverts attention from the dubious (and embarrassing) premises on which they seem to rest. This is also why a singularly important slippage in Pinsker's logic is so easy to miss and so obvious when it comes to one's notice. The problem is this: Whether Pinsker's understanding of Judeophobia is persuasive on its own terms, the diagnosis does not, in any obvious way, lead to the conclusion that the Jews "*must become a nation*" (*AE*, 4; Blondheim, 2, emphasis in the original). To make the necessary leap from Pinsker's concept of Judeophobia to this conclusion, the reader is required to accept that "among the living nations of the earth Jews occupy the position of a nation long since dead" (*AE*, 4; Blondheim, 2). The case for Judeophobia—the pathology of Jew hatred rooted in a natural fear of ghosts (German, *Gespensterfurcht*)—rests on a Jewish "secret" that Pinsker unveils as though to the sound of trumpets: With the loss of political independence, Jewish life has become nothing short of pathological, the Jews having fallen "into a state of decomposition [German, *Zersetzung*] which is incompatible with existence as an integral, living organism" (*AE*, 4; Blondheim, 2). As Pinsker sees it, the reason that non-Jews congenitally fear and despise Jews is that Jews present to the world "the uncanny [Ger. *unheimliche*] form of one of the dead walking among the living."

> This ghostly apparition of the dead wandering among the living, of a people without land or other bond of union, no longer alive and yet walking about among the living—this strange form, the like of which is not to be found in history, unlike any that has preceded or followed it, could not fail to make a strange and singular impression upon the imagination of the nations. (*AE*, 4; Blondheim, 3, translation slightly altered)

The "secret" turns out to be that it is because Jews are really "ghostlike" that they "could not fail" to provoke the irrational and dangerous fear of ghosts in other people, presumably themselves members of nations that are very much alive. The eerie form of Jewish being induces in non-Jews a pathological but entirely "understandable" response. The "sight" of Jewish zombies raises an instinctive ("innate") and incorrigible antipathy that Pinsker endorses as having "a certain justification in the psychic life of humanity." But this "certain justification" derives from Pinsker's view of Jewish history, not from his view of humanity.

Judeophobia, Pinsker says, may be a universal disorder, "an inherited aberration of the human mind," but it is a Jewish problem, in the sense that both its cause and its treatment rest with Jews. This is Pinsker's essential point, and it is the exact reverse of the historicist position on the persistence of anti-Jewish hostility that *Autoemancipation* means to call into question: namely, that although this hostility vitiates the quality of Jewish life and may have adverse effects on the Jewish psyche, ultimately the problem and its solution originate in the non-Jewish world.[23] Such a position (that Judeophobia is not a problem for Jews to solve) does not necessarily exclude Pinsker's secondary claim about the psychological peculiarity of *Judenhass*. The non-Jewish world may indeed be prone to Judeophobia because people have an innate tendency to fear ghosts, but their fears are their own business; no doctor (with the possible exception of Springfield's Dr. Nick Riviera) would attribute acrophobia to the excessive height of mountains and skyscrapers. The believers might be instructed not to be afraid of ghosts because ghosts do not exist, but this task should not fall, so to speak, to the ghosts themselves; fear of ghosts does not "prove" their existence. If the attempt to correct spurious beliefs and alleviate the anxieties they produce should fail, as Pinsker says it must, incurable Judeophobes ought to be restrained from attacking their neighbors. People who decide to take a couple of floors off the top of the Empire State Building because they harbor an innate pathological hatred of tall buildings *get arrested* and, if they are lucky, placed under a doctor's care. No one, least of all the doctor, would blame the Empire State Building. Pinsker, in fact, admits that the only practical way to keep the "sinister powers" of "prejudice [and] instinctive ill will . . . within bounds" is by the exercise of "material coercion" (*AE*, 7; Blondheim, 4). But he still blames the ghosts.

To entertain such a response on the part of Pinsker's imagined opponents is not a frivolous exercise in *pilpul*. It demonstrates quite clearly that Pinsker's understanding of Judeophobia rests on his perception of the Jewish condition, not, as historians tend to assume, the other way around. What drives the writing of *Autoemancipation* is not Judeophobia, the imperishable fear lurking in the hearts of "all the peoples of the earth," but Pinsker's horror at the spectral half-life to which *modernity* has, to his way of thinking, reduced the Jewish people. Indeed, even though Pinsker locates the origins of this disaster as far back as 70 CE, when the Jewish state was "crushed under the weight of Roman rule and disappeared from before the eyes of the nations" (*AE*, 4; Blondheim, 2), the concept of Judeophobia derives its force from his analysis of contemporary Jewish behavior. Although the "disease" has ostensibly been "transmitted for two thousand years," Pinsker represents Judeophobia as a response to the degenerate condition of modern Jewry, subject to its own secret pathology that cannot be defined, only obliquely described by what it is not. Speaking of Jewish life "under present conditions," Pinsker says:

> They [Jews] lack most of those attributes which are the hallmarks of a nation. They lack that characteristic national life which is inconceivable without a common language, common customs, and a common

land. The Jewish people have no fatherland . . . they have no rallying point, no center of gravity, no government of their own, no accredited representatives. They are everywhere in evidence but nowhere at home. . . . The Jews are not a nation because they lack a certain distinctive national character. (*AE*, 2; Blondheim, 2)

Eleven lines of German text contain *fifteen* words of negation.

The word for this modern Jewish *kenosis* (emptying-out), this condition of self-abnegation, this madness that cannot speak its name, this abject state of collective ego-renunciation, is *emancipation*. Emancipation induces a form of radical self-denial, an illness that its sufferers do not even know they have: "The strongest fact . . . operating to prevent the Jews from striving after an independent national existence is that that they feel no need for such an existence. Not only do they feel no need for it, but they even deny the reasonableness of such a need" (*AE*, 3; Blondheim, 3). In this formulation it is precisely the success of emancipation, not its descent into antisemitic reaction, that makes Pinsker see Judeophobia everywhere, "whether it appears in the form of deeds of violence, as envious jealousy, or under the guise of tolerance and protection." For Jews, emancipation constitutes a moral failure and produces a "lack" [German, *fehle*]—a word that Pinsker presses relentlessly in his description of "self-forgetting" emancipated Jews—which is both disgraceful and suicidal. It threatens to make Jews disappear. Thus it is to the beneficiaries of emancipation, "the Jews in the West" [German, *der Juden im Occident*], that the "Russian Jew" addresses his "admonition" [German, *Mahnruf*]. They are the ones who require the moral tonic of a reminder that their disorder has gone tragically undiagnosed, even unnoticed; Judeophobia is both their disease and their cure. *They*—a ghostly people without a self—are the intended object of self-help evoked in Pinsker's revised quotation from *m. Avot* 1:14 that serves as the epigraph to *Autoemancipation* and suggests a possible source of its memorable title.

The fact that Pinsker, whose primary language of communication with his Jewish audience was Russian, wrote *Autoemancipation* in German and addressed it to "the Jews in the West" has not escaped the attention of scholars. The most recent analysis of this feature of the text focuses on the significance of German as a "'prestige language' [which] served non-Germans as a pathway to the realms of knowledge and politics."[24] In this account, "Pinsker's choice of the German language reflected an attempt to mobilize German's prestige in order to give greater resonance to the national cause of Eastern European Jews."[25] The argument follows in the footsteps of the generally held view that Pinsker set out to write a political manifesto, meant to appeal to the sensibilities of secular-minded progressive people, people, that is to say, like himself. It is perfectly true that in choosing to write in German, Pinsker meant to address German-speaking Jews, although, of course, most educated Russian Jews also read German; but it does not, by any means, follow that he identified with his German Jewish audience. Pinsker writes to his "Occidental" *Stammesgenossen* as a "Russian Jew" in their "language of prestige" not because he is seeking their approval but to register his disapproval *of them*. He speaks to "the Jews in the West" as an "oriental" Jewish prophet, through a text that presents itself as a *Mahnruf*, an exhortation, a warning, a wake-up call; the purport of *Autoemancipation* is neither political nor scientific but ethical. It is, in other words, a sermon—which is precisely how it was read. *Autoemancipation*, wrote one of its German-speaking readers to another, "is rooted in the mundane but [it] has been consecrated by its holy belief in the vocation of our prophets."[26]

From the opening pages of *Autoemancipation*, prophetic hectoring seeps out between the lines of medical language: "Close your eyes and hide your heads ostrich-fashion as you will," warns Pinsker. "*Lasting peace* will not be granted to you unless you make use of this fleeting moment of calm to devise more *radical* remedies than those palliatives with which our unhappy people have been troubled for a thousand years" (AE, ii; Blondheim, 1, translation altered; emphasis in the original). Passages like this make it impossible to isolate Pinsker's analysis of the Jewish condition from his judgment of privileged emancipated Jews as sick and wicked. "The Jews are not a nation because they lack a certain distinctive national character," he declares, as though it were a matter of fact. As the reader moves through the text, however, such assertions morph into normative statements of value. It becomes clear that Pinsker's conclusions follow from moral principles that have a venerable Jewish pedigree rather than from neutral-sounding descriptions. Let us take that same sentence again and put it back in its place: "The Jews are not a nation because they lack a certain distinctive national character. . . . Thanks to their ready adaptability, they have all the more easily acquired the alien traits of the peoples among whom they have been cast by fate." This is still within the bounds of evolutionary theory. But then: "Moreover, to please their protectors, they often divested themselves of their traditional individuality." What is being described is a deliberate act of self-betrayal, undertaken for unsavory motives. It gets worse: "They acquired, *or persuaded themselves that they had acquired*, certain cosmopolitan tendencies." And, finally, "In seeking to fuse with other people, *they deliberately renounced, to a certain extent, their own nationality*" (*AE*, 3; Blondheim, 2, emphasis added).

Pinsker moves smoothly from a naturalistic account in which Jews have simply adapted to conditions imposed on them by fate to an indictment of willful apostasy, deliberate self-renunciation, if only to a "certain extent" (Jews who are reading *Autoemancipation* cannot be entirely beyond redemption). Although he compares this condition to an unacknowledged illness, its cause is ultimately not an unfortunate lack of certain qualifications for nationhood but a "lack of desire for national independence," a healthy need vitiated by a contrary and perverse inclination of "Jews in the West" to want to "please their [Gentile] protectors." The "hidden cause" of Jewish misery is not the ineluctable rejection of Jews by non-Jewish society but Jewish self-betrayal. Such guilt is signified by the "stigma" of Jewish social embarrassment—Gentile violence is the "bloody" signature of emancipation. Here, Pinsker's argument runs close to rabbinic theodicy, in which Gentile persecution is the scourge of God, divine punishment for the Jewish proclivity to go whoring after strange gods. Indeed, Pinsker goes on to define *Judenhass* as the historical instrument of divine election, analogous in its social meaning to the "traditional individuality" that "Jews in the West" have "renounced."

Under present historical circumstances, when emancipation enables Jews to repudiate their "traditional individuality," the real danger is not the persistence of Jew hatred but the possibility of its disappearance. The tocsin of Judeophobia is the historical call to Jewish resistance, not to the resurgence of "prejudice or instinctive will"—which, Pinsker says, ought to be "simply ignored"—but to the most insidious manifestation of Jew hatred in "the guise [German, *der Maske*] of tolerance and protection" (*AE*, 7; Blondheim, 4). Jew hatred is to be left alone not merely because it is useless to fight it but because it provides emancipated Jews with incontestable proof of their own Jewish individuality, now a lost article of faith. Emancipated and enlightened "fallen Jews" require positive evidence of their chosenness.[27] Jew hatred is, in the final analysis, morally instructive. Exposed to "bloody deeds of violence" against Jews, "he must be blind, indeed, who will assert that the Jews are not the chosen people, chosen for universal hatred" (*AE*, 6; Blondheim, 3). Before the lesson of Judeophobia can be translated into "practical" terms, its singularity as an "abstract . . . Platonic hatred" must be lifted above its present reality ("bloody scenes of violence") and promoted to the permanent status of a "universal" metaphysical truth (*AE*, 5; Blondheim, 3). Like God (Pinsker suggests), Judeophobia, whatever its specific historical manifestations, is One.[28]

Gentile "tolerance and protection" is, in itself, a disguised form of "antipathy." Pinsker applies this maxim to emancipation: What appears to be a legal elevation to the status of citizen is, in fact, a reduction to the social condition of beggar. Pinsker concedes that the "*legal* emancipation of the Jews is the crowning achievement of our century," but "it remains a rich gift, splendid alms, willingly or unwillingly flung to the poor humble beggars whom no one, however, cares to shelter because a homeless wandering beggar wins confidence and sympathy from none" (*AE*, 9; Blondheim, 5). Pinsker's point is not that legal emancipation fails to provide adequate protection against the social effects of prejudice; rather, emancipation is, in and of itself, a gesture of contempt that lowers Jews to the subject position of "negroes" and "women" who are, likewise, "persecuted, tolerated, protected, *emancipated*" (*AE*, 8; Blondheim, 4, emphasis in the original). Their freedom (and, one would suppose, the freedom of "women" and "negroes" too) is an illusion, an expression of their "degrading dependence" (*AE*, 10; Blondheim, 5). It is also a source of constant anxiety, because what is granted by law can, by law, be taken away. Whatever constitutional guarantees emancipated "Jews in the West" may presently enjoy, they are far from secure. "The Jew," Pinsker says, "is not permitted to forget that the daily bread of civil rights must be given to him" (*AE*, 10; Blondheim, 5). Any personal gains attained under emancipation must be transient and uncertain. Emancipated Jews are constantly at risk of slipping back into the social depths from which they have been permitted to rise, but they refuse to see it. This is a singularly important point. It is surely "Jews in the West," with an impressive but relatively recent record of social and economic improvement who are vulnerable to being reminded (by an unemancipated "Russian Jew") that their hard-won achievements are not merely precarious but a source of distress and shame: "We have sunk so low," Pinsker charges his readers,

> that we become almost jubilant when, as in the Occident, a small fraction of our people is put on an equal footing with non-Jews. But he who must be *put* on a footing assuredly stands insecurely. If no notice is taken of our descent and we are treated like others born in the country, we are thankful to the point of actually turning renegades. For the sake of the comfortable position we are granted, for the fleshpots which we may enjoy in peace, we persuade ourselves and others that we are not Jews any longer but full-blooded sons of the fatherland. (*AE*, 14–15; Blondheim, 7)

In this view of emancipation the material signs of personal freedom are preeminent signifiers of devastating psychological and cultural debility. The Egyptian "fleshpots" of plenitude are portents of nonbeing. Ten years later, Ahad Ha'am (1856–1927) would expand on this point in his well-known essay "Slavery in Freedom" [Hebrew, *avdut betokh ḥerut*]. Along the same lines as Pinsker, he describes the condition of French Jews as the "exact opposite" of "exaltation" and reminds his Russian Jewish readers that the "privileges of emancipation are not worth the price."[29] On the question of emancipation, there is little to distinguish Pinsker's practical Zionism from the spiritual variety associated with Ahad Ha'am. This is not necessarily because Ahad Ha'am's essay was indebted in some specific way to *Autoemancipation*, which it certainly was, but because Jewish nationalism in Russia leaned heavily on well-established textual commonplaces.

Pinsker dwells with singular feeling on the absence of "national self-respect" (*AE*, 12; Blondheim, 6) that characterizes the paradoxical condition of inner subjugation to which *Autoemancipation* seeks to awaken its emancipated audience. Although he represents himself as a "realist" adopting a "rational line of conduct" in response to a "*natural antagonism*," for which he does not (he says) hold "either of the parties seriously responsible" (*AE*, 11; Blondheim, 6, emphasis in the original), he appeals directly and unambiguously to the meaning of Jewish liturgical tropes. Echoing a familiar passage (which is also a song) from the Passover Haggadah, "God's promise has stood by us and by our fathers" [Hebrew, *vehi she'amda le'avoteinu velanu*], Pinsker sums up the entirety of Jewish history as the "most glorious of all partisan struggles with all the peoples of the earth who, with one accord, desired to exterminate us" (*AE*, 12; Blondheim, 6). His ostensibly "unbiased" (*AE*, 11; Blondheim, 6) account of the Jewish present is grounded in a reading of the Jewish past as *Heilsgeschichte*, the main theme of which is unremitting Jewish struggle against ceaseless Gentile persecution. The same persistence of tradition has been observed in the work of academically trained nineteenth-century German Jewish historians, chiefly in the writing of Heinrich Graetz (1817–1891), a prolific and popular author.[30] Pinsker knew his audience; whatever their metaphysical or spiritual commitments, their Jewish sentiments were educated by the likes of Graetz, who depicted the sweep of Jewish history as a magnificent morally inspiring *Trauerspiel* and saw himself as a Jewish prophet, engaged in "reconciling the hearts of parents to their children."[31] Indeed, throughout the *longue durée* of Jewish textuality, the primary function of rehearsing stories of Jewish suffering at the hands of non-Jews was not etiological but moral: The point of such literary intervention was not to account for the hatred of the Gentiles but to provide cultural prophylaxis against the temptations of apostasy and to deliver a "message of pride for future generations."[32] It is along these lines that *Autoemancipation* presents itself to its modern Jewish readers, to impress upon them an awareness that they "have a past, a history a common, unmixed descent, an indestructible vigor, an unshakeable faith and an unexampled history of suffering" (*AE*, 20; Blondheim, 10).

Notwithstanding Pinsker's insistence that the "basis of [his] reasoning . . . rests upon anthropological and social principles, innate and ineradicable" (*AE*, 18; Blondheim, 9) and the reputation of *Autoemancipation* as a primary source in the history of secular Zionism, the text lends itself to an unambiguously pietistic Jewish reading. It belongs to the enduring commemorative tradition that David Roskies calls the literature of destruction, which includes masterpieces of devotional and homiletical writing such as the midrash on Lamentations, medieval martyrological poetry, the Hebrew chronicles of the First Crusade, and Natan Hanover's *Abyss of Despair* (1653).[33] Its resonance with its first Jewish readers depended less on the plausibility of Pinsker's proofs from nineteenth-century anthropology and psychology and more on its connections with the commonplaces of Jewish collective memory. The implicitly Jewish framework of explanation is what makes Pinsker's explicit appeal "purely and simply to the operation of those general forces based on human nature" (*AE*, 21; Blondheim, 10) intelligible, not to say self-evident. In fact, throughout *Autoemancipation*, natural Judeophobia appears to be interchangeable with Christian *Judenhass*, Edom's eternal hatred of Israel that will not disappear until the arrival of the messiah (*AE*, 1; Blondheim, 1). Tellingly, Pinsker never actually uses the word *antisemitism*, perhaps because it had too contemporary a ring. His "unbiased" view of emancipation as impracticable, contrasted to a view of the world "judged" according to the "principles of an Utopian Arcadia" (*AE*, 11; Blondheim, 6), was underwritten by his conviction that emancipation must be renounced as a false god. In the end, Pinsker proclaimed, the turn to nationalism requires of Jews an ethical rather than a political commitment: "It is our bounden duty to devote all our remaining moral force [German, *moralische Kraft*] to re-establishing ourselves as a living nation" (*AE*, 18; Blondheim, 9).

Pinsker mobilized the threat of antisemitism in response to the shame of Jewish apostasy; in *Autoemancipation* the pathological Jew hater becomes a stalking horse for the modern emancipated "Occidental" Jew, a "patriotic fanatic," debased by the necessity of "sacrificing every claim upon independent national life to [his] loyalty as citizen" (*AE*, 15–16; Blondheim, 8). Although he represents the pathology of Judeophobia as the problem to which nationalism is the only possible solution, Pinsker's insistence on incurable Gentile hatred makes a much better case against the lure of Gentile love. The rhetorical target of *Autoemancipation* is not antisemitism but emancipation; Pinsker's insistence that emancipation is an "idle delusion" (*AE*, 15; Blondheim, 7), because Judeophobia is incurable, should be read as an exhortation to reject emancipation, because it is morally dangerous and socially undesirable *for Jews*.

At the heart of *Autoemancipation* lay a Jewish problem that had first arisen in maskilic literature in response to the promise of Jewish citizenship: the fracture of Jewish society and the loss of collective discipline entailed in the shift from communal to personal autonomy.[34] What historians of Zionism have described as Pinsker's awakening to the realities of antisemitism was the upshot of a deep-seated suspicion of emancipation that "bloody deeds of violence" served to confirm. Both the contrarian desire to restore Jewish collective authority and the urgent call to reassert Jewish self-respect had their origins in Jewish ambivalence toward the modern social contract, which proposed to "refuse everything to the Jews as a nation and accord everything to the Jews as individuals."[35] From a perspective informed by an acute sensitivity toward policies that rested on this distinction (ultimately rooted, it must be said, in Christian hostility toward Judaism and a commanding interest in converting Jews), Pinsker saw the modern resurgence of *Judenhass* as both historically inevitable and psychologically indispensable.[36] For him, antisemitism was morally rather than politically significant. Indeed, the secular politics (if that is what they are) of *Autoemancipation* make the most compelling historical sense as a species of Jewish ethics.

Notes

1 Most of the literature on Simone Weil appears to be relentlessly apologetic, but see Hans Meyerhoff, "Contra Simone Weil: The Voice of Demons for the Silence of God," *Commentary* 24 (1957): 240–49; Susan Sontag, "Simone Weil," *New York Review of Books* (1 February 1963); and Stanislawski's own essay, Michael Stanislawski, "Simone Weil et Raissa Maritain," *Cahiers du Judaisme* 11 (2001–2002): 97–107. On secular trends and economic causes of Jewish migration from Russia to the United States, see Jacob Lestschinsky, "Jewish Migrations, 1840–1946," in *The Jews: Their History, Culture, and Religion*, ed. Louis Finkelstein (New York: Harper, 1949), 2: 1198–238; Simon Kuznets, "Immigration of Russian Jews to the United States: Background and Structure [1975]," in *Jewish Economies: Development and Migration in America and Beyond*, ed. E. Glen Weyl and Stephanie Lo (London: Routledge, 2017), 2: 143–232; and Yannay Spitzer, "Pogroms, Networks, and Migration: The Jewish Migration from the Russian Empire to the United States, 1881–1914," *Maurice Falk Institute for Economic Research in Israel Discussion Paper Series* 3 (2021): 1–83.

2 For the most recent example, see Kenneth B. Moss, *An Unchosen People: Jewish Political Reckoning in Interwar Poland* (Cambridge, MA: Harvard University Press, 2021).

3 The last three years have seen the publication of several books on the subject, greeted with rave reviews. All of them advance large conceptual claims on behalf of antisemitism. See Steven J. Zipperstein, *Pogrom: Kishinev and the Tilt of History* (New York: Norton, 2018); Götz Aly, *Europe Against the Jews, 1880–1945*, trans. Jefferson S. Chase (New York: Metropolitan, 2020); and

Jeffrey Veidlinger, *In the Midst of Civilized Europe: The Pogroms of 1918–1921 and the Onset of the Holocaust* (New York: Metropolitan, 2021).

4 Enzo Traverso, *The End of Jewish Modernity*, trans. David Fernbach (London: Pluto, 2016), 9. Traverso characterizes antisemitism as "*the* source of the mixture of particularism and cosmopolitanism *that characterizes Jewish modernity*" (emphasis mine).

5 See Scott Ury, "Strange Bedfellows? Anti-Semitism, Zionism, and the Fate of 'the Jews,'" *American Historical Review* 123 (2018): 1151–71.

6 On the limited usefulness of the term *antisemitism* in historical explanation, see the brilliant critique by David Engel, "Away from a Definition of Anti-Semitism: An Essay in the Semantics of Historical Description," in *Rethinking European Jewish History*, ed. Jeremy Cohen and Moshe Rosman (London: Littman Library of Jewish Civilization, 2009), 30–53. On the philological origins of the concept, see Maurice Olender, *The Languages of Paradise: Race, Religion, and Philology in the Nineteenth Century*, trans. Arthur Goldhammer (Cambridge, MA: Harvard University Press, 1992). On the term's entry into the political vocabulary of late nineteenth-century Europe, see Albert S. Lindemann, *Esau's Tears: Anti-Semitism and the Rise of the Jews* (Cambridge, UK: Cambridge University Press, 1997). On the connection between "race" and "religion" in antisemitic discourse, see Susannah Heschel, *The Aryan Jesus: Christian Theologians and the Bible in Nazi Germany* (Princeton, NJ: Princeton University Press, 2008).

7 Israel Bartal and Jonathan Frankel, "From Ḥibbat Ẓion to Zionism: The Zionist Movement in the Russian Empire, 1881–1917" [Hebrew], in *World Regional Zionism: Geo-Cultural Dimensions*, ed. Allon Gal (Jerusalem: Zalman Shazar Center for Jewish History, 2009), 1: 52.

8 Stuart Clark, "Inversion, Misrule, and the Meaning of Witchcraft," *Past and Present* 87 (1980): 99e. For the methodological context of Clark's remarks, see Quentin Skinner, "Meaning and Understanding in the History of Ideas," *History and Theory* 8 (1969): 3–53.

9 [Leo Pinsker], *Autoemancipation! Mahnruf an seine Stammesgenossen von einem russischen Juden* (Berlin: W. Issleib [G. Schuhr], 1882). Pinsker's name did not appear on the cover or anywhere else in the original publication. The best available English translation is by David Blondheim. It was first serialized and, immediately upon completion, issued as an off-print by *The Maccabaean*, a monthly journal published by the Federation of American Zionists. See Leo Pinsker, *Auto-Emancipation*, trans. D. S. Blondheim (New

York: The Maccabaean, 1906). Readers who rely on the generally accepted version of Blondheim's translation published in *The Zionist Idea: A Historical Analysis and Reader*, ed. Arthur Hertzberg (Philadelphia: Jewish Publication Society, 1997), should be aware that this version is based on a subsequent reprint (1944) of Blondheim's translation and is marred by several editorial changes and substantial cuts to the text. Future citations from *Autoemancipation* will appear as parenthetical references within the body of the text; I refer to the English translation as Blondheim and to the original German as *AE*.

10 Actually, the first explicit argument for the restoration of Jewish self-government appeared in 1868–1869, in an essay on Jewish law written by M. L. Lilienblum (1843–1910) and serialized in the Odessa Hebrew weekly *Ha-meliz*. Lilienblum argued that Jewish sovereignty was embodied and preserved in the institution of rabbinic jurisprudence and referred to the law as an expression of Jewish general will. In describing the social function of rabbinic legislative power, he used political terms such as *shilton* (government) and *memshalah* (dominion). See M. L. Lilienblum, "Orḥot ha-talmud," *Ha-meliz* 8 (1868): 99–100, 122–23, 139, 154–55, 178–79, 186–87, 203, 211, 215–17; and M. L. Lilienblum, "Nosafot l'ha-ma'amar orḥot ha-talmud," *Ha-meliz* 9 (1869): 61–63, 67–69, 76–77, 86–87, 91–92. There are interesting parallels between Lilienblum's argument and one that was formulated in 1873 by the young Hungarian rabbi Akiva Yosef Schlesinger (1837–1922). See Michael K. Silber, "Alliance of the Hebrews, 1863–1875: The Diaspora Roots of an Ultra-Orthodox Proto-Zionist Utopia in Palestine," *Journal of Israeli History* 27 (2008): 119–47. Silber places Schlesinger's ideas in context, but he does not mention Lilienblum's excursus as a possible source. Given that "Orḥot ha-talmud" was something of a *succès de scandale* when it appeared, it is entirely possible that Schlesinger read it, even though he would not have found it expedient to allude to it in his own work. Significantly in the present context, neither Lilienblum nor Schlesinger referred to anti-Jewish animus as a motive force or even a stimulus of Jewish national awakening. Neither Schlesinger's work nor Lilienblum's "Orḥot ha-talmud" ever appears as a source for the history of the "Zionist idea," whereas *Autoemancipation* has become canonic.

11 On Pinsker's career before 1881, see Dimitry Shumsky, "Leon Pinsker and *Autoemancipation!* A Reevaluation," *Jewish Social Studies* 18 (2011): 33–62.

12 The definitive work on the subject remains Jonathan Frankel, *Prophecy and Politics: Socialism, Nationalism, and the Russian Jews, 1862–1917* (Cambridge, UK: Cambridge University Press, 1981).

13 For an assessment of the violence, its causes, progress, and repercussions of pogroms, see I. Michael Aronson, *Troubled Waters: Origins of the 1881 Pogroms in Russia* (Pittsburgh: University of Pittsburgh Press, 1991).

14 The most dramatic version of Pinsker's conversion from "enlightenment" to "nationalism" appears in David Vital, *The Origins of Zionism* (Oxford, UK: Oxford University Press, 1975).

15 For the latest interpretation of Herzl's story of his Zionist awakening, precipitated by antisemitism, see Derek Penslar, *Theodor Herzl: The Charismatic Leader* (New Haven, CT: Yale University Press, 2020), 66–69. Penslar says that Herzl's supremely convincing act of narrative self-fashioning "appears not to have been conscious." Like other biographers of Herzl, Penslar takes his subject's word that he had known nothing of Pinsker and had not read *Autoemancipation* before his own "invention" of Zionism in 1895.

16 Bartal and Frankel, "From Ḥibbat Zion to Zionism: The Zionist Movement in the Russian Empire," 1: 52.

17 Gideon Shimoni, *The Zionist Ideology* (Hanover, NH: Brandeis University Press, 1995), 33.

18 The "revisionism" of recent writing in Jewish cultural history that Shumsky discusses in his article on Pinsker (see Shumsky, "Leon Pinsker") is, to my mind, greatly overstated. Although Zipperstein and Bartal have pushed the so-called crisis of Russian Jewry back to the 1870s (before the pogroms), their work does not challenge the consensus explanation of modern Jewish politics that Frankel expounded on at great length in *Prophecy and Politics*. Jewish history remains tethered to the idea that Zionism is a postliberal response to what Shumsky characterizes as the "ineffectuality of emancipation-oriented maskilic Jewish ideology." If there is a substantial difference between this proposition and the consensus that Zionism was a response to antisemitism, I cannot see it.

19 But see Peter Schäfer, *Judeophobia: Attitudes Toward Jews in the Ancient World* (Cambridge, MA: Harvard University Press, 1997). Schäfer defines Judeophobia as a toxic combination of "fear and hatred," a feeling that Jewish misanthropy and xenophobia constitute a "constant threat to the civilized world" (205–9). This usage is quite different from Pinsker's.

20 M. L. Lilienblum, "Obshcheevreiskii vopros i Palestina," *Razsvet* 3, no. 41 (9 October 1881), 1597–1600, and no. 42 (16 October 1881), 1637–42. As I have already noted, Lilienblum's ideas about Jewish nationalism were formed in the late 1860s, predating the emergence of modern antisemitism by a

decade; see Shumsky, "Leon Pinsker." For other possible sources, see Mark Volovici, "Leon Pinsker's *Autoemancipation!* and the Emergence of German as a Language of Jewish Nationalism," *Central European History* 50 (2017): 44–45.

21 Ury, "Strange Bedfellows," 1154.
22 For a discussion of Judeophobia within the context of late nineteenth-century psychology, see Sander L. Gilman and James M. Thomas, *Are Racists Crazy? How Prejudice, Racism, and Antisemitism Became Markers of Insanity* (New York: New York University Press, 2016), 33–38. Gilman and Thomas attribute Pinsker's unprecedented interest in "the inherent racism of Judeo-phobes" to his primary concern: to trace the "etiology of the madness of the Jews" to "the Enlightenment demand that Jews become 'like everyone else' in a national society while repressing their own Jewish national identity" (36). Although I am not persuaded by Gilman and Thomas that this concern was grounded in Pinsker's reading of contemporary "critical literature about European Jewry" (37), their only evidence of which is Nietzsche's highly ambiguous and not altogether apposite fragmentary text about Spinoza, a text that reached publication only in 1884–1885 (37n55) and which Pinsker could not possibly have read before writing *Autoemancipation*, the parallels between their argument and mine will be readily apparent.
23 This was the position held by "major medical figures" of the time, including Cesare Lombroso (1835–1909), "the Jewish founder of the Italian school of positivist criminology." Lombroso "denied any inherent biological weakness in the Jewish psyche but rather saw the inheritance of such predispositions as the result of '2,000 years of oppression.'" See Gilman and Thomas, *Are Racists Crazy*, 31.
24 Volovici, "Leon Pinsker's *Autoemancipation*," 41. Volovici's article is the latest installment in a historiographic tradition dedicated to normalizing Jewish nationalism by making it as un-Jewish as possible. Because I object to the fundamental assumptions on which this tradition rests, there is no point in belaboring Volovici's argument here. I would say only this: Although it is not clear from Volovici's own evidence that any of Pinsker's German readers responded enthusiastically to the elements of German nationalism, German philosophy, and German science that Volovici distills from *Autoemancipation*, what his evidence does show quite clearly is that Russian Jews read *Autoemancipation* as a Jewish text. They also seemed to have endorsed Pinsker's critique of their German *Stammesgenossen*. Volovici's more ambitious

claim that *Autoemancipation* is a "radical text" (44) rests on its apparent affinities with the work of Marx and Bakunin; if so, contemporary readers likewise overlooked this connection. In fact, one reader at least saw Pinsker's arguments as being "rooted in religion" (52). "These are essentially mystical and fantastic views," wrote I. A. Rubanovich of *Autoemancipation*, "which prevent the examination of the real conditions of life and which therefore cannot be subjected to rational arguments" (cited in Frankel, *Prophecy and Politics*, 128). Rubanovich (1859–1920) was one of the founders of the Socialist Revolutionaries, a party that attracted more Jewish radicals than any other within the broad stream of the Russian revolutionary movement. In the 1880s he was a *narodovolets* (a member of the People's Will, the group that was responsible for the assassination of Alexander II); if there was one reader of Pinsker who had also read both Bakunin and Marx and would have been primed to connect the dots, it was Rubanovich.

25 Volovici, "Leon Pinsker's *Autoemancipation*," 41.

26 Letter from David Gordon to Rabbi Isaac Rülf, cited in Volovici, "Leon Pinsker's *Autoemancipation*," 54. David Gordon (1831–1886) was the editor of the Hebrew weekly *Ha-magid*, published in Lyck, East Prussia, between 1856 and 1903 and widely circulated in Russia. Gordon was an early supporter of Zionism, as was Rülf (1831–1902), who was born and educated in Germany and served as communal rabbi in Memel (now Klaipėda in Lithuania). After reading *Autoemancipation*, Rülf was moved to compose his own Zionist manifesto, which was explicitly in the prophetic mode; see Isaac Rülf, *Aruchas Bas-Ammi: Israels Heilung* (Frankfurt: J. Kauffmann, 1883). It is altogether remarkable how many rabbis were drawn to a movement informed by a text that ostensibly "subverted the religious dimension of the national question in Eastern European Jewish societies" (Volovici, "Leon Pinsker's *Autoemancipation*," 58). Reading Volovici, one gets the distinct impression that all of Pinsker's German acquaintances were rabbis, although Volovici somehow fails to notice this fact.

27 The famous phrase "fallen Jews" comes from Yosef Hayim Yerushalmi, *Zakhor: Jewish History and Jewish Memory* (Seattle: University of Washington Press, 1982), 85. Yerushalmi refers to "history" as the "arbiter of Judaism" in an age given to the "ever-growing decay of Jewish group memory." Yerushalmi does not say this explicitly, but it is difficult to avoid the conclusion that what nineteenth-century Jewish "appellants" to history were seeking was not all that different from Jewish "memory."

28 Here, Pinsker's argument follows directly in the path laid down by rabbinic sources, where the "essentializing of Israel's enemies and generalizing them in the figure of the *goy* is part of the response to God's withdrawal from history." According to Adi Ophir and Ishay Rosen-Zvi, the "generalized *goy* of the aggadic narrative" is both "a signifier of God and a substitute for Him." See Adi Ophir and Ishay Rosen-Zvi, *Goy: Israel's Multiple Others and the Birth of the Gentile* (Oxford, UK: Oxford University Press, 2018), 234–35.

29 Ahad Ha'am, "Slavery in Freedom [1891]," in *Selected Essays by Ahad Ha'am*, ed. and trans. Leon Simon (Philadelphia: Jewish Publication Society, 1962), 176–77, 193.

30 See Nils Roemer, *Jewish Scholarship and Culture in Nineteenth-Century Germany: Between History and Faith* (Madison: University of Wisconsin Press, 2005); and Jeffrey Blutinger, "Writing for the Masses: Heinrich Graetz, the Popularization of Jewish History, and the Reception of National Judaism," PhD diss., University of California, Los Angeles, 2003.

31 See Nils Roemer, "Turning Defeat into Victory: *Wissenschaft des Judentums* and the Martyrs of 1096," *Jewish History* 13 (1999): 65–80; and Amos Bitzan, "The Problem of Pleasure: Disciplining the German-Jewish Reading Revolution, 1770–1870," PhD diss., University of California, Berkeley, 2011, 111–31. Graetz was citing Malachi 4:6; for the quotation in its context, see Roemer, *Jewish Scholarship*, 103.

32 Adam Teller, "Jewish Literary Responses to the Events of 1648–1649 and the Creation of a Polish-Jewish Consciousness," in *Culture Front: Representing Jews in Eastern Europe*, ed. Benjamin Nathans and Gabriella Safran (Philadelphia: University of Pennsylvania Press, 2008), 33. See also Jeremy Cohen, *Sanctifying the Name of God: Jewish Martyrs and Jewish Memories of the First Crusade* (Philadelphia: University of Pennsylvania Press, 2006).

33 David G. Roskies, ed., *The Literature of Destruction: Jewish Responses to Catastrophe* (Philadelphia: Jewish Publication Society, 1988). Roskies does not include *Autoemancipation* in his anthology.

34 On maskilic emancipation anxiety, see Shmuel Feiner, "The Pseudo-Enlightenment and the Question of Jewish Modernization," *Jewish Social Studies* 3 (1996): 62–88.

35 Comte de Clermont-Tonnerre, "Speech on Religious Minorities and Questionable Professions (23 December 1789)," in *The French Revolution and Human Rights: A Brief Documentary History*, ed. and trans. Lynn Hunt (Boston and New York: Bedford/St. Martin's, 1996), 88.

36 This sensitivity is ultimately traceable to Moses Mendelssohn and the beginning of public debate about the prospect of Jewish emancipation in Prussia. See Olga Litvak, *Haskalah: The Romantic Movement in Judaism* (New Brunswick, NJ: Rutgers University Press, 2012), 106–12. I follow Salo Baron's caution against assuming that emancipation "brought the Golden Age." It was Baron who first proposed that "left to themselves, the Jews might for long have clung to their corporate existence" and who, in the same landmark article, referred to "national Judaism" as "medievalism on a higher plane." See Salo Baron, "Ghetto and Emancipation," *Menorah Journal* 14 (1928): 515–26. So far as I know, Jewish scholarship on the modern period in general and on "national Judaism" in particular has yet to grapple with the implications of Baron's argument.

PART III
THE DISPLACEMENTS OF EUROPE'S GREAT WARS

9

East, West, and a Gendering of Jewish Tradition During the First World War

Nils Roemer

World War I reshaped German and Jewish cultures in many ways. The collapse of the Ottoman, Austrian-Hungarian, and Russian Empires at the end of the war, the promulgation of the Balfour Declaration in 1917, a renewal of antisemitism in the West, and violence in the East profoundly challenged and refashioned European Jewry. Men and women experienced these political, social, cultural, and religious transformations differently. In Germany and Austria World War I accelerated and amplified an existing transformation in art, literature, culture, politics, and gender relations. The experience of military conflict offered an opportunity for many Germans and Austrians to fantasize about and fashion a new warlike masculinity, xenophobic nationalism, and militant racism.[1] Yet men who participated in World War I not only came to envision new models of military masculinity but also, as Joanna Bourke suggests in *Dismembering the Male*, found that the war experience exposed a greater fluidity and ambiguity in men's experiences in all-male settings, one characterized by complex and fragile constructions of male identity.[2]

Already before the war, Jews and other Germans feared the decline of ideals of masculinity and advocated their renewal; this fear affected both genders. By the turn of the twentieth century, Jewish women in Austria-Hungary and Germany had often been held responsible for Jews' radical assimilation.[3] These assertions acquired a new virulence at the beginning of the twentieth century with the massive growth of modern consumerism, which placed the individual pursuit of happiness at the center of modernity. In the century's first decade, anxiety about the stability of the aristocratic notion of masculinity that had existed during the extended period of peace could be felt; perhaps the lack of military necessity had weakened German men.[4] In 1907, Elias Auerbach, a physician, Bible scholar, and Zionist activist, published the article "On the Military Fitness of Jews" in the *Jüdische Rundschau*; in the essay Auerbach advocated the making of a new Jewry of muscle.[5] Zionists, who often embraced ascetic and spiritual ideals in their national movement, denounced women for their association with consumer cultures (i.e., conspicuous consumption and materialism). In a 1901 essay Martin Buber not only coined the concept of a Jewish renaissance but also fostered among German-speaking Jews a greater appreciation for Eastern European culture while at the same time rebuking German Jewish women for their sensual and material attraction to material culture. He blamed the disintegration of tradition on Jewish women who sought to re-emasculate Judaism.[6] The artist Ephraim Lilien, a Zionist artist par excellence, portrayed not only an idealized version of the Jewish woman of valor but also a new Jewish male aesthetic. Lilien sought to combat existing stereotypes of Jewish men and women by fashioning new Jewish men in line with their muscular biblical ancestors. These corporeal Jewish men had their counterparts in the new Jewish women, pictured as oriental and chaste beauties.[7]

When the war broke out, German Jews embraced the opportunity to prove their patriotism by symbolically, emotionally, and actively participating in the military effort.[8] About 100,000 Jews served Germany in the war, with the vast majority on the front lines. More than 12,000 Jews died fighting; 35,000 Jews were decorated in the war; and 2,000 Jews became officers.[9] Their initial enthusiastic responses to participating in the war effort reflected new ideals of military masculinity among Jews.[10] To many male German Jews, the war proved not only an opportunity to display their patriotism but also a way to enact the ideal of masculinity. Claims to masculinity had been dislodged from being the exclusive possession of the nobility, thereby making it available to a broader class of men who could qualify for prized membership in the officer corps. Based on Bavarian case studies, David J. Fine suggests that Jewish officers were well integrated into and openly identified as both Jews and Germans in the German army. Tim Grady convincingly demonstrates that even well into the early 1930s, many German non-Jews had retained at least a grudging if fading respect for the record of Jewish soldiers who had fought in the German army.[11] Even during the Third Reich period German Jewish war veterans reminded themselves and their fellow German citizens of their combat record to fend off the daily experience of humiliation.[12]

Current scholarship on modern Jewish cultures has become more attuned to studying shifting gender roles and shifting concepts of masculinity and femininity.[13] Less explored is how the ideals of gender shaped encounters with Eastern European Jewry during the war, a meeting between East and West that is often credited for intensifying the already blossoming renaissance of Jewish cultures.[14] The *Ostjude* had featured prominently in German Jewish debates and served in the nineteenth century as an argument in favor of modernization as a way of distancing German Jewry from the legacy of the life and culture of the allegedly benighted "ghetto." Whereas previously the East had been cast as the backward other of the modernizing Western European Jewish communities, at the turn of the century the East was rediscovered—particularly for Zionist-oriented writers and artists—as a place of "authentic" Jewish culture, presumably untainted by the process of emancipation and assimilation.[15] This reevaluation was partly made possible by the westward migration of Eastern European Jews, which initiated a process of exchange between East and West, intensified by World War I.

From the perspective of cultural exchange, World War I represented not only confrontation and destruction but also an important moment "in terms of foreign encounters," in the words of Ute Frevert.[16] During the war, crossing borders brought individuals to the battlefield and thus into contact with different customs, languages, and traditions. This was particularly true for Jewish combatants who encountered Polish Jewish life while serving in the German army.

Here, the experience of World War I aided in gendering Jewish authenticity. Critical of modern life and Jewish culture in the West and simultaneously informed by male angst, German Jewish travelogues of Poland during the war used a gendered representation of Eastern European Jews in their search for "Jewish authenticity." Their textual and visual representations of Eastern European Jews reverberated with the gender politics of the fin de siècle and with their intensified quest for ideals of masculinity during the war.

These ambivalent gender politics that cast Jewish women as oriental, desirable, and yet virginal informed the sense of crisis among German Jews as well as aspirations for cultural renewal.[17] This revival affected men and women differently, and many early twentieth-century commentators constructed their views of what they deemed authentic in a highly gendered manner. Before World War I women significantly redefined their social roles as universities opened to them and as many entered the workforce. Unsurprisingly, backlash ensued. German Zionist and physician Felix Theilhaber, for one, did not welcome these changes. Almost a third of all Jewish women worked outside the home in 1907, which, according to Theilhaber, adversely affected the life of the family. He claimed that women were not, in fact, supporting their families economically. Many women, he charged, actually strained family finances with their intense desires for consumer goods. A widely respected demographer and pioneer in the sex reform movement, Theilhaber nonetheless insisted that Jewish female consumerism and materialism, together with a decline in religiosity, were major causes of the weakening of Jewish life and culture.[18] Whereas emancipation and professional training appeared to other observers as indications of progress toward greater possibilities for women, Theilhaber viewed that change as undermining traditional societal roles—and the traditional Jewish patriarchal family expectations—of women as mothers and wives.[19] In the debate over marriage and family, independent women appeared as the culprits, threatening masculinity and undermining healthy sexual constraints.

During the war, German Jewish soldiers brought such perceptions with them to the Eastern European landscape—along with their male anxieties and desires. Young male commentators imported the criticisms of Jewish women from their home country and applied them to Eastern European Jewish women while at the same time sexually objectifying those women. Conversely, they invested Jewish men with the qualities of authenticity. Already before the start of World War I, the artist Herman Struck, born to a middle-class Orthodox Jewish family in Berlin, had idealized Jewish patriarchs as the embodiment of Jewish tradition. Struck exhibited several graphic prints of Eastern European Jews at the first Jewish art exhibition at the Fifth Zionist Congress in 1901.[20] His evocative images of three older Polish Jewish men cast these figures as pensive and weary but also with an aura of distinction, embodying Jewish cultural and religious life. These images celebrate the enduring power of these Eastern European Jewish patriarchs, as does his famous *Polnischer Rabbiner* (1900), sketched apparently of a Polish rabbi who was then visiting Berlin. These works exhibit key characteristics of Struck's other etchings of Eastern European Jews.[21] Along with the three sketches of Eastern European men, Struck exhibited a self-portrait at the Congress that presented the 25-year-old artist as aged and with a trimmed beard, thereby forging a link between himself and the portrayed Eastern European Jews.

During World War I, many German-speaking Jews met Eastern European Jews as soldiers of the German army in the East. Crossing borders brought individuals not only to the battlefield but also into contact with different customs, languages, and traditions. This was particularly true for Jewish combatants, who experienced Eastern European Jews while soldiers of the German army in the East. The Zionist Adolf Friedemann observed how soldiers were seized by curiosity in Warsaw. After visiting the Gerer Rebbe, they did not know any longer whether they had encountered the Middle Ages or the Orient, he contended.[22] Celebrated Austrian Jewish writer Stefan Zweig noted in his diary in July 1915 that it was strange to encounter Eastern European Jews who were coachmen, donkey drivers, and servants, lower-class professions that he associated with penury: "I saw the unsuspected misery of the Jews in ghettos."[23]

These meetings between German and Eastern European Jews were refracted through a highly sexualized lens. For example, Hugo Natt from Frankfurt, a Jewish army staff physician, observed how, in a Polish village filled with German and Austrian troops, a Jewish daughter presented herself seductively, showing off her hair and figure while her father in a caftan and ear locks remained unperturbed.[24] German Jewish philosopher Franz Rosenzweig recorded in his letters to his mother the profound impression Eastern European Jews had made on him. He thought that the Jewish boys were "magnificent" and confessed that in Poland he "felt something I rarely feel, pride in my race, in so much freshness and vivacity." Rosenzweig's newly found veneration still reverberated with the uncertainty that had brought him only a few years earlier close to conversion to Christianity. He noted that in comparison Western European Jews had become "philistine, bourgeois."[25] In contrast, he found in the Eastern European Jews an affirmation of his own newly constructed identity. Even the 5-year-old Eastern European Jewish children live in the "context of three thousand years."[26] He was also struck by the "masculine character" of the Hasidic pupils and by the overall sense of psychological comfort and confidence with which the Eastern European Jews moved around.[27] Rosenzweig's confessional letters illustrate the intersection of his German and Jewish cultural, religious, and gender identity formation.

At times, the conflicting identities pulled at each other, for example, when the Austrian Jewish journalist and Zionist Robert Weltsch assessed the disastrous effect of war on Jewish communities in the East. The war, he contended, had "destroyed the inner structure of the Jewish people."[28] Women suffered not only as objects of violence but also as objects of lust.[29] In Lublin the streets were populated by Jewish soldiers and "Jewish girls."[30] He was appalled by a German officer's advances toward the "beautiful Jewesses" and felt a sense of degradation, shame, and, above all, powerlessness.[31] Weltsch perceived not just prostitution but even mere social, lighthearted, or flirtatious interactions between Jewish women and soldiers as degrading, where women gave up on the "dignity of their royal blood."[32] The presence of young women in Zionist youth groups eventually consoled him. He hoped that these proud and strong women would be able to create beautiful homes in which to raise "masses of gorgeous, healthy, lively Jewish children."[33]

Other German Jews' encounters with their East European Jewish brethren led to an exoneration of them, especially of the women. Sammy Gronemann, a Berlin attorney who had become a Zionist and writer, served the German press office as a translator during World War I. In the Lithuanian town of Kovno, he discovered, as did many other German Jews, something original and authentic in Eastern European Jews. Attending religious services repeatedly in the East estranged him from the modernized Western religious practice. He confessed that he had felt at home there.[34] In Vilna he, along with Hermann Struck, who had volunteered to serve in the infantry and became part of the press office (with many other writers and artists) of the German Army Supreme Command for the East in 1915, guided the German poet Richard Dehmel to the Jewish quarter and to a synagogue. He found the Jewish quarter exhilarating. "But everywhere faces! Faces, that tell history—the history of the people," he later wrote.³⁵ Unlike other Germans, Gronemann's homecoming experience was less misogynistic, and he dismissed reports about Jewish prostitution as exaggerated and exceptional.³⁶

These varied personal impressions acquired new meaning when the German press office expressed an intent to cast the territory as suitable for Germany's annexation and promoted the Germanization of the local population. During the war, Struck and German playwright Herbert Eulenberg published an illustrated travel account about Lithuania, White Russia, and Courland.³⁷ Dedicated to the infantry of General Erich Ludendorf, the book vividly sketched, for those at home, the location of the German army's operations.

Struck's portrayal became an exercise in imagining and representing the diversity of the Eastern European landscape and its people. In the midst of a wide canvas of Lithuanian farmers combined with depictions of Latvian and Polish women and mothers, Struck detailed in broad strokes the Jews of Eastern Europe by relying on several iconographic traditions: the wooden synagogue of Grodno, the grave of Ger Zedek of Vilna, and Vilna's bustling Jewish lane, where he believed he heard the echo of the ancient Temple's wall and found a people who had remained true to themselves. Interspersed with these symbolic places were highly stylized portraits of individuals, both women and men. His sketch *Rahel* depicts a woman with dark brown hair, lending her a confident appearance. The accompanying text describes her as soft, dreamy, and wistful, a creature who does not understand politics, or Yiddish, but speaks only Russian and French and is familiar with Heinrich Heine and Friedrich Nietzsche. She appears as a stereotype of a highly educated and assimilated Jewish woman, whose dark eyes, however, also embody sorrow. Playing Chopin exhibits not her cultural finesse but rather causes tears to flow down her cheeks. Alongside this evocative portrayal, Struck chose several men to foreground the extent to which the social and political circumstances could be discerned in their appearance. Toward this end, Struck presents a Jewish luggage carrier and carter and an old, bearded, and slightly hunched Jewish man, both of whom evoke the manifold troubles, disappointments, and disillusionments of Eastern European Jewish masculinity.³⁸

Struck's images of the downtrodden existence of Eastern European Jews during the war became transformed into icons of endurance and strength in a collaborative publication project when he became the expert for Jewish affairs in the German Army Supreme Command for the East in 1917. That same year, German Jewish writer Arnold Zweig (no relation to Stefan) joined the press department of the Supreme Command. The two eventually collaborated on *Das ostjüdische Antlitz* (The Face of East European Jewry), which appeared in 1920.[39] The book makes obvious that World War I acted to galvanize prewar anxieties over changing gender roles, intensifying concerns over male identities and the family.

The war experiences no doubt initially provided opportunities for Jewish men to assert their masculinity, alongside already existing programs for Jewish physical renewal.[40] Yet Jewish men did not always succeed in preserving their status as wartime antisemitism escalated, culminating in a census in October 1916 to document whether Jews proportionately fulfilled their responsibilities on the front lines. In fact, the census's evidence dispelled these charges, but anti-Jewish hostility prevented its publication. Confronted with the challenges to their patriotism and military honor, some German Jewish soldiers adamantly sought to latch on to ideals of a corporeal Jewish tradition embodied in the Eastern European Jewish male.

Zweig's *Face of East European Jewry* idealized Eastern European Jews textually and figuratively. Neatly divided into distinct units, the book portrays various types of Eastern European Jews, their institutions, religious services, work, politics, and family, culminating in an account of Jewish youth. Following theories of environmental determinism, Zweig contrasts the urban dweller in the West who has "no direct access to the passing of the year" with Eastern European Jews' life in an organic environment.[41] He juxtaposes the Eastern European Jewish youth's endurance, authenticity, and spiritual vitality with those of Jews of the West. Writing in the first-person plural, he describes German Jews as "we" who had "traded part of our soul with Europe, giving up part of our Jewishness."[42] The Eastern European pastoral trumped the West's urbanism and urbanity. In contrast to "our" bustling metropolitan centers, he wrote, their houses of worship are made of "weathered wooden boards" on "hilly streets or in a valley, in the middle of a village or in an outlying town . . . [where] old trees are always nearby."[43]

Zweig's prose aimed to document the Jews' indestructibility and their devotion to purity, as he explained in a letter to Martin Buber.[44] Zweig also appreciated Eastern European male Jews' sturdiness, their ability to endure, their lack of insecurity and inferiority complexes, and, above all, their patriarchal role in their society. For Westerners like Zweig, sexuality had become a "destructive and menacing demon of the bourgeois world,"[45] and the sensual would become something impure if it were not for the purpose of marriage and procreation. Indeed, Zweig admired Eastern European Jewish men's control of sexual desire, which was channeled only toward procreation in the marital union. He apparently deemed an "erotically tepid" relationship an ideal marriage and looked at religious Jews, who "dance naturally without women" in the prayer halls, with some measure of envy.[46]

Zweig's and Struck's portrayal of Eastern European Jewish life also reasserted traditional domestic female virtues, making women responsible for the Jewish people's vitality but elevating men as the representatives of spiritual values. Struck particularly admired older Jews for their sturdiness, endurance, and lack of insecurity, suggesting that their faces were "sincere and dreamy and pure."[47] This reification of older Jewish men enabled the authors to invert the stereotyped image of the old talmudic scholar, the icon of Jewish learning, which had come to be associated with a feeble, almost neutered masculinity.[48] These older men united elements of Jewish spirituality and learning with an ability to endure and persist. In his comments on the illustration Zweig described an older man, who "turns his eye away from me and into the distance, distance that is nothing but time."[49] These were individuals who have "eaten from the bitter bread of exile" but have nevertheless "no sense of hopelessness" and do not feel confronted by degradation.[50]

Despite the text's infatuation with Eastern European Jewish culture, Zweig was keenly aware that secularizing forces had also affected Eastern European Jews. The young generation in Poland has thrown itself into political activism, embracing socialism, other forms of collectivism, and breaking with traditional Jewish culture.[51] Zweig feared that these trends were assimilationist and would lead to Judaism's impoverishment.[52] He placed his hope on those sections of Left-oriented Eastern European Jewish youth who had turned toward Zionism, which would allow them to fulfill their socialist ideals in a Jewish community in Palestine.[53]

For German Jews such as those who experienced other Jewish cultures on the Eastern front, those encounters became a template onto which to formulate and test views of culture and ideals of gender at home. German Jewish soldiers—and the artists and writers who became soldiers—brought their male anxieties and desires to the Eastern European landscape. They often projected their own fears and unstable gendered identities onto women, accusing them of rushing to assimilate and of neglecting their duties as mothers and preservers of tradition. At the same time, they elevated Eastern European Jewish men as the embodiment of Jewish spiritual values.

Notes

1 See Klaus Theweleit, *Male Fantasies*, vol. 1, *Women, Floods, Bodies, History*; and vol. 2, *Male Bodies: Psychoanalyzing the White Terror*, trans. Stephen Conway (Minneapolis: University of Minnesota Press, 1989); and, more recently on this subject, Jason Crouthamel, *An Intimate History of the Front: Masculinity, Sexuality, and German Soldiers in the First World War* (London: Palgrave, 2014); Karen Hagemann and Stefanie Schüler-Springorum, eds., *Home/Front: The Military, War and Gender in Twentieth-Century Germany* (New York: Berg, 2002); Marsha L. Rozenblit and Jonathan Karp, eds., *World War I and the Jews: Conflict and Transformation in Europe, the Middle East, and America* (New York: Berghahn, 2017); and Edward Madigan and Gideon Reuveni, eds., *The Jewish Experience of the First World War* (London: Palgrave-Macmillan, 2019).
2 Joanna Bourke, *Dismembering the Male: Men's Bodies, Britain, and the Great War* (London: Reaction, 1996).
3 In many ways this was old wine in new bottles. Already in the late eighteenth century, Jewish women who embraced acculturation were accused of destroying traditional Jewish society. See Steven M. Lowenstein, *The Berlin Jewish Community: Enlightenment, Family, and Crisis, 1770–1830* (New York: Oxford University Press, 1994); and Natalie Naimark-Golddberg, *Jewish Women in Enlightenment Berlin* (Oxford, UK: Littman Library of Jewish Civilization, 2012).
4 Marcus Funck, "Ready for War? Conceptions of Military Manliness in the Prusso-German Officer Corps Before the First World War," in *Home/Front: The Military, War and Gender in Twentieth-Century Germany*, ed. Karen Hagemann and Stefanie Schüler-Springorum (New York: Berg, 2002), 58.

5 Elias Auerbach, "Die Militärtauglichkeit der Juden," *Jüdische Rundschau* 50 (1908): 491–92; Todd Samuel Presner, *Muscular Judaism: The Jewish Body and the Politics of Regeneration* (London: Routledge, 2007), 192.
6 Martin Buber, "Das Zion der jüdischen Frau," *Die Welt* 5, no. 17 (1901): 3–5; David Biale, *Eros and the Jews: From Biblical Israel to Contemporary America* (Berkeley: University of California Press, 1997), 180–82.
7 Michael Stanislawski, *Zionism and the Fin de Siècle: Cosmopolitanism and Nationalism from Nordau to Jabotinsky* (Berkeley: University of California Press, 2001); Lynne M. Swarts, *Gender, Orientalism, and the Jewish Nation: Women in the Work of Ephraim Moses Lilien at the German Fin de Siècle* (London: Bloomsbury, 2020).
8 Derek Jonathan Penslar, *Jews and the Military: A History* (Princeton, NJ: Princeton University Press, 2013), 439.
9 Presner, *Muscular Judaism*, 199.
10 Presner, *Muscular Judaism*, 187–216; Gregory Caplan, "Germanising the Jewish Male: Military Masculinity as the Last Stage of Acculturation," in *Towards Normality? Acculturation and Modern Germany*, ed. Rainer Liedtke and David Rechter (Tübingen: Mohr Siebeck, 2003), 159–84.
11 David J. Fine, *Jewish Integration in the German Army in the First World War* (Berlin: de Gruyter, 2012); Tim Grady, "Fighting a Lost Battle: The Reichsbund jüdischer Frontsoldaten and the Rise of National Socialism," *German History* 28, no. 1 (2010): 1–20; Tim Grady, "'They Died for Germany': Jewish Soldiers, the German Army, and Conservative Debates About the Nazi Past in the 1960s," *European History Quarterly* 39, no. 1 (2009): 27–46; Tim Grady, "A Common Experience of Death: Commemorating the German Jewish Soldiers of the First World War," in *Between Mass Death and Individual Loss: The Place of the Dead in Twentieth-Century Germany*, ed. Paul Betts, Alon Confino, and Dirk Schumann (New York: Berghahn, 2008), 179–96.
12 Michael Geheran, "Remasculinizing the Shirker: The Jewish Frontkämpfer Under Hitler," *Central European History* 51, no. 3 (2018): 440–65.
13 The late Paula E. Hyman's work was pioneering. See Paula E. Hyman, *Gender and Assimilation in Modern Jewish History* (Seattle: University of Washington Press, 1995); and the Festschrift in her honor, Marion A. Kaplan and Deborah Dash Moore, eds., *Gender and Jewish History* (Bloomington: Indiana University Press, 2011). See also Benjamin Maria Baader, Sharon Gillerman, and Paul Lerner, *Jewish Masculinities: German Jews, Gender, and History*

(Bloomington: Indiana University Press, 2012); and Benjamin Maria Baader, "Jews, Women, and Germans: Jewish and German Historiographies in a Transatlantic Perspective," in *Gendering Modern German History: Themes, Debates, Revisions*, ed. Karen Hagemann and Jean H. Quataert (New York: Berghahn, 2007), 169–89.

14 Steven E. Aschheim, *Brothers and Strangers: The East European Jew in German and German Jewish Consciousness, 1800–1923* (Madison: University of Wisconsin Press, 1982), 139–84; Michael Brenner, *The Renaissance of Jewish Culture in Weimar Germany* (New Haven, CT: Yale University Press, 1996), 32–35; Fine, *Jewish Integration*, 94.

15 Aschheim, *Brothers and Strangers*; Mordechai Breuer, *Modernity Within Tradition: The Social History of Orthodox Jewry in Imperial Germany*, trans. Elizabeth Petuchowski (New York: Columbia University Press, 1992), 50–53.

16 Ute Frevert, "Europeanizing German History," *GHI Bulletin* 36 (Spring 2005), 13.

17 Brenner, *Renaissance of Jewish Culture*.

18 Felix Theilhaber, *Der Untergang der deutschen Juden* (Munich: E. Reinhardt, 1911), 75, 125–26.

19 Theilhaber, *Der Untergang der deutschen Juden*, 125.

20 Gilya Gerda Schmidt, *The Art and Artists of the Fifth Zionist Congress, 1901: Heralds of a New Age* (Syracuse, NY: Syracuse University Press, 2003).

21 Schmidt, *Art and Artist*, 35. On the identity of the rabbi, see Max Friedeberg, "Ein jüdischer Künstler," *Allgemeine Zeitung des Judentums* 65, no. 38 (20 September 1901): 455.

22 Adolf Friedemann, "Von einer Reise nach Warschau," *Süddeutschen Monatsheften* 14, pt. 1 (January 1915): 561.

23 Stefan Zweig, *The World of Yesterday: An Autobiography by Stefan Zweig* (Lincoln: University of Nebraska Press, 1964), 248.

24 Fine, *Jewish Integration*, 77.

25 Nahum N. Glatzer, ed. *Franz Rosenzweig: His Life and Thought* (New York: Schocken, 1961), 74.

26 Glatzer, *Franz Rosenzweig*, 77.

27 Glatzer, *Franz Rosenzweig*, 75, 77.

28 Robert Weltsch, "Ein Feldpost aus dem Osten," *Der Jude* 8 (1916): 529.

29 Weltsch, "Ein Feldpost aus dem Osten," 529–30.

30 Weltsch, "Ein Feldpost aus dem Osten," 530.

31 Weltsch, "Ein Feldpost aus dem Osten," 530.
32 Weltsch, "Ein Feldpost aus dem Osten," 530.
33 Weltsch, "Ein Feldpost aus dem Osten," 533.
34 Samuel Gronemann, *Hawdoloh und Zapfenstreich: Erinnerungen an die Ostjüdische Etappe, 1916–1918* (Berlin: Jüdischer Verlag, 1984), 60, 70.
35 Gronemann, *Hawdoloh und Zapfenstreich*, 78.
36 Gronemann, *Hawdoloh und Zapfenstreich*, 169–72; Sammy Gronemann, "Eine Dehmel-Erinnerung," *Neue jüdische Monatshefte* 4, no. 11 (1920): 261–63.
37 Hermann Struck and Herbert Eulenberg, *Skizzen aus Litauen, Weissrussland und Kurland* (Berlin: G. Stilke, 1916), no pagination.
38 Schmidt, *Art and Artist*, 104–9.
39 Arnold Zweig and Hermann Struck, *Das ostjüdische Antlitz* (Berlin: Weltverlag, 1920).
40 Gideon Reuveni, "Sports and the Militarization of Jewish Society," in *Emancipation Through Muscles*, ed. Michael Brenner and Gideon Reuveni (Lincoln: University of Nebraska Press, 2006), 44–61; Caplan, "Germanising the Jewish Male"; Todd Presner, "Muscle Jews and Airplanes: Modernist Mythologies, the Great War, and the Politics of Regeneration," *Modernism/Modernity* 13, no. 4 (2006): 701–28.
41 Arnold Zweig, *The Face of East European Jewry, with Fifty-Two Drawings by Hermann Struck*, ed. and trans. Noah Isenberg (Berkeley: University of California Press, 2004), 45.
42 Zweig, *Face of East European Jewry*, 1.
43 Zweig, *Face of East European Jewry*, 31.
44 Arnold Zweig to Martin Buber, 13 May 1918, in Martin Buber, *Briefwechsel aus sieben Jahrzehnten, 1897–1918*, ed. Grete Schaeder (Gerlingen: Lambert Schneider, 1972), 1: 534; Zweig, *Face of East European Jewry*, 25.
45 Zweig, *Face of East European Jewry*, 61.
46 Zweig, *Face of East European Jewry*, 46, 60–61, 83. I differ here from Steven Aschheim's observation that Zweig castigated Eastern European Jews for denial of their body and repression of their sexuality, which could only be redeemed in a socialist Palestine. See Aschheim, *Brothers and Strangers*, 202.
47 Zweig, *Face of East European Jewry*, 2.
48 See Daniel Boyarin, *Unheroic Conduct: The Rise of Heterosexuality and the Invention of the Jewish Man* (Berkeley: University of California Press, 1997).

49 Zweig, *Face of East European Jewry*, 1.
50 Zweig, *Face of East European Jewry*, 9, 12.
51 Zweig, *Face of East European Jewry*, 95.
52 Zweig, *Face of East European Jewry*, 97, 108.
53 Zweig, *Face of East European Jewry*, 100, 131–50.

10

The Yiddish Chair in Weimar Germany That Wasn't

Kalman Weiser

The project to establish Germany's first academic Yiddish chair on the eve of Hitler's ascent to power remains an intriguing yet almost completely unknown chapter in the history of Yiddish studies. The position was to be part of a proposed institute for the study and promotion of languages closely related to German for the mutual cultural and economic benefit of their speakers. The idea of uniting experts in Dutch, Afrikaans, Yiddish, Pennsylvania German, and Frisian under one academic roof was the brainchild of Heinz Kloss, a young researcher for the Institute for Germans Abroad. But he relied heavily on the Yiddish expertise of Solomon (Salomo) Birnbaum, Yiddish lector at the University of Hamburg, and the political connections of Franz Thierfelder, director of the German Academy for the Scholarly Research and Fostering of Germandom, to pursue what amounted to an ambitious private project.[1]

Little documentation has survived in German archives to explain the genesis and evolution of the project for a Yiddish chair or to account for its failure beyond the advent of Hitler's antisemitic reign of terror. However, the extensive correspondence contained in Birnbaum's personal archives allows us to reconstruct it chiefly from Birnbaum's perspective with the help of additional sources. Though leaving many questions unanswered, the letters tell the story of an unlikely alliance of brilliant young researchers and their institutions—Jewish and non-Jewish, nationalist and antinationalist, socialist and conservative, religious and secular—united in the promotion of Yiddish studies in the land where Yiddish was born yet had long ceased to be the mother tongue of Jews, apart from Eastern European migrants.

The episode sheds light on the early careers of Birnbaum and Kloss, seminal figures in the fields of Jewish language studies and sociolinguistics, respectively. Their collaboration also complicates our understanding of the forces that have shaped Yiddish studies, a field whose pre–World War II historiography is dominated by ideologically secular activists committed to Yiddish as part of programs for the political and cultural transformation of Jewish society. The Orthodox Birnbaum did not work for YIVO (the Yiddish Scientific Institute), a private research institute in Vilna, Poland, conceived as a Yiddish language authority and university for a diasporic Jewish nation; nor did he hold a position at a state-supported research institute functioning in the context of Soviet nationalities policy.[2] Committed to preserving Yiddish as part of a religion-centric Jewish identity, Birnbaum eschewed institutions associated with Jewish socialist parties and communism. Instead, he traveled the more conservative but no less difficult path of German academia, struggling to establish himself and Yiddish amid the mounting antisemitism and anguishing political and economic turmoil of the Weimar Republic.

In contrast, Kloss, a researcher for a German nationalist institution, arrived at Yiddish through his activity to promote German interests internationally in the wake of World War I. His plan to create a Yiddish chair as part of a Germanic languages institute points to a long tradition of German Gentile scholarly engagement with Yiddish for the promotion of religious, economic, or political aims that did not necessarily coincide with those of its speakers. It recalls the vexing question of the relationship between Yiddish and German and, by extension, between their speakers—what Kloss described as "the tension between being related and foreign"[3]—that had long been central to Yiddish studies' self-definition and emancipation from a subordinate position in German studies.[4] Birnbaum's complicated and troubled relationship with Kloss lies at the heart of this story of complementary and conflicting personal and political motivations for the support of Yiddish scholarship on the eve of what we know in retrospect as the cruelest chapter in German-Jewish relations.

A Short History of Yiddish Research in Germany

Scholarship about Yiddish in Germany begins in the sixteenth century. Viewing Yiddish as a halfway point between German and Hebrew, Christian Hebraists wrote instructional guides to Yiddish as a means to facilitate acquisition of the holy tongue. They were joined in their investigations of the language and its literature by missionaries, who recognized the utility of Yiddish for imparting their salvific message to ordinary Jews. Outside universities, where instruction in Yiddish was offered by the eighteenth century, merchants produced practical guides to commerce with Yiddish speakers. Criminologists also took an interest in Yiddish, especially as an aid in deciphering German thieves' cant, which borrowed heavily from it, thanks to collaboration between Jewish and Gentile criminal bands.[5]

Although greater familiarity with Yiddish and Jewish practices helped dispel superstitions about Jews and even inspired appreciation among some Christians, for others it only confirmed prejudices about Jews' antagonisms toward the dominant society. Indeed, Yiddish was often perceived not as the natural language of a distinct community but as a deliberate and malevolent distortion of the German language. Knowledge of it was therefore necessary to reveal and counter Jews' blasphemy and deception, even though their conversion was unlikely. In contrast, eighteenth-century Enlightenment thinkers typically argued against the necessity of converting Jews to "improve" them but found little inherent or instrumental value in Yiddish. To them, it was an ugly language incompatible with higher thought, because of its "impure" hybrid nature, and a barrier to social integration. Along their path to emancipation in the nineteenth century, Jews themselves commonly came to accept such views. Yiddish was seen as a degenerate German, a product of ghetto seclusion best left behind as they acculturated and entered the middle class.[6]

As the language declined among most German Jews, so too did practical interest in it. By the late nineteenth century, however, a new wave of interest arose among scholars—this time in the living varieties of the language spoken chiefly in Eastern Europe. The interest drew on advances in historical linguistics and from the romantic interest in language as the reflection of the unique genius of a people and therefore as a means to define membership in a given ethnic nation across political boundaries. From this perspective contemporary Yiddish was a medieval German dialect carried eastward by Jews and fossilized through isolation from the main branch of the language. It was a museum piece useful for elucidating German's historical development, even though its speakers were not considered part of the German nation. A few dissertations about Yiddish language or literature, chiefly by Jewish students who did not speak it, appeared in German-language universities by the early twentieth century.[7]

Interest in Yiddish intensified as a result of the encounter between German soldiers and masses of Yiddish-speaking Jews in Poland and Lithuania during World War I. This contact inspired a large number of articles in Germany that described this strange people whose tongue afforded a degree of mutual intelligibility and evaluated the utility of the language for the war effort and Germany's postwar future in Eastern Europe. German troops, officials, and businessmen took an interest in the language and culture of a significant part of the local population in whose hands resided so much commerce and whose émigré population was believed to hold decisive political influence in the United States. This prompted the use of Yiddish in official proclamations aimed at the Jewish population, the creation of a Yiddish-German dictionary, the tolerance of Yiddish as a language of instruction in Jewish secular schools with an eye toward Germanization (especially where Germany entertained the possibility of annexing territory), and the sponsorship of a pro-German Yiddish press. The purported affinity of German and Jewish interests was particularly encouraged by German Zionists' propaganda, which argued—paradoxically—that Jews were the historic carriers of German culture to the primitive Slavic East and therefore deserved recognition as a distinct people. Such claims contributed to accusations by their detractors that Eastern European Jews served as eager agents of German imperialism despite their vocal opposition to such notions.[8]

Though still a marginal phenomenon among the general public, this wave of interest enabled Solomon Birnbaum (1891–1989) to secure a publisher in 1915 for his *Praktische Grammatik der jiddischen Sprache*, the first modern scientific grammar of Yiddish in any language. A native of Vienna, Birnbaum encountered Yiddish through the engagement of his father, the famous Jewish cultural and political activist Nathan Birnbaum (1864–1937),[9] in the movement for Jewish national cultural autonomy in the Habsburg monarchy. He mastered it while attending high school in Czernowitz in the Austrian province of Bukovina, where his father presided over the First Yiddish Language Conference in 1908. He returned to the Austrian capital in 1910, and in 1912 relocated again to Berlin, where his father had moved the family following a religious awakening that caused him to grow increasingly estranged from what he came to see as the "idolatry" of the secularist Yiddishist movement. Encouraged by his father, Birnbaum published translations of Yiddish literature and folk songs to help familiarize German-speaking Jews with the intellectual and cultural creativity of Eastern European Jews. To facilitate German speakers' learning of the language, he devised his own systems for Yiddish spelling and the romanization of Yiddish texts, which he later applied in his Yiddish grammar.[10]

After convalescing from a bullet wound in the throat during his service in the Austro-Hungarian army during World War I, Birnbaum began a doctorate in Oriental studies at the University of Vienna in 1919. As was then the custom, he took semesters at several other universities, studying in Zurich, Berlin, and finally Würzburg, to benefit from instruction from specific professors. His 1921 dissertation, which explored the Hebrew-Aramaic component of Yiddish, helped lay the foundations for the study of Ashkenazic Hebrew as well as Yiddish, which Birnbaum insisted on referring to as "Jiddisch" rather than "Judendeutsch" or some other commonly used designation that suggested that it was a variety of German. His dissertation, along with Max Weinreich's thesis about the history of Yiddish research (Marburg University, 1923), was one of about half a dozen dissertations about Yiddish completed by students from Eastern Europe (or with close ties to it) who arrived in German-language universities after the war. Native or near native Yiddish speakers, they were influenced by developments in Jewish nationalism in Eastern Europe that accorded Yiddish a central place in Jewish life and in programs for national-cultural autonomy there. Hence they studied Yiddish not as a subset or aid to German philology but as a field in itself.[11]

But it was Birnbaum's Yiddish grammar, not his dissertation, that drew the attention of Conrad Borchling, director of the German Philology Seminar at the University of Hamburg. With little hope as a Jew for a professorship, let alone one in a field such as Yiddish or Judaica that did not yet formally exist in universities, Birnbaum came to Hamburg in 1921 to work as the secretary for a Jewish welfare organization. Upon making Birnbaum's acquaintance, Borchling invited him to teach Yiddish language and literature, the first position for Yiddish in a modern university and an opportunity that changed the course of Birnbaum's life.[12]

Birnbaum's work was held in universally high esteem by colleagues and was largely responsible for the growing recognition of Yiddish as an autonomous language in German academia in the 1920s. Yet his two attempts at habilitation (about contemporary Hebrew literature in 1926 and Hebrew paleography in 1929), a necessary step toward becoming a *Privatdozent* and then professor in German academia, were declined, despite predominantly positive evaluations by reviewers. This was a staggering disappointment that effectively blocked his career advancement through conventional channels; Birnbaum privately attributed these rejections to the professional jealousy of a colleague, although antisemitic motives are not to be ruled out.[13]

Having followed in his father's footsteps of religious "return" during his adolescence, Birnbaum acquired a profound knowledge of classical Jewish texts without the benefit of a yeshiva education. He also became active in the circles of the Orthodox antinationalist organization Agudas Yisroel, for which his father served as general secretary from 1919 to 1921. He argued in the organization's publications and in other publications that Yiddish, which was in a complementary relationship with traditional *loshn-koydesh* (holy language, i.e., Hebrew-Aramaic) in traditional Ashkenazic society, was the expression of an all-encompassing religious-cultural way of life. Yiddishism, the movement to create a modern Jewish identity focused on secular Yiddish culture, was in his eyes a form of European nationalism like any other and served to disconnect Yiddish and Jews from Judaism. It reflected Jews' spiritual assimilation and was thus liable to divert Jews from their divinely ordained religious mission, ultimately destroying the foundations of their uniqueness.[14]

Birnbaum was willing to publish in YIVO journals, hoping to have some influence in its circles, but he refused repeated entreaties to join the institute's philological section in order not to lend his name to a secularist institution. He also resented YIVO's efforts to undo the success of his "traditionalist" spelling system, which had been adopted by schools and publications affiliated with Agudas Yisroel. In the 1930s YIVO attempted to convince Agudas Yisroel to introduce YIVO's own system, adopted by secular Yiddish schools, in the name of unity among Yiddish speakers. Based on conventions that predated the Haskalah (Jewish Enlightenment), which introduced spelling and vocabulary modeled on literary German into Yiddish, Birnbaum's system not only eliminated modern Germanisms but also could be read equally well by speakers of any major Yiddish dialect. In contrast, Birnbaum argued, YIVO's system removed some Germanisms while unwittingly introducing new ones, thereby furthering assimilation. Moreover, he claimed that YIVO's orthography sought to impose the Vilna-centric spelling and pronunciation norms of its core members on all Yiddish speakers, most of whom spoke other dialects.[15]

Although Birnbaum derived prestige and satisfaction from his position at the university, the salary he earned as an adjunct lector was grossly inadequate to support his growing family. He consequently undertook a wide variety of freelance jobs to make ends meet in the 1920s: book sales, commissioned scholarly writing, journalism, lecturing, translation, teaching Jewish refugee children from Eastern Europe in a religious school, and private English lessons. In the exhausting pursuit of a livelihood, he was

Figure 10.1. Birnbaum family, 1932. From the left, Eleazar, Irene, Eva, Jacob, and Solomon. Courtesy David Birnbaum.

assisted by his Viennese-born, London-raised wife, Irene, who gave private English lessons and worked as a translator in addition to helping raise their three young children. As Birnbaum described to his father in the late 1930s, palpable antisemitism more than the deteriorating economic conditions of Germany in the wake of what we now call the Great Depression and its aftershocks made him an eager candidate for emigration.[16] But where could Birnbaum, a lone Orthodox scholar of Yiddish active in a field dominated by left-leaning and ideologically secular Jews, find adequate and stable employment? Even though he considered other careers, he was convinced that scholarship was the only one for which he was suited and the only one that truly appealed to him.

Heinz Kloss's Plans for a German-Yiddish Alliance

While pursuing his doctorate in law and economics at the University of Halle, Heinz Kloss (1904–1987) worked on contract as an editorial assistant for the Institute for Germans Abroad (Deutsches Ausland-Institut, DAI), a private organization with close ties to the country's political and economic elites. Following World War I, 30 million Germans lived in the new states that had emerged from the wreckage of empires—both prewar German citizens living in territory lost in the war and ethnic Germans who had never resided in the prewar German Reich. The government of Weimar Germany supported the cause of *Auslandsdeutsche* as part of a larger policy of championing national minorities, including Jews, throughout Europe to remedy the inadequacy of their protection by the League of Nations. Such a policy was motivated both by general humanitarian principles and by a specific concern for the often precarious situation of German minorities, who faced assimilation and/or discrimination in the new states of Europe. Not only could the position of ethnic Germans be strengthened through alliances with other minorities, but championing all minorities also would strategically help to defend Germany against suspicions of irredentism.[17]

The DAI was but one of several organizations in Germany spanning the spectrum from liberal to right-wing nationalists committed to assisting German minorities. It worked to strengthen their cultural and economic position and, depending on the circumstances, forestall or direct their emigration. Some supporters of the DAI also recognized in Germans abroad an asset for conducting foreign policy aimed at restoring Germany's dominance in Central Europe and the prewar political and territorial status quo without resorting to force. The DAI's chief activities were to maintain contact between *Auslandsdeutsche* and the German state and to gather information about German communities around the world. For comparative purposes it also gathered information about nationality problems faced by other peoples, a practice reflected in Kloss's publications about Yiddish-speaking Jewry in *Nation und Staat*, a prestigious journal for minority problems funded by the German Foreign Office.[18]

Kloss first introduced himself by letter to Solomon Birnbaum in 1927, reporting that he sought the assistance of a scholar commended to him by YIVO's Max Weinreich and others as "the single best expert in Yiddish."[19] He had acquired a reading knowledge of the language thanks to Birnbaum's grammar but turned to Birnbaum and Weinreich to answer his queries and to acquire additional resources and contacts for his research about Yiddish. His articles about Yiddish as a minority language in Eastern European states won praise from Weinreich, who described him as having "penetrated the Yiddish literary language and the development of the Yiddish language in general (both in the linguistic and cultural-political senses) more deeply than a large number of Jewish writers about these topics."[20]

As reflected in his letters to Birnbaum, Kloss evinced a keen philological interest in Yiddish, including recondite matters such as transcription and spelling that preoccupied Birnbaum as much for their practical as their ideological significance. But his plans for the language, which he outlined in the programmatic essays *Nebensprachen* (1929) and *Deutsche und Jidden* (1930), were motivated more by cultural-political aims than by academic ones. He hoped to establish a university department or chair for Yiddish as part of a proposed *Nebenspracheninstitut*, an institute devoted to cognate languages of German for the mutual political and economic benefit of their speakers.

Although he echoed arguments made during World War I about Yiddish's utility for spreading German influence, Kloss did not adopt their advocacy of Yiddish as a stepping-stone to Jews' linguistic and cultural Germanization. On the contrary, his plan relied on the indefinite preservation of the language's distinctiveness. Yiddish had more speakers in 1930—10–12 million in his estimation[21]—than nearly any other Germanic language and was spoken across a vast territory in Europe, the Americas, and elsewhere. Moreover, he argued, Yiddish-speaking Jews frequently knew German as a second language, extending the language's reach. Like the Germans, they were a people both widely envied and mistrusted by others, who held them in contempt for their rather one-sided display of talent and skills, such as was the case with immigrant Jewish speculators in London's East End and German farmers in America. Further, he argued that a large degree of formal linguistic similarity and mutual comprehensibility existed between the two languages despite the "racial" differences between their speakers.[22] Hence both sides could benefit from gaining at least a passive knowledge of the other's language, which they could acquire at an accelerated pace, to exchange skills in each group's respective areas of strength or to share resources in, for example, a technical school teaching farming and business administration in Yiddish to Jews and Germans in South America.[23]

Despite his enthusiasm for extensive cooperation between German speakers and Yiddish speakers, Kloss recognized in his published essays and privately that there would be numerous challenges. He lamented to Birnbaum that it would be difficult to convince the haughty Germans of the cultural and practical value of Yiddish so long as they considered it a jargon or deformation of German. A significant obstacle to acquainting "we" Germans with the treasures of Yiddish literature, he explained, was "your" Hebrew alphabet. He therefore inquired about texts Birnbaum had already transcribed into roman letters and asked him to translate and romanize a German-language text for inclusion in his essay *Nebensprachen* so that Germans could "see" and not just "hear" Yiddish.[24] It is unclear whether Kloss, who corresponded exclusively in German with Birnbaum, was aware at this time that his interlocutor was as much a product of the German linguistic and cultural sphere as he. Birnbaum felt no need to challenge his implicit exclusion from the German nation.

However, Birnbaum objected to the term *Nebensprachen*, because it suggested to his ears that Yiddish was somehow inferior to German; instead, he proposed *Nahsprachen*, to emphasize linguistic proximity rather than subordination. He also disapproved of *Jidde*, the phonetically inaccurate term that Kloss proposed to refer to Yiddish-speaking Jews so as to avoid the "ghetto notions" associated with the term *Ostjude*; he recommended *Jid* in its place.[25] Birnbaum otherwise raised few objections to the aims or general content of the proposal for *Deutsche und Jidden* that he reviewed at Kloss's request, including Kloss's use of what may strike us today as racialized language. For example, Kloss pointed to the lesser linguistic and racial difference separating Spaniards from speakers of "Spaniolish (Ladino, Dzudezmo)" than that separating Germans from speakers of Yiddish.[26] Although he rejected essentializing notions of biological race common to nationalists of the day, Birnbaum nonetheless viewed Jews as a distinct people rather than merely a religious category, in contradistinction to the dominant view among liberal Jews in Germany.[27]

Birnbaum, however, maintained that Kloss underestimated the difficulty with which even highly educated non-Jews could acquire a passive comprehension of Yiddish. He attributed this difficulty not primarily to the barrier of the Hebrew alphabet or non-Germanic elements in Yiddish's vocabulary, as Kloss suggested. Rather, it was a lack of familiarity with Jewishness as a cultural system and the Jewish way of seeing the world that represented the greatest barrier to Gentile comprehension of Yiddish.[28] Although he hailed Kloss's ideas as an attempt "to make a breach in a strong wall" of prejudice, Birnbaum remained skeptical of the "utopian" project's chances for success. It would be difficult, he argued, to convince Jews not to view such plans as evidence of German cultural imperialism, which could aggravate their relationship with the majority peoples among whom they lived. Moreover, in his estimation, the larger part of German people regarded Jews at worst with disdain and at best with indifference, making cooperation with Jews unlikely. "The only interest that has existed so far in Yiddish, has been academic," he judged, "and that, of course, doesn't suffice."[29]

Despite these reservations, Birnbaum agreed to prepare a Yiddish translation of *Deutsche und Jidden* and, later, to help Kloss find a publisher for it when YIVO declined to print it.[30] YIVO's reasons are unknown, but its leadership likely saw the project's political thrust as outside its scholarly purview. Weinreich, for one, publicly acknowledged the potential for Jews to derive a number of economic and cultural benefits through close cooperation with speakers of cognate languages. But he made clear that he bore no illusions about Kloss's German-centric motivations and the ammunition his plan would furnish Jews' enemies.[31]

Fund-Raising for a *Nebenspracheninstitut*

As the secretary-general of the German Academy, Franz Thierfelder sought to strengthen the position of the German language internationally and spread German cultural and economic influence through educational endeavors, above all, schools teaching German. Intrigued after reading Kloss's *Nebensprachen*, he sought him out and published Kloss's *Deutsche und Jidden* in the German Academy's organ along with his own essay emphasizing the value of Yiddish for expanding the reach of German as a lingua franca. He too emphasized that it was incumbent on Germans to overcome their racial prejudices and groundless ideas about linguistic purity to undertake research about Yiddish and to cooperate with Yiddish speakers.[32]

From Kloss, Birnbaum learned that he and Thierfelder had worked out a plan in November 1929 to expand the existing Holland Institute at the University of Frankfurt into a *Nebenspracheninstitut*. Their ambition was to fund positions for Dutch, Afrikaans, and Yiddish scholars with an estimated budget of 15,000 to 20,000 marks (about US $3,550 to $4,730) annually, shared equally between the Holland Institute, the German Academy and German Language Association, Jewish circles, and Boer groups in South Africa. The plan called for transforming the Holland Institute, which was primarily occupied with teaching the Dutch language and enjoyed funding from the government of the Netherlands, into a predominantly research-oriented institution that would publish belletristic works in each of the institute's languages, linguistics and literary studies about them, and an annual bibliography of writings in them. Ideally, it would also teach Yiddish and Afrikaans.[33]

As exciting as these plans were to Birnbaum, the fact that he first learned of them through a press communication more than six months after their hatching aroused his concerns that he was to be excluded from a position in the proposed institute. These conclusions were reinforced by the failure of Kloss, with whom he was in regular contact, to acknowledge him in his articles or to give him credit for translations of German texts included in *Nebensprachen*. He worried that Kloss, whom he correctly identified to his father as both a nationalist and a socialist but about whom he knew little else, would introduce someone from YIVO's "Leftist" circles to occupy the position rather than an Orthodox Jew. Or perhaps

Kloss would recommend a Gentile Germanist for the position to avoid a Jew altogether or even appoint himself, despite what Birnbaum deemed his glaring lack of philological qualifications.[34] Finally, he feared that attempts to win the financial support of prominent German Jewish donors would be sabotaged by a "clique" of Eastern European intellectuals residing in Berlin who would seek to win the project for YIVO.[35]

Birnbaum's anxieties were temporarily quieted when Kloss paid personal visits to his home in Hamburg in September 1930 before embarking on a nine-month trip to the United States to establish ties and research the language of the Pennsylvania German community. The visit convinced Birnbaum that he was essential to the project for his knowledge of Yiddish and to attract the support of Jewish donors among New York's Yiddish cultural elite.[36] Writing to his father, he commented that Kloss was "a strange person" but "you can't say that he's not likeable." Kloss, however, irritated him by making what Birnbaum considered excessive demands of his time and showing little gratitude—not even offering Irene Birnbaum a bouquet of flowers—for the hospitality extended to him by Birnbaum's household during lengthy visits. By the time of Kloss's departure from Hamburg in October, Birnbaum was more convinced than ever that Kloss was not only a charming ingrate but a shrewd careerist who was using Birnbaum to establish himself, a contract researcher, as the director of a funded research institute.[37] As he expressed to his father, "Kloss tortures me every second day for hours on end, simply takes up half days and nights. I even have to give him food. And, in the end, it won't be easy with him. He wants to hold the whole matter in his hands. . . . He is some kind of exploiter."[38]

Regardless of his suspicions about Kloss's personal intentions and his lack of familiarity with Thierfelder, whom he had never met, Birnbaum continued to afford them every possible assistance as their plan gained momentum in 1930–1931. His efforts, which were assisted by his father, included an extensive letter-writing campaign to facilitate their introduction to Jewish organizations and seeking private sources of funding. Upon their request, Birnbaum also wrote an article, which was published in the Germany Academy's organ in 1930, that provided readers with an overview of Yiddish and its place in contemporary Jewish life. In addition, he outlined a plan for the teaching and research activities of the Yiddish department of the proposed *Nebenspracheninstitut* (as noted earlier, he preferred the term *Nahspracheninstitut*).[39] The department's activities would parallel some of the philological research conducted by YIVO and Soviet Yiddish research institutions, but it would emphasize making the language and its culture accessible to German rather than Yiddish speakers. The specific themes for linguistic research outlined by Birnbaum were those to which he dedicated his own work, such as the history of the language and of Yiddish Bible translations.

Birnbaum was thus heartened by news from Thierfelder in January 1931 that the regional Jewish associations of southern Germany had pledged 5,000 marks (about US $1,200), constituting about a third of the proposed budget for the project. The reasons that German Jews, notoriously indifferent if not hostile toward Yiddish, contributed are not specified but likely had more to do with eagerness to support Jewish culture allied to a German cause than interest in Yiddish per se. This fund-raising news offered hope for the success of the project, but it also confirmed Birnbaum's sense of being an outsider despite his contributions. Moreover, his initial discomfort with the political ramifications of the planned institute intensified as matters began to assume more concrete dimensions. Nazi electoral victories, armed conflict in the streets between Communists and the paramilitary Sturmabteilung (SA), and thuggish violence directed at Jews and any Nazi opponents were cause for growing existential fear. Given the circumstances, he confided to his father, "You know that work in such an institute is not ideal for me. It is, in the end, a German political matter. Jews really can't afford not to remain neutral."[40]

News soon after arrived from Kloss about his fund-raising efforts, above all his meeting with David Shapiro, the wealthy publisher of the liberal Zionist daily *Der Tog* in New York. With only weeks remaining before his return to Europe, Kloss hastened Birnbaum and Thierfelder to send him additional copies of publications about the institute for distribution in America. He also requested that either Solomon Birnbaum or his father write directly to Shapiro to assure him that German Jewish circles supported the project and that his financial contributions would find their way exclusively into "competent Jewish hands for the purpose of Yiddish research." Similarly, he urged Thierfelder to write to Shapiro to demonstrate "that leading non-Jewish cultural-political circles support this matter and that the time has come to spread understanding of *Ostjuden* in Germany through expert research conducted by *Ostjuden* but in close cooperation with, as well as with the moral and organizational backing of, responsible non-Jewish German circles."[41]

Lacking confidence in Kloss's intentions, Birnbaum urged his father to write to Shapiro to fund not an institute but a lectureship or chair for Yiddish at a German university. In this way, he reasoned, research about Yiddish would not be explicitly linked to German nationalist goals and he would be assured the position. Birnbaum encouraged his father to emphasize Gentile interest in Yiddish as a positive sign of the timeliness of such a position as well as its value as a weapon against antisemitism. The difficulty lay not in making a case for the relevance of Yiddish but in making clear that Solomon Birnbaum was the only appropriate candidate without outright insisting that any donation be conditional on his appointment.[42] In the absence of documentary evidence, it is unclear what precisely David Shapiro, who previously offered to fund a Yiddish chair in Jerusalem,[43] thought of what must have seemed conflicting messages emerging from the efforts of Kloss, Thierfelder, and the Birnbaums. We know only that Kloss returned from America empty-handed in mid-1931.[44]

But that summer Kloss shared with Birnbaum the most promising news yet: Boer parties, as represented by Dr. M. L. Du Toit, senior lector in German at the University of Pretoria,[45] had taken an interest in his proposal for the project thanks to Thierfelder's mediation. Thierfelder had also convinced the German Foreign Office of the plan's merits, and it was almost certain to give money. The Foreign Office advised, however, that the site of the institute be changed from the Holland Institute in Frankfurt, considering the German and Dutch governments' mutual lack of interest in systematic collaboration and the Dutch government's rather jaundiced view of the other *Nebensprachen*, which it considered beneath its own. The Oriental Seminar at the University of Berlin was recommended instead.[46]

The Oriental Seminar, Kloss pointed out, would make an ideal home for the institute because it already possessed a lector for Dutch and Afrikaans; therefore it would only be a matter of creating a position for a Yiddish lector, which could possibly be paid for with existing money from the seminar, freeing up monies for other uses by the institute. Among the proposed activities of the institute were research, the publication of books and a scholarly quarterly devoted to all the institute's languages, and the establishment and maintenance of a library. The institute would also conduct external "cultural mediation work," such as facilitating study by Boer and Eastern European Jewish students in German universities, organizing lecture tours and exhibits, and promoting research among doctoral candidates in German philology. Birnbaum, Kloss conveyed, would assume the Yiddish position and should write directly to Thierfelder in Munich to express his minimum salary requirements in preparation for upcoming meetings with the Foreign Office.[47]

His hopes revived, Birnbaum eagerly waited for news of further developments but was to be sorely disappointed. After nearly half a year of silence, a letter from Kloss arrived in January 1932 requesting information about books. It concluded with an unadorned comment: "I am now rather pessimistic about the prospects for our institute."[48] Nathan Birnbaum, who had himself endured a life of frequent penury while pursuing often iconoclastic ideas, agonized over his son's straits. "I know you ought to get out of Germany," he wrote to Solomon in the summer 1932. "But it is more difficult precisely for you than for others: not a Zionist, not a Communist. An Orthodox scholar of Yiddish [*Yidishist*] with no influence."[49]

Solomon Birnbaum's *Institutum Ascenezicum*

By November 1932, after months without any contact, Birnbaum had all but given up on their common endeavor and began to draw up plans to launch his own institute. He was convinced that self-reliance was the only path to success, especially in such trying times. To his father he explained, "But no matter how bad the times, a way must be found. . . . It will be impossible to obtain large sums. But bigger money grows out of small amounts too for merchants."[50]

Shifting tack from Kloss's arguments about Yiddish's value as a cognate language for German political and economic interests abroad, Birnbaum aimed instead to "sell" his institute to German Jewish donors by emphasizing Yiddish's value for understanding German's linguistic history—an approach departing from his usual insistence on Yiddish for Yiddish's sake—and its cultural role as the historic language of Germany's Jews, thus reaffirming Jews' attachment to Germany. His initial strategy was to approach leading Gentile Germanists, Hebraists, and Bible scholars to secure statements attesting to the value and desirability of a proposed "Institutum Germano-Judaicum" under his direction. The support of respected Gentiles could then be used to entice Jewish scholars and, most important, wealthy and prominent German Jews across the ideological spectrum—Zionists, liberals, and Orthodox alike—to support the institute morally and financially in their own self-interest. In his draft proposals directed at a Jewish audience, Birnbaum emphasized that Yiddish, once the language of German Jews and still that of their descendants beyond Germany's borders, provided a historical link between Germans and Jews. German Jews' aversion to the language, a product of their struggle for emancipation in the nineteenth century, assured that they remained ignorant of their own history and culture, whereas Gentile Germans had begun to take an interest in it, especially for its philological and cultural-political value. Funding the proposed institute in a time of great material distress was thus justified not only to fill a scholarly void in the realm of German Jewish history and culture but also as a means to combat the "long unabating flood" of hatred against Jews. Although justified with somewhat different ideological goals, the Yiddish-focused research program for his institute would be substantially the same as that which he had outlined for the *Nebensprancheninstitut*.[51]

Birnbaum's resolve in going his own way was reinforced by news of an unexpected visit by Kloss to his father in January 1933, when Kloss and Thierfelder came to Berlin to attend a conference of the newly formed South Africa Committee of the German Academy. As Nathan Birnbaum conveyed to his son, Kloss reported to him that "for psychological reasons," Yiddish and Afrikaans institutes would necessarily be pursued separately, with the latter to be established immediately and the former by January 1934. Further, "for psychological reasons"—which Nathan Birnbaum interpreted as meaning antisemitism—a future Jewish institute would necessarily have a Gentile public director and administrator in addition to an internal academic director. Kloss himself would thus function as the public face and head of the institute. When asked directly about Solomon Birnbaum's place in the institute, Kloss offered an evasive answer. He was also meeting with representatives of YIVO in Berlin, "but it could be understood that they will take you," Nathan Birnbaum assured his son, "because they don't want a Leftist."[52] Kloss's expectation that the German Academy would establish a *Nebensprancheninstitut* with Yiddish as its focus by the new year is confirmed by his correspondence with Jacob Lestschinsky of YIVO in Berlin requesting that he and his Vilna colleagues prepare a volume of Yiddish-language scholarly materials in roman script for publication by the institute.[53]

For Solomon Birnbaum this was the final straw. It confirmed his darkest suspicions that Kloss intended the institute as a means to establish his own career on stable footing and would likely hire people affiliated with YIVO instead of him. In his eyes this latest revelation of Kloss's treachery, coupled with Thierfelder's distance from the project, vindicated his actions: "If I'm not for myself, who is? Other people don't budge."[54] To Birnbaum's satisfaction, 60 signatures arrived from Gentile scholars in support of his project, even after Hitler's appointment as chancellor; prominent Jews, citing the difficulty of financially maintaining existing Jewish academic institutions and the uncertain conditions of the time, were decidedly less inclined to sign.[55] Nonetheless, though Birnbaum labored intensively in the early months of 1933 to canvass support for his Institutum Germano-Judaicum, he harbored no illusions about the future of Jews in Germany. "In a generation," he wrote to his father that February, "all Jews will probably be pushed out of any place in German life except perhaps economic life, where there will perhaps remain a tenth of their former situation."[56]

Cooperation between Kloss, Thierfelder, and Birnbaum came to its decisive end not long thereafter. Kloss wrote to Birnbaum in late February 1933 with his customary coolness, confirming changes in plans in light of "the worsening of the economic situation, which makes raising money harder, the psychological worsening in the Jewish Question in general, and finally the impossibility of putting off further the donors of the sum of RM 5000" raised in the German Jewish community. He then reprimanded the Birnbaums for not informing him of private efforts to create an institute, which he had learned of through another party and from which he requested Birnbaum desist. "Any attempt to pursue Jewish matters publicly, whether funded by the state or not," Kloss warned, "runs the risk of being stopped at first attempt in light of the current situation of the Jewish Question in Germany."[57] He no doubt knew of what he spoke: Fritz Wertheimer, the DAI's secretary general, a German nationalist of "Jewish descent," was barred from entry into its premises by the SA only a few days later and subsequently removed from his position.[58]

In his response to Kloss, Birnbaum restrained the fury and indignation he expressed in private letters to his father. With language equaling Kloss's for politeness, Birnbaum unabashedly confirmed that he was pursuing a long-standing aspiration to create an institute of his own after receiving no communications from Thierfelder's German Academy for more than a year and a half. He also confronted Kloss about what he perceived as the former's dishonesty and manipulation, noting the personal insult inflicted in seeking "to exclude me, to whose pioneering work a part of the scholarly and other interest in Yiddish is due, from this undertaking."[59]

Without denying Birnbaum's accusations, Kloss pronounced that further collaboration with the German Academy was now impossible, and he expressed regret that he and Birnbaum had "maneuvered apart from each other" in a field in which the number of actively interested parties is "too small to afford such divisions." Kloss concluded his letter by asking Birnbaum to send him publications about his institute and to keep him informed, as he did not wish to lose contact with Birnbaum.[60]

Correspondence between Kloss and Birnbaum abruptly ended in March 1933, and there is no evidence that the two ever resumed direct contact. Gifted with prescience, both Nathan and Solomon Birnbaum left Germany a few weeks later, the former spending his final years in Holland and the latter settling in England. An impoverished refugee, Solomon Birnbaum struggled to establish himself in a new land. It took time but his achievements were recognized by the late 1930s in the form of lectureships in Yiddish and in Hebrew epigraphy and paleography arranged for him at the University of London by Professor Norman Jopson with the financial assistance of local Jewish groups.[61] He also helped mentor a postwar generation of Yiddish researchers in Germany, whose efforts would culminate in the country's first Yiddish chairs in the 1990s.[62] In contrast, Heinz Kloss continued his career in a Nazified DAI, becoming one of the Third Reich's leading *Volkstumsforscher* and a propagandist for its *Blut und Boden* ideology before pursuing a postwar career as an expert in national minority language rights.[63]

Conclusion

In retrospect, the Orthodox Birnbaum, an ardent opponent of secular nationalism of any kind, hardly seems an obvious partner for Kloss, a socialist-turned-nationalist who embraced conventional racialized conceptions of peoplehood, in the pursuit of pro-German cultural-political work. However, they shared not only an academic interest in Yiddish but also ambitions to advance their respective careers. They were also initially united by a concern for the disappearance of their own diasporic ethnolinguistic minority through assimilation, whether through secularization (Birnbaum) or the culturally homogenizing policies (Kloss) of the new ethnic nation-states that had emerged from the ruins of the old empires in the aftermath of World War I. Indeed, Solomon Birnbaum was reluctant to collaborate too closely with other Jewish scholars of Yiddish, most of whom identified as ideologically secular Jews. Given his need to preserve boundaries between religious Jewry and other Jewish groups, it is not surprising that he was more inclined to form a pragmatic alliance with Kloss, a Gentile affiliated with a quasi-governmental institution and with whom he had no ideological conflicts, than with Weinreich and his colleagues in YIVO, a poorly financed private institute in an impoverished country that he viewed as a rival for influence.

Moreover, unlike most German academics, whose interest in Yiddish was limited to its presumed value in reconstructing the history of German, Kloss took Yiddish seriously in itself, even if primarily as a tool in the service of German political and economic interests. His plan for a *Nebenspracheninstitut* emerged at a time when German foreign policy saw the benefit of cultivating allies for Germany and *Auslandsdeutsche* among other national minorities. Yiddish's utility for his plans rested on his understanding of it as the stable autonomous language of a national community whose replacement with German in Jewish communities was neither likely nor desirable. Indeed, according to this conception, Yiddish-speaking Jews were valuable to Germany precisely because of their linguistic proximity while remaining distinct—culturally and racially—from Germans.

Such an alliance was, however, no longer conceivable once the Nazi regime began to exclude Jews as racial enemies. In its hands, Yiddish became a tool not primarily to serve German religious, political, economic, or academic interests but for the plunder and destruction of Jewish life and culture. Such was the fate of YIVO and other Jewish institutions looted by the self-professed Judaica experts of the notorious *Einsatzstab Reichsleiter Rosenberg*.[64] Kloss's 1944 German-language guide to North American Jewry and its organizations, a copy of which was acquired in 2018 by Library and Archives Canada from Hitler's personal library, serves as a grim reminder of the application of the expert knowledge that he amassed in part thanks to Birnbaum and YIVO.[65]

Most cynically perhaps, Kloss made use of Yiddish scholarship to new ends again in the post–World War II era, this time, to signal philosemitism and distance from Nazi ideology. A decade after the war, he worked with Thierfelder for West Germany's Institute for Foreign Relations, the DAI's successor institute now dedicated to promoting intercultural understanding. Writing in a journal devoted to the revival of Yiddish studies in German-speaking lands, he recalled how he and Thierfelder were close to creating an institute with a position for Yiddish when Hitler came to power. Though omitting Birnbaum's role in the endeavor, he stressed that German speakers bore a moral responsibility to "look after the remains of Yiddish language culture and its bearers" and to promote Yiddish research to help reduce the "alienation" between Jews and Germans after the Holocaust.[66] Like the journal's editor Franz Beranek, a prolific Yiddish researcher and fellow *Volkstumsforscher*, he made no mention of his own Nazi past.[67]

Notes

1 My interest in the remarkable Birnbaums—Solomon and his father, Nathan—dates from a seminar paper I wrote for Michael Stanislawski, who encouraged my interest in the intersection of language and ideology in modern Jewish history. I benefited immeasurably from his insightful readings of hagiographic works produced by movements about their leaders and his analysis of memoirs and autobiographical writings as acts of careful self-fashioning.

2 On YIVO, see Cecile Esther Kuznitz, *YIVO and the Making of Modern Jewish Culture: Scholarship for the Yiddish Nation* (New York: Cambridge University Press, 2014). On Yiddish academia in the USSR, see David Shneer, *Yiddish and the Creation of Soviet Jewish Culture* (Cambridge. UK: Cambridge University Press, 2004) and Elissa Bemporad, *Becoming Soviet Jews: The Bolshevik Experiment in Minsk* (Bloomington: Indiana University Press, 2013), ch. 4.

3 Heinz Kloss, "Deutsch und Jiddisch," *Mitteilungen aus dem Arbeitskreis für Jiddistik* 1, no. 2 (1955): 4.

4 On the relationship of Yiddish studies to Germanistik, see Neil G. Jacobs and Dagmar C. G. Lorenz, "If I Were King of the Jews: Germanistik and the

Judaistikfrage," in *Transforming the Center, Eroding the Margins: Essays on Ethnic and Cultural Boundaries in German-Speaking Countries*, ed. Dagmar C. G. Lorenz and Renate S. Posthofen (Columbia, SC: Camden House, 1998), 185–98.
5 See Aya Elyada, *A Goy Who Speaks Yiddish: Christians and the Jewish Language in Early Modern Germany* (Stanford, CA: Stanford University Press, 2012).
6 Jeffrey Grossman, *The Discourse on Yiddish from the Enlightenment to the Second Empire* (Rochester, NY: Camden House, 2000).
7 Gabriele Strauch, "Methodologies and Ideologies: The Historical Relationship of German Studies to Yiddish," in *Studies in Yiddish Linguistics*, ed. Paul Wexler (Tübingen: Max Niemeyer, 2000), 83–100.
8 Kalman Weiser, *Jewish People, Yiddish Nation: Noah Prylucki and the Folkists in Poland* (Toronto: University of Toronto Press, 2011), 120–39; Marcos Silber, "Yiddish Language Rights in Congress Poland During the First World War: The Social Implications of Linguistic Recognition," *Polin* 27 (2015): 335–65; Tobias Grill, "'Pioneers of Germanness in the East'? Jewish-German, German, and Slavic Perceptions of East European Jewry During the First World War," in *Jews and German in Eastern Europe*, ed. Tobias Grill (Berlin: De Gruyter, 2018), 125–59.
9 On Nathan Birnbaum, see Jess Olson, *Nathan Birnbaum and Jewish Modernity: Architect of Zionism, Yiddishism, and Orthodoxy* (Stanford, CA: Stanford University Press, 2013).
10 See Kalman Weiser, "*Yiddish: A Survey and a Grammar* in Its Historical and Cultural Context," in Solomon Birnbaum, *Yiddish: A Survey and a Grammar*, 2nd ed., ed. Eleazar Birnbaum, David Birnbaum, Kalman Weiser, and Jean Baumgarten (Toronto: University of Toronto Press, 2016), xxix–xxxiv.
11 Hans Peter Althaus, "Yiddish," in *Current Trends in Linguistics*, vol. 9, *Linguistics in Western Europe*, ed. Thomas A. Sebeok (The Hague: De Gruyter Mouton, 1972), 1355–56.
12 Althaus, "Yiddish," xxxiv.
13 David Birnbaum, "Salomo Birnbaum's Experiences at Hamburg University," in *Key Documents of German-Jewish History*, 22 August 2018, dx.doi.org/10.23691/jgo:article-206.en.v1 (accessed 13 April 2021).
14 On Birnbaum's attitudes toward YIVO, see Weiser, "*Yiddish*."
15 On Birnbaum's Yiddish spelling system, see Kalman Weiser, "The 'Orthodox' Orthography of Solomon Birnbaum," *Studies in Contemporary Jewry* 20 (2004): 275–95.

16 Solomon Birnbaum to Nathan Birnbaum, 30 December 1930, family correspondence, Nathan and Solomon Birnbaum Archives (NSBA), Toronto.
17 Carole Fink, *Defending the Rights of Others: The Great Powers, the Jews, and International Minority Protection, 1878–1938* (Cambridge, UK: Cambridge University Press, 2004), 296–309.
18 Martin Seckendorf, "Deutsches Ausland-Institut," in *Handbuch der völkischen Wissenschaften: Personen, Institutionen, Forschungsprogramme, Stiftungen*, ed. Ingo Haar and Michael Fahlbusch (Munich: K. G. Saur, 2008), 140–49; Christopher Hutton, *Linguistics and the Third Reich: Mother-Tongue Fascism, Race, and the Science of Language* (London: Routledge, 1999), 153–55.
19 Heinz Kloss to Solomon Birnbaum, 29 June 1927, folder Kloss, NSBA.
20 M. Vaynraykh, "Deutsche Akademie, Mitteilungen, 1930, 1–6 (399 p.); 1931, 1–4 (380 p.)," *YIVO-Bleter* 3 (1932): 71.
21 Heinz Kloss, *Nebensprachen: Eine Sprachpolitische Studie über die Beziehungen eng verwandter Sprachgemeinschaften* (Vienna: Wilhelm Braumüller, 1929), 4.
22 Even as a socialist Kloss felt that natural bonds between members of the "white," "black," and "yellow" races took priority over class bonds across races, but he did not argue for the superiority or inferiority of any race. Where Jews fit into this scheme is unclear. See Heinz Kloss, "Proletariat und Rasse," *Die Grüne Fahne* 7 (October 1924): 214–16.
23 See Heinz Kloss, "Deutsche und Jidden," *Mitteilungen der Akademie zur wissenschaftlichen Erforschung und zur Pflege des Deutschtums: Deutsche Akademie* 1 (1930): 1–13; Kloss, *Nebensprachen*; and Hutton, *Linguistics and the Third Reich*, 201–4.
24 Heinz Kloss to Solomon Birnbaum, 15 August 1927, folder Kloss, NSBA; Hutton, *Linguistics and the Third Reich*, 204.
25 Kloss recognized that *Jidde* was phonetically incorrect but thought that "Jide or, more precisely, Jiede, would, however, be even uglier German." Heinz Kloss to Solomon Birnbaum, 20 December 1927, folder Kloss, NSBA. See also Solomon Birnbaum to Heinz Kloss, 28 December 1927 (draft), folder Kloss, NSBA. Presumably, *Jidde* was meant to be a back-formation from *Jidden* (*Yidn* in Yiddish means "Jews," whereas a *Yid* is a "Jew") on the analogy of *Jude* ("Jew" in German) and *Juden* (Jews).
26 Kloss, *Deutsche und Jidden*, 13.
27 For example, Birnbaum wrote to his father, "There are no doubt millions of people running around Europe today whose forefathers were Jews. . . . 'Blood'

is only there where there remains some connection to Jews or Jewishness. As soon as there is no more trace, as soon as the people have gone over completely to other cultures, you no longer hear from their blood." Solomon Birnbaum to Nathan Birnbaum, 14 April 1932, family correspondence, NSBA.

28 Solomon Birnbaum to Heinz Kloss, 28 December 1927 (draft), folder Kloss, NSBA.
29 Solomon Birnbaum to Heinz Kloss, 19 December 1927 (draft), folder Kloss, NSBA.
30 Heinz Kloss to Solomon Birnbaum, 23 February 1930, folder Kloss, NSBA.
31 M. Vaynraykh, "In daytshland hot oyfgevakht gor a nayer interes tsu der yidisher shprakh," *Forverts* (17 August 1930), 10.
32 Franz Thierfelder, "Neue Wege zur Verbreitung der deutschen Sprache im Ausland," *Mitteilungen der Akademie zur wissenschaftlichen Erforschung und zur Pflegung des Deutschtums: Deutsche Akademie* 1 (1930): 14–40; Eckard Michels, "Deutsch als Weltsprache? Franz Thierfelder, the Deutsche Akademie in Munich, and the Promotion of the German Language Abroad, 1923–1945," *German History* 22, no. 2 (2004): 206–28.
33 Heinz Kloss to M. J. Van der Meer, 19 September 1930, folder Kloss, NSBA. On the Holland Institute, see Helmut Gabel, "Zwischen Mythos und Logos: Niederlande-Forschung in Deutschland zur Zeit der Weimarer Republik," *Jahrbuch des Zentrums für Niederlande Studien* 10–11 (1999–2000): 69–100.
34 Solomon Birnbaum to Nathan Birnbaum, 11, 15, 19, and 23 May 1930, family correspondence, NSBA.
35 Solomon Birnbaum to Nathan Birnbaum, 26 and 28 May 1930, family correspondence, NSBA.
36 Solomon Birnbaum to Nathan Birnbaum, 22 September 1930, family correspondence, NSBA.
37 Solomon Birnbaum to Nathan Birnbaum, 30 September 1930, family correspondence, NSBA.
38 Solomon Birnbaum to Nathan Birnbaum, 28 September 1930, family correspondence, NSBA.
39 Salomo A. Birnbaum, "Die Stellung der jiddischen Sprache," *Mitteilungen der deutschen Akademie* 5 (1930): 355–64; Lilian Türk, "Der Plan für ein Aschkenasisches Zentrum: Vortrag anlässlich des 20. Jubiläums der Salomo-Birnbaum-Gesellschaft für Jiddisch in Hamburg, e.V.," paper presented at the twentieth anniversary celebration of the Salomo-Birnbaum-Gesellschaft in Hamburg, 27 September 2015, www.academia.edu/19837012/

Der_Plan_f%C3%BCr_ein_Aschkenasisches_Zentrum (accessed 25 September 2023).

40 Solomon Birnbaum to Nathan Birnbaum, 24 January 1931, family correspondence, NSBA.

41 Kloss to Solomon Birnbaum and Franz Thierfelder, 28 February 1931, folder Kloss, NSBA.

42 Solomon Birnbaum to Nathan Birnbaum, 21 March 1931, family correspondence, NSBA.

43 On the attempt to create a Yiddish chair at the Hebrew University, see Arieh Leyb Pilowsky, *Tsvishn yo un neyn: yidish un yidish-literatur in erets-yisroel, 1907–1948* (Tel Aviv: Veltrat far yidish un yidishe kultur, 1986), 141–91.

44 Solomon Birnbaum to Nathan Birnbaum, 18 June 1931, family correspondence, NSBA.

45 P. G. Nel, "Du Toit, Marthinus Lourens," in *Dictionary of South African Biography*, ed. C. J. Beyers and J. L. Basson (Pretoria: Human Sciences Research Council), 5: 223.

46 Kloss to Solomon Birnbaum, 12 July 1931, folder Kloss, NSBA; Ref. L. S. Dr. Freudenberg to Franz Thierfelder, 20 May 1931, R61129 (Bestand RZ 514), Aktenzeichen Kult prop 1, Afrika: Deutsche Kulturpropaganda in Afrika, Politisches Archiv, Auswärtiges Amt, Berlin.

47 Heinz Kloss to Solomon Birnbaum, 12 July 1931, folder Kloss, NSBA.

48 Heinz Kloss to Solomon Birnbaum, 5 January 1932, folder Kloss, NSBA.

49 Nathan Birnbaum to Solomon Birnbaum, 16 August 1932, family correspondence, NSBA.

50 Solomon Birnbaum to Nathan Birnbaum, 24 November 1932, family correspondence, NSBA.

51 See Birnbaum's drafts, especially "Einige Bemerkungen zu den gegenwärtigen Aufgaben der aschkenazischen Studien," December 1932, folder Institutum Ascenezicum, NSBA. For Birnbaum's account of the genesis of the institute, see S. A. Birnbaum, "Institutum Ascenezicum," *Leo Baeck Institute Year Book* 17 (1972): 243–49.

52 Nathan Birnbaum to Solomon Birnbaum, 12 January 1933, family correspondence, NSBA.

53 Heinz Kloss to Jacob Lestschinsky, 2 February 1933, RG 1.1, folder 679, YIVO Institute for Jewish Research.

54 Solomon Birnbaum to Nathan Birnbaum, 16 January 1933, family correspondence, NSBA.

55 Birnbaum, "Institutum Ascenezicum," 244–47. For Jewish responses to Birnbaum's appeal, see folder Institutum Ascenezicum, NSBA.
56 Solomon Birnbaum to Nathan Birnbaum, 2 February 1933, family correspondence, NSBA.
57 Heinz Kloss to Solomon Birnbaum, 28 February 1933, folder Kloss, NSBA.
58 Seckendorf, "Deutsches Ausland-Institut," 143; Tammo Luther, *Volkstumspolitik des Deutschen Reiches 1933–1938* (Stuttgart: F. Steiner, 2004), 54–55.
59 Solomon Birnbaum to Heinz Kloss, 3 March 1933, folder Kloss, NSBA.
60 Heinz Kloss to Solomon Birnbaum, 9 March 1933, folder Kloss, NSBA.
61 David Birnbaum and Eleazar Birnbaum, "A Brief Account of Solomon Birnbaum's Life," in Solomon Birnbaum, *Yiddish: A Survey and a Grammar*, 2nd ed., ed. Eleazar Birnbaum, David Birnbaum, Kalman Weiser, and Jean Baumgarten (Toronto: University of Toronto Press, 2016), xi, xvii–xix.
62 Erika Timm, "Salomo Birnbaums Leben und Werk," in *Salomo/Solomon A. Birnbaum: Ein Leben für die Wissenschaft / A Lifetime of Achievement*, ed. E. Timm, E. Birnbaum, and D. Birnbaum (Berlin: De Gruyter, 2011), 1: xxvi; Marion Aptroot, "Yiddish Studies in Germany Today," in *Yiddish in the Contemporary World*, ed. G. Estraikh and M. Krutikov (Oxford, UK: Legenda, 1999), 50.
63 On Kloss's Nazi activity, see Hutton, *Linguistics and the Third Reich*, ch. 6; Cornelia Wilhelm, "Nazi Propaganda and the Uses of the Past: Heinz Kloss and the Making of a 'German America,'" *Amerikastudien / American Studies* 47, no. 1 (2002): 55–83; and Terence G. Wiley, "Heinz Kloss Revisited: National Socialist Ideologue or Champion of Language-Minority Rights?" *International Journal of the Sociology of Language* 154 (2002): 837. Max Weinreich, in his 1946 study *Hitler's Professors: The Part of Scholarship in Germany's Crimes Against the Jewish People* (New York: Yiddish Scientific Institute), was the first to identify Kloss's Nazi association.
64 On the fate of YIVO and its staff, see David Fishman, *The Book Smugglers: Partisans, Poets, and the Race to Save Jewish Treasures from the Nazis* (Lebanon, NH: ForeEdge, 2017).
65 Edith Pütter and Heinz Kloss, eds., *Statistik, Presse und Organisationen des Judentums in den Vereinigten Staaten und Kanada* (Stuttgart: Selbstverlag der Publikationsstelle, 1944).
66 Kloss, "Deutsch und Jiddisch," 5.
67 On Beranek's postwar reception by Yiddish scholars, see Kalman Weiser, "'One of Hitler's Professors': Max Weinreich and Solomon Birnbaum Confront Franz Beranek," *Jewish Quarterly Review* 108, no. 1 (2018): 106–24.

11

The Jewish Postwar

Gil Rubin

In his seminal study *Postwar*, Tony Judt portrayed the postwar period not as a specific historical time frame but as a state of mind, defined by the way European societies grappled with the moral and political ramifications of the war and by a visceral sense of living in a decidedly post-1945 world.[1] Norman Naimark examined the diversity of the concept of the postwar in European history, noting how the fighting began and ended and new political orders emerged in vastly different moments across Europe. For the Czechs the war started with Munich in 1938, for the French only in July 1940. Yugoslavia's postwar government began to function in November 1943, whereas the Communist-dominated Polish Provisional Government was given increasing control of the country after January 1945. "There was no all-European '*Stunde Null*' [zero hour]," Naimark writes, "at which the war began and, despite the enormous historical significance of the defeat of Nazi Germany, there was no '*Stunde Null*' when it ended and the postwar began."[2] In this chapter I draw on these insights to explore the concept of the Jewish postwar. I argue that the Jewish postwar was not only the historical period that immediately followed the end of the war in Europe but also a state of mind and a political concept that shaped the way Jewish leaders and thinkers thought about the future of Jews during World War II and in its aftermath.

* * *

From the start of World War II dozens of Jewish leaders and intellectuals in New York, London, and Palestine, many of whom had been recent refugees from Europe, began to plan for the Jewish postwar. The assumption of practically all Jewish leaders engaged in postwar planning was that the war, much like the Great War, would end with a major international peace conference that would offer them an opportunity to radically reshape the political and legal position of Jews in this second postwar world. The extensive Jewish wartime discussion on the postwar order initially took place in the Jewish press but was soon institutionalized through the establishment of various Jewish postwar planning institutes. In November 1940 the American Jewish Committee founded the Institute on Peace and Postwar Problems, the first Jewish research institute dedicated exclusively to planning for the coming peace. The American Jewish Congress and the World Jewish Congress followed suit in February 1941, establishing the Institute of Jewish Affairs. Several months later the Jewish Labor Committee set up its own postwar planning body, and the Board of Deputies of British Jews began to draft its postwar agenda. The Executive of the Jewish Agency in Jerusalem dedicated many of its wartime meetings to plan for the postwar order. Other Jewish postwar planning activities took place on a smaller scale within organizations such as YIVO and the Bund (both organizations relocated to New York shortly after the outbreak of war) and among various national committees organized by Jewish refugees from Eastern Europe. These disparate Jewish postwar planning institutes reflected diverse Jewish political agendas, from a commitment for new minority rights guarantees for Jews in postwar Eastern Europe, to the defense of emancipation, to support for socialism and Zionism.[3]

Jewish planning for the postwar order took place within a broader postwar planning frenzy in the Allied capitals. In 1942 the Council of Foreign Relations listed more than 300 groups engaged in postwar planning; these groups laid out plans on issues as diverse as reforming the international monetary system, rebuilding a more robust international organization, and eradicating hunger and unemployment. The Allied capitals were full of representatives of European governments-in-exile and leaders of various European political parties who hoped to win over US and British support for their role in rebuilding their countries after the war.[4]

The Jewish postwar planning scene was marked by a sense of optimism about the future. Indeed, during the first years of the war, Jewish leaders envisioned the Jewish postwar not so much as a specific historical period but as the dawn of a new and positive era of political redemption for the Jews. This optimism about the future was apparent in the way Jewish leaders spoke about the postwar order, a discourse that at times took on religious overtones. As Joseph Tenenbaum, president of the American Federation of Polish Jews, observed in a 1942 speech on Jewish postwar planning, "Rarely in the history of the last two thousand years did we have such an urgent call to participate in the dynamic forces molding our own future."[5] "The main problem of European Jewry," declared Nahum Goldman, president of the World Jewish Congress, in November 1941, "is the problem of its future, after Hitlerism has been destroyed and the democratic victory will have opened the way to the establishment of a new world."[6] One *Haaretz* commentator was baffled by the obsession of Jewish leaders with the future. Everyone these days has assumed the ungrateful role of a prophet, he noted, attempting to predict the shape of the postwar order and peek behind the "the veil of the future."[7]

Jewish optimism about the postwar was shaped by two frameworks of historical interpretation. The first was the memory of Jewish achievements at the 1919 Paris Peace Conference, where Jews secured minority rights for Jewish communities in Eastern Europe and the Great Powers soon established a mandatory regime committed to developing a Jewish national home in Palestine. Many Jewish leaders who engaged in postwar planning during World War II either took part in shaping the Jewish agenda at Versailles or had become politically active in the years immediately following the peace conference. These leaders and thinkers all remembered the previous postwar moment as one of great political advancement for the Jews. After World War I Jewish legal equality was extended throughout Europe; Jews in Eastern Europe were granted collective guarantees for minority rights under the supervision of the League of Nations, and the British Empire issued the Balfour Declaration and committed to developing Palestine as a national homeland for the Jews. Catastrophic war and political rebirth were thus intertwined in the Jewish political imagination. Just days after the Nazi invasion of Poland, David Ben-Gurion reminisced about Jewish achievements in World War I and declared "the World War of 1914–1918 brought us the Balfour Declaration, this time we need to bring about a Jewish state."[8] Speaking from Vilna in March 1940, Russian Jewish historian Simon Dubnow emphasized this historical parallel, urging Jewish leaders to bear the experiences of 1919 in mind as they prepared to fight for Jewish rights in the postwar world.[9] In an article he wrote shortly after the outbreak of war, Dubnow envisioned the postwar peace conference as a courtroom of sorts that would be forced to deal with the "Jewish problem" "in its full magnitude" and to which "Jewish representatives from every country throughout the world" would come and "demand justice from the 'New Europe' for that people which suffered more than anyone from Hitler's terrors."[10]

The second historical framework that shaped Jewish thinking about the postwar was the experience of Jews in the 1930s. The Holocaust has overshadowed the fact that during the 1930s Jewish leaders and thinkers were overwhelmingly convinced that European Jewry was headed toward imminent catastrophe. Indeed, during the 1930s the Jewish birthrate in Europe rapidly declined and fewer Jews identified with the Jewish religion or national cause. In Eastern Europe Jews were rapidly losing their economic positions in the middle class in the face of nationalist economic reforms. Jewish legal equality was revoked in Germany, and Jewish rights were being assaulted throughout Eastern Europe. At the same time, the 3 million Jews in the Soviet Union were cut off from Jewish communities around the world.[11] Jewish historian Lewis Namier thus observed in 1927 that "dissolution and ultimate disappearance seem the inevitable future of the Jews of West and Central Europe."[12] Surveying the position of Jews in Europe in the epilogue of his 1937 study *A Social and Religious History of the Jews*, historian Salo W. Baron concluded that "the Jewish people are passing through one of the greatest of their historical crises." No other period in the history of Jews was "fraught with more danger to Jewish survival than are contemporary developments.... One must go back perhaps to the First Exile to find a situation equally threatening."[13] Dubnow shared Baron's analysis, lamenting before the outbreak of war that "we are now passing through one of the gravest crises in our history."[14] At around the same time German-born Zionist sociologist Arthur Ruppin ominously declared that "much as primitive peoples lose their traditional way of living... the Jews in these countries are trending toward 'race suicide.'"[15]

In Palestine, too, the Yishuv leadership was gripped by a sense of imminent collapse of the Zionist enterprise. After the outbreak of the 1929 riots, Zionist leaders increasingly feared that the British government would soon renege on the promise of establishing a "Jewish national home" in Palestine and turn the mandate into an Arab nation-state in which Jews would remain a minority. Facing a growing Arab nationalist movement and rising anticolonial sentiment across the empire, the British authorities pushed for the establishment of a legislative council in Palestine, an elected body that was to gain significant control over internal affairs in which the Arab population was to enjoy majority representation. After the 1936 Arab riots, the British laid out a new immigration policy, stipulating that Jews in Palestine would at no point exceed 30% of the total population. In December 1937 Chaim Weizmann predicted that the British might soon publicly accept "the Arab demand for the establishment in Palestine of an independent Arab State and the reduction of the Jews to the status of a permanent minority, to be guaranteed by the euphemistically termed 'minority rights.'"[16] A few months later, Ben-Gurion lamented that Zionism might soon become devoid of its "political value" and "fall off the international stage" as a solution to the "Jewish question."[17] In May 1939, just four months before the Nazi invasion of Poland, Zionist leaders' greatest fears came true. The British government issued the 1939 White Paper, which effectively halted further Jewish immigration to Palestine and stipulated steps that should be taken to turn Palestine within ten years into an independent state in which the Arab population would remain an overwhelming majority and Jews a minority, not to exceed about a third of the population.[18] For a long moment it seemed that Zionism had become a road not taken.

The outbreak of war thus appeared to Jewish leaders and thinkers as a break in historical time, an opportunity to radically reshape the disastrous course of events of the 1930s. It allowed Jewish leaders and thinkers to shift from a secular conception of time—Jewish history—to a religious conception—Jewish memory, which envisioned persecution and redemption as twin historical events.[19] This point was powerfully articulated by Jacob Flaizser (later known as the historian Jacob Talmon), a young student at the Hebrew University of Jerusalem, in an essay published in a student paper in May 1939. Flaizser shared the widespread conviction among Jewish leaders of his day that the foundations of Jewish existence across the Diaspora have "already been shattered or are pacing toward a catastrophe." He yearned for a historical framework that would allow him to make sense of what he, some four months before the outbreak of war, already called the Shoah of the Jewish Diaspora: "In previous times there was meaning to the sufferings of the Diaspora . . . every wave of violence and persecution was considered as the last trial by God, an act in a marvelous historical vision . . . the historiosophical chain of choice-sin-galuth-and-redemption. . . . There were times . . . [in which] the persecution of Jews seemed like the last vestige of an evil world that was about to disappear into darkness. But today, who hasn't lost faith in this vision?"[20] Several months after writing this piece, Flaiszer left for Paris to pursue his doctorate at the Sorbonne. After the German invasion of France in March 1940, he escaped to London, where he spent the rest of the war working for the Board of Deputies of British Jews and with Zionist leaders planning for the postwar Jewish world.

Jewish optimism about the postwar was shaped not only by these historical attitudes but also by a specific analysis of the scale and form of the Jewish problem in postwar Europe. Indeed, during the first years of the war Jewish leaders were overwhelmingly convinced that the war would end with an unprecedented Jewish refugee problem, some 3–5 million "floating Jews" in postwar Europe, as Weizmann prophesied in 1942.[21] Although Jewish leaders expected that masses of Jews would perish in the war, they envisioned the scale of destruction in similar terms to the violence of World War I, in which 250,000 Jews were murdered in a series of pogroms in Ukraine, rather than a methodical, industrial killing. In the summer of 1940 Baron thus concluded that even a "Nazi victory in the war" did not imply the end of European Jewry.[22] In May 1942, after reports of Nazi massacres of Jews in the Soviet Union were already being discussed in the Allied capitals, Weizmann insisted that in the worst-case scenario "25% of European Jewry" would perish in the war.[23]

The postwar Jewish problem was thus perceived as the problem of the Jewish refugee, and the postwar Jewish refugee problem would be the largest of the many refugee problems in postwar Europe. The Nazis displaced millions of Jews throughout Eastern Europe, and the local population had taken their homes and professions. During the 1930s, Eastern European governments advocated for the "evacuation" of millions of their Jewish citizens. In a series of meetings early in the war, the leaders of the Polish and Czech governments-in-exile told Jewish leaders that they would in fact prevent the reintegration of masses of Jewish refugees after the war.[24] Jewish leaders believed that this postwar effort to prevent Jewish reintegration would take place at the same time that Eastern Europe states would expel Germans and other minorities in postwar Europe and would be part of a new ethnic reordering in postwar Eastern Europe. As Zionist leader Yitzhak Gruenbaum observed in January 1942, "World leaders have all recognized that the Jewish question has become the question of the refugee."[25] As Europe emerged from the rubble, declared the authors of the wartime study *The Jewish Refugee*, Jewish leaders would be faced with an enormous task: turning millions of floating Jews "from refugees to builders of a Jewish future."[26] In her 1943 essay "We Refugees," Hannah Arendt analyzed the social experience of the Jewish refugee and observed how the gaze of the refugee is turned only toward the future: "Even among ourselves we do not speak about this past. Instead, we have found our own way of mastering an uncertain future. Since everybody plans and wishes and hopes, so do we.... We leave the earth with all its uncertainties behind, and we cast our eyes up to the sky."[27]

Although Jewish leaders agreed on the scale of the postwar Jewish refugee problem, they were sharply divided about the solution. During the 1920s, a widespread consensus emerged among Jewish leaders and thinkers that the Jewish masses in Eastern Europe would develop in two national centers: first, as a protected minority community in Eastern Europe and, second, as a state-in-the-making in Palestine. The Yishuv in Palestine was thus to develop alongside, rather than instead of, the major center of Jewish life in Eastern Europe. However, after the outbreak of war, this consensus began to unravel as Jewish leaders debated whether Jews would have a future in Eastern Europe at all after the war.

A group of primarily Eastern European Jewish leaders and thinkers who were active in promoting the vision of minority rights between the wars insisted that there was no other solution but to reintegrate the vast majority of Jewish refugees into their prewar homes after the war and to provide them with new and extensive guarantees for equality and minority rights.[28] Even as they recognized that a great number of Jews would seek to immigrate to Palestine, they envisioned a postwar world remarkably similar to the one they dreamed about in 1919 but built on a firmer and more lasting foundation. These leaders thus sought to counter the plans of the Polish and Czech governments-in-exile to prevent the postwar reintegration of Jews by applying public and diplomatic pressure on these governments through British and American intervention. As Jacob Robinson, head of the Institute of Jewish Affairs, later reminisced, "Our focus [early in the war] was on minority protection in a new world order that would basically follow the same pattern—but with greater preparation—that emerged in Versailles."[29]

Zionist leaders promoted a radically different vision. They argued that Jewish life in Eastern Europe had been irrecoverably shattered. Given that Eastern European states had planned to expel millions of minorities after the war, they argued, there was no basis on which to expect a return to a system of minority protection in postwar Europe. The only solution to the large-scale postwar Jewish refugee problem lay in the mass immigration of millions of Jews from Eastern Europe to Palestine within a few short years after the war. This Jewish population transfer would take place alongside other population transfers in postwar Europe and would lead to the establishment of a Jewish majority in Palestine larger than Zionist leaders had ever before anticipated. Although the Great Powers sidelined the problem of Jewish refugees from Nazi Germany in the 1930s, Zionist leaders argued that they would be forced to find an immigration solution for a refugee problem that they expected to be eight times as large. At the May 1942 Biltmore Conference in New York, the Zionist leadership publicly laid out its postwar program, calling for "Palestine to be established as a Jewish Commonwealth integrated into the structure of the new democratic world."[30] The Biltmore program marked the first moment in which the Zionist leadership publicly called for the establishment of a majority Jewish state in the entire territory of the British mandate. During the 1930s such a vision seemed preposterous. Jews at no point constituted more than 30% of the population of Mandatory Palestine, and even under conditions of favorable British immigration policy, the Yishuv would require several decades of Jewish immigration to offset the overwhelming Arab demographic majority in Palestine.

* * *

Beginning in late 1942, however, as news of the extermination of Jews had begun to reach the Allied capitals, many Jewish leaders started to realize that they should prepare for a radically different Jewish postwar than they had initially expected. Jewish leaders grappled with a series of grave new questions. Would enough Jews survive the war to justify new demands for minority rights or for the establishment of a Jewish majority state in Palestine? Jewish leaders and thinkers grappled with the Holocaust not just as a collective catastrophe or as a question of rescue but also as a geopolitical question with wide ramifications for the Jewish future.

The debate over the implications of the mass murder of European Jewry on the Jewish future started as soon as Jewish leaders recognized that a Nazi mass extermination plan was underway. In August 1942 Richard Lichtheim, head of the Jewish Agency office in Geneva, concluded that the Nazis were carrying out a systematic killing operation. In a report he sent to Zionist leaders just a month later, Lichtheim argued that, in light of the events in Europe, the Zionist movement should abandon the Biltmore program it had adopted just a few months earlier. After the war, Lichtheim argued, there would not be millions of Jewish refugees in need of emigration, but most likely no more than half a million to a million Jewish survivors. Such a small number of Jews could easily be reintegrated into their former homes. Moreover, such a small number of survivors would not suffice for the establishment of a Jewish majority in Palestine. Zionism, Lichtheim declared, "is finished. . . . Let us stop talking of Palestine as 'the solution of the Jewish problem.' . . . It is now too late."[31]

Ben-Gurion and Weizmann shared Lichtheim's analysis that the destruction of European Jewry might bring about the end of the Zionist movement. In an October 1942 speech, Ben-Gurion observed that it was possible that every single Jew would be exterminated before the end of the war, in which case "there will be no *Aliyah*, and our future here will be like the future of Yemenite Jews or the Assyrians of Iraq or that of Jews in Germany before the rise of Hitler."[32] Weizmann lamented in an April 1944 letter that, when the facts about the scale of the extermination become widely known, "they will speak for themselves. And any demand of ours based on the imperative necessity of transferring large number of Jews speedily to Palestine will then fall off the ground."[33] Still, both Ben-Gurion and Weizmann remained committed to the Biltmore program throughout the war, hoping that they could still establish a Jewish majority in Palestine by culling enough Jewish survivors from Eastern Europe alongside Jewish immigrants from North African and Muslim countries and the United States. Both Weizmann and Ben-Gurion also increasingly considered the expulsion of a large segment of the Arab population as a method for the establishment of a Jewish majority in Palestine.

Reports on the murder of Jews also deeply preoccupied Jewish supporters of minority rights. In June 1943 Robinson sent a memo to the leadership of the World Jewish Congress, arguing that they should abandon the vision of minority rights after the war.[34] Several studies carried out by the Institute of Jewish Affairs in 1943 painted a grim picture of Jewish life in postwar Europe. In August the Institute published a widely discussed report according to which 3 million Jews had already been murdered in Europe.[35] Moreover, Robinson argued, large-scale wartime deportations of ethnic groups by the Nazis and other Axis powers, as well as Allied plans for the expulsion of Germans after the war, would create a new ethnic landscape in Europe in which Jews, in some countries, would remain the only sizable minority after the war. Under such conditions, Robinson insisted, it would be implausible to expect that the Allies would enforce new minority rights guarantees. Similarly, sociologist Jacob Lestschinsky argued in a series of essays that there could be no future for Jews as a minority community in Eastern Europe because the Jewish economy had been irreparably shattered. In Poland, for example, the local population had taken many positions previously occupied by middle-class Jews. Moreover, the Jewish interwar economy had been significantly based on inter-Jewish commerce and commerce with other minorities, such as Germans and Ukrainians, but the Jewish population had been depleted and the Polish government intended to expel the Germans after the war.[36] "One thing is clear and that is the most important thing for us," Lestschinsky observed, "the minority question had disappeared from politics. It had almost vanished from the minds of political thinkers and planners."[37] Lestschinsky pondered the implications of the genocide on the Jewish future in a subsequent essay: "If Jewish life is completely destroyed ... and we must build everything anew, then we must ask—where and how? If we are to be reborn again as a group, a collective, then history says the change will have to be radical."[38]

Many Jewish leaders rejected these conclusions. Goldman decried the call to abandon minority rights as a fringe right-wing Zionist position.[39] During 1944 and 1945, several of Robinson's colleagues in fact published new proposals for the restoration of an international system of minority protection after the war. The most famous of these was published by Polish Jewish lawyer Raphael Lemkin. In his book *Axis Rule in Occupied Europe*, Lemkin coined the term *genocide* as both a descriptive legal term for categorizing the Nazi crimes of the physical, economic, social, and cultural destruction of national groups and a prescriptive legal category that should shape the future of international law for the protection of minorities.[40] Lemkin's study drew extensively on the publications of the Institute of Jewish Affairs, and Lemkin in fact informed Robinson in 1946 the he had "been the great inspiration for [the coinage of the term] genocide."[41]

Jewish leaders remained committed to minority rights in part because, even as they learned about the extermination of Jews, they were divided over its magnitude. In the final years of the war, it was a figure in the realm of 3–4 million (the figure published by the Institute of Jewish Affairs)—rather than 6 million—that served as the basis for Jewish thinking on the postwar order. This figure allowed for imaging of a future for minority rights. Moreover, after two years of advocacy against Polish and Czech plans to prevent the reintegration of parts of their Jewish population after the war, beginning in mid-1941 Jewish leaders were registering some success. The Polish government-in-exile issued a series of declarations on Jewish equality after the war, and the Czech government-in-exile agreed to add a Jewish national member to its national council. For Jewish leaders this was a sign that they could secure lasting guarantees for Jewish rights in postwar Europe.

It was only after the end of the war that Jewish leaders entirely abandoned their early wartime visions for the postwar Jewish world. By 1945 Jewish leaders had become aware of the full magnitude of the catastrophe. Across Eastern Europe Jewish survivors faced dire economic straits, and governments took few measures to restore their economic positions. A series of pogroms in Poland, culminating in the June 1946 Kielce pogrom, prompted tens of thousands of Jews to flee the country. With Eastern European states under Soviet influence—and the chilling of the Cold War in the air—it seemed as though there was little prospect for new guarantees for international oversight over the treatment of minorities. In addition, a series of Allied-supported large-scale population transfers of millions of minorities, primarily ethnic Germans, from Poland, Czechoslovakia, Hungary, and Yugoslavia, transformed Eastern European states into ethnically homogeneous polities. As a representative of the American Jewish Committee in Europe observed in 1946, postwar Europe was marked by "mass expulsions, population exchanges, and boundary alterations.... Millions of Germans in Poland and Czechoslovakia had been expelled."[42]

In Palestine, too, the wartime dream of a Jewish state seemed a matter of the past. During the war, Zionist leaders planned for a Jewish refugee problem on the scale of millions, but the postwar Jewish refugee problem turned out to be one of the smallest refugee problems in postwar Europe. And rather than preventing the reintegration of Jews after the war, as Zionist leaders believed would be the case, the new regimes across Eastern

Europe quickly extended citizenship and equality to their Jewish populations. By the summer of 1946 the problem of stateless Jews in Eastern Europe had become tantamount in international discussions to the fate of some 250,000 Jews who lingered in displaced persons camps in Germany and Austria, a number far smaller than the German Jewish refugee problem in the 1930s. With the Jewish population in Mandatory Palestine numbering 600,000–650,000 and 2 million Palestinian Arabs, there was no scenario in which the math added up for the establishment of a Jewish majority in the entire territory. Moreover, in 1945 the British government reaffirmed its commitment to the 1939 White Paper: Palestine was to become an Arab state with a Jewish minority. The US government also opposed Jewish statehood, pushing for the emigration of 100,000 Jews to Palestine as a humanitarian gesture. An armed Jewish campaign in Palestine against the British authorities was severely repressed by the British in the summer of 1946, with the arrest of thousands of Yishuv officials and with several prominent Yishuv leaders—among them Ben-Gurion—fleeing Palestine to Europe.

Two events in the summer of 1946 symbolically marked the end of the vision of the postwar as a moment of political redemption for the Jews. The first was the 1946 Paris Conference. The Paris Conference was convened by the Allied victors to settle the terms of peace with Nazi Germany's wartime European allies—Hungary, Rumania, Bulgaria, and Italy—home to over 700,000 Jewish survivors. Representatives of nine Jewish organizations arrived in Paris in early July, hoping to repeat the success of Jewish leaders at the 1919 Paris Peace Conference. This was the moment Jewish leaders had prepared for throughout the war, and they laid out demands for new minority rights, human rights guarantees, and financial reparations. Yet, unlike in 1919, in 1946 none of the demands of Jewish leaders were accepted, or even officially discussed, by the Allies. The Jewish question—which since the nineteenth century had been a key diplomatic and political question in Europe—was absent from the conference agenda. Robinson lamented that none of the states at the conference had even taken "the slightest note" of the various memoranda submitted by Jewish groups. The word *Jew*, he observed, had become taboo at the conference.[43] "The special sufferings of the Jewish people at the hands of Hitler, their exposed position as a minority in each of the European countries are well-known," noted a Jewish delegate in his report on the conference, "but it is not apparent that any nation represented in Paris is ready to take diplomatic action . . . to protect the Jews who will continue to remain in Europe."[44] Flaiszer (Talmon) attended the conference as a representative of the Board of Deputies of British Jews. In a report he wrote in late 1946, he summarized the mood of humiliation among Jewish representatives in Paris and their failure to secure any meaningful guarantees for Jewish rights in Europe. "The morality of the world," he declared, "had greatly declined from 1919 to 1946."[45]

At the same time as Jewish representatives in Paris witnessed the vision of a future for Jewish collective rights in Eastern Europe vanish, the executive committee of the Jewish Agency for Palestine met just a few miles away and decided to bury the Biltmore program without officially repudiating it. In July 1946 the Zionist leadership saw no way out of its political crisis and feared that US president Truman would soon throw his support behind the Morrison-Grady plan—a British plan for limited Jewish provincial autonomy alongside a larger Arab autonomy in a federated Palestine under British control. Moreover, Zionist leaders recognized that, unless they managed to facilitate the immigration of Jewish displaced persons imminently to Palestine, these refugees would find other avenues for immigration. As Ben-Gurion observed toward the end of the war, there is a factor of "fateful significance for the future of Zionism. It is the factor of time." If the small remnant of European Jewry were not transferred to Palestine immediately, they might begin to find other avenues for immigration and destinations for resettlement.[46]

Sharing this pessimistic outlook, Goldman laid out a radical compromise proposal that was eventually adopted in the meeting. The Zionist movement would negotiate with the British and American governments on the basis of the Morrison-Grady scheme, with the goal of achieving control over immigration to Palestine and expanding the allotted Jewish territory. This would serve as a first step toward a Jewish state in a future partitioned Palestine. This decision reflected the recognition that, as Goldman concluded in the meeting, the dream of establishing a Jewish state in the whole of Palestine, as the Biltmore program called for, was "no realistic policy, because we have no Jewish majority." Extensive autonomy within a federated or partitioned Palestine as a precursor for a state was the most the Zionist movement could achieve in the new postwar realities.[47] In 1946 the Zionist leadership thus adopted a new post-Holocaust vision of Jewish statehood: a small state in a partitioned Palestine. This plan, in turn, was never adopted. A Jewish state emerged almost abruptly, after the British simply left Palestine and Jews won the ensuing war with Palestinian Arabs and Arab armies. It was not the Jewish majority state that Zionists planned for. If not for the flight and expulsion of 750,000 Palestinian refugees, Jews would have been a minority even in a small, partitioned Palestine.

* * *

The concept of the Jewish postwar emerged with the outbreak of war as a vision of political redemption. As news of the extermination of Jews reached the Allied capitals during and in the immediate aftermath of the war, the Jewish postwar turned into the recognition that the Eastern European Jewish center had vanished and that the political projects that were designed to ensure Jewish security and legal equality in the modern period had failed. Still, although the Holocaust shattered the redemptive vision of the Jewish postwar, it is remarkable that within a few short years after the war it became the basis of new narratives of the postwar as an era of political redemption for the Jews. In this sense the Jewish postwar is unique among the many European postwars in how quickly the crisis of the war years and its aftermath was succeeded by narratives of political triumphs. The way the Jewish postwar had been conceptualized in Jewish public thinking post-1948 is thus far more similar to the redemptive vision of 1939–1943 than to the vision of an unprecedented crisis of 1944–1947.

The most prominent example of this is the establishment of the State of Israel in 1948. As we have seen, the Holocaust almost destroyed the prospects for Zionism. When the State of Israel emerged in 1948, the Jewish population in Palestine was not significantly larger than it had been in 1939, and Jews still remained an overwhelming minority throughout the territory of the former British Mandate. Nonetheless, the war and the Holocaust soon became the basis of a redemptive narrative that explained the origins of the State of Israel as a consequence of the catastrophe. The Holocaust was said to have proven the moral necessity for a Jewish state, which in turn also brought about its actual historical creation. The Israeli national calendar is centered around this narrative, exemplified in the concept of "From the Holocaust to National Rebirth" (Hebrew, *Mi-sho'ah le-tekumah*), in which Holocaust Remembrance Day (Yom HaShoah) is followed by the Memorial Day for the Fallen Soldiers (Yom HaZikaron), which is immediately followed by Independence Day (Yom Ha'atzmaut). The traditional religious period known as *sefirat ha-omer* (counting of the *omer*), which marks the seven weeks between the Exodus from Egypt celebrated at Passover and the revelation at Sinai celebrated on Shavuot, shapes a public memory in which persecution and redemption are intertwined events.

There is also another, much less discussed way in which the Holocaust serves as the basis of a narrative of the postwar as a moment of Jewish political redemption. The post-1945 period ushered in an unprecedented era of Jewish legal equality, social integration, and physical security throughout the world, a period in which religious anti-Jewish hatred and racial antisemitism were considered beyond the pale across Western culture and in which attitudes toward Jews in the public space were increasingly shaped by a philosemitic culture that viewed Jews as the face of humanity rather than as a religious and political threat to the possibility of a common humanity and universalism.[48] In a series of essays written in 1947 and 1948, Baron insisted that the most significant development of Jewish life in the postwar period was in fact the emergence of a new era of Jewish legal equality and physical security as well as new prospects for successful Jewish social integration throughout the world. "Only now, in these years after World War II," Baron observed in these essays, "we perceive the first glimmerings of a universal Jewish emancipation." This development, Baron argued, was a result of the Holocaust. After Hitler's assault on the Jews, it became clear that any attack on Jewish rights was an attack on civilization as a whole, a threat to both democratic life and political stability throughout the world. Baron lamented the fact that Jews seemed unaware of the gravity of this postwar historical development, either because they "still are under the impact of the great tragedy" or because their gaze is turned exclusively to events in Palestine. "There is a deep reason for the absence of elation among Jews of all lands with the present, almost millennial achievement of universal Jewish emancipation. Had constitutional equality [for Jews] been proclaimed throughout the world only half a century ago," Baron dramatically argued, "many Jews would have [labeled] it as almost the ushering in of the messianic era." He continued, "Today, however, the widespread mood of despondency is not lessened by this apparent realization of a century-old dream." And he declared, "The prediction seems... not too rash that future historians may well consider the present post-war period as the incipient stage of a truly world-wide Jewish equality."[49] Baron wrote his essay with American Jewry in mind, reflecting his belief that the center of Jewish life after the war would develop in America, which by 1948 boasted a Jewish population of roughly 5 million compared to around 700,000 in Palestine. Baron argued that it was legal discrimination in Eastern Europe and American Jewry's fight for their rights that preserved Jewish collective identity in the past. He feared that Jewish collective identity, particularly in America, would dissipate without a common cause. The challenge Jews would face in the postwar period, Baron argued in these essays, was how to preserve Jewish collectivity under conditions of worldwide equality.

It is striking that Baron's views have had so little resonance on Jewish public perceptions of the postwar period. Baron's views are echoed in David Sorkin's recent book *Jewish Emancipation: A History Across Five Centuries*. Sorkin argues that emancipation was "the principal event" of modern Jewish history. The Holocaust and the establishment of the State of Israel, he writes, have "obstructed our field of visions and overwhelmed our cognitive capacities." They were invariably construed as "the culmination of Jewish history" or as evidence for the failure of Jewish emancipation. But as Baron convincingly argued, the postwar period marked not the failure but the triumph of Jewish emancipation.[50]

Notes

1 Tony Judt, *Postwar: A History of Europe Since 1945* (New York: Penguin, 2005).

2 Norman Naimark, "The Persistence of 'the Postwar': Germany and Poland," in *Histories of the Aftermath: The Legacies of the Second World War in Europe*, ed. Frank Biess and Robert G. Moller (New York: Berghahn, 2010), 14.

3 There remains the question of when exactly the war began for Jews. In a major 1943 publication, the Institute of Jewish Affairs suggested that the war on Jews had started in 1933. See Boris Schub, ed., *Hitler's Ten-Year War on the Jews* (New York: Institute of Jewish Affairs of the World Jewish Congress, 1943).

4 For scholarship on postwar planning in the United States and Britain, see, for example, Or Rosenboim, *The Emergence of Globalism: Visions of World Order*

in Britain and the United States, 1939–1950 (Princeton, NJ: Princeton University Press, 2016); Stephen A. Wertheim, *Tomorrow, the World: The Birth of US Global Supremacy* (Cambridge, MA: Harvard University Press, 2020); and Christopher D. O'Sullivan, *Sumner Welles, Postwar Planning, and the Quest for a New World Order, 1937–1943* (New York: Columbia University Press, 2002). For an analysis of British and American competing postwar visions for the Middle East, see Aiyaz Husain, *Mapping the End of Empire: American and British Strategic Visions in the Postwar World* (Cambridge, MA: Harvard University Press, 2014).

5 Joseph Tenenbaum, "The Great Emergency," 1942, YIVO Archives, Joseph L. Tenenbaum Papers, RG 283, box 1, folder 1.
6 Nahum Goldman, "Post-War Problems," *Congress Weekly* 8, no. 39 (28 November 1941): 5–7. Goldman's essay was first delivered as an address at the Inter-American Jewish Conference in November 1941.
7 S. Goralik, "When One Raises the Tip of the Veil of the Future," *Haaretz* (21 February 1941) (Hebrew).
8 David Ben-Gurion, "Lecture," 8 September 1939, Ben-Gurion University of the Negev, Ben-Gurion Archives and Library, item 87879.
9 "Dubnow Urges Jews to Learn from Last War in Fighting for Rights," *Jewish Telegraphic Agency* (5 May 1940). See also "The Future of European Jewry: Professor Dubnow's Views, Lessons from 1920," *Jewish Chronicle* (24 May 1940).
10 Simon Dubnow, "Inter arma (1940): Thoughts by a Jewish Historian About the Goals of War and Peace," *Oyfn sheydveg* 3, YIVO Archives, Tcherikower Collection, RG 80–89, folder 12–83. I am using Joshua Karlip's translation. For the examination of Dubnow's article and the journal *Oyfn sheydveg* (At the Crossroads), see Joshua Karlip, "At the Crossroads Between War and Genocide: A Reassessment of Jewish Ideology in 1940," *Jewish Social Studies* 11, no. 2 (2005): 170–201.
11 For an examination of the discourse about the perceived imminent extinction of the Jewish collective in the 1930s, see Bernard Wasserstein, *On the Eve: The Jews of Europe Before the Second World War* (New York: Simon & Schuster, 2012), 8–28. See also Ezra Mendelsohn, *The Jews of East Central Europe Between the World Wars* (Bloomington: Indiana University Press, 1983).
12 Cited in Wasserstein, *On the Eve*, 10.
13 Salo W. Baron, *A Social and Religious History of the Jews* (New York: Columbia University Press, 1937), 364–65.

14 Simon Dubnow, "What Should We Do in Haman's Time?" (letter to the editors of *Oyfn sheydveg*, 1939), republished in Simon Dubnow, *Nationalism and History: Essays on the Old and New Judaism* (Philadelphia: Jewish Publication Society of America, 1958), 354–59.

15 Wasserstein, *On the Eve*, 13.

16 Chaim Weizmann to Sir John Schukburgh, 31 December 1937, in Chaim Weizmann, *The Letters and Papers of Chaim Weizmann*, series A, ed. Leonard Stein (Piscataway, NJ: Transaction, 1975), 18: 281; and Chaim Weizmann to Sir Osmond d'Avigdor-Goldsmid, 31 December 1937, in Weizmann, *Letters and Papers*, 18: 279.

17 David Ben-Gurion, "Our Role in This Moment," lecture delivered at the fourth convention of Mapai, 7 May 1938, Ben-Gurion University of the Negev, Ben-Gurion Archives and Library, item 87969.

18 "The objective of His Majesty's Government is the establishment within 10 years of an independent Palestine State. . . . Jewish immigration during the next five years will be at a rate which, if economic absorptive capacity permits, will bring the Jewish population up to approximately one third of the total population of the country. . . . After the period of five years, no further Jewish immigration will be permitted unless the Arabs of Palestine are prepared to acquiesce in it." British White Paper of 1939, avalon.law.yale.edu/20th_century/brwh1939.asp (accessed 11 May 2023).

19 This terminology draws of course on Yerushalmi. See Yosef Hayim Yerushalmi, *Zakhor: Jewish History and Jewish Memory* (Seattle: University of Washington Press, 1982).

20 "A Painful Conversation: An Account of Our Generation," *Niv ha-student* (February and May 1939), republished in Jacob Talmon, *The Riddle of the Present and the Cunning of History* (Jerusalem: Bialik Institute, 2000), 377–90 (Hebrew). For a biographical overview of Talmon's life, see Arie Dubnov, "Priest or Jester? Jacob L. Talmon (1916–1980) on History and Intellectual Engagement," *History of European Ideas* 34, no. 2 (2008): 133–45.

21 Chaim Weizmann, "Speech at Extraordinary Zionist Conference of the American Emergency Committee for Zionist Affairs," 9 May 1942, Biltmore Conference Stenographic Protocol, Central Zionist Archive (CZA), Jerusalem.

22 Salo Baron, "Reflections on the Future of the Jews of Europe," *Contemporary Jewish Record* 3, no. 4 (1940): 362. This address was first delivered to the joint session of the National Conference of Jewish Social Welfare, Pittsburgh, 25 May 1940.

23 Weizmann, "Speech at Extraordinary Zionist Conference."
24 The early wartime discussions over the plans of the Polish and Czech governments-in-exile to prevent the reintegration of masses of Jews after the war are explored in detail in Gil Rubin, "The Future of the Jews: Planning for the Postwar Jewish World, 1939–1946," PhD diss., Columbia University, 2017, pp. 41–86.
25 Meeting of the Zionist Executive, Protocol, Central Zionist Archive, 5 January 1942.
26 Cited in Arieh Tartakower and Kurt Grossman, *The Jewish Refugee* (New York: Institute of Jewish Affairs, 1944), 524. The book was originally written in 1942.
27 Hannah Arendt, "We Refugees," *Menorah Journal* 31 (1943): 66–77, reprinted in Hannah Arendt, *The Jewish Writings*, ed. Jerome Kohn and Ron H. Feldman (New York: Schocken Books, 2007), 265.
28 On this milieu of Eastern European Jewish internationalists, see James Loeffler, *Rooted Cosmopolitans: Jews and Human Rights in the Twentieth Century* (New Haven, CT: Yale University Press, 2018).
29 Cited in Daniel Greenberg, "Jacob Robinson as a Person: The Human Side of One of the Great Figures of the 20th Century," paper presented at the Life, Work, and Times of Jacob Robinson Conference, Kaunas, Lithuania, 22 October 2007. I thank Philipp Graf for sharing these materials with me.
30 "Zionist Congresses: The Biltmore Conference (May 6–11, 1942)," www.jewishvirtuallibrary.org/the-biltmore-conference-1942 (accessed 11 May 2023).
31 Richard Lichtheim to Nahum Goldman, 9 September 1942, Ben-Gurion University of the Negev, Ben-Gurion Archives and Library, item 204842.
32 Protocol of the Fifth Convention of Mapai in Kfar Vitkin, 27 October 1942, Ben-Gurion University of the Negev, Ben-Gurion Archives and Library, item 5827.
33 Chaim Weizmann to Meyer W. Weisgal, 13 April 1944, in Weizmann, *Letters and Papers*, 21: 165–71.
34 Jacob Robinson, "Minority Rights as Part of Our Peace Program: Notes Submitted to the Peace Aims Planning Committee," 29 June 1943, World Jewish Congress Records, American Jewish Archives, Cincinnati, C118 8 (records from the World Jewish Congress were accessed as copies at the United States Holocaust Memorial Museum Archive).
35 Institute of Jewish Affairs, *Hitler's Ten-Year War on the Jews* (New York: Institute of Jewish Affairs, 1943).
36 Jacob Lestschinsky, "How Will Jews Live in Europe," *Davar* (26 September 1944) (Hebrew).

37 Jacob Lestschinsky, "Jews in the Coming Europe," *Idisher kempfer* (14 March 1941), 4–6 (Yiddish).
38 Jacob Lestschinsky, "The *Shoah* of European Jewry," *Davar* (15 January 1943) (Hebrew).
39 Minutes of the World Jewish Congress Peace Planning Committee Meeting, 1943, World Jewish Congress Records, C118 8.
40 Raphael Lemkin, *Axis Rule in Occupied Europe: Laws of Occupation, Analysis of Government, Proposals for Redress* (Washington, DC: Carnegie Endowment for International Peace, 1944).
41 Memorandum and letter by Raphael Lemkin to Jacob Robinson, 28 August 1946, World Jewish Congress Record, C14 21. For a recent examination of Lemkin in the context of interwar Eastern European Jewish minority politics, see James Loeffler, "Becoming Cleopatra: The Forgotten Zionism of Raphael Lemkin," *Journal of Genocide Research* 19, no. 3 (2017), 340–60.
42 Zacharia Schuster, *The Paris Peace Conference* (New York: American Jewish Committee Institute on Peace and Postwar Problems, 1947), 4.
43 Jacob Robinson, "Amendments Submitted by the Delegation to the Paris Conference," 30 August 1946, World Jewish Congress Records, C98 26.
44 Saul Hays, "Jewish Representation at the Peace Conference in Paris," 5 December 1946, World Jewish Congress Records, C99 2, p. 2.
45 Jacob Flaiszer, "The Jewish Question in the 1946 Paris Peace Conference," *Mezuda* 5, no. 6 (1947–1948): 166 (Hebrew). For more on Jewish representatives at the 1946 Paris Conference, see Nathan Kurz, *Jewish Internationalism and Human Rights After the Holocaust* (Cambridge, UK: Cambridge University Press, 2020), 19–38.
46 David Ben-Gurion, "The Time Factor in Zionism," speech before the Fourth Annual Wartime Zionist Conference in Tel Aviv, 28 December 1944; reprinted in *Davar* (1 January 1945).
47 "Minutes of the Meeting of the Executive of the Jewish Agency, Paris, Friday, August 2, 1946," Ben-Gurion Papers, item 228880; and address of Dr. Nahum Goldman before the Executive of the Jewish Agency, Paris, France, 3 August 1946, Ben-Gurion University of the Negev, Ben-Gurion Archives and Library, item 228883. See also Michael J. Cohen, *Palestine and the Great Powers, 1945–1948* (Princeton, NJ: Princeton University Press, 1982), 145.
48 On postwar philosemitism, see Malachi Hacohen, *Jacob and Esau: Jewish European History Between Nation and Empire* (Cambridge, UK: Cambridge University Press, 2019), 584–89; and Daniel Cohen, "Good Jews:

Philosemitism in Post-Holocaust Europe," in *SIMON: Shoah: Intervention, Methods, Documentation* 7, no. 3 (2020): 118–27.

49 There are several drafts of the essays in which Baron makes this argument, and it is not clear which one he considered the final version. See, for example, "Final Stages of Jewish Emancipation," "The Crisis of Emancipation," "The Delayed Crisis of Emancipation," and "The World Looks to America," Salo W. Baron Papers, Stanford University Libraries, Department of Special Collections and University Archives, M0580, Box 412.

50 See David Sorkin, *Jewish Emancipation: A History Across Five Centuries* (Princeton, NJ: Princeton University Press, 2019), 2.

12

Temporalities of Postwar Jewish Emigration

Rebekah Klein-Pejšová

Jewish survivors sought not only to protect their bare right to exist in the aftermath of World War II but also to find an adequately safe environment in which to rebuild their shattered worlds. They sought geographies of protection, paths out of grotesquely familiar landscapes of dehumanization. The Israeli Sinologist Irene Eber writes of her own experience as a displaced person (DP) in the United States occupation zone in Germany as "returning to life, relearning to make choices, confronting the empty reality of [one's] new existence, trusting other human beings, and becoming trustworthy [of oneself]."[1] Further, she writes about "learning to live again as a human being among other human beings, all of them strangers."[2] Eber captures a process of restoring, or rehabilitating, one's self and one's personhood in displacement through decision making and interactions with others in her work on what she calls learning to live again in human society after the war. A preponderance of postwar decision making among Jewish survivors centered on movement. They pondered whether to rebuild their lives in their countries of origin or whether, how, and when to emigrate.

Would-be émigrés confronted the capricious temporality of emigration bureaucracy at every step. When would they be able to exit one sovereign state and enter another, and when would they gain authorization for transit across the territories in between? What sort of documentation would they need to cross the necessary borders? Which country would be first to approve a visa? How soon would it be possible to set out? Their ability to obtain exit visas was determined by the destination countries' reluctant immigration policies and by diplomatic connections between their countries of origin or of sojourn and the receiving countries. They waited to be able to submit their paperwork—in a form the relevant authorities deemed acceptable—and followed up on the status of their cases like clockwork. They waited for their visas to come through, in the right order, and ached for the ability to make good on them before they expired. Using the hard-won transit visas while they remained valid depended on the receiving country's immigration policies, their ability to secure transportation, and a travel ticket stamped with a viable departure date. They gathered at embarkation sites and waited anxiously for the moment when they might board their designated vessel.

Meanwhile, Jewish survivors who had made their way to the DP camps experienced time in excruciating parcels of waiting. More than 250,000 Jewish survivors sojourned in the DP camps administered by the Allied authorities and the United Nations Relief and Rehabilitation Administration (UNRRA) in Germany, Austria, and Italy between 1945 and 1952.[3] In these way stations to an undefined future destination over which they could exert minimal influence, they waited for aid packages of food and clothing, educational programming, vocational training (and the materials necessary to undertake it), for meals, for cigarette distribution, for winter to be over. All waited for news and information, especially concerning the fate of family and friends. Inescapable waiting permeates the material relating to the lives of Jewish survivors in the DP camps of postwar Germany, Austria, Italy, and elsewhere. The stark protractedness of the camps sank into their bones. It affected their morale, their moods, and their ability to cope with their daily existence.

The DP camp became a place of temporal struggle, where Jewish survivors strove to regain, or gain, control over their lives. My consideration of the relationship between the temporal forces, both external and internal to the DP camp regime, acting on Jewish DPs and their ability to exert control over their own time, and thus over their personal autonomy, is indebted to anthropologist Katherine Verdery's work on Ceaușescu's Romania. Verdery defines and draws out the implications of "the ways in which the Romanian state seized time from the purposes many Romanians wished to pursue," especially those connected with unbearable austerity policies and coerced leadership veneration.[4] Her work helps us to better understand the link between how one experiences time and one's personhood, bound up with one's decision-making ability. Fluctuations in immigration policy, quotas, the restrictive elements built into those policies, and so on heightened the uncertain and provisional nature of the DP camp and so too the struggle with time and with regaining one's sense of self.

The idea of "lived time," as used by historian Guy Miron in his work on how German Jews experienced their removal from collective "synchronized time" under the Nazi regime, is also valuable for examining the continued experience of Jews' passive waiting in the DP camps.[5] The psychiatrist Eugène Minkowski conceived of the term *lived time* in the 1930s to distinguish between activity and expectation, or between controlling and shaping events, and "[awaiting] passively a future dictated by external forces more powerful than he."[6] In her study of the intertwined relations between Jews, Germans, and Americans in the American-occupied zone, historian Atina Grossmann writes that Jewish survivors in the DP camps in Germany appeared in publicity and fund-raising films produced by DPs and American Jewish aid organizations "restlessly walking up and down the streets of DP camps, exchanging rumors, devouring newspapers, making shady deals, and everywhere pushing baby carriages, holding toddlers by the hand, 'waiting, waiting, waiting,' for the world to take notice."[7] DPs filled their hours with activities that underscored the imposed passivity of their lived time.

When we forget the geographic extent of the scattered postwar Jewish Diaspora by centering our attention on the mass migration to the United States and Israel, we diminish our understanding of Jews as individuals whose overall emigration experience was shaped by temporality. Expanding our imagination of postwar Jewish geography draws in the story of personal rehabilitation and reclaiming of personhood behind the challenges, opportunities, and arduous decisions embedded in the paths of emigration as well as the choices many Jews made to remain in their countries of origin and rebuild their lives there. Those paths of emigration, particularly before the transformations in immigration possibilities to the United States and Israel in 1948, created a new far-flung, widely dispersed postwar global Jewish diaspora.

Even in 1947 the United States still clung to a policy put in place in 1924 by the Johnson-Reed Act, including the Asian Exclusion Act and the National Origins Act, which restricted the number of immigrants by country of origin to 2% of the number for that group in the United States in 1890. However, President Truman's 1945 directive gave priority to DPs, which allowed 16,000 Jewish DPs to enter the United States. In the following year the United States passed the limited 1948 Displaced Persons Act, which allowed in 200,000 DPs, although only those who had acquired official DP status before 22 December 1945 were eligible. A reform to that law passed in 1950 allowed in additional DPs who had acquired official status by 1 January 1949. The United Nations partition of Palestine on 29 November 1947 paved the way for the establishment of the State of Israel on 15 May 1948 and subsequent mass migration there. Nearly 140,000 Jewish survivors emigrated to the newly established State of Israel after May 1948. The United States approved immigration of 400,000 Jewish survivors between 1945 and 1952. Another 20,000 Jewish survivors gained entry in other destination countries around the world.[8]

In this chapter I investigate the experience of emigration for Jewish survivors whose paths led them into the prolonged uncertainty of the DP camp and then into far-flung dispersion, where they created a new postwar global Jewish diaspora. I seek to understand the paths of Jewish postwar displacement and dispersion against a global backdrop by tracing Jews' movement, with special attention to the forces of temporality at work on them. I uphold Rebecca Kobrin's assertion that it is crucial "to locate this profound population shift in the larger global context."[9] Jewish survivors who chose to migrate did so into an emerging postwar geopolitical order defined by Cold War divisions between a Soviet-dominated East and a United States–dominated West. Their mobility with relation to the state, the international community, and Jewish philanthropic organizations engaged in Jewish survivor support and resettlement was shaped by their citizenship status, nationality status, place of residence before the war and after with reference to wartime border changes, and, above all, the experience of persecution.

When the World Jewish Congress (WJC) met in Montreux, Switzerland, in July 1948, it largely measured Jewish survivors' progress toward self-rehabilitation, the main theme of its proceedings, through emigration. The WJC's Political Commission praised the efforts that Jewish DPs sojourning in the DP camps in Allied-occupied postwar Germany and Austria and in Italy and Cyprus had made toward that end.[10] Emigration, understood this way, was a means by which to retake control over one's life and fate, to reconstruct the narrative of one's existence after emerging from wartime persecution.

As such, it complemented the long-established view espoused by a broad range of political actors, humanitarian organizations, and Jews themselves that emigration represented the "solution" to social, economic, and demographic questions.[11] Postwar Jewish emigration was the latest wave of large-scale population movement in response to existential crisis. For a hundred years by the 1940s, Tara Zahra writes, 55–58 million Europeans and Eurasians had made the transatlantic migration to the Americas to seek answers to their fates. Further, millions of people migrated from India and China to Southeast Asia and islands in the Indian Ocean and South Pacific, and another 46–51 million left northeast Asia and Russia for Manchuria, Siberia, Central Asia, and Japan.[12] For Central Europeans coming to the United States, migration was not always a one-way street but often a strategy to work hard abroad for a few years in order to bring some good money back home and in that way pay off debts and improve one's economic position.[13]

The 2.5 million Jews from Eastern and Central Europe who chose transatlantic migration in response to dire conditions of economic distress and antisemitic discrimination arising from modern mass political movements between 1881 and 1924 largely sought geographies of security and opportunity.[14] It was not uncommon for them to break up long-distance overseas migration to the United States into smaller intermediary steps, heading first to larger cities and then across the Atlantic.[15] After World War I the terms of Jewish migration shifted as physical security took precedence over other concerns for the great majority of the world Jewish population.[16] The Habsburg, German, Russian, and Ottoman Empires had collapsed. A new state system emerged from the radically redrawn European map based on the principle of national self-determination and on territorially defined citizenship. The antisemitic politics and violence of this interwar reality, combined with the lingering experience of Jewish wartime dislocation, catalyzed Jewish migration largely for destinations in the Americas.[17]

The intensified persecution of the interwar years, followed by the policies and practices intended to destroy European Jewry during World War II, led to the cataclysmic conditions confronting Jewish migration choices in the war's aftermath. In making their decisions, they sought not only their physical security but the very right to exist. They sought their right to personhood in an unrelenting struggle with time.

Bulging Roads

The "emigration question" dominated discussion among Jewish survivors after the war in memoirs, testimonials, and fictional representations. For example, in Arnošt Lustig's novel *Dita Saxová*, the question of whether to stay in or leave one's country of origin, in this case Czechoslovakia, is woven into every aspect of this work of period literature, providing multiple layers of profound and tragic meaning to Dita's own heartbreaking story.[18] In 1946, as we learn from the records of the Budapest branch office of the Hebrew Immigrant Aid Society (HIAS), an American Jewish immigrant aid organization, the many Jewish survivors who had returned to Hungary determined that for them "emigration was an inevitable and existential necessity." Those who emigrated cut ties to their former country in order to immigrate anywhere else on earth. The Budapest HIAS office explained with despair that "this symptom is known [by] the name 'Black Alijah.'"[19] The term was intended to turn traditional meanings of *aliyah* upside down and inside-out. Not the idea of physical, altitudinal ascent to Jerusalem, neither the honor of being called up to bless and/or read from the Torah nor even emigration to the Land, "Black Aliyah" was meant to indicate a desperate exit from one's country of origin in a quest for a willing unknown destination. Although many Hungarian Jewish survivors opted to return home to Hungary as soon as they were able after liberation and although many chose to stay and rebuild their lives at home, their circumstances after arrival were often devastating. "The whole Jewish population of Hungary sank into utter distress," concluded the Budapest HIAS office; they had lost their financial assets, their apartments, furniture, utensils, clothing—they were destitute.[20] Return made clear just how much the Nazis and their helpers had destroyed.[21] It was an unbearable landscape of loss.

In March 1946 the Budapest HIAS office determined that two main groups of Jews wanted to leave Hungary for good: those who were old or infirm and wished to reunite with relatives abroad who would care for them;

and those who were young, had no relatives "whatsoever" abroad, but were able to work. The first group was in a good position to leave, and, according to HIAS, the Hungarian government aided in the procedure. Prospects for the second group were more uncertain, because the postwar Hungarian government saw their youth and ability to work as valuable for rebuilding the country.[22] For them, leaving Hungary would require obtaining a Hungarian emigration passport. Potential émigrés had to produce evidence that they possessed the relevant entry permits for their final destination countries before the Hungarian administration would grant them an emigration passport. This requirement was nearly impossible to fulfill. Before Hungary entered into the peace treaty in March 1946, only the United Kingdom and the United States maintained consulates on Hungarian territory.[23]

HIAS implemented the workarounds necessary to handle the visas and financial issues for the clients it took under its wing. The ability to work with HIAS, an organization with 62 years of experience and expertise by 1946, was a godsend for Jews who wanted to emigrate.[24] HIAS elaborated a workflow by which it procured an official statement from the necessary consulate declaring that the entry permit for that individual was available for them to pick up without delay; the emigrant would then use this letter to travel to another state where the relevant consulate was located and would then continue on their way to their destination. HIAS managed to gain a promise from the head of the Office for Hungarian Emigrants that he would cooperate with this complicated but workable procedure. HIAS helped would-be emigrants put together the documentation they would need for transit, as most people had lost all their papers during the war. In this way, HIAS handled the complication that the Allied Control Commission was responsible for issuing exit permits from Hungary before the peace of March 1947. Finally, HIAS organized how each journey would be financed. When a relative abroad was not able to sponsor the emigrant, HIAS would determine whether the emigrant really needed their funding. To avoid having funds paid out in-country in Hungarian forints, HIAS would provide the emigrant with an expense letter with their photo and signature, which they would present at all necessary offices along the journey.[25]

As the spaces of sojourn following the initial decision to emigrate, the DP camps in Germany, Austria, and Italy became the locus of high-order emigration calculus by late 1946, when roads in Czechoslovakia "bulged" with refugees heading toward them.[26] Czechoslovakia became the ultimate catalyst for the heightened number of refugees when it recognized the *Brihah*—the illegal emigration movement operated by local Jews in Central and Eastern Europe before the establishment of the State of Israel—whose operations had been blocked until March 1946. The Czechoslovakian government allowed *Brihah* to transport Jews across state territory with the proviso that no Jewish refugees remain in the country. The United States blocked further Jewish refugee influx into the DP camps in April 1947. At the time, US policy distinguished between Jewish DPs and Jewish "infiltrees"; the latter could enter Germany and Austria but not the DP camps themselves. The percentage of Jews in the DP population rose from 3.7% in September 1945 (18,361) to 25% in 1947 (122,313).[27]

The situation of Jewish DP camps and centers in the American occupation zones in Austria and Germany differed considerably with regard to local contexts, American refugee policy, and assistance provided by the American Jewish Joint Distribution Committee (the Joint). Germany, in broad strokes, seemed to be a "liberal haven" in contrast to conditions in Austria. Jewish survivors preferred to sojourn in Germany, as it was well-known and evident that Austria hosted them only with great reluctance.[28] We learn from the work of historian Susanne Rolinek that Austria was a more transitory environment than Germany overall, which, for example, saw a "daily mass migration" of 1,000 Jewish refugees from Austria to the American occupation zone in Germany between July 1946 and September 1946.[29] In her book *Jüdische Lebenswelten, 1945–1955: Flüchtlinge in der amerikanischen Zone Österreichs*, Rolinek analyzes the meaning and function of networks and social relations in the American occupation zone in Austria, with special attention to the *Brihah*.[30] In Germany the American military sought to cease this illegal movement of Jewish refugees, whereas in Austria the *Brihah* worked substantially with the Jewish Affairs Desk organized by the United States Military Government in Salzburg. The Joint, too, understood Austria above all as a key transit country for the *Brihah* and provided financial backing for its operations.[31]

Best Chance

In the summer of 1946 General Mark W. Clark, head of the United States occupation forces in Austria, called on Jewish DPs sojourning in the

American zone of Allied-occupied Austria to carefully ponder their present position and where their best chance for future security and economic independence might lie.[32] For General Clark, the "best chance" available to Jewish DPs to regain control of their own fate was repatriation back to their countries of origin in Central and Eastern Europe. His chief arguments for repatriation were the prohibitively small immigration quotas for countries in North and South America, which were usually reserved for people with desired occupational skills, and the difficult linguistic and cultural barriers to their integration in Austria.[33] Repatriation was indeed the long-standing policy solution followed by states with refugee inflows resulting from the first mass civilian displacements catalyzed by World War I.[34] Mark Wyman, a historian of postwar displacement, reminds us that Jewish writers referred to the period from late 1945 through mid-1947 under the governance of General Clark as the "humanitarian period" in relations between the Jews and the US Military Administration in the DP camps, as he believed Jews were entitled to first consideration because of their wartime experiences.[35] As Atina Grossmann notes, people knew that General Clark was at least partly Jewish.[36]

Yet because of the steep rise in the number of Jews fleeing their countries of origin after their returns following liberation and sojourning in the DP countries—Germany, Austria, and Italy in 1946 and 1947—UNRRA came to recognize that many DPs could not safely return home, nor could they be forced to do so.[37] International organizations came to see Jews as a nonrepatriable group by December 1946. Poles, Ukrainians, and Baltic nationals also did not wish to return home to an increasingly Soviet-dominated Eastern Europe because of fear of Soviet retribution, strong national feeling, anti-Communist sentiment, and economic concerns. Even before the establishment of the International Refugee Organization (IRO) in 1947, UNRRA had begun to aid in resettlement for nonrepatriable DPs, which ran bluntly counter to the wishes of Eastern European countries.[38] The IRO also recognized Roma from Germany as eligible for assistance, as they had been stripped of their citizenship during the Nazi period and were therefore stateless. According to historian Ari Joskowicz, sometimes administrators deliberately brought in the derogatory category "Gypsy" to describe Roma applicants, as the term signified statelessness and wartime persecution and qualified the applicant for resettlement aid. However, he notes that the term rapidly returned to undesirable usage when national governments returned to power.[39] Overall, the creation of the IRO represented a shift toward resettlement practices and largely became the province of the Western Allied powers, who provided over half of its funding, including a fleet of ships for refugee movement.[40] The shift to resettlement away from dominant practices of repatriation underscores emigration as a key solution to the problem of postwar Jewish rightlessness.[41]

Although resettlement became standard practice for qualifying groups, personal circumstances determined potential destination countries' willingness to receive individual emigrants. The case of Ivan, a young Hungarian Jewish war orphan with relatives in the United States who was sojourning in the Bad Gastein DP camp in the US zone of Austria, is instructive for understanding the forces acting on emigration potential. Fay Calkins, an enthusiastic recent graduate of Haverford College in Pennsylvania who was working as an UNRRA Welfare Officer at Bad Gastein, assiduously transcribed the relevant details of Ivan's life narrative for his stateless identity documentation. Ivan would need that documentation to obtain his entry visa for the United States. It was the summer of 1946. Ivan had relatives on his father's side on Southern Boulevard and on Tremont Avenue in the Bronx, whom he said he was looking forward to living with, and they were anxious to sponsor and house him.[42] His uncle had submitted an affidavit of support for Ivan, his mother Kato, and his father Dezső back in May 1938, 10 days before the Hungarian government enacted its first set of explicitly anti-Jewish laws. Ivan's uncle Alexander swore to the US government that he was gainfully employed and would sponsor the emigration and sponsorship for the family of three. Alexander had immigrated to the United States in 1913 and was naturalized on 11 June 1924, less than a month after President Calvin Coolidge signed the infamously restrictive Immigration Act of 1924, also known as the Johnson-Reed Act, into law.[43] Kato and Dezső perished during the war.[44] This tragic circumstance facilitated Ivan's emigration to the United States under President Truman's immigration policy directive of December 1945 that hastened to admit 39,000 DPs beginning in the spring of 1946, giving preference to orphans whose sponsorship was guaranteed.[45] By December 1947, about 22,950 DPs, of whom two-thirds were Jewish, entered the United States under the Truman immigration visa directive.[46] Ivan arrived in the United States on 16 September 1946.[47]

Which factors account most closely for Ivan's ability to immigrate to the United States? His guaranteed sponsorship certainly unlatched the heavy entry door. The sponsorship requirement was a key feature in the addendum to the US administration's immigration policy. Yet Ivan's entry was not determined by economic questions alone. His relatives had guaranteed his—and his murdered parents'—support since before the outbreak of the war, to no effect. Nor was it solely his war orphan status, which gave his case preference but did not decide the outcome. The principal factor contributing to his ability to emigrate was his status as a DP residing at the Bad Gastein camp, aided by UNRRA in preparing his documentation, at the moment when the revised US emigration policy came into force. Truman's policy directly focused on DPs and was a step toward an extension of their conditional and limited entry permission to the United States. Ivan's sponsorship and war orphan status pushed his case within the parameters of the modified DP entry quotas effective from spring 1946. In other words, had Ivan's parents survived, none of them may have qualified for emigration. Ivan's exceptional case demonstrates General Clark's point. The attractiveness of the United States as an emigration destination was nearly inversely proportional to one's potential to get there. The many DPs still willing to seek emigration scoured their resources to pull together the information they needed to act on potential paths of migration.

In the early fall of 1946 Brazil offered DPs hope as another realizable emigration destination from Italy. HIAS had been successful in convincing the Brazilian consulate in Florence to issue Brazilian entry visas to DPs without special formalities. HIAS also cooperated with the International Red Cross in Rome to speed the issuance of 100 travel documents, in lieu of passports, for Jewish DPs. The International Red Cross in Rome agreed to deliver the said travel documents to Florence, where the DPs sojourned, thus sparing the cost of their travel to Rome to pick them up. HIAS emigration data from the Central Office for Italy in Rome from the end of September 1946 show that out of 118 emigration cases from Italy for the month, 66 Jewish DPs found entry in Brazil, 35 of whom embarked together on 9 September aboard the SS *Campana*. The United States allowed entry for 16 DPs, ranking a distant second. Other destinations lay predominantly in South America but also in Africa, Western Europe, and Palestine, including but not limited to France (accepting 2), the United Kingdom (7), Colombia (1), Uruguay (3), Argentina (2), Chile (7), Bolivia (1), Palestine (4), Sweden (1), Venezuela (2), (then) Belgian Congo (4), Cuba (1), and Egypt (1).[48]

Many Jewish DPs who had previously registered for emigration to the United States switched their paperwork to Brazil in September 1946. This destination appeared to offer a quicker route to the Western Hemisphere and the chance to get to the United States from there. Rapidity was certainly the decisive factor. Italian authorities urged Jewish DPs to leave "the sooner the better," as they came around to check identity documentation with increasing frequency. The HIAS office in Rome noted matter of factly that "Brazil is the only country nowadays which at present time pretty willingly accepts European refugees."[49]

By the following month, immigration to Brazil became a less viable option. When Brazil changed its immigration policies in October 1946 to admit only those DPs who had secured an in-country employment contract, HIAS and UNRRA began a fight against time on behalf of the DPs for whom visas had already been granted. Shipping space was the key variable in making good on those visas before they expired. "If by miraculous good luck a vessel bound for South America is found during November, everything can be straightened, but should we not succeed, the DPs will run the risk of losing their chances: their visas will become invalid."[50] Brazilian consulates in Europe suspended granting visas overall in March 1947. Without the entry visas from Brazil, local consulates refused to grant transit visas, which made it nearly impossible to make one's way to sites of sojourn in Paris or Zurich or elsewhere where HIAS might be able to assist emigrants as they waited for new regulations. HIAS Budapest implored the Jewish Colonization Association in Brazil to let the relatives know of the delays, even as Brazil continued to encourage potential emigrants and to blame HIAS for delaying family reunifications.[51]

As a result of the change in Brazil's emigration policies and the heightened pressure to leave Italy, Paraguay became an increasingly attractive emigration target. HIAS New York concluded an agreement with the Paraguayan government for the entry of 100 Jewish families. "The DPs have of course immediately (and also through UNRRA Headquarters, Rome) learnt of the existence of that agreement and consequently rushed to our offices in order to be registered," remarked the HIAS Rome office.[52] DPs promptly acted on the capricious bureaucracy of emigration through bits of precious policy news they culled from their information environment.

In 1947 the Joint detailed an increasingly bleak emigration situation. Their reports related the increasingly stringent conditions from the United

States consul for obtaining a visa, particularly regarding documentation requirements. Joint representatives found the US demands for documentation "extremely difficult for persons who lost all the required documents during their years of wandering from concentration camp to concentration camp."[53] The United States Consul recognized the level of difficulty and drew the not-untrue conclusion that some applicants had submitted false documentation because of it. Only significant intervention from the US adviser on Jewish affairs saved forgers from prosecution. The Joint indignantly described the situation in this way: "It is indeed difficult for these people who for long have lived by their wits alone, who often owe their survival to some devious means, to understand that a dateline, the accident of birth at one side of a border rather than the other, should determine their destiny."[54]

The height of Jewish DP numbers in 1947 corresponded with the low point of emigration possibilities. The total number of Jewish DPs sojourning in camps in Germany, Austria, and Italy in the summer of 1947 hovered around 250,000 people. Morale was low. Some DPs made the painful decision to return to their countries of origin, taking General Clark's advice.[55]

The DP camp was always a site of sojourn, assessment, and waiting, always waiting. The displaced considered where it would be possible to go, by what means, and with what kind of help while factoring in migration quotas and policies in a bifurcating world and balancing their destination preferences with the transforming realities of postwar territoriality. Emigration documentation shows that the pressure of tightly constricted emigration possibilities plus the intensity of emigration need combined with aid toward that end from the IRO and Jewish philanthropic organizations resulted in widely dispersed emigration from 1946 through 1947.

Way Stations

In contrast to the imposed passivity of the DP camps, undertaking emigration was a central way that Jewish survivors expressed their agency. When Jews decided to leave their countries of origin, they reasserted control over their lives. This made it all the more difficult to become marooned in a holding pattern of waiting as part of the emigration process. The trying relationship between passive waiting and active personal autonomy frustrated and angered emigrants, especially when they were given misleading information that resulted in more waiting than they anticipated, as in the following example. The European hub office of the HIAS in Paris wrote to its Budapest office to reproach the director there for making unfounded promises to emigrants on their way to Australia and the United States, a passage for which it took more time than usual to arrange shipboard accommodation. Facing a longer wait than they were expecting and for which they were ill-equipped, emigrants who had been promised an early departure to their final destination became unhappy and dissatisfied, and unspecified "incidents" occurred. The emigrants told the Paris HIAS office that they would have preferred waiting in their homes in Hungary, in which, it should be stated, they could no longer bear to remain, rather than be caught portside in a limbo of uncertain duration.[56]

Aware of the damage that protracted waiting could wreak on the traumatized DPs, including the depressive effects of boredom and idleness on morale, DP camp administrators and Jewish aid workers together sought to create schedules and routines to reintegrate survivors into normal patterns of everyday socialization. When visiting camps in the British zone in March 1946, diplomat Thomas Brimelow urged camp staff to create some kind of useful employment for the DPs, "in order that they should not go to pieces as a result of forced inactivity."[57] Atina Grossmann described the nervous condition of the Jewish DP population in the American occupation zone in Germany as a highly mobile, stateless, traumatized population in transit. The officials and workers—the military government and local German officials, Jewish aid workers from the United States and UNRRA, Zionist emissaries from Palestine, DP teachers and leaders—saw and labeled the DPs as "jittery, excitable, anxiety prone," on edge, unable to "tolerate any contradiction," susceptible to rumors and quick to panic, and "allergic to authority or change."[58] Wanting the best for the DPs and aspiring to help rehabilitate and restore this damaged population, administrators and aid workers sought to organize and make sense of the DPs' time in the camps.

Camp administrators turned their attention to creating activity schedules after the immediate postwar needs, such as accommodation, food, and medical care, had been addressed. In the American zone US military authorities first handled pressing housing issues. They had not at first recognized Jews as a distinct group to be handled separately, and Jewish DPs were heedlessly housed together in poor conditions under military guard with people who had persecuted them during the war. This changed after Earl G. Harrison's condemnatory report to President Truman concerning the mistreatment and poor care of nonrepatriable Jews and the outraged public response to it following its publication in the *New York Times* on 30 September 1945. Jews were then accommodated in separate Jewish camps with greater attention to the specific nature of Jewish wartime suffering.[59] In the American zone, then, these DP camps became a separate Jewish space, where Jews could struggle with the realities of their sojourn together.

The United States Military Administration oversaw the camp system in the American zone and worked together with the Joint and the Jewish Agency for Palestine, which arrived in the last weeks of 1946, to create a "concerted program of vocational, educational, and social activities to interest and stimulate activity among the people in the months to come." They aligned their efforts with the goals of facilitating emigration, strengthening morale, and improving provision for the DPs' daily needs. The Joint recognized that morale was low because "until now there has been so little of an activity program to occupy the people, and because they are so deeply disappointed in their enforced delay here."[60] The triad of agencies intensified their energies in late 1946 to involve the camp population in regimented educational and vocational activity and in the work needed to run the camp, including police work, serving on a People's Court to hear complaints about misbehavior, employment in the PX (army base retail store) and the clothing store, and work in the kitchen and the warehouse, in the camp office of the UNRRA, and in manual sanitation labor.[61]

Scarcity of equipment and supplies, however, was a terrible obstacle mitigating against the fulfillment of the benevolently minded educational and vocational programs. We know from Verdery's work just how far-reaching the implications of scarcity and shortages could be.[62] In this case, even though the organization of time in the camp was meant to improve DP living conditions and morale and prepare DP camp inhabitants for their eventual successful emigration, problems connected to scarcity had the unintended consequences of enforcing idleness, fomenting competition for resources and accusations of favoritism in resource access and distribution, triggering rash reactions to situations that reminded them of conditions under Nazism, and, above all, contributing to their passive rather than active or controlled experience of lived time. That is, scarcity issues represented a complex deterrent to achieving control over their time, their personal autonomy, and their ability to plan for the future. Beyond enforced conformity to the regimentation of a daily schedule, which the camp administration meant positively as a path to reintegrating traumatized people into some semblance of normal life, scarcities compounded survivors' frustrations and inhibited their rehabilitation. Scarcity seized their time and with it their control over their activities.

The "point system" is an example of how the relationship between scarcity and agency through control over one's time worked. As a means of promoting involvement in the running of the DP camp, the administration instituted a point system, by which people earned points that could be used to purchase necessities at the PX or the clothing store based on the number of hours per week of employment. The program was meant to foster initiative and to improve material status. Accommodations were made for those unable to work. However, scarcity of equipment limited the number of people who could participate in the work program, which led to idleness for many and lowered morale. The People's Committee enjoined Leon Fisher of the AJC to help them with four demands: (1) obtaining a weekly ration pack of cigarettes and a cake of soap weekly without points for all residents, (2) eliminating favoritism in the PX and clothing store, where, they argued, employees held better items for friends, (3) giving a separate shopping hour to teachers, and (4) installing a member of the People's Council in the PX to keep an eye on inventory and to make sure those without points to spend, such as children, the sick, and expectant mothers, would still receive the resources they needed. Nearly all these demands were met—except for the free distribution of cigarettes and soap—yet there was no letup in the documentation of low morale, restlessness, and frustration for the duration of the DP camps' existence.[63]

Even more than scarcity, Jewish survivors' long-term suffering and postwar emotional state inhibited their rehabilitation in relation to the DP camps' organization of time. According to a report by the UNRRA Council for Jewish Affairs near Munich, Jewish DPs could not adjust to the crowded group living conditions with inadequate facilities. "It is recognized by all authorities," read the council's report, "that Jewish persons, after their privations are emotionally handicapped and quickly react to any situation which reminds them of their lives under Nazism." Jewish DPs could not abide any form of restraint, the report continued, and "violent repercussions result" from trying. Furthermore, living as they were in Germany contributed to their anxiety. Overall, the DP camp staff expressed the greatest concern over potential "security incidents," or violent outbreaks, arising from Jewish emotional disorders related to DP Nazi-era traumas if they were not actively engaged in a program for education, training, employment, and rehabilitation. The UNRRA Council for Jewish Affairs urged the camp administration to improve living conditions to the greatest extent possible, with an emphasis on eliminating overcrowding and creating "normal community activities."[64] The council's report makes clear that they believed folding the Jewish DPs into as normal and busy a routine as possible would aid their recovery, bring them back to everyday life, and reduce the risk of unspecified security incidents. Yet Jewish DPs struggled with the imposed "temporal discipline" of the DP camp that sought to control their lives rather than allow them to regain control over their lived time.

The transitory nature of the camp sojourn was, of course, the greatest temporal force acting on the Jewish DPs. Although the decision to emigrate was an act of seizing personal agency, the unpredictable waiting time and the uncertainty of destination drained the DPs' ability to maintain active control over their choices. Vast documentation points to countries' shifting immigration policies, the difficulties in securing transportation, the mountains of required—and often impossible to obtain—documentation for visa acquisition, and then the hopes of being able to embark on the emigration before the visas expired. DPs often considered emigration destinations based on potential waiting time before commencing the journey. Would it be months, or years, and how many? In September 1948, three months after the establishment of the new state of Israel, the US Military Administration together with Jewish aid organizations issued the following statement on potential paths of emigration for Jewish DPs:

> Since, under the most optimistic conditions, it will take the better part of a year and a half for Israel to absorb the DPs, there will be those who consider it to their advantage to wait the necessary period for US visas, in sufficient numbers to absorb the entire quota allowed to DPs. . . . It looks like 15,000 will go to countries other than the US or

Israel, about 20,000 will be admitted to the US in the following two years, the remaining 115,000 will have to be resettled in Israel.[65]

It was impossible to know the answer to the question of how much time one would personally wait. The uncertainty dragged on their souls. They were out of place and lived out of time.

Place the Displaced

News of the UN partition at the end of November 1947 boosted Jewish DP morale and brought joy to emigration aid workers.[66] Yet they were also pragmatic enough to recognize that mass emigration had not yet begun, that further difficulties might yet arise, and that it was imperative to continue to pursue broad emigration goals with members of the following three groups: (1) immigrants to the United States under the 1945 Truman directive, (2) immigrants to other countries based on specific skills, and (3) immigrants to other countries for family reunification.[67] Concerning its activities to assist emigration to countries other than the United States or Palestine, the Joint wrote that "soon after liberation, the overwhelming majority of Jews in the [American] zone expressed their desire to emigrate to Palestine." Nevertheless, because of severe restrictions on that desired emigration destination, "a growing interest in resettlement to the Americas, South Africa, and Australia has become manifest."[68] Between 1946 and 1950, 165,000 European Jews emigrated to countries other than Palestine/Israel, compared with the 339,100 European Jews who emigrated to Israel between 1948 and 1951.[69]

At the World Jewish Congress plenary session in Montreux in 1948, the assembly produced a resolution on DPs affirming that Jewish DPs "found consolation in the fact that the Jewish State of Israel has become an unshakable reality," and they urged the "nations of the world" to afford them a "speedy and large-scale resettlement" there.[70] Yet the WJC also made it clear that it was "aware of the fact that some Jewish DPs wish to be admitted to countries other than Israel, especially where the reunion of scattered Jewish families is concerned."[71] The WJC recorded its displeasure with those countries that carried out "discriminatory policies toward Jews and Jewish DPs, a policy in contradiction to the letter and spirit of the United Nations Charter and all the basic concepts of human rights, as embodied in the draft Bill of Human Rights."[72] The organization urged these countries to admit Jewish DPs. That is, the countries should recognize that Israel was not the sole resettlement option for Jews. Emigration out of Germany remained a top priority for the WJC, which wished to protect Jewish DPs from the intensification of postwar antisemitism there. The WJC feared that other countries "washed their hands" of the Jewish DP "problem" after the creation of the State of Israel.[73]

Israel alone could not handle the entirety of Jewish DP postwar resettlement. As "the curtain rung down on calendar year 1949," Jewish aid organizations struggled to "place the displaced."[74] Henry Ortner, director of HIAS operations in Germany and Austria, estimated in early 1950 that 20,000 Jewish DPs under his management still sought resettlement in countries around the world other than Israel.

> The emigration to Israel is very slow, and less than four hundred monthly leave Germany and Austria for that country. Much of the reason can be given to the fact that housing is inadequate and industry up to now cannot absorb all that have gone there. Many who have gone there are now returned and are in Germany and Austria at this time.[75]

Ortner recorded the number of Jewish DPs sponsored by HIAS in 1949 who had been resettled in the countries of their choice. Of the 14,851 Jewish DPs directly sponsored by HIAS, 13,225 had gone to the United States, 1,300 to Canada, 189 to Australia, and 37 to other countries. A further group of HIAS protégées included 435 resettled through mass migration to Canada, 154 to Australia, and 63 to other countries.[76]

Nevertheless, we know that mass immigration to the United States and the newly established State of Israel after May 1948 accounted for the greatest postwar resettlement of European Jewish survivors. But the speed by which Jewish DP youth, the largest segment of the Jewish DP population, became keen adherents of the Zionist project remains an improbable feature of the early postwar landscape. The work of historian Avinoam Patt provides a compelling explanation for that eventuality: Zionism gave the youth grounding and purpose by offering vocational training, personal rehabilitation, and a sense of family.[77] He writes of the thousands of young kibbutz members, adherents to the full range of Zionist streams, working on 40 training farms in the DP camps in Germany by the middle of 1946, numbers that accounted for the majority of Jewish youth overall who sojourned in the camps, who looked hopefully toward emigration to Palestine, later Israel.[78] And they were ready to fight. Between 1948 and 1949, Patt tells us, about 22,000 DPs left the DP camps for Palestine and were enlisted into the Haganah, the Zionist defense force in Mandatory Palestine.[79] The explanation speaks to the keen sense of agency, meaning, and decision-making control that the Zionist movement provided. In this way, it offered a restoration of personhood. Patt's work points to the fact that it was not as much the ideology that drew in adherents but the positive rehabilitative space it opened for a return to their own active lived time.

* * *

Framing the postwar Jewish emigration experience within its broad geographic parameters, in which Jews sought to seize active control over their lived time but confronted both the imposed time regime of the camp and the capricious temporality of the emigration process, highlights the forces with which they struggled to recover themselves. The postwar Jewish story moves from displacement, to dispersion, to the formation of a new global diaspora. Jews, Jewish and non-Jewish humanitarian organizations, and political actors built on previous paths of global Jewish migration and settlement to place a population claiming its right to reclaim and rehabilitate itself in the aftermath of the war.

Notes

It is a privilege to contribute to this volume in honor of my adviser, Michael Stanislawski, whose transformative approach to Jewish historiography taught me how to write expansive, creative, integrative history with discipline and gratitude and to leave out the "mushy" parts. Many thanks to the anonymous manuscript reviewers for their valuable suggestions.

1 Irene Eber, "Holocaust Education and Displaced Persons (DP) Camps," *Contemporary Review of the Middle East* 3, no. 3 (2016): 231. *Displaced person* (DP) was a term created by the United States for use in handling the

large-scale civilian population displacement in the aftermath of the war through UNRRA and the United States Army. See Gerard Daniel Cohen, *In War's Wake: Europe's Displaced Persons in the Postwar Order* (Oxford, UK: Oxford University Press, 2011), 4.

2. Eber, "Holocaust Education," 235.
3. "Displaced Persons," *Holocaust Encyclopedia*, United States Holocaust Memorial Museum, Washington, DC, encyclopedia.ushmm.org/content/en/article/displaced-persons (accessed 1 April 2023).
4. Katherine Verdery, in developing the concept of how the self is defined through temporal patterns, offers many penetrating insights into how the Romanian state functioned. See Katherine Verdery, "The 'Etatization' of Time in Ceaușescu's Romania," in her *What Was Socialism, and What Comes Next?* (Princeton, NJ: Princeton University Press, 1996), 40, 53.
5. Guy Miron, "The 'Lived Time' of German Jews Under the Nazi Regime," *Journal of Modern History* 90, no. 1 (2018): 117.
6. Eugène Minkowski, *Lived Time: Phenomenological and Psychological Studies* (Evanston, IL: Northwestern University Press, 1970), 6, 87–88, cited in Miron, "Lived Time," 135–36.
7. Atina Grossmann, *Jews, Germans, and Allies: Close Encounters in Occupied Germany* (Princeton, NJ: Princeton University Press, 2009), 147.
8. "Displaced Persons," United States Holocaust Memorial Museum; "Refugees," *Holocaust Encyclopedia*, United States Holocaust Memorial Museum, Washington, DC, encyclopedia.ushmm.org/content/en/article/refugees (accessed 1 April 2023).
9. Rebecca Kobrin, *Jewish Bialystok and Its Diaspora* (Bloomington: Indiana University Press, 2010), 3–4.
10. "World Jewish Congress, Political Commission: Resolution on Displaced Persons," 4 July 1948, YIVO Institute for Jewish Research, Records of the Displaced Persons Camps and Centers in Germany, 1945–1952, Subseries II: Presidium of the Central Committee, 1945–1950, RG 294.2, microfilm reel 6, folder 67.
11. Tara Zahra, *The Great Departure: Mass Migration from Eastern Europe and the Making of the Free World* (New York: Norton, 2016), 18.
12. Zahra, *Great Departure*, 3–4.
13. At least one-third of Central European migrants to America returned home. Zahra, *Great Departure*, 14.
14. John M. Efron, Steven Weitzman, and Matthias B. Lehmann, *The Jews: A History*, 2nd ed. (Boston: Pearson, 2014), 359.

15 Kobrin, *Jewish Bialystok*, 14. Kobrin indicates that this was especially true for Jews from Bialystok.
16 David Engel, "World War I and the Problem of Security in Jewish History," in *World War I and the Jews: Conflict and Transformation in Europe, the Middle East, and America*, ed. Marsha L. Rozenblit and Jonathan Karp (New York: Berghahn, 2017), 26.
17 Peter Gatrell, *The Making of the Modern Refugee* (Oxford, UK: Oxford University Press, 2013), 2; Rebekah Klein-Pejšová, *Mapping Jewish Loyalties in Interwar Slovakia* (Bloomington: Indiana University Press, 2015), 1, 42. Brazil was one of the main receiving countries for Jewish emigrants from Eastern Europe in this period. See Jeff Lesser, *Immigration, Ethnicity, and National Identity in Brazil, 1808 to the Present* (Cambridge, UK: Cambridge University Press, 2013), ch. 5.
18 Arnošt Lustig, *Dita Saxová*, rev. ed. (Evanston, IL: Northwestern University Press, 1993).
19 "Report on the Activity of the Office of the HICEM/HIAS-ICA Emigration Association in Budapest, Hungary from April til December 31, 1945," YIVO Institute of Jewish Research, HIAS, France IV, RG 245.5, microfilm reel 19, folder 228; Rebekah Klein-Pejšová, "Across the Iron Curtain: Hungarian Jewish Refugees in Austria, 1945–1949—The Letters to Enns," in *The Holocaust in Hungary: Seventy Years Later*, ed. Randolph L. Braham and Andras Kovacs (New York: Central European University Press, 2016), 201. I have not yet found evidence to indicate use of "Black Aliyah" elsewhere.
20 "Report on Our Activity," HIAS, YIVO Institute of Jewish Research.
21 Michael Robert Marrus, *The Unwanted: European Refugees in the Twentieth Century* (New York: Oxford University Press, 1985), 335. There is much excellent recent literature on the problem of return. See, in particular, Anna Cichopek-Gajraj, *Beyond Violence: Jewish Survivors in Poland and Slovakia, 1944–48* (New York: Cambridge University Press, 2014).
22 Julius Kovacs of the Budapest HIAS office to HIAS, Paris, 4 March 1946, p. 2, YIVO Institute of Jewish Research, HIAS/HICEM, France IV, RG 245.5, microfilm reel 19, folder 229.
23 Julius Kovacs of the Budapest HIAS office to HIAS, Paris, 4 March 1946, YIVO Institute of Jewish Research.
24 Letter from the British Political Mission about Hungarian Jewish Emigration to Australia, October 1946, YIVO Institute of Jewish Research, HIAS/HICEM, France IV, RG 245.5, microfilm reel 19, folder 229.

25 Julius Kovacs of the Budapest HIAS office to HIAS, Paris, 4 March 1946, pp. 2–5, YIVO Institute of Jewish Research.
26 Mark Wyman, *DPs: Europe's Displaced Persons, 1945–1951* (Ithaca, NY: Cornell University Press, 1998), 148.
27 Wyman, *DPs*, 149.
28 Tara Zahra, "Prisoners of the Postwar: Expellees, Displaced Persons, and Jews in Austria After World War II," *Austrian History Yearbook* 41 (2010): 191. For comparison with DP camps in Italy, see Danielle Willard-Kyle, "Living in Liminal Spaces: Jewish Refugees in Italian Displaced Persons Camps, 1945–1951," PhD diss., Rutgers University, 2020.
29 Susanne Rolinek, "Clandestine Operators: The *Bricha* and *Betar* Network in the Salzburg Area, 1945–1948," *Journal of Israeli History* 19, no. 3 (1998): 46.
30 Susanne Rolinek, *Jüdische Lebenswelten, 1945–1955: Flüchtlinge in der amerikanischen Zone Österreichs* (Innsbruck: Studienverlag, 2007).
31 Rolinek, "Clandestine Operators," 50, 58.
32 Mark W. Clark, "General US Army: Proclamation to the Displaced Persons in the US Zone Austria," YIVO Institute of Jewish Research, Records of the Displaced Person Camps and Centers of Austria, RG 294.4, microfilm reel 21, folder 541.
33 Clark, "General US Army."
34 Gatrell, *Making of the Modern Refugee*, 7.
35 Wyman, *DPs*, 137.
36 Grossmann, *Jews, Germans, and Allies*, 166.
37 Pamela Ballinger, "Impossible Returns, Enduring Legacies: Recent Historiography of Displacement and the Reconstruction of Europe After World War Two," *Contemporary European History* 22 (2013): 128–29.
38 G. Daniel Cohen, "Between Relief and Politics: Refugee Humanitarianism in Occupied Germany, 1945–1946," *Journal of Contemporary History* 43, no. 3 (2008): 444–45.
39 Ari Joskowicz, "Romani Refugees and the Postwar Order," *Journal of Contemporary History* 51, no. 4 (2016): 764, 774–75.
40 Marrus, *The Unwanted*, 343.
41 James B. Loeffler, "On Writing and Routing Rights," *Shofar: An Interdisciplinary Journal of Jewish Studies* 37, no. 1 (2019): 197.
42 For the obituary for Fay Gilkey Calkins Ala-ilima, see Ellen Brenna, "Fay Gilkey Calkins Ala-Ilima," *Western Friend*, 17 November 2016, westernfriend.org/memorials/fay-gilkey-calkins-ala-ilima (accessed 19 May 2021). See

also Fay Calkins, UNRRA Welfare Officer, "UNRRA Correspondence, 1946–1947," YIVO Institute for Jewish Research, DP Camps and Centers in Austria, RG 294.4; folder 306.

43 Affidavit of Support, United States Holocaust Memorial Museum Archives, Washington, DC, Becker Family Papers (2018.359.2). The Hungarian parliament passed the *numerus clausus* law of 1920 to restrict the enrollment of students of racial and national minorities in the university to that group's percentage of the population. Although the law was directed at the Jewish population, it did not explicitly mention them. Nathaniel Katzburg, "Hungarian Jewry in Modern Times," in *Hungarian-Jewish Studies*, ed. Randolph L. Braham (New York: World Federation of Hungarian Jews, 1966), 155. See also "United States Immigration and Refugee Law, 1921–1980," encyclopedia.ushmm.org/content/en/article/united-states-immigration-and-refugee-law-1921-1980 (accessed 1 June 2021).

44 Fay Calkins, UNRRA Welfare Officer, "UNRRA Correspondence, 1946–1947," YIVO Institute for Jewish Research.

45 Mark Wischnitzer, *Visas to Freedom: The History of HIAS* (Cleveland: World Publishing, 1956), 207–8. Of the 39,000 total DPs, 16,000 were Jewish; see "Displaced Persons," United States Holocaust Memorial Museum.

46 "New Directive on Immigrant Visas to the US," United States Holocaust Memorial Museum, www.ushmm.org/learn/timeline-of-events/1942-1945/truman-directive-on-immigrant-visas (accessed 21 June 2019).

47 Transcript of Ivan Becker, United States Holocaust Memorial Museum Archives, Washington, DC, Becker Family Papers (2018.359.2), RG-50.106*0016.

48 "Monthly Activity Report, September 1946," p. 1, October 1946, YIVO Institute of Jewish Research, HIAS, France IV, RG 245.5, microfilm reel 19, folder 234.

49 "Monthly Activity Report, September 1946," p. 1, October 1946, YIVO Institute of Jewish Research.

50 "Monthly Activity Report, October 1946," p. 1, November 1946, YIVO Institute of Jewish Research, HIAS, France IV, RG 245.5, microfilm reel 19, folder 234.

51 Julius Kovacs, HIAS Budapest, to Dr. Leitchio, the Jewish Colonization Association in Rio de Janeiro, 27 March 1947, YIVO Institute of Jewish Research, HIAS, France IV, RG 245.5, microfilm reel 19, folder 231.

52 "Monthly Activity Report, October 1946," p. 1, November 1946, YIVO Institute of Jewish Research, HIAS, France IV, RG 245.5, microfilm reel 19, folder 234.

53 "Annual Report of the AJDC," December 1947, YIVO Institute of Jewish Research, Records of the Displaced Persons Camps and Centers in Germany,

1945–1952, Series XIV: AJDC, 1945–1952, RG 294.2, microfilm reel 107, folder 1497.
54 "Annual Report of the AJDC," December 1947, YIVO Institute of Jewish Research.
55 For Jewish DP numbers in June 1947, see Marrus, *The Unwanted*, 335.
56 Mr. Lewis Neikrug in Paris to Julius Kovacs in Budapest, 12 December 1946, YIVO Institute for Jewish Research, Records of the HIAS-HICEM Offices in Europe, RG 245.5, folder 229.
57 Peter Gatrell, *The Unsettling of Europe: How Migration Reshaped a Continent*, 1st ed. (New York: Basic, 2019), 43.
58 Grossmann, *Jews, Germans, and Allies*, 149.
59 Michael Brenner, *A History of Jews in Germany Since 1945: Politics, Culture, and Society* (Bloomington: Indiana University Press, 2018), 63–66.
60 "Report on the AJDC, Salzburg Area, Activities," from Leon Fisher, Field Director, AJDC Salzburg, to American Joint Distribution Committee, 10 December 1946, YIVO Institute for Jewish Research, DP Camps and Centers in Austria, RG 294.4, folder 6.
61 "Report on Visits to Camp Bad Gastein, Austria," from Leon D. Fisher of the AJDC in Salzburg, to Mr. Rice in New York, 11 March 1946, report on first two visits to Camp Bad Gastein, 22–24 February 1946 and 6–7 March 1946, YIVO Institute for Jewish Research, DP Camps and Centers in Austria, RG 294.4, folder 6.
62 Verdery, *What Was Socialism*, ch. 2.
63 "Report on Visits to Camp Bad Gastein, Austria," YIVO Institute for Jewish Research.
64 "Staff Study Relating to Winter Care and Planning for Jewish Displaced Persons in Germany by the UNRRA Jewish Council," UNRRA Council for Jewish Affairs, Pasing-Munich, August 1946, YIVO Institute for Jewish Research, DP Camps and Centers in Germany, RG 294.2, folder 65.
65 "Report on Certain Aspects of Jewish Problems in the US Zone, Germany, and Austria," submitted by Harry Greenstein and Maj. Abraham S. Hyman, 15 September 1948, YIVO Institute for Jewish Research, DP Camps and Centers in Austria, RG 294.4, folder 12.
66 "Monthly AJDC Reports," November 1947, YIVO Institute of Jewish Research, Records of the Displaced Persons Camps and Centers in Germany, 1945–1952, Series XIV: AJDC, 1945–1952, RG 294.2, microfilm reel 107, folder 1498.

67 "Monthly AJDC Reports," November 1947, YIVO Institute of Jewish Research.
68 "Organization Bulletin No. 7," November 1947, YIVO Institute of Jewish Research, Records of the Displaced Persons Camps and Centers in Germany, 1945–1952, Series XIV: AJDC, 1945–1952, RG 294.2, microfilm reel 107, folder 1500.
69 Marrus, *The Unwanted*, 155; "Population and Migration: Migration Since World War I," in *The YIVO Encyclopedia of Jews in Eastern Europe*, www.yivoencyclopedia.org/article.aspx/Population_and_Migration/Migration_since_World_War_I#id0ezwbi (accessed 21 June 2019).
70 "World Jewish Congress, Political Commission: Resolution on Displaced Persons," 4 July 1948, YIVO Institute of Jewish Research.
71 "World Jewish Congress, Political Commission: Resolution on Displaced Persons," 4 July 1948, YIVO Institute of Jewish Research.
72 "World Jewish Congress, Political Commission: Resolution on Displaced Persons," 4 July 1948, YIVO Institute of Jewish Research.
73 "World Jewish Congress, Political Commission: Resolution on Displaced Persons," 4 July 1948, YIVO Institute of Jewish Research.
74 "Report from Germany and Austria for the Calendar Year 1949, Henry Ortner, HIAS Director for Germany and Austria, to Lewis Neikrug, HIAS, Paris," 4 January 1950, YIVO Institute for Jewish Research, Records of the HIAS-HICEM Offices in Europe, RG 245.5, microfilm reel 19, folder 352.
75 "Report from Germany and Austria for the Calendar Year 1949," 4 January 1950, YIVO Institute for Jewish Research.
76 "Report from Germany and Austria for the Calendar Year 1949," 4 January 1950, YIVO Institute for Jewish Research.
77 Avinoam J. Patt, *Finding Home and Homeland: Jewish Youth and Zionism in the Aftermath of the Holocaust* (Detroit: Wayne State University Press, 2009).
78 Avinoam J. Patt, "Living in Landsberg, Dreaming of Deganiah: Jewish Displaced Youths and Zionism After the Holocaust," in *"We Are Here": New Approaches to Jewish Displaced Persons in Postwar Germany*, ed. Avinoam J. Patt and Michael Berkowitz (Detroit: Wayne State University Press, 2010), 99.
79 Avinoam J. Patt, "Stateless Citizens of Israel: Jewish Displaced Persons and Zionism in Post-War Germany," in *The Disentanglement of Populations*, ed. Jessica Reinisch and Elizabeth White (London: Palgrave Macmillan, 2011), 162–82.

PART IV

LEGACIES OF EUROPEAN JEWISH CULTURE AND HISTORY

13

The Rise of Yiddish Religious Revolutionary Socialism, 1926–1941

Daniel B. Schwartz

In the standard biography of the Eastern European Jewish socialist of the late nineteenth and early twentieth centuries, becoming a revolutionary thinker and activist was part of a thoroughgoing secularization. The surreptitious reading of Marxist and anarchist literature, the joining of radical and subversive movements, the embrace of atheism or at least agnosticism—all were either accompanied by or followed on the heels of an abandonment of Jewish law and tradition.[1] In some cases, such as the notorious Yom Kippur Balls in Jewish anarchist circles in turn-of-the-twentieth-century New York, hostility to religion went so far as to manifest in a deliberate and public flouting of the sacred.[2] But even those socialists who spurned such displays as unseemly and developed a commitment to reconciling Jewish cultural creativity and even nationalism (*yidishe kultur*) with leftist politics generally construed this as a secular project.[3] Ḥayim Zhitlovsky, one of the foremost theoreticians of Yiddishism as a Diaspora cultural identity, denied the necessity of a connection between Jewish religion and Jewish nationality, or at the very least subordinated the former to the latter.[4] Simply put, to be a socialist with roots in Eastern European Judaism and Yiddish culture was, as a general rule, to be estranged from Jewish religion and observance.[5]

This association of Russian Jewish socialists in their transnational contexts with secularism has, to date, not been seriously challenged in scholarship.[6] Many have interpreted the disproportionate Jewish attraction to and leadership within socialism (not to mention Marxism itself) as a form of secularized messianism,[7] but few have studied concrete examples of Jewish socialist thinkers who advocated a distinctively Jewish religious socialism. In his analysis of a strain of Jewish messianic, mystical, and anarchist thought among a wide range of twentieth-century Central European Jewish intellectuals, Michel Löwy pointedly rejects the existence of any equivalent tendency among Eastern European Jewish socialists. He claims that these socialists, whether they endorsed a radical cosmopolitanism or a national and cultural Jewish identity, "still had one element in common: rejection of the Jewish religion. Their world-view was always rationalist, atheist, secular, *Aufklärer*, materialist." The "writings of radical Russian-Jewish intellectuals," he concludes, "unlike those of many Central European Jewish revolutionaries, did not make the least reference to religion, nor did they display the least trace of a messianic/religious dimension."[8]

This unequivocal assertion is contradicted by the emergence, in the interwar period, of a growing number of radical Russian- and Polish-born Jewish intellectuals who not only made reference to religion but also argued for religious socialism in general and Jewish religious socialism in particular. They vouched for the primacy of an ethical and idealistic socialism that was staunchly antimaterialist, anti-Marxist, and anti-Bolshevik yet avowedly revolutionary and not reformist. In this regard they were not entirely new, as there were others in this mold, such as Naḥman Syrkin and Zhitlovsky himself, who espoused similar views. Where they differed was not in their integration of socialism and ethics per se but in their mooring of this ethical socialism in Jewish religious texts and sources. These Jewish religious socialists were a mixed bunch. Some, probably the majority, hailed from anarchist and socialist parties and came to religion as adults, even if a few had always been personally observant; others were Orthodox Jews who came to socialism.[9] Although clustered around specific journals and in specific circles and factions, they never bound together to create a cohesive movement. Yet starting in 1925 and lasting some two decades, the existence of a Jewish religious yet revolutionary socialist current was so evident that contributors to a journal as left-wing as the anarchist New

York-based *Fraye Arbeter Shtime* could speak of "penitent moods" (*ba'al tshuve shtimungen*) and "the 'pious' moods of our radicals" (*di "frumkayt"-shtimungen fun undzere radikaln*) in the workers movement.[10] Observers took note of the novelty of a Jewish religious socialism, especially compared with Christian socialism, long in existence.[11]

In what follows, I analyze the contributions to this emergent discourse of three of its leading exponents: the former Russian revolutionary Isaac Naḥman Steinberg (1888–1957), the Chicago anarchist and philosopher William Nathanson (1883–1963), and the "red rabbi" Abraham Bick (1913–1990). Their work shared certain themes—an embrace of Jewish messianism as a prototype or model for socialism, an insistence on the need for "religiosity" over mere religion, and a mining of classical sources for socialist prooftexts—but they varied in the degree to which they were activists, the concreteness of their programs, and the nature of the radical Judaism they pursued. Together, however, they served as an alternative to a freethinking anarchism, a reformist socialism and trade unionism, and Bolshevik (increasingly Stalinist) communism. The map of Yiddish socialism from the 1920s to the 1940s should include this prominent if minority current.

Isaac Naḥman Steinberg

Isaac Naḥman Steinberg had the most colorful past of all the new-wave ethical and religious socialists.[12] Born in 1888 in Dinaburg (Dauguvpils) in what is today Latvia into an affluent family, Steinberg combined a talmudic education with study at a Russian gymnasium and an immersion in radical revolutionary literature. Following his graduation in 1906, he studied law at Moscow University, where he joined the Social Revolutionary Party. Arrested in 1907 for the spread of illegal revolutionary propaganda, he was imprisoned and sent into exile for a time. Steinberg chose to continue his study of law at the University of Heidelberg, while also carrying on his tutelage in Talmud. Returning to Moscow in 1910, he began practicing Jewish law and became a pillar of the Jewish community. He returned to revolutionary activity in 1916.

The Socialist Revolutionary Party to which Steinberg belonged was an outgrowth of Russian populism and the *narodniki*. Contrary to the Russian

Marxist Social Democratic Party, it did not champion the urban proletariat as the class of the future, nor did it believe that the revolution was historically inevitable. Instead, the Socialist Revolutionary Party looked to the traditional Russian peasant community as the nucleus of future revolution. The task of the revolutionary was to "go to the people," to educate the oppressed peasants in agrarian reform and revolutionary propaganda, and to be educated by their idealized communalist morality in turn.

In the aftermath of the February Revolution, Steinberg broke with the majority of the Socialist Revolutionary Party members, who were cooperating with the liberal bourgeois parties in the Constituent Assembly, and formed a new faction, the Left Social Revolutionaries (LSRs). The LSRs clamored for a much more sweeping socialist revolution than the mainstream party, arguing for a socialist government without any reliance on the liberal parties. After the October Revolution, the Bolsheviks realized that they were still too weak to rule alone and invited the LSRs to form a coalition with them. As part of the deal, Steinberg became the people's commissar of justice. In this role he supported the dissolution of the Constituent Assembly out of opposition to its vision of a Russian liberal democratic state. Troubled by the mounting state-sponsored Bolshevik terror of the Cheka (secret police), he sought to exercise greater control over their activities and purges but enjoyed only intermittent success. The seeds for the ultimate break between the LSRs and the Bolsheviks came as a result of the Treaty of Brest-Litovsk of March 1918, which ended the Russian war with Germany and Austria-Hungary in what was widely seen as a capitulation. Steinberg and the LSRs opposed the treaty as a sign of Russian realpolitik and a concession of the utopian hope of fostering revolutionary aspirations among the German workers. The LSRs mounted an unsuccessful revolt against the Bolsheviks in July 1918, though Steinberg escaped the immediate consequences as a result of having been sent abroad by his party to drum up support among German and Swiss socialists. (This represented the termination of his nearly six-month tenure as minister of justice.) Upon returning to Russia, he was swept up in a wave of arrests of LSRs. Even though he was ultimately freed, in 1921 the Bolsheviks permitted him to leave Russia on the condition that he did not return. In 1922 he settled in Berlin, where he continued work for an LSR party that he eventually came to realize was essentially hopeless. He began applying himself to conceiving a distinctively Jewish socialism that would live up to the ethical maximalism of his own vision. In 1926, together with his brother Aaron Steinberg and Ḥayim Zhitlovsky, he launched the first issue of the Yiddish *Free Writings* (*Fraye shriftn*), a journal committed to featuring and disseminating Jewish socialist thought. Steinberg wrote articles for practically all 18 of the volumes printed between 1926 and 1937, when the journal ceased to publish.[13]

Three main themes pervaded Steinberg's articles and his brand of ethical Jewish socialism. First, he polemicized against both social democratic reformism and Bolshevism. The social democratic reformers, having opted to collaborate with liberalism and capitalism in securing greater rights and protections for workers, betrayed the cause of socialist revolution. The Bolsheviks stood accused of a greater range of crimes. In addition to supposedly elevating the proletariat as the chosen class and excluding the peasantry, Bolshevism was in fact an elitist clerisy that viewed citizens as human sheep to be pastored and led, shorn of individual conscience, down history's unswerving line based on ironclad economic laws to socialism. "The bearer of the consciousness [of this line] is ... one—the proletariat, or the communist party, or perhaps most accurately the central committee of the party," who alone were entitled to shepherd the masses through the historical process.[14] Bolshevism had accordingly yielded not socialist revolution but the power principle in politics. It had crushed the hopes for a decentralized state organized around workers' soviets (councils) and confiscated the free consciousness of the individual.

Second, Steinberg issued a pointed critique of Jewish national formalism. Although applauding the spirit of the creation of a national culture and language (Yiddish or Hebrew), he took issue with those (like, he believed, Zhitlovsky) who placed the preservation of the nation (*kiyum ha-umah*) above all other values and marginalized the need for the nation to contain a clear socio-ethical and social-revolutionary content.[15] For example, in Yiddishism, which he had once regarded as a pathbreaking movement for the cultural education of the Jewish masses, Steinberg lamented the conversion of the cause of perpetuating Yiddish to a goal unto itself. The Yiddishists and Hebraists sought to forestall "national assimilation" but failed to reckon with the dangers of what Steinberg called "human assimilation," symbolized in the extensive technological and material advances of "civilization" (a critique Steinberg probably borrowed from Nathanson, as will be seen) and the stagnancy and even decline of moral progress. As he wrote in "Politics and Morality in the Eyes of Jews" (*Politik un moral bay yidn*), the Jewish nation was not simply "a natural family-union, connected through instinctive relations of blood and memories"; it was "a *living spiritual unity*, a unique dynamic power, a power that leads not only back to an already closed history, but forward to new world-historical tasks."[16] Steinberg applied this same standard to Zionism. Although he approved of the small communes (*kevuzot*) that the socialist Zionists were establishing, he expressed concern about their collaboration with bourgeois Zionists who espoused a capitalist-statist ideology—reservations that would ultimately lead Steinberg to create the territorialist "Freeland" movement in the late 1930s. Jews wandered for 40 years in the wilderness, Steinberg wrote, before they arrived in the Land of Israel. In between, they had a profound nation-building experience that left an indelible stamp on their consciousness—the giving of the Torah (*matan torah*), with its conferral of a complete worldview and a concrete program of life and morality. The point was that Jews became a unity not with the conquest of a land or kingdom but on its threshold; they constituted themselves as a nation through the spiritual self-understanding and ethical determination of the blueprint for life they obtained at Sinai.[17]

A third element of Steinberg's outlook was his belief that complete devotion to an ethical socialist revolutionary ideal was possible here and now, if only there was the will to freely choose it. Jewish workers had to learn to fight *against* the historical current, against its supposedly lawfully flowing waters, for their liberation. "Organizing the Jewish will, deepening and unifying its ideal, transforming the 'impossible' of today into a possible tomorrow—is this not the main task of Jewish socialism?" he proclaimed.[18] The ethical-activist spirit necessary for the advent of socialism was seeded in the prophetic and self-sacrificial Jewish religious past, in the Jewish common man's passionate yearning, in response to the deepest suffering, for social justice and right. "A people," Steinberg wrote, "which has borne (and continues to bear) in itself the hope for a messiah . . . can connect its daily worries with a revolutionary ideal."[19]

From his renegade youth through his term as the first Soviet commissar of justice and continuing with his long period as a Jewish socialist and eventually territorialist, Steinberg combined revolutionary maximalism with strict religious observance. In 1924 the pioneering Eastern European Jewish historian and Diaspora autonomist Simon Dubnow attended

Steinberg's seder in Berlin and was struck by the "unusual circumstances" of "the family of the former Commissar of Justice Steinberg" holding fast to religious rituals. Dubnow's uncle, Victor Erlich, who was also in attendance, called it "the longest and most 'orthodox' seder, in which I have participated."[20] Still, most of Steinberg's essays for *Fraye shriftn*, while invoking Judaism's prophetic heritage and messianic belief, tended more toward an ethical than a religious socialism per se. In other articles, however, he did broach the possibility that the "religious Jew as such had something decisive and for him obligatory to say regarding the social question."[21] In a piece he wrote for a small German Jewish Orthodox publication in 1932, Steinberg noted attempts to create a religious socialism while questioning why such efforts had made little inroads among Jewish socialists. The key symbol for Steinberg was the giving of the Torah at Mount Sinai. This was not a circumscribed historical and geographic event but an ongoing revelation of absolute character, to the point that "in every generation, the Jewish people stands once again before Mount Sinai, in order to receive anew the pronouncement and obligation and to proclaim, 'We will do and we will listen.'"[22] On the basis of this everlasting Sinai, Judaism was capable of mounting a trenchant critique of the chief evils of the age, including war, social and material want, and modern civilization. With regard to the social question, Steinberg conceded that the path of charity encouraged by Judaism was too accommodating of capitalism and incapable of uprooting the social order. In general, the biblical laws in areas such as agriculture and slavery "did not contain in and of themselves a social revolutionary effect." However, it was necessary

> to recognize the *spirit* of this legislation, which was always ready to undertake social upheavals, which had no reverence for human property relations ("indeed all the earth is Mine"),[23] and which subordinated material goods to the ethical-religious. Those laws are the expression of a timeless social-ethical spirit, which in our particular epoch can also assume the particular historical forms of social liberation.[24]

Steinberg thus discerned in the spirit of the Torah a revolutionary potential whose further elaboration, as we will see, he would welcome in the work of Abraham Bick.

William Nathanson

Born in Kyiv, Nathanson's given name was certainly not William, though none of the lexicon entries or obituaries appear to have any notion of it. At the age of 13, he left home for Bielozerkov and Zhitomir to study in preparation for university, but eventually he became sidetracked by involvement in the Bund, where he received a grounding in Marxism.[25] At about age 20, Nathanson immigrated to the United States, settling in Chicago. He began studying medicine but soon gave himself completely over to the study of philosophy, which, along with psychology, he studied in university for three years. While beginning to write, primarily in Yiddish, on a broad range of philosophical and artistic topics, he made a living by teaching in Jewish schools in Chicago. The year 1923 was an especially prolific one for Nathanson; in addition to publishing a translation of Henri Bergson's *Introduction to Metaphysics* in Yiddish and producing the first Yiddish translation of Spinoza's *Ethics*, he came out with his magnum opus, *Culture and Civilization* (*Kultur un tsivilizatsye*), a book of over 400 pages that was a major addition to the limited library of Yiddish philosophical works.[26] Here, he outlined the principles of his "Neo-Socialism" for the first time and laid out many of the key themes that would mark his voluminous future writings.

If Nathanson had once been a Marxist or at least a member of a Marxist party, he wrote *Culture and Civilization* as a fervent opponent of Marx and his socialist legacy. Materialism was not only wrong on its face but also had lost the prestige it had possessed in the second half of the nineteenth century, when it was the dominant philosophical outlook. In its place, a new idealistic direction, embodied by Nathanson's beloved Bergson, was emerging. In contrast to the older idealism of Kant, which restricted itself to reason and intellectualism and thus was susceptible to relativism, the new idealism recognized the primacy of feeling and the will, even the irrational. As opposed to intellectualism, this idealism was based in intuitionism, which was capable of apprehending absolute, divine, eternal, and infinite truth and set for itself the ultimate task of absolute freedom of speech and writing and absolute social and economic equality.

This assessment of the changing Zeitgeist of philosophy and the respective legacies of materialism and intuitionism was the basis for Nathanson's duality of culture and civilization. Civilization was marked by the achievement in society of more material wealth, more bodily comforts, and greater technical power over the forces of matter, and its privileged fields of knowledge production were the natural sciences and technology. Humanity was understood chiefly as *Homo faber*, the mechanic who fabricates and invents tools that enhance the mastery of nature and make life more comfortable. Culture, on the other hand, encompassed the realm of spirit, in which the driving aim was to enrich the life of the human soul and to discover the meaning and purpose of life. These strivings found their expression in art, philosophy, morality, and religion. Culture's model of the human was *Homo sapiens*, the seeker of knowledge who struggles to understand the problems of life more deeply.[27] Civilization, whose chief emphasis was the practical and material dimension of existence, cared only about the uses of objects and events, whereas culture was predominantly concerned with values. Civilization predominated in the second half of the nineteenth century, when *Homo faber* threw itself headlong into scientific discovery and the manufacturing of things, all with the goal of conquest of the external world and improving the creature comforts of life. Culture, and its speculative quest for the divine essence and the spiritually beautiful and eternal, Nathanson argued, must regain the upper hand.

For Nathanson, all the socialist movements to date had failed to transcend the limits of civilization and reach the heights of culture. Marxism was based on philosophical materialism and determinism and reduced everything spiritual and ethical to the prevailing economic conditions. The social democrats were Marxist, materialist, intellectualist, and relativist. The Socialist Revolutionaries in Russia renounced Marxism and materialism but remained beholden to the old intellectualist idealism. The Bolsheviks were Marxist and materialist, intellectualist, and relativist, and since coming to power, they had betrayed the socialist principle of absolute freedom of speech and writing and, through measures such as the New Economic Policy of 1921, with its more market-oriented economic policy, absolute social and economic equality as well.

Neosocialism was to be built not on the materialist, civilization-encrusted foundations of the nineteenth century but on the new culture-based idealism of the twentieth. Its goals were absolute and uncompromising: freedom of speech and writing and social and economic equality for all members of society. Even if their achievement spelled a diminishment of overall material wealth and a lower level of civilization, that should be no obstacle, for only a life lived in the light of culture was truly worthy of humanity.

Twelve years and several books and articles later, amid the burgeoning catastrophe for European Jews, Nathanson directed his call for neosocialism to Jewish radical thought specifically. In *Toward the Revision of National-Radical Thought* (*Tsu der revizye fun natsyonal-radikaln gedank*), published in 1935, Nathanson called for a return to religion among Jewish socialists and within their schools and institutions: "The newest research and discoveries in the realm of culture and the new feelings and convictions, which now predominate in a few radical camps, have placed in the foreground the need and the impetus to *revise everything* that goes under the name *radical thought*."[28] True to his arguments in *Culture and Civilization*, this radicalism would realize "that spirituality and not materiality is the source and goal of the world and humanity, and that the foundation and content of everything—in the world as in humanity—is God."[29] Nathanson made many appeals to belief in God and to a reversion to the "old religious-moral foundations" as well as to a recognition "of the great role of religiosity" and the "profound influence and impact of the ethical feelings."[30] For Jews, this meant finding a way back to Mount Sinai and the words and inspiration of the Torah and the prophets. Nathanson castigated the system of Jewish socialist schools that had failed to transmit the message of Sinai and the prophets, a failing that ultimately accrued to the teachers and parents who had banished *Yidishkayt* from their midst.[31]

Nathanson laced his argument with quotations and paraphrases from the biblical prophets, Isaac Nachman Steinberg and his brother Aaron Steinberg, Y. L. Peretz, the literary critic Baruch Rivkin, and others. Yet his most extended engagement was with Ḥayim Zhitlovsky, in particular, with an article Zhitlovsky had written in 1911, "The National-Poetic Rebirth of the Jewish Religion."[32] Nathanson regarded this essay as a pioneering, if ultimately unsuccessful attempt to persuade radicals to reclaim the sacred energies embedded in their Jewish heritage. "Every religion," Nathanson quoted Zhitlovsky as arguing, "has created moments, which call forth in the soul of believers feelings of holiness. It [religion] has holy personas . . . holy places . . . holy sources . . . holy times . . . and also holy actions."[33] Zhitlovsky argued that radicals could relate positively to these so long as they transposed them to a poetic key. Religious images, representations, myths, and ceremonies "will become holy and dear to us not because we believe in their supernatural divinity, but rather because our mood will be moved by their human beauty and they evoke in us poetic feelings and thoughts, which we regard as humanly holy."[34] This would, in short, be a secular rehabilitation of religious ceremonies and symbols. "Passover," Zhitlovsky wrote, "is the *yom-tov* of the revolutionary struggle for freedom."[35] Shavuot could be celebrated even by nonbelievers in the unity and divinity of Mosaic Torah, who nevertheless saw the Torah as a "treasure of knowledge and justice," in which a people

> for the first time declared before humanity that the treasure of knowledge and justice is the *holiest* thing that a people possesses, the most *important* thing, about which a person must think day and night ("you shall recite it day and night") and which he must transmit as an inheritance to the coming generation ("impress them on your children").[36]

According to Nathanson, despite this earnest appeal, Zhitlovsky remained "a lonely voice in the desert."[37] He attributes this in part to the fact that Zhitlovsky mostly shied away from the theme of revitalizing religion in his later writings and placed greater emphasis on Yiddishism, the secularization of Jewish nationalism, and his rejection of the belief that Israel and the Torah are one. In addition, Zhitlovsky's call for a poetic transformation failed to grasp the power of *religiosity* and collapsed under its own secularism. Religion is only religiosity, Nathanson claims, when it designates a sense of being subject to an "all-providential, guiding spirit," when it "influences the individual and the community to [an appreciation of] the most beautiful, the highest and deepest." Contrary to the radicals, "God ... is not ... a product of the yearning of the human soul for something higher, more beautiful, and supernatural"; he is "the cause of everything," and "if He did not exist, there would be no yearning." The goal, then, should not have been to foster a "national-*poetic*, but a national-radical-*religious* rebirth," for "poetry has never taken and will never take the place of religiosity."[38]

Nathanson frequently remonstrates with the ethical and religious socialists he cites for their failure to offer a concrete program for change. But Nathanson himself is exceedingly vague on this question; he mentions belief in God and the need for a return to Judaism's "religious-moral foundations" repeatedly, but he has little to say about what, beyond greater spirituality, he wishes to revive. At one point, he argues that only that in venerable antiquity which can withstand and endure the sharp penetration of reason, and which can additionally kindle the feelings and soothe the emotions, can be renewed and will once again be felt with intentionality [*kavone*] and be hoisted on a beam for the building and construction of a new and higher way of life and content of life.[39]

For all his emphasis on God and Torah, Nathanson proves here to be skeptical about the divinity of the law, claiming that what will survive of the tradition must be in accord with reason and feeling. In that sense, he is perhaps not so distant from Zhitlovsky. Even his credo for the new Jewish national religious radical culture union he clamors for—the feeling that an omnipotent and universal spiritual force named God is present, combined with the belief that religion and religiosity are not only individual but also social—is devoid of Jewish content. Nathanson eventually gets around to providing his vision with some Jewish subject matter and detail. He calls for students in the Jewish socialist-radical schools to be educated about the God idea through Jewish legends (Aggadah) and the teachings of the sages. He insists that students be taught Hebrew, "the language in which the God-revolution and God-understanding of the Jewish people was revealed and formulated," so that they are able to read the Hebrew Bible in the original.[40] He invokes the need to reclaim Talmud and midrash, speculative and *musar* literature, and Kabbalah and Hasidism for Jewish religious-national radicalism. Yet he demonstrates no familiarity in the book with any of these. About one thing he is clear, however: No revolution for absolute social and economic equality is possible if those who fight for it are not deeply rooted in religious and ethical ground. He makes a sharp division between the radical and nonradical segments of the Jewish people. "For us [radicals]," he asserts, "the prophets with their demand for justice is of greatest significance, not the priests with their pleasure from burnt offerings, meal offerings, and voluntary offerings."[41] Nathanson's project of revision and rebuilding is intended for Jewish radicals alone.

Abraham Bick

The first thing that distinguishes Abraham Bick from the previous ethical and religious socialists examined is that he was an Orthodox rabbi, who signed his books and articles with the honorific Rav. Born in Kobrin, Poland, Bick moved to the United States at the age of 14 in 1927, before immigrating to Palestine four years later. There, he studied at Yeshivat Merkaz Ha-Rav Kook, the seminary created and permeated by the teachings of Abraham Isaac Kook, the towering Jewish thinker and chief Ashkenazic rabbi of Mandatory Palestine. In 1936 Bick returned to the United States and eventually took a position as rabbi of an Orthodox congregation in Brooklyn.[42] During his years in Palestine, Bick became involved in a political party of religious socialist Zionists called Dat ve-Avodah (Religion and Labor). Founded in Poland in 1929 as a more radical offshoot of the chief movement of the religious Zionist left, Ha-Po'el Ha-Mizrahi (which itself had branched off from the religious Zionist party Mizrahi in 1922 in the name of reconciling Torah values with the Zionist labor movement's commitment to pioneering and rural settlement), Dat ve-Avodah was ultimately destroyed in Europe because of the Holocaust, and, with the creation of the State of Israel, it disappeared there too.[43]

In 1938, from his base in Brooklyn, Bick published his most programmatic work, *Fundamental Principles of Religious Socialism* (*Gruntprintsipn fun religyezn sotsyalizm*).[44] The volume contained a foreword by Isaac Nahman Steinberg, who wrote that he had "prayed for this book." Steinberg also noted his pride that the ideas of *Fraye shriftn* had found in Bick "such a strong and esteemed adherent."

The principal argument of *Fundamental Principles* is that socialism is not only reconcilable with the Torah but also forms its ultimate aim and realization. It is not simply that one *could* be but that one *had* to be an Orthodox Jew and also a socialist. The book is divided into three main sections. In the first, Bick explains the ethical foundations of Mosaic Torah while also demonstrating that various traits and teachings of revolutionary (indeed, Marxian) socialism were foreshadowed by the Jewish religious tradition. The second section is a polemic against the philosophical underpinnings of Marxism, and the third is a critique of "official Orthodoxy."

Bick opens by arguing that the Torah proclaims a radical ethics rooted in monotheism. If one affirms the eternality of the one and only God, the "foundation of foundations," one must acknowledge that the concepts of justice and morality are similarly absolute and eternal and commit oneself to practicing only such deeds as can have an eternal existence. Here, Bick cites the interpretation of Job 29:14 by one of his intellectual heroes, the nineteenth-century rabbi and renowned Tanakh commentator Meir Lebush ben Yehiel Michel (aka the Malbim). The verse begins "I clothed myself in righteousness and it robed me"; the Malbim, changing the first person from Job to God, interprets this as "I wear justice and justice wears me"—meaning that justice is God's garb. "It is clear," Bick writes, "that Mosaic Torah is above all a moral philosophy; its foundation is ethics." Moreover, the sources for this outlook are not merely the Torah and the prophets but also the Talmud, the *Zohar*, Jewish philosophy, Kabbalah, and Hasidism. All constitute "the ethical source . . . for a complete overthrow of all the present-day social conditions in the world."[45]

There follows a long (and not entirely persuasive) discussion of revolutionary socialist positions for which alleged support in the Torah and classical rabbinic literature can be found. These include opposition to private property, slavery, the belief in class struggle, and the commitment to internationalism. Perhaps the most striking instance of this tendency is Bick's explanation of the halakhic perspective on Marx's theory of surplus value, the engine of capitalism. According to Marx, under the conditions of capitalism, the surplus value created by workers—the value above what is necessary for them to reproduce their labor-power—contractually belongs to the proprietor or factory owner.[46] Bick, however, discerns in the Babylonian Talmud an alternative concept of surplus value and invokes a *sugya* in *Baba Kama* 98b discussing the case of a carpenter commissioned to build a chest, a box, or a cabinet with wood supplied by the purchaser. According to Rav Asi, in the event the carpenter causes irreparable harm to the wood before building anything, he is liable for full damages. But if he builds the chest, box, or cabinet, and before giving it to the buyer breaks it, he is liable only for the damage caused to the wood but is exempt from paying for the vessel. The reason for this is that "the craftsman acquires through the enhancement of the vessel."[47] In other words, the craftsman is considered to have acquired the vessel through his work, which enhances its value, and it remains in his possession until he returns it to the buyers. Consequently, if he damages the vessel in any way, he is damaging his *own* item and must return only the value of the raw materials to the owners. From this premise (which the Gemara proceeds to debate), Bick claims that, according to the Talmud, the one who creates the surplus value is the one who owns it. He asserts that Judaism upholds "the importance of the worker against the work-provider in relation to value, and it will be clear to us that modern socialism proceeds without knowledge and unwittingly in the footprints of the Torah, and justifies unconsciously the foundations of Talmudic Halakha."[48]

As a proponent of socialist revolution, albeit one driven by the ethical teachings of the Torah rather than by notions of historical determinism, Bick felt the need to devote several pages to the problem of revolutionary violence. On one hand, he claims that the Jewish idealistic approach to revolution is quite different from the Marxist-Bolshevik example with its embrace of violence, terror, and bloodshed. The latter violates the basic commandment "You shall not kill" and is unworthy of the name socialism. On the other hand, Bick does allow that violence may be required in some instances. Drawing on one of Isaac Naḥman Steinberg's postmortems on the October Revolution, Bick argues that in a situation when the revolution is in full throttle and facing belligerent reaction, violence may be required, citing the talmudic dictum of "he who comes to kill you, rise up and kill him first."[49] Violence, in this case, is essentially a matter of self-defense. That differs significantly from the situation under the Bolsheviks, where the revolutionaries, having seized power, held onto it through a mixture of "sadistic revenge and brutality." After claiming that "the Tanakh is in general permeated by the spirit of revolution" and developing an argument grounded in Jewish texts for the importance in Judaism of God's "principle of judgment" (*midat ha-din*) alongside God's "principle of mercy" (*midat ha-raḥamim*), Bick backtracks somewhat. He allows that revolutionary violence may fall under the legal category of "a commandment that is fulfilled through a sinful act" (*miẓvah ha-ba'ah be-averah*), according to which, in most cases, the end is invalidated through the means. He returns to his earlier argument for self-defense but admits that "in no case can a revolution be justified a priori as a mitzvah."[50] Yet after contending that a religious socialist revolution based on love can counter the cruelty that revolution entails, Bick ultimately concludes that, whether driven by love or fear, revolution is necessary. "As religious socialists," he avers, "we must fight to achieve socialism only out of love, but if not, it must come through fear, but come it must."[51]

The second part of the book is a critique of Marx and specifically of his historical materialism, which Bick views as utterly incommensurate with the idealistic and ethical socialism authorized by the Torah. Bick offers a more nuanced assessment of Marx in an essay published two years after *Fundamental Principles* in his anthology *World and Home* (*Velt un heym*).[52] There, Bick considers the question of what is Jewish in Marx. He asserts that the "holy wrath" of the *Communist Manifesto* bears traces of the tenor of ancient Jewish prophecy. Marx's tirades against the injustice of the social order, his ability to foretell other possibilities for historical development than the prevailing social order, even his theory that labor is the only source for the human creation of value—all are cited as evidence that "Marx was nourished on the milk of Judaism."[53] Where Marx broke with Judaism was in his reduction of the world of ideas and spiritual values to economic relations.[54] This made truth, justice, and even Judaism itself no more than reflections of the material conditions of the ruling system. "It is certain," Bick writes, "that Marxism's posing of the problem stems from a Jewish ethos, from Jewish morality and its rootedness, but its solution to the problem is in opposition to Judaism."[55] Although Bick concedes that economic circumstances help shape the emergence of a philosophy or theory, he balks at the notion that they also condition its truthfulness. Marxist-Leninism, he goes on to say, deprives the human of an eternal soul, a personality that is created in the image of God. Everything in the world, including humankind, is simply a mirroring of material forces, an outlook Bick deems responsible for the "monstrous cruelty" and "tyranny" that has lasted a quarter century "in the land of the Marxist-Leninist revolution." Marxism, according to the title of Bick's essay, is the "warped face of Jewish ideology."[56]

On a few occasions in *Fundamental Principles*, Bick cites his teacher Rav Kook, in one case partly to redeem materialism. In a passage recorded by one of his interlocutors, Kook praised the then strengthening materialist outlook for its lucidity: "The good spark in the materialist inclination . . . is the effort to perceive the real world without the admixture of images."[57] In that lies its truth, Kook claimed, because the spiritual concepts must at the outset be grasped through images that do not accord with reality. And materialism does a great deal of good initially by overturning the weak and false images to clear a place for pure faith in the reality of God, who is higher than all images and whose name is likewise more certain than the entirety of material reality. Only such an absolute denial—only such a heresy—can give rise to the light of a stronger faith, in which the spiritual forces will once again prevail.[58] Whereas elsewhere in his work Kook stresses the necessity of imaginative representations and treats the imagination as a vessel of truth, here he portrays images as obstacles to understanding and materialism as a dialectical counterpoint that can cut out the middleman of the imagination and make way (once transcended) for an apprehension of divinity.[59] His approach to materialism echoes his attempt to rescue the modern revolutionary heretics of the Second Aliyah, despite their antagonism to Judaism, by regarding their rebellion against the Exile as part of the unfolding of the messianic redemption; materialism is similarly "saved," but it is also not appreciated on its own terms.[60] Although Kook does not specifically mention Marxism, it may in fact have been his intended referent, given its potency among the socialist Zionists in the Yishuv.

Bick reserves his final attack for what he calls bourgeois or official Orthodoxy. This is the Orthodoxy that proclaims the opposition of the Torah to socialism, which it deems *treyf* and heretical. Proponents of official Orthodoxy cite biblical passages such as "for there will never cease to be poor in the land" (Deuteronomy 15:11) to claim that poverty and wealth are foreordained in heaven, by special providence. Judaism, they claim, knows only of charity and mercy, not of social revolution. This prompts Bick's most blistering dissent.

> This theory is essentially anti-religious and blasphemous. . . . The inclination to make the Creator of the World a partner to wickedness and hatefulness is not new. To hold that poor people must remain so, in order to permit one to practice the mitzvah of mercy, only means to deprive the poor not only of this world [*Oylam hazeh*] but also the world to come [*Oylam habo*]. Because if we shall assume that without charity and mercy one cannot fulfill God's commandment in the world, and therefore the present social order must be preserved, so that the mitzvah of charity will not be lacking, how will the poor fulfill this mitzvah? They cannot have mercy on the notables, they cannot divvy charity up among the rich. It follows then, that poor people cannot fulfill the entire Torah, if one robs them in this way of the world beyond.[61]

Bick thus demands a "radical change of values" of "official Orthodoxy," a transformation that will realize "that religion does not mean belief in God, and carrying out by rote the mitzvot," but a commitment to the ethical foundations of Torah. While asserting that religious socialists stand side by side with the official Orthodox in their defense of the mitzvot "between man and God," he insists that the religious socialists demonstrate a deeper understanding of and devotion to the mitzvot "between man and his comrade."[62]

Bick concludes with a twelve-point program that presumably represents his party of religious socialists. Among the points made, he declares that "they are the sharpest opponents of the present capitalist regime," which is "an explicit contradiction to the fundamental principles of the Torah." They reject the philosophical teachings of Marxism, arguing that "socialism is not an outcome of economic materialism, but an eschatological messianic striving that draws its sustenance from the moral sources of the Torah and prophetic justice."[63] They are against reformism and its acquiescence to the capitalist order but will nevertheless agitate for labor reforms such as unemployment insurance, compensation, and a six-hour workday. They prefer, as religious ethical socialists, a planned rebuilding of society but will not shy away from bloody resistance if there is no alternative. For all their differences with official Orthodoxy, they are also opposed to any kind of religious reform and will brook not even the slightest weakening of the practical mitzvot. In short, they equate social liberation with religious redemption.

Bick's *Fundamental Principles* was positively reviewed in the *Forverts*.[64] His views—including those about forerunners of Jewish religious social (even socialist) thought, which he assembled in a book published one year later, *Fighters and Guardians* (*Kempfer un hiter*)—were made known through the numerous freelance articles he published in the *Forverts* and other Yiddish newspapers. In 1945 Bick founded a school in today's East Village for Jewish radical thought called the Institut far Yidisher Bildung (Institute for Jewish Education), which at its peak had 400 students. Courses included "The Jewish People Under Capitalism, Imperialism, and Socialism," "The National Question and the Jewish People," "Marxism, the Jews, and the National Question," "The History of the Jews in the American Labor Movement," "The Bible, a Social Analysis," "American Jewish Life Today," "On Jewish Children and Their Problems," and "Teachers in the Struggle Against Anti-Semitism."[65] Starting around 1950, Bick became a regular contributor to the Yiddish communist newspaper *Morgn Frayhayt*. Exactly when he had modified his earlier critical opinions of Bolshevism is unknown, but in his articles for the *Morgn Frayhayt* he consistently defended the treatment of Jews in the Soviet Union and the Eastern Bloc, contradicting rumors (and, indeed, especially in the early 1950s, the reality) of antisemitic persecutions. In 1956 Bick was subpoenaed by the House Committee on Un-American Activities to answer questions about his political convictions, writings, and travels.[66] He invoked the Fifth Amendment 73 times, refusing to confirm information about his passport renewals, his trips to Europe and Brazil to participate in peace conferences funded by the Soviets, and whether he was a communist. The rabbinic establishment denounced him to the committee, and enrollment figures plummeted in his yeshiva, ultimately requiring its closure. Yet Bick continued writing for the *Morgn Frayhayt* until 1968. At that point, he broke with the newspaper and the communist movement more generally over its position on the State of Israel, where he subsequently settled. Throughout his life he remained a prolific writer in Yiddish, Hebrew, and English, and in his final decade he even published a short work on Jewish influences in Marx's thought.[67]

* * *

It should be underscored that the various streams of Jewish socialism, even when they consciously sought to break decisively with Jewish religion, generally bore its imprint. This was as true for movements such as the Bund as it was for the Palestine labor movement. In an essay written for a volume on Marx on the occasion of the centennial of his birth in 1918, Baruch Charney Vladeck, a celebrated Bundist activist in Eastern Europe who immigrated to the United States in 1908 (and became a notable leader of the Jewish labor movement there as well), highlighted the degree to which socialism and Marxism had substituted for traditional Judaism in the Jewish street. "The strike," he wrote, "has taken the place of a fast [*taanis*], the assembly—the place of prayer [*davenen*], the socialist pamphlet—the place of '*En Ya'akov*.'"[68] For Vladeck, Jewish Marxism retained the same religious sense of the sacred and enchanted, only displaced from traditional objects of veneration, such as the Torah and the Talmud and rites such as fasts and prayer, onto the new forms of socialist literature and activity. The entire frame of reference, however, remained Jewish. Without ever positing a Jewish core to Marx's philosophy (though he may in fact have subscribed to such a belief), Vladeck nevertheless argued for the profound influence of a Jewish cultural and religious inheritance in Marx's Jewish reception. As Anita Shapira has shown, the Palestine labor movement, for all its fierce anticlericalism, was awash in "kabbalistic and messianic terminology."[69] And Gerald Sorin, in his study of American Jewish immigrant radicals, has argued that Jewish socialists were a "prophetic minority" stamped by their earlier immersion in "the moral commandments of the Torah and Talmud, in messianic belief-systems, traditions of *tzedaka* . . . mutual aid, and communal responsibility."[70] Indeed, all the streams of modern Jewish politics—liberal integrationist, Diaspora nationalist, secular Zionist, and Orthodox—have invoked or reworked the religious tradition in some fashion.[71] Still, the Jewish religious socialist current introduced here represented something novel. In his 1911 essay Zhitlovsky aimed to redeem nearly all the Jewish holidays—including Shabbat, "the sacred *socialist* yom-tov"—but questioned whether "the purely-individual High Holidays [could] be included in the system of national-poetic Judaism."[72] The socialist-Zionists of the Yishuv similarly ignored Rosh Hashanah and Yom Kippur; "their exclusively religious character, and the lack of some other rationale, prevented them from being adapted to the secular arena, as the other holidays had been."[73] Thinkers such as Nathanson and Bick, on the other hand, grounded their neosocialism and religious socialism in a belief in a transcendent and omnipotent God and, in the case of Bick, in the strict observance of the commandments as well. The closest analogue to this Jewish religious socialism was the religious Zionist Ha-Po'el Ha-Mizrahi movement in Palestine, but this movement was much less committed to internationalism and global revolution. The same could be said for the Haredi workers' movement (and eventually political party) Poale Agudat Yisrael. Rabbi Yehuda Leib Orlean, a Ger Hasid who was one of Poale Agudat Yisrael's founders, wrote that "it is not man's task to make revolutions" and that total upheavals of society can be brought about only by God alone.[74]

Most studies of Jewish socialism have focused on its pre–World War I phase and have devoted relatively little attention to its evolution in the interwar period.[75] Perhaps this accounts for the dearth of awareness of this religious turn in Yiddish revolutionary socialism, which A. Almi, in his introduction to Bick's *Fundamental Principles*, described as an increasingly conspicuous phenomenon by the late 1930s. None of those who "returned" to religion revealed their motivations, though we might speculate that it reflects a profound disenchantment with the Bolshevik Revolution, a theme that traverses the works examined here. Nor is there an obvious explanation for the turn to socialism among some Orthodox Jews like Bick. Perhaps it suggests that socialism had grown so compelling in the interwar period that even some Orthodox Jews felt compelled to arrive at some sort of synthesis. Further research is necessary to determine the degree to which socialism made inroads into the Orthodox community. What is clear, however, is that the notion that the Yiddish revolutionary left was staunchly secularist needs to be qualified. The effort to ground Jewish socialism in religious faith and practice extended beyond the efforts of Steinberg, Nathanson, and Bick and remains to be more fully studied.[76]

Notes

My thanks to Tony Michels for introducing me to this revolutionary religious current in Yiddish socialism that originated in the 1920s. And, of course, I am deeply indebted to Michael Stanislawski for mentoring me in Eastern European Jewish thought and for training me to see the nuances in the relationship between the religious and the secular.

1 Perhaps the paradigmatic example of such a Jewish socialist biography is that of Abraham Cahan, the Russian Jewish immigrant to America who became the longtime editor of the *Forverts*. See Abraham Cahan, *Bleter fun mayn leben*, vol. 1 (New York: Forverts, 1926); and Leon Stein, ed., *The Education of Abraham Cahan* (Philadelphia: Jewish Publication Society, 1969).
2 N. Goldberg, "Die antireligyeze bavegung," in *Geshikhte fun der yidisher arbeter bavegung in di faraynikte shtatn*, ed. Elias Tcherikover (New York: YIVO, 1945), 2: 418–57.
3 On the idea of *yidishe kultur*, see Tony Michels, *A Fire in Their Hearts: Yiddish Socialists in New York* (Cambridge, MA: Harvard University Press, 2005), 125–77.
4 David Fishman, *The Rise of Modern Yiddish Culture* (Pittsburgh: University of Pittsburgh Press, 2005), 101.
5 Virtually none of the myriad Jewish socialists discussed in such classical studies as Jonathan Frankel's *Prophecy and Politics: Socialism, Nationalism, and the Russian Jews, 1862–1917* (Cambridge, UK: Cambridge University

Press, 1981), Irving Howe's *World of Our Fathers* (New York: Simon & Schuster, 1976), and Norah Levin's *While Messiah Tarried: Jewish Socialist Movements, 1871–1917* (New York: Schocken, 1977)—whatever their relationship to Jewishness—would have defined themselves as religious and certainly not as observant.

6 For some exceptions, see Lilian Türk and Jesse Cohn, "Yiddish Radicalism, Jewish Religion: Controversies in the Fraye Arbeter Shtime," *Essays in Anarchism and Religion*, vol. 2, ed. Alexander Christoyannopoulos (Stockholm: Stockholm University Press, 2018); Hayyim Rothman, "Rediscovering Rabbi Abraham Bick at the Site of the Former *Institut far Yidishe Bildung*," 12 January 2020, ingeveb.org/blog/rediscovering-radical-rabbi-abraham-bick-at-the-site-of-the-former-institut-far-yidisher-bildung (accessed 2 August 2021); and Hayyim Rothman, *No Masters but God: Portraits of Anarcho-Judaism* (Manchester, UK: Manchester University Press, 2021).

7 See Adam Weisberger, *The Jewish Ethic and the Spirit of Socialism* (New York: Peter Lang, 1997); and Anita Shapira, "The Religious Motifs of the Labor Movement," in *Zionism and Religion*, ed. Shmuel Almog, Jehuda Reinharz, and Anita Shapira (Waltham, MA: Brandeis University Press, 1998), 251–72.

8 Michel Löwy, *Redemption and Utopia: Jewish Libertarian Thought in Central Europe*, trans. Hope Heaney (Stanford, CA: Stanford University Press, 1992), 42, 43.

9 A list of the anarchists and socialists who came to religion would include Isaac Nachman Steinberg and his brother Aaron Steinberg, William Nathanson, H. Wolf, Jacob Babinsky, Abba Gordin, and Baruch Rivkin; the Orthodox Jews who came to socialism included Meir Hertzberg, Pinchas Wasserman, and Abraham Bick.

10 A. Almi, "Ober davenen muz men dokh . . . teme: 'tsurik tsu got'—Baaltshuve shtimungen bay a teyl idishe inteligents—emeser globin order derniderung," *Fraye Arbeter Shtime* (10 November 1940), 5, 7; Tuvye Eyges, "Di 'frumkayt'-shtimungen fun undzere radikaln," *Fraye Arbeter Shtime* (21 March 1941), 3.

11 S. Niger, "A religye on a Shulkhan Arukh," *Der Tog* (3 March 1935), 4.

12 This survey of Steinberg's revolutionary activity is based on Isaac Naḥman Steinberg, *Zikhroynes fun a folks-komisar* (Warsaw: H. Bshozha, 1931); Mikhail Krutikov, "Isaac Nahman Steinberg: From Anti-Communist Revolutionary to Anti-Zionist Territorialist," *Jews in Eastern Europe* 1–2 (1999): 5–24; and Leyzer Podryatshik, "Yitskhok Nakhmen Shteynberg," *Yiddish*

Lexicon, yleksikon.blogspot.com/2019/08/yitskhok-nakhmenshteynberg-isaac.html (accessed 7 May 2021). Most recently, Hayyim Rothman's *No Masters but God* includes an excellent chapter on Steinberg's intellectual biography.

13 On *Fraye shriftn*, see S. Niger, "*Fraye Shriftn*," *Der Tog* (11 August 1929); Eliyahu Shulman, "Di 'Fraye Shriftn,'" in *Yitskhok Nakhmen Shteynberg: Der mentsh, zayn vort, zayn oyftu*, ed. Benjamim Bialostotzky (New York: I. N. Steinberg Bukh-Komitet, 1961), 267–83; and Leybl Bayan, "Shteynberg's etisher sotsyalizm in der krayz 'Fraye Shriftn,'" in *Yitskhok Nakhmen Shteynberg: Der mentsh, zayn vort, zayn oyftu*, ed. Benjamim Bialostotzky (New York: I. N. Steinberg Bukh-Komitet, 1961), 284–93.

14 I. N. Steinberg, "Politik un moral," in his *In kampf far mentsh un yid* (Buenos Aires: Dr. I. N. Steinberg Kabalas Ponim Committee, 1962), 35. The article was originally published in *Fraye shriftn* 4 (November 1928): 3–29.

15 I. N. Steinberg, "Politik un moral bay yidn," in his *In kampf far mentsh un yid* (Buenos Aires: Dr. I. N. Steinberg Kabalas Ponim Committee, 1962), 187. The article was originally published in *Fraye shriftn* 5 (April 1929): 3–43.

16 Steinberg, "Politik un moral bay yidn," 188; emphasis in original.

17 Steinberg, "Politik un moral bay yidn," 210.

18 I. N. Steinberg, "Alte verter oyfsnay" [Old Values Anew], in his *In kampf far mentsh un yid* (Buenos Aires: Dr. I. N. Steinberg Kabalas Ponim Committee, 1962), 21. Originally published in *Fraye shriftn* 1 (September 1926): 5–12.

19 I. N. Steinberg, "Vegn sotsyaln basis fun yidishn sotsyalizm" [On the Social Basis of Jewish Socialism], in his *In kampf far mentsh un yid* (Buenos Aires: Dr. I. N. Steinberg Kabalas Ponim Committee, 1962), 232. Originally published in *Fraye shriftn* 2 (May 1927): 3–22.

20 Quoted in Tobias Grill, "Kampf für Sozialismus und Judentum auf vier Kontinenten: Isaac Nachman Steinbergs rooted cosmopolitanism," *BIOS: Zeitschrift für Biographieforschung, Oral History und Lebensverlaufanalysen* 28, nos. 1–2 (2015): 52.

21 I. N. Steinberg, "Über jüdische Religiosität," *Nachalath Z'wi: Eine Monatschrift für Judentum in Lehre und Tat* 2, nos. 9–10 (April 1932): 268.

22 Steinberg, "Über jüdische Religiosität," 266.

23 This verse comes from Exodus 19:5–6: "Indeed, all the earth is Mine but you shall be to Me a kingdom of priests and a holy nation."

24 Steinberg, "Über jüdische Religiosität," 269.

25 Leyb Vaserman, "William Natanson," in *Yiddish Lexicon*, trans. David Wollins, yleksikon.blogspot.com/search?q=nathanson (accessed 11 May 2023).

The only discussion of Nathanson in a scholarly article I have been able to track down concerns his translation of Spinoza's *Ethics*. See Shlomo Berger, "Undzer Bruder Spinoza: Yiddish Authors and the Freethinker," *Studia Rosenthaliana* 30 (1996): 255–68.

26 William Nathanson, *Kultur un tsivilizatsye* (Chicago: Naye Gezelshaft, 1923).

27 This assignation of priority to *Homo sapiens* over *Homo faber* is precisely the opposite of Marx's conception, as first articulated in the *Economic and Philosophical Manuscripts* (1844). See Shlomo Avineri, *Karl Marx: Philosophy and Revolution* (New Haven, CT: Yale University Press, 2019), 65.

28 Willam Nathanson, *Tsu der revizye fun natsyonal-radikaln gedank* (Chicago: L. M. Stein, 1935), 5.

29 Nathanson, *Tsu der revizye*, 5–6.

30 Nathanson, *Tsu der revizye*, 15.

31 As opposed to Irving Howe, who defined "the culture of *Yiddishkeit*" as increasingly secular, albeit indebted to the religious past, Nathanson associated *Yidishkayt* with a Jewish way of life that was traditional and marked by deep religiosity. See Howe, *World of Our Fathers*, 16; and Nathanson, *Tsu der revizye*, 18.

32 Hayim Zhitlovsky, "Di natsyonal-poetishe vidergeburt fun der idisher religye," in his *Gezamelte shriftn* (New York: Ḥayim Zhitlovsky ferlag gezelshaft, 1912), 4: 219–78.

33 Nathanson, *Tsu der revizye*, 32.

34 Zhitlovsky, "Di natsyonal-poetishe vidergeburt," 224.

35 Zhitlovsky, "Di natsyonal-poetishe vidergeburt," 252.

36 Zhitlovsky, "Di natsyonal-poetishe vidergeburt," 252; emphasis in original.

37 Nathanson, *Tsu der revizye*, 34.

38 Nathanson, *Tsu der revizye*, 38, 39, 61; emphasis in original.

39 Nathanson, *Tsu der revizye*, 30.

40 Nathanson, *Tsu der revizye*, 52–53.

41 Nathanson, *Tsu der revizye*, 26.

42 "Avrom (Avraham) Bik," *Yiddish Lexicon*, yleksikon.blogspot.com/2016/01/avrom-avraham-bik.html (accessed 11 May 2023).

43 Abraham Bick, "'Dat ve-Avodah': zerem smoli be-tsionut ha-datit," in *Sefer Shragay: Perakim be-ḥeker ha-tsionut ha-datit ve-ha-aliyah le-Eretz Yisrael*, ed. Mordechai Eliav and Yitzhak Refael (Jerusalem: Mosad Ha-Rav Kuk, 1981), 127–32.

44 Abraham Bick, *Grunt-printsipn fun religyezn sotsyalizm* (New York: Bafrayung, 1938).

45 Bick, *Grunt-printsipn*, 23.
46 Karl Marx, *Capital*, trans. Ben Fowkes (New York: Vintage, 1977), 1: 300–301.
47 BT *Baba Kama* 98b, www.sefaria.org/Bava_Kamma.98b?lang=bi (accessed 11 May 2023).
48 Bick, *Grunt-printsipn*, 39.
49 The work by Steinberg is I. N. Steinberg, *Der moralishe ponim fun der revolutsye* (Warsaw: H. Bzshoza, 1927). The maxim appears in various places in rabbinic literature, including in BT *Sanhedrin* 72a.
50 Bick, *Grunt-printsipn*, 56.
51 Bick, *Grunt-printsipn*, 57.
52 Abraham Bick, "Dos oysgekrimte ponim fun der yidisher ideologye," in his *Velt un heym: esseyen* (New York: M. S. Slarsky, 1941), 59–72.
53 Bick, "Dos oysgekrimte ponim," 64.
54 The understanding of Marx as an economic determinist ("vulgar Marxism") is of course controversial. Friedrich Engels himself sought to challenge this reputation in an 1890 letter written after Marx's death. There, he wrote that "Marx and I are ourselves partly to blame for the fact that the younger people sometimes lay more stress on the economic side than is due to it. We had to emphasise the main principle *vis-à-vis* our adversaries, who denied it, and we had not always the time, the place or the opportunity to allow the other elements involved in the interaction to come into their rights." See Friedrich Engels, "Letters on Historical Materialism," in *The Marx-Engels Reader*, 2nd ed., ed. Robert C. Tucker (New York: Norton, 1978), 762.
55 Bick, "Dos oysgekrimte ponim," 66.
56 Bick, "Dos oysgekrimte ponim," 59.
57 Abraham Isaac Kook, *Ma'amarei Ha-Re'iyah: kovez ma'amarim* (Jerusalem: Ha-Keren a. sh. Goldah Kats, 1984), 40–41, under the heading "Perurim mi-shulhan gavoah" (Crumbs from a High Table).
58 Bick, *Grunt-printsipn*, 74.
59 On Kook's understanding of the imagination, see Yehudah Mirsky, *Towards the Mystical Experience of Modernity: The Making of Rav Kook, 1865–1904* (Boston: Academic Studies, 2021), 201–18.
60 On Kook's attitude to these "seeming sinners," see Yehudah Mirsky, *Rav Kook: Mystic in a Time of Revolution* (New Haven, CT: Yale University Press, 2014), 97–99.
61 Bick, *Grunt-printsipn*, 92–93.

62 Bick, *Grunt-printsipn*, 112.
63 Bick, *Grunt-printsipn*, 110.
64 Hillel Rogoff, "A rav shraybt a bukh zu bavayzen az frume yidn darfn zayn sotsyalistn," *Forverts* (26 February 1939).
65 Rothman, "Rediscovering Rabbi Abraham Bick."
66 "Investigation of the Unauthorized Use of United States Passports—Part 4," Hearing before the Committee on Un-American Activities, House of Representatives, Eighty-Fourth Congress, Second Session, 16 June 1956 (Washington, DC: US Government Printing Office, 1956), 4597–622.
67 Abraham Bick, *Nezer mi-shorashav mozaʾo ve-olamo ha-yehudi shel Karl Marks* (Tel Aviv: Hakibbutz Hameuchad, 1984).
68 B. Vladeck, "Tsum bild fun Karl Marks," in *Karl Marks: zayn leben, zayn virken un zayne lehren: 1818–1918*, ed. Tsivyon [Ben-tsien Hoffman] (New York: Jewish Socialist Federation, 1918), 14. *ʿEn Yaʿakov* is the canonical anthology of legendary stories (*aggadot*) from the Babylonian Talmud, compiled and edited in the sixteenth century by Jacob ibn Habib of Salonika.
69 Shapira, "Religious Motifs," 255.
70 Gerald Sorin, *The Prophetic Minority: American Jewish Immigrant Radicals, 1880–1920* (Bloomington: Indiana University Press, 1985), 3.
71 Ezra Mendelsohn, *On Modern Jewish Politics* (New York: Oxford University Press, 1993), 3–36.
72 Zhitlovsky, "Di natsyonal-poetishe vidergeburt," 254.
73 Shapira, "Religious Motifs," 269.
74 See Yehuda Leib Orlean, *Tsu zate un tsu hungerike* [The Satiated and the Hungry] (Warsaw: Undzer Bukh, 1930–1931), 35. On the history of Poale Agudat Yisrael more broadly, see Yosef Fund, *Proletarim datiyim hitʾahdu! Polaei Agudat Yisrael, ideʾologyah u-medinut* (Jerusalem: Yad Yitzhak Ben-Zvi, 2018); and Ada Gebel, *Ḥaredim ve-anshe maʿaseh: Poale Agudat Yisraʾel, 1933–1939* (Jerusalem: Yad Yitzhak Ben-Zvi, 2017).
75 Examples include Frankel, *Prophecy and Politics*, and Levin, *While Messiah Tarried*. A notable exception to this phenomenon is studies of the Bund in interwar Poland. See, for example, Jack Jacobs, *Bundist Counterculture in Interwar Poland* (Syracuse, NY: Syracuse University Press, 2009); and Bernard Goldstein, *Twenty Years with the Jewish Labor Bund: A Memoir of Interwar Poland*, trans. and ed. Marvin S. Zuckerman (West Lafayette, IN: Purdue University Press, 2016).

76 Hayyim Rothman's *No Masters but God* is a groundbreaking step in this direction. The book consists of a series of eight illuminating biographical studies of Jewish religious (and frequently rabbinic) anarchists of Eastern European descent. Although Rothman locates the origins of this "anarcho-Judaism" in the late nineteenth century, I see the interwar era as the period when this current of Eastern European Jewish religious socialism and anarchism began to manifest more prominently (reflected in the fact that its appearance registered as a surprise in so much of the Yiddish press at the time).

14

The Fires of Hell, or *azoy vi got in ades*?

Revisiting Jewish Odessa from Mendoza, Argentina, 1964

Israel Bartal

"Inside" and "Outside" in Modern Jewish History

Only several decades after the Holocaust did scholars of late nineteenth-century Jewish history begin to distance themselves from the political-ideological discourse that had held sway in Poland and Russia early in the twentieth century. Eastern European Jews, constituting nearly 90% of world Jewry (including immigrants to other parts of the world) on the eve of World War II, exported a historiographic legacy written along party lines. Despite the fading of the political, social, and cultural realities that had shaped the historians' mind, highly politicized discourse continued to have an impact in the new lands where both writers and readers had immigrated. This dissonance, often accompanied by overt or covert rebellion against influential academic institutions and by challenges to authoritative venerated historians, took place simultaneously on both sides of the Atlantic.

Together with a group of young Israeli historians, I participated in this intellectual rebellion, which began on the academic campuses of Jerusalem, Tel Aviv, Haifa, and Be'er Sheva after the 1967 Arab-Israeli war. A similar group appeared in American and Canadian universities, and they

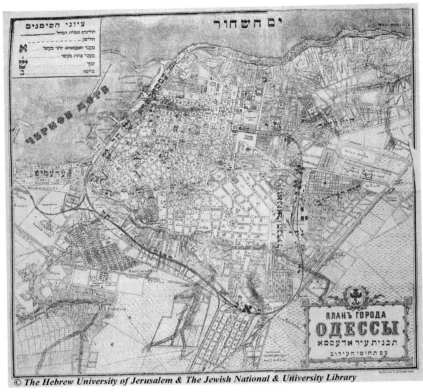

Figure 14.1. Map of Odessa. Source: Eran Laor Cartographic Collection, National Library of Israel.

played a key role in the flourishing of Jewish studies in North America. Both groups, separated by thousands of miles and spawned in completely disparate academic (and political) environments, shared a sweeping objection to the relatively simplistic historical imagery instilled in historians of Eastern European Jewry by social and/or national radical traditions. Thus, for example, Israeli and North American historians simultaneously "discovered" new forms of Jewish "Orthodoxy" as a distinctly modern phenomenon. They soon began liberating the study of Hasidism from Marxist-nationalist socioeconomic labels and uncovering the "external" and "internal" sources of modern Jewish nationalism.

In the 1970s and 1980s Israeli academe opened up to North American influences, and relations between historians in the United States and Israel became closer. This is the backdrop to my relationship with Michael Stanislawski, which began more than four decades ago. I first met Michael in Jerusalem, when he was visiting the various libraries and archives that housed the Jewish cultural treasures that had survived the greatest disaster in modern Jewish history. Along this journey he had the privilege of learning from the great Jewish historians who had escaped from Eastern Europe and were then at the peak of their academic careers in North American and Israeli universities. At the time, Michael was hard at work completing his research on the history of Russian Jews under Tsar Nicholas I.[1]

Michael specialized in two areas of Eastern European Jewish history that were central to my professional work: the emergence of the Haskalah movement in the Russian Empire and the roots of European Zionism. Meeting with him in Jerusalem and Boston, I was deeply impressed by his skills as a historian, particularly his fine critical acumen and intellectual integrity, which were reflected in how he expressed his dissent from the works and methods of other leading scholars. Michael forthrightly questioned politically or ideologically motivated messages and astutely comprehended shifting historical images.

His scholarly work on the cultural history of the Jews in the Russian Empire surveys the "long nineteenth century," ranging over the vast Jewish expanse between the northwestern regions of the Pale of Settlement and the capital St. Petersburg, the provinces of New Russia, and the cosmopolitan metropolis of Odessa. Michael's remarks on the place of Odessa in the emergence of Russian Jewish modernism were in the back of my mind when I was writing the present essay: "Odessa's Jews made up the largest group after the Russians and were far more Russified than those in any other part of the Russian Empire, save the tiny numbers allowed to live in St. Petersburg, Moscow, and Kiev. In their homes, schools, and theaters, and increasingly in the street, Russian was the language of choice and culture."[2]

Michael found common ground with other historians of his generation who were trying to decipher the riddle of Jewish modernism and thereby anchor Zionist European thought in its social and cultural contexts. He was one of the first scholars of Russian Jewry to challenge the binary separation between Jewish "assimilation" and the conscious preservation of Jewish identity widely made by many of his predecessors, such as Simon Dubnow and Shmuel Ettinger. This dichotomy has sometimes been described as centrifugal (moving away from Jewish identity) versus centripetal (moving toward Jewish identity). This duality and the challenges it faced from the new historiography were the subject of Jonathan Frankel's seminal article, in which he cites Michael's work.[3]

Michael was keenly aware of the complex contradictions inherent in the embourgeoisement and acculturation of Jews in the Russian Empire at the end of the tsarist period. Zionist ideology, much like the Orthodox position, has struggled with these contradictions, often discounting them for an all-embracing, simplistic, if not blatantly politicized adaptation of the term *assimilation*. Thus, for example, Michael could easily reconcile Ze'ev Jabotinsky's childhood indifference to anything Jewish with his social affinity to his Jewish schoolmates: "On the one hand, as a child, teenager, and young adult, Jabotinsky had virtually no interest in anything Jewish, never read a book on a Jewish topic, never studied any ancient Jewish lore. And yet, on the other hand, in school, the Jewish children sat together and played together, barely associating with the non-Jewish children."[4]

Like many scholars of Jewish nationalism in Israel and the United States, Michael looked to Haskalah, the Jewish Enlightenment, for the roots of modern nationalism. He did not reject the dialectic established by Simon Dubnow, on which generations of historians were educated—among them my teachers from the "Jerusalem School," Ben-Zion Dinur and Shmuel Ettinger[5]—addressing the tension between the desire for social and political integration and the commitment for continued Jewish communal existence, a tension that accompanied the various streams of Jewish nationalism well into the twentieth century. Michael was well aware of the powerful link between the Haskalah movement in its Eastern European form, the development of the new national idea, and the emergence of Zionism at the end of the nineteenth century. Characterizing those who agreed with Jabotinsky's political program yet who came to Zionism not from the outside, as he did, but from the inside, Michael wrote, "They were heirs of, and in some cases, former contributors to, the Haskalah movement and continued to ponder the central problems of Jewish faith and identity debated for over a century in the Hebrew, Yiddish, German, and more recently, Russian and Polish writings of the Jewish Enlightenment. . . . Not so Jabotinsky, who knew nothing and cared less about this Jewish Enlightenment tradition and the religious faith it aimed to supersede."[6]

This essay is dedicated to Michael, the scholar of Eastern European Jewish modernism: a modernism that emerged from the encounter of Imperial Russian Jewry with the Enlightenment and their physical and cultural path from provincial shtetls to metropolitan centers. This study presents an infrequently studied Odessan autobiography that engages with the historical research stations in Michael's career and is meant as a token of appreciation for his contribution to the study of Jewish biography and the inroads he made into the world of Russian Jewish culture. In the following study of the memoir of Isaac Ze'ev Spivakoff, the reader will find a path of Russian Jewish modernization that, while passing through Odessa and exposing the autobiographer to its metropolitan culture, nonetheless affected him differently than it did the young Ze'ev Jabotinsky. For Spivakoff, this cosmopolitan city would emerge as a place where traditional shtetl life could seemingly "continue" while new connections were forged with Russian culture.[7]

"The Life of Every Person of Culture"

The memoirs written by Jewish emigrants who left Eastern Europe after World War I are often incredibly rich. These writers grew up in a multilingual environment where they experienced extensive processes of cultural change during the decades preceding the war and the disintegration of the old political order. When these emigrants decided to record their memories, some of them chose to maintain their allegiance to the language of the countries they had left behind, documenting their lives in either Russian or Polish. Many others chose to write in the languages of their new homes, mainly in English, French, Spanish, and German. Some of this autobiographic literature was composed in Yiddish, and other memoirs were written in Hebrew, a liturgical language that had undergone a radical process of desacralization, ultimately becoming the state language of Israel.

Isaac Ze'ev Spivakoff (1874–1968),[8] born in Odessa, was a poet, translator, teacher, and linguist whose mother tongue was Yiddish. Educated in a Russian Jewish high school, he became fluent in Hebrew, Russian, and German. In his later years, as an émigré in Mendoza, Argentina, Spivakoff learned Spanish. After some years in South America, he mastered this language so well that he was able to compile a voluminous Spanish-Hebrew dictionary.⁹ It was in Hebrew—a sacred tongue recently modernized by the Haskalah movement—that he chose to write the story of his life for future generations. Spivakoff's decision to tell his life's story in a language that played a limited and marginal role (to say the least) in the Argentinean cultural context invites us to delve into a fascinating multicultural and multilingual document. His memoir was written in outdated literary Hebrew that was used by some of the Eastern European Jewish intelligentsia during the early decades of the twentieth century. Although Spivakoff corresponded with childhood friends who had emigrated to Palestine and had quickly become immersed in the newly revitalized spoken form of Hebrew and although he also read Hebrew writings published into the mid-1960s, he barely modified the more archaic Hebrew he had learned in Odessa. The linguistic process that led Spivakoff to write this way was both a central component and an influential factor in the process of historical change that Eastern European Jews underwent in modern times. The Hebrew used in his memoir was the product of a process of acculturation that took place in the time and space separating the imperial Russian city of Odessa and the Argentinean provincial city of Mendoza. Within this autobiography lies the tale of the unique acculturation processes that Spivakoff experienced.

Spivakoff's memoir is not a comprehensive record of his life; it is instead a choice selection of events he saw fit to preserve for posterity. Already in his introduction, he informs the reader of previously published fragments of his story—of matters and events that he had written about at length—that he chose to omit from the present work: "I did not include these memories in my biography, as I had used them previously as biographical elements embedded in my writings and monographs that were published in various journals and periodicals."¹⁰ Thus, for example, anyone examining the 1947 article published by Yitzhak Spivakoff in an Argentinean newspaper about his membership in the Odessan Association for the Advancement of the Hebrew Language will discover a wealth of information not included in his later autobiography.¹¹

In several cases Spivakoff explicitly mixes early and later events, lightly skipping back and forth between the decades. Anyone seeking to derive accurate historical facts, dates, and the sequence of events from this memoir runs the risk of historical anachronism.¹²

In a short preface Spivakoff explains what motivated him to set down his memories: "In a biography we can see the development, progress, and true character [of the subject], noting all of the facets that interest us in their elemental forms, before we find them in his literary works."[13] According to this testimony, Spivakoff selected the axis along which he wrote his autobiography so as to best portray his unique personal life story. The author is the hero of his own memoir, and his actions and experiences take center stage. Spivakoff explicitly admits the mixed impact of autobiographic writing in the spirit of both Enlightenment and Romanticism. In the introduction to his memoir, written in the 1960s, he notes two autobiographies that stand out as masterpieces of European literature that deal with the formation of an individual's character: "The most complete and comely autobiographies are those of Rousseau and Goethe. That, at least, is the position of noted writers. Whereas in my opinion, the life of every person of culture, without exception, presents us with no less significant moments that are also worthy of publication.... When one composes a biography, one must include not only the bright, innocent sides of the man ... but also his darker, negative aspects. Even if it is harmful, the truth must be told."[14]

Much like authors of early Hebrew autobiographies that preceded his work, among them Mordekhai Aharon Gintsburg (1795–1846) and Moshe Leib Lilienblum (1843–1910), Spivakoff decided to dedicate a large part of his life story to exploring how his personality and his spiritual world developed. Whereas Gintsburg and Lilienblum, both of whom were members of the Haskalah movement, are rather didactic in their memoirs, which are replete with sharp social critiques about the society in which they had grown up, Spivakoff chooses another path. A large part of his autobiography is devoted to his religious education, first in his parents' house and later in Jewish educational institutions.

In contrast to what was common in many maskilic autobiographies, Spivakoff's autobiography completely lacks their confessional element, where the author recognizes the severe wrongs inflicted on him by the traditional, religious Jewish society that irreparably damaged his young soul, hindering the development of his full, adult personality.[15] As Gintsburg put it, the maskilic author was expected to recount the history of his soul (*Selbstbiografie*): "to show the distress of his soul as shaped by his tutors, teachers, friends, and other contemporaries."[16] This was a far cry from Spivakoff's approach. In this sense, he can be considered a clearcut anachronistic example of a post-maskilic Hebrew writer. Alongside the axis of personal development, the plot of Spivakoff's written life progresses down a second track, which ultimately dictates the unfolding of the narrative. His is a collective biography of the ethnic-religious community into which he was born, whose spirit he imbibed, and whose collapse, over which the Jews had no control, swept him away, along with everyone else. In short, these personal memories are part of the historical story shared by the largest Jewish community in the world.

The autobiography portrays five periods in Spivakoff's life: his childhood in Odessa; his service in the Russian army; his travel to Paris and subsequent return to Odessa, including his stint as a successful businessman (which ended with the 1917 revolution); his life in Odessa during the civil war and the beginning of the Soviet era; and, finally, his long exile—a voyage across the ocean and his establishment of a permanent residence in Mendoza, Argentina. However, the autobiography does not devote equal attention to all subjects or periods in the author's life. In some chapters Spivakoff goes into great detail, providing nuanced descriptions of events, whereas in others, he is brief, almost curt. The disparity between the number of pages devoted to his earlier and his later years is striking. About a third of the texts deals expansively with Spivakoff's early days in Odessa until his enlistment in the Russian army, whereas the period of his life following his escape from the Soviet Union takes up merely an eighth of the text. Spivakoff's biographical periodization tends to blur the boundaries of conventional historiography. The facts that the October Revolution and the Balfour Declaration were five days apart and that two generations after the "end" of the Haskalah a maskil's grandson could meet Spivakoff who still wrote maskilic Hebrew are not just serendipity. These historical simultaneities and overlaps suggest that periodization is, as we know, a heuristic device necessary for historians. But historical agents do not stay in their periods and events and personalities collide.[17] When looking for change, historians should be mindful that the conservative, traditional, and seemingly outdated trends do not disappear. The cutting edge may, in the longue durée, not be the defining factor of an era.

This focus on the maturation of the hero lends the first part of the autobiography a semblance of a coming-of-age novel (bildungsroman). However, the narrative arc is dramatically altered by the ramifications of the disintegration of the Russian Empire and the collapse of the world order in which Spivakoff was raised. As a result, the second part of his book reads like a tale of migration, a narrative in which the memories of his youth, gleaned in his far-flung abandoned hometown, have no place in the reality of his new land, a world in which the elder Spivakoff feels "foreign and estranged."[18] His life in Odessa, the trials and tribulations he endured there, did little to prepare him for life in Argentina, a country that served as a sanctuary from formidable political forces beyond his control. Unlike his contemporaries who emigrated to the Land of Israel after the 1917 revolution, for whom the cultural traditions they had acquired under tsarist rule in Russia became a relevant part of their experience of the renewed Hebrew culture, Spivakoff felt alone, stranded at the edge of the world.

Spivakoff carefully weighed what to include in the memoir and what to omit: "I have endured many hardships in my life, but I have not included them in the biography."[19] His business career, which is certainly of interest to those seeking to understand the connection between the commercial activities of the Jews in the emerging capitalist markets of Eastern Europe and how they integrated into the imperial Russian culture, takes up only a modest portion of the book. The sparse details embedded in the memoir of imperial Russian business trips serve as a background for descriptions of meetings with people of various ethnic origins, classes, and religions. Thus, for example, Spivakoff spent some time in a Russian monastery, where he spoke with priests and nuns and examined up close a world that was, for him, completely alien and distant. A business trip he conducted with the purpose of selling lighting oil for illuminating saints' icons has left us with a satirical portrait written in an anticlerical spirit about corruption, sexual libertinism, and superstition.[20]

Spivakoff's business enabled him to speak before Jewish audiences in various cities, thereby helping to spread the Jewish cultural and national revival. He was hardly unique in this, and in fact many members of the Russian Jewish intelligentsia who traveled for business purposes also used these trips to hold public lectures, albeit under the watchful eye of the tsarist secret police. Spivakoff presents himself as a kind of "itinerant Zionist preacher" (in Russian), an occupation whose circumstances and messages he expands on far more than the industrial products he was selling to his clients.

> I sought out opportunities far and wide to speak about the nature of Zionism and of the Jewish national revival slowly emerging in the Land of the Patriarchs—about the Jewish question, which had caused us so much grief and troubled us for ages; about religion and life; about happiness; about enlightenment and backwardness; about love and jealousy; about the Hebrew language and its nature, and the necessity to tie Jews together by their tongue—a people cannot be separated from their tongue. . . . All of this I did in Russian, our common language.[21]

Spivakoff, who considered himself a person who upheld the culture in which he was raised but also rebelled against it, writes monologues delivered by a gallery of characters with different worldviews, or he enters into dialogues with them, in which past positions, opinions, and views appear. Thus, for example, the figure of a Jewish grandmother interrupts his description of his impressions from the Kishinev pogrom (1903) and proceeds to make a speech upholding the conservative values of the "previous generation" and expressing complete loyalty to the tsarist regime: "After all, in their day there were no pogroms . . . and the government recognized its duty to protect its children and defended the Jews. During the period of Tsar Nicholas I, when pogroms threatened to break out somewhere, they whipped the unruly gentiles publicly—in the streets!—and punished them severely. Thus, calm was achieved, and our forefathers were spared."[22]

In a number of places Spivakoff incorporates descriptions of men and women who reflected the socioeconomic reality of Eastern European Jewry. His portraits cover several ethnic groups, from the Ashkenazic Jewish residents of the Pale of Settlement, to the Bukharan Jews from Russian Turkestan,[23] to the "Judaized" Russian-speaking peasants in a large village in central Russia.[24] Anyone who studies these scenes, and particularly Spivakoff's memories as a soldier in the Russian army wandering the markets and alleys of destitute suburbs of Białystok,[25] will be reminded of similar depictions of the everyday and familiar from Hebrew literary realism; and indeed, these works were composed precisely during the years in which Spivakoff fulfilled his military service in northeastern Poland.[26]

In this regard, Spivakoff is preserving a long-standing literary tradition of Jewish ethnography. This tradition can be traced back to nineteenth-century maskilic texts written in Hebrew and Yiddish (such as the short atmospheric sketches composed by Isaac Meir Dik and Israel Aksenfeld's novel *Dos shterntikhl*)[27] and was influenced by contemporary Russian literary criticism. Yet, unlike works in both languages written by fellow maskilim, Spivakoff's portraits of people and situations rarely present us with ideological calls for social amelioration and reeducation. (The exceptions to this rule are the sketches of his meeting with the Bukharan Jews,[28] in which a paternalistic "European" gaze, with Zionist Russian characteristics, can be clearly discerned.) Reading these depictions today, one gains the impression that they were written as part of research expeditions designed to study particular communities in depth. At the end of the nineteenth century, during Spivakoff's service in the Russian army, there was a great awakening of interest in radical nationalist anthropological studies focusing on the Jewish communities of Eastern Europe. On the face of things, Spivakoff's insistence on the idea of the rebirth of the Hebrew language and his use of Hebrew for ethnographic purposes seem to contradict the documentation of a lived culture in which Jewish traditions, life-cycle events, and popular art in its various genres were primarily conducted in Yiddish.[29] Yet Spivakoff, like his schoolmate from the Jewish gymnasium in Odessa, Naḥum Slouschz (1872–1966),[30] successfully used archaic Hebrew to reflect facts and impressions he had gathered in the vernacular.

Heaven and Hell in the Big City

Odessa, where Spivakoff spent nearly half his life, was established less than a hundred years before he was born. There was the "lower city of Odessa"—a bustling port situated at a central trade junction between East and West that attracted immigrants from far and wide—and there was what might be called a "heavenly Odessa," a literary convention referring to a utopian destination, an intangible place yearned for by lovers of culture and knowledge and feared by God-fearing Jews. The maskilim gave this second city the high-flown Hebrew name *Ashdot*; but for the average Jews, there was the Yiddish saying: "The fires of hell burn for ten miles around the city of Odessa" (with alternative versions explicating how far beyond the city's limits these fires burned). When those who pursued the vision of a heavenly city met with Odessa's actual realities, discovered the alienation of city life, and experienced firsthand its cultural superficiality, they were gripped by a passion to return, at least in spirit, to the "premodern world" they had left behind. The depth of the crisis wrought by the shattering of the illusion of a heavenly Odessa is poignantly expressed in Lilienblum's "great confession," *The Sins of Youth*, a revealing autobiographical document that was published when Spivakoff was 2 years old.[31]

It seems that the Odessan reality in which Spivakoff grew up and was educated and the image of this city, whether utopian or dystopian, with which he became acquainted by reading maskilic writings and listening to ultra-Orthodox sermons, reinforced each other. The tension between what Spivakoff recollected and what was written about the city by others, both admirers and critics, is consistently present throughout his autobiography.

What set apart the city of Odessa in Russian history and the Odessa found in the history of the Jews in Eastern Europe? This metropolis grew out of an ambitious imperial project conducted by Catherine the Great during the second half of the eighteenth century in which the borders of Russian sovereign territory were expanded far into the steppe region north of the Black Sea, called New Russia. In 1783, when Catherine the Great's forces arrived at the shores of the Black Sea, they found only a remote village, Khadjibey, guarded by a small Ottoman fortress. The Russian Empire transformed some of the small harbors in the newly annexed territory into modern port cities, with Russian (and sometimes Greek) names, to promote its international trade. Of all these newly developed cities, Odessa emerged as the most economically successful port city in the southern part of the empire.

From the middle of the eighteenth century until the last decades of the nineteenth century, settlers from different ethnic and religious groups poured into New Russia, including many Jews from provinces that had been annexed after the partitions of Poland. During Odessa's early years, there were hardly any Jews in the city. The census for the first decade of the nineteenth century counted less than 250 Jews in the whole city. But by 1897, when Spivakoff was 23 years old, the census indicated that Odessa, with its 140,000 Jews, was the largest Jewish community in the Russian Pale of Settlement.

Odessa played a major role in the transformation of the Jews from a semi-autonomous ethnoreligious corporation into an urban nation. In the empire's cities a new type of Jewish bourgeoisie emerged, one that often identified itself with the empire and would serve as the socioeconomic basis for the development of Jewish culture in a Russian—as well as a Jewish—urban proletariat. At the beginning of the twentieth century the Jewish group numbered in the hundreds of thousands and was the main audience of radical movements promoting social reform and opposition to the tsarist regime.

The acculturation processes that took place in the major cities had different effects on the various groups in Jewish society. The impact of diverse cultural alternatives threatening the premodern heritage—a number of imperial identities, Western influences, and "national" cultures—grew, and the competition between them became sharper and more pronounced in the city than in the provincial towns. But, as attested to by Spivakoff's memories of his childhood and adolescence, modernization and urbanization did not cause Jews to vanish as an ethnoreligious group distinct from other immigrants who arrived in the big city. Quite the reverse: One could argue that the conditions of the metropolis were those that encouraged the preservation of the separate nature of the Jewish communities while concomitantly Jewish identity experienced a flourishing of new identities unprecedented in the history of Eastern European Jewry. The urban context in which Spivakoff grew up also contained the Jewish provincial town, both the imagined shtetl, as preserved in the memories of those who left it for the big city, and genuine social and cultural shtetl phenomena that were transplanted to Odessa with the immigrants and survived in the metropolis.

Spivakoff's memories present us with a traditional Jewish family, one that stood apart from its surroundings in its faith, opinions, and customs. Thus, for example, he relates that his mother traveled from Odessa to visit the Tsadik of Talne (Rabbi David Twersky, 1808–1882) to ask for a blessing for her newborn son that he would live a long life, in return for fair remuneration, of course.[32] Tensions between Jews and their Gentile neighbors were high in cities, doubtlessly a contributing factor to the rise of Jewish nationalism, as was the case in Odessa. The large and different ethnoreligious groups did not blend in with each other; they reinforced old prejudices and economic competition, leading to an increase in interethnic tensions. Ironically, it was in Odessa—the destination of choice for Jewish intellectuals enraptured by the charms of Western culture and seeking civil equality, those who hoped to overcome the ancient superstitions by means of reason—where violent clashes between these different groups broke out. Particularly tense were the relations between the large Greek and Jewish communities. These tensions erupted in the first pogrom in the southern port city in 1821, harking back to residual religious animosity from as far back as the Byzantine period, the Greek national awakening (one of whose centers was located in Odessa!), and the intense economic rivalry between Greek entrepreneurs and their Jewish competitors for control of the grain export trade and civic commerce. Odessa would for the next hundred years be the site of violent riots against Jews. Between 1821 and 1919 there were at least six waves of such pogroms! Spivakoff experienced three of these violent riots while living in the city, which he documented in his memoir: in May 1881, when he was 7 years old; in October 1905, when he was 31; and in 1919, a few years before his emigration. The pain resulting from the gap between the heavenly city of Odessa, his birthplace, and the seething demographic volcano that cast its shadow of terror on the Jewish population haunted him for the rest of his life.

In his memoir Spivakoff weaves together events from the earliest days of the Odessa-style Hebrew nationalism, many of which were later transferred from the shores of the Black Sea, in part or in full, to the Land of Israel. This brand of Jewish nationalism had emerged during a period when the Ashkenazic cultural legacy specific to the Pale of Settlement had to come to terms with an imperial Russian version of Western culture. The first Jewish nationalists in Odessa, in whose circle Spivakoff found himself, experienced a process of acculturation where Hebrew, an ancient liturgical tongue, served, surprisingly enough, as the means of communication with Western Europe, alongside Russian. The new Hebrew-language gateway to the West that was built in Odessa also served as a gateway to the Middle East, Palestine included. All this took place in a city that literally linked East and West.

Spivakoff's autobiography depicts the emergence of a Jewish nationalism whose heart was, supposedly, in the East, in the Land of Israel, but which faced westward, a nationalism whose basis was firmly planted in the world of business ventures and financial activities. And even though Spivakoff genuinely and deeply advocated for the Land of Israel (as a historical homeland), the circumstances of his life ultimately led him in a direction diametrically opposed to the desired objective of Hebrew nationalism.

A Child of Odessa

Many members of the so-called Odessa group (Hebrew, *Ḥavurat Odesa*) who were present in the city when the local version of new Hebrew culture was born were in reality only drops of water in a great sea of Jewish immigrants flooding the metropolis, many arriving from far distant shores. Some arrived in Odessa as children, brought by their parents. Mendele Moykher Sforim (Sholem Yankev Abramovitsh), Moshe Leib Lilienblum, Ahad Ha'am (Asher Ginzberg), Ḥayim Naḥman Bialik, Ḥayim Tchernowitz (Rav Ẓa'ir), Yosef Klausner, Naḥum Slouschz, and many others were born in small or medium-size communities in Lithuania, Belarus, and Ukraine. Even though (for them) the transition from a conservative environment to a modern metropolis was a major revolutionary step, Odessa was ultimately only a stepping-stone, a chapter in their biographies and a station in their literary or political careers. Spivakoff, by contrast, was a child of Odessa. Odessa was his childhood, adolescence, and much of his adulthood. His life in this city continued into the first years of the Soviet era and, aside from his military service and a few years in France, he only left it when he was close to 50! One could say, then, that Spivakoff was as much an Odessan as one could be.

Spivakoff's identification with the city, which had existed for only about 80 years when he was born, appears in his memoir in conjunction with his sense of belonging to the Russian Empire. Spivakoff presents himself in his memoir as the grandson and great-grandson of observant Jews who took part in a century-long project of extending the empire's borders to the shores of the Black Sea.

One of Spivakoff's treasured family memories, passed down to him from his father, was that his grandfather had won a high imperial honor, "the silver medal with the emblem of Vladimir," as he put it.[33] This same grandfather had had the honor of shaking the hand of Tsar Alexander II during his 1863 state visit to Odessa to inaugurate a monument to the legendary governor-general of New Russia, Mikhail Vorontsov (1782–1856). Vorontsov, a Russian nobleman and field marshal, had gained renown during Napoleon's invasion of Russia in 1812. Spivakoff's grandfather was honored for his part in creating a military facility in Ochakov. The name Ochakov (today, Ochakiv) was of great significance in the imperial discourse during the tsarist period because in 1788, a few years before

Odessa was founded, the Russians conquered the fortress of Ochakov, which caused the complete removal of Turkish forces from the areas north of the Black Sea. This victory was memorialized in a famous poem by Gavrila Derzhavin (1743–1816) that was recited in gymnasiums across Russia during Spivakoff's adolescence, which strengthened the national connection to New Russia.

The sense of belonging to the empire was congruent with a kind of "local Odessan patriotism," which influenced Jewish writers and thinkers of Spivakoff's generation to varying degrees. The best known of them was Vladimir (Ze'ev) Jabotinsky (1880–1940), a Russian writer, Hebrew poet, and Zionist statesman who was also born in Odessa.[34] Though quite different, these two men shared a number of characteristics that might be connected to their common upbringing in Odessa. First among these, in my eyes, was their combination of modern Hebrew culture, at times outspokenly secular, and their strong identification with Russian culture.[35] This local Odessan patriotism did not contradict the identification of the local Jewish intelligentsia with Jewish nationalism in general and Zionism in particular. Throughout his entire life, Spivakoff treasured those Odessan sites that were for him most connected to his childhood memories of the city, his sense of belonging to the Russian imperial culture, his love for the Hebrew language, and his allegiance to the idea of Jewish national revival. And what could better exemplify the connection to the Russian imperial context than a ceremony Spivakoff and his companions performed at the foot of a statue to a famous Russian poet?

"On a certain Saturday afternoon, our group of twelve teenage boys gathered at Pushkin's feet, at the base of this poet's statue, facing the Black Sea. And there we swore an oath to devote ourselves to the Hebrew language forever."[36] These adolescents chose Pushkin, the Russian poet who manifested Odessa's cosmopolitan spirit, to witness the creation of their clandestine society. This was a fitting expression of the challenge the group meant to pose to the traditional Jewish Ashkenazic culture identified with the Pale of Settlement, not the least of which was due to the rhymed Hebrew oath that Spivakoff composed for the occasion.[37]

The group's decision to pursue a radical-nationalist line was inspired by their teacher at the Jewish gymnasium, Jehuda Leib Dawidowicz (1855–1898), who published widely on educational matters in the Zionist journal *Ha-shilo'aḥ* and translated the writings of the English philosopher

Herbert Spencer into Hebrew. The description of this society brings to mind similar nationalist-minded groups, inspired by Romanticism, created by teenagers and university students from other nations in the multiethnic empires of Central and Eastern Europe. Although Pushkin's statue lent a cosmopolitan nuance to the group's Odessan identity, the monument of Mikhail Vorontsov added their parents' prenationalist affinity to the register of ethnic heterogeneity that was part and parcel of this local identity.

Spivakoff's cultural world took shape, as it were, between these two civic monuments and their historical provenance. They were erected in the city by the tsarist regime, which shaped the map of the city along the contours of the various ethnic groups of which it was composed, naming streets after Italians, Greeks, Jews, and others from the founding communities. The geography of memory etched out in the Odessan chapters in Spivakoff's autobiography gives insight into an additional dimension in the elusive reciprocal relationship between continuity and change, and tradition and revolution, a relationship that accompanied the initiators of modern Jewish nationalism.

Many of the members of the Odessa group, who went on to spread the legacy of the Jewish cultural creation in Odessa around the world, had already undergone the process of extricating themselves from their traditional Jewish background before arriving in the city. Spivakoff, by contrast, underwent this process—a well-known and almost essential part of the collective biography of tens of thousands of members of the Jewish intelligentsia in Eastern Europe, which even became a literary convention—without ever leaving the city of his birth. For Spivakoff, the metropolis was never a utopia; it was simply his hometown. Moreover, as the son of a family that maintained a traditional Jewish life in the big city, his memories do not link the old-fashioned Jewish lifestyle with a shtetl childhood experience.

A Russian Melting Pot?

Spivakoff's memories amply demonstrate the highly heterogeneous, complex, and volatile nature of the cultural melting pot into which Russian Jewry was thrown when modernization swept the country at the end of the tsarist period. He opens a window through which we can glimpse something of the ethnolinguistic blend that reigned in the period preceding World War I. Spivakoff experienced many of the acculturating forces ubiquitous in this period: Russian imperial culture, Polish culture (which he encountered during his time in the northeast of the Pale), and German culture. Together, these influences were part of a multiethnic cacophony in which not one but two modern and emergent Jewish cultures were involved, the one chasing the heels of the other: Hebrew and Yiddish. Until 1917 all options were still on the table.

Any of the cultural paths listed could be chosen as a route to Jewish modernity. One could even progress along two or three parallel routes at the same time, or, alternatively, remain entrenched in the conservative Orthodox position and reject some or all modernist options altogether. Jewish cultural life in Eastern Europe had fluctuated between monolingual, bilingual, trilingual, and other multilingual options. Spivakoff, who wrote in Russian and Hebrew, was also fluent in German; in this he was like legions of his contemporaries who wrote in these languages as well as in Yiddish and Polish. And there was, of course, also a political background that had a great influence on the choices made by Jews in various regions from among the cultural options available to them.

Russian imperial politics toward various ethnic groups, the restrictions they imposed on certain languages, and the incentives granted to use the language of the empire are recurrent themes in Spivakoff's autobiography. He taught the official state language (Russian) during his military service, acting as an imperial cultural agent. Spivakoff's account of his military service sketches a precise synchronic and diachronic picture of the state of affairs in Białystok, a local case study in the aforementioned dynamic chain of cultural-linguistic processes. In the spring of 1899 he published in *Ha-zefirah* a Hebrew poem eulogizing one of the first pro-Russian proponents of Jewish Enlightenment, Abraham Ber Gottlober (1811–1899), a well-known bilingual writer (Hebrew and Yiddish) noted for his translations from German.[38] At the time, Spivakoff was staying in the house of Gottlober's daughter, Sofia Gottlober-Bornstein, and her son, Yasha [Jacob] Bornstein. Gottlober's grandson was a Polish nationalist poet pursued by the tsarist secret police for writing in this then-persecuted language (Polish). Yasha, the young Polish patriot, an offspring of one of the founders of pro-Russian Haskalah, tried to convince Spivakoff to read the poetry of Adam Mickiewicz (1798–1855), widely recognized as one of the symbols of Polish nationalism. Spivakoff, the Jewish soldier from Odessa, turned him down, saying, "Everything having to do with Poles is forbidden in the barracks. Polish books are a real danger to any soldier who reads them. We are not even free to read the classic Russian writers."[39]

Thanks largely to his education at the gymnasium in Odessa, whose curriculum offered Jewish studies alongside general, secular education, Spivakoff was trained as an imperial cultural agent for the provinces. In other words, the cultural Russian element of his education enabled the military to confer upon Spivakoff the task of Russification of the ethnic groups in the western part of the empire. This led to the paradox of a Jewish soldier from Odessa, who had devoted himself to the revival of the Hebrew language from an early age and had mastered Russian, teaching illiterate Slavic soldiers the state language while simultaneously working to advance the Russian-language prowess of his Jewish brethren living in northeast Poland. According to Spivakoff's testimony, around the turn of the twentieth century, "Russian was only seldom heard. The masses spoke Polish; and Jews knew their Yiddish as well as Polish. Russian was required only by those who had business with the state institutions or the military."[40]

The Stolen Piano

For many Jews living in the crumbling Russian Empire, the interim period between the 1917 February Revolution and the establishment of a stable Soviet regime at the beginning of the 1920s was semi-apocalyptic in nature. In Spivakoff's memories this period was marked by a mixture of hope for redemption and scenes of destruction, and his impressions are strongly colored by both anticipation and terror. On the one hand, millions of Jews had instantly gained political equality and, with it, the complete freedom to develop a national culture according to their own views. This brief moment gave rise to an outburst of unrestrained Jewish cultural creation unfettered by censorship. Yet, at the same time, the interethnic tensions that in the southern provinces had led to mass murder intensified, and the threatening face of Bolshevik totalitarianism was first exposed. The publication of the Balfour Declaration, promising the Jews a national home in Palestine, and the October Revolution, which opened the Soviet period in Russian history, occurred only five days apart! During these fateful days,

Spivakoff took part in a ceremony the likes of which a Russian Jew could have never imagined before the fall of the tsar, not even in his wildest dreams: The English consul in Odessa congratulated the Zionists on the occasion of the Balfour Declaration. But the burst of national awakening and the joy many Jews felt in 1917 at finally being granted equal rights and the freedom of speech abated within just a few months.[41]

Spivakoff, a property-holding industrialist with Zionist views, was not among those who supported Russian social democracy in the prerevolutionary period. His scenes of everyday Odessa bear witness to his loathing of the new Soviet rule, a regime that decimated everything he had held precious in his beloved city. Spivakoff focused his memory on recording property the Bolsheviks confiscated from Jews of different socioeconomic classes. The confiscation of his daughter's piano—an instrument that fulfilled a key role in the bourgeois house and symbolized for many Jews their integration into Western culture—marked for him the end of an era. He experienced this event as catastrophic on many levels simultaneously: It had both cultural and financial ramifications and marked the necessity for a complete change of mind. Indeed, for Spivakoff, the event had an almost religious connotation, echoing the great catastrophes of the Jewish people: "The day they stole our piano was like Tisha b'Av [the memorial day for the destruction of the First and Second Jewish Temples] in my house, a day of mourning. My wife and only daughter cried bitterly and were inconsolable. When they removed the piano, we felt as though we were watching a living man being led away to his execution."[42]

In one government warehouse, Spivakoff saw dozens of confiscated pianos, lying beside organs that had been uprooted from city churches as well as the organ of the synagogue built by immigrants from Brody. For him, the destruction of the Jewish bourgeois home and the decimation of the symbols of Christian-Jewish civilization that had marked the cosmopolitan metropolis were an apocalyptic episode foretelling his forthcoming exile from this city of his birth.

A Nobel Encounter in Astrakhan

Spivakoff's memoir contains details of great historical value about dozens of people he met throughout his life, including Jewish teachers, fellow students who went on to make names for themselves in Hebrew literature, science, and public life, community leaders, writers, poets, and political activists. The variety of men and women who inhabit his memoir is extremely wide, a broad arc of the representatives of Russian Jewry at the end of the tsarist period, stretching between Orthodox Judaism, on the one hand, to examples of different forms and extents of Russification on the other—an impressive variety that he felt compelled to document and pass down to future generations. Rabbi David Shlomo (d. 1918), the Tsadik of Kobrin, a radically conservative Hasidic leader, is a good example of Orthodox Judaism, whereas Bialik's brother-in-law Jan Gamarnik (1894–1937), a sworn Bolshevik, represents the Russified Jew. Other figures worked into this arc are the poet Hayim Nahman Bialik (1873–1934), the historian Hayim Yonah Gurland (1843–1890), the doctor and book collector Joseph Hazanovitch (1844–1919), the poet Shaul Tchernichowsky (1875–1943), the progressive rabbi Shimon Aryeh Schwabacher (1820–1889), and the historian and literary scholar Yosef Klausner (1874–1858).

Among his teachers at the gymnasium-yeshiva in Odessa were such formative figures as the writer and teacher Elimelekh Wexler-Bezredka (1842–1919), who inspired Spivakoff's primary relationship to the Bible and the Hebrew language. Wexler, who was a member of the Hebrew Enlightenment in Odessa, wrote in both Hebrew and Yiddish under the pen name Ish Naomi (Naomi's husband). He is a recurring figure in this autobiography, appearing in different periods, beginning with Spivakoff's childhood memories in the 1880s and ending with a description of his funeral during the turbulent days that followed the 1917 revolution.

Throughout his life Wexler was an adherent of biblical purism. He adamantly refused the post-maskilic forms of writing that mixed later historical strata of the Hebrew language, beginning with Mishnaic Hebrew and ending with the Ashkenazic Hebrew of rabbinic and Hasidic literature. For many of the writers in the Odessa circle of the 1890s—who abandoned the archaic maskilic, "overly flowery" way of writing and adopted instead a Hebrew prose styled after Mendele Moykher Sforim, while simultaneously taking an active part in the fostering of literary writing in Yiddish—Wexler's position as a biblical purist seemed outdated.[43]

Spivakoff, on the other hand, never ceased to admire his teacher, whom he called "the purist writer."[44] Inspired by Wexler's lifelong commitment to the revival of the Hebrew language and for being an intellectual whose secular approach to the biblical scriptures influenced his choice to abandon the traditional way of life in which he had been brought up, Spivakoff remembered his teacher fondly for his support of the Hebrew journal published by Spivakoff and his fellow students, *Ha-Gan*: "We never forgot the great spirit of this teacher, even long after having left the yeshiva. He asked us for one thing only: 'Use the Bible, use its beautiful idioms and expressions. You will find everything there; nothing is missing in the Bible.'"[45]

Here Spivakoff's memoir challenges modern Hebrew culture's long-established literary canon.[46] According to him, Wexler was the last link in a maskilic-nationalist tradition that took hold in cosmopolitan Odessa, namely, the secular reliance on biblical scripture. And indeed, a similar spirit of return to the biblical text with secular-humanistic intentions is a trait that marks the works of several Russian Jewish writers and scholars who, influenced by Jewish nationalism, took up the revision of ancient Jewish history (e.g., Slouschz, Jabotinsky).[47] Apparently, they were fulfilling Wexler's spiritual last will and testament, which Spivakoff recounts. In describing Wexler's modest funeral in 1919, Spivakoff writes, "The spirit of God hovers over the Holy Scripture, yet the writer of these letters is not God."[48] When writing about Wexler, Spivakoff clearly identifies himself as the upholder of an Odessan maskilic school of thought sharply opposed to the group composed of Bialik, Yehoshua Ravnitski, and Sholem Aleichem. This went well with his pronounced anti-Yiddish battles. As he remarks, citing the poet Shaul Tchernichowsky, proper Jewish bilingualism was "either Hebrew or Russian."[49]

Of great interest is a random meeting Spivakoff had in 1910 with Nobel Prize winner Dr. Ilya Mechnikov (1845–1916).[50] This noted scientist was the grandson of Yehudah Leib Nevakhovich (1776–1831), one of the first proponents of the Haskalah in Russia and author of the pro-Russian Hebrew-language composition *Kol shave'at bat Yehudah* (The Crying Voice of the Daughter of Judah), published in Shklov in 1804.[51] This meeting between Spivakoff and Mechnikov embodies more than a hundred years' acculturation of Jews from the partitioned Polish-Lithuanian Commonwealth to Russian culture. Jewish exposure to the new imperial culture began after the first partition in 1772, when a handful of Jews relocated from Belarus to St. Petersburg, and continued with the acculturation of their progeny (some of whom converted). They successfully became part of the political and scientific elite in imperial Russia. Spivakoff's Russian education was part of an advanced stage of this cultural process.

From the description of the conversation between Spivakoff and Mechnikov, it would appear that, only a few generations after Nevakhovich left the Belarusan province for St. Petersburg, the acculturation of those early maskilim seemed like a distant episode. Yet this is not how Spivakoff, who, like his Odessa schoolmates, connected Russification with a desire to become part of Western culture, saw matters. When Spivakoff and Mechnikov met by chance in a post office in Astrakhan, they conversed in Russian, each having no prior knowledge of his interlocutor's religious or ethnic identity. For all intents and purposes, they were Russian. But when Mechnikov was asked by Spivakoff about an acquaintance of his, a Jewish scientist working at the Institut Pasteur in Paris, the distinguished scholar remarked that the person was "A Jew from Odessa," adding, "Is it perhaps the case that you too, sir, are a Jew?" "I am indeed a Jew," said Spivakoff. "My mother too," replied Mechnikov, "is a Jew. She is now 85 years old."[52]

The acquaintance about whom Spivakoff had asked Mechnikov was the immunologist Shmaryahu (Alexander) Wexler-Bezredka (1870–1940), the son of Ish Naomi, Spivakoff's admired teacher mentioned earlier. Shmaryahu, the son-in-law of the famous Odessan cantor Pinḥas Minkowski (1859–1954),[53] also emigrated from tsarist Russia to take up a position at a leading scientific institution in Paris, working alongside Mechnikov, the Christian grandson of a Shklov maskil! In many cases the Russification of provincial Jews, who climbed the social ladder, received higher education, and established scientific careers, led to Paris, one of the great cities of the West. In other cases members of the same group, including Spivakoff's schoolmates, reached Jerusalem, Tel Aviv, or Haifa, where they brought other cultural elements of imperial Russia. The meeting between the Odessan Jewish industrialist and the Russian French scientist of Jewish extraction that took place in a far-flung postal office provides the readers of Spivakoff's autobiography with a passage in which one can glimpse the great story of Jewish modernism as it spread across the expanses of the Russian Empire, along the roads and sea lanes leading to Palestine, to Western Europe, and to North and South America.

Even in Mendoza, an Odessan

Historians and students of modern Hebrew literature who wish to examine the complex entangled roots of the various forms of Jewish cultural modernity will find great value in Spivakoff's memoir, a tale of the Odessan Hebrew enthusiast who was uprooted from a cosmopolitan metropolis in the southern part of the Russian Empire—an important, formative center in the annals of modern Jewish culture—and spent more than four decades of his life in a provincial Argentinean town. His Hebrew autobiographical materials are replete with records of his experiences with Western culture in its Eastern European iterations. His memoir evokes the enthusiasm of modern national awakening, encapsulating the frightful shock of meeting a newly established totalitarian regime. It also shares poignant memories immersed in the pain of exile, emigration, and acculturation to an unknown culture. The experiences of Spivakoff, whose Odessa childhood was spent in the final days of Tsar Alexander II and whose later years were lived out in a provincial Argentinean city in the 1960s, are valuable components of a multicultural and multilingual biographical mosaic spanning the entire globe. This is a group portrait of millions of Jews who were born in one of Europe's multinational empires, were uprooted with the collapse of the old political order, and carried the cultural heritage of prestate nationalism with them across the ocean. This cultural heritage, a product of the Hebrew renaissance (which was doomed, as in the title *For Whom Do I Toil?*, Michael Stanislawski's biography of Judah Leib Gordon), had in fact a strange afterlife well into the second half of the twentieth century for Spivakoff and many others on both sides of the Atlantic.

Notes

1 Michael Stanislawski, *Tsar Nicholas I and the Jews: The Transformation of Jewish Society in Russia, 1825–1855* (Philadelphia: Jewish Publication Society of America, 1983).

2 Michael Stanislawski, *Zionism and the Fin de Siècle: Cosmopolitanism and Nationalism from Nordau to Jabotinsky* (Berkeley: University of California Press, 2001), 126.

3 Jonathan Frankel, "Assimilation and the Jews in Nineteenth Century Europe: Toward a New Historiography?" in *Crisis, Revolution, and Russian Jews*,

ed. Jonathan Frankel (Cambridge, UK: Cambridge University Press, 2009), 276–310.
4. Stanislawski, *Zionism*, 123.
5. On the "Jerusalem School," see David N. Myers, *Re-Inventing the Jewish Past: European Jewish Intellectuals and the Zionist Return to History* (New York: Oxford University Press, 1995).
6. Stanislawski, *Zionism*, 183.
7. Stanislawski, *Zionism*, 183.
8. Sometimes transliterated in Spanish as Itzjak Spivacoff.
9. Isaac Spivakoff, "Diccionario-completo Español-Hebreo: Mendoza, Argentina, 1924–1927, 1934–1940," unpublished manuscript, hebrew-academy.org.il/2020/05/20/מילון-ספרדי-עברי-מאת-יצחק-ספיבקוב/ (accessed 11 May 2023). Besides a digitized version of this dictionary, the website has other documents from Spivakoff's literary estate.
10. Isaac Spivakoff's memoir has been published recently: Isaac Spivakoff, *Sirati al penei ha-okyanos* [My Boat on the Ocean Waves], ed. Yael Mishor and Mordechai Mishor (Jerusalem: Mosad Bialik, 2022), 66–67.
11. Isaac Spivakoff, "Hasar hasin ha-ru'aḥ," *Darom: yarḥon le'inyenei haẓibur vedivrei sifrut* (January 1947): 11–12.
12. Michael Stanislawski alerted credulous readers to the perils of taking the historicity of autobiographies and memoirs at face value. Michael Stanislawski, *Autobiographical Jews: Essays in Jewish Self-Fashioning* (Seattle: University of Washington Press, 2004).
13. Spivakoff, *Sirati al penei ha-okyanos*, 66.
14. Spivakoff, *Sirati al penei ha-okyanos*, 65–66.
15. On maskilic autobiographies, see Alan Mintz, *"Banished from Their Father's Table": Loss of Faith and Hebrew Autobiography* (Bloomington: Indiana University Press, 1989).
16. Mordekhai Aharon Gintsburg, *Viduyo shel maskil Avi'ezer*, ed. Shmuel Werses (Jerusalem: Mosad Bialik, 2009), 29, see also 68.
17. On this point, see Stanislawski, *Tsar Nicholas*, 51.
18. Spivakoff, *Sirati al penei ha-okyanos*, 69.
19. Spivakoff, *Sirati al penei ha-okyanos*, 66.
20. Spivakoff, *Sirati al penei ha-okyanos*, 241–48.
21. Spivakoff, *Sirati al penei ha-okyanos*, 283.
22. Spivakoff, *Sirati al penei ha-okyanos*, 201.
23. Spivakoff, *Sirati al penei ha-okyanos*, 296–302.

24 Spivakoff, *Sirati al penei ha-okyanos*, 252–54.
25 Spivakoff, *Sirati al penei ha-okyanos*, 175–82.
26 For a collection of some examples of these works, see Yosef Even, ed., *Niẓanei ha-reʾalizm basifrut ha'ivrit*, 2 vols. (Jerusalem: Mosad Bialik, 1972). Spivakoff's depictions of socioeconomic reality brings to mind Y. L. Peretz's Yiddish short stories published after his tour of several Jewish towns in Poland around 1890: Y. L. Peretz, *Bilder fun a provints-rayze in Tomashover poviyat in yor 1890* (Warsaw: Halter & Eisenstadt, 1894). On these stories, see Marc Caplan, "The Fragmentation of Narrative Perspective in Y. L. Peretz's *Bilder fun a Provints-Rayze*," *Jewish Social Studies* 14, no. 1 (2007): 63–88.
27 Dan Miron, *Ben ḥazon leʾemet: nitzanei ha-roman ha'ivri vehayidi bameʾah hatesha-esreh* (Jerusalem: Mosad Bialik, 1979), 184–91.
28 Spivakoff, *Sirati al penei ha-okyanos*, 296–97.
29 This tensioned contradiction has continued well into the study of Jewish folklore and ethnography of the interwar period. See Dani Schrire, *Isuf shivre hagolah: ḥeker hafolklor haẓiyoni lenokhaḥ haShoʾah* (Jerusalem: Magnes Press, 2018), 52–98.
30 Slouschz, like Spivakoff, toured the Lithuanian provinces of the Pale in 1897. He published his impressions in Hebrew: Naḥum Slouschz, *Masa beLita baderekh meAshdot* (Vilnius, 1898). Ashdot was one of the Hebrew biblical names given by maskilim to Odessa.
31 Moshe Leib Lilienblum, *Ḥatʾot neʾurim* [The Sins of Youth], in *Ketavim otobiyografiyim*, ed. Shelomoh Breiman (Jerusalem: Mosad Bialik, 1970), 2: 13.
32 Spivakoff, *Sirati al penei ha-okyanos*, 71–72.
33 Spivakoff, *Sirati al penei ha-okyanos*, 72.
34 Dmitry Shumsky, "An Odessan Nationality? Local Patriotism and Jewish Nationalism in the Case of Vladimir Jabotinsky," *Russian Review* 79, no. 1 (2020): 64–82.
35 On Jabotinsky's autobiography, see Stanislawski, *Zionism*; and Brian J. Horowitz, *Vladimir Jabotinsky's Russian Years, 1900–1925* (Bloomington: Indiana University Press, 2020).
36 Spivakoff, *Sirati al penei ha-okyanos*, 113.
37 The members of this clandestine group included Yosef Klausner, Naḥum Slouschz, and Ester Yevin (then Yunis, 1877–1975), who went on to become one of the leaders of the struggle for women's rights in Mandatory Palestine, a member of the Assembly of Representatives (the prestate parliamentary assembly), and the Jewish National Council.

38 Spivakoff, "Aḥare mot hameshorer," *Ha-ẓefirah* (17 April 1899); Spivakoff, *Sirati al penei ha-okyanos*, 172.
39 Spivakoff, *Sirati al penei ha-okyanos*, 174.
40 Spivakoff, *Sirati al penei ha-okyanos*, 165.
41 Spivakoff, *Sirati al penei ha-okyanos*, 303–8.
42 Spivakoff, *Sirati al penei ha-okyanos*, 309.
43 Ido Bassok, *Layofi velanisgav libo er, Shaul Tchernihovski* (Jerusalem: Carmel, 2017), 82–83, 120, 193, 264. This is how the young, innovative poet Shaul Tchernichovsky treated the veteran maskil whom he met browsing through the Hebrew newspapers in the Odessa library.
44 Spivakoff, *Sirati al penei ha-okyanos*, 34.
45 Spivakoff, *Sirati al penei ha-okyanos*, 111.
46 This "alternative" canon has been discussed in recent years by several scholars. See Jörg Schulte, "Der hebräische Humanismus in Odessa und Warschau," in *Mitteleuropa denken: Intellektuelle Identitäten und Ideen*, ed. Walter Pape and Jiri Subrt (Berlin: De Gruyter, 2019), 245–57.
47 In a way, these young fervent Hebrew secularists had been the forerunners of the Israeli Canaanite movement. See Yaacov Shavit, *The New Hebrew Nation: A Study in Israeli Heresy and Fantasy* (London: Cass, 1987), 79; and Schrire, *Isuf*, 62–68.
48 Spivakoff, *Sirati al penei ha-okyanos*, 262.
49 Spivakoff, *Sirati al penei ha-okyanos*, 158.
50 Mechnikov, a noted physician, was a professor at the University of Odessa when Spivakoff was growing up. He later moved to Paris and was awarded the Nobel Prize in 1908, with Paul Ehrlich, for their research on the immune system.
51 This work was first published in Russian as *Vopl' dshcheri iudeyskoy* (St. Petersburg, 1803). For a photocopy of the rare 1804 Hebrew treatise, see *He'avar* 2 (1918): 197–201.
52 Spivakoff, *Sirati al penei ha-okyanos*, 269. The age of Mechnikov's mother given here is hard to reconcile with her biography.
53 Spivakoff, *Sirati al penei ha-okyanos*, 269–70. Anat Rubinstein, "The Cantor of the *Haskalah*: Life and Work of Hazzan Pinkhas Minkowski, 1859-1924," PhD diss., Hebrew University, 2018. Minkowski's daughter was a pianist who lived in Paris with her husband, Dr. Shmaryahu Wexler-Bezredka. Spivakoff cites from the letters she sent to her father in Odessa.

15

Biography as *Hesped*

S. L. Shneiderman's Homage to Ilya Ehrenburg

Nancy Sinkoff

On 12 August 1981, on a sultry New York City summer evening, I attended a memorial for the Soviet Yiddish writers murdered by Stalin. The memorial was sponsored by *Jewish Currents*, which was still edited by the older ex-Communist guard Morris Schappes (1907–2004), who also presided over the event. Without any sense of irony (compounded by the fact that the memorial was held on the campus of Hebrew Union College, the Reform movement's seminary), Schappes began the evening by saying in Yiddish, "Haynt iz undzer tishabov" (Today is our Tisha B'Av), thus linking Stalin's purge of the Sovietized Yiddish intelligentsia to the traditional Jewish calendar's marking of the destruction of the two ancient temples. Aggrieved by the memory of the murder of members of the Jewish Anti-Fascist Committee (JAFC), including its leaders, the actor Solomon Mikhoels (1890–1948) and the poet Itsik Fefer (1900–1952), Schappes reached back into the Jewish past to express his anguish, endeavoring to sacralize a definitively secular event to embed the murder of the Yiddish writers into contemporary Jewish memory.[1] Although his appeal to a traditional religious signifier obscured the relationship of the victims to their executioners, most of those murdered were not observant Jews and had in fact supported the regime's attack on "bourgeois clericalism." Nonetheless, Schappes's words sounded like a *hesped* (eulogy), albeit voiced in a secular context.[2]

One can view this event as part of a continuum of the Jewish engagement with Communism that since 1922 has twisted and turned with Soviet policy (and that of its satellites and Western adherents) and continues today in the historiography and memory culture of those dark years.[3] The collapse of the Soviet Union in 1991, which allowed for the declassification of party documents, the possibility of liberal, democratic politics in Eastern Europe, and the more recent political backlash in the form of the resurgence of right-wing integral nationalism in the region, with its concomitant toxic association of Jews and Communism, make these issues still resonant in writing the history of the Jews of Eastern Europe.[4] The *Jewish Currents* event can also be seen as evidence of the deep transnational cultural ties between diasporic Eastern European Jewry—which could be composed of Jews from the lands of Russia, Poland, Austria, Ukraine, Romania, and later the Soviet Union—and the European homeland that began in the late nineteenth century and also continues today.

I do not recall if Schappes mentioned Ilya Ehrenburg (1891–1967), a member of the JAFC and one of the few survivors of the persecutions. As a Russian-language poet, novelist, and journalist of Jewish origin, Ehrenburg was spared Stalin's predations. But his survival became, tautologically, proof of his complicity. During his life and posthumously, a vast historiography emerged to assess his role in the alleged destruction of Soviet Jewish culture under Stalin, with a specific focus on his putative role in the murder of the Yiddish writers in 1952.[5]

A little-known assessment of Ehrenburg is the eponymous 1968 Yiddish biography *Ilye Erenburg*, by Sh. L. Shnayderman (1906–1996),[6] himself a neglected figure in twentieth-century Polish Jewish history. Shneiderman's life intersected with interwar Polish Jewish literary modernism in both Warsaw and Paris, leftist politics, the Spanish Civil War, the Holocaust, the founding of Israel, and the continuities of Eastern European Jewish life in the post–World War II world. In other words, his own biography incorporated many of the same events that shaped Ehrenburg's life, making him a compelling and engaged, even implicated, interlocutor for Ehrenburg. Library shelves are filled with books addressing the genre of biography and its convergences with literary narrative, autobiography, and memoir. Suffice it to say here that I view the biographer as akin to the memoirist or autobiographer, one who makes selective choices when writing someone else's life, guided by the biographer's own distinct concerns.[7] In Shneiderman's case, he brought his leftist Jewish nationalist commitments to his reading of and writing on Ehrenburg's life. *Ilye Erenburg* is a biography of a Russian Jewish internationalist written by a Polish Jewish nationalist.

Ilye Erenburg is also a text that offers readers today the opportunity to reflect on the intertwined yet divergent fates of Russian and Polish Jewry. **Ilye Erenburg** reverberates with the complexity of identity mirroring Polish and Soviet Jews as distinct modern iterations of eastern Ashkenazic history and culture.[8] The House of Ashkenazic Judaism[9] had many rooms, but in all of them the Yiddish language—the mother tongue of so much of Eastern European Jewry and the symbolic marker of Ashkenazic civilization—was (and still is) a symbol of both consonance with and distance from Ashkenazic Jewry's premodern past, evidenced not only by Schappes's proclamation but also by Shneiderman's language choice.[10]

Doppelgängers

Shneiderman and Ehrenburg were modern Eastern European Jewish doppelgängers of a sort, living almost parallel lives until the outbreak of World War II. After 1939, however, their geographies shifted dramatically. But until then, they traversed similar if distinct modern Eastern European Jewish terrain: Both were students of modernist literature and poets, both lived in interwar Paris, and both covered the internecine antifascist struggles in Spain. With the German invasion of France, their lives diverged, with Ehrenburg returning to Moscow and Shneiderman immigrating to New York City (after a six-month sojourn in South Africa). Yet, as witnesses to prewar Polish Jewish and Soviet Jewish life, the two remained connected, intellectually and personally. This connection is a testament to the foundational early modern history of eastern Ashkenazic Jewry, later separated by the processes of partition and modernization in the long nineteenth century and the revolutionary twentieth century. In the catastrophic last century, Polish and Soviet Jews encountered and reencountered one another at several critical historical junctures. The stories and diary of Isaac Babel, the great Russian writer of Jewish descent who embedded with a Cossack cavalry unit of the Red Army, provide evidence of such meetings, often in the wake of violence, between Russian and Polish Jews.[11] After the Polish-Soviet war, when the eastern borders were fixed and the

Soviet Union was consolidated, Polish and Russian Jews remained acutely aware of each other's communities over the border. Any Yiddishist in the interwar years knew that the language was initially supported by the Soviet government; in fact, several Polish Yiddishists, facing the dire economic straits of the fledgling Polish Second Republic, immigrated to the USSR.[12] The occupation of eastern Poland by the Soviet Union after 1939 with the concomitant Sovietization of Polish and Polish Jewish life, enacted another form of encounter. Likewise, the flight eastward through Soviet lands of many Jews who found themselves under Nazi rule effected yet another reunion of these two communities of Eastern European Jews.[13] In June 1941, when the mobile killing squads victimized both former Polish Jews and Soviet Jews, their political, cultural, religious, and linguistic diversity was homogenized into a shared genocidal fate. After the war, amid the ruins of cities once home to Jews and in displaced persons camps, Polish and Soviet Jews met again.

Although separated physically during the war years and in its aftermath, both the Soviet writer Ehrenburg and the Polish writer Shneiderman responded to the emergence of modern political and racial antisemitism and the destruction of Jewish life in the Holocaust through their work. Both writers promoted the publication of memoirs and testimonies of the victims. Shneiderman edited Mary Berg's *Warsaw Ghetto: A Diary* in 1940 and Ehrenburg was instrumental in issuing the Russian edition of *The Diary of Anne Frank* in the 1960s.[14] As we will see, Ehrenburg, along with the writer Vasily Grossman (1905–1964), was central to the project of collecting testimonies and eyewitness accounts of the murder of the Jews in German-occupied Soviet (formerly Polish) territory in 1941, and Shneiderman documented the "new Poland" that was mostly absent of Jews in 1946.[15] Still, in the postwar period they wrote not only on opposite sides of the postwar Cold War divide but also from the vastly different ideological positions of their prewar lives: Shneiderman the Polish Yiddishist nationalist and Ehrenburg the Russified Soviet cosmopolitan.

Shneiderman and Ehrenburg: Early Lives

Shneiderman was born in Kazimierz nad Wisłą (Yiddish, Kuzmir), about 150 kilometers southeast of Warsaw. He was educated at both a religious

Jewish school and a Polish middle school and later moved to the capital to study literature at the Free Polish University (Wolna Wszechnica Polska). Shneiderman wrote in both Yiddish and Polish, and his oeuvre includes literary studies, film criticism, stories, poetry, war and travel reportage, and translations. In Warsaw he was coeditor of the magazine *Shprotsungen* (Sprouts) and contributed to *Ilustrirter magazin* (Illustrated Magazine),[16] publishing two poetry collections, *Gilderne feygl* (Gilded Birds, 1927) and *Fayren in shtot* (Fires in the City, 1932), as well as film criticism in the short-lived magazine *Film Velt* (Film World).[17] In his youth Shneiderman identified with the Linke Poalei Tsiyon, the Left Marxist-Zionist movement inspired by the theoretician Ber Borochov, yet he wrote for both left and right blocs of the Labor Zionist spectrum.[18] In 1932 he and his wife, Eileen (née Chaja Szymin, known as Halina and as Hala), went to Paris, where he became coeditor of the bimonthly journal *Bleter* (Pages) and edited the weekly *Pariz* (Paris). During the Spanish Civil War between 1936 and 1938, Shneiderman served as a correspondent for both Yiddish and Polish newspapers, later publishing *Krig in Shpanyen: Hinterland* (The War in the Spanish Hinterland), accompanied by photographs taken by his brother-in-law David Seymour (b. Dawid Szymin, aka "Chim"), earning him the moniker "The first Yiddish war reporter."[19] Caught up in the maelstrom of German aggression in Central Europe, Shneiderman considered taking a permanent editorship for the Yiddish newspaper *Afrikaner Idishe Tsaytung* (African Jewish Newspaper) in Johannesburg. World War II thwarted those plans, and he settled with his wife and their young daughter in New York City in 1940, where he spent most of the rest of his life, authoring hundreds of articles, travelogues, reportage, and translations in the Yiddish and Anglo-Jewish press. Shneiderman was a regular contributor to *Morgn-zhurnal* (Morning Journal), *Tog-morgn-zhurnal* (Day-Morning Journal), and later the *Forverts* (Forward); in the 1950s several of his articles were translated into Hebrew for *Davar* (Word), the organ of the Histadrut (the General Organization of Workers in Israel) in Mandatory Palestine. His travelogues included *Tsvishn shrek un hofenung* (Between Fear and Hope), about his visit to postwar Poland in 1946, and *Ven di vaysl hot geredt yidish* (When the Vistula Spoke Yiddish).[20]

Ehrenburg was born in Kiev in 1891 when the empire was still ruled by Alexander III. His family moved to Moscow in 1895, and in his youth he was drawn to the Bolshevik underground. Arrested in 1908, he spent

Figure 15.1. Hala Szymin (Eileen Shneiderman) and S. L. Shneiderman, Paris 1931–1933. Photo by David Seymour-Chim/Magnum, www.davidseymour.com.

five months in prison and then left for France, which was a geographic magnet and cultural muse throughout his life. Ehrenburg became disillusioned with Bolshevism and devoted himself to writing literature and poetry and essays about modernist art. He also covered the Western front for Russian newspapers during World War I. Ehrenburg returned to Russia five months after the abdication of Tsar Nicholas II. During the Russian Civil War, his lyric poetry attacked the Bolsheviks and illuminated the horrifying anti-Jewish violence in Ukraine, observing in 1919, "If Jewish blood could cure, then Russia would be a flourishing country. But blood cannot cure, it only infects the air with malice and discord."[21]

Ehrenburg went to Paris in 1921, where he was expelled by the French police, so he proceeded to Belgium and then Berlin, a hub of Russian émigré life in the interwar years, and only returned to Paris in 1924. There, he completed his first novel, *The Adventures of Julio Jurenito and His Disciples*, followed by *The Stormy Life of Lasik Roitschwantz* in 1929. In 1932 he became the Paris correspondent for *Izvestia* and covered the Spanish Civil War from 1936 to 1939. Joshua Rubenstein, Ehrenburg's English-language biographer, relates that Ehrenburg suffered a crisis with the signing of the Hitler-Stalin Pact and could not eat for eight months.[22] After the Germans invaded France in the spring of 1940, Ehrenburg returned to Moscow—the same year that Shneiderman made his way to New York. Ehrenburg had broken with the Bolsheviks in 1909, but after the fateful summer of 1941, when Germany abrogated the non-aggression pact with the Soviet Union, his patriotism married with support for Stalin's war against the Germans.

The brutal incursion of the Germans into Soviet territories, which started the "Great Patriotic War," offered loyal Communists in both the Soviet Union and abroad the opportunity to reinvigorate the antifascist ideology that had been compromised by the treaty. It also made the choice between Stalin and Hitler clear. Secure in their opposition to Nazi Germany, Soviet citizens could faithfully fight to protect the motherland and to defend its political-economic system. In June 1941 Ehrenburg was offered a position writing for *Red Star*, and over a period of four years more than 2,000 of his articles appeared.[23] With his articles widely circulated on the front, Ehrenburg became a beloved figure for soldiers; anecdotes relate that the paper from his articles was not used for rolling cigarettes.[24] An ideological problem existed, however, because in fighting the Germans, the Soviets became allies of the capitalist Western powers, previously the regime's arch enemies. Stalin needed loyal supporters to rally domestic support for an alliance with the United States and Britain and to secure foreign aid for the Great Patriotic War.

In the first winter after the German invasion, Stalin created five antifascist committees, propaganda arms of the regime whose purpose was to encourage support from the West. The Jewish Anti-Fascist Committee was founded as the Jewish Anti-Hitler Committee in 1942 in Kuibyshev (today, Samara), with two veteran Polish Bundists, Henryk Erlich (1882–1942) and Viktor Alter (1890–1942), as its organizers—both Erlich and Alter were imprisoned by Stalin's orders before the committee's formal establishment—with the express purpose of raising money from world Jewry, particularly from Jews in the United States.[25] Ehrenburg and Vasily Grossman represented the Russian language, and the theater actor Solomon Mikhoels and writers Dovid Bergelson (1884–1952) and Itsik Fefer, among others, the Yiddish. After Mikhoel's and Fefer's fundraising tours in 1943, the JAFC authorized Ehrenburg and Grossman to compile material for what would eventually be called *The Black Book*, which was to include firsthand documentation, including testimonies, photographs, newspaper clippings, and eyewitness accounts of the destruction of the Jews in Soviet-occupied Poland by the Einsatzgruppen. However, the book was censored amid the anticosmopolitan campaign starting in 1948 and did not appear in Russian until 1980, in Ukrainian in 1991, and in English in 2002.[26] *The Black Book* contained official documents, dozens of testimonies, and other personal documents, including letters sent directly to Ehrenburg. During the war, Ehrenburg's articles highlighted Jewish suffering, and the JAFC's house organ, *Eynikayt* (Unity), published material from *The Black Book*. Ehrenburg contributed a brief foreword to *Merder fun felker* (Murderer of Peoples), a Yiddish compilation of materials from *The Black Book*, published in Moscow by Der Emes in 1945.[27] Deputized to produce a work that would mobilize domestic and international Jewish support for the Soviet war effort, Ehrenburg and Grossman's book dutifully served the aims of the Soviet government while expressing the editors' identification with the Jewish victims.[28]

The JAFC was liquidated in 1948, the same year that Mikhoels was called to Minsk and murdered, although the regime dissembled and reported his death as the result of a car accident. In May 1952, at the height of Stalin's paranoia and antisemitism, 15 Jews associated with the JAFC, including 5 Yiddish writers, were put on trial for antigovernmental activities. Interrogated and tortured, 12 of the defendants were shot, including Fefer, Bergelson, Peretz Markish, Dovid Hofshteyn, and Leib Kvitko.[29] Ehrenburg managed to survive Stalin's purges and wrote the novel *The Thaw* after the dictator's death, the title becoming a marker of a whole historical period in the Eastern Bloc. He also later survived Khrushchev's denunciations. Ehrenburg died a natural death from cancer in Moscow in 1967—his wife at his side, one of his lovers waiting for him in Sweden—in an apartment on Gorky Street not far from the infamous Lubyanka prison where the Yiddish cultural activists had perished.

Shneiderman and Ehrenburg knew each other from interwar Paris and the Spanish front and were acquainted enough for the Russian writer to open his home in Moscow to his Polish peer in 1965 shortly before the former's death in 1967.[30] A year later, Shneiderman published his biography, with the iconic portrait of Ehrenburg made by Pablo Picasso on the cover[31] (Figure 15.2). Its dustjacket reads:

> After Ehrenburg's death in September 1967, passionate debate about his so-called role in the liquidation of Yiddish culture in the Soviet

Figure 15.2. Book jacket of Shneiderman's biography of Ilya Ehrenberg.

Union was renewed. Voices were also heard about Ehrenburg's bold defense of artistic expression and especially about his courageous fight against antisemitism. This study of Ilya Ehrenberg is an attempt towards an objective confrontation of facts about the stormy life and works of this leading Jewish-Russian writer with whom the author met in the course of thirty years in various circumstances in Western Europe. In the winter of 1965 [he] held long conversations with him in his home in Moscow.[32]

Shneiderman's decision to write a biography of Ehrenburg emerged for a variety of reasons. In 1964 an English translation of the first six volumes of the Russian writer's memoirs were translated and published as a prestigious Borzoi book by Alfred A. Knopf, allowing Ehrenburg to ruminate on the questions on every observers' tongue: "How did you survive?" and "What were the ethical costs of that survival?"[33] Shneiderman's biography, which unfolds in 18 chapters that are not always chronological—with the chapter on the Popular Front coming after

Ehrenburg's tangles with Khrushchev—squarely faces those questions. The biography is interspersed with literary criticism and political observations and is particularly attentive to Ehrenburg's complex modern Jewish identity. It begins with Shneiderman's reflections on the aesthetics of Ehrenburg's apartment and concludes with commentary on Ehrenburg's incomplete confessional memoirs. Shneiderman positions himself and his transnational Jewish nationalist sensibilities almost immediately, telling his readers that when he met with Ehrenburg in 1965, the Egyptian flags hoisted in Nasser's honor were still flying near the Kremlin.[34] He situates Ehrenburg as a rebellious modernist, living in a Russian apartment house that nonetheless felt like a Parisian home, its walls and shelves filled with extraordinary modern French art and the afternoon meal served on elegant Sèvres porcelain.

Shneiderman's biography exonerates Ehrenburg for his role in the destruction of Jewish culture, consistently emphasizing that the only way to understand Ehrenburg was as a modern form of Russified Jewish intellectual, whose ties to Jewishness and the Jewish people were primarily activated by anti-Jewish hatred, a poison that did not distinguish between the national origin (i.e., that of the Gentile state in which the Jews lived). Contrasting his own Jewish national consciousness with Ehrenburg's "assimilated," cosmopolitan identity, Shneiderman concluded that for Ehrenburg the "only unifying factor for Jews all over the world was their struggle against antisemitism and their defense against persecution. [It is] antisemitism that makes a Jew from Tunis connected to a Jew from Chicago. It is a solidarity of insult and rage."[35]

Shneiderman's Defense of Ehrenburg

In 1963 Galina Serebriakova, a rehabilitated gulag survivor, publicly accused Ehrenburg of collaborating with the regime to destroy the JAFC. Her denunciation lacked evidence; she likely never met with her purported source, Alexander N. Poskrebyshev, Stalin's personal secretary, who, she claimed, fingered Ehrenburg as giving testimony against the Yiddish writers at their trial. But the 1952 trial was closed with no witnesses and no testimony. Nonetheless, her accusation found fertile ground in the West, and the accusations haunted Ehrenburg.[36]

Shneiderman's defense of Ehrenburg rested on several points. He insisted, first, that Ehrenburg's oft-quoted article in *Pravda*, "Because of a Certain Letter," published on 21 September 1948, must be read in the context of the visit of Golda Meir, Israel's representative to the Soviet Union, to the Great Synagogue that month. Her visit was notable for the surprisingly enthusiastic reception of Soviet Jews following the establishment of the State of Israel earlier in May. Ehrenburg's posture in the *Pravda* article was a calculated move, argued Shneiderman, to emphasize where the loyalties of Soviet Jews should lie. In the article Ehrenburg addressed a fictitious disillusioned German Jewish anti-Nazi named Alexander R. who had reencountered antisemitism in the postwar period; Ehrenburg endeavored to persuade him that only socialism, not Zionist state nationalism, would solve the Jewish question. Ehrenburg emphasized the Russian patriotism of Moscow's Jews and their commitment to Marxism. Shneiderman reminded his readers that Ehrenburg was loyal to the Marxist understanding of antisemitism as an extreme form of racism, citing the Soviet writer's comment that antisemitism was the result of "the most dangerous vestige of cannibalism" (*di same-geferlekhste iberblaybenish fun kanibalizm*).[37] By January 1949 the hostility to Jews as "rootless cosmopolitans" was being widely disseminated. Ehrenburg's arrest was announced in March of that year. Although he was spared (he was able to trade on Stalin's need for him to represent the Soviet Union at the World Peace Congress in Paris to showcase the USSR's critique of racism and national chauvinism to the world), the next two years were filled with the bizarre oscillations of sycophancy and terror. In 1951 Ehrenburg received the Stalin Prize. In August 1952 the Yiddish writers and the other members of the JAFC were murdered.[38] That November the Slansky trial falsely accused Czech Communists of Jewish origin of plotting against the regime in cahoots with the Joint Distribution Committee. And in 1953 the so-called Doctors' Plot targeted Jewish physicians for allegedly conspiring to kill prominent Soviet public figures. Ehrenburg is reported to have slept with a packed suitcase by his bedside, ready for the terrifying knock on the door.[39] Shneiderman's biography stressed the paralyzing tightrope walk that Soviet Jews like Ehrenburg took over the abyss of Stalin's arbitrary, murderous policies.

He wasn't alone. An exculpatory view of Ehrenburg had emerged already before his death: that his accuser, Serebriakova, was being used by the regime. Victor Erlich, Henryk Erlich's son, exonerated Ehrenburg of responsibility in the murder of the Yiddish writers in his assessment in the State Department organ *Problems of Communism*.[40] Even Esther Markish, widow of the liquidated writer Peretz Markish, remained close to Ehrenburg throughout their lives, if not exactly proof of Ehrenburg's innocence, at least evidence of her enduring trust in him. In his biography Shneiderman concluded that Khrushchev successfully deployed Serebriakova to foist the blame on a Jew for extinguishing Yiddish culture in the USSR in order to kill two birds with one stone: to make a Jew responsible for the murder of his brethren and thus deflect the regime's culpability and to warn Ehrenburg not to promote any more dissent against the regime.[41]

Given Shneiderman's Yiddishist and Jewish nationalist commitments, how can we account for his sympathy to Ehrenburg? The two men shared an optimistic faith in modernism, artistic creativity and openness, and a vocabulary of social justice, albeit one defined by patriotism to a state (Ehrenburg) and the other by a commitment to socialist expressions of equality (Shneiderman). But there is something else. Shneiderman felt a kinship with Ehrenburg, a tie between modern Polish Jewry and Soviet Jewry, despite their vastly different histories, societal contexts, and languages. The same complex negotiation of kinship shaped the experience of Polish and Soviet Jews from the beginning of the division and occupation of the Polish Republic in 1939. Polish Jews escaping the Germans encountered Soviet Jews, some of whom offered them shelter and food and others who both informally and formally adopted orphaned children.[42] Yet some Soviet Jews kept their distance from their Polish Jewish "brethren," refraining from speaking Yiddish or acknowledging knowledge of Jewish ritual. Natalie Belsky concluded that Polish Jews generally found Soviet Jews emotionally closed, reluctant to open up in conversations with the Polish refugees, a result of their social and linguistic acculturation and patriotic identification with the Soviet state.[43] The feelings of kinship were not always mutual.

But in *Ilye Erenburg*, Shneiderman expressed a sense of deep empathy with his Soviet Jewish peer and emphasized Ehrenburg's Eastern European Jewish identity and their common inheritance. Two short examples support this view.

Ehrenburg and Tuwim

In Chapter 11 of *Ilye Erenburg*, "Ehrenburg and Tuwim," Shneiderman highlights Ehrenburg's affinity with Julian Tuwim (1894–1953), the modernist Polish poet of Jewish origin whose poem "My, Żydzi Polscy" (We, Polish Jews) announced Tuwim's identification with the fate of the Jews on the anniversary of the Warsaw Ghetto Uprising. Appearing in April 1944 when Tuwim was living in New York and published in an American Polish language newspaper, the poem was a bold assertion of empathy; this was a contrast with most of Tuwim's previous work, which had expressed ambivalence to Jewish national identity.[44] Tuwim's powerful lyric indicted Nazi racism by distinguishing between two kinds of blood (that which flows in the veins and that which flows from the veins), and he syncretistically announced his baptism with the second kind of blood, the blood of murdered Jews.

Ehrenburg had excerpted parts of Tuwim's poem in *Pravda* in 1948, and on 26 January 1961 he gave a talk on Moscow radio on his seventieth birthday in which he again invoked Tuwim. Ehrenburg used the radio address to criticize Stalinist socialist realism's postulate that the task of the writer was to engineer souls—an explicit goal of the 1935 International Congress for the Defense of Culture.[45] Rather, Ehrenburg insisted, writers should be "teachers of life." He next defended his self-definition as a Russian writer, even though his passport stamped him as a Jew, a statement that, in Shneiderman's words, lifted "a stone off the heart of not only one embittered Jew in this period of sharpened discriminations against Jews in all domains of public life in Soviet Russia."[46] The evocation of Tuwim, who, from his position in American exile, could express his rage at the extent of Polish collaboration in the murder of the Jews, allowed Ehrenburg to deflect his criticism of the Soviet regime onto the past and through the voice of a Polish citizen. Yet his radio interview was the first time in the USSR that the passport designation of Jewish nationality—that paradoxical symbol of the Bolsheviks' reluctant recognition of Jewish nationality on par with other ethnicities in the nascent Soviet state (even as the policy contravened communist internationalism)—which had become a marker in the post-war years of the Jews' unassimilability, was publicly mentioned. In so doing, Ehrenburg exposed the inconsistencies of Soviet nationality policy; what had originally been intended as recognition and legitimization of Jewish nationality evolved into a discriminatory label.[47] Ehrenburg's radio address was evidence for Shneiderman of his Soviet peer's strong identification with Polish Jewry, especially with those who shared the Russian's integrationist stance.

Ehrenburg, Bialik, and Sutzkever

In Chapter 16 of *Ilye Erenburg*, "This Is How Jews Fight," Shneiderman underscores the ways in which he conceptualized Ehrenburg's Jewish identity as quintessentially Soviet and proudly Jewish, emblematic of the acculturated Soviet Jewish intelligentsia and yet linked to an older Eastern European Jewish identity. Shneiderman emphasizes that Soviet Jewish identity was marked by an emphasis on physical heroism, on the affirmation of the universalist values that comported with being patriotic Soviet citizens, and on being resolutely brave in the face of antisemitism, which Soviet Jews never hesitated to combat. Ehrenburg was the embodiment of that triad. In "This Is How Jews Fight," Shneiderman references an article on Jewish resistance by Ehrenburg with the same title, which was published in *Eynikayt* on 7 November 1942. Shneiderman cites the Soviet writer's linking Jewish heroism during World War II to the venerable Jewish past.[48] Indeed, during the war years, the Soviet Jewish intelligentsia, writing in both Russian and Yiddish, was allowed to emphasize Jewish heroism, in keeping with the propagandistic goals of the Central Committee and the JAFC to encourage a patriotism rooted in ethnic specificity, combining, in Arkadi Zeltser's phrase, "ethnocentrism and etatism."[49] Articles in *Eynikayt*—many but not all of which were translated from Russian originals—could refer to a pantheon of Jewish figures from the "religious" past, including Bar Kokhba and Rabbi Akiva, who were positioned as icons of resistance to fit with Soviet ideology.[50] Shneiderman quotes Ehrenburg as writing, "The grandchildren of the Maccabees were, however, no cowards. The Jews embraced the battle."[51] His chapter claims that Ehrenburg did not merely deploy the rebellious Maccabees as symbols of Jewish heroism but referred directly to their descendants' courage and empowerment in the face of the slaughter. Shneiderman's citation is a clear allusion to and inversion of the famous lyric poem "In the City of Slaughter" by the Russian Zionist Hebrew poet Chaim Nachman Bialik (1873–1934). In "In the City of Slaughter," the poetic voice of God chastises the men of the city of Kishinev, the site of pogrom violence in 1903, for their cowardice: "Come, now, and I will bring thee to their lairs / The privies, jakes and pigpens where the heirs / Of Hasmoneans lay, with trembling knees, / Concealed and cowering,—the sons of the Maccabees!"[52] Yet, although Bialik's poem was translated into Russian in 1911 by Vladimir Jabotinsky (the poet's work was never reprinted in the Soviet period), there is no evidence that Ehrenburg directly referenced the Maccabees in his article in *Red Star*.[53] Ehrenburg's original Russian article, simply titled "Jews," highlighted the Jews' bravery, spirit of sacrifice, and their embrace of battle, but it does not mention the Maccabees.[54] Contrasting the heroism of Soviet Jewish soldiers to Bialik's condemnation of diasporic Jewish male passivity may well have been the translator's choice alone. It was then affirmed in 1968 by Shneiderman, who imputed a connection to religious symbolism of the ancient Jewish rebels to Ehrenburg.

Nonetheless, Ehrenburg was certainly familiar with Bialik's work.[55] Shneiderman relates that Ehrenburg would often listen to the recitation of the works of Bialik and Saul Tchernichovsky by the poet-partisan Avrom Sutzkever (1913–2010), who, with his wife, was airlifted from the Narocz forest to safety in Moscow in August 1944.[56] Shneiderman tells his readers that Ehrenburg loved the "prophetic sound" of the Hebrew he could not understand.[57] The persona of Sutzkever, the Polish Jew, not only as a modernist poet but also as a partisan willing to take up arms in the struggle against Hitler, affirmed Ehrenburg's modern Soviet Jewish values: physical agency, internationalist antifascist activism on the part of all peoples, and resistance to Nazi antisemitism.[58] Their friendship, emphasized by Shneiderman in his biography, wove together the different pieces of the modern Soviet and Polish Jewish experiences.

Conclusion

In his nuanced evaluation of Ehrenburg written only a year after the Soviet writer's death, Shneiderman's biography functions like a *hesped*, a commemorative appraisal of Ehrenburg's life, especially as it relates to his public-facing support of the Soviet Union under Stalin. In its analysis and tone, Shneiderman's book anticipated both the revisionist and subjectivity turns in Soviet studies of the 1980s.[59] His view of Ehrenburg is gray, not black and white.[60] Shneiderman recognized Ehrenburg's complex and liminal identity as a modernist Russian poet, writer, and war reporter more at home in Paris than in Moscow and as a Jew deeply affected by the destruction of Jewish life in German-occupied Soviet territory after Operation Barbarossa. He recognized Ehrenburg's limited agency, the constraints of being an advocate of free expression, a modernist, a writer, and a Jew in a totalitarian state.[61] Shneiderman concluded, "Ehrenburg always found himself on the edge of two worlds, which he tried to conjoin, and at the same time he aroused suspicions in both worlds about the authenticity of his intentions. Within Ehrenburg's three-way split personality, the Jew, the Russian, and the Westernized cultural figure struggled. In the period of Stalinist insanity, this struggle—which was characteristic for not [only] one assimilated Jewish Soviet intellectual—was labeled with the curse word: cosmopolitanism."[62]

Shneiderman's ultimate assessment of Ehrenburg's life always emphasized his role as a writer, asserting that "in his last years, [Ehrenburg] was the standard bearer for freedom and artistic expression" for Soviet writers.[63] Although he was fiercely anti-Stalinist,[64] Shneiderman's biography rejects a triumphalist Western Cold War anticommunist narrative; rather, it reads today as a prescient, even sympathetic analysis of the entangled ideological commitments of a Communist Soviet Jew and as an affirmation of the ties that bound an explicitly nationalist, or ethnically conscious, Polish Jew to a Soviet Jew.

Together, the lives of Shneiderman and Ehrenburg represent the dynamism, complexity, and divergences of Eastern European Jewish modernity. A signal tragic feature of this modernity on both sides of the Iron Curtain was the impact of Eastern European Jewry's encounter with the modern state on Yiddish culture and language.[65] The use of Yiddish declined in the nineteenth and twentieth centuries. This was due, first, to the natural attrition of voluntary linguistic modernization and assimilation in Polish and Soviet lands,[66] but, second, to the fact that it was mercilessly annihilated with most of its native speakers. In writing his biography of Ehrenburg in Yiddish, Shneiderman asserted the legitimacy and normalcy of writing a modern prose work about a modern Eastern European Jew in a language that increasingly few Jews could read. Ironically, his own subject could not have read the book. By composing in Yiddish, Shneiderman affirmed the linguistic particularity of his commitment to Jewish nationalism, a belief in "the existence of a common destiny for the Jewish people."[67] By writing about Ehrenburg in Yiddish, Shneiderman inserted his subject into a more blatant Jewish substrate, enveloping, as it were, the Soviet writer into his, Shneiderman's, own identification with Ehrenburg as a fellow Eastern European Jew. Although the community of Jewish internationalists at the *Jewish Currents* memorial mourned the murdered Yiddish poets of 1952, they curiously forgot that most internationalist of Russian Jews, Ilya Ehrenburg. It took S. L. Shneiderman, the Polish Jewish Yiddishist, to insist on the shared bonds of their Eastern European Jewish past.

Notes

I am grateful for the research assistance of Julija Levin and Brooke Ramos, the suggestions of my fellow editors, the email exchanges with Helen Sarid, Ben A. Shneiderman, Magdalena Kozłowska, and Joshua Rubenstein, and the Zoom conversations I had with Shimon Redlich.

1 For a contemporary echo of Schappes's appropriation of tradition, see Rokhl Kafrissen, "Night of the Murdered Poets," *Tablet*, 13 August 2019, www.tabletmag.com/sections/community/articles/night-of-the-murdered-poets (accessed 11 May 2023). For the ways in which Communist-affiliated Yiddish writers Judaized the experience of other minorities, such as Black Americans and Palestinian Arabs, through Hebrew and Yiddish expressions to affirm solidarity with them, see Amelie M. Glaser, *Songs in Dark Times: Yiddish Poetry of Struggle from Scottsboro to Palestine* (Cambridge, MA: Harvard University Press, 2020).

2 It is likely that Schappes was still following party dictate. In 1976 an international Yiddish conference held in Jerusalem had appealed to Jews worldwide to mark the execution of the Yiddish writers. Gennady Estraikh, "The Life, Death, and Afterlife of the Jewish Anti-Fascist Committee," *East European Jewish Affairs* 48, no. 2 (2018): 145.

3 Dan Diner and Jonathan Frankel, "Introduction: Jews and Communism—The Utopian Temptation," in *Dark Times, Dire Decisions: Jews and Communism*, ed. Dan Diner and Jonathan Frankel (London: Oxford University Press, 2004), 3–12. For a new, revisionist view of Soviet *Yidish-kayt*, see Miriam Schulz, "*Keyner iz nit fargesn*: Soviet Yiddish Antifascism and the Holocaust," PhD diss., Columbia University, 2021.

4. See Paul Hanebrink, *A Specter Haunting Europe: The Myth of Judeo-Bolshevism* (Cambridge, MA: Harvard University Press, 2018); Michael Shafir, "Four Pitfalls West and East: Universalization, Double Genocide, Obfuscation, and Competitive Martyrdom as New Forms of Holocaust Negation," *Revista de Istorie a Evreilor Din Romania* 4–5, nos. 20–21 (2020): 443–75; and Jeffrey Herf, "Putin's Continuities: From 'Israelis as Nazis' to 'Denazifying' Ukraine," *Times of Israel* (11 March 2022), blogs.timesofisrael.com/putins-continuities-from-israelis-as-nazis-to-denazifying-ukraine/ (accessed 11 March 2022).

5. See, for example, Joshua Rubenstein, *Tangled Loyalties: The Life and Times of Ilya Ehrenburg* (New York: Basic, 1996); Shimon Redlich, *Propaganda and Nationalism in Wartime Russia: The Jewish Antifascist Committee in the USSR, 1941–1948* (Boulder, CO: East European Quarterly, 1982); Gennady Estraikh, *Yiddish in the Cold War* (London: Legenda, 2008); and Harriet Murav, *Music from a Speeding Train: Jewish Literature in Post-Revolution Russia* (Stanford, CA: Stanford University Press, 2011).

6. Sh. L. Shnayderman, *Ilye Erenburg* (New York: Yidisher kempfer, 1968). Shneiderman translated and excerpted sections of his biography in S. L. Shneiderman, "Ilya Ehrenburg Reconsidered," *Midstream* 14, no. 8 (1968): 47–67. For this chapter, I transliterate Shneiderman's name as Sh. L. Shnayderman according to its Yiddish spelling when the text was written in Yiddish. For his English works, I use S. L. Shneiderman, as he did.

7. The recent controversies over the new biographies of Bill Cosby and Philip Roth are evidence of the problematics of considering a biography as an "objective," unmediated source of truth. Biographers make choices, even when endeavoring to honor the historian's quest for some kind of "qualified objectivity." On that term, see Joyce Appleby, Lynn Hunt, and Margaret Jacob, *Telling the Truth About History* (New York: Norton, 1994), 254–69. On Cosby's biography, see Michael Schaub, "Bill Cosby Biography Loses Celebrity Blurbs, Won't Be Published in Paperback," *Los Angeles Times* (23 July 2015), www.latimes.com/books/jacketcopy/la-et-jc-cosby-biography-loses-celebrity-blurbs-20150723-story.html (accessed 11 May 2023); on Roth's, see Alexandra Alter and Rachel Abrams, "Sexual Assault Allegations Against Biographer Halt Shipping of His Roth Book," *New York Times* (21 April 2021), www.nytimes.com/2021/04/21/books/philip-roth-blake-bailey.html (accessed 11 May 2023). On the subjectivity of the autobiographical narrative, see Michael Stanislawski, *Autobiographical Jews: Essays in Jewish Self-Fashioning* (Seattle: University of Washington Press, 2004).

8   For the uncoupling of Prussian (western) Ashkenazic Jews from Polish and Russian (eastern) Ashkenazic Jews, see Ismar Schorsch, "The Myth of Sephardic Supremacy," in his *From Text to Context: The Turn to History in Modern Judaism* (Hanover, NH: University Press of New England, 1994), 71–92. The classic studies on the mirroring relationship between western and eastern Ashkenazic Jews are still Steven E. Aschheim, *Brothers and Strangers: The East European Jew in German and German Jewish Consciousness, 1800–1923* (Madison: University of Wisconsin Press, 1982) and Steven E. Aschheim, Brothers and Strangers *Reconsidered* (Rome: Archivio Guideo Izzi, 1998).

9   For the phrase "House of Ashkenazic Judaism," see Schorsch, "Myth of Sephardic Supremacy," 71.

10 Naomi Seidman, *A Marriage Made in Heaven: The Sexual Politics of Hebrew and Yiddish* (Berkeley: University of California Press, 1997); Jeffrey A. Grossman, *The Discourse on Yiddish in Germany: From the Enlightenment to the Second Empire* (Rochester, NY: Camden House, 2000).

11 Isaac Babel, *1920 Diary*, ed. and trans. Carol J. Avins (New Haven, CT: Yale University Press, 2002); I. (Isaak) Babel', *Red Cavalry*, trans. Boris Dralyuk (London: Pushkin, 2014).

12 Puah Rakovsky spent a half-year there in 1928 to see her son, who had settled in the Soviet Union after the Bolshevik revolution. Puah Rakovsky, *My Life as a Radical Jewish Woman: Memoirs of a Zionist Feminist in Poland*, ed. Paula E. Hyman, trans. Barbara Harshav and Paula E. Hyman (Bloomington: Indiana University Press, 2002), 172–81. The writer Der Nister (né Pinkhes Kahanovich, 1884–1950) returned to Soviet Russia from Berlin in 1926. See Mikhail Krutikov, *Der Nister's Soviet Years: Yiddish Writer as Witness to the People* (Bloomington: Indiana University Press, 2019). On other Russian returnees, including Dovid Bergelson (1884–1952) and Leib Kvitko (1890–1952), see Gennady Estraikh, *In Harness: Yiddish Writers' Romance with Communism* (Syracuse, NY: Syracuse University Press, 2005), 83–84.

13 Sheila Fitzpatrick, "Annexation, Evacuation, and Antisemitism in the Soviet Union, 1939–1946," in *Shelter from the Holocaust: Rethinking Jewish Survival in the Soviet Union*, ed. Mark Edele, Sheila Fitzpatrick, and Atina Grossmann (Detroit: Wayne State University Press, 2017), 133–60; Eliyana R. Adler and Natalia Aleksiun, "Seeking Relative Safety: The Flight of Polish Jews to the East in the Autumn of 1939," *Yad Vashem Studies* 46, no. 1 (2018): 41–71. Among the refugees was the Polish historian Bernard (Beryl) Mark. Shimon Redlich, *War, Holocaust, and Stalinism: A Documented History of the Jewish*

Anti-Fascist Committee in the USSR (Luxembourg: Harwood Academic, 1995), 68.

14 Mary Berg, *Warsaw Ghetto: A Diary*, ed. S. L. Shneiderman, trans. Sylvia Glass (New York: L. B. Fischer, 1945); Jeffrey Shandler, "From Diary to Book: Text, Object, Structure," in *Anne Frank Unbound: Media, Imagination, Memory*, ed. Barbara Kirshenblatt-Gimblett and Jeffrey Shandler (Bloomington: Indiana University Press, 2012), 38–39.

15 Sh. L. Shnayderman, *Tsvishn shrek un hofenung* (Buenos Aires: Tsentralfarband fun Poylishe Yidn in Argentine, 1947); S. L. Shneiderman, *The Warsaw Heresy* (New York: Horizon Press, 1959).

16 Sh. L. Shnayderman, "From the Book, *Kazimierz*," *Ilustrirter magazin* 1 (1927): 10–11.

17 J. Hoberman, *Bridge of Light: Yiddish Films Between Two Worlds* (New York: Museum of Modern Art, 1991), 8–9.

18 Samuel D. Kassow, "The Left Poalei Tsiyon in Interwar Poland," in *The Emergence of Modern Jewish Politics: Bundism and Zionism in Eastern Europe*, ed. Zvi Gitelman (Pittsburgh: University of Pittsburgh Press, 2003), 71–84.

19 Shloyme Shaynberg, "A vort fun farlag," in Sh. L. Shnayderman, *Krig in Shpanyen* (Warsaw: Jewish Universal Library, 1938). There is renewed interest in Shneiderman in contemporary Poland. See Szmuel Lejb Sznajderman, *Wojna w Hiszpanii: Reportaż z Głębi Kraju*, trans. Magdalena Kozłowska (Wołowiec: Czarne, 2021).

20 Shnayderman, *Tsvishn shrek un hofenung*; Sh. L. Shnayderman, *Ven di vaysl hot geredt yidish* (Tel Aviv: Urli, Perets, 1970). Both works were published in English translation. See S. L. Shneiderman, *Between Fear and Hope* (New York: Arco, 1947); and S. L. Shneiderman, *The River Remembers* (New York: Horizon, 1978). On Shneiderman's postwar trip back to Poland, see Jack Kugelmass, "Strange Encounters: Expat and Refugee Polish-Jewish Journalists in Poland and Germany Shortly After World War II," in *Juden und Nichtjuden nach der Shoah: Begegnungen in Deutschland (Europäisch-Jüdische Studien-Beiträge)*, ed. Stefanie Fischer, Nathanael Riemer, and Stefanie Schüler-Springorum (Oldenberg: De Gruyter, 2019), 31–47. See also Eileen (Hala) Szymin-Shneiderman, "S. L. Shneiderman: Decades Together," www.lib.umd.edu/slses/donors/decades (accessed 11 May 2023).

21 Cited in Rubenstein, *Tangled Loyalties*, 58. On anti-Jewish violence during World War I and the Russian civil war, see Jeffrey Veidlinger, *In the Midst of*

Civilized Europe: The Pogroms of 1918–1921 and the Onset of the Holocaust (New York: Metropolitan, 2021).

22 Rubenstein, *Tangled Loyalties*, 181. See also Ehrenburg's comment about his ill health in the winter of 1940 in Paris: Ilya Ehrenburg, *Memoirs, 1921–1941*, trans. Tatania Shebunina (Cleveland: World, 1964), 31.

23 Redlich, *War, Holocaust, and Stalinism*, 5, 97.

24 Rubenstein, *Tangled Loyalties*, 193–94.

25 Redlich, *Propaganda and Nationalism*.

26 Rubenstein, *Tangled Loyalties*, 212–17; Ilya Ehrenburg and Vasily Grossman, *The Complete Black Book of Russian Jewry*, ed. and trans. David Patterson (New Brunswick, NJ: Transaction, 2002). Rubenstein later published a volume of materials that were not chosen to be in the original *Black Book*, which had first appeared in 1993 in Israel in Russian as *Neizvestnaya Chyornaya Kniga*. Joshua Rubenstein and Ilya Altman, eds., *The Unknown Black Book: The Holocaust in German-Occupied Soviet Territories*, trans. Christopher Morris and Joshua Rubenstein (Bloomington: Indiana University Press, 2008).

27 Ilye Erenburg, "Foreword," in *Merder fun felker* (Moscow: Der Emes, 1945), 2: 3–6; Redlich, *Propaganda and Nationalism*, 92. Ehrenburg had earlier published a Russian article that excerpted victim testimony, "Narodoubiytsy" (Murderers of Peoples), in the journal *Znamya*. He wrote: "Those who hide from the truth are cowards." Cited in Hannah Pollin-Galay, "Avrom Sutzkever's Art of Testimony: Witnessing with the Poet in the Wartime Soviet Union," *Jewish Social Studies: History, Culture, Society* 21, no. 2 (2016): 9. See also Estraikh, "Life, Death, and Afterlife."

28 On the dialogic relationship between the editors and collectors of the testimonies and the victims and eyewitnesses, see Polly Zavadivker, "Preserving 'Events That Are Vanishing Like Smoke': *The Black Book* as Community of Survivors and Writers, 1943–1946," *Zutot: Perspectives on Jewish Culture* 11 (2014): 1–12.

29 Estraikh, "Life, Death, and Afterlife," 145; Joshua Rubenstein and Vladimir P. Naumov, eds., *Stalin's Secret Pogrom: The Postwar Inquisition of the Jewish Anti-Fascist Committee*, trans. Laura Esther Wolfson (New Haven, CT: Yale University Press, 2001).

30 Shnayderman, *Ilye Erenburg*, 14; Shneiderman, "Ilya Ehrenburg Reconsidered," 47. The two men were more than acquaintances but less than friends. Ehrenburg's memoirs mention Shneiderman only once, and then only in

passing. My thanks to Jochen Hellbeck for this information. The language of their conversations was likely French, as Ehrenburg did not know Yiddish and Shneiderman did not know Russian.

31 A metal reproduction of the image, etched by the sculptor Lev Slonim, graces Ehrenburg's headstone in Moscow. Rubenstein, *Tangled Loyalties*, 395.

32 Shnayderman, *Ilye Erenburg*, dustjacket. On page 16 of the book, however, Shneiderman relates that he visited Ehrenburg on a warm September day. See also Shneiderman, "Ilya Ehrenburg Reconsidered," 47.

33 Ilya Ehrenburg, *People and Life, 1891–1921* (New York: Knopf, 1962); Ehrenburg, *Memoirs*.

34 See also Shneiderman's aside regarding the threat to Israel during the Six Day War: "Barely twenty years after that [the appearance of Ehrenburg's article in *Pravda*], as if from the same words that came from Ehrenburg's pen, that apocalyptic vision would be brought about completely in June 1967 with the destructive tools and support of the 'socialist fatherland'" (Shnayderman, *Ilye Erenburg*, 40–41).

35 Shnayderman, *Ilye Erenburg*, 31.

36 Rubenstein, *Tangled Loyalties*, 346–48.

37 Shnayderman, *Ilye Erenburg*, 32.

38 The preparation for the trial against the JAFC and the Yiddish writers began in earnest in early 1952, and a list of 200 additional names of allegedly disloyal subjects, including Ehrenburg, was drawn up. Redlich, *War, Holocaust, and Stalinism*, 151–52.

39 Shnayderman, *Ilye Erenburg*, 20.

40 Victor Erlich, "The Metamorphoses of Ilya Ehrenburg," *Problems of Communism* 12, no. 4 (1963): 15–24; Victor Erlich, "Ilya Ehrenburg Takes a Bow," *Problems of Communism* 14, no. 5 (1965): 72–74.

41 Shnayderman, *Ilye Erenburg*, 80–83.

42 Ehrenburg himself adopted an orphan, Fanya Fishman, from Pinsk. See Rubenstein, *Tangled Loyalties*, 211; and Redlich, *Propaganda and Nationalism*, 92.

43 Natalie Belsky, "Fraught Friendships: Soviet Jews and Polish Jews on the Soviet Home Front," in *Shelter from the Holocaust: Rethinking Jewish Survival in the Soviet Union*, ed. Mark Edele, Sheila Fitzpatrick, and Atina Grossmann (Detroit: Wayne State University Press, 2017), 161–84; Eliyana Adler, *Survival on the Margins: Polish Jewish Refugees in the Wartime Soviet Union* (Cambridge, MA: Harvard University Press, 2020). See also Schulz, "*Keyner iz nit fargesn*," 110–56.

44 See also Rubenstein, *Tangled Loyalties*, 204–5, 259.
45 In notes to his unpublished autobiography, selections of which his wife later compiled, Shneiderman noted that he conferred with Ehrenburg at the 1935 International Congress for the Defense of Culture: "Realizing that the aim had been to eliminate any spokesman for the Yiddish writers in the Soviet Union, a fact ignored by the Jewish Communists in Paris, I felt moved to approach the directors of the Congress with an offer to give an informative lecture on Yiddish literature. I conferred with Ilya Ehrenburg, one of the organizers of the Congress, about the lecture. To my great surprise and delight, Ehrenburg supported my proposal and tacitly confirmed my suspicion about the reasons for the exclusion of the Soviet Yiddish writers" (S. L. Shneiderman, "Notes for an Autobiography," trans. Fannie Peczenik, 2001; this source was available on 4 January 2022 through the University of Maryland library archive; it is now housed at the Weitzman National Museum of American Jewish History, theweitzman.org/university-of-md-archive).
46 Shnayderman, *Ilye Erenburg*, 77.
47 Shnayderman, *Ilye Erenburg*, 79. See Michael Stanislawski, "Russian Jewry, the Russian State, and the Dynamics of Jewish Emancipation," in *Paths of Emancipation: Jews, States and Citizenship*, ed. Pierre Birnbaum and Ira Katznelson (Princeton, NJ: Princeton University Press, 1995), 281; and Zvi Gitelman, *A Century of Ambivalence: The Jews of Russia and the Soviet Union, 1881 to the Present* (Bloomington: University of Indiana Press, 2001).
48 Ilye Erenburg, "Ot azoy shlogn zikh Yidn," *Eynikayt* 16–17 (November 1942): 6; Shnayderman, *Ilye Erenburg*, 109.
49 Arkadi Zeltser, "How the Jewish Intelligentsia Created the Jewishness of the Jewish Hero: The Soviet Yiddish Press," in *Soviet Jews in World War II: Fighting, Witnessing, Remembering*, ed. Harriet Murav and Gennady Estraikh (Boston: Academic Studies, 2014), 109.
50 Zeltser, "How the Jewish Intelligentsia Created." The appropriation of figures from the Jewish "religious" past for secular aims was characteristic not only for Jews on the left but also for Zionist ideologues on all points on the political spectrum in their construction of a usable past. See Ezra Mendelsohn, *On Modern Jewish Politics* (Oxford, UK: Oxford University Press, 1993), 19–20.
51 Shnayderman, *Ilye Erenburg*, 109. See also Ehrenburg's pronouncement about the Jews' loyalty to the USSR and their military prowess as soldiers in the Red Army: "Now the Jews of the Soviet Union are on the front lines. The country

knows a lot of the names of Jewish heroes. Courage cannot be measured, victims cannot be fully counted. Blood cannot be weighed. We will say, in brief: 'Jews fulfill their [military] duty!'" (cited in Ehrenburg, "Foreword," 6).

52 Paul Mendes-Flohr and Jehuda Reinharz, *The Jew in the Modern World: A Documentary History*, 3rd ed. (Oxford, UK: Oxford University Press, 2010), 391.

53 Il'ia Ehrenburg, *Voina: 1941–1945*, ed. B. Ia. Frezinskii (Moscow: Olimp, AST, Astrel', 2004), 317–18.

54 Ehrenburg, *Voina*, 317–18. My thanks to Marat Grinberg for several emails in the winter and spring of 2022 regarding Ehrenburg and the original Russian version of the article.

55 Brian J. Horowitz, *Vladimir Jabotinsky's Russian Years, 1900–1925* (Bloomington: Indiana University Press, 2020), 32. On the power of Jewish literature to shape Soviet Jewish identity, see Marat Grinberg, *The Soviet Jewish Bookshelf: Jewish Culture and Identity Between the Lines* (Waltham, MA: Brandeis University Press, 2023). Grinberg also makes special note of Ehrenburg's memoirs as a source of Jewish collective memory for Soviet readers. See Grinberg, *Soviet Jewish Bookshelf*, 35–40, 82.

56 Pollin-Galay, "Avrom Sutzkever's Art of Testimony"; David Fishman, *The Book Smugglers: Partisans, Poets, and the Race to Save Jewish Treasures from the Nazis* (Lebanon, NH: ForeEdge, 2017), 129–31.

57 Shnayderman, *Ilye Erenburg*, 92.

58 Ehrenburg had met with partisans in liberated Vilna in 1944. Rubenstein, *Tangled Loyalties*, 209–12. See also Fishman, *Book Smugglers*, 131–32.

59 On the shifts in Soviet historiography that critiqued the Cold War "totalitarian" school's political-science-informed perspective on the USSR as a completely closed authoritarian system with no room for human agency "from below," including active support for the regime for socially mobile workers, see Sheila Fitzpatrick, "Revisionism in Soviet History," *History and Theory* 46, no. 4 (2007): 77–91; Anna Krylova, "Soviet Modernity: Stephen Kotkin and the Bolshevik Predicament," *Contemporary European History* 23, no. 2 (2014): 167–92; Julie Hessler, "Sheila Fitzpatrick: An Interpretive Essay," in *Writing the Stalin Era: Sheila Fitzpatrick and Soviet Historiography*, ed. Golfo Alexopoulos, Julie Hessler, and Kiril Tomoff (New York: Palgrave MacMillan, 2011), 21–35; and Jochen Hellbeck, *Revolution on My Mind: Writing a Diary Under Stalin* (Cambridge, MA: Harvard University Press, 2006).

60 For a similar assessment of a Polish Jew living under communism, see the portrait of Bernard Mark: Joanna Nalewajko-Kulikov, "Sylwetki: Trzy Kolory:

Szary—Szkic Do Portretu Bernarda Marka," *Zagłada Żydów: Studia i Materiały* 4 (2008): 263–84.

61 See also Joshua Rubenstein, "Letter to the Editor," *Commentary* (January 1983), 10, where he emphasizes Ehrenburg's independence from Stalinism.
62 Shnayderman, *Ilye Erenburg*, 10–11.
63 Shnayderman, *Ilye Erenburg*, 128.
64 S. L. Shneiderman, "Yiddish in the USSR," *New York Times Book Review* (15 November 1970); S. L. Shneiderman, "*Sovietish Heimland* and Its Editor, Aron Vergelis," *Midstream* (October 1971): 28–42.
65 Max Weinreich, *History of the Yiddish Language*, ed. Paul Glasser, trans. Shlomo Noble and Joshua A. Fishman (New Haven, CT: Yale University Press, 2008); Jeffrey Shandler, *Yiddish: Biography of a Language* (London: Oxford University Press, 2020).
66 The paradoxes of linguistic assimilation in the Soviet Union included the efforts of Soviet Communist Yiddishists to modernize the morphology of the language by de-Hebraizing its Hebrew-component words in an effort to de-Judaize it. Soviet Yiddish, however, was still printed in the *alef-bays*.
67 Shneiderman, "Ilya Ehrenburg Reconsidered," 64.

16

The Wall and the Mountain

Symbols of Two Israels

Michael Brenner

In an essay titled "Hakir vehahar" (The Wall and the Mountain) Israeli writer A. B. Yehoshua juxtaposed the two most prominent sites of national commemoration in his country: The Western Wall and Mount Herzl.[1] For Yehoshua, these two places symbolize two opposing modes of memory in the State of Israel. The Kotel (Hebrew, Western Wall) is for him a purely religious symbol, which calls to mind the destructions of the Jewish past. It has neither redeeming value nor aesthetic quality. Mount Herzl, on the other hand, Yehoshua continues, is a place that emanates pride for the whole nation. As opposed to the Western Wall, which is dominated by the commanding sight of the two mosques on top of it, Mount Herzl is, "a complete place, an autonomous unit, which is not hit or threatened by any foreign element" (*har Herzl hu makom shalem, yeḥida otonomit asher eyna pegu'a o me'uyemet al yedei element zar*).[2] In his 1980s vision of a future Jewish-Palestinian commonwealth Yehoshua sees the Western Wall reduced to minor status as part of the religious landscape of East Jerusalem, whereas Mount Herzl becomes the undisputed symbol of memory for secular Israel.

In this chapter tracing the history of these two sites of Israeli national commemoration from early statehood to the present day, I argue that Yehoshua's vision was not realized. With the possible brief exception of the years between 1949 and 1967, when Jerusalem's Old City was part of

Jordan and inaccessible to Jewish visitors, the mountain remained in the shadow of the wall. Today more than ever, not only is the Western Wall the image that emotionally appeals to a growing number of religious Israelis and to Jews around the world but it has also become an icon of Jewish nationalism. On the other hand, the burial site of the founder of political Zionism has been relegated to an important but less central place in Israeli collective memory than the founders of the state, or for that matter Yehoshua, had envisioned.[3]

It is hard to tell when exactly the Western Wall received its status as the most sacred place for Jews all over the world. Built in the late Second Temple period in about 19 BCE by King Herod, it served originally as a retaining wall to support his extensive renovations of the Temple. During the Middle Ages, this last remnant of the ancient Temple complex was not yet singled out as the most sacred site for Jews.[4] But soon after Jerusalem became part of the Ottoman Empire in the sixteenth century, more and more reports appeared about the site being identified as a gathering point for Jews, who would bemoan the fall of the two temples (therefore the term *Wailing Wall*).[5] With an increasing number of travelers visiting Jerusalem in the nineteenth century, the Western Wall received an iconic status through postcards, artworks, and tourist brochures in Jewish communities worldwide.[6] By the early twentieth century, depictions of the wall, such as that by the artist E. M. Lilien, were widespread in the Jewish Diaspora.[7] However, for many Zionists the Kotel remained a piece of *galut* (Hebrew, exile) in the Land of Israel. They identified it also with the old Yishuv, the pre-Zionist past of the Land of Israel that was superseded by the modern Zionist movement. Yehoshua's essay echoed earlier Zionist sentiments concerning the Western Wall and the Old City of Jerusalem, including the voice of Herzl himself. In a diary entry the founder of political Zionism expressed his disgust at the dirty Old City of Jerusalem: "When I will remember you, oh Jerusalem, in days to come, it won't be with pleasure. The dark residues of two millennia full of inhumanity, intolerance, and uncleanliness are engrained in your foul-smelling alleys."[8] Modern Zionist institutions, such as the Bezalel Art School established in 1906, rather than the Western Wall became popular icons to be used in Zionist depictions of Jerusalem. The Zionist socialist newspaper *Hapo'el Haza'ir* of 1910 quoted "one of the important tourists" juxtaposing the two principal sights in the city: "The dead Western Wall and the living Bezalel; the remembrance of the past and the harbinger of the future."[9]

It was the tumultuous events of the 1920s that turned the Kotel into a cornerstone of Zionist awareness. Under British rule the wall remained in Muslim possession. As under Ottoman rule before, Jews had the right to access it freely. However, they were not allowed to change the status quo. When just before Yom Kippur in 1928 Orthodox Jews erected a screen to separate women from men, local Arab authorities regarded this as a violation of the status quo. Jews who came to pray at the site, on the other hand, felt that the construction of a throughway by Arabs was a disturbance of their sacred space. After months of negotiations the British high commissioner notified the mufti in June 1929 that the Jews were entitled to worship without being disturbed and that the Muslims were allowed to continue their building activities in close proximity to the wall. Neither side was satisfied. Tensions ensued, with militants on both sides continuing their agitation, culminating in violent clashes in Jerusalem on 23 August 1929 and the annihilation of the Jewish community of Hebron one day later.[10]

By then, the wall was in the process of becoming a national symbol in addition to being a religious symbol. Thus the British Western Wall Committee, established in 1930, stated that the Western Wall had become a national symbol for Jews and Arabs alike and that the question of its rights was no longer a purely religious issue.[11] Increasing restrictions by the British authorities and conflicts with local Arabs around the wall transformed the struggle over the wall into a central element in the struggle for Jewish statehood. Starting in 1931, Jewish youth made it an annual ritual to violate the prohibition to blow the shofar at the wall at the conclusion of Yom Kippur. These efforts became part of the Revisionist Zionist focus on linking the wall's perilous status to attempts to provoke conflict with Palestinians. When the wall, and the whole Old City, was lost to Jordan in the 1948 Israeli War of Independence, Jews were not able to enter the area for the next nineteen years, between 1948 and 1967.[12]

The newly established State of Israel needed a site of national commemoration. Traditionally, Jewish sacred spaces were tombs of biblical and talmudic figures.[13] The Zionists added places of national heroism, such as Masada and Tel Hai, the site of an early battle between Jews and Arabs in 1920.[14] After the loss of the Old City, King David's alleged tomb on Mount Zion was turned into the top Jewish religious site for pilgrimage. It was also the closest place from which Jews could view the wall and the Temple Mount.[15]

The first secular memorials emerging after Israel's independence in 1948 were war memorials and military cemeteries. Most prominent were battle remnants, such as the Syrian tank symbolizing the defense of Kibbutz Degania, remains of armored vehicles along the Burma Road to Jerusalem, and the water towers of Negba and Yad Mordechai.[16] In the 1950s alone, approximately 150 memorials to commemorate the victims of the War of Independence were erected (1 monument for every 40 fallen soldiers), most of them initiated by the prestate military movements (Hagana, Palmach, Etzel, Lehi) or local councils.[17]

But none of these local religious and military monuments were deemed appropriate for a national site of commemoration. Such a site would have to serve the purpose, together with other centralizing elements, of forming one nation out of many diverse immigrant groups. What could serve this purpose better than to evoke the spirit of a deceased leader for such a site of commemoration! Just as Lenin's tomb in Russia or Mao's tomb in China or the Pantheon in Paris fulfilled similar functions, the young state of Israel was to build its national site of commemoration in its capital and around the grave of the founder of political Zionism, Theodor Herzl. Other Zionist leaders, among them Leon Pinsker, Max Nordau, and Herzl's successors as presidents of the World Zionist Organization, David Wolffsohn and Otto Warburg, had already been reinterred in the Land of Israel, but Theodor Herzl's remains were still in the family grave in the Jewish cemetery of the Mödling district of Vienna.[18]

Herzl's last will of 1903 stated that he wanted himself and his family (he mentioned explicitly his parents, his sister, and his children, but his wife only if she wished so) to be reinterred in "Palestine." But, as noted, Herzl had no great love for Jerusalem. In *Old-New Land* he alluded to what could have been interpreted as a preference for Mount Carmel in Haifa, overlooking the Mediterranean on the one side and the Land of Israel on the other, as an eternal place of rest. Indeed, during the 1920s and 1930s, the municipal administrations of Haifa and Tel Aviv competed over the reinterment place for Herzl.[19] For the first Israeli government, however, there was no doubt that the burial place of Herzl had to be in the country's future capital. Interior Minister Yitzhak Gruenbaum underlined this position: "I think that specifically now, when our intention is to strengthen Jerusalem and to turn it into a spiritual center . . . the most appropriate place for Herzl's tomb is in Jerusalem."[20] The next step, then, was to determine an appropriate space in Jerusalem.

After much deliberation it was decided to bestow upon the city's highest elevation, located at the western entrance of Jerusalem, the name Mount Herzl. Here, Theodor Herzl was reinterred in an official state ceremony in August 1949. At that time, Jerusalem had not yet been officially declared Israel's capital, and the provisional Knesset was still situated at the Kessem Cinema in Tel Aviv; the reburial ceremony was planned to help underline Jerusalem's role as Israel's future capital, which was finally announced by the Israeli government on 5 December 1949.

The Israeli army oversaw the transport of Herzl's body from Vienna to Israel, the so-called Operation Herzl. When his coffin was placed in front of the Knesset in Tel Aviv, up to 200,000 people came to pay their respects; and in Jerusalem, in front of the Jewish Agency building, another 50,000 people appeared. Herzl's reburial was the first state funeral in Israel. It was attended by 6,000 invited guests. During the ceremony, psalms were sung by a choir, the sound of a shofar was heard, and earth from almost every Jewish settlement in Israel was thrown into the open grave. Mount Herzl thus became, in the words of historian Maoz Azaryahu, the sacred epicenter of the nation.[21]

However, a closer look reveals that Mount Herzl was actually never the unified place of commemoration that some politicians envisioned and

Figure 16.1. Herzl's reburial in Jerusalem, 1949.

some historians claimed it was. Even the reports on the first ceremony on Mount Herzl, Herzl's reburial, reveal a lot of controversy. The left-leaning press envisioned more involvement of the ordinary people and criticized the fact that the public was kept out. The Revisionists, condemning the ruling Labor Party for appropriating Herzl in their paper *Herut*, called the center-left government gravediggers who buried Herzl's ideas together with the man. And the religious paper *Ha-zofe*, expressing their rejection of elevating a secular Jew to quasi-messianic status, distanced itself altogether from the ceremony, maintaining that the cult of the dead is foreign to Judaism.[22]

The Israeli government tried hard to make Mount Herzl the new symbol of the state. Independence Day ceremonies started there, world leaders were brought there, and in the 1950s regular tourists were handed a little present with the following text:

> Dear Visitor, On the occasion of your visit to Mount Herzl, the resting-place of the great Prophet and Founder of the State of Israel, BENJAMIN ZEEV (THEODOR) HERZL, we hand you as a souvenir
>
> 1) a handful of earth
>
> 2) a bag with the aromatic flowers and plants grown on the spot.
>
> Take it with you wherever you go, for good luck and blessings.[23]

Initial plans, which had called for a monumental mausoleum, gave way to a more modest tombstone, seen as more appropriate for a poor and struggling young state. After many years, in 1960, the provisional tomb was replaced by a flat black gravestone with Herzl's name inscribed in golden letters. It was designed by Ossip (Yosef) Klarwein, who later also became the architect for the original design of the modern Knesset building (opened in 1966 in close proximity).[24]

Mount Herzl was soon expanded as a national site of commemoration: first, by a military cemetery, consisting of terraces with large rows of uniform graves of over 4,000 soldiers, and, second, by the government-initiated establishment of the graves of the Great of the Nation (*ḥelkat gedolei ha-umah*). If one were to draw a comparison with the United States, one might say that Mount Herzl was designed as a place to combine Mount Vernon, Arlington National Cemetery, and the presidential memorials on the National Mall.

Mount Herzl was to be the central place of national commemoration, and Herzl himself was to be the one hero of the Zionist enterprise everyone could agree on. Herzl's image was present at the moment the state he had envisioned was declared. When David Ben-Gurion read the Declaration of Independence, a larger-than-life portrait of Theodor Herzl could be seen behind him. In this document Herzl is called "the visionary of the Jewish state" (*ḥozeh ḥazon ha-medinah ha-yehudit*).

But despite their efforts to celebrate Herzl, the founders of the state were at a loss when it came to determine how exactly to commemorate his legacy in the new state. In the early years of the state, the anniversary of his death on 20 Tammuz was still an officially proclaimed holiday. In 1948 it was named Yom Ha-medinah (State Day) and became the occasion for the first big military parade. However, this new holiday was so little ingrained in people's minds that in the following year it was renamed Yom Ha-zava (Army Day). Under this name, however, it was also celebrated only once. After 1950 the day stopped playing any role in the official state calendar. Just as before 1948, Herzl Day celebrations were left to the World Zionist Organization.[25]

On 20 Tammuz 1960, Herzl's 100th birthday, the small Herzl Museum, containing his original workroom, which had previously been kept at the World Zionist Organization's headquarters, opened in close vicinity to his grave. Similar to textbooks used in Israeli schools or official speeches on the occasion of Herzl Day, the museum chose to portray certain aspects of Herzl's personality while disregarding others. His assimilated background was downplayed, as was his original plan to solve the Jewish question by mass conversion. Even his name, Theodor, hardly appeared and was replaced by the Hebrew Binyamin Ze'ev, which was never used by Herzl himself. The fact that he did not know Hebrew and never thought a Jewish state would be viable with a language "in which one could not buy a train ticket" was hardly mentioned.

And then there was the issue of his children. Hardly anyone in Israel knew about their existence until the early 2000s. In his last will, Herzl made it clear that he wanted his children reinterred together with him in Palestine. But in 1949 only his sister and his parents were reburied in Jerusalem. His daughter Trude, who lived most of her life in an asylum and was murdered by the Nazis in the Terezin concentration camp, did not have a grave. But Herzl's other daughter, Pauline, and his son, Hans, were both buried in Bordeaux in 1930. Their story, however, was too troublesome to be included in the official Zionist narrative. Pauline was an unstable person addicted to morphine and other drugs for many years. She died, probably of an overdose, a lonely and impoverished woman at age 40 in a hotel room in Bordeaux. Her brother, Hans, who made critical remarks about Zionism and had converted to several Christian churches before returning to Judaism, killed himself a few days after he found his sister dead. They were buried in the same ceremony at the Jewish cemetery in Bordeaux. It took the private initiative of one Herzl scholar, Dr. Ariel Feldstein, to fulfill Herzl's last will finally in 2006, when his children were reburied in Jerusalem on Mount Herzl.[26]

Just as it remained unclear for decades who of Herzl's family would be reburied on Mount Herzl, another controversy arose about the question of who belonged to the "Great of the Nation" and had the right to be buried near Herzl. The first person to be laid to rest there was finance minister Eliezer Kaplan, when he died in 1952. He was the last government minister to receive this honor, however. The site was subsequently reserved for presidents and prime ministers, Knesset speakers, and presidents of the World Zionist Organization. The discrepancy between the vision and the reality of Mount Herzl is illustrated by the fact that many, if not most, of those who were entitled to be buried there chose other places of eternal rest. The founder of the state, David Ben-Gurion, is buried in his old-age retreat, the kibbutz of Sde Boker; his first successor as prime minister, Moshe Sharett, chose to be laid to rest in Tel Aviv; the first Likud prime minister, Menachem Begin, preferred Jerusalem's Mount of Olives; and Ariel Sharon's grave is outside his old house in the Negev. Out of seven deceased presidents only three (Zalman Shazar, Chaim Herzog, and Shimon Peres) chose to be buried on Mount Herzl; others chose different locations, beginning with the gravesite of Israel's first president, Chaim Weizmann, near his house in Rehovot. The most controversial burial on the site was that of Revisionist leader Vladimir Ze'ev Jabotinsky, who was reinterred on Mount Herzl only after Ben-Gurion was no longer prime minister and while his successor, Levi Eshkol, was on a state visit in France, in 1964, so he did not have to be present (although he stood guard at Jabotinsky's coffin during a memorial ceremony in Paris during a stopover of the coffin from New York). Jabotinsky's grave is located at the margins of the central area reserved for the Great of the Nation.[27]

When Herzl's tomb was built, it was deliberately placed on an axis with the Western Wall. The intention was to juxtapose the symbol of national destruction with the symbol of national revival. However, with the reunification of Jerusalem in 1967 and Israeli control over the holy places, the wall became both the religious *and* the national symbol of the new and enlarged Israeli state. More than any other symbol, the wall was used to underscore Israel's age-old claim to sovereignty over the whole city. As we have seen, the reinterpretation of the wall from a symbol of national destruction to a symbol of national renewal had already begun in the late 1920s, after *political* clashes concentrated around *religious* sites. It intensified as a result of the conquest of the Old City of Jerusalem by Israeli troops in the 1967 war.

The recapturing of the wall was a central, perhaps *the* central element of Israel's military triumph of 1967, as described in an address to the Knesset in 1995 by then prime minister Yitzhak Rabin, who in 1967 had been chief of staff of the Israeli Defense Forces.

> There was one moment in the Six-Day War which symbolized the great victory: that was the moment in which the first paratroopers . . . reached the stones of the Western Wall, feeling the emotion of the place; there never was, and never will be, another moment like it. Nobody staged that moment. Nobody planned it in advance. Nobody prepared it and nobody was prepared for it; it was as if Providence had directed the whole thing: the paratroopers weeping—loudly and in pain—over their comrades who had fallen along the way, the words of the Kaddish prayer heard by Western Wall's stones after 19 years of silence, tears of mourning, shouts of joy, and the singing of "Hatikvah" [the Israeli national anthem].[28]

Religious and national elements were intertwined from the very moment the wall was captured by Israeli troops. When the staff of the Israeli army loaded the command car in which they were to follow the paratroopers to the Western Wall, they took along a Torah scroll, a shofar, and a bench—to perform exactly the acts the British authorities had prohibited in 1931. Performing them showed Israel and the world that the Jews had returned to the Western Wall and were in full control of it.[29]

The centrality of the capture or, in official Israeli language, "liberation," of the Western Wall was further strengthened by the visual images of the Israeli military appearing at this site in the middle of the Six Day War. David Rubinger's iconic photographs of Israeli paratroopers being moved by the 2,000-year-old stones and of Military Chief Rabbi Shlomo Goren blowing the shofar show a blending of military and religious messages, especially considering the prohibition of blowing the shofar at this site during Ottoman and British rule. They helped to turn the wall from a symbol of national destruction into a symbol of military triumph.

In this spirit the term *Wailing Wall* was suppressed and replaced by symbols of heroism. As Kobi Cohen-Hattab and Doron Bar wrote, "Amid the struggles that have occurred in Israeli society in recent decades over the character of the state, the Western Wall received a new identity that turned it into a battleground between religious and national aspirations. It also became a place where religion and nationality blended, a symbol of the national-religious symbiosis that flourished in the wake of the Six-Day War."[30]

This blending of national and religious elements was clearly reflected by an article in the *Jerusalem Post* in 1971: "Tisha B'Av [the fast day in memory of the destruction of both temples] at the Western Wall is becoming ever more an international Jewish Holiday and ever less a day of mourning. To the tens of thousands of Israelis and tourists who swarmed to the Old City last night when the fast commenced, The Wall was obviously more of a reminder of the Israeli victory four years ago, than of the Jewish defeat and destruction of the Temple 1,901 years ago."[31] The swearing-in ceremonies for Israeli soldiers (first for paratroopers in September 1967) and the official beginning ceremony of Yom Hazikaron, the memorial day for Israel's fallen soldiers and victims of terrorism, held at the wall contributed further to the merging of its religious and military significance. In 1968 Jerusalem Day (Yom Yerushalayim) was introduced as a national holiday celebrating Israel's capture of East Jerusalem during the Six Day War. This new symbolism of the wall for Jews around the world was expressed well in the lines that Eliezer Wiesel, later better known as Elie Wiesel, wrote in

Figure 16.2. Israeli paratroopers at the Western Wall (June 1967).

Yediʿot Aharonot on 16 June 1967: "It is me standing and looking at [the Western Wall], as if struck by a dream. Looking at it, holding my breath, as looking at a living body, omnipotent and almighty. A human essence that transcended itself—and those observing it—beyond and above time. An essence that transferred me into a far away and uncanny place, in which stones too, have their own will, their own fate and memory."[32]

Of course, there were also dissenting voices to this attitude that elevated the Kotel to the most important national symbol of the State of Israel. Most prominent among them was the iconoclastic religious thinker and philosopher Yeshayahu Leibowitz, who warned, in a scathing letter to *Haaretz*, of the Western Wall becoming an idolatrous symbol with people praying to stones and pushing notes through its cracks: "Here is my proposal. The square in front of the *kotel* should be revamped as the largest discotheque in the State of Israel, named the Divine Disco. This will satisfy everybody." *Haaretz* printed his letter under the title "DisKotel."[33] Leibowitz was referring to the square, the plaza, in front of the wall that had replaced the old Mugrabi (Moroccan) Arab residential quarter, which was torn down only two days after the end of the war in June 1967 on the order of mayor Teddy Kollek. This action happened without any official authorization and constituted an attempt to erase the Arab Palestinian presence in front of the holiest Jewish site and a symbolic response to the Jordanian destruction of much of the Jewish quarter after the conquest in the war of 1948–1949.[34]

One-time deputy mayor of Jerusalem Meron Benvenisti, who supervised public planning in the city in the 1970s, observed that besides the practical considerations of creating space for hundreds of thousands of people who streamed to the Western Wall, the post-1967 transformation of the plaza reflected "an irrational impulse was at work. The move was a settling of an historic account with those who had harassed the Jewish people over the centuries, restricting and humiliating it at its holiest place, as well as with those who had prevented access to the Wall for 19 years." On 14 June 1967 the plaza in front of the wall was opened for the holiday of Shavuot. In a single 24-hour period a quarter of a million people visited the wall, a phenomenon the city had not seen since the days of the Second Temple.[35]

Instead of the narrow alley, which gave access to 120 square meters in front of the wall, the new plaza covered 20,000 square meters and could hold up to 400,000 people. The new space was, in the words of one scholar:

> A carefully planned double dimension. . . . The space in front of the Wall is composed of two distinct zones: the area closest to the wall, for prayer, is the focus of traditional religious devotion and falls under the aegis of the rabbinate. The more distant expanse of the plaza, controlled by the government, became the representation of Israeli "civic religion": military parades, swearing-in ceremonies, commemoration of the soldiers fallen in war, Jerusalem Day, and so on.[36]

Indeed, national and religious interests were intertwined in the area around the wall, and for a while there existed an unsolved conflict of interest between secular and religious authorities, especially between the National Nature and Park Authority and the Chief Rabbinate, over the control of the wall plaza. Ultimately, attempts by Moshe Dayan and other Israeli politicians to make the area around the Western Wall part of the National Nature and Park Authority failed, and control over the area was delegated to the Ministry of Religion, which appointed a specific rabbi responsible for the Kotel. The idea that the Western Wall would become a museum or a "park" horrified the Orthodox religious establishment. Once they had taken control of the area, they implemented rules of behavior and exterior alterations, the most important of which was the setting up of a barrier between the (larger) men's section and the (smaller) women's section.[37] This became just one more element in the power-sharing arrangement between the secular majority and political elite and the religious minority in the state, a process that had begun long before with Ben-Gurion's status quo agreements.

The Six Day War was a crucial element but certainly not the only one in the changing perception of Israel's main monuments of national commemoration. The profound transformation of Israeli society played its role too. For Ben-Gurion and the parties on the left, *mamlakhtiyut* (statism) had been an important governing principle in the 1950s and parts of the 1960s. It meant that the state was to be omnipresent in the social, economic, and cultural ways of life. A unified state culture, to be built out of a certain interpretation of Jewish history, was a central element of the doctrine of *mamlakhtiyut*. A strong image of the founding father of the state and his grave helped to shape such a unified culture and, in addition, helped to depict Ben-Gurion as a modern-day Herzl. In the words of Ben-Gurion, Herzl represented all the virtues of previous heroes of Jewish history in one person. He connected "the might of the Maccabees, the cunning of David, the bravery of Rabbi Akiva . . . with the humility of Hillel, the beauty of Hanassi and the burning love of Judah Ha-levi. It's one in several million that such a wondrous man is born."[38] So long as Ben-Gurion's idea of a unified state culture was viable, the Herzl cult remained a central part of the young state.

However, with the increasing weight of the voices of immigrants from Arab countries, of the political right, and of the Orthodox, this vision gave way to deeper rifts in Israeli society. To be clear, they all paid lip service to Herzl: Mizraḥim ("Eastern" Jews, i.e., Jews from North Africa and the Middle East) often gave Herzl as a first name to their children;[39] the religious paper *Ha-zofe* called on Jewish women to pray at the grave of Herzl's mother; and the labor federation of the right-wing Revisionists declared Herzl's day of death, instead of the socialist May 1, as the national Day of the Workers.

But for most Revisionist Zionists, Orthodox Jews, and Jews from Arab countries, Herzl's grave and the monument built by Ben-Gurion on the western outskirts of the city could not compete with the ancient stones of the Western Wall in its historical heart. The rise of the political right after the 1977 elections, combined with the increasingly messianic undertones of religious Zionism, helped hasten the displacement of Mount Herzl by the wall as Israel's most important space of national commemoration. The fact that Prime Minister Menahem Begin chose to be buried close to the former Temple site on the Mount of Olives with its messianic-religious meaning rather than on the relatively recent and secular cemetery for the Great of the Nation on Mount Herzl is telling in itself.

Mount Herzl did not entirely lose its part in the memory culture of the State of Israel. Yitzchak Rabin was buried there among the Great of the Nation after his assassination. Every year, right after the end of Yom Hazikaron, the commemoration of which begins at the Kotel, the ceremonies of Yom Ha'atsma'ut, the Day of Independence, start on Mount Herzl, and in 2005 a new multimedia Herzl Museum opened its doors. A year earlier, on the 100th anniversary of his death, the Knesset passed the Herzl Law with the purpose "to inculcate future generations with the vision, legacy and activity of Binyamin Ze'ev Herzl, to honor his memory, to teach future generations and to effect the creation of the State of Israel in accordance with his Zionist vision." The Knesset stated in the law that

Herzl Day would have the status of a national day of mourning and that therefore "once a year on the 10th of Iyar, Herzl's birthday, Herzl Day will be observed."[40] Herzl Day had so much slipped out of memory that hardly anyone even noticed that it had been switched from the day of Herzl's death to his birthday. The state commemoration, the museum, and the Herzl Law underlined the character of Mount Herzl as an official memorial site built for official purposes by official authorities rather than pointing to its place in the hearts of the people.

Furthermore, with the steady expansion of Yad Vashem, the national memorial to the victims of the Holocaust established in 1953, the increasing sacralization of the Holocaust just below Mount Herzl, and the completion of a "connecting path" between Yad Vashem and Mount Herzl, the mountain has been dominated more and more by its slopes. In this respect, Yad Vashem constitutes an intriguing parallel to the Western Wall, which after its expansion in 1967 has risen to compete with the once dominant view of the two holy Muslim places on top of the Temple Mount.[41]

The Western Wall and the mountain represent, *en miniature*, the changes within Israeli society itself since its establishment. Mount Herzl was the most sacred space of Israel's civil religion so long as the state itself was held sacred under Ben-Gurion's policy of *mamlakhtiyut*. With the revival of religious and nationalistic ideals and the unification of Jerusalem, the need for an all-embracing statist society to turn to a recently created secular sacred space disappeared. By the 1980s political scientists Charles Liebman and Eliezer Don-Yehiya called the Western Wall "the most sacred of all places in the Israeli civil religion," evoking "everything that is Jewish-Israeli," both the national and religious glory of the past.[42]

Historians usually adhere to a somewhat ironic detachment from national myths, in the vein of Eric Hobsbawm's notion of the invention of tradition or Pierre Nora's concept of *lieux de mémoire*. In their important works on Zionist and Israeli national myths, Yael Zerubavel, Maoz Azaryahu, and others have applied these ideas to the Zionist movement and the State of Israel. But this detachment seems to have little resonance with the actual feeling of the people on the ground, in this case with the majority of Israel's Jewish citizens.

This gap between intellectual concepts and popular opinion is also obvious when we reflect today on A. B. Yehoshua's call for Israelis to focus on a less disputed site in a less disputed part of Jerusalem than its Old City.

In his vision, we recall, the Kotel would ultimately be reduced to a part of the religious landscape of East Jerusalem and Mount Herzl would become the undisputed symbol of memory for secular Israel. Today such a vision sounds like a nostalgic view of a secular Zionist idea, in which religious symbols have little value. What Yehoshua failed to grasp is the power of tradition when it comes to collective symbols and myths—a power that proved greater than the rational decision behind the construction of a modern national site of commemoration.

The wall and the mountain have become sites of contestation between religious and secular elements on the battleground for the soul of the Jewish polity. The Kotel remains the most important symbolic place in Israel for Jews visiting from abroad.[43] Its continuing appeal within Israeli society also reflects the growth of its religious sector and its major political and religious transformations. But, just like Mount Herzl, the wall did not become the undisputed symbol of memory for all Israelis. Many secular Israelis keep their distance from the Kotel, as it represents in their minds the growing influence of religion in society. Similarly, non-Orthodox Jewish religious groups have come to see the holiest Jewish site first and foremost as a constant battleground over women's rights to practice their religion equally to men.[44]

In stark contrast to Yitzchak Rabin's 1967 emotional moment at the Kotel and A. B. Yehoshua's 1980s powerful vision of a mostly secular nation gathering around the united symbol of Mount Herzl, Israeli president Reuven Rivlin made clear in his 2015 speech just how difficult it has become in a fragmented society to find a common denominator. He spoke about the four tribes of Israel (secular, national-religious, ultra-Orthodox, Arab), who interact very little in everyday life and who do not share common values.[45] So long as this fragmentation—which intensified during the protests against the planned judicial overhaul in 2023—continues, neither the wall nor the mountain has the power to unite a divided society.

Notes

1 A major inspiration for this essay was the classes I took with Michael Stanislawski at Columbia University in the late 1980s. He introduced me to the importance of the symbolic language of Zionism, ranging from the iconic

art of Ephraim Moses Lilien to Herzl's drawing of a flag with seven stars for the aspirational seven working hours in a future Jewish state. Moreover, my understanding of the significance of symbols such as the Western Wall and Mount Herzl in Jerusalem grew out of studying the Haskalah and nationalism among Eastern European Jews with him.

2 A. B. Yehoshua, "Hakir vehahar," in his *Ha-kir veha-har: Mezi'uto halo sifrutit shel ha-sofer biYisrael* (Tel Aviv: Zmora Bitan, 1989), 217. I want to thank Kobi Cohen-Hattab for his insightful comments on an earlier draft of this article.

3 Of course, there are other possible sites of Israeli national commemoration, but they never enjoyed the same popularity. See, for example, the inclusion of Giv'at Hatakhmoshet outside Jerusalem as a memorial site dedicated to the "liberation of Jerusalem" in 1967. Maoz Azaryahu, "(Re)Locating Redemption: Jerusalem—The Wall, Two Mountains, a Hill, and the Narrative Construction of the Third Temple," *Journal of Modern Jewish Studies* 1, no. 1 (2002): 22–35. On the secularization of Israeli collective memory in general, see Yael Zerubavel's now-classic book, *Recovered Roots: Collective Memory and the Making of Israeli National Tradition* (Chicago: University of Chicago Press, 1995).

4 For a historical overview, see Kobi Cohen-Hattab and Doron Bar, *The Western Wall: The Dispute over Israel's Holiest Jewish Site, 1967–2000* (Leiden: Brill, 2020), 16–44.

5 Meir Ben Dov, Mordechai Naor, and Zeev Aner, *The Western Wall* (New York: Adama, 1983), 68.

6 See Kobi Cohen-Hattab and Ayelet Kohn, "The Nationalization of Holy Sites: Yishuv-Era Visual Representations of the Western Wall and Rachel's Tomb," *Jewish Quarterly Review* 107, no. 1 (2017): 66–89.

7 See especially the chapter on Lilien in Michael Stanislawski, *Zionism and the Fin de Siècle: Cosmopolitanism and Nationalism from Nordau to Jabotinsky* (Berkeley: University of California Press, 2001).

8 Theodor Herzl, *The Complete Diaries of Theodor Herzl*, ed. Raphael Patai, trans. Harry Zohn (New York: Herzl Press, 1960), 2: 741.

9 Quoted in Arieh Bruce Saposnik, "Wailing Walls and Iron Walls: The Western Wall as Sacred Symbol in Zionist National Iconography," *American Historical Review* 120, no. 5 (2015): 1659.

10 Hillel Cohen, *Year Zero of the Arab-Israeli Conflict, 1929*, trans. Haim Watzman (Waltham, MA: Brandeis University Press, 2015).

11 See Cohen-Hattab and Bar, *Western Wall*, 29–40.

12 Cohen-Hattab and Bar, *Western Wall*, 40–44.
13 On the spatial turn in Jewish studies, see Barbara E. Mann, *Space and Place in Jewish Studies* (New Brunswick, NJ: Rutgers University Press, 2012); and Julia Brauch, Anna Lipphardt, and Alexandra Nocke, *Jewish Topographies: Visions of Space, Traditions of Place* (Aldershot, UK: Ashgate, 2008).
14 Zerubavel, *Recovered Roots*.
15 Doron Bar, "Reconstructing the Past: The Creation of Jewish Sacred Space in the State of Israel, 1948–1967," *Israel Studies* 13 (2008): 8.
16 Maoz Azaryahu, "The Topography of National Remembrance: Two Israeli Cases," in *The Mosaic of Israel Geography*, ed. Yehuda Gradus and Gabriel Lipshitz (Beer Sheva: Ben-Gurion University of the Negev, 1996), 254.
17 Mooli Brog, "Victims and Victors: Holocaust and Military Commemoration in Israeli Collective Memory," *Israel Studies* 8, no. 1 (2003): 68–71.
18 Otto Warburg's burial posed a special problem with the religious authorities, as he was cremated after his death in 1938. His ashes were reinterred in Kibbutz Deganiah after other cemeteries were ruled unfit in 1940. See Doron Bar, *Landscape and Ideology: Reinterment of Renowned Jews in the Land of Israel (1904–1967)* (Berlin: De Gruyter, 2016), 97–98.
19 Bar, *Landscape and Ideology*, 22–24.
20 Cited in Andrea Livnat, *Der Prophet des Staates: Theodor Herzl im kollektiven Gedächtnis Israels* (Frankfurt: Campus, 2011), 109.
21 Azaryahu, "Topography," 52. See also Bar, *Landscape and Ideology*, 36–41.
22 Livnat, *Prophet des Staates*, 108.
23 Livnat, *Prophet des Staates*, 126.
24 Azaryahu, "Topography," 51–52. For more details, see Michal Naor-Wiernik and Doron Bar, "The Competition for the Design and Development of Herzl's Tomb and Mount Herzl, 1949–1960," *Cathedra* 144 (2012): 107–36 (Hebrew); and Myra Warhaftig, *They Laid the Foundation: Lives and Works of German-Speaking Jewish Architects in Palestine, 1918–1948* (Tübingen: Wasmuth, 2007), 294–95.
25 Livnat, *Prophet des Staates*, 79–79, 90, 113–14.
26 Vered Levy-Barzilai, "One Historian's Vision Fulfilled the Zionist Visionary's Last Wishes," *Haaretz* (15 September 2006).
27 Bar, *Landscape and Ideology*, 139–56.
28 Yitshak Rabin, "Address to the Knesset by Prime Minister Rabin on Jerusalem, 29 May 1995," Israel Ministry of Foreign Affairs. This address is ex post facto but is presented as truth of the moment. The speech needs to be understood not in its 1967 context but in its 1995 context, when Rabin was

prime minister. For almost immediate responses to the recapturing of the Old City, see Avraham Shapira, ed., *Si'aḥ Loḥamim: Pirkei Hakshavah vehitbonenut* [Fighters' Talk: Chapters in Listening and Introspection] (Tel Aviv: Be-hotsa'at Kevutsat Ḥaverim Tse'irim mehatenu'at hakibutsit, 1968).

29 Meron Benvenisti, *Jerusalem: The Torn City* (Minneapolis: University of Minnesota Press, 1976), 305.

30 Kobi Cohen-Hattab and Doron Bar, "From Wailing to Rebirth: The Development of the Western Wall as an Israeli National Symbol After the Six-Day War," *Contemporary Jewry* 38 (2018): 284.

31 D. Landau, "70,000 at Western Wall; Little Mourning Observed," *Jerusalem Post* (1 August 1971).

32 Cited in Edith Zertal, "From the People's Hall to the Wailing Wall," *Representations* 69 (Winter 2000): 113.

33 Tom Segev, *1967: Israel, the War, and the Year That Transformed the Middle East* (New York: Metropolitan, 2005), 433.

34 See the detailed account in Doron Bar and Rehav Rubin, "The Jewish Quarter After 1967: A Case Study on the Creation of an Ideological-Cultural Landscape in Jerusalem's Old City," *Journal of Urban History* 37, no. 5 (2011): 775–92.

35 Benvenisti, *Jerusalem*, 307.

36 Simone Ricca, "Heritage, Nationalism, and the Shifting Symbolism of the Wailing Wall," *Archives de Sciences Sociales des Religions* 151 (2010): 179.

37 See Cohen-Hattab and Bar, *Western Wall*, 90–97.

38 Quoted in Ze'ev Tzahor, "Ben-Gurion's Mythopoetics," in *The Shaping of Israeli Identity: Myth, Memory, and Trauma*, ed. Robert S. Wistrich and David Ohana (London: Taylor & Francis, 1995), 70.

39 One example is the poet Herzl Hakak, whose twin brother is named Balfour.

40 See the official Knesset website, knesset.gov.il/vip/herzl/eng/Herz_Bio_eng.html (accessed 8 May 2023).

41 On the new Yad Vashem Museum and its relationship to Zionist ideology, see most recently Doron Bar, *Yad Vashem: The Challenge of Shaping a Holocaust Remembrance Site, 1942–1976* (Berlin: De Gruyter, 2021); and Grace Wermenbol, *A Tale of Two Narratives: The Holocaust, the Nakba, and the Israeli-Palestinian Battle of Memories* (Cambridge, UK: Cambridge University Press, 2021), esp. 211–19.

42 Charles S. Liebman and Don Yehiya, *Civil Religion in Israel: Traditional Judaism and Political Culture in the Jewish State* (Berkeley: University of California Press, 1983), 158.

43 As there is no entrance fee to the Western Wall, it is hard to come by exact visitor numbers. According to one count, in 2008, 50% of all 3.6 million tourists to Israel visited the Western Wall, making it by far the most popular tourist attraction in the country. See Wendy Pullan, Maximilian Sternberg, Lefkos Kyriacou, Craig Larkin, and Michael Dumper, eds., *The Struggle for Jerusalem's Holy Places* (Abington, UK: Routledge, 2013), 83. See also Kobi Cohen-Hattab and Noam Shoval, *Tourism, Religion, and Pilgrimage in Jerusalem* (Abington, UK: Routledge: 2015).

44 See Lihi Ben Shitrit, *Women and the Holy City: The Struggle over Jerusalem's Sacred Space* (New York: Cambridge University Press, 2021); and Yuval Jobani and Nahshon Perez, *Women of the Wall: Navigating Religion in the Sacred Sites* (New York: Oxford University Press, 2017).

45 On Rivlin's speech, see Tommy Steiner, *President Rivlin's "Four Tribes" Initiative: The Foreign Policy Implications of a Democratic and Inclusive Process to Address Israel's Socio-Demographic Transformation* (Herzliya: IPS Publications, 2016).

17

Past and Present

Modern Jewish Historiography, Premodern
History, and the Politics of History

Magda Teter

The question Yehuda Leib Gordon asked in 1865 in his poem "For Whom Do I Toil?"—or, as he would recast it twenty years later, "For whom do I toil and for what should I toil?"—is one that Jewish intellectuals and scholars of Jewish history and culture have been asking at least since the nineteenth century.[1] As Michael Stanislawski argued, Gordon was reflecting on "the meaning of his life" and "on the frustration he felt as a lonely campaigner for a moderate reform of the life and culture of Jews of Russia" that would provide balance for the participation of Jews in public and civic life and their Jewishness. He articulated this ideal in his famous poem "Awake, My People" in the poem's memorable line "Be a man in the street and a Jew at home."[2] Gordon believed that, to quote Stanislawski, it was "the duty of educated Jews to devote themselves to the enlightenment of Jewish society as a whole."[3]

Modern scholars in Jewish studies have faced similar questions and dilemmas, pondering whether their work should be part of a broader scholarly conversation or a service to the Jewish public. In the 2010s, the Association for Jewish Studies (AJS) revised its mission statement, declaring that the "AJS's mission is to advance research and teaching in Jewish Studies at colleges, universities, and other institutions of higher learning, *and to foster greater understanding of Jewish Studies scholarship among the wider public.*"[4] This statement represented a major change for the AJS. The AJS was established in 1969, and for decades, in efforts to establish the academic legitimacy of Jewish studies, it had sought to secure the "boundaries between academic Jewish studies and the Jewish community and Jewish foundations, which had begun to see the potential for Jewish studies as a source of community revival and identity formation."[5] Irving "Yitz" Greenberg, one of the AJS's founding members and himself a prominent Orthodox rabbi, stressed that "to achieve academic respectability, they should not attain 'too close an identification with the concerns of the Jewish community and for the Jewish civilization.'"[6] These Jewish studies scholars wanted to be, as Bible scholar Samuel Sandel put it, "relatively [speaking], objective, dispassionate, and—above all—committed to the impartial search for the truth and not to some antecedent convictions."[7]

The AJS's ethos reflected both a recognition of "a spread of Jewish studies as an accepted academic discipline in the American liberal-arts colleges and universities" and the need for the field to fit the academic ethos of objectivity and detachment from parochial communal concerns in the midst of a politically charged moment in American history, when other groups—for example, women and Black Americans—in the United States were unapologetically challenging, to the chagrin of some historians, the academic status quo.[8] Although modern historians at no point in time were "objective" and "detached," they subscribed to the idea that, as Peter Novick averred, they should be guarded "from social pressure or political influence" and should "purge themselves of external loyalties" in order to pursue "the objective historical truth."[9] According to Novick, this was all but a "founding myth," or, in David Myers's phrasing, a "dispassionate modern façade."[10] Scholarship has always been engaged and has always, explicitly or implicitly, served political and contemporary concerns and, sometimes, was "a source of community revival and identity formation."[11] And in the field of Jewish studies this idea of objectivity and detachment has often been infused with the explicit or implicit need to respond to antisemitism. This has been manifested in the subjects chosen by Jewish historians or the questions they asked of topics ostensibly far removed from their contemporary world. The present-day concerns, sometimes even specific events, have loomed large in the scholarship that has ultimately shaped the field of Jewish studies.

The anxiety over the influence of such contemporary and community concerns on scholarship, which clashed as recently as 1998, is not limited to Jewish historians.[12] But, if scholars in the fields of the majority culture—known in Jewish historiography as "general history" though there is nothing "general" about them—could labor under the cloak of universal, or "general," concerns and search for "universal" truths, then for minority scholars, including scholars in Jewish studies, the bar of objectivity seemed even higher. They were always charged with subjectivity and, with their political commitments laid bare, often asked to carry the weight of their identity.[13] At the same time that the dominant scholarship could be deemed detached and objective, the scholarship of marginalized groups has been viewed with suspicion and has needed to justify itself to the dominant fields. Jewish studies was no different. Since its earliest years, Jewish studies had been linked to and funded by the Jewish community,[14] and its scholarship had been responsive to contemporary events and social needs, especially to antisemitism. In the second half of the twentieth century, as American Jewry was integrating into the white majority, the newly founded AJS, without the imprimatur of the American Academy for Jewish Research and its senior scholars, was struggling to be recognized within the ecosystem of respectable academic professional organizations, away from parochialism. Trying to join the American Council of Learned Societies, its founders and members felt that they needed to guard the boundaries between the "impartial search for truth" and "some antecedent convictions," often looking inward and avoiding the pressures of the present. But this seems to have been a relatively brief interlude between the community-engaged scholarship of the first century of modern Jewish historiography and the recent revision of the AJS mission that turned the discipline's gaze back toward the broader public and recognized the need to re-engage with the Jewish public's interests and concerns.

The Founding Myth of Objectivity and the Early Years of Jewish Historiography

In his preface to *Histories of the Latin and Germanic Peoples* (1824), Leopold von Ranke famously wrote, "To history has been given the function of judging the past, of instructing men for the profit of future years. The present attempt does not aspire to such a lofty undertaking. It merely wants to show how it essentially was [*wie es eigentlich gewesen*]."[15] This came to be one of the most misunderstood passages in historiography, comparable in Jewish historiography with Salo Baron's famous statement about "the lachrymose conception of Jewish history." The misinterpretation of Ranke's statement as rigid objectivity was due to a late nineteenth-century American misunderstanding and mistranslation of the German *Wissenschaft* as "science" and to neo-Rankian positivist German scholars who rejected the politically engaged nationalist historians who came after Ranke.[16] But Ranke did not show "just how it essentially was"; he chose to present a limited slice of history that aligned with his political views. Just a few paragraphs before this much quoted sentence, Ranke acknowledged that "the intention of a historian depends on his viewpoint."[17] And that very viewpoint circumscribed the scope of his work: the Latin and Germanic peoples, "a unit," according to Ranke. The historian rejected "the concept of universal Christendom," because it would force him to "embrace even the Armenians." He similarly dismissed the concept of "the unity of Europe," reasoning that, "since the Turks are Asiatics and since the Russian Empire comprises the whole north of Asia, their situations could not be thoroughly understood without penetrating and drawing in the total Asian situation." Ranke also rejected the concept "of a Latin Christendom," because that would include "Slavic, Latvian, and Magyar tribes," which had "a peculiar and special nature." Ranke explicitly identified "with the tribally related peoples of either purely Germanic or Germano-Roman origin [*rein germanischer oder germanisch-romanischer Abukunft*], whose history is the nucleus of all recent history, and touches on what is foreign only in passing as something peripheral."[18] If Ranke rejected even other Christian peoples who were "tribally" not related to his "people," he certainly did not think to include Jews in his history, though they may have lived in the same towns and villages as his "Germanic and Latin" peoples. The book would get him a job at the University of Berlin. And, although Ranke was not an integral nationalist, he studied history and institutions and staunchly supported the Prussian state, arguing, as Georg Iggers put it, that "the task of Germans" was "to create a genuinely German state," a state that corresponded to "the spirit of the nation."[19] If Ranke's marriage of political commitments and his scholarship might have been relatively subtle, those who followed him were not—they created a more overtly politically engaged German nationalist historiography.[20] But the ideas of impartiality that Ranke embraced continued to live on, albeit in a somewhat distorted form.

Ranke was neither first nor alone in his thinking. Five years *before* Ranke published these words, a group of seven young Jewish men in Berlin formed the Verein für Cultur und Wissenschaft der Juden, a society devoted to academic studies of Jewish history and culture, later known as the Wissenschaft des Judentums.[21] They also had embraced "a scientific" approach to the study of Judaism and Jewish history, stating as their goal "the dissemination of clear, objective knowledge" and "purely scholarly" (*reinwissenschaflitche*) activities in their statutes.[22] Despite these ideals, what the men proposed was not divorced from current social needs. When, after Napoleon's fall, it became clear that "the prospects" of political equality for Jews were "rapidly receding," with violent attacks on them erupting across German lands in the summer of 1819 and with some Jews even converting to Christianity, they decided to do something in response to this crisis.[23] They were seeking a new way to "unite" Jews as a people and to "preserve our Jewishness" in light of fear that "in the future we, as individuals, will not be able to continue to live as Jews, or at least not in the way we would like to."[24] Many nineteenth-century Jewish studies scholars, as Salo Baron observed in his study of scholars during the 1848 revolution, "took up the cudgels for their people."[25] For example, in Eastern Europe Jewish intellectuals turned to history, as Natalia Aleksiun and Brian Horowitz put it, "to support the project of Jewish emancipation and integration in Congress Poland by demonstrating the depth of Jewish roots in Polish lands."[26] The study of Jewish history, as Isaac Bernfeld wrote in 1881 in Lemberg (now Lviv, Ukraine), was to help affirm a positive Jewish identity "to acquire a solid reputation among the family of nations" and "a mantle of praise in place of the mantle of shame and disgrace."[27] Historiography was for many early Jewish historians "an expression of communal identity."[28] Therein lay the strong link between the community and scholarship and between social and political needs and "scientific scholarship." As the Polish Jewish Marxist historian Emanuel Ringelblum observed, an "objective historical presentation" has a relevant political function "in the present."[29] Present concerns, Ringelblum seems to have argued, did not have to be in conflict with objective historical research.

But that link between social needs and scholarship was a cause of anxiety and tensions. A goal to "decrease antisemitism," balanced with "the new objective theory of historical science," was what lay, for example, behind the creation of the Jewish Historical Society of England in 1893 and elsewhere.[30] Its focus was to highlight Jewish accomplishments and contributions; at the same time, as the historian Israel Abramson declared, "its methods must be severely scientific—critical, systematic, minutely analytical of sources."[31] In France the first issue of the *Revue des études juives* declared that the concern of the journal was "scientific truth," and the editors stated that they did not wish to engage in "religious propaganda, nor pursue a goal of edification."[32] Fifteen years later, in 1895, in the early days of the Dreyfus affair, Theodore Reinach, the president of the Société des études juives in France, said in his address to the members of the Société, "I use my authority as president one last time to remind myself of the question. The Société des études juives need not concern itself with the present trials of Judaism, however poignant the interest [in doing so] may be."[33] The Société, Reinach asserted, "dwells in the quieter sphere of history," and it was "only by dispelling the accumulated errors about ancient Judaism that [the Société] can indirectly contribute to rehabilitating or consoling Judaism today." And yet, in 1898, just three years later, Joseph Reinach—also a member of the Société and Theodore's brother—published a book titled *Une erreur judiciaire sous Louis XIV: Raphaël Levy*, about the trial of Raphaël Levy, a Jewish man from Lorraine accused of killing a Christian boy near Metz in 1669.[34] Although the subject of a seventeenth-century trial may seem to have "dwelled in the quieter sphere of history," the book's title betrayed that it was very much influenced by the contemporary crisis engulfing France.

The title *Une erreur judiciaire sous Louis XIV* was not accidental. In 1896 Bernard Lazare, a French Jewish intellectual, published a book about the Dreyfus affair: *Une erreur judiciaire: La vérité sur l'affaire Dreyfus*. The book was then republished in 1897 and 1898, and the phrase entered French vocabulary, among both the Dreyfussards and the antisemites.[35] That Joseph Reinach would publish a book related to the Dreyfus affair should not be surprising—he was a staunch defender of Alfred Dreyfus and would later write one of the most definitive histories of the affair. But what is important here about this work is that it was about a seventeenth-century affair ostensibly far removed from the Dreyfus affair. And yet it was a work of historical scholarship—still used by historians—that was a product of and a response to the Dreyfus affair.

Reinach's book is not the only example of the influence of present concerns and specific events on scholarship. As David Myers has recently shown, most Jewish studies scholars have always toiled with the recognition of the utilitarian value of their work,[36] whether it was Diaspora historians, those committed to what Shulamit Volkov called "liberal history," which presented Jews as integral to the societies within which they lived, or, later, Zionist historians, those committed to, as Volkov has argued, "inventing" a Zionist, national Jewish narrative.[37] Even committed Zionist historians were able to deploy modern critical historical methods to their scholarship while centering Eretz Yisrael in their narrative and contributing to the recovery of sources to study the Jewish past in Palestine. A prime example of that was Ben-Zion Dinur and the journal *Zion*, which he cofounded with Yitzhak Baer and which was devoted, originally, to the archeological, historical, and anthropological study of the Jewish past in Eretz Yisrael.[38]

But even scholars whose work was seemingly most detached, judicious, and dispassionate had strong political, social, and communal commitments. Among them was Salo Baron, whose scholarship, marked by meticulous and seemingly neutral research, became and remains a model for historians of the Jews.[39] Although Baron at times wrote about Jewish history in such a way that would lead to a pushback from the general public, he remained deeply committed to the Jewish community. In 1939 Baron reflected on "the practical dangers of historical iconoclasm."[40] Iconoclastic Baron certainly was pushing to move away from the assumption of his German predecessors in the Verein für Cultur und Wissenschaft der Juden that the medieval Jewish experience was a "lachrymose" history of persecution and suffering. He favored a more complex picture of the past that challenged the popular beliefs of his readers. "Time and again," Baron wrote, he "had the perhaps tragi-comic experience of finding the Jewish public sort of enamored with the tales of ancient and modern persecutions."[41] A scholar, Baron was also a community leader, demonstrating that scholars could be politically and communally engaged without being tendentious and pandering to communal emotions.

Baron's iconoclastic push against the "lachrymose conception of Jewish history" has been one of the most misunderstood phrases written by modern Jewish historians. As with Leopold von Ranke's famous phrase, Baron's is also more widely known than his vast scholarship. If it was the neo-Rankians who misinterpreted Ranke's approach decades after he articulated it, so too was Baron's work, as David Engel has observed, misconstrued through "neobaronianism." According to Engel, Baron was not as iconoclastic as that phrase—taken out of context—suggests: He did not deny or minimize Jewish persecution and suffering.[42]

Baron's work was in fact animated by questions dear to the Jewish community and Jewish communal organizations. His own work is permeated with questions about the role historians play within the community.[43] Baron was interested in the "perseverance" and "survival" of Jews, and for that reason he understood that historians needed to study more than moments of defeat and destruction.[44] As I have argued elsewhere, Baron's strategy was to expand the perspective on the Jewish historical experience and the vocabulary deployed to describe it in order to fight antisemitism.[45] Baron's balance of meticulous scholarship with communal leadership illustrated Thomas Haskell's point that "objectivity is not neutrality."[46]

This stress on vitality and survival appears repeatedly in Baron's work, both before World War II and after its devastation became apparent. In the introduction to *Social and Religious History of the Jews*, published in 1937, Baron notes, "What really matters in Jewish religion is not the immortality of an individual Jew, but that of the Jewish people."[47] In 1945 Baron insisted that "without an inner determination to survive, without strong beliefs and rich culture and powerful institutions, the Jewish people could not possibly have come down the ages."[48] He refused to see Jews as "mere objects" of historical developments; as he put it in 1963, "Were Jews mere objects of general historical evolution, they could not possibly have survived the successive waves of hostility throughout the ages."[49] Baron's interest in the survival of Jews was not that dissimilar from that of other early scholars, even if his methods became more sophisticated and the depth of his studies more profound and in line with the increasingly professionalizing academic studies of Jews. Indeed, in 1873 the early Italian Jewish journal *L'Educatore Israelita* ran a long series of essays on the Jewish community, which it called *il self government*, in which it explored the "wonderous continuity" of Judaism.[50]

As a community activist and leader who remained deeply connected with the Jewish community and its concerns, Baron was very much informed by contemporary events and communal needs—intellectual, spiritual, and political. Baron, as Michael Stanislawski has noted, was "rooted in tradition."[51] He was rooted in tradition but not in the religious sense imbibed in his observant Jewish natal home in Tarnów. Baron himself was not religiously observant in his adult life, but he remained connected with the Jewish community as the chair of the Council of Jewish Relations. All the while, he protected his academic pursuits and promoted the academic legitimacy of Jewish studies from his perch as the Miller Chair in Modern Jewish History at Columbia University.[52] Baron was not among the cohort of founders of the Association for Jewish Studies, the young scholars who were looking to detach themselves from the Jewish community and to create a new vibrant community of Jewish studies scholars reflective of the contemporary American academic world. He had, after all, advocated for both the appreciation of scholarship in the Jewish community and for the communal support of that scholarship.[53] By the time the AJS was founded, Baron had retired from Columbia, but he remained actively engaged in the American Academy for Jewish Research, which remained a strictly scholarly organization.

Salo Baron cofounded and then coedited the journal *Jewish Social Studies*, today one of the preeminent journals in Jewish studies. The journal was created in 1939 from an urge to respond to Nazism and antisemitism. In its efforts to balance both historical works and contemporary events, both framed in a scholarly language and approach, it harkened back to the earlier Jewish scholarly journals published in Europe. In the opening pages, Morris Cohen, the president of the Council of Jewish Relations that published the journal, defined the Council's goals: "In view of the tumult of prejudice and pseudo-scientific assertions in regard to the questions thus raised, it is certainly the duty of all thoughtful men and women to seek the basic truths relevant to these issues. To serve this end, to help to bring about a better understanding of the position of the Jews in the modern world, is the aim of the Conference on Jewish Relations."[54] The Council of Jewish Relations was, the editors asserted, "committed to no particular solution or panacea but seeks to promote scholarly research in the field of Jewish anthropological, economic, political and cultural problems, and to make the results of such study available to a wide circle of serious readers." And with "the destruction of important centers of Jewish learning in Eastern and Central Europe," it was "imperative that the United States, with the largest and richest Jewish community in the world today, should do its share to see to it that Jewish studies and research do not perish."[55]

The journal then published historical research and reported on contemporary events, albeit framed in a more scholarly language and approach. In the second issue of *Jewish Social Studies*, Rudolph Stahl published the lengthy article "Vocational Retraining of Jews in Nazi Germany, 1933–1938."[56] And Joel Cang published the article "The Opposition Parties in Poland and Their Attitude Towards the Jews and the Jewish Problem," in which he noted the recent transformation in attitudes toward Jews, claiming that the Endeks, the Polish Nationalist Party, "no longer advocate[d] the assimilation of the Jews, although this used to be a point in their program in the days when Catholicism came before politics"; their new platform was "the complete elimination through expulsion or otherwise, of all Jews from Poland."[57] The party, Cang observed, was "the strongest, best organized, and most vital political opposition party in the country." It was "responsible for most of the antisemitism in Poland," and its "propaganda, carried on long before Hitler but greatly intensified since, has served to so magnify the Jewish problem in Poland as to become, even in the eyes of non-Endeks, the most vital problem in Poland, which calls for immediate and drastic solution. A whole generation of young Poles is now being brought up under the influence of Endek doctrines preaching hostility towards the Jews."[58]

Over the course of the 1940s *Jewish Social Studies* continued to publish works by scholars responding to contemporary events through a mix of scholarly analysis, reporting, and even political advocacy.[59] What was happening in Europe was on the minds of the scholars writing about the premodern past as well. In 1940 Samuel Blumenfeld began his article celebrating the nine-hundredth anniversary of Rashi's birth by connecting it to the ongoing events in Europe.

> The nine-hundredth anniversary of the birth of Rashi coincides with a most critical and ominous period in Jewish history, the culmination of seven tragic years of brutality and humiliation. There is a rabbinic dictum: "Do not comfort thy fellow-man in the hour when his dead lies before him." With scores of thousands dying in Europe, Jewry has been in no mood to celebrate this anniversary of the birth of Rabbi Solomon ben Isaac in any but a subdued spirit. The lack of enthusiasm may also be due to the fact that there is nothing so striking about Rashi as to arouse general interest and that he is too familiar to

evoke intense feeling among those acquainted with his contribution. Nevertheless, the Rashi anniversary presents a rare opportunity to re-examine the contribution of a great spirit whose teachings and ideals and, above all, whose personality and achievement can still serve as a beacon of light to Jewry.[60]

As Blumenfeld's article illustrates, the study of the premodern era was not immune to the impact that the war and the Nazi regime had on Jewish scholarship. That same year, *Jewish Social Studies* published an essay by Cecil Roth that directly connected the experiences of Jews in Iberia with what was happening in Germany. The essay ended with a suggestion "that if research workers and public leaders of today desire to anticipate the probable outcome of the persecution which is disgracing Germany today, they might do worse than turn for guidance to the record of the racial persecution in the Iberian peninsula, in which contemporaneous conditions were so ludicrously foreshadowed."[61] And in 1941, in response to "denaturalization" of Jews in Romania the previous year, Joshua Starr published an essay about the history of Jewish citizenship in Romania. Even Baron's bibliography related to Jewish studies bore the marks of concerns with contemporary events.[62] In 1941 the journal adopted a new tag line: "A quarterly journal devoted to contemporary and historical aspects of Jewish life." As in the earlier Jewish scholarly journals, in *Jewish Social Studies*, the past was never far from the present.

Past and Present in Jewish Studies

An unequivocal declaration of the link between past and present came from Ignacy Schiper, who, like Salo Baron, was born in Tarnów.[63] "Our aim is always the present," Schiper stated.[64] "It is the understanding of the present that we seek in our history. One must want something from the past." In many earlier journals in Jewish studies that connection between past and present was manifested in separate sections devoted to reporting on contemporary events and to the publication of historical research and primary sources from the archives that were linked to the pressing issues of the day. For example, in 1855–1856 the case of Giuditta Castilliero, who accused Jews of trying to sacrifice her in Italy, captured the attention of *L'Educatore Israelita*. Known as the Badia affair, one of the six blood libels in nineteenth-century Italy, it led to the publication of court proceedings.[65] Similarly, the journals *Voskhod* and *Evreiskaia Starina* in Russia tracked other blood libels of the late nineteenth century and early twentieth century and also published primary sources related to the trials.[66] During the Tiszaeszlár affair, which erupted in 1882 and lasted through 1883, *Voskhod* published a review of a pamphlet by Michael Levi Rodkinson, *Maẓat-miẓvah va-alilat ha-dam*, which connected the rise of ultra-Orthodox Jews and the misunderstanding of the fastidiousness with which they produced matzo with the rise of blood accusations and an extensive report on the Tiszaeszlár affair.[67] When another libel erupted, this time in Xanten in Germany in 1891, *Voskhod* followed the affair and then published historical research related to past blood libels, with articles by Sergei Bershadskii on the history of Jews in Poland and his work on the blood libel in Różany in 1659.[68] When the Beilis affair blew up, *Evreiskaia Starina*, another prominent Russian-language Jewish journal, published several pioneering articles about anti-Jewish libels in Dunajgród in 1748 and Zasław in 1747 that are still cited by scholars of blood accusations in the Polish-Lithuanian Commonwealth.[69] French scholars publishing in *Revue des études juives* were not far behind.[70] Although these journals published other kinds of work, including literature, poetry, scholarship, and book reviews and essays about Jewish life around the world, there is no question that antisemitism and persecution played an important role in shaping their contents and the questions that the field of Jewish studies would subsequently engage.

Antisemitism and the Framing of Jewish History

The first Jewish scholarly association was partly formed in response to antisemitism. As Michael Brenner has observed, "Wissenschaft des Judentums could not be separated from the battle against exclusion and for the emancipation of the Jews."[71] For Immanuel Wolf, a member of the Verein für Cultur und Wissenschaft der Juden, "scholarly knowledge about Judaism" would help "decide regarding the Jews' worthiness or unworthiness, their ability or inability to have the same respect and rights as other citizens."[72] Eduard Gans, one of the founders of the Verein für Cultur und

Wissenschaft der Juden, recalled the association's roots: "It was toward the end of 1819 that we met for the first time. In many cities of the German fatherland dreadful scenes occurred that made some people suspect an unanticipated return to the Middle Ages. We came together to help discuss, when necessary, how best to escape the deeply rooted damage."[73] Gans's statement also revealed his view of the premodern era, the Middle Ages, as a woeful and violent time.

With the past and the present so interconnected, the influence of antisemitism on Jewish studies was not far behind; after all, the field emerged and matured as modern antisemitism gradually developed into a fully articulated movement. Glancing through the topics covered by the early scholarly Jewish journals, we can see the striking role that antisemitism played in shaping the narrative of Jewish history and the contents of the journals. In 1909, Ludwig Phillipson observed, "Antisemitism dominates directly and indirectly the whole history of the Jewish community in the last quarter of the nineteenth century," and he included in his multivolume history of Jews a significant section devoted to the history of modern antisemitism.[74]

But this concern and influence were not limited to accounting for Jewish persecution or to writing the history of antisemitism—a new field that emerged in the 1880s—but also included the framing of Jewish scholarship.[75] Even when not explicitly referring to anti-Jewish sentiments and persecution, these topics were always in the back of scholars' minds. In Italy, for example, the journal *L'Educatore Israelita*, founded in 1852, wanted to bring knowledge about Jews, Judaism, and Jewish history to lessen hatred against Jews. The first volume started with a declaration: "Whoever walks in darkness draws fear from everything he encounters."[76] And thus people "in ignorance distrust and fear everyone and everything; and since hatred is the natural fruit of fear," so the nations, not knowing much about each other, have hated each other "to the very grave damage of each and every one." In the early years *L'Educatore Israelita* focused its historical studies on antiquity—biblical and postbiblical—and on prominent Jews, such as Moses Mendelssohn, and some eighteenth-century Italian intellectuals.[77] Among the news reported in the early years were books published, advances of Jews in other countries, enumerations of successful Jews as university professors, doctors, and so on, reports about Moses Montefiore, epidemics, and even conversions *to* Judaism.[78]

L'Educatore Israelita was notably less lachrymose than journals and publications elsewhere in Europe. Still, the backdrop of its articles was often the challenges of Jewish-Christian relations, subtly providing tools for positive interactions. Crescenzo Altri's 1856 article about Jews and the papacy related that the popes were said to have been the Jews' protectors, but the notorious Counter-Reformation Pope Paul IV, who established the Roman ghetto, was not mentioned at all.[79]

Even in the 1880s, when antisemitism was on the rise across Europe, some of that same political sentiment remained. For example, in 1881 *Il Vessillo Israelitico*, the successor of *L'Educatore Israelita*, published the short piece "Popes and Princes, Defenders of the Jews," in which the author asserted, "The Jews have always had enemies, the envious among the vulgar and the ignorant. But the learned men, the enlightened princes have judged them on other principles. They have always welcomed or sought them for their ability in the sciences, no less than for their intelligence in commerce and in affairs useful for the general good of the state."[80] The physical proximity to the pope and the close, if sometimes hostile and invasive, relations between the Holy See and Roman Jews meant that the accounts of these relations were not as unsympathetic as those penned elsewhere. In German Jewish historiography, in part because of Germany's dominant Protestantism and its implicit anti-Catholicism, the focus on a lachrymose history of relations between Jews and the Catholic Church might have worked. In Italy, less so—the political dominance of the Catholic Church and Catholics would make such emphasis alienating for Jews. Still, because of the emergence of more explicit political antisemitism in the 1870s, more explicit concern with rising antisemitism began to seep into Jewish historiography, and not just in Italy.

In Eastern Europe Jewish scholarly journals did not shy away from exploring the themes of anti-Jewish animosity and Jewish survival, though they also tried to provide other models from Western Europe by publishing works of Western scholars.[81] The editors of these journals bemoaned that Russia produced the likes of Iacov Brafman, a notorious Russian Jewish convert to Christianity who was responsible for writing books advancing theories of Jewish conspiracies, and not "Roschers, Schleidans, or Amyntors," references to Western non-Jewish scholars who were far more inclined to see "the beneficial influence of Jews."[82] The journals *Evreiskaia Biblioteka*, *Evreiskaia Starina*, and *Voskhod* routinely published scholarly pieces that directly addressed contemporary issues. Some were explicitly apologetic; some provided content that was not directly responding to specific issues but rather was related to broader contemporary concerns. For example, after years of increasing anti-Jewish propaganda in Russia, during which Richard Wagner's essay "Das Judenthums in der Musik" was published in Russian translation in 1869 and other German antisemitic works followed in the 1870s, *Evreiskaia Biblioteka* republished the lengthy article "The Jewish Question and Russian Interests," which had originally appeared in 1862.[83] In the introduction the editors noted that, though the article had been published so many years before, the recent anti-Jewish attacks proved all-too-familiar: "All the same arguments are repeated in all sorts of ways" and "only the names of the authors are different." The lengthy republished essay explored historical issues in defense of the Talmud.[84] As debates challenging the legal status of Jews continued in Russia, the journal also published lengthy treatises on the history of laws concerning Jews, using legal history to illuminate the present. Such was a three-part and nearly book-length history of Jewry laws in Russia by the young scholar and lawyer Ilya Orshanskii.[85]

But it was not just journals that responded to antisemitism with scholarship. As Joseph Reinach's *Erreur judiciaire* demonstrates, books were also deployed. According to Ismar Schorsch, for Leopold Zunz, "a defense of Judaism was always an occasion to advance the frontiers of scholarship."[86] And so, when the Prussian state imposed restrictions on naming Jewish children, forbidding Jews to use "Christian proper names," Zunz published a book on the history of names Jews used as a scholarly polemic against the law.[87] Zunz documented the names used by Jews over centuries and concluded that there were "no Christian names," just as there was no "Christian language"; names "always belong at first to a people and a language, never to a church and a dogma, never to this or that political or religious opinion."[88]

Although the work of the preeminent German Jewish historian Heinrich Graetz, as Michael Brenner concluded, "can be understood only in the context of confrontation with the dominant trends within contemporary Wissenschaft des Judentums as well as German historiography," so many works of historians, then and now, can only be understood in the context of specific events.[89] Zunz's *Namen der Juden* and Reinach's *Erreur judiciaire* are such examples. But so is Auguste Molinier's study of the anti-Jewish murder libel in 1247 in Valréas, an accusation that led to the first papal condemnation of such accusations.[90] Published in 1883, Molinier's study has to be located in the context of the Tiszaeszlár affair, to which Molinier only gestured in the introduction, saying that the legend that Jews killed Christian children still found "credence" today "in several European countries" among "the popular, ignorant and fanatical masses." Molinier's study remains to date the most detailed and authoritative work about the 1247 accusation. Cecil Roth's *Ritual Murder and the Jew*, published in 1935, was a response to the May 1934 issue of *Der Stürmer*, which focused on "ritual murder."[91] In this book Roth published the famous 1759 report by Cardinal Lorenzo Ganganelli, in which the cardinal demonstrated the absurdity of blood accusations against Jews.[92] Nazism inspired other scholars to delve more deeply into the issues of antisemitism and Jewish-Christian relations.[93]

These nineteenth- and early twentieth-century journals and publications in Jewish studies influenced generations of scholars and scholarly projects. In light of the destruction of many archives and buildings during the wars of the twentieth century, these primary sources, texts, or images are now invaluable, living on beyond their own period.[94] Studies and primary sources published in *Archives Israelites de France*, *Revue des études juives*, *Voskhod*, *Evreiskaia Starina*, or *Monatsschrift für Geschichte und Wissenschaft des Judentums*, for example, have been used and cited even in the most recent works by scholars in Jewish studies, including my own. And yet we modern scholars have sometimes used these sources uncritically, neglecting to reflect on how these primary texts and images entered circulation, what might be missing from them, and of what contemporaneous conversation these sources were a part. As a result, we might also be missing how that conversation influenced the way these historical sources and studies were framed. Lisa Leff has gestured toward this question in her study of Zosa Szajkowski, noting how the documents that Szajkowski obtained, removing them from their original archival context, shaped the historiography of French Jewry.[95] Jacqueline Jung, a medievalist, has begun to examine the role that Nazi aesthetics and ideology have played in the documentation of Gothic sculpture ubiquitously used by scholars of medieval studies even today.[96]

These are important questions. How the past was told and what was told about it have shaped all historiography, including Jewish studies.[97] For instance, Jewish studies might have looked quite different if Jewish historiography had drawn more robustly from the roots of Italian or British scholarship and from the questions they asked rather than those explored by German and Eastern European Jewish scholars. The Italian journals were far more attuned to non-European Jews than northern European Jewish journals, perhaps with the exception of the *Jewish Chronicle* published in London. The *Chronicle* also reported on Jews in North Africa, the Ottoman Empire, even Ethiopia and Abyssinia, regions and cultures that only in recent decades have garnered scholarly attention as the field began to shift away from the study of the Ashkenazic Jewish past.[98] Of course, both the Italian and the British publications have to be seen in the context of British and Italian colonialism.

A glimpse of that focus on non-European Jews might be found in the popular work of Cecil Roth, a British Jewish historian, who, like Baron, also adamantly insisted on breaking with earlier Jewish historiography that tended to overstress "the traditional tale of woe" to "prevent the wood from being obscured by the undergrowth, and to convey above all the glorious sweep and continuity which makes Jewish history the most fascinating."[99] His influence on Jewish studies as a field was limited, his scholarship considered too populist. But today his intellectual roots in Italian and British Jewish historiography are clear; his questions and methodologies were different, some, such as book history or material culture, we have only recently begun to appreciate.[100]

What this bird's-eye view over these works also reveals is that the fears that the founders of the AJS and the Jewish studies scholars of the late twentieth century had of being accused of parochialism were not unfounded. They guarded their academic detachment and boundaries between the public and their scholarship and wanted to be seen, to paraphrase Yehuda Leib Gordon, as "scholars in the academic world and Jews at home," because historically this boundary was much more fluid. In fact, one could argue that in Jewish historiography the claims of objectivity, detachment, and insulation from, to use Salo Baron's words, "the mainstream of Jewish life . . . had no foundations at all."[101] The aspirations to it existed from the earliest days, but its institutional fulfillment did not take root.

The debates about what Yiddish literary scholar Ruth Wisse called the applicability of scholarship to social needs and about community connections in the early years of the AJS took place at the time when

Jewish studies as a discipline was seeking academic respectability in the midst of major cultural and political upheavals. Other minority groups or groups less represented in the mainstream academy—most notably women and African Americans—were fighting for inclusion and recognition in the profession. Activist students were clamoring for ethnic studies courses.[102] As a result, scholars who appeared to engage with public questions or to respond to social movements in their work were sometimes disparaged—creating tensions between scholarship and activist concerns. And although some scholars, including those in Jewish studies, rejected "the traditional university model of detached, third-person critical inquiry and analysis," others sought to "retreat" from an "identity-based position," fearing it "would compromise the critical analytic approach central to scholarship" and "undermine scholar's credibility."[103] To achieve academic respectability, Jewish studies scholars needed to show detachment from "the concerns of the Jewish community and for the Jewish civilization," as Irving Greenberg put it.[104]

But just as the AJS's origins were a sign of a shift of Jewish studies from internal Jewish intellectual spheres into the dominant academic world, so too today the recently revised statement affirming the organization's commitment both to "advanc[ing] research and teaching in Jewish Studies at colleges, universities, and other institutions of higher learning, and to foster[ing] greater understanding of Jewish Studies scholarship among the wider public" represents another shift. In the recent past the ivory tower has been pushed to demonstrate that it matters, and scholars, especially those in the humanities and social sciences, have increasingly been asked to explain why what they do matters. This also applied to scholars in Jewish studies. Many have begun to make their case to the public, speaking to the public and trying to write for the public as well. The last several years amplified that need for applying scholarly knowledge to explain the present. With the Trump era and the accompanying resurgence of violence, antisemitism, and racism and with the pandemic and the crisis it wrought, we are beginning to see a return to publicly engaged scholarship, with historians stressing "the importance of history as an ingredient in informed civic debate."[105]

But what the last years have also laid bare is "the specter of presentism," throwing into full display the impact that specific events have on scholarship.[106] With so many Jewish studies scholars turning to Jewish history and exploring questions of disease and epidemics and race and racial relations within the Jewish community and without and, beyond Jewish studies, with the crop of studies covering race, violence, and epidemics, we are confronted with the questions of the role that social and political concerns have in the study of the past and the interrelation between the past, the present, and the future. This interrelation has vexed Jewish studies scholars since the founding of the field, and their work has reflected it even when veiled behind scholarly detachment.

Notes

In my second year of graduate studies, I took Michael Stanislawski's course on Jewish historiography that focused on the periodization of Jewish history. This course set the trajectory for my academic career, first and foremost in terms of raising questions of how Jewish history was written and conceptualized. It was also in that course that I examined how the relations between Jews and the Catholic Church have been covered in historiography. This chapter is an early fruit of a difficult year, when I was a National Endowment for the Humanities scholar-in-residence at the Center for Jewish History, yet unable to access the Center's physical collections because of COVID-19. I am grateful to the Center's staff for making many materials accessible to me online. I want to thank, in particular, Rachel C. Miller, Lauren Gilbert, Malgorzata Bakalarz Duverger, and Julie Kaplan. I also want to thank Deborah Dash Moore for joining me for a conversation about Jewish studies scholars and political engagement at the Center for Jewish History.

1 Michael Stanislawski, *For Whom Do I Toil? Judah Leib Gordon and the Crisis of Russian Jewry* (New York: Oxford University Press, 1988), 4. The poem was discussed on pages 104–5.
2 Stanislawski, *For Whom Do I Toil*, 49–52.
3 Stanislawski, *For Whom Do I Toil*, 48.
4 Emphasis mine. "AJS Mission and History," www.associationforjewishstudies.org/about-ajs/mission-and-history (accessed 4 September 2023).
5 Kristen Loveland, "The Association for Jewish Studies: A Short History," paper presented at the 40th Annual Conference of the Association for Jewish Studies, 21–23 December 2008, p. 10, www.associationforjewishstudies.org/docs/default-source/ajs-history/ajs-history.pdf (accessed 5 May 2023).

6 Loveland, "Association for Jewish Studies," 4.
7 Loveland, "Association for Jewish Studies," 4. On the AJS concerns, see "Interview with Robert Chazan," American Academy for Jewish Research, February 2018, aajr.org/centennial-project/interview-with-robert-chazan/ (accessed 5 May 2023).
8 Arnold J. Band, "Jewish Studies in American Liberal-Arts Colleges and Universities," *American Jewish Yearbook* 67 (1966): 3, quoted in Loveland, "Association for Jewish Studies," 2. See also Marc Dollinger, *Black Power, Jewish Politics: Reinventing the Alliance in the 1960s* (Waltham, MA: Brandeis University Press, 2018), 113–15. For a provocative study of the crisis of objectivity, see Peter Novick, *That Noble Dream: The "Objectivity Question" and the American Historical Profession* (Cambridge, UK: Cambridge University Press, 2009), esp. ch. 14, on women's history and Black history. For a critique arguing for detachment rather than neutrality as a goal for scholarly objectivity, see Thomas L. Haskell, "Objectivity Is Not Neutrality: Rhetoric vs. Practice in Peter Novick's *That Noble Dream*," *History and Theory* 29, no. 2 (1990): 129–57.
9 Novick, *That Noble Dream*, 2–3.
10 Novick, *That Noble Dream*, 3. David N. Myers, *The Stakes of History: On the Use and Abuse of Jewish History for Life* (New Haven, CT: Yale University Press, 2018), 62.
11 Loveland, "Association for Jewish Studies," 10.
12 In 1998, in a plenary speech at the AJS, Hava Tirosh-Samuelson condemned the "conceit of objectivity" and Jewish studies scholars' pursuit of detachment, urging them, the *Chronicle of Higher Education* reported, "to return to their founding mission: 'the well-being of Judaism and the Jewish people.'" Scott Heller, "The New Jewish Studies: Defying Tradition and Easy Categorization," *Chronicle of Higher Education* (29 January 1999), www.chronicle.com/article/the-new-jewish-studies-defying-tradition-and-easy-categorization/ (accessed 4 September 2023). In an op-ed published a month later in the *Chronicle*, Tirosh-Samuelson argued that Jewish studies scholars "did not have to play" by the rules of American academy; in fact, they could challenge its assumptions by not living "like an intellectual Marrano, hiding what he or she believes because it is uncouth or not academically correct. If we wish to instill in our students (both Jews and non-Jews) a love of the Jewish people and the Jewish religious civilization, we cannot hide behind the persona of the cool, uninvolved academic researcher, who only

observes from afar but does not get too close to the material he or she studies." Hava Tirosh-Samuelson, "The Academic Study of Judaism," *Chronicle of Higher Education* (26 February 1999), www.chronicle.com/article/the-academic-study-of-judaism-2041/ (accessed 4 September 2023).

13 For example, Leopold von Ranke may have claimed a new detached approach while promoting a political vision of history and the nation that was deeply committed to a Prussian state. See Georg G. Iggers, *The German Conception of History: The National Tradition of Historical Thought from Herder to the Present* (Middletown, CT: Wesleyan University Press, 1969), 63–89. In the United States, for example, the Dunning school of American history at Columbia University actively promoted the Southern version of the Reconstruction era in US history and, as Eric Foner noted, "helped freeze the white South for generations in unalterable opposition to any change in race relations." According to Foner, the example of Reconstruction scholarship illustrates "how historical interpretation both reflects and helps shape current policies." Eric Foner, *Who Owns History? Rethinking the Past in a Changing World* (New York: Hill & Wang, 2003), 17.

14 David Hollinger, "Rich, Powerful, and Smart: Jewish Overrepresentation Should Be Explained Instead of Avoided or Mystified," *Jewish Quarterly Review* 94, no. 4 (2004): 595–602.

15 Leopold von Ranke and Georg G. Iggers, *The Theory and Practice of History*, trans. Wilma A. Iggers (London: Routledge, 2011), 86.

16 Iggers, *German Conception of History*, esp. 90, 130–31. On the American scientism and the misinterpretation of Ranke, see Novick, *That Noble Dream*, ch. 1.

17 Ranke and Iggers, *Theory and Practice of History*, 85.

18 Leopold von Ranke, *Geschichten der Romanischen und Germanischen Völker von 1494 bis 1535, Erster Band* (Leipzig: Bey G. Reimer, 1824), iv. I slightly modified the English translation from Ranke and Iggers, *Theory and Practice of History*, 85.

19 Iggers, *German Conception of History*, 73.

20 Iggers, *German Conception of History*, 91–92.

21 Ismar Schorsch, *Leopold Zunz: Creativity in Adversity* (Philadelphia: University of Pennsylvania Press, 2017), ch. 2.

22 *Entwurf von Statuten des Vereins für Cultur und Wissenschaft der Juden* (Berlin: F. Nietack, 1822), 6. Sections published in English in Paul R. Mendes-Flohr and Jehuda Reinharz, eds., *The Jew in the Modern World*, 3rd ed. (Oxford, UK: Oxford University Press, 2011), 238–39.

23 Schorsch, *Leopold Zunz*, 29–30.
24 Joel Abraham List, "A Society for the Preservation of the Jewish People (1819)," in *The Jew in the Modern World*, 3rd ed., ed. Paul R. Mendes-Flohr and Jehuda Reinharz (Oxford, UK: Oxford University Press, 2011), 236–37.
25 Salo W. Baron, "The Revolution of 1848 and Jewish Scholarship, Part I: France, the United States, and Italy," *Proceedings of the American Academy for Jewish Research* 18 (1948): 4.
26 Natalia Aleksiun and Brian J. Horowitz, "Introduction," in *Writing Jewish History in Eastern Europe*, ed. Natalia Aleksiun, Brian J. Horowitz, and Antony Polonsky (Oxford, UK: Littman Library of Jewish Civilization, 2017), 5. Also see Natalia Aleksiun, *Conscious History: Polish Jewish Historians Before the Holocaust* (London: Littman Library of Jewish Civilization, 2021).
27 Quoted in Rachel Manekin, "Constructing Polish Jewry's 'Shrine of History': Galician Beginnings," in *Writing Jewish History in Eastern Europe*, ed. Natalia Aleksiun, Brian J. Horowitz, and Antony Polonsky (Oxford: Littman Library of Jewish Civilization, 2017), 77. See also Aleksiun, *Conscious History*.
28 Aleksiun, *Conscious History*, 12.
29 Michael Brenner, *Prophets of the Past: Interpreters of Jewish History* (Princeton, NJ: Princeton University Press, 2010), 112.
30 Brenner, *Prophets of the Past*, 48. On Eastern European Jewish historiography as an implicit or explicit response to antisemitism, see, for example, the essays by Ela Bauer, Brian Horowitz, Rachel Manekin, and Sarah Ellem Zarrow in Natalia Aleksiun, Brian J. Horowitz, and Antony Polonsky, eds., *Writing Jewish History in Eastern Europe* (Oxford, UK: Littman Library of Jewish Civilization, 2017); and Aleksiun, *Conscious History*.
31 Brenner, *Prophets of the Past*, 48.
32 Quoted in André Lemaire, "Les Reinach et les études sur la tradition juive," *Comptes rendus des séances de l'Académie des Inscriptions et Belles-Lettres* 151, no. 2 (2007): 1106–7.
33 Theodore Reinach, "Allocution prononcée a l'Assemblée Générale de la Société des Études Juives," *Revue des études juives* 30 (1895): viii.
34 See Joseph Reinach, *Une erreur judiciaire sous Louis XIV: Raphaël Levy* (Paris: Delagrave, 1898). On the Levy trial, see Pierre Birnbaum, *A Tale of Ritual Murder in the Age of Louis XIV: The Trial of Raphaël Lévy, 1669*, trans. Arthur Goldhammer (Stanford, CA: Stanford University Press, 2012); and Magda Teter, *Blood Libel: On the Trail of an Antisemitic Myth* (Cambridge,

MA: Harvard University Press, 2020), 250–56. On the Reinach brothers and Jewish studies in France, see Lemaire, "Les Reinach."
35 "Erreur judiciaire," *La Libre Parole*, no. 175 (14 November 1898). The cover image is based on Edgar Degas's painting *Portraits at the Bourse*.
36 Myers, *Stakes of History*.
37 Shulamit Volkov, "Ha-yehudim be-ḥay ha-amim: sipur le'umi o perek be-historiyah meshulevet" [Jews Among the Nations: A Unique National Narrative or a Chapter in National Historiographies], *Zion* 91, no. 1 (1996): 91–111; David N. Myers, *Re-Inventing the Jewish Past: European Jewish Intellectuals and the Zionist Return to History* (Oxford, UK: Oxford University Press, 2005).
38 Judith Bronstein, "Reviving Forgotten Jewish Heroes: An Aspect of the Early Twentieth-Century Zionist Perception of the Crusader Period in Palestine," *Jewish Quarterly Review* 109, no. 4 (2019), 637. On Dinur, see David Myers, "History as Ideology: The Case of Ben Zion Dinur, Zionist Historian 'Par Excellence,'" *Modern Judaism: A Journal of Jewish Ideas and Experience* 8, no. 2 (1988): 167–93; Uri Ram, "Zionist Historiography and the Invention of Modern Jewish Nationhood: The Case of Ben Zion Dinur," *History and Memory* 7, no. 1 (1995): 91–124; and Arielle Rein, "Defusei ha-historiografiyah ha-le'umit be-yeẓirto shel Ben-Ẓiyon Dinur" [Patterns of National Historiography in Ben-Zion Dinur's Works], *Zion* 68, no. 4 (2003): 425–66.
39 For a recent retrospective on Salo Wittmayer Baron and his impact on Jewish studies, see Rebecca Kobrin, ed., *Salo Baron: The Past and Future of Jewish Studies in America* (New York: Columbia University Press, 2022).
40 Salo W. Baron, "Emphases in Jewish History," *Jewish Social Studies* 1, no. 1 (1939): 37.
41 Baron, "Emphases in Jewish History," 37.
42 David Engel, "Crisis and Lachrymosity: On Salo Baron, Neobaronianism, and the Study of Modern European Jewish History," *Jewish History* 20, no. 3 (2006): 243–64. See also, more recently, David Engel, "Salo Baron on Anti-Semitism," in *Salo Baron: The Past and Future of Jewish Studies in America*, ed. Rebecca Kobrin (New York: Columbia University Press, 2022), 115–31. Cf. Adam Teller, "Revisiting Baron's 'Lachrymose Conception': The Meanings of Violence in Jewish History" *AJS Review* 38, no. 2 (2014): 431–39.
43 Baron's essays on the 1848 revolution published just years after the end of World War II read as an implicit reflection on the role scholars play during historical upheavals. See Baron, "Revolution of 1848, Part I," 1–66; and

Salo W. Baron, "The Revolution of 1848 and Jewish Scholarship, Part II: Austria," *Proceedings of the American Academy for Jewish Research* 20 (1951): 1–100.

44 See, for example, Baron, "Emphases in Jewish History," 37. See also Magda Teter, "The Pandemic, Antisemitism, and the Lachrymose Conception of Jewish History," *Jewish Social Studies* 26, no. 1 (2020): 20–32.

45 Teter, "Pandemic."

46 Haskell, "Objectivity Is Not Neutrality."

47 Salo Wittmayer Baron, *A Social and Religious History of the Jews* (New York: Columbia University Press, 1937), 1: 13. See also Elisabeth Gallas, *A Mortuary of Books: The Rescue of Jewish Culture After the Holocaust* (New York: New York University Press, 2019), 198.

48 Quoted in Gallas, *Mortuary of Books*, 216.

49 Salo W. Baron, "Newer Emphases in Jewish History," *Jewish Social Studies* 25, no. 4 (1963): 244.

50 Giuseppe Levi, "Il self government e la durata maravigliosa del giudaismo," *L'Educatore Israelita* (1873): 129.

51 Michael Stanislawski, "Salo Wittmayer Baron: Demystifying Jewish History," *Columbia Magazine* (5 January 2005), magazine.columbia.edu/article/salo-wittmayer-baron-demystifying-jewish-history (accessed 5 May 2023). The most comprehensive to-date biography of Salo Wittmayer Baron is Robert Liberles, *Salo Wittmayer Baron: Architect of Jewish History* (New York: New York University Press, 1995). See also Robert Chazan, "Salo Wittmayer Baron (1895–1989)," *Proceedings of the American Academy for Jewish Research* 58 (1992): 7–13.

52 Rebecca Kobrin, "Introduction: Salo Baron, Columbia University, and the Expansion of Jewish Studies in Twentieth Century America," in *Salo Baron: The Past and Future of Jewish Studies in America*, ed. Rebecca Kobrin (New York: Columbia University Press, 2022), 1–24.

53 Salo W. Baron, "Communal Responsibility for Jewish Social Research," *Jewish Social Studies* 17, no. 3 (1955): 242–45. See also Salo W. Baron, "Opening Statement," *Jewish Social Studies* 17, no. 3 (1955): 175–76.

54 Morris R. Cohen, "Publisher's Foreword," *Jewish Social Studies* 1, no. 1 (1939): 3–4.

55 Cohen, "Publisher's Foreword," 3–4.

56 Rudolph Stahl, "Vocational Retraining of Jews in Nazi Germany, 1933–1938," *Jewish Social Studies* 1, no. 2 (1939): 169–94.

57 Joel Cang, "The Opposition Parties in Poland and Their Attitude Towards the Jews and the Jewish Problem," *Jewish Social Studies* 1, no. 2 (1939): 243.

58 Cang, "Opposition Parties," 244.
59 For an example of advocacy, see Koppel S. Pinson, "Antisemitism in the Post-War World," *Jewish Social Studies* 7, no. 2 (1945): 99–118.
60 Samuel M. Blumenfield, "Rashi, the Teacher in Israel (1040–1105)," *Jewish Social Studies* 2, no. 4 (1940): 391.
61 Cecil Roth, "Marranos and Racial Antisemitism: A Study in Parallels," *Jewish Social Studies* 2, no. 3 (1940): 248. This connection between Iberian *limpieza de sangre* and racial antisemitism was addressed years later by Salo Baron's student Yosef Hayim Yerushalmi, who acknowledged some phenomenological parallels but refused to make direct causal connections between the two. See Yosef Hayim Yerushalmi, *Assimilation and Racial Anti-Semitism: The Iberian and the German Models* (New York: Leo Baeck Institute, 1982).
62 Salo W. Baron, "Jewish Social Studies, 1938–39: A Selected Bibliography," *Jewish Social Studies* 2, no. 3 (1940): 305–88.
63 Brenner, *Prophets of the Past*, 106–14. On Schiper in the context of the history of Polish Jewish historiography, see Aleksiun, *Conscious History*.
64 Aleksiun, *Conscious History*, 218; Brenner, *Prophets of the Past*, 112. Other Polish Jewish historians also advocated "linking the past and the present" (Aleksiun, *Conscious History*, 218).
65 *L'Educatore Israelita* (1856), 303–14, 364–68. The defense of Jews draws on early modern defenses (367).
66 See also Brian J. Horowitz, "'Building a Fragile Edifice': A History of Russian Jewish Historical Institutions, 1860–1914," in *Writing Jewish History in Eastern Europe*, ed. Natalia Aleksiun, Brian J. Horowitz, and Antony Polonsky (Oxford, UK: Littman Library of Jewish Civilization, 2017), 61–75, esp. 72–73.
67 Michael Levi Rodkinson, *Maẓat-miẓvah va-alilat ha-dam* [*Das Ungesäuerte Brod und Die Anklage des Blutgebrauchs am Passah-Feste*] (Pressburg: D. Löwy, 1883). See "Literaturnaia litopis," *Voskhod* 2 (1883): 22–28; and "Sudebnaia khronika" [Court Chronicle], *Voskhod* 10–12 (1883). The Italian journal *Vessillo Israelitico* hardly reported on the Tiszaeszlár affair; in 1883 it briefly mentioned the pamphlet *The "Blood Accusation": Its Origin and Occurrence in the Middle Ages*, by Asher I. Myers, published in London about the affair, among other bibliographic notices, noting that the trial in Tisza Eszlar had given rise to "many writings" about blood accusations against Jews ("Bulletino bibliografico," *Vessillo Israelitico* 20 [1883]: 224); see Asher I. Myers, *The "Blood Accusation": Its Origin and Occurrence in the Middle*

Ages—An Historical Commentary on the Tisza-Eszlar Trial (London: Asher I. Myers, 1883).

68 On the Xanten affair, see *Voskhod* 13, no. 7 (1893): 36–56; 13, no. 11 (1893): 44–73; and 13, no. 12 (1893): 24–59. For the Różany blood libel, see Sergei Aleksandrovich Bershadskii, "Ruzhanskiye muzhchiny," *Voskhod* 13, no. 7 (1893): 13–22. Bershadskii's work on blood accusations continued in *Voskhod* 14, no. 9 (1894).

69 For the Beilis affair, see, for example, I. Galant, "Ritual'nyi protsess v Dunaigorode v 1748," *Evreiskaia Starina* 4 (1911): 268–85; I. Galant, "Zhertvy ritual'nogo obvineniia v Zasalave v 1747 G: po aktam Kievskago Tsentralnago Arkhiva," *Evreiskaia Starina* 5, no. 2 (1912): 202–18; and I. D. Kuzmin, *Materialy k voprosu ob obvineniakh evreev ve ritual'nykh prestupleniakh* (St. Petersburg: A. Smolinskii, 1913). See also Horowitz, "Building a Fragile Edifice," 73.

70 Salomon Reinach, "L'accusation du meurtre rituel," *Revue des études juives* 25, no. 50 (1892): 161–80.

71 Quoted in Brenner, *Prophets of the Past*, 29.

72 Brenner, *Prophets of the Past*, 29.

73 Brenner, *Prophets of the Past*, 29.

74 Brenner, *Prophets of the Past*, 80.

75 On the history of the historiography of antisemitism, see Jonathan Judaken, "Anti-Semitism (Historiography)," in *Key Concepts in the Study of Antisemitism*, ed. Sol Goldberg, Scott Ury, and Keith Ian Weiser (Basingstoke, UK: Palgrave Macmillan, 2020), 25–38.

76 "Due parole di prefazione," *Annuario Israelitico Italiano*, Anno Primo (1852): 3.

77 For example, *L'Educatore Israelita* (1852–1853, 1855, 1856).

78 For example, *L'Educatore Israelita* (1855): 186–190, 287.

79 Crescenzo Altri, "Gl'Israeliti a Roma," *L'Educatore Israelita* (1856): 262–66. Altri's was a classic articulation of what Yosef Hayim Yerushalmi would later call "the vertical alliance," in which Jews in the premodern period almost invariably sought security through an alliance with the highest authorities in a given society. See Yosef Hayim Yerushalmi, *The Lisbon Massacre of 1506 and the Royal Image in the Shebet Yehudah* (Cincinnati: Hebrew Union College, Jewish Institute of Religion, 1976).

80 "Papi e principi, difensori degli ebrei," *Il Vessillo Israelitico* (1881): 9.

81 See, for example, V. Rosher (Roscher), "Evrei v srednίe veka s tochki zreniya torgovoy politiki," *Evreiskaia Biblioteka* (1878), 37–60.

82 "Znachenie evreev dlia vozrozhdeniia i sokhranenia nauk v srednix vekakh," *Evreiskaia Biblioteka* (1878), 1–2.
83 On the publication of antisemitic literature in Russia, see John D. Klier, "German Antisemitism and Russian Judeophobia in the 1880s: Brothers and Strangers," *Jahrbücher für Geschichte Osteuropas* 37, no. 4 (1989): 524–40.
84 "Evreiskii vopros i interesy Rossii," *Evreiskaia Biblioteka* 2 (1875): 1–47. The Italian *Vessillo Israelitico* also published articles about the Talmud in 1883. Although they were ostensibly informative, they explicitly or implicitly countered antisemitic attacks on this key rabbinic work.
85 Ilya Grigorevich Orshanskii, "Russkoe zakondatel'stvo o evreiakh proshlogo stoletya," *Evreiskaia Biblioteka*, vols. 3–5 (1873–1875). See, also in the 1875 issue, B. Pavlovich, "Plan reformy pol'skikh evreev v kontse proshlogo stoletiia," *Evreiskaia Biblioteka* 5 (1875): 89–100.
86 Schorsch, *Leopold Zunz*, 69.
87 Schorsch, *Leopold Zunz*, 69–70; Brenner, *Prophets of the Past*, 31–32.
88 Quoted in Brenner, *Prophets of the Past*, 31.
89 Brenner, *Prophets of the Past*, 65.
90 Auguste Molinier, *Enquête sur un meurtre imputé aux Juifs de Valréas* (Paris: H. Champion, 1883).
91 Cecil Roth, *The Ritual Murder Libel and the Jew* (London: Woburn Press, 1935). On ritual murder, see Teter, *Blood Libel*, Epilogue.
92 On the Ganganelli report, see Teter, *Blood Libel*, chaps. 9–10.
93 For example, James William Parkes, *The Conflict of the Church and the Synagogue: A Study in the Origins of Antisemitism* (New York: Atheneum, 1969 [1934]).
94 Brenner, *Prophets of the Past*, 49.
95 Lisa Moses Leff, *The Archive Thief: The Man Who Salvaged French Jewish History in the Wake of the Holocaust* (New York: Oxford University Press, 2018).
96 Jacqueline Jung, "The Work of Gothic Sculpture in the Age of Its Photographic Reproduction," in *The Lives and Afterlives of Medieval Iconography*, ed. Pamela A. Patton and Henry D. Schilb (University Park: Penn State University Press, 2021), 161–94.
97 Brenner, *Prophets of the Past*, 49.
98 *L'Educatore Israelita* 3 (1855): 255–60, 297–301, 370–71; 4 (1856): 7–11, 21, 164–75. In 1877 *Il Vessillo* reported the publication of an edition of prayers of Ethiopian Jews in Amharic with a Hebrew translation, asking at the end, "In what way, if not through the press, can we make known the beauties of our

literature, the facts of our history" (*Il Vessillo* [1877], 175). See Joseph Halevy, *Seder Tefillot Ha-Falashim* (Paris: D. Jouaust, 1877),

99 Cecil Roth, *A Short History of the Jewish People, 1600 BC–AD 1935* (London: Macmillan, 1936), vii.

100 On Roth, see David B. Ruderman, "Cecil Roth, Historian of Italian Jewry: A Reassessment," in *The Jewish Past Revisited*, ed. David N. Myers and David B. Ruderman (New Haven, CT: Yale University Press, 1998), 128–42.

101 Baron's comment comes in regard to Jewish studies scholars during the 1848 revolution, a lengthy study he published in the *Proceedings of the American Academy for Jewish Research* in 1948–1949 and 1951, quoted in Myers, *Stakes of History*, 39.

102 Dollinger, *Black Power, Jewish Politics*, 113–15.

103 Dollinger, *Black Power, Jewish Politics*, 114.

104 Loveland, "Association for Jewish Studies," 4. See also Dollinger, *Black Power, Jewish Politics*, 114.

105 Myers, *Stakes of History*, 20.

106 Myers, *Stakes of History*, 22.

Acknowledgments

The editors wish to acknowledge the individuals and institutions who helped to bring this volume to fruition. The staff at Wayne State University Press, especially Sandra Korn, Emily Gauronskas, and Carrie Teefey, have been terrific, and we were so fortunate to benefit from their professionalism. Likewise, that of our indexer, Rachel Lyon. Shoshana Norman of the Ghetto Fighters' House Museum aided us in locating Yosef Raviv, who provided the permission for the photographic image on the spine of the book in a period of enormous instability in Israel in the fall of 2023. We are grateful to them both. Anaïs Faurt did a superb job helping to finalize the book's submission to the press while working on her doctorate at Rutgers University. Finally, we thank the Cohn-Haddow Center for Judaic Studies at Wayne State University and the Institute for Israel and Jewish Studies at Columbia University for providing generous funding for the book's publication.

Contributors

Jonathan Karp is associate professor of Judaic studies and history at Binghamton University of the State University of New York (SUNY). He is the author of *The Politics of Jewish Commerce: Economic Thought and Emancipation in Europe* and has edited or coedited five volumes, including *The Cambridge History of Judaism in the Early Modern Period* (with Adam Sutcliffe) and *Classic Essays on Jews in Early Modern Europe* (with Francesca Trivellato). His forthcoming monograph is *Chosen Surrogates: How Blacks and Jews Changed American Popular Music*.

James Loeffler is professor of history at Johns Hopkins University. He is the author of *Rooted Cosmopolitans: Jews and Human Rights in the Twentieth Century* and *The Most Musical Nation: Jews and Culture in the Late Russian Empire*. He is coeditor of *The Law of Strangers: Jewish Lawyer and International Law* and of the *Association for Jewish Studies Review*.

Howard Lupovitch is professor of history and director of the Cohn-Haddow Center for Judaic Studies at Wayne State University. He is the author of *Transleithanian Paradise: A History of the Budapest Jewish Community, 1738–1938* and a coeditor, with François Guesnet and Antony Polonsky, of *Polin: Poland and Hungary—Jewish Realities Compared*, vol. 31.

Nancy Sinkoff is professor of Jewish studies and history and the academic director of the Allen and Joan Bildner Center for the Study of Jewish Life at Rutgers University, New Brunswick. She is the author of *Out of the Shtetl: Making Jews Modern in the Polish Borderlands* and *From Left to Right: Lucy S. Dawidowicz, the New York Intellectuals, and the Politics of Jewish History*. She is coeditor of *Sara Levy's World: Gender, Judaism, and the Bach Tradition in Enlightenment Berlin* (with Rebecca Cypess) and of

Polish Jewish Culture Beyond the Capital: Centering the Periphery (with Halina Goldberg).

* * *

David Assaf is professor of Jewish history at Tel Aviv University. He is the author of *The Regal Way: The Life and Times of Rabbi Israel of Ruzhin*, *Beguiled by Knowledge: Anatomy of a Hasidic Controversy*, and *A Song Is More Than Words: Chapters in the History of the Hebrew Songs*.

Israel Bartal is the Avraham Harman Professor of Modern Jewish History, emeritus, at the Hebrew University of Jerusalem. He is the author of *Poles and Jews: A Failed Brotherhood* (with M. Opalski), *The Jews of Eastern Europe, 1772–1881*, and *Tangled Roots: The Emergence of Israeli Culture*.

Michael Brenner is distinguished professor and the Abensohn Chair in Israel Studies at American University and holds the Chair of Jewish History and Culture at the University of Munich. He is the author of *In Hitler's Munich: Jews, the Revolution, and the Rise of Nazism* and *In Search of Israel: The History of an Idea*.

Elisheva Carlebach is the Salo W. Baron Professor of Jewish History, Culture, and Society at Columbia University. She is the author of *The Pursuit of Heresy*, *Divided Souls: Converts from Judaism in Early Modern Germany*, *Palaces of Time: Jewish Calendar and Culture in Early Modern Europe*, and *Confronting Modernity*, volume 6 in the Posen Library of Jewish Culture and Civilization.

Edward Fram is professor of Jewish history and holds the Solly Yellin Chair in Lithuanian and East European Jewry at Ben-Gurion University of the Negev. He is the author of *The Codification of Jewish Law on the Cusp of Modernity* and *Ideals Face Reality: Jewish Law and Life in Poland, 1550–1655*.

Jonathan Marc Gribetz is associate professor of Near Eastern studies and Judaic studies at Princeton University, where he directs the Program in Near Eastern Studies. He is the author of *Defining Neighbors: Religion, Race, and the Early Zionist-Arab Encounter* and of the forthcoming *Reading Herzl in Beirut: The PLO Effort to Know the Enemy*.

Gershon David Hundert (1946–2023) was professor of history and Leanor Segal Professor of Jewish Studies at McGill University. He is the author of *Jews in Poland-Lithuania in the Eighteenth Century: A Genealogy of Modernity*, *The Jews in a Polish Private Town: The Case of Opatow in the Eighteenth Century*, and a critical edition of the writings of Dov Ber Birkenthal.

Rebekah Klein-Pejšová is associate professor of history and Jewish studies and co-director of the Human Rights Program at Purdue University. She is the author of *Mapping Jewish Loyalties in Interwar Slovakia* and coeditor of *Shofar: An Interdisciplinary Journal of Jewish Studies*.

Olga Litvak is the Laurie B. and Eric M. Roth Professor of Modern European Jewish History at Cornell University. She is the author of *Conscription and the Search for Modern Russian Jewry* and *Haskalah: The Romantic Movement in Judaism*.

Natan M. Meir is the Lorry I. Lokey Professor of Judaic Studies in the Harold Schnitzer Family Program in Judaic Studies at Portland State University. He is the author of *Kiev, Jewish Metropolis: A History, 1859–1914* and *Stepchildren of the Shtetl: The Destitute, Disabled, and Mad of Jewish Eastern Europe, 1800–1939*.

Michael L. Miller is head of the Nationalism Studies Program and director of the Jewish Studies Program at Central European University in Vienna, Austria. He is the author of *Rabbis and Revolution: The Jews of Moravia in the Age of Emancipation* and, as a co-author, *Prague and Beyond: Jews in the Bohemian Lands*.

Nils Roemer holds the Arts, Humanities, and Technology Distinguished University Chair is the Stan and Barbara Rabin Professor and dean of the School of the Arts, Humanities, and Technology, and is the director of the Ackerman Center for Holocaust Studies, all at the University of Texas at Dallas. He is the author of *Jewish Scholarship and Culture in Nineteenth-Century Germany: Between History and Faith* and *German City, Jewish Memory: The Story of Worms*. He is the coeditor of *Germanic Review*.

Gil Rubin is head of academic programs at the Fortunoff Video Archive for Holocaust Testimonies, Yale University. He was a postdoctoral fellow at the Center for Jewish Studies at Harvard University and at the Fortunoff Video Archive at Yale.

Daniel B. Schwartz is professor of history at George Washington University. He is the author of *The First Modern Jew: Spinoza and the History of an Image* and *Ghetto: The History of a Word*.

Magda Teter is the Shvidler Chair in Judaic Studies and professor of history at Fordham University. She is the author of several books, most recently, *Christian Supremacy: Reckoning with the Roots of Antisemitism and Racism* and *Blood Libel: On the Trail of an Antisemitic Myth*.

Kalman Weiser is associate professor and the Silber Family Chair of Modern Jewish Studies in the Departments of History and Humanities at York University, where he directs the Koschitzky Centre for Jewish Studies. He is the author of *Jewish People, Yiddish Nation: Noah Prylucki and the Folkists in Poland* and coeditor of *Key Concepts in the Study of Antisemitism* (with Sol Goldberg and Scott Ury).

Index

Note: Page numbers appearing in *italics* refer to figures.

Abolition of the State, The (Engländer), 161
Abramson, Israel, 424
Abyssinia/Ethiopia, 59–61, 64, 72n28
acculturation: of Hungarian Jews, 171–73, 181, 187; of Jews in Odessa, 356–57, 366–67; of Spivakoff, 350; women's role in Jewish, 227–28, 236n3. *See also* assimilation
Achtundvierzigerplatz ('48er Square), 151, 154, 162
activism, traditional or religious, 93, 100n45
ad hoc courts, 124–25, 128, 140n18, 140n20
afterlife and martyrdom, 34, 37–38, 39, 51n52, 52n56, 53n59
agency: of Jewish refugees, 301–2, 304, 305; and Steinberg's ethical socialist revolutionary ideal, 322
agents, in Jewish small claims courts, 130–32, 143nn45–47
Agudas Yisroel, 246, 336
Ahasuerus, 88
Akiva, Rabbi, 37, 386, 412
Aleksiun, Natalia, 423
Alexander I, Tsar, 88, 92
Alexander II, Tsar, 93, 99n41, 203, 221n24, 359
Alexander III, Tsar, 100n47
Almi, A., 336

Alphabet of Sirach, 108
Alter, Viktor, 129, 132–36, 379
Altona, 122, 126, 136. *See also* Jewish courts
Altri, Crescenzo, 432, 444n79
American Jewish Joint Distribution Committee (the Joint), 296, 300–301, 303, 306, 383
anarchism, 161, 317, 318–19, 343n76
An-sky, S., 88–89, 101, 102
antisemitism: Bick on, 335; blood accusations against Jews, 179, 429–30, 433–34, 443n67; Blumenfeld on, 428–29; Ehrenburg on, 378; etiological function of, 201–3, 219n18; experienced by Birnbaum in Germany, 248; influence on Jewish history, 430–31; and Jewish involvement in Revolutions of 1848, 151; and Jewish migration, 201–2, 293; Jewish studies and responding to, 420–21; Judeo-centrism in modern imagery of, 92; Marxist understanding of, 383; in Odessa, 358; of Polish National Party, 428; during post-WWII period, 281; response to nineteenth-century, 423–24; Roth on, 429; in Shneiderman and Ehrenburg works, 376; Shneiderman on connection through, 382; Stanislawski and new historiography of, 3–5, 7;

antisemitism (*continued*)
and state protection in Subcarpathian Rus', 179–80; Traverso on, 217n4; WWI-era, 234; and Zionism in *Autoemancipation*, 203–9, 213–16. See also Holocaust; Jew hatred (*Judenhass*); Judeophobia
archives, and nature of truth, 68
Arendt, Hannah, 273
Aschheim, Steven, 239n46
Ashkenization, 30, 38
Ashton, Rosemary, 150
Asi, Rav, 330
assimilation: Polish National Party's position on Jewish, 428; Stanislawski on, 6, 348. See also acculturation
Association for Jewish Studies (AJS), 419–20, 421, 427, 435–36
Auerbach, Elias, 228
Auslandsdeutsche, 248, 249, 260
Austria, 150–62, 227, 296
Autobiographical Jews (Stanislawski), 7, 69n3, 369n12, 390n7
Autoemancipation (Pinsker), 203–16, 217n9, 220n24
"Awake, My People!" (Gordon), 1–2, 22n1, 419
Azaryahu, Moaz, 403

Babel, Isaac, 375
Babylon, 61, 62–63
Bad Gastein DP camp, 298, 299
Badia affair, 429–30
Baer, Yitzhak, 425
Bak, Nissan, 89
Bakunin, Mikhail, 221n24
Balfour Declaration (1917), 227, 269, 352, 363, 364
Bar, Doron, 408
Barbi, Meir, 183
Baron, Salo W.: on conception of Jewish history, 3–4, 22n4, 422, 425–26; on danger facing Jews in interwar period,

270; on detachment of Jewish life, 435; on Jewish emancipation, 223n36; on Jewish postwar, 272, 281–82; on Revolutions of 1848, 151, 155, 423, 441n43; scholarship of, 425–27; Stanislawski and, 3–4, 22n4
Bartal, Israel, 219n18
Bartha, Miklós, 176–77
Basnage, Jacques, 57
Bauernfeld, Eduard von, 154
Becher, Alfred Julius, 154
Begin, Menachem, 406, 412
Beilis affair, 430
beit tifleh, 62, 73n38
Belsky, Natalie, 384
Ben-Gurion, David, 269, 271, 275, 278, 279, 405, 406, 411–12, 413
Benvenisti, Meron, 410
Beranek, Franz, 261
Bereg Megyei Izraelita Magyar Egylet (The Bereg County Magyar Society), 191–92
Bereg Megyei Izraelita Magyar Nőegylet (Bereg County Jewish Women's Aid Society), 182
Bergelson, Dovid, 379, 380
Berger, Anna, 194n2
Berkovitz, Jay, 125, 142n35, 143n45
Bernfeld, Isaac, 423
Ber of Bolechów (Birkenthal, Dov Ber), 55–69, 72n28, 184–85
Bershadskii, Sergei, 430
bet din zuta, 126, 128–30. See also Jewish courts
Bialik, Hayim Nahman, 365, 386–87
Bible: biblical purism, 365–66; and *Shalosh Nashim* incantation, 110–12
Bick, Abraham, 323, 328–35, 336
Bidermann, Hermann, 177
Bikhovsky, Rabbi Haim Eliezer, 99n41
Biltmore Conference (1942), 274, 275, 279
biography: of Judah Leib Gordon, 5; as "objective" source of truth, 390n7;

Stanislawski's work on Jewish, 7. See also *Ilye Erenburg* (Shneiderman)
Birnbaum, Irene, 247–48, 253
Birnbaum, Nathan, 244, 245, 255, 256, 257, 259–60
Birnbaum, Solomon (Salomo): background of, 242; and fund-raising for *Nebenspracheninstitut*, 252–56; on Jewishness as ethnicity, 251, 263n27; and Kloss's plans for German-Yiddish alliance, 241, 249, 250–51; plans for *Institutum Ascenezicum*, 256–59; work and studies in Yiddish, 244–48
"Black Aliyah" / "Black Alijah," 294
Black Book, The, 379–80, 393n26
Blondheim, David, 217n9
blood libels, 179, 429–30, 433–34, 443n67
Blumenfeld, Samuel, 428–29
Bolshevism/Bolsheviks, 319, 320, 321, 325, 331, 363–64
Borchling, Conrad, 245–46
borders, fluctuating, 167–69, 194n1
Bornstein, Yasha (Jacob), 362–63
Botero, Giovanni, 59–61, 64, 72n28
Bourke, Joanna, 227
Bozóky, Edina, 106, 112
Brafman, Iacov, 432
Brawer, Abraham Ya'akov, 56–57, 69n2
Brazil, as emigration destination, 299–300, 310n17
Brenner, Michael, 430, 433
Brihah, 295–96
Brimelow, Thomas, 302
British Western Wall Committee, 401
Buber, Martin, 83, 228
Buchheim, Adolf, 152, 155, 156, 158, 159

Cahan, Abraham, 337n1
Calkins, Fay, 298
Camarilla, 153. *See also* Revolutions of 1848
Cang, Joel, 428
capitalism, 330
Castilliero, Giuditta, 429–30

Catherine the Great, Empress, 84, 356
Central Committee of Radical Clubs (Central-Comité der radikalen Vereine), 154
Chaisés, Adolf, 152, 153, 154, 155, 156, 158
charity, 49n34, 132, 135, 138, 333
Christianity, as idolatry, 39, 52n59
Christianization, of *Yeven mezulah* Yiddish translation, 38, 39–40, 41
Christians, Birkenthal and Jewish debates against, 56, 57–58, 63, 64–66, 67
Chronicle of Higher Education, 438n12
circumcision, 60, 107–8
civilization, William Nathanson's duality of culture and, 324–25
Clark, Mark W., 296–97
clock time, Birkenthal's references to, 67
Cohen, Gerson, 51n50
Cohen, Morris, 427
Cohen-Hattab, Kobi, 408
commerce: disputes in Jewish courts, 132–33; Hungarian Jewish community and economic activity, 171, 175–79
conscription: into Hungarian National Guard, 188, 200n68; into Russian army, 88, 93
consumerism, 228, 230
contract disputes, 133–36, 142n34
Coram iudicio (Kleyn), 56
Cosby, Bill, 390n7
cosmopolitanism, 217n4, 318, 388
Cossacks. *See Yeven mezulah* (Hannover)
Council of Four Lands, abolishment of, 79, 96n8
Council of Jewish Relations, 427
courts. *See* Jewish courts
Culture and Civilization (Nathanson), 324, 326
Cyrus, 62
Czechoslovakia: ethnic Germans in, 277; fluctuating borders of, 167–69, 194n1; Jewish refugees in, 294, 295–96. *See also* Munkács; Ungvár

Dat ve-Avodah (Religion and Labor), 329
David, King, 63, 87, 401
Dawidowicz, Jehuda Leib, 360–61
Dayan, Moshe, 411
death, blamed on evil eye, 102
Dehmel, Richard, 232
De Medicamentis (Marcellus Empiricus), 106, 113
demonopathy, Judeophobia as form of, 206
Der Radikale (The Radical), 152–53
Der Salon (Sunday Papers), 152
Derzhavin, Gavrila, 360
destruction, literature of, 214
detachment, in Jewish studies, 435–37, 438nn12–13
Deutsch, David, 183
Deutsch, Simon, 152, 153–54, 155–56, 158, 159–61
Deutsche und Jidden (Kloss), 249, 251, 252
Dinur, Ben-Zion, 348, 425
Dionisopoulos-Mass, Regina, 105
displaced persons (DP) camps, 290–91, 296, 298, 299, 301–6. *See also* Jewish refugees / displaced people
Displaced Persons Act (1948), 292
Dita Saxová (Lustig), 294
Divrei binah (Birkenthal), 55, 56, 57, 65–66, 69n2
Doctors' Plot (1953), 383
domestic service, contract disputes concerning, 133–35, 137, 142n34
Don-Yehiya, Eliezer, 413
Dorfjuden (village Jews), 175
Dov Ber Schneur (Mitteler Rebbe), 85–86
Dreyfus affair, 204, 424
Dubnow, Simon, 95, 96n11, 98n27, 101, 269–70, 322–23, 347, 348
Dundes, Alan, 105, 113
Du Toit, M. L., 255
Dynner, Glenn, 181

East-Central Europe: fluctuating borders of, 167–69, 194n1; following World War I, 192–93, 194n5. *See also* Czechoslovakia; Hungary; Subcarpathian Rus'
Eastern European Jews: encounter with modern state on Yiddish culture and language, 388; experience of, preceding WWII, 270; '48ers (Jewish revolutionaries), 150–62; German Jews' encounters with, 230–36, 239n46; and Holocaust, 274–76, 277; memoirs of, 349–55; and predicted postwar Jewish refugee problem, 272–74, 277–78; secularizing influences on, 235; Stanislawski's study of history of, 347. *See also* Ehrenburg, Ilya; Hungary; Odessa; Spivakoff, Isaac Ze'ev
Eber, Irene, 289
Edict of Tolerance (1782), 80
Edom, 36, 50n48
education, advocacy for changes to Hungarian Jewish, 187–89
Eeghen, I. H. Van, 46n13
Egan, Ede, 176
Ehrenburg, Ilya, 374, 387–89; confers with Shneiderman at International Congress for the Defense of Culture, 394n45; connection between Shneiderman and, 375–76; early life of, 376–82; on Holocaust, 393n27; on Jews in Red Army, 395n51; Shneiderman's defense of, 382–87; Shneiderman's relationship with, 393n30; Tuwim and, 384–85. See also *Ilye Erenburg* (Shneiderman)
Einhorn, Edward, 187
Einsatzstab Reichsleiter Rosenberg, 260
Eisenstadter, Meir (MaHaRam Eysh), 182–83, 184, 185, 189–90
Eisenstadter, Menachem, 183
Elijah, prophet, 105, 114

Elimelekh, son of King Solomon, 61
emancipation, 209, 211–13, 215, 223n36.
  See also *Autoemancipation* (Pinsker)
emigráció, 149–62
emigration. See *emigráció*; Jewish
  refugees / displaced people
Endeks (Polish National Party), 428
enemies, forgiveness for, 40–41, 48n30,
  54n68
Engel, David, 426
Engels, Friedrich, 157, 158, 341n54
Engländer, Sigmund, 152, 155, 156,
  157–58, 161–62
Eötvös, Károly, 179, 198n38
Erlich, Henryk, 379
Erlich, Victor, 323, 383–84
Eshkol, Levi, 407
Ettinger, Shmuel, 348
Eulenberg, Herbert, 233
evil eye, 102–3, 105. See also *Shalosh
  Nashim* incantation
Evreiskaia Biblioteka, 432–33
Evreiskaia Starina, 430, 432–33

Face of East European Jewry (Zweig),
  234–35
Fanheim, Hirsch, 134
Fates, the, 106, 108, 118n46
Fefer, Itsik, 379, 380
Feldstein, Ariel, 406
Fényes, Elek, 173
Feuer, Hirsch, 134–35
Fine, David J., 229
First World War. See World War I
Fischhof, Adolf, 155
Fisher, Leon, 304
Fishman, Fanya, 394n42
Flaiszer, Jacob (Jacob Talmon), 271–72,
  279
Foner, Eric, 439n13
forgiveness, in *Yeven mezulah*, 40–41,
  48n30, 54n68
formalism, Jewish national, 321–22

Forty-eighters (German émigrés), 150
'48ers (Jewish revolutionaries), 150–62
"For Whom Do I Toil?" (Gordon), 419
For Whom Do I Toil? (Stanislawksi), 5
Franco-German communist plot, 158
Frank, Jacob, 56
Frankel, Jonathan, 219n18, 348
Frankl, Ludwig August, 151, 152, 158,
  159
Franz I, Emperor, 94
Franz Joseph, Emperor, 94, 159, 200n68
"Freeland" movement, 322
Free Writings (*Fraye shriftn*), 321, 323,
  329
Freitag, Sabine, 150
French workers' movement, Engländer's
  history of, 161
Frevert, Ute, 229
Friedemann, Adolf, 231
Fuks, Lajb, 46n14
Fuks-Mansfeld, Renate, 46n14
*Fundamental Principles of Religious
  Socialism* (Bick), 329–34

Gamarnik, Jan, 365
Ganganelli, Lorenzo, 434
Gans, Eduard, 430–31
Ganzfried, Solomon, 184
genocide, 276. See also Holocaust
German language: learned by Birkenthal,
  58; Pinsker writes in, 209–10
Germany: émigrés from, 150; Franco-
  German communist plot, 158;
  Greater Germany, 151–52; history of
  Yiddish research in, 243–48; impact
  of First World War in, 227–28;
  invasion of Soviet Union, 379; Jewish
  historiography on, 430, 432–33;
  Jewish refugees in, 296, 305; military
  service of Jews during WWI, 228–29.
  See also Yiddish chair, project to
  establish Germany's first
German-Yiddish alliance, 248–51

gezerah (decree), 49n34
Gilman, Sander L., 220n22
Gintsburg, Mordekhai Aharon, 351, 369n16
Goldman, Nahum, 269, 276, 279
Gordon, David, 221n26
Gordon, Judah Leib, 1–2, 5, 6, 7, 22n1, 368, 419, 435
Goren, Rabbi Shlomo, 408
Gottesman, Abraham, 183
Gottlober, Abraham Ber, 79, 80, 92–93, 362
Gottlober-Bornstein, Sofia, 362
Gotzmann, Andreas, 123, 136, 142n35, 144n67
goy, 222n28
Grady, Tim, 229
Graetz, Heinrich, 214, 433
Great Britain: as destination for Austrian fugitives, 157; Jewish historiography in, 434–35; and pre-WWII Zionist enterprise, 270–71; White Paper (1939), 271, 278, 284n18
Greater Germany, 151–52
Great Migration, 202
Greek community, tensions between Jews and, in Odessa, 358
Greek Orthodox, 33, 34–35, 36, 40, 48n30, 52n59, 180
Greenberg, Irving "Yitz," 420, 436
Gronemann, Sammy, 232–33
Grossman, Vasily, 376, 379–80
Grossmann, Atina, 291, 297, 302
Gruenbaum, Yitzhak, 272–73, 402–3
Grunwald, Yekutiel, 175
Güdeman, Moritz, 107
Guide for the Perplexed (Maimonides), 47n19
Gurland, Ḥayim Yonah, 365

Ha'am, Ahad, 213, 359
Habsburg neoabsolutism, 187
Hadarshan, David ben Manasseh, 52n59

Hahn, Seligman, 142n34
Haim of Kosov, 94
"Hakir vehahar" (Yehoshua), 399
HaKohen, Rabbi Shabbetai ben Meir, 108
Halberstadt, R. Joel, 130
Haman, 49n36, 88
Hammer, Jill, 118n42
Handlerjuden, 176
Hannover, Nathan Neta, 30–31, 33. See also *Yeven meẓulah* (Hannover)
Ha-Po'el Ha-Mizrahi movement, 329, 336
Hapo'el Haẓa'ir, 400
Harrison, Earl G., 303
Hartmann, Moritz, 152, 155, 156, 157, 158–59
Hasidism: controversy between Mitnagdim and, 82; in Munkács, 185, 186–87; opponents of, 90; worldview of, 91; Schneur Zalman on background of growth of, 84–85. See also meetings between Hasidic and secular leaders, tales of
Haskalah (Jewish Enlightenment), 1–2, 4, 19, 246, 347, 348, 350–52, 362, 366
Haskell, Thomas, 426
Ha-ẓefirah (Spivakoff), 362
Hausjuden, 176
Hazanovitch, Joseph, 365
Ha-ẓava (Army Day, Israel), 405
Hebrew / Hebrew texts: Nathanson on teaching, 328; in Odessa, 358; significance of, 32; Spivakoff's use of, 350, 355
Hebrew Immigrant Aid Society (HIAS), 294–95, 299, 300, 302, 307
Hebrew nationalism, 358
Helfert, Joseph Alexander von, 154–55
Heller, Rabbi Zvi Hirsch, 198n50
Helmers, Helmer, 50n42
Herodotus, 61, 66
heroism, Jewish, 386–87, 395n51
Herzl, Hans, 406
Herzl, Pauline, 406

Herzl, Theodor, 7, 204, 219n15, 400, 402–3, 404, 405–6, 411–12. *See also* Mount Herzl
Herzl, Trude, 406
Herzl Day, 405, 412–13
Herzl Law (2004), 412–13
Herzl Museum, 405, 412
hesped, 373, 387
Hess, Moses, 158
Hezekiah, 112
Highlands Commission (Hegyvidéki akció), 176
Histories of the Latin and Germanic Peoples (Ranke), 421–22
historiography. *See* Jewish historiography
historiola, 106
Hitler, Adolf, 16, 241, 258, 260, 261, 270, 275, 278, 281, 378, 379, 387, 428
Hitler-Stalin Pact, 379
Hofshteyn, Dovid, 380
Holland Institute, 252, 255
Holle, Frau, 107–8, 118n42
Hollekreisch/holekrash, 107–8
Holocaust, 272, 274–77, 280–81, 282, 376, 379–80, 393n27, 413
Homo faber, 325
Hopstein, Israel (Maggid of Kozhniẓ), 103
Horowitz, Brian, 423
Horowitz, Shemuel Shmelke Halevi, 103
House Committee on Un-American Activities, 335
housing, for Jewish refugees, 302–3
Howard, John, 107
Howe, Irving, 340n31
Hungarian National Guard, 188, 200n68
Hungary: antisemitism and state protection of Jews in, 179–80; competing traditionalist outlooks in, 180–85; émigrés from, 149–50, 294–95, 298–99; following World War I, 192–93, 194n5; Jewish economic activity in, 171, 175–79; and Jewish migration, 173–74, 176–77, 294–95; and Jewish national consciousness, 169–72; Magyarization of Jews in, 171–73, 176, 181, 185–92; *numerus clausus* law (1920), 312n43
husband, separation of wife and, 39–40

Iberian peninsula, antisemitism in, 429, 443n61
iconography, 7
idolatry, 39, 51n50, 52n59
Iggers, Georg G., 422
illness, blamed on evil eye, 102, 105
Il Vessillo Israelitico, 432, 443n67, 445n84, 445n98
Ilye Erenburg (Shneiderman), 374–75, 380–89
imagination, Kook on, 332–33
Immigration Act (1924), 291–92, 298
incantations. *See Shalosh Nashim* incantation
Informationsbüro (Bureau of Information, Austria), 151
Institute for Germans Abroad (Deutsches Ausland-Institut, DAI), 248–49
Institute of Jewish Affairs, 268, 275–76, 277
Institute on Peace and Postwar Problems, 268
Institut far Yidisher Bildung (Institute for Jewish Education), 334
Institutum Ascenezicum, 256–59
International Congress for the Defense of Culture, 394n45
International Red Cross, 299
International Refugee Organization (IRO), 297–98
International Workingmen's Association, 158
"In the City of Slaughter" (Bialik), 386
Israel, State of, 280–81, 282, 292, 306, 307, 399–414
Israel Ba'al Shem Tov (the Besht), 92

Israel Friedman of Ruzhin, Rabbi, 81, 86–91
Israel of Koznicz, 93–94
Isserles, Moses, 108
Istóczy, Viktor, 179
Italy: blood libels in, 429–30; Jewish historiography in, 431, 432, 434–35; and Jewish migration, 299, 300, 301
Ivan (Hungarian Jewish war orphan), 298–99

Jabotinsky, Vladimir (Ze'ev), 7, 348, 360, 406–7
jealousy, 102
Jellinek, Hermann, 154, 155, 156
Jerusalem. *See* Old City of Jerusalem
Jerusalem Day (Yom Yerushalayim), 408
Jesus of Nazareth, Birkenthal on, 64
Jew hatred (*Judenhass*), 205, 207–8, 211–12, 215, 216. *See also* antisemitism; Judeophobia
Jewish Agency for Palestine, 279, 303
Jewish Anti-Fascist Committee (JAFC), 373, 379–80, 382, 386, 394n38
Jewish authenticity, gendering of, 229–30
Jewish Chronicle, 435
Jewish collective identity, 282
Jewish courts, 121–24, 136–38; agents in, 130–32, 143nn45–47; business disputes in, 132–33; contract disputes in, 133–36, 142n34; logistics of, 128–30; records of, 126–28, 137; standing courts versus ad hoc courts, 124–25
Jewish Currents, 373–74, 388–89
Jewish Diaspora. *See* Jewish refugees / displaced people
Jewish Enlightenment (Haskalah), 1–2, 4, 347, 348
Jewish equality, postwar, 277, 282
Jewish ethnography, Spivakoff as preserving literary tradition of, 354–55

Jewish heroism, 386–87, 395n51
Jewish Historical Society of England, 424
Jewish historiography, objectivity and early years of, 421–29. *See also* Jewish studies
Jewish national consciousness, 169–72
Jewish national formalism, 321–22
Jewish nationalism: and ethnoreligious tensions in Odessa, 357–58; Western Wall as icon of, 400–401. *See also* Zionism
Jewish patriarchs, Struck's idealization of, 230–31, 235
Jewish politics, emergence of, 4–5
Jewish postwar, 267, 280–82; abandonment of early wartime visions for, 277–80; early wartime planning for, 267–69; historical framework shaping thinking about, 268–72; Holocaust's impact on visions for, 274–77; Jewish refugees in, 272–74, 277–78. *See also* Jewish refugees / displaced people
Jewish postwar planning institutes, 268
Jewish psyche, Judeophobia's impact on, 220n23
Jewish refugees / displaced people, 289–94, 308; in Czechoslovakia, 295–96; in DP camps, 301–6; in Germany and Austria, 296; from Hungary, 294–95; and Jewish postwar visions, 272–74, 277–78; repatriation of, 297; resettlement of, 296–301, 306–8
Jewish religious socialism. *See* Yiddish religious socialism
Jewish Social Studies, 427–29
Jewish sovereignty: first argument for restoration of, 203, 218n10; following Roman defeat, 62–63. *See also Autoemancipation* (Pinsker); emancipation; Zionism
Jewish studies, 345–46, 419–21; antisemitism's influence on, 430–31;

connection between past and present in, 429–30; detachment in, 435–37, 438nn12–13. *See also* Jewish historiography
Jewish tradition, gendering of, during First World War, 227–36
Jidde, 250–51, 263n25
Jobbaszty, Gyula, 182
Johnson-Reed Act (1924), 291–92, 298
Jopson, Norman, 259
Joseph, and *Shalosh Nashim* incantation, 110–11
Joseph II, 78–81, 96n11, 97n13
Josephus Flavius, 61
Joskowicz, Ari, 297–98
journalists, and Revolutions of 1848, 152–62
Judenhass. *See* Jew hatred (*Judenhass*)
Judeo-Bolshevism, 151
Judeo-centrism, in tales of meetings between Hasidic and secular leaders, 92
Judeophobia, 151, 205–9, 212, 215, 219n19, 220n22, 220n23. *See also* antisemitism; *Judenhass* (Jew hatred)
Judt, Tony, 267
Jung, Jacqueline, 434

Kaplan, Eliezer, 406
Kav ha-yashar (Koidanover), 51n52
Kertbeny, K. M., 149–50
Khmelnytsky, Bogdan, and Khmelnytsky massacres (1648–1649), 30, 40–41, 54n68. See also *Yeven meẓulah* (Hannover)
Kielce pogrom (1946), 277
Kishinev pogrom (1903), 354, 386
Klarwein, Ossip (Yosef), 404
Klausner, Yosef, 359, 365, 370n37
Kleyn, Franciszek, 56
Klier, John, 23n7
Kloss, Heinz: background of, 242; as Birnbaum's partner, 259–60; and Birnbaum's plans for *Institutum Ascenezicum*, 257–59; and fundraising for *Nebenspracheninstitut*, 252–56; plans for German-Yiddish alliance, 241, 248–51; on racial and class bonds, 263n22; use of Yiddish scholarship, 260–61
Kobrin, Rebecca, 292
Koidanover, Zevi Hirsch, 51n52
Kolisch, Sigmund, 152, 155, 156, 157, 158, 159
Kollek, Teddy, 410
Konrád, Miklós, 191
Kook, Rav Abraham Isaac, 329, 332–33
Kornjuden, 176
Koselleck, Reinhart, 67
Kotel (Western Wall), 399–401, 407–11, 413–14, 418n43
Kryvonis, Maksym, 49n36
Kvitko, Leib, 380

language learning, Birkenthal and, 57–58, 64, 65, 68
Lattek, Christine, 150
lay court, 128–29, 145n74. *See also* Jewish courts
Lazare, Bernard, 424
Lazarus and the rich man, 37–38
L'Educatore Israelita, 426, 429–30, 431–32
Leff, Lisa, 434
Left Social Revolutionaries (LSRs), 320
Leibowitz, Yeshayahu, 410
Leib Surehs, 78–81, 95n5, 96n11, 97nn12–13
Lemkin, Raphael, 276
Lestschinsky, Jacob, 257, 276, 285n36, 286nn37–38
Letter of Rabbi Samuel, 64
Levy, Raphaël, 424
libraries, and nature of truth, 68
Lichtheim, Richard, 275
Liebes, Yehuda, 52n58
Liebman, Charles, 413
Lilien, Ephraim, 228, 400

Lilienblum, Moshe Leib, 205, 218n10, 219n20, 351, 356, 359
Lilith, 11, 107, 108, 114, 117n38, 118n40
Lindemann, Mary, 137
liquid, and *Shalosh Nashim* incantation, 105–6, 107, 111–13
literature of destruction, 214
Litt, Stefan, 142n40
lived time, 291
Lombroso, Cesare, 220n23
lottery drawings, 132–33
"Lovers of Zion," 203
Löw, Eleazar, 186
Löwy, Michel, 318
Ludendorf, Erich, 233
Luria, Rabbi Isaac, 38, 52n57
Lustig, Arnošt, 294
Luther, Martin, 40

Maccabees, 386–87
Maggid of Kozhniz (Israel Hopstein), 103
Magi, 60–61
magical charms and remedies, 101–2. See also *Shalosh Nashim* incantation
Magyarization of Hungarian Jews, 171–73, 176, 181, 185–92, 195n7
Magyar language, 189–92
maidservants, contract disputes concerning, 133–35, 137, 142n34
Maimonides, Moses, 47n19, 190
malkhut, 111–12
mamlakhtiyut, 411, 413
Marcellus Empiricus (Marcellus of Bordeaux), 106, 113
March Revolution (1848), 150–51
Markel-Mosessohn, Miriam, 22n1
Markish, Esther, 384
Markish, Peretz, 380
marriage, and separation of husband and wife, 39–40
martyrdom: Rabbi Samson on, 52n58; redefinition of Jewish, 52n59; in *Yeven mezulah*, 37–40, 52n54, 52n56

Marx, Karl, 157, 158, 220n24, 330, 331–32, 341n54
Marxism, 202, 324, 325, 332, 335, 383
masculinity: and gendering of Jewish tradition during WWI, 227–29; and reification of older Jewish men, 235
maskilim, 90. See also Spivakoff, Isaac Ze'ev
materialism, 228, 230, 324, 331, 332–33
Mazat-mizvah va-alilat ha-dam (Rodkinson), 430
Mechnikov, Ilya, 366–67, 371n50
meetings between Hasidic and secular leaders, tales of, 77–78, 92–95; Rabbi Israel of Ruzhin and Tsar Nicholas I, 86–91; Rabbi Schneur Zalman of Lyady and Tsar Paul I, 82–86; Leib Surehs and Emperor Joseph II, 78–81, 96n11
Meir, Golda, 383
Melilah, 60
Meltzer, Shimson, 95n5, 97n12
Memoirs (Birkenthal), 55–69
Mendel, Menachem, 86, 87, 186
Mendelssohn, Moses, 22n1, 223n36
Merder fun felker (Murderer of Peoples), 380
messianism, 10, 55, 56, 64, 88, 318, 319
Michelet, Jules, 156–57
Mickiewicz, Adam, 362–63
microcredit court cases, 132
Mikhoels, Solomon, 379, 380
military service: German, during WWI, 228–29; Hungarian conscription into, 188, 200n68
Mindel, Rabbi Nissan, 91
Minkowski, Eugène, 290
minority rights, 275–77
Miriam's Well, 111–12
Miron, Guy, 291
Mitnagdim, controversy between Hasidism and, 82
Mitteler Rebbe (Dov Ber Schneuri), 85–86

Möbeljuden, 176
Moinier, Auguste, 433–34
Mondshine, Yehoshua, 84
Montefiore, Moses, 89
months, Birkenthal's translation of names of, 60, 62, 66–67
Mordechai of Kuzmir, 100n47
Morgen Frayhayt, 334–35
Morrison-Grady scheme, 279
Moses ben Aaron, 46n14
Moses ben Abraham, 31, 32, 34, 45n10, 46n11, 46n14, 51n52. See also *Yeven mezulah* (Hannover)
Mount Herzl, 399, 402–7, 412–14
Mount Sinai, 323
Munkács, 167; antisemitism and state protection of Jews in, 179–80; as case study in development of national consciousness, 169; competing traditionalist outlooks in, 180–85; following World War I, 192–93; Hasidism in, 171; Jewish economic activity in, 171, 175–79; Jewish immigrants in, 173–74, 176–77; Magyarization of Jews in, 171–73, 176, 181, 185–92
Munkács and Ungvár Commercial Association, 178
Murder in Lemberg, A (Stanislawski), 6
mursheh, 130–32, 143nn45–47
Myers, David, 420, 425

Nahmanides, 51n52
Nahman of Bratslav, Rabbi, 80, 92
Nahsprachen, 250
Nahspracheninstitut. See *Nebenspracheninstitut*
Naimark, Norman, 267
names, Prussian restrictions concerning, 433
Namier, Lewis, 270
Napoleonic wars, 85
Nathan of Nemirov, 96n10
Nathanson, William, 324–28, 336
national consciousness. See Jewish national consciousness
National Education Fund Act (1851), 187–88
"National-Poetic Rebirth of the Jewish Religion, The" (Zhitlovsky), 326–27
Natt, Hugo, 231
Nazi regime, 260–61, 272, 304–5, 428–29. See also Holocaust; Jewish postwar; Jewish refugees / displaced people
Nebensprache, 250
Nebenspracheninstitut, 252–56, 257–58, 260
nefesh (soul), 39
Neolog Judaism, 185–87, 195n9
neosocialism, 325–26, 336
Nevakhovich, Yehudah Leib, 366
New and Old Testament Connected in the History of the Jews, The (Prideaux), 59, 61–63, 66, 72n31
New Ottomans, 160
New Russia, 356, 360
Nicholas I, Tsar, 81, 86–91, 93, 99n41, 200n68, 347, 354
Niemirów, Cossack attack on, 38, 52n54
Nister, Der, 391n12
No Masters but God (Rothman), 343n76
nonviolence, rabbinic, 6
Nordmann, Johann(es), 158–59
Novick, Peter, 420

oaths, 129
objectivity: and early years of Jewish historiography, 421–29; in Jewish studies, 420–21
Ochakov, 359–60
October Revolution (1848), 154, 155–56, 352, 363
Odessa, 346; acculturation of Jews in, 356–57; cultural mixing in, 361–63; history of, 356; perception versus reality of, 355–56; prerevolutionary

Odessa (*continued*)
  period in, 363–64; Spivakoff on, 349; Spivakoff's encounters in, 364–67; Spivakoff's identification with, 359–61; Spivakoff's life in, 352, 353; Stanislawski's study of Jews in, 347; tensions between Jews and Gentile neighbors in, 357–58
Odessa group, 359, 361
Odile, St., 109
Old City of Jerusalem: Herzl on, 400; Russian land purchases in, 89–90. *See also* Mount Herzl; Western Wall (Kotel)
Oliel-Grausz, Evelyne, 121–22
Operation Herzl, 403
Ophir, Adi, 222n28
optimism, about Jewish postwar, 268–70, 272
Oriental Seminar, 255–56
Orshanskii, Ilya, 433
Orthodox Judaism: Bick on, 333–34; in Ungvár, 185–87
Ortner, Henry, 307
Ostjuden, 177, 179, 229, 251, 254–55

Palestine, 270–71, 273, 278–80, 306, 308. *See also* Zionism
Palestine labor movement, 336
Paradise, 37–38, 51n52
Paraguay, 300
Paris, as destination for Austrian fugitives, 156–57
Paris Commune (1871), 160
Paris Conference (1946), 278–79
Paris Peace Conference (1919), 269
Patt, Avinoam, 307–8
Paul I, Tsar, 82–86
Paul IV, Pope, 432
Penslar, Derek, 219n15
Peretz, Y. L., 370n26
periodization, 352
Phillipson, Ludwig, 431

Phoebus, Uri, 31, 47n17
piano(s), Bolshevik confiscation of, 364
Pikulski, Gaudenty, 56
pinkas takanot, 140n20, 144n64
Pinsker, L. S., 203–16, 217n9, 220n22, 220n24, 222n28
Plater, Wladyslaw, 160
Podolia, 56
pogroms, 277, 354, 358. *See also* Holocaust
"point system," in DP camps, 304
Polish, learned by Birkenthal, 57–58, 65, 68
Polish Jews, encounters with Soviet Jews, 375–76, 384
Polish National Party (Endeks), 428
Polish writing, 362–63
political clubs, and Jewish involvement in Revolutions of 1848, 153–54
Polnischer Rabbiner (Struck), 231
Poniatowski, Stanisław August, 79, 96n8, 98n20
Poskrebyshev, Alexander N., 382
Posner, Samuel, 134
postwar. *See* Jewish postwar
poverty: and Orthodoxy, 334; and Russian Jews' immigration to America, 201
Pravda, 383
Pressburg Orthodoxy, 183
Prester John, 59–60, 72n28
Prideaux, Humphrey, 59, 61–63, 66, 72n31
Proudhon, Pierre-Joseph, 161–62
Pulszky, Ferenc, 157
Pushkin, Alexander, 360, 361

rabbinic court, 128–29. *See also* Jewish courts
rabbinic nonviolence, 6
Rabbi Samuel (Radliński), 63–64
Rabin, Yitzhak, 6, 407, 412, 414, 416n28
Radliński, Jakub, 63–64

Rahel (Struck), 233
Rákóczi family, 174
Rakovsky, Puah, 391n12
Ranke, Leopold von, 421–22, 425–26, 439n13
Rapoport, Ḥayim, 56
Rappoport, Samuel, 109
Rashi, 39, 110, 428–29
Rath, R. John, 153
rebbes. *See* meetings between Hasidic and secular leaders, tales of
Rechtman, Avrom, 110
Reconstruction scholarship, 439n13
Red Star, 379
Reinach, Joseph, 424, 433
Reinach, Theodore, 424
Reinberger, Aaron, 192
Relazioni Universali (Botero), 59–61, 64, 72n28
religiosity, 230, 319, 326, 327
representatives, in Jewish small claims courts, 130–32, 143nn45–47
Reuter, Paul Julius, 158
revenge, in *Yeven meẓulah*, 40–41, 48n30, 54n68
Revolutions of 1848, 150–62, 352, 363, 423, 441n43
Revue des études juives, 424, 430
rhyme, in Yiddish literature, 32–33
Ringelblum, Emanuel, 423
Ritual Murder and the Jew (Roth), 434
Rivlin, Reuven, 414
Robinson, Jacob, 273, 275, 276, 278
Rodkinson, Michael Levi, 78–79, 82–83, 430
Rolinek, Susanne, 296
Roma refugees, 297–98
Rosen-Zvi, Ishay, 222n28
Rosenzweig, Franz, 231–32
Roskies, David, 214
Roth, Cecil, 429, 434, 435
Roth, Philip, 390n7
Rothman, Hayyim, 343n76

Rubanovich, I. A., 220n24
Rubenstein, Joshua, 378–79, 393n26
Rubinger, David, 408
Ruge, Arnold, 158
Rülf, Rabbi Isaac, 221n26
Ruppin, Arthur, 270
Russian Compound, 90
Russian Empire: prerevolutionary period in, 363–64; in Spivakoff's memoirs, 353–54; Stanislawski's study of Jews in, 347–48. *See also* Odessa

Sabbatean movement, 56, 65–66
Samson ben Pesaḥ, Rabbi, 38, 52nn57–58
Sandel, Samuel, 420
Sattelzeit (saddle time), 67
scarcity, in DP camps, 303–4
Schäfer, Peter, 219n19
Schappes, Morris, 373, 389n2
Schick, Moses, 185
Schiper, Ignacy, 429
Schlesinger, Akiva Yosef, 218n10
Schneur Zalman, Rabbi, 82–86, 99n41
Schonborn family, 174
schools: advocacy for changes to Hungarian Jewish, 188–89; laws concerning, in Hungary, 187–88
Schorsch, Ismar, 433
Schreiber, Reuven ben Zalman, 131
Schutzjuden (protected Jews), 175
Schwabacher, Shimon Aryeh, 365
Schwarzer, Ernest von, 154
Second Aliyah, 333
Second French Republic, 156–57
Second World War. *See* World War II
secularism, socialism and, 317–18
secular leaders. *See* meetings between Hasidic and secular leaders, tales of
Sefer ha-orah (Solomon ben Isaac [Rashi]), 112
Sefer Raziel Ha-malakh, 118n40
sefirah, 111–12
Segel, David, 31

Serebriakova, Galina, 382, 383, 384
servants, contract disputes concerning, 133–35, 137, 142n34
sexuality: and *Shalosh Nashim* incantation, 105–6; Zweig on, 235
Seymour, David, 377
Sha'ar ha-gemul (Naḥmanides), 51n52
Shalosh Nashim incantation, 101, 113–14; biblical verses included in, 110–12; and evil eye, 102–3; medieval antecedents to, 106–10; stone and water in, 112–13; text of, 103–6
shamash, 133, 134, 141n28
Shapira, Anita, 336
Shapira, Shlomo, 184
Shapira, Zvi Elimelech, 183–84
Shapira family, 171, 182–84
Shapiro, David, 254–55
Sharett, Moshe, 406
Sharon, Ariel, 406
Shevet yehudah, Stanislawski's analysis of translation of, 29–30, 41
Sheyris Yisroel, 57
Shlomo, David, 365
Shneiderman, Eileen, 377, *378*
Shneiderman, S. L., 374–75, *378*, 387–89; confers with Ehrenburg at International Congress for the Defense of Culture, 394n45; connection between Ehrenburg and, 375–76; defense of Ehrenburg, 382–87; early life of, 376–82; Ehrenburg's relationship with, 393n30; on Six Day War, 394n34
Shumsky, Dimitry, 219n18
sickness, blamed on evil eye, 102, 105
Silber, Michael K., 218n10
Sinai, 323
Six Day War, 394n34, 407–8, 411
Slansky trial (1952), 383
"Slavery in Freedom" (Ha'am), 213
Slouschz, Naḥum, 355, 370n30, 370n37

small claims courts, 123–24. *See also* Jewish courts
Smolenskin, Perez, 203
Social Democratic movement, 158, 160
social democratic reformism, 321
socialism. *See* Yiddish religious socialism
Socialist Revolutionary Party, 319–20, 325
Société des études juives, 424
Sofer, Chaim, 184, 186
Sofer, Moses, 171, 183, 189, 190–91
Solomon ben Isaac (Rashi), 112
Sonntagsblätter (Sunday Papers), 152
Sophia, St., 109
Sorin, Gerald, 336
Sorkin, David, 282
soul (*nefesh*), 39
sovereignty, Jewish. *See* Jewish sovereignty
Soviet Jews, encounters with Polish Jews, 375–76, 384
Soviet Union: and fluctuating boundaries, 167–69, 194n1; German invasion of, 379; Jews' military enlistment in, 395n51; linguistic assimilation in, 397n66; Spivakoff on, 364; Yiddish writers murdered in, 373–74, 383–84, 388–89. *See also* Czechoslovakia; Hungary
Spivakoff, Isaac Ze'ev, 349–55, 358; and cultural mixing in Odessa, 361–63; identification with Odessa, 359–61; languages spoken by, 349–50, 362; people encountered by, 364–67; on Soviet rule, 364; value of memoir of, 368
Stahl, Rudolf, 428
Stalin, Joseph, 373–74, 379, 380, 383–84, 388–89
standing courts, 124–25
Stanislawski, Michael: analysis of *Shevet yehudah* translation, 29–30, 41; on antisemitism, 3–5; on assimilation, 6;

Autobiographical Jews, 7, 69n3, 369n12, 390n7; on autobiographies and memoirs, 369n12; on Baron, 426–27; career of, 347–48; *For Whom Do I Toil?*, 5; on Gordon's "Awake, My People!," 1–2; on Gordon's "For Whom Do I Toil?," 419; influence on Jewish historians, 7–8; on Jewish enlightenment, 419; *A Murder in Lemberg*, 6; and new historiography of antisemitism, 7; on Russian Jews' immigration to America, 201; themes shaping writings of, 8–9; *Tsar Nicholas I and the Jews*, 3; on Simone Weil, 201–2; work on Jewish biography, 7; on Zionism, 5–6; *Zionism and the Fin de Siècle*, 5–6, 7; *Zionism: A Very Short Introduction*, 6
Starr, Joshua, 429
State of Israel, 280–81, 282, 292, 306, 307, 399–414
statism (*mamlakhtiyut*), 411, 413
Steele, Eric, 124
Steinberg, Aaron, 321
Steinberg, Isaac Naḥman, 319–23, 329, 331
stone, and *Shalosh Nashim* incantation, 112–13
Struck, Herman, 230–31, 232, 233–34, 235
Subcarpathian Rus', 168, 169–72; following World War I, 192–93, 194n5; Jews in, *170*, 171, 176–77. *See also* Hungary
Sumner, William, 102
surplus value, theory of, 330–31
Sutzkever, Avrom, 387
synchronized time, 291
Syrkin, Naḥman, 318
Szajkowski, Zosa, 434
Sziget, 181

Talmon, Jacob (Jacob Flaiszer), 271–72, 279

Tausenau, Karl, 152, 153, 154, 155, 156, 158, 159
Tchernichowsky, Shaul, 365, 366, 371n43, 387
teachers, contract disputes concerning, 135
Teller, Adam, 52n56
temporality: Jewish emigration experience as shaped by, 291, 292; and waiting in DP camps, 301–2. *See also* time
Tenenbaum, Joseph, 269
Thaw, The (Ehrenburg), 380
Theilhaber, Felix, 230
Thierfelder, Franz, 241, 252, 253, 254–55, 256, 257, 258, 261
Thomas, James M., 220n22
three sisters motif, 106–10. *See also Shalosh Nashim* incantation
Tiferet Israel Synagogue, 89
time: in Birkenthal's translations, 60, 62, 66–67; in DP camps, 290, 301–2; lived, 291; standardization of, 66; synchronized, 291. *See also* temporality
Tirosh-Samuelson, Hava, 438
Tiszaeszlár affair, 179, 430, 434, 443n67
Torah, 323, 327, 329–30
Tóth, Heléna, 150
Toward the Revision of National-Radical Thought (Nathanson), 326
traditional activism, 93
trauma, caused by Nazi regime, 304–5
Traverso, Enzo, 217n4
Treaty of Brest-Litovsk (1918), 320
Trevelyan, G. M., 151
Truman, Harry, 279, 292, 298, 299, 303
Tsar Nicholas I and the Jews (Stanislawski), 3
Tsiyon, Linke Poalei, 377
Tuszewicki, Marek, 111
Tuwim, Julian, 384–85
Twersky, Abraham, 93

Ukaz, 84–85
Une erreur judiciaire: La vérité sur l'affaire Dreyfus (Lazare), 424
Une erreur judiciaire sous Louis XIV: Raphaël Levy (Reinach), 424
Ungvár: antisemitism and state protection of Jews in, 179–80; as case study in development of national consciousness, 169; competing traditionalist outlooks in, 180–85; following World War I, 192–93; Jewish economic activity in, 171, 175–79; Jewish immigrants in, 173–74, 176–77; Magyarization of Jews in, 171–73, 176, 181, 185–92; Orthodoxy in, 171
Ungvár Israelite Women's Mutual Sick Aid Society, 182
United Nations Relief and Rehabilitation Administration (UNRRA), 290, 297, 299, 300; Council for Jewish Affairs, 304, 305
United States: and DP camps, 303; as emigration destination, 150, 298–301, 307; Kloss's visit to, 253
United States Military Administration, 303, 305–6
University of Frankfurt, 252
University of Hamburg, 245–46, 247
Ury, Scott, 206
Ushits case, 86–88, 89
Ussher, James, 72n31
uterine pain, 106, 107

Valréas murder libel, 433–34
Veltri, Giuseppe, 106, 107
vengeance, in *Yeven meẓulah*, 40–41, 48n30, 54n68
Verdery, Katherine, 290–91, 303, 309n4
Verein für Cultur und Wissenschaft der Juden, 423, 425, 430–31
"vertical alliance," 444n79
Viennese revolution, 150–62

Vladeck, Baruch Charney, 335–36
Volkov, Shulamit, 425
Volovici, Mark, 220n24, 221n26
Vorontsov, Mikhail, 359, 361
Voskhod, 430, 432–33

Wachnacht, 107–8
Wagner, Richard, 433
Warburg, Otto, 416n18
War of Independence (Israel, 1948), 401, 402
Wasserman, Jacob, 81
wasser-polaken, 173–74
water, and *Shalosh Nashim* incantation, 105–6, 107, 111–13
Weil, Simone, 201–2
Weinreich, Max, 245, 249
Weiser, Abraham David, 185
Weizmann, Chaim, 270–71, 272, 275, 406
well of the chieftains, 111–12
Weltsch, Robert, 232
Wertheimer, Fritz, 258
Western Wall (Kotel), 399–401, 407–11, 413–14, 418n43
Wexler-Bezredka, Elimelekh, 365–66
Wexler-Bezredka, Shmaryahu (Alexander), 367
White Paper (1939), 271, 278, 284n18
Wiesel, Elie, 181, 408–10
wife, separation of husband and, 39–40
Windmill, Fogel, 129
Wischnitzer, Mark, 55–56, 66
Wisse, Ruth, 435–36
Wissenschaft des Judentums, 423, 430
Wolf, Immanuel, 430
womb incantations, 107
women: ambivalent gender politics concerning, 230; Gordon's commitment to equality for, 22n1; and Jewish assimilation, 227–28, 236n3; and Jewish claims courts, 129–30; pre-WWI social roles of, 230; WWI's impact on Jewish, 232, 235

women's associations, 182
World and Home (Bick), 332
World Jewish Congress (WJC), 292–93, 306–7
World War I: gendering of Jewish tradition during, 227–36; impact on ethnic Germans, 248, 260; Jewish achievements in, 269
World War II: experience of Jews preceding, 270–72; German invasion of Soviet Union, 379; impact on Jewish scholarship, 428–29; Shneiderman and Ehrenburg on Jewish heroism during, 386; starting points of, 267, 282n3. *See also* Jewish postwar; Jewish refugees / displaced people
World Zionist Organization, 405, 406
Wyman, Mark, 297

Xanten affair, 430
Xenophon, 61, 66

Yad Vashem, 413
yawning, as protection against evil eye, 105
Yehoshua, A. B., 399, 400, 413–14
Yeruḥam ben Mushullam, Rabbi, 108
Yerushalmi, Yosef Hayim, 221n27, 443n61, 444n79
Yeven meẓulah (Hannover): audience of, 32; author and Yiddish translator of, 30–32, 45–46nn10–11; claims of earlier Yiddish translations of, 44n5; differences between original and translation of, 33–34; frame of references for original versus translation of, 34–36; martyrdom in, 37–40, 52n54, 52n56; popularization and sanitation of, 41–44; purpose of Yiddish translation of, 32–34; vengeance in, 40–41, 48n30, 54n68
Yevin, Ester, 370n37

Yiddish: in existing memoirs, 57; German-Yiddish alliance, 248–51; history of German research on, 243–48; and linguistic assimilation in Soviet Union, 397n66; under Nazi regime, 260–61; perception of, 243–44, 257; post-war speakers of, 250; Shneiderman's use of, 388. *See also* Yiddish chair, project to establish Germany's first; Yiddish literature; Yiddish religious socialism; Yiddish studies
Yiddish chair, project to establish Germany's first, 241–42, 259–61; and Birnbaum's plans for *Institutum Ascenezicum*, 256–59; and fundraising for *Nebensprachinstitut*, 252–56; and history of Yiddish research in Germany, 243–48; and Kloss's plans for German-Yiddish alliance, 248–51
Yiddishism, 321, 327
Yiddishkeit, 340n31
Yiddish literature, 32–33, 47n18, 394n45. See also *Yeven meẓulah* (Hannover); Yiddish writers
Yiddish religious socialism, 317–19, 335–37; Bick and, 328–35; Nathanson and, 324–28; Steinberg and, 319–23
Yiddish studies, 241, 242; history of, in Germany, 243–48; Kloss's use of, 260–61. *See also* Yiddish chair, project to establish Germany's first
Yiddish writers: excluded from International Congress for the Defense of Culture, 394n45; murdered by Stalin, 373–74, 383–84, 388–89. *See also* Yiddish literature
YIVO (Yiddish Scientific Institute), 242, 246–47, 251, 253, 260
Yom Ha-medinah (State Day, Israel), 405
Young Ottoman Society, 160

zaddikim. *See* meetings between Hasidic and secular leaders, tales of
Zahra, Tara, 293
Zederbaum, Aleksander, 82
Zeltser, Arkadi, 386
Zhitlovsky, Hayim, 317, 318, 321, 326–27, 336
Zion, 425
Zionism: and antisemitism in *Autoemancipation*, 203–9, 213–16; and contradictions in embourgeoisement and acculturation of Russian Jews, 348; and emancipation in *Autoemancipation*, 212–13; and etiological function of antisemitism, 202–3, 219n18; Gordon as early supporter of, 221n26; and Jewish postwar visions, 273, 275, 277–80; and Jewish self-betrayal in *Autoemancipation*, 210–11; pre-WWII sense of collapse of, 270–71; Stanislawski on, 5–6, 348; Stanislawski's study of roots of, 347; Steinberg on, 322; Western Wall as icon of, 400–401; White Paper (1939), 271, 278, 284n18. *See also* Jewish nationalism
Zionism and the Fin de Siècle (Stanislawski), 5–6, 7
Zionism: A Very Short Introduction (Stanislawski), 6
Zionist historians, 425
Zipperstein, Steven J., 219n18
Złość żydowska (Pikulski), 56
Zohar Hadash, 111–12, 117n38, 118n40
Zunz, Leopold, 433
Zvi, Shabbetai, 56, 65
Zweig, Arnold, 234–35
Zweig, Stefan, 231, 239n46